D0940153

THE *unofficial* GUIDE®
TO Walt Disney World® with Kids

2011

THE *unofficial* GUIDE®

TO Walt Disney World® with Kids

2011

BOB SEHLINGER *and* LILIANE J. OPSOMER
with LEN TESTA

(Walt Disney World® is officially known as Walt Disney World® Resort.)

WILEY

Produced by Menasha Ridge Press

Cover design by Paul Dinovo

Interior design by Vertigo Design

For information on our other products and services or to obtain technical support, please contact our Customer Care Department within the United States at 800-762-2974, outside the United States at 317-572-3993, or by fax at 317-572-4002.

John Wiley & Sons, Inc., also publishes its books in a variety of electronic formats. Some content that appears in print may not be available in electronic formats.

ISBN 978-0-470-63237-6

Manufactured in the United States of America

5 4 3 2

CONTENTS

LIST *of* MAPS

ACKNOWLEDGMENTS

THANKS TO OUR TEAM OF YOUNG PUNDITS, Idan Menin, Ian Geiger, Hannah Testa, Katie Sutton, and Shelton Siegel for their unique wisdom and fun-loving attitude (gotta have attitude, right?). Lou Mongello created the theme-park trivia quizzes, and Disney historian Jim Hill provided insightful and funny glimpses of the World behind the scenes. Cartoons in the guide were created by artist Tami Knight, possibly the nuttiest person in Canada. Much appreciation to Eve Zibart for her characteristically droll comments concerning Walt Disney World attractions, hotels, and dining. For research and contributions concerning family dynamics and child behavior, thanks to psychologists Karen Turnbow, Susan Corbin, Gayle Janzen, and Joan Burns. Kudos also to *Unofficial Guide* Research Director Len Testa and his team for the data collection and programming behind the touring plans in this guide. To the Ortiz family, *gracias* for your help during our research trip. Getting 28 crazy Disney fans to ride the major attractions together is more difficult than herding cattle!

Many thanks also to Holly Cross, Ritchey Halphen, Amber Kaye Henderson, Molly Merkle, Ashley M. Arthur, Jenny Cromie, Steve Millburg, Holly B. Smith, Carla Stec, and Emily C. Beaumont for production and editorial work on this book. Annie Long earned our appreciation for her fine work in providing the typography. Cartography was provided by Steve Jones, and the index was prepared by Ann Cassar.

INTRODUCTION

HOW COME "UNOFFICIAL"?

DECLARATION OF INDEPENDENCE

THE AUTHORS AND RESEARCHERS OF THIS GUIDE specifically and categorically declare that they are and always have been totally independent of the Walt Disney Company, Inc.; of Disneyland, Inc.; of Walt Disney World, Inc.; and of any and all other members of the Disney corporate family not listed.

The authors believe in the wondrous variety, joy, and excitement of the Walt Disney World attractions. At the same time, we recognize that Walt Disney World is a business, with the same profit motivations as businesses the world over. In this guide we represent and serve you, the consumer. If a restaurant serves bad food, or a gift item is overpriced, or a certain ride isn't worth the wait, we can say so, and in the process we hope to make your visit more fun, efficient, and economical.

YOUR UNOFFICIAL WALT DISNEY WORLD TOOLBOX

YOU NEED DIFFERENT TOOLS TO WORK ON YOUR CAR than you do to fix your DVD player or trim the azaleas. It's much the same when it comes to a Walt Disney World vacation. If we think of information as tools, a couple with two toddlers in diapers will need different tools than a party of seniors going to the Epcot Flower and Garden Festival. Likewise, adults touring without children, families with kids of varying ages, and honeymooners all require their own special tools.

To meet the varying needs of our readers, we have created a very comprehensive guide, *The Unofficial Guide to Walt Disney World*. At about 850 pages, we call this guide the Big Book. The Big Book contains the detailed information anyone traveling to Walk Disney World needs to have a super vacation. It's our cornerstone guide.

As thorough as we try to make *The Unofficial Guide to Walt Disney World*, there isn't sufficient space for all the tips and valuable information that may be important and useful to certain readers. Thus, we've developed five additional Disney World guides, each designed to work in conjunction with the Big Book. All provide information tailored to specific Disney World visitors. Although some tips from the Big Book (such as arriving early at the theme parks) are echoed in these guides, most of the information is unique. You could think of the Big Book as a vacuum cleaner and the other guides as specialized attachments that certain users might need for a particular job (back to tools, you see).

So here's what in the toolbox:

This guide, *The Unofficial Guide to Walt Disney World with Kids* by Bob Sehlinger and Liliane J. Opsomer with Len Testa, presents detailed planning and touring tips for a family vacation, along with more than 20 special touring plans for families that are not published anywhere else. *The Unofficial Guide to Walt Disney World with Kids* is a complete guide and contains a wealth of family-specific information, tips, and advice not available in the Big Book or anywhere else. It's the only *Unofficial Guide* that is created with the guidance of a panel of kids, all of varying ages and backgrounds.

The Unofficial Guide: The Color Companion to Walt Disney World is a full-color visual feast that proves that a picture is worth 1,000 words. You can read everything you need to know about Disney's Wilderness Lodge Resort in the Big Book (even learn the best rooms to request), but in the *Color Companion* you can see the guest rooms, the pool, and the magnificent lobby. For the first time photos illustrate how long the lines are at different times of day, how drenched riders get riding Splash Mountain, and how the parks are decked out for various holidays. The *Color Companion* whets your appetite for Disney fun, pictures all the attractions, serves as a keepsake, and as always, helps make your vacation more enjoyable. Most of all, the *Color Companion* is for fun. For the first time we are able to use photography to express our zany *Unofficial Guide* sense of humor. You might think of it as Monty Python meets Walt Disney in TechniColor.

The Unofficial Guide to Walt Disney World for Grown-Ups by Eve Zibart focuses on adult pursuits and helps adults traveling without children make the most of their Disney vacation.

Mini Mickey: The Pocket-Sized Unofficial Guide to Walt Disney World, by Bob Sehlinger and Len Testa, is a portable *CliffsNotes*-style version of *The Unofficial Guide to Walt Disney World.* It distills information from the Big Book to help short-stay or last-minute visitors decide quickly how to plan their limited hours at Disney World.

Beyond Disney: The Unofficial Guide to Universal Orlando, Sea-World, and the Best of Central Florida, by Bob Sehlinger and Grant Rafter, is a guide to non-Disney attractions, restaurants, outdoor recreation, and nightlife in Orlando and central Florida.

THE MUSIC OF LIFE

ALTHOUGH IT IS COMMON in our culture to see life as a journey from cradle to grave, Alan Watts, a noted late–20th-century philosopher, saw it somewhat differently. He viewed life not as a journey but as a dance. In a journey, he said, you are trying to get somewhere, and are consequently always looking ahead, anticipating the way stations, and thinking about the end. Though the journey metaphor is popular, particularly in the West, it is generally characterized by a driven, goal-oriented mentality: a way of living and being that often inhibits those who subscribe to the journey metaphor from savoring each moment of life.

When you dance, by contrast, you hear the music and move in harmony with the rhythm. Like life, a dance has a beginning and an end. But unlike a journey, your objective is not to get to the end but to enjoy the dance while the music plays. You are totally in the moment and care nothing about where on the floor you stop when the dance is done.

As you begin to contemplate your Walt Disney World vacation, you may not have much patience for a philosophical discussion about journeys and dancing. But you see, it is relevant. If you are like most travel guide readers, you are apt to plan and organize, to anticipate and control, and you like things to go smoothly. And truth be told, this leads us to suspect that you are a person who looks ahead and is outcome-oriented. You may even feel a bit of pressure concerning your vacation. Vacations, after all, are special events and expensive ones as well. So you work hard to make the most of your vacation.

We also believe that work, planning, and organization are important, and at Walt Disney World they are essential. But if they become your focus, you won't be able to hear the music and enjoy the dance. Though a lot of dancing these days resembles highly individualized seizures, there was a time when each dance involved specific steps, which you committed to memory. At first you were tentative and awkward, but eventually the steps became second nature and you didn't think about them anymore.

Metaphorically, this is what we want for you and your children or grandchildren as you embark on your Walt Disney World vacation. We want you to learn the steps ahead of time, so that when you're on your vacation and the music plays, you will be able to hear it, and you and your children will dance with grace and ease.

YOUR PERSONAL TRAINERS

WE'RE YOUR WALT DISNEY WORLD PERSONAL TRAINERS. We will help you plan and enjoy your Walt Disney World vacation. Together we will make sure that it really is a vacation, as opposed to, say, an ordeal or an expensive way to experience heatstroke. Our objective, simply put, is to ensure that you and your children have fun.

Because this book is specifically for adults traveling with children, we'll concentrate on your special needs and challenges. We'll share our

IDAN   IAN   HANNAH   SHELTON

most useful tips as well as the travel secrets of more than 37,000 families interviewed over the years we've covered Walt Disney World.

So who are *we*? For starters, there's a bunch of us. Your primary trainers are Liliane and Bob. Helping out big time are Idan and Ian—also known as the I-Boys—as well as Hannah and Shelton. Idan is 19 years old and comes from the Queens borough of New York. He plays rock guitar (loudly), has kind of a sweetly grunge style (secondhand clothes are the coolest, right?), and wears shoes large enough for eagles to nest in. Ian is a 15-year-old from Tampa, Florida. His surfer mop-headed hair nearly covers his hazy blue peepers. He gets a kick out of playing soccer and hanging with his pet gecko, Iggie (not part of the I-Boys), and is addicted to saying "Sweet!" and "Awesome!"—punctuated with an occasional "Dude!" Hannah, age 11, lives near Winston-Salem, North Carolina, really knows Disney, and will read you the riot act if you mess up. The rest of us work for her. Our most recent team member is Shelton, who is a high school sophomore in Arlington, Virginia. He sings, plays keyboard, and loves to chow down on ethnic food. Maybe he'll team up with Idan to form an *Unofficial* rock band. The I-Boys, Shelton, and Hannah, needless to say, have a lot of opinions when it comes to Disney. So many, in fact, that they think Liliane and Bob are largely superfluous.

Liliane comes from Belgium and works in New York City. She's funny, very polite in the best European tradition, and puts more energy into being a mom than you'd think possible without performance-enhancing drugs. Optimistic and happy, she loves the sweet and sentimental side of Walt Disney World. You might find her whooping it up at the *Hoop-Dee-Doo Revue,* but you'll never see her on a roller coaster with Bob.

Speaking of whom, Bob is not exactly a curmudgeon, but he likes to unearth Disney's closely guarded secrets and show readers how to beat the system. His idea of a warm fuzzy might be the Rock 'n' Roller Coaster, but he'll help you save lots of money, find the best hotels and restaurants, and return home less than terminally exhausted. The caricatures on the next page pretty much sum up the essence of Bob and Liliane.

If you're thinking that the cartoons paint a somewhat conflicted picture of your personal trainers, you're right. Bob and Liliane—it must be admitted—have been known to disagree on a thing or two. Together,

BOB   **LILIANE**

however, they make a good team. You can count on them to give you both sides of every story. As an analogy, Liliane will help you bask in the universal brotherhood theme of *It's a Small World*. Bob will show up later and help you get the infernal song out of your head. You get the idea.

Oops, almost forgot: There's another team member you need to meet. Called a Wuffo, she's our very own character. She'll warn you when rides are too scary, too dark, or too wet. You'll bump into her throughout the book doing, well, what characters do.

 Why did we create our own character when Disney has dozens just sitting around? Simple—Disney characters toe the company line. We needed a tough (but lovable) independent character who would give you the straight skinny on what Disney rides do to your stomach and central nervous system. Incidentally, if you work for Disney, you're probably licking your chops at the thought of getting a Wuffo to star in one of your animated features. Yeah? I thought so. Have your agent call our agent, and we'll do lunch.

ABOUT *this* GUIDE

WALT DISNEY WORLD HAS BEEN OUR BEAT for more than two decades, and we know it inside out. During those years we have observed many thousands of parents and grandparents trying—some successfully, others less so—to have a good time at Walt Disney World. Some of these, owing to unfortunate dynamics within the family, were handicapped right from the start. Others were simply overwhelmed by the size and complexity of Walt Disney World; whereas still others fell victim to a lack of foresight, planning, and organization.

Walt Disney World is a better destination for some families than for others. Likewise, some families are more compatible on vacation than others. The likelihood of experiencing a truly wonderful Walt Disney World vacation transcends the theme parks and attractions offered. In fact, the theme parks and attractions are the only constants in the equation. The variables that will define the experience and determine its success are intrinsic to your family: things like attitude, sense of humor, cohesiveness, stamina, flexibility, and conflict resolution.

The simple truth is that Walt Disney World can test you as a family. It will overwhelm you with choices and force you to make decisions about how to spend your time and money. It will challenge you physically as you cover miles on foot and wait in lines touring the theme parks. You will have to respond to surprises (both good and bad) and deal with hyperstimulation.

This guide will forewarn and forearm you. It will help you decide whether a Walt Disney World vacation is a good idea for you and your family at this particular time. It will help you sort out and address the attitudes and family dynamics that can affect your experience. Most important, it will provide the confidence that comes with good planning and realistic expectations.

THE SUM OF ALL FEARS

EVERY WRITER WHO EXPRESSES an opinion is accustomed to readers who strongly agree or disagree: it comes with the territory. Extremely troubling, however, is the possibility that our efforts to be objective have frightened some readers away from Walt Disney World or made others apprehensive. For the record, if you enjoy theme parks, Disney World is as good as it gets, absolute nirvana. It's upbeat, safe, fun, eye-popping, happy, and exciting. If you arrive without knowing a thing about the place and make every possible mistake, chances are about 90% that you'll have a wonderful vacation anyway. In the end, guidebooks don't make or break great destinations. Rather, they are simply tools to help you enhance your experience and get the most for your money.

 Be prepared to read experienced Disney World visitors' opinions of the parks in this book and to apply them to your own travel circumstances.

As wonderful as Walt Disney World is, however, it's a complex destination. Even so, it isn't nearly as challenging or difficult as New York, San Francisco, Paris, Acapulco, or any other large city or destination. And, happily, there are numerous ways to save money, minimize hassle, and make the most of your time. That's what this guide is about: giving you a heads-up regarding potential problems or opportunities. Unfortunately, some *Unofficial Guide* readers add up the warnings and critical advice and conclude that Walt Disney World is too intimidating, too expensive, or too much work. They lose track of the wonder of Disney World and focus instead on what might go wrong.

Our philosophy is that knowledge is power (and time and money too). You're free to follow our advice—or not—at your discretion. But you can't exercise that discretion if we fail to present the issues.

With or without a guidebook, you'll have a great time at Walt Disney World. If you let us, we'll help you smooth the potential bumps. We're certain that we can help you turn a great vacation into an absolutely superb one. Either way, once there, you'll get the feel of the place and quickly reach a comfort level that will allay your apprehensions and allow you to have a great experience.

LETTERS AND COMMENTS FROM READERS

MANY OF THOSE WHO USE *The Unofficial Guide to Walt Disney World with Kids* write us to make comments or share their own strategies for visiting Walt Disney World. We appreciate all such input, both positive and critical, and encourage our readers to continue writing. Readers' comments and observations are frequently incorporated into revised editions of the *Unofficial Guide* and have contributed immeasurably to its improvement.

Privacy Policy

If you write us, you can rest assured that we won't release your name and address to any mailing-list companies, direct-mail advertisers, or other third party. Unless you instruct us otherwise, we will assume that you do not object to being quoted in a future edition.

How To Write or E-mail the Authors

Bob and Liliane
The Unofficial Guide to Walt Disney World with Kids
P.O. Box 43673
Birmingham, AL 35243
UnofficialGuides@MenashaRidge.com

When you write, be sure to put a return address on your letter as well as the envelope; sometimes envelopes and letters get separated. It's also a good idea to include your phone number.

Remember, our work often requires that we be out of the office for long periods of time, and *Unofficial Guide* mail and e-mail are not forwarded to us when we're traveling. So forgive us if our response is a little slow; we will respond as soon as possible when we return.

READER SURVEYS

A READER SURVEY IS LOCATED at the end of this guide. You'll notice throughout the book that we quote readers and publish the results of our several surveys. We'd love to hear from you and register your opinions. To this end you can either complete and mail the forms at the back of he book or take the Walt Disney World survey online at **touringplans.com.** We're betting that you'll really like the advice and opinions of readers included in *The Unofficial Guide to Walt Disney World with Kids.* Be a contributor: Let us know what you think.

continued on page 12

South Orlando & Walt Disney World Area

Orlando

Florida's Turnpike

Windermere

Lake Butler

Universal Studios Florida

Vineland Rd

Universal's Islands of Adventure

74-B

Wet 'n Wild

74-A

Universal Blvd

429

Winter Garden-Vineland Rd.

535

S. Apopka-Vineland Rd.

Orange County Convention Center

72

1

Magic Kingdom

SeaWorld Orlando

71

Fort Wilderness Campground

Discovery Cove

The Walt Disney World Resort

Aquatica

International Dr.

Western Way

Lake Buena Vista

Epcot Center Dr.

World Dr.

Downtown Disney

Epcot

68

To 27 & Ocala

Disney's Hollywood Studios

Buena Vista Dr.

536

417

Disney's Animal Kingdom

Osceola Pkwy.

67

W. Irlo Bronson Memorial Hwy.

192

65

535

ESPN Wide World of Sports Complex

3

64

Celebration

2

192

429

Poinciana Blvd.

Western Beltway (toll road)

62

4

58

532

To Busch Gardens & Tampa

17

27

92

To Davenport

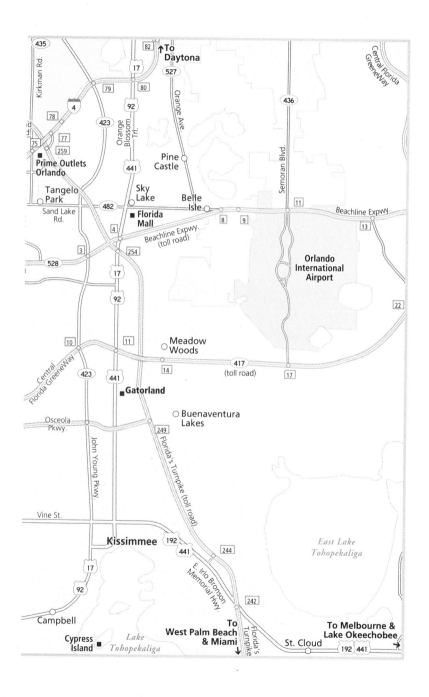

Walt Disney World

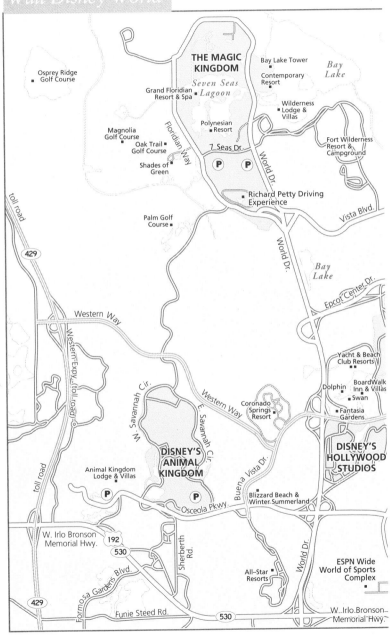

Osprey Ridge
Golf Course

**THE MAGIC
KINGDOM**

Bay Lake Tower

*Bay
Lake*

Contemporary
Resort

*Seven Seas
Lagoon*

Grand Floridian
Resort & Spa

Wilderness
Lodge &
Villas

Polynesian
Resort

Magnolia
Golf Course

Oak Trail
Golf Course

7 Seas Dr.

Fort Wilderness
Resort &
Campground

Floridian Way

World Dr.

Shades of
Green

Richard Petty Driving
Experience

Vista Blvd.

Palm Golf
Course

World Dr.

*Bay
Lake*

Epcot Center Dr.

toll road

429

Western Way

Western Expy. (toll road)

Yacht & Beach
Club Resorts

W. Savannah Cir.

Western Way

BoardWalk
Inn & Villas

Dolphin

Swan

E. Savannah Cir.

Coronado
Springs
Resort

Fantasia
Gardens

**DISNEY'S
HOLLYWOOD
STUDIOS**

**DISNEY'S
ANIMAL
KINGDOM**

Animal Kingdom
Lodge & Villas

Buena Vista Dr.

Blizzard Beach &
Winter Summerland

toll road

Osceola Pkwy.

W. Irlo Bronson
Memorial Hwy.

192

Sherberth Rd.

World Dr.

**ESPN Wide
World of Sports
Complex**

530

Formosa Gardens Blvd.

All-Star
Resorts

429

Funie Steed Rd.

530

W. Irlo Bronson
Memorial Hwy.

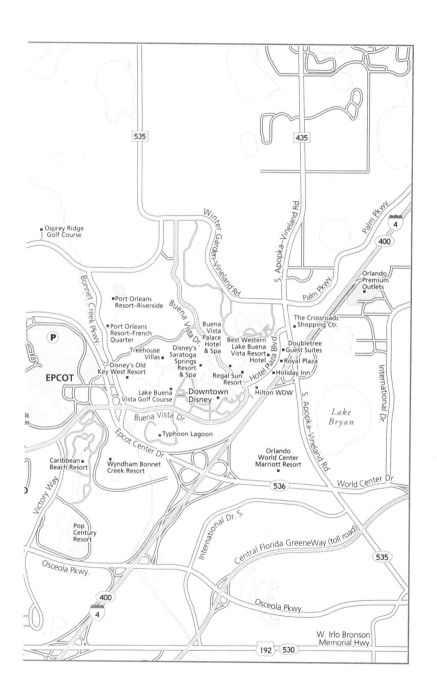

continued from page 7

A **QUICK TOUR** *of a* **BIG WORLD**

WALT DISNEY WORLD ENCOMPASSES 43 SQUARE MILES, an area twice as large as Manhattan and roughly the same size as Boston. Situated strategically in this vast expanse are the Magic Kingdom, Epcot, Disney's Hollywood Studios, and the Animal Kingdom theme parks; two water parks; two nighttime entertainment areas; a sports complex; several golf courses, hotels, and campgrounds; almost 100 restaurants; four large, interconnected lakes; a shopping complex; three convention venues; a nature preserve; and a complete transportation system consisting of four-lane highways, elevated monorails, and a system of canals.

THE MAJOR THEME PARKS

The Magic Kingdom

When people think of Walt Disney World, most think of the Magic Kingdom. It comprises Cinderella Castle and the collection of adventures, rides, and shows symbolizing the Disney cartoon characters. Although the park is only one element of Disney World, it remains its heart. The Magic Kingdom is divided into seven areas or lands, six of which are arranged around a central hub. First encountered is Main Street, U.S.A., which connects the Magic Kingdom entrance with the central hub. Clockwise around the hub are Adventureland, Frontierland, Liberty Square, Fantasyland, and Tomorrowland. Mickey's Toontown Fair, the first new land in the Magic Kingdom since the park opened, is situated along Walt Disney Railroad on 3 acres between Fantasyland and Tomorrowland. (Mickey's Toontown Fair will also be the Magic Kingdom's first land to go out of business. It will close forever sometime in 2010 to make way for an expanded Fantasyland.) Access is through Fantasyland, from Tomorrowland, or via the railroad. The Contemporary, Polynesian, and Grand Floridian Beach resorts are close to the Magic Kingdom and are directly connected to it by monorail and boat. Two additional hotels, Shades of Green (operated by the Department of Defense) and Wilderness Lodge Resort, are nearby but aren't served by the monorail.

Epcot

Epcot opened in October 1982. Divided into two major areas, Future World and World Showcase, the park is twice as big as the Magic Kingdom and comparable in scope. Future World consists of futuristic pavilions relating to different themes concerning humankind's creativity and technological advancement. World Showcase, arranged around a 41-acre lagoon, presents the architectural, social, and cultural heritages of almost a dozen nations, with each country represented by replicas of famous landmarks and local settings familiar to world travelers. Epcot is more education-oriented than the Magic Kingdom and has been repeatedly characterized as a sort of permanent World's Fair.

The five Epcot resort hotels—Disney's Beach Club and Villas, Disney's Yacht Club Resort, Disney's BoardWalk Inn and Villas, the Walt Disney World Swan, and the Walt Disney World Dolphin—are within a 5- to 15-minute walk of Epcot's "back door," the International Gateway entrance. The hotels are also linked to the park by boat. Disney's Caribbean Beach Resort is near Epcot but not linked to it. Epcot is connected to the Magic Kingdom and its resort hotels by monorail.

Disney's Hollywood Studios

This 100-acre theme park opened in 1989 and is divided into two areas. The first is a theme park focusing on the past, present, and future of the motion picture and television industries. This section contains movie-theme rides and shows and covers about half of the Studios complex. Highlights include a re-creation of Hollywood and Sunset boulevards from Hollywood's Golden Age; movie stunt demonstrations; a children's play area; and four high-tech rides: The Twilight Zone Tower of Terror, Star Tours, the Rock 'n' Roller Coaster, and Toy Story Mania.

The second area is a working motion picture and television production facility encompassing three soundstages, a back lot of streets and sets, and creative support services. Public access to this area is limited to studio tours, which take visitors behind the scenes for crash courses on Disney animation and moviemaking, including (on occasion) the opportunity to witness the actual shooting of a feature film, television show, or commercial.

Disney's Hollywood Studios is linked to other Walt Disney World areas by highway and canal but not by monorail. Guests can park in the Studios' pay parking lot or commute by bus. Patrons staying in Epcot resort hotels can reach the Studios by boat.

Disney's Animal Kingdom

More than five times the size of the Magic Kingdom, the Animal Kingdom combines zoological exhibits with rides, shows, and live entertainment. The park is arranged somewhat like the Magic Kingdom, in a hub-and-spoke configuration. A lush tropical rain forest called The Oasis serves as Main Street, funneling visitors to Discovery Island at the center of the park. Dominated by the park's central icon, the 14-story-tall, hand-carved Tree of Life, Discovery Island is the park's center, with services, shopping, and dining. From Discovery Island, guests can access the theme areas: Africa, Asia, DinoLand U.S.A., and Camp Minnie-Mickey. Africa, the largest of the theme areas at 100 acres, features free-roaming herds in a re-creation of the Serengeti Plain. Guests tour in open-air safari vehicles. Rafiki's Planet Watch, unlike the other themed areas, is accessed from Africa.

Animal Kingdom has its own pay parking lot and is connected to other Disney World destinations by the Disney bus system. Although no hotels are at the Animal Kingdom, the Animal Kingdom Lodge and Villas, All-Star, and Coronado Springs resorts are nearby.

THE WATER THEME PARKS

THERE ARE TWO MAJOR SWIMMING THEME PARKS in Walt Disney World: Typhoon Lagoon and Blizzard Beach. Typhoon Lagoon is distinguished by a wave pool capable of making 6-foot waves. Blizzard Beach features more slides than Typhoon Lagoon. Both parks are beautifully landscaped, with great attention to aesthetics and atmosphere. Typhoon Lagoon and Blizzard Beach have their own adjacent parking lots and can be reached by Disney bus.

OTHER WALT DISNEY WORLD VENUES

Downtown Disney (Downtown Disney Marketplace, Pleasure Island, and Downtown Disney West Side)

Downtown Disney is a large shopping, dining, and entertainment complex encompassing the Downtown Disney Marketplace on the east, Pleasure Island in the middle, and Downtown Disney West Side on the west. Downtown Disney Marketplace is home to the largest Disney character merchandise store in the world, upscale resort-wear and specialty shops, and several restaurants, including the tacky but popular Rainforest Cafe. Pleasure Island was converted in 2008 from an admission-required collection of nightclubs to a shopping-and-dining venue.

Downtown Disney West Side combines nightlife, shopping, dining, and entertainment. Dan Aykroyd's House of Blues serves Cajun-Creole dishes in its restaurant and electric blues in its music hall. Bongos, a Cuban nightclub and cafe created by Gloria and Emilio Estefan, offers Caribbean flavors and rhythms. Wolfgang Puck Café, sandwiched among pricey boutiques, is the West Side's prestige eatery. In the entertainment department, you'll find a 24-screen cinema; a permanent showplace for the extraordinary, 70-person cast of Cirque du Soleil; and DisneyQuest, a high-tech, interactive virtual reality and electronic games venue. Downtown Disney can be accessed via Disney buses from most Walt Disney World locations.

Disney's BoardWalk

Located near Epcot, Disney's BoardWalk is an idealized replication of an East Coast turn-of-the-20th-century waterfront resort. Open all day, the BoardWalk features upscale restaurants, shops and galleries, a brewpub, an ESPN sports bar, a nightclub with dueling pianos (New Orleans Pat O'Brien's–style), and a dance club. Although there is no admission fee for the BoardWalk per se, individual clubs levy a cover charge at night. Besides the public facilities, the BoardWalk fronts a 378-room deluxe hotel and a 532-unit time-share development. The BoardWalk is within walking distance of the Epcot resorts and the International Gateway of the Epcot theme park. Boat transportation is available to and from Epcot and Disney's Hollywood Studios, with buses serving other Disney World locations.

ESPN Wide World of Sports

Covering 200 acres, ESPN Wide World of Sports is a state-of-the-art competition and training facility consisting of a 7,500-seat ballpark, a field house, and venues for baseball, softball, tennis, track and field, beach volleyball, and more than 50 other sports. In addition to being the spring-training home of the Atlanta Braves, the complex hosts a mind-boggling calendar of professional and amateur competitions. Although Walt Disney World guests are welcome at the complex as paid spectators, none of the facilities are available for use by guests unless they are participants in a scheduled competition.

The Mouse at Sea

The Disney Cruise Line fleet consists of the **Disney Magic** and the **Disney Wonder.** Two new larger ships, the **Disney Dream** and the **Disney Fantasy,** enter service in 2011 and 2012 respectively. Though the foundation of its business is built on 3-, 4-, 5-, and 7-day Bahamian and Caribbean cruises out of Port Canaveral (about a 90-minute drive from Walt Disney World), the Disney Cruise Line also offers Alaska, Mediterranean, Baltic Sea, Pacific Coast, and Mexican Riviera cruises, as well as transatlantic and Panama Canal repositioning cruises. All cruises originating in Port Canaveral make at least one port call at Disney's private island, Castaway Cay, and all can be combined in a land-sea package with a stay at Walt Disney World.

If you go for the cruise and Disney World package, visit the parks first; then sail away for more fun, as well as some much-deserved rest. *La dolce vita,* here I come.

Liliane

The Disney cruises are perfect for families and for kids of all ages. Although the cruises are family-oriented, extensive children's programs and elaborate child-care facilities allow grown-ups plenty of opportunities to relax and do adult stuff. The ships are modern ocean liners with classic steamship lines. Cabins are among the most spacious in the cruise industry, and the staff is very attentive and accommodating. From the waitstaff at breakfast, lunch, and dinner to the cabin stewards, yours truly has not experienced any better.

Cabin design reveals Disney's finely tuned sense of the needs of families and children and offers a cruise-industry first: a split bathroom with a bathtub and shower combo and sink in one room, and toilet, sink, and vanity in another. This configuration, found in all but standard inside cabins, allows any family member to use the bathroom without monopolizing it. All bathrooms have a tub and shower, except disabled rooms (shower only). Decor includes unusual features such as bureaus

The room service gets a thumbs-up! Drinking pink lemonade and eating hot dogs, pizza, and cookies while watching a movie with friends is awesome.

Idan

designed to look like steamer trunks. Cabins also have a telephone with voice mail, TV, hair dryer, and a cooling box. In some cabins, pull-down Murphy beds or drop-down bunk beds allow for additional daytime floor space. Storage is generous, with deep drawers and large closets. Premium H2O Plus spa products are available in all cabins; bathrobes, unfortunately, are not available in all categories.

A big party with appearances by Mickey and Minnie marks departures, when the ship's horn toots "When You Wish upon a Star." Halfway through your voyage Disney throws a deck party, where Mickey saves all passengers from Captain Hook and his evil plans. For the "Pirates IN the Caribbean" evening, guests are encouraged to dress up like pirates.

Dining is a true pleasure. Each night, passengers move to a different family restaurant—each with its own unique theme and menu—and take their table companions and waitstaff with them. In addition to the family restaurants, the ships have a range of cafes offering pizza, burgers, sandwiches, and ice-cream bars. Room service is available 24/7.

All the suits and ties in the world did not get me into Palo. I am still feeling the need for revenge, as I was denied access as a 17-year-old looking like Johnny Depp with a 20-year-old beauty on my arm.

For a night out without kids, Palo, which offers tables with a view, is a must. Reservations are also a must, and a surcharge of $15 is added for this service to your onboard bill. The food is excellent, and the ambience sophisticated. Disney enforces a strict policy for diners at Palo to be 18 years of age or older.

The Disney ships offer 15,000-plus square feet of playrooms and other kids' facilities. Programs include interactive activities, play areas supervised by trained counselors, and a children's drop-off service in the evening. Passengers can register their children for the nursery, and group babysitting is available for select hours every day. Cost is $6 per child per hour. The Oceaneer Club program with its Never Land theme is perfect for kids ages 3–7, though children up to age 10 can participate. (Programs on the *Wonder* allow children up to age 12.) Oceaneer Lab offers high-tech play. Kids wear ID bracelets, and parents receive pagers. There's a special club for teens.

Big with kids of all ages are the pools and the nightly entertainment on board, which show Disney at its best. The Walt Disney Theatre stages several musical productions each cruise, and the Buena Vista Theatre with its full-screen cinema shows first-run and digital 3-D movies as well as classic Disney films. Movies are also played poolside on a state-of-the-art 24- by 14-foot LED screen affixed to the forward funnel in the Goofy's Pool area.

Vista Spa & Salon (known as Senses on the *Dream* ship) is an area reserved exclusively for adults and is a great place to relax when the kids are occupied at Oceaneer Club or spending time at the nursery. The treatments are pricey, and there's a surcharge of $15 per day for the use of the saunas and steam rooms, as well as two aromatic showers. (The fitness center's showers and lockers are free of charge.)

Shore excursions depend on the itinerary, but all Cape Canaveral sailings make at least one call at **Castaway Cay,** Disney's 1,000-acre private island. The natural environment and miles of white-sand beaches have been nicely preserved. The best way to enjoy the island is to disembark first thing in the morning and secure a prime spot at the beach complete with hammock and shade. **Castaway** family beach is served by a tram running every 5 minutes. We walked the quarter mile to the beach, but realize that it could be tiresome to walk in the blistering summer heat. **Cookie's BBQ** serves a buffet lunch of burgers, pork ribs, hot dogs, baked beans, slaw, corn on the cob, fruits, and potato chips. Programs for kids on Castaway Cay give parents a chance to enjoy **Serenity Bay,** the adults-only beach. Not to be missed is Davy Jones's ship the *Flying Dutchman,* the pirate ship seen in the film *Pirates of the Caribbean.* The 175-foot "ghost ship" anchored off the island provides a scenic photo opportunity.

The Disney Cruise Line fared better than most during the recession, but throughout the industry, demand has declined and capacity, with the introduction of a number of new ships, has gone up. Disney Cruise Line offers a distinctive product and has a loyal client base. When other cruise lines heavily discount their cruises, the deals are often so good that Disney Cruise Line is forced to struggle to hang onto its market share. When you can buy a seven-night Alaska cruise on another line for less than a four-day Disney cruise to Nassau and Castaway Cay, it strains the loyalty of even the most ardent Mouseketeer. Disney, therefore, has been discounting and offering Kids Sail Free specials for children who share a cabin with their parents.

The bottom line is that cruises are unequivocally the best deal in travel right now and for the foreseeable future. Deals abound. Check Web sites such as **cruisecritic.com, cruisemates.com, vacationstogo. com, lastminutetravel.com,** and **disneycruiseline.com** for the latest discounts. Search engine **kayak.com** is a great resource for uncovering cruise bargains. If you prefer to buy directly from Disney, here's how to get in touch:

Disney Cruise Line
800-951-6499 or 800-951-3532
disneycruise.com

Disney Cruise Line offers a free planning DVD that tells you all you need to know about Disney cruises and then some. To obtain a copy, call 888-D CL-2500, or order online at **disneycruise.com.**

DISNEYSPEAK POCKET TRANSLATOR

ALTHOUGH IT MAY COME AS A SURPRISE to many, Walt Disney World has its own somewhat peculiar language. Here are some terms that you are likely to bump into:

DISNEYSPEAK	ENGLISH DEFINITION
Adventure	Ride
Attraction	Ride or theater show
Attraction Host	Ride operator
Audience	Crowd
Backstage	Behind the scenes, out of view of customers
Bull Pen	Queuing area
Cast Member	Employee
Character	Disney character impersonated by an employee
Costume	Work attire or uniform
Dark Ride	Indoor ride
Day Guest	Any customer not staying at a Disney resort
Face Character	A character who does not wear a head-covering costume (Snow White, Cinderella, Jasmine, and the like)
General Public	Same as day guest
Greeter	Employee positioned at an attraction entrance
Guest	Customer
Hidden Mickeys	Frontal silhouette of Mickey's head worked subtly into the design of buildings, railings, vehicles, golf greens, attractions, and just about anything else
In Rehearsal	Operating, though not officially open
Lead	Foreman or manager, the person in charge of an attraction
On Stage	In full view of customers
Preshow	Entertainment at an attraction prior to the feature presentation
Resort Guest	A customer staying at a Disney resort
Role	An employee's job
Security Host	Security guard
Soft Opening	Opening a park or attraction before its stated opening date
Transitional Experience	An element of the queuing area and/or preshow that provides a story line or information essential to understanding the attraction

PART ONE

BASIC CONSIDERATIONS

IS WALT DISNEY WORLD *for* YOU?

ALMOST ALL VISITORS ENJOY WALT DISNEY WORLD on some level and find things to see and do that they like. In fact, for many, the theme park attractions are just the tip of the iceberg. The more salient question, then (because this is a family vacation), is whether the members of your family basically like the same things. If you do, fine. If not, how will you handle the differing agendas?

A mother from Toronto wrote a couple of years ago describing her husband's aversion to Disney's (in his terms) "phony, plastic, and idealized version of life." Touring the theme parks, he was a real cynic and managed to diminish the experience for the rest of the family. As it happened, however, dad's pejorative point of view didn't extend to the Disney golf courses. So mom packed him up and sent him golfing while the family enjoyed the theme parks.

If you have someone in your family who doesn't like theme parks or, for whatever reason, doesn't care for Disney's brand of entertainment, it helps to get the attitude out in the open. Our recommendation is to deal with the person up front. Glossing over or ignoring the contrary opinion and hoping that "Tom will like it once he gets there" is naive and unrealistic. Either leave Tom at home, or help him discover and plan activities that he will enjoy, resigning yourself in the process to the fact that the family won't be together at all times.

DIFFERENT FOLKS, DIFFERENT STROKES

IT'S NO SECRET THAT WE AT THE *Unofficial Guides* believe thorough planning is an essential key to a successful Walt Disney World vacation. It's also no secret that our emphasis on planning rubs some folks the wrong way. One author's sister and her husband, for example, are spontaneous people and do not appreciate the concept of detailed planning or, more particularly, following one of our touring plans when they visit the theme parks. To them the most important thing is to relax, take things as they come, and enjoy the moment. Sometimes they arrive at Epcot at 10:30 in the morning (impossibly late for us *Unofficial Guide* types), walk around enjoying the landscaping and architecture, and then sit with a cup of espresso, watching other guests race around the park like maniacs. They would be the first to admit that they don't see many attractions, but experiencing attractions is not what lights their sparklers.

Not coincidentally, most of our readers are big on planning. When they go to the theme park, they want to experience the attractions, and the shorter the lines, the better. They are willing to sacrifice some spontaneity for touring efficiency.

We want you to have the best possible time, whatever that means to you, so plan (or not) according to your preference. The point here is that most families (unlike my sister and her husband) are not entirely in agreement on this planning versus spontaneity issue. If you are a serious planner and your oldest daughter and husband are free spirits, you've got the makings of a problem. In practice, the way this and similar scenarios shake out is that the planner (usually the more assertive or type-A person) just takes over. Sometimes daughter and husband go along and everything works out, but just as often they feel resentful. There are as many ways of developing a win-win compromise as there are well-intentioned people on different sides of this situation. How you settle it is up to you. We're simply suggesting that you examine the problem and work out the solution *before* you go on vacation.

THE NATURE OF THE BEAST

THOUGH MANY PARENTS DON'T REALIZE IT, there is no law that says you must take your kids to Walt Disney World. Likewise, there's no law that says you will enjoy Walt Disney World. And although we will help you make the most of any visit, we can't

Sehlinger's Law postulates that the number of adults required to take care of an active toddler is equal to the number of adults present, plus one.

change the basic nature of the beast . . . er, mouse. A Walt Disney World vacation is an active and physically demanding undertaking. Regimentation, getting up early, lots of walking, waiting in lines, fighting crowds, and (often) enduring heat and humidity are as intrinsic to a Walt Disney World vacation as stripes are to a zebra. Especially if you're traveling with children, you'll need a sense of humor, more than a modicum of patience, and the ability to roll with the punches.

KNOW THYSELF AND NOTHING TO EXCESS

THIS GOOD ADVICE WAS MADE AVAILABLE to ancient Greeks courtesy of the oracle of Apollo at Delphi, who gave us permission to pass it along to you. First, concerning the "know thyself" part, we want you to do some serious thinking concerning what you want in a vacation. We also want you to entertain the notion that having fun and deriving pleasure from your vacation may be very different indeed from doing and seeing as much as possible.

You can enjoy a perfectly wonderful time in the World if you are realistic, organized, and prepared. *Liliane*

Because Walt Disney World is expensive, many families confuse "seeing everything" in order to "get our money's worth" with having a great time. Sometimes the two are compatible, but more often they are not. So, if sleeping in, relaxing with the paper over coffee, sunbathing by the pool, or taking a nap ranks high on your vacation hit parade, you need to accord them due emphasis on your Disney visit (are you listening?), even if it means you see less of the theme parks.

Which brings us to the "nothing to excess" part. At Walt Disney World, especially if you are touring with children, less is definitely more. Trust us, you cannot go full tilt dawn to dark in the theme parks day after day. First you'll get tired, then you'll get cranky, and then you'll adopt a production mentality ("we've got three more rides and then we can go back to the hotel"). Finally, you'll hit the wall because you just can't maintain the pace.

Plan on seeing Walt Disney World in bite-size chunks with plenty of sleeping, swimming, napping, and relaxing in between. Ask yourself over and over in both the planning stage and while you are at Walt Disney World: What will contribute the greatest contentedness, satisfaction, and harmony? Trust your instincts. If stopping for ice cream or returning to the hotel

Get a grip on your needs and preferences before you leave home, and *Bob* develop an itinerary that incorporates all the things that make you happiest.

for a dip feels like more fun than seeing another attraction, do it—even if it means wasting the remaining hours of an expensive admissions pass.

The AGE THING

THERE IS A LOT OF SERIOUS COGITATION among parents and grandparents in regard to how old a child should be before embarking on a trip to Walt Disney World. The answer, not always obvious, stems from the personalities and maturity of the children, as well as the personalities and parenting style of the adults.

Walt Disney World for Infants and Toddlers

We believe that traveling with infants and toddlers is a great idea. Developmentally, travel is a stimulating learning experience for even the youngest of children. Infants, of course, will not know Mickey Mouse from a draft horse but will respond to sun and shade, music, bright colors, and the extra attention they receive from you. From first steps to full mobility, toddlers respond to the excitement and spectacle of Walt Disney World, though of course in a much different way than you do. Your toddler will prefer splashing in fountains and clambering over curbs and benches to experiencing most attractions, but no matter: He or she will still have a great time.

Somewhere between 4 and 6 years of age, your child will experience the first vacation that he or she will remember as an adult. Though more likely to remember the comfortable coziness of the hotel room than the theme parks, the child will be able to experience and comprehend many attractions and will be a much fuller participant in your vacation. Even so, his or her favorite activity is likely to be swimming in the hotel pool.

As concerns infants and toddlers, there are good reasons and bad reasons for vacationing at Walt Disney World. A good reason for taking your little one to Walt Disney World is that you want to go and there's no one available to care for your child during your absence. Philosophically, we are very much against putting your life (including your vacation) on hold until your children are older.

Especially if you have children of varying ages (or plan to, for that matter), it's better to take the show on the road than to wait until the youngest reaches the perceived ideal age. If your family includes a toddler or infant, you will find everything from private facilities for breast-feeding to changing tables in both men's and women's restrooms to facilitate baby's care. Your whole family will be able to tour together with fewer hassles than on a picnic outing at home.

Traveling with infants and toddlers sharpens parenting skills and makes the entire family more mobile and flexible, resulting in a richer, fuller life for all.

Liliane

An illogical reason, however, for taking an infant or toddler to Walt Disney World is that you think Walt Disney World is the perfect vacation destination for babies. It's not, so think again if you are contemplating Walt Disney World primarily for your child's enjoyment. For starters, attractions are geared more toward older children and adults. Even designer play areas like Tom Sawyer Island in the Magic Kingdom are developed with older children in mind.

By way of example, one author has a friend who bought a camcorder when his first child was born. He delighted in documenting his son's reaction to various new experiences on video. One memorable night when the baby was about 18 months old, he recorded the baby eating a variety of foods (from whipped cream to dill pickles) that he had never tried before. While some of the taste sensations elicited wild expressions and animated responses from the baby, the exercise was clearly intended for the amusement of Dad, not junior.

That said, let us stress that for the well prepared, taking a toddler to Walt Disney World can be a totally glorious experience. There's truly nothing like watching your child respond to the color, the sound, the festivity, and, most of all, the characters. You'll return home with scrapbooks of photos that you will treasure forever. Your little one won't remember much, but never mind. Your memories will be unforgettable.

Along similar lines, remember when you were little and you got that nifty electric train for Christmas, the one Dad wouldn't let you play with? Did you ever wonder who that train was really for? Ask yourself the same question about your vacation to Walt Disney World. Whose dream are you trying to make come true: yours or your child's?

If you elect to take your infant or toddler to Walt Disney World, rest assured that their needs have been anticipated. The major theme parks have centralized facilities for infant and toddler care. Everything necessary for changing diapers, preparing formula, and warming bottles and food is available. Dads in charge of little ones are welcome at the centers and can use most services offered. In addition, men's rooms in the major theme parks have changing tables.

Baby supplies—including disposable diapers, formula, and baby food—are for sale, and there are rockers and special chairs for nursing mothers.

Liliane

Infants and toddlers are allowed to experience any attraction that doesn't have minimum height or age restrictions. A Minneapolis mom suggests using a baby sling:

> *We used a baby sling on our trip and thought it was great when standing in the lines—much better than a stroller, which you have to park before getting in line (and navigate through crowds). My baby was still nursing when we went to Walt Disney World. The only really great place I found to nurse in the Magic Kingdom was a hidden bench in the shade in Adventureland in between the freezee stand (next to Tiki Birds) and the small shops. It is impractical to go to the baby station every time, so a nursing mom better be comfortable about nursing in very public situations.*

Two points in our reader's comment warrant elaboration. First, the rental strollers at all of the major theme parks are designed for toddlers and children up to 3 and 4 years old but are definitely not for infants. If you bring pillows and padding, the rental strollers can be made to work. You can bring your own stroller, but unless it's collapsible, you will not be able to take it on Disney trams, buses, or boats.

Even if you opt for a stroller (your own or a rental), we nevertheless recommend that you also bring a baby sling or baby/child backpack. Simply put, there will be many times in the theme parks when you will have to park the stroller and carry your child. As an aside, if you haven't checked out baby slings and packs lately, you'll be amazed by some of the technological advances made in these products.

The second point that needs addressing is our reader's perception that there are not many good places in the theme parks for breastfeeding unless you are accustomed to nursing in public. Many nursing moms recommend breast-feeding during a dark Disney theater

Liliane

In addition to providing an alternative to carrying your child, a stroller serves as a handy cart for diaper bags, water bottles, and other items you deem necessary.

presentation. This only works, however, if the presentation is long enough for the baby to finish nursing. *The Hall of Presidents* at the Magic Kingdom and *The American Adventure* at Epcot will afford you about 23 and 29 minutes, respectively.

Many Disney shows run back to back with only a minute or two in between to change the audience. If you want to breast-feed and require more time than the length of the show, tell the cast member on entering that you want to breast-feed and ask if you can remain in the theater and watch a second showing while your baby finishes. Also keep in mind that many shows may have special effects or loud soundtracks that may make children even as old as 7 uncomfortable.

If you can adjust to nursing in more public places with your breast and the baby's head covered with a shawl or some such, nursing will not be a problem at all. Even on the most crowded days, you can always find a back corner of a restaurant or a comparatively secluded park bench or garden spot to nurse. Finally, the Baby Care Centers, with their private nursing rooms, are centrally located in all of the parks except the Studios.

Walt Disney World for 4-, 5-, and 6-Year-Olds

Four-, five-, and six-year-olds vary immensely in their capacity to comprehend and enjoy Walt Disney World. With this age group, the go/no-go decision is a judgment call. If your child is sturdy, easygoing, fairly adventuresome, and demonstrates a high degree of independence, the trip will probably work. On the other hand, if your child tires easily, is temperamental, or is a bit timid or reticent in embracing new experiences, you're much better off waiting a few years. Whereas the travel and sensory-overload problems of infants and toddlers can be addressed and (usually) remedied on the go, discontented 4- to 6-year-olds have the ability to stop a family dead in its tracks, as this mother of three from Cape May, New Jersey, attests:

> My 5-year-old was scared pretty bad on [the] Snow White [ride] our first day at Disney World. From then on, for the rest of the trip, we had to coax and reassure her before each and every ride before she would go. It was like pulling teeth.

If you have a tiring, clinging, and/or difficult 4- to 6-year-old who, for whatever circumstances, will be part of your group, you can sidestep or diminish potential problems with a bit of pretrip preparation. Even if your preschooler is plucky and game, the same prep measures (described later in this section) will enhance his or her experience and make life easier for the rest of the family.

Parents who understand that a visit with 3- to 6-year-old children is going to be more about the cumulative experience than it is about seeing it all will have a blast and wonderful memories of their children's amazement.

The Ideal Age

Although our readers report both successful trips as well as disasters with children of all ages, the consensus ideal children's ages for family compatibility and togetherness at Walt Disney World are 8–12 years. This age group is old enough, tall enough, and sufficiently stalwart to experience, understand, and appreciate practically all Disney attractions. Moreover, they are developed to the extent that they can get around the parks on their own steam without being carried or collapsing. Best of all, they are still young enough to enjoy being with mom and dad. From our experience, ages 10–12 are better than 8 and 9, though what you gain in maturity is at the cost of that irrepressible, wide-eyed wonder so prevalent in the 8- and 9-year-olds.

Walt Disney World for Teens

Teens love Walt Disney World, and for parents of teens the World is a nearly perfect, albeit expensive, vacation choice. Although your teens might not be as wide-eyed and impressionable as their younger sibs, they are at an age where they can sample, understand, and enjoy practically everything Walt Disney World has to offer.

For parents, Walt Disney World is a vacation destination where you can permit your teens an extraordinary amount of freedom. The entertainment is wholesome, the venues are safe, and the entire complex of hotels, theme parks, restaurants, and shopping centers is accessible via the Walt Disney World transportation system. The transportation system allows you, for example, to enjoy a romantic dinner and an early bedtime while your teens take in the late-night fireworks at the theme parks. After the fireworks, a Disney bus, boat, or monorail will deposit them safely back at the hotel.

Because most adolescents relish freedom, you may have difficulty keeping your teens with the rest of the family. Thus, if one of your objectives is to spend time with your teenage children during your Disney World vacation, you will need to establish some clear-cut guidelines regarding togetherness and separateness before you leave home. Make your teens part of the discussion, and try to meet them halfway in crafting a decision everyone can live with. For your teens, touring on their own at Walt Disney World is tantamount to being independent in a large city. It's intoxicating, to say the least, and can be an excellent learning experience, if not a rite of passage. In any event, we're not suggesting that you just turn them loose. Rather, we are just attempting to sensitize you to the fact that for your teens, there are some transcendent issues involved.

Most teens crave the company of other teens. If you have a solitary teen in your family, do not be surprised if he or she wants to invite a friend on your vacation. If you are invested in sharing intimate, quality time with your solitary teen, the presence of a friend will make this difficult, if not impossible. However, if you turn down the request to bring a friend, be prepared to go the extra mile to be a companion to your teen at Walt Disney World. Expressed differently, if you're a teen, it's not much fun to ride Space Mountain by yourself.

One specific issue that absolutely should be addressed before you leave home is what assistance (if any) you expect from your teen in regard to helping with younger children in the family. Once again, try to carve out a win-win compromise. Consider the case of the mother from Indiana who had a teenage daughter from an earlier marriage and two children under age 10 from a second marriage. After a couple of vacations where she thrust the unwilling teen into the position of being a surrogate parent to her stepsisters, the teen declined henceforth to participate in family vacations.

Many parents have written the *Unofficial Guide* asking if there are unsafe places at Walt Disney World or places where teens simply should not be allowed to go. Although the answer depends more on your family values and the relative maturity of your teens than on Walt Disney World, the basic answer is no. Though it's true that teens (or adults, for that matter) who are looking for trouble can find it anywhere, there is absolutely nothing at Walt Disney World that could be construed as a precipitant or a catalyst.

As a final aside, if you allow your teens some independence and they are getting around on the Walt Disney World transportation system, expect some schedule slippage. There are no posted transportation schedules other than when service begins in the morning and when service terminates at night. Thus, to catch a bus, for example, you just go to a bus station and wait for the next bus to your Disney World destination. If you happen to just miss the bus, you might have to wait 15–45 minutes (more often 15–20 minutes) for the next one. If punctuality is essential, advise your independent teens to arrive at a transportation station an hour before they are expected somewhere in order to allow sufficient time for the commute.

About **INVITING** *Your* **CHILDREN'S FRIENDS**

IF YOUR CHILDREN WANT TO INVITE FRIENDS on your Walt Disney World vacation, give your decision careful thought. There's more involved here than might be apparent. First, consider the logistics of numbers. Is there room in the car? Will you have to leave something at home that you had planned on taking to make room in the trunk for the friend's luggage? Will additional hotel rooms or a larger condo be required? Will the increased number of people in your group make it hard to get a table at a restaurant?

If you determine that you can logistically accommodate one or more friends, the next step is to consider how the inclusion of the friend will affect your group's dynamics. Generally speaking, the presence of a friend will make it harder to really connect with your own children. So if one of your vacation goals is an intimate bonding experience with your children, the addition of friends will probably frustrate your attempts to realize that objective.

If family relationship building is not necessarily a primary objective of your vacation, it's quite possible that the inclusion of a friend will make life easier for you. This is especially true in the case of only children, who may otherwise depend exclusively on you to keep them happy and occupied. Having a friend along can take the pressure off and give you some much-needed breathing room.

If you decide to allow a friend to accompany you, limit the selection to children you know really well and whose parents you also know. Your Walt Disney World vacation is not the time to include "my friend Eddie from school" whom you've never met. Your children's friends who have spent time in your home will have a sense of your parenting style, and you will have a sense of their personality, behavior, and compatibility with your family. Assess the prospective child's potential to fit in well on a long trip. Is he or she polite, personable, fun to be with, and reasonably mature? Does he or she relate well to you and to the other members of your family?

Because a Walt Disney World vacation is not, for most of us, a spur-of-the-moment thing, you should have adequate time to evaluate potential candidate friends. A trip to the mall including a meal in a sit-down restaurant will tell you volumes about the friend. Likewise, inviting the friend to share dinner with the family and then spend the night will provide a lot of relevant information. Ideally this type of evaluation should take place early on in the normal course of family events, before you discuss the possibility of a friend joining you on your vacation. This will allow you to size things up without your child (or the friend) realizing that an evaluation is taking place.

By seizing the initiative, you can guide the outcome. Ann, a Springfield, Ohio, mom, for example, anticipated that her 12-year-old son would ask to take a friend on their vacation. As she pondered the various friends her son might propose, she came up with four names. One, an otherwise sweet child, had a medical condition that Ann felt unqualified to monitor or treat. A second friend was overly aggressive with younger children and was often socially inappropriate for his age. Two other friends, Chuck and Marty, with whom she had had a generally positive experience, were good candidates for the trip. After orchestrating some opportunities to spend time with each of the boys, she made her decision and asked her son, "Would you like to take Marty with us to Disney World?" Her son was delighted, and Ann had diplomatically pre-empted having to turn down friends her son might have proposed.

We recommend that you do the inviting, instead of your child, and that you extend the invitation to the parent (to avoid disappointment, you might want to sound out the friend's parent before broaching the issue with your child). Observing this recommendation will allow you to query the friend's parents concerning food preferences, any medical conditions, how discipline is administered in the friend's family, how the friend's parents feel about the way you administer discipline, and the parents' expectation regarding religious observations while their child is in your care.

Before you extend the invitation, give some serious thought to who pays for what. Make a specific proposal for financing the trip a part of your invitation, for example: "There's room for Marty in the hotel room, and transportation's no problem because we're driving. So we'll just need you to pick up Marty's meals, theme park admissions, and spending money."

A FEW WORDS *for* SINGLE PARENTS

BECAUSE SINGLE PARENTS GENERALLY are also working parents, planning a special getaway with your children can be the best way to spend some quality time together. But remember, the vacation is not just for your child—it's for you too. You might invite a grandparent or a favorite aunt or uncle along; the other adult provides nice company for you, and your child will benefit from the time with family members. You might likewise consider inviting an adult friend.

Though bringing along an adult friend or family member is the best option, the reality is that many single parents don't have friends, grandparents, or favorite aunts or uncles who can make the trip. And while spending time with your child is wonderful, it is very difficult to match the energy level of your child if you are the sole focus of his or her world.

One alternative: Try to meet other single parents at Walt Disney World. It may seem odd, but most of them are in the same boat as you; besides, all you have to do is ask. Another option, albeit expensive, is to take along a trustworthy babysitter (18 or up) to travel with you.

The easiest way to meet other single parents at the World is to hang out at the hotel pool. Make your way there on the day you arrive, after traveling by car or plane and without enough time to blow a full admission ticket at a theme park. In any event, a couple of hours spent poolside is a relaxing way to start your vacation.

If you visit Walt Disney World with another single parent, get adjoining rooms; take turns watching all the kids; and, on at least one night, get a sitter and enjoy an evening out.

Throughout this book we mention the importance of good planning and touring. For a single parent, this is an absolute must. In addition, make sure that you set aside some downtime back at the hotel every day.

Finally, don't try to spend every moment with your children on vacation. Instead, plan some activities for your children with other children. Disney educational programs for children, for example, are worth considering. Then take advantage of your free time to do what you want to do: Read a book, have a massage, take a long walk, or enjoy a catnap.

While pricey, one of the best ways for single parents to relax is to add a three- or four-night cruise to their Disney stay. Onboard activities will keep your child occupied and give you time to relax.

"HE WHO HESITATES IS LAUNCHED!" *Tips and Warnings for Grandparents*

SENIORS OFTEN GET INTO PREDICAMENTS caused by touring with grandchildren. Run ragged and pressured to endure a blistering pace, many seniors just concentrate on surviving Walt Disney World rather than enjoying it. The theme parks have as much to offer older visitors as they do children, and seniors must either set the pace or dispatch the young folks to tour on their own.

An older reader from Alabaster, Alabama, writes:

The main thing I want to say is that being a senior is not for wussies. At Disney World particularly, it requires courage and pluck. Things that used to be easy take a lot of effort, and sometimes your brain has to wait for your body to catch up. Half the time, your grandchildren treat you like a crumbling ruin and then turn around and trick you into getting on a roller coaster in the dark. What you need to tell seniors is that they have to be alert and not trust anyone. Not their children or even the Disney people, and especially not their grandchildren. When your grandchildren want you to go on a ride, don't follow along blindly like a lamb to the slaughter. Make sure you know what the ride is all about. Stand your ground and do not waffle. He who hesitates is launched!

If you don't get to see much of your grandchildren, you might think that Walt Disney World is the perfect place for a little bonding and togetherness. Wrong! Walt Disney World can potentially send children into system overload and can precipitate behaviors that pose a challenge even to adoring parents, nevermind grandparents. You don't take your grandchildren straight to Disney World for the same reason you don't buy your 16-year-old son a Ferrari: Handling it safely and well requires some experience.

Begin by spending time with your grandchildren in an environment that you can control. Have them over one at a time for dinner and to spend the night. Check out how they respond to your oversight and discipline. Most of all, zero in on whether you are compatible, enjoy each other's company, and have fun together. Determine that you can set limits and that they will accept those limits. When you reach this stage, you can contemplate some outings to the zoo, the movies, the mall, or the state fair. Gauge how demanding your grandchildren are when you are out of the house. Eat a meal or two in a full-service restaurant to get a sense of their social skills and their ability to behave appropriately. Don't expect perfection, and be prepared to modify your behavior a little too. As a senior friend of mine told her husband (none too decorously), "You can't see Walt Disney World sitting on a stick."

If you have a good relationship with your grandchildren and have had a positive one-on-one experience taking care of them, you might consider a trip to Walt Disney World. If you do, we have two recommendations. First, visit Walt Disney World without them to get an idea of what you're getting into. A scouting trip will also provide you with an opportunity to enjoy some of the attractions that won't be on the itinerary when you return with the grandkids. Second, if you are considering a trip of a week's duration, you might think about buying a Disney package that combines four days at Walt Disney World with a three-day cruise. In addition to being a memorable experience for your grandchildren, the cruise provides plenty of structure for children of almost every age, thus allowing you to be with them but also to have some time off. Call the Disney Cruise Line at ☎ 800-951-3532 or visit **disneycruise.com**.

A Dozen Tips for Grandparents

1. It's best to take one grandchild at a time, two at the most. Cousins can be better than siblings because they don't fight as much. To preclude sibling jealousy, try connecting the trip to a child's milestone, such as finishing the sixth grade.
2. Let your grandchildren help plan the vacation, and keep the first one short. Be flexible, and don't overplan.
3. Discuss mealtimes and bedtime. Fortunately, many grandparents are on an early dinner schedule, which works nicely with younger children. Also, if you want to plan a special evening out, be sure to make the reservation ahead of time.
4. Gear plans to your grandchildren's age levels, because if they're not happy, you won't be happy.
5. Create an itinerary that offers some supervised activities for children in case you need a rest.
6. If you're traveling by car, this is the one time we highly recommend headphones. Kids' musical tastes are vastly different from most grandparents'. It's simply more enjoyable when everyone can listen to his or her own preferred style of music, at least for some portion of the trip.
7. Take along a night-light.

8. Carry a notarized statement from parents for permission for medical care in case of an emergency. Also be sure you have insurance information and copies of any prescriptions for medicines the kids may be on. Ditto for eyeglass prescriptions.

9. Tell your grandchildren about any medical problems you may have so they can be prepared if there's an emergency.

10. Many attractions and hotels offer discounts for seniors, so be sure you check ahead of time for bargains.

11. Plan your evening meal early to avoid long waits. And make advance reservations if you're dining in a popular spot, even if it's early. Take some crayons and paper to keep kids occupied.

12. If planning a family-friendly trip seems overwhelming, try Grandtravel, a tour operator/travel agent aimed at kids and their grandparents (call ☎ 800-247-7651 or visit **grandtrvl.com**).

ORDER *and* DISCIPLINE *on the* ROAD

OK, OK, WIPE THAT SMIRK OFF YOUR FACE. Order and discipline on the road may seem like an oxymoron to you, but you won't be hooting when your 5-year-old launches a screaming stem-winder in the middle of Fantasyland. Your willingness to give this subject serious consideration before you leave home may well be the most important element of your pretrip preparation.

Discipline and maintaining order are more difficult when traveling because everyone is, as a Boston mom put it, "in and out" (in strange surroundings and out of the normal routine). For children, it's hard to contain excitement and anticipation that pop to the surface in the form of fidgety hyperactivity, nervous energy, and sometimes, acting out. Confinement in a car, plane, or hotel room only exacerbates the situation, and kids are often louder than normal, more aggressive with siblings, and much more inclined to push the envelope of parental patience and control. Once in the theme parks, it doesn't get much better. There's more elbow room, but there's also overstimulation, crowds, heat, and miles of walking. All this coupled with marginal or inadequate rest can lead to meltdown in the most harmonious of families.

The following discussion was developed by leading child psychologist Dr. Karen Turnbow, who has contributed to the *Unofficial Guides* for years and who has spent many days at Walt Disney World conducting research and observing families.

Sound parenting and standards of discipline practiced at home, applied consistently, will suffice to handle most situations on vacation. Still, it's instructive to study the hand you are dealt when traveling. For starters, aside from being jazzed and ablaze with adrenaline, your kids may believe that rules followed at home are somehow suspended when traveling. Parents reinforce this misguided intuition by being inordinately lenient in the interest of maintaining peace in the family. While some of your home protocols (cleaning your plate, going to bed at a set time, and such) might be relaxed to good effect on vacation, differing from your normal approach to discipline can precipitate major misunderstanding and possibly disaster.

Children, not unexpectedly, are likely to believe that a vacation (especially a vacation to Walt Disney World) is expressly for them. This reinforces their focus on their own needs and largely erases any consideration of yours. Such a mind-set dramatically increases their sense of hurt and disappointment when you correct them or deny them something they want. An incident that would hardly elicit a pouty lip at home could well escalate to tears or defiance when traveling.

Discuss your vacation needs with your children and explore their wants and expectations as well before you depart on your trip.

Liliane

The stakes are high for everyone on a vacation; for you because of the cost in time and dollars, but also because your vacation represents a rare opportunity for rejuvenation and renewal. The stakes are high for your children too. Children tend to romanticize travel, building anticipation to an almost unbearable level. Discussing the trip in advance can ground expectations to a certain extent, but a child's imagination will, in the end, trump reality every time. The good news is that you can take advantage of your children's emotional state to establish pre-agreed rules and conditions for their conduct while on vacation. Because your children want what's being offered sooooo badly, they will be unusually accepting and conscientious regarding whatever rules are agreed upon.

According to Dr. Turnbow, successful response to (or avoidance of) behavioral problems on the road begins with a clear-cut disciplinary policy at home. Both at home and on vacation, the approach should be the same and should be based on the following key concepts:

1. LET EXPECTATIONS BE KNOWN. Discuss what you expect from your children but don't try to cover every imaginable situation. Cover expectations in regard to compliance with parental directives, treatment of siblings, resolution of disputes, schedule (including wake-up and bedtimes), courtesy and manners, staying together, and who pays for what.

2. EXPLAIN THE CONSEQUENCES OF NONCOMPLIANCE. Detail very clearly and firmly the consequences of unmet expectations. This should be very straightforward and unambiguous. If you do X (or don't do X), this is what will happen.

3. WARN YOUR KIDS. You're dealing with excited, expectant children, not machines, so it's important to issue a warning before meting out discipline. It's critical to understand that we're talking about one unequivocal warning rather than multiple warnings or nagging. These undermine your credibility and make your expectations appear relative or less than serious. Multiple warnings or nagging also effectively pass control of the situation from you to your child (who may continue to act out as an attention-getting strategy).

4. FOLLOW THROUGH. If you say that you're going to do something, do it. Period. Children must understand that you are absolutely serious and committed.

5. BE CONSISTENT. Inconsistency makes discipline a random event in the eyes of your children. Random discipline encourages random behavior, which translates to a nearly total loss of parental control. Long-term, both at home and on the road, your response to a given situation or transgression must be perfectly predictable. Structure and repetition, essential for a child to learn, cannot be achieved in the absence of consistency.

Although the above are the five biggies, there are several corollary concepts and techniques that are worthy of consideration.

First, understand that whining, tantrums, defiance, sibling friction, and even holding the group up are ways in which children communicate with parents. Frequently the object or precipitant of a situation has little or no relation to the unacceptable behavior. A fit may on the surface appear to be about the ice cream you refused to buy little Robby, but there's almost always something deeper, a subtext that is closer to the truth (this is the reason why ill behavior often persists after you give in to a child's demands). As often as not the real cause is a need for attention. This need is so powerful in some children that they will subject themselves to certain punishment and parental displeasure to garner the attention they crave.

To get at the root cause of the behavior in question requires both active listening and empowering your child with a "feeling vocabulary." Active listening is a concept that's been around a long time. It involves being alert not only to what a child says, but also to the context in which it is said, to the language used and possible subtext, to the child's emotional state and body language, and even to what's not said. Sounds complicated, but it's basically being attentive to the larger picture, and more to the point, being aware that there is a larger picture.

Helping your child to develop a feeling vocabulary consists of teaching your child to use words to describe what's going on. The idea is to teach the child to articulate what's really troubling him, to be able to identify and express emotions and mood states in language. Of course learning to express feelings is a lifelong experience, but it's much less dependent on innate sensitivity than being provided the tools for expression and being encouraged to use them.

It all begins with convincing your child that you're willing to listen attentively and take what he's saying seriously. Listening to your child, you help him transcend the topical by reframing the conversation to address the underlying emotional state(s). That his brother hit him may have precipitated the mood, but the act is topical and of secondary importance. What you want is for your child to be able to communicate how that makes him feel and to get in touch with those emotions. When you reduce an incident (hitting) to the emotions triggered (anger, hurt, rejection, and so on), you have the foundation for helping him to develop constructive coping strategies. Not only are being in touch with one's feelings and developing constructive coping strategies essential to emotional well-being, but they also beneficially affect behavior. A child who can tell his mother why he is distressed is a child who has discovered a coping strategy far more effective (not to mention easier for all concerned) than a tantrum.

Children are almost never too young to begin learning a feeling vocabulary. And helping your child to be in touch with, and try to communicate, his emotions will stimulate you to focus on your feelings and mood states in a similar way.

SIX MORE TIPS

UNTIL YOU GET THE ACTIVE LISTENING and feeling vocabulary going, be careful not to become part of the problem. There's a whole laundry list of adult responses to bad behavior that only make things worse. Hitting, swatting, yelling, name calling, insulting, belittling, using sarcasm, pleading, nagging, and inducing guilt (as in: "We've spent thousands of dollars to bring you to Disney World and now you're spoiling the trip for everyone") figure prominently on the list.

Responding to a child appropriately in a disciplinary situation requires thought and preparation. Following are key things to keep in mind and techniques to try when your world blows up while waiting in line for Dumbo.

1. BE THE ADULT. It's well understood that children can punch their parents' buttons faster and more lethally than just about anyone or anything else. They've got your number, know precisely how to elicit a response, and are not reluctant to go for the jugular. Fortunately (or unfortunately) you're the adult, and to deal with a situation effectively, you must act like one. If your kids get you ranting and caterwauling, you effectively abdicate your adult status. Worse, you suggest by way of example that being out of control is an acceptable expression of hurt or anger. No matter what happens, repeat the mantra, "I am the adult in this relationship."

2. FREEZE THE ACTION. Being the adult and maintaining control almost always translates to freezing the action, to borrow a sports term. Instead of a knee-jerk response (at a maturity level closer to your child's than yours), freeze the action by disengaging. Wherever you are or whatever the family is doing, stop in place and concentrate on one thing and one thing only: getting all involved to calm down. Practically speaking, this usually means initiating a time-out. It's essential that you take this action immediately. Grabbing your child by the arm or collar and dragging him toward the car or hotel room only escalates the turmoil by prolonging the confrontation and by adding a coercive physical dimension to an already volatile emotional event. If, for the sake of people around you (as when a toddler throws a tantrum in church), it's essential to retreat to a more private place, choose the first place available. Firmly sit the child down and refrain from talking to him until you've both cooled off. This might take a little time, but the investment is worthwhile. Truncating the process is like trying to get on your feet too soon after surgery.

3. ISOLATE THE CHILD. You'll be able to deal with the situation more effectively and expeditiously if the child is isolated with one parent. Dispatch the uninvolved members of your party for a Coke break or have them go on with the activity or itinerary without you (if possible) and arrange to rendezvous later at an agreed time and place. In addition to letting the others get on with their day, isolating the offending child with one parent relieves him of the pressure of being the group's focus of attention and object of anger. Equally important, isolation frees you from the scrutiny and expectations of the others in regard to how to handle the situation.

4. REVIEW THE SITUATION WITH THE CHILD. If, as discussed above, you've made your expectations clear, stated the consequences of failing those expectations, and have administered a warning, review the situation with the child and follow through with the discipline warranted. If, as often occurs, things are not so black and white, encourage the child to communicate his feelings. Try to uncover what occasioned the acting out. Lecturing and accusatory language don't work well here, nor do threats. Dr. Turnbow suggests that a better approach (after the child is calm) is to ask, "What can we do to make this a better day for you?"

5. FREQUENT TANTRUMS OR ACTING OUT. The preceding four points relate to dealing with an incident as opposed to a chronic condition. If a child frequently acts out or throws tantrums, you'll need to employ a somewhat different strategy.

Tantrums are cyclical events evolved from learned behavior. A child learns that he can get your undivided attention by acting out. When you respond, whether by scolding, admonishing, threatening, or negotiating, your response further draws you into the cycle and prolongs the behavior. When you accede to the child's demands, you reinforce the effectiveness of the tantrum and raise the cost of capitulation next time around. When a child thus succeeds in monopolizing your attention, he effectively becomes the person in charge.

To break this cycle, you must disengage from the child. The object is to demonstrate that the cause and effect relationship (that is, tantrum elicits parental attention) is no longer operative. This can be accomplished by refusing to interact with the child as long as the untoward behavior continues. Tell the child that you're unwilling to discuss his problem until he calms down. You can ignore the behavior, remove yourself from the child's presence (or visa versa), or isolate the child with a time-out. The important thing is to disengage quickly and decisively with no discussion or negotiation.

Most children don't pick the family vacation as the time to start throwing tantrums. The behavior will be evident before you leave home, and home is the best place to deal with it. Be forewarned, however, that bad habits die hard, and a child accustomed to getting attention by throwing tantrums will not simply give up after a single instance of disengagement. More likely, the child will at first escalate the intensity and length of his tantrums. By your consistent refusal over several weeks (or even months) to respond to his behavior, however, he will finally adjust to the new paradigm.

Liliane

Tantrums are about getting attention. Giving your child attention when things are on an even keel often preempts acting out.

Children are cunning as well as observant. Many understand that a tantrum in public is embarrassing to you and that you're more likely to cave in than you would at home. Once again, consistency is the key, along with a bit of anticipation. When traveling, it's not necessary to retreat to the privacy of a hotel room to isolate your child. You can carve out space for time-out almost anywhere: on a theme park bench, in a park, in your car, in a restroom, even on a sidewalk. You can often spot the warning signs of an impending tantrum and head it off by talking to the child before he reaches an explosive emotional pitch.

6. SALVAGE OPERATIONS. Children are full of surprises, and sometimes the surprises are not good. If your sweet child manages to make a mistake of mammoth proportions, what do you do? This happened to an Ohio couple, resulting in the offending kid pretty much being grounded for life. Fortunately there were no injuries or lives lost, but the parents had to determine what to do for the remainder of the vacation. For starters, they split the group. One parent escorted the offending child back to the hotel where he was effectively confined to his guest room for the duration. That evening, the parents arranged for in-room sitters for the rest of the stay. Expensive? You bet, but better than watching your whole vacation go down the tubes.

A family at Walt Disney World's Magic Kingdom theme park had a similar experience, although the offense was of a more modest order of magnitude. Because it was their last day of vacation, they elected to place the child in time-out, in the theme park, for the rest of the day. One parent monitored the culprit while the other parent and the siblings enjoyed the attractions. At agreed times the parents would switch places. Once again, not ideal, but preferable to stopping the vacation.

PART TWO

GETTING *Your* ACT TOGETHER

Visiting Walt Disney World is a bit like childbirth—you never really believe what people tell you, but once you have been through it yourself, you know exactly what they were saying!

—Hilary Wolfe, a mother and *Unofficial Guide* reader from Swansea, United Kingdom

GATHERING INFORMATION

IN ADDITION TO THIS GUIDE, our first recommendation is to visit our Web site, **touringplans.com,** which has essential tools for planning your trip and saving you time and money.

One of the most popular parts of **touringplans.com** is our crowd calendar, which shows crowd projections for each Disney and Universal theme park for every day of the year. Look up the dates of your visit, and the calendar will not only show the projected wait times for each day but will also indicate which theme park will be the least crowded.

We've also written more than 140 Disney-theme-park touring plans in addition to those in this book, featuring variations for holidays, seniors, Extra Magic Hours, and those who like to sleep in. If our plans aren't quite what you're looking for, **touringplans.com** lets you create your own, either from scratch or by using one of ours as a template (we'll automatically include restaurant information, hidden Mickeys, attraction trivia, park hours, and weather forecasts), and share them with family and friends. As of this writing, around 40,000 reader-contributed plans are available free of charge.

To help you select the best resort for your family, we've also provided thousands of photos and dozens of online videos covering every inch of every Disney resort, plus many off-site accommodations.

Our most popular new Web feature is Lines, a mobile application providing continuous real-time updates on wait times at the Walt Disney World, Universal, and Disneyland parks. Using a combination of our in-park researchers and updates sent in by readers, this new feature allows you to see all current wait and Fastpass-distribution times at every attraction in every park, as well as our estimated wait times for these attractions for the rest of that day and the next. If you have a Web-enabled cell phone, you'll be able to see instantly where the shortest lines are at any time of day. Apps are available via iTunes App Store (search for "touring plans") and Android App Store. Owners of other phones can use the Web-based version at **m.touringplans.com.**

And as long as you've got that smart phone handy while visiting the World, we and your fellow *Unofficial Guide* readers would love it if you could report on the wait times you see while you're there. Go to **m.touringplans.com,** log in to your user account, and click the button labeled "+Time" in the upper right corner to help everyone out.

A big money-saving feature of the Web site is our Ticket Calculator, which tells you the least-expensive combination of tickets to buy (and where) to see everything you want in the theme parks and water parks.

In 2011 **touringplans.com** will provide computer-optimized touring plans for every day of your Walt Disney World visit. Simply select the attractions you wish to experience, the restaurants at which you plan to dine, and any breaks you plan to take. Our Web site will determine the best order to do these activities to minimize your waits in line and avoid backtracking through the parks. If you're in a park, we can provide an updated touring plan via your phone using the most current wait times available to adjust the order of the steps, based on what's actually happening in the park that day.

 Request information as far in advance as possible and allow six weeks for delivery. Make a checklist of information you request, and follow up if you haven't received your materials within six weeks.

Much of our Web content—including the online trip planner, resort photos and videos, and the Ticket Calculator—is completely free for anyone to use. Access to part of the site, most notably the crowd calendar, additional touring plans, and in-park wait times, requires a small subscription fee (current-book owners get 50% off). This nominal charge helps keep us online and costs less than a sandwich at Flame Tree Barbecue in the Animal Kingdom. Plus, **touringplans.com** offers a 45-day money-back guarantee—something we don't think Flame Tree can match.

Next, we recommend that you obtain the following:

1. **THE WALT DISNEY TRAVEL COMPANY FLORIDA VACATIONS BROCHURE AND DVD** These cover Walt Disney World in its entirety, list rates for all Disney resort hotels and campgrounds, and describe Disney World package vacations. They're available from most travel agents by calling the Walt Disney Travel Company at ☎ 407-828-8101 or 407-934-7639 or by visiting **disneyworld.com.** Be prepared to hold. When you get a representative, ask for the DVD vacation planner.

2. **THE DISNEY CRUISE LINE BROCHURE AND DVD** This brochure provides details on vacation packages that combine a cruise on the Disney Cruise Line

with a stay at Disney World. Disney Cruise Line also offers a free DVD that tells all you need to know about Disney cruises and then some. To get a copy, call ☎ 800-951-3532 or order at **disneycruise.com.**

3. **ORLANDO MAGICARD** If you're considering lodging outside Disney World or if you think you might patronize out-of-the-World attractions and restaurants, obtain an Orlando Magicard, a Vacation Planner, and the *Orlando Official Vacation Guide* (all free) from the Orlando Visitors Center. The Magicard entitles you to discounts for hotels, restaurants, ground transportation, shopping malls, dinner theaters, and non-Disney theme parks and attractions. The Orlando Magicard can be downloaded for printing at **orlandoinfo.com/magicard.** To order the accommodations guide, call ☎ 800-643-9492. For more information and materials, call ☎ 407-363-5872 weekdays during business hours or 9 a.m.–3 p.m. on weekends, or go to **visitorlando.com.**

4. **FLORIDA TRAVELER DISCOUNT GUIDE** Another good source of discounts on lodging, restaurants, and attractions statewide is *Florida RoomSaver*, published by Trader Publishing Company. The guide is free, but you pay $3 for handling ($5 if shipped to Canada). Call ☎ 386-418-6800 or 800-332-3948, Monday through Friday, 8 a.m.–5 p.m. Eastern Time, or visit **travelerdiscountguide.com** for more information. Similar guides to other states are available at the same number. You can also print hotel coupons and reserve rooms free at the **roomsaver.com** Web site.

5. **"CHOOSE KISSIMMEE" GUIDE** This full-color visitors guide is one of the most complete resources available and is of particular interest to those who intend to lodge outside of Disney World, featuring ads for hotels, rental houses, time-shares, and condominiums, as well as a directory of attractions, restaurants, special events, and other useful info. For a copy, call the Kissimmee Convention and Visitors Bureau at ☎ 800-327-9159 or 407-944-2400, or view it online at **floridakiss.com.**

6. **GUIDEBOOK FOR GUESTS WITH DISABILITIES** Pick one up at Guest Relations at any of the parks. Additional information is also available online at **disneyworld.disney.go.com/plain-text.**

7. **QUEENS IN THE KINGDOM: THE ULTIMATE GAY AND LESBIAN GUIDE TO THE DISNEY THEME PARKS** ($17.95) by Jeffrey Epstein and Eddie Shapiro.

PASSPORTER'S GUIDE

A SUPER RESOURCE FOR ANYONE WITH SPECIAL NEEDS is *Pass-Porter's Open Mouse for Walt Disney World and the Disney Cruise Line* by Deb Wills and Debra Martin Koma. The book covers everything from ADHD to asthma and is available from PassPorter Travel Press at ☎ 877-929-3273 or **passporter.com.**

WALT DISNEY WORLD ON THE WEB

SEARCHING THE INTERNET for Disney information is like navigating an immense maze for a very small piece of cheese: There's a lot of information available, but you may have to wade through list after list until you find the Internet addresses you want and need.

Many individuals maintain elaborate Disney-related Web sites and chat groups that can provide both correct and incorrect information, depending on who's chatting.

Recommended Web Sites

Unofficial Guide coauthor Len Testa has combed the Web looking for the best Disney sites. See his picks below.

BEST OFFICIAL THEME-PARK SITE We're not sure if it's some sort of make-work program for underemployed Web designers, but the official **Walt Disney World Web site (disneyworld.com** or **disneyworld. disney.go.com)** recently underwent its third major overhaul in four years. While it still has room for improvement, it gets our nod as the best official park Web site, over the official sites for Universal Studios (**universalorlando.com**) and SeaWorld (**seaworld.com**). On the minus side, however, the site remains bogged down by multimedia gimmickry that causes pages to load slower than Space Mountain's standby line in July. (Maybe they're just conditioning you?)

BEST GENERAL UNOFFICIAL WALT DISNEY WORLD WEB SITE Besides **touringplans.com,** Deb Wills's **allears.net** is the Web site we recommend to friends who are interested in making a trip to Disney World. It contains information on virtually every hotel, restaurant, and activity in the World. Want to know what a room at a Disney resort looks like before you book one? This site has photos—sometimes for each floor of a resort. The site is updated several times per week and includes information for guests with special needs, menus from Disney restaurants, ticketing information, maps, and such.

BEST MONEY-SAVING SITE Mary Waring's **mousesavers.com** is the kind of site for which the Web was invented. It keeps an updated list of discounts and reservation codes for use at Disney resorts. The codes are separated into categories such as "For the general public" and "For residents of certain states." Anyone who calls Disney's central reservation office (☎ 407-W-DISNEY) can use a current code and get the discounted rate. Savings can be considerable—up to 40% in many cases. The site also displays discounts for AAA members and Disney Annual Pass holders, making it easy to determine if those options make sense for your trip. Two often-overlooked site features are the discount codes for rental cars and non-Disney hotels in the area.

BEST WALT DISNEY WORLD PREVIEW SITE If you want to prepare your children for the attractions, or if you just want to see what a particular attraction is like, visit **YouTube (youtube.com)**. Enter the name of the desired attraction in the search bar at the top of the page, and several videos should come up. Videos of indoor ("dark") rides are usually inferior to those of outdoor rides due to poor lighting, but even the videos of indoor rides generally provide a good sense of what the attraction is about.

SOCIAL NETWORK SITES Social network sites such as Facebook and Twitter are popular forums for Disney fans to gather online and share comments, tips, and photos. Following fellow Disney fans as they share their experiences while they're in the parks can make you feel as if you're there, even if you're stuck in a cubicle at work.

BEST DISNEY DISCUSSION BOARDS   The best online discussions of all things Disney can be found at **disboards.com.** With tens of thousands of members and millions of posts, these discussion boards are the most active and popular on the Web. For boards that feel more familiar than your neighborhood bar, try **disneyecho.emuck.com.** Disney visitors from the United Kingdom can say "cheerio" to one another whilst online at **thedibb. co.uk** or at **wdisneyw.com/forums,** where tips on transatlantic-airfare discounts, visa requirements, American customs, and more can be found.

MOBILE MAGIC   Apps are the latest buzz, and Disney certainly knows when to seize an opportunity. Disney, together with Verizon, developed the Mobile Magic App, which for $9.99 is all yours for 180 days. Simply text MAGIC to 2777 on your Verizon phone, and the app will let you keep track of where to meet your kids' favorite characters. The app also lets you check the wait times and Fastpass return times for the park you're in. Finding a restaurant is part of the deal, and Disney will gladly help you plan the rest of your trip. For more information, go to **disneyparks. com/mobilemagic.**

Also check out the $4.99 Undercover Tourist app for the iPhone. The popular app gives you ride wait times, opening hours, and parade times, as well as restaurant and events information. The Traffic Light System helps you find the least-crowded attractions and parks. Interactive maps include Locate Me and Find a Friend features. The GPS tool can even help you find your car. For more information, visit **undercovertourist.com/ united-states/florida/orlando/attractions/avoid-the-lines.html.**

GOING HIGH-TECH WITH LILIANE

Podcasts

If you just can't make it through the year without the Mouse, don't despair. Sounds, images, and news from the World are available in abundance online. Here are some of our favorites.

WDW TODAY   *Unofficial Guide* Research Director Len Testa cohosts three Podcasts a week (Monday, Wednesday, and Friday) on all things Disney. Subscriptions are available free through iTunes. These programs consistently rank among the top 10 iTunes travel Podcasts, drawing 8,000–10,000 listeners per show. Visit **wdwtoday.com.**

PASSPORTER MOMS PODCAST   Two moms, Jennifer and Sara, share tips and chat with friends and guests about Walt Disney World, Disneyland, Disney Cruise Line, and general travel. So get some coffee and listen to some of the best advice out there at **passporter. com/podcast/home.php.**

WINDOW TO THE MAGIC   Paul Barrie, your smooth-voiced host, brings you all the magic with his weekly Podcast. The show includes a game called "Where in the Park?" and delivers sounds, pictures, prizes, and more. Check it out at **windowtothemagic.com/podcast.html.**

SOUNDS OF DISNEY Every other Sunday you can join Jeff Davis, also known as The Sorcerer, as he delights his audience with music, news, and Disney songs right from the parks. In addition to the Podcast, Davis's Web site, **srsounds.com,** provides music, videos, pictures, and a message board.

Blogs

Our all-time favorite blogger is Jim Hill, who has been writing about Disney for years at **jimhillmedia.com.** Although Jim undoubtedly loves the Mouse, he tempers his enthusiasm with the right dose of criticism and is perfectly attuned to what's going on behind the scenes.

Another fun place for the latest rumors is **thedisneyblog.com.** We especially like how easy it is to navigate the different categories. From A to Z, it's the way to go! The site is really on top of things, so much so that the *Orlando Sentinel* monitors it regularly and is even known to report on the posts.

BEST SITE FOR BREAKING NEWS AND RUMORS We try to check **wdwmagic. com** every few days for the latest news and rumors about Disney World. The site is popular with Disney fans and park cast members, who often provide insider information on upcoming attractions and developments. It also features pages dedicated to major rides, parades, and shows in each park, including audio and video clips. User forums allow you to read and post messages.

BEST TRIVIA SITES Louis Mongello's excellent *The Walt Disney World Trivia Book* has an equally good online companion **disney worldtrivia.com**—with message boards, Disney theme park news, and more. Lou hosts live Internet chats at his Web site, usually on Tuesdays, and also hosts the WDW Radio Show Podcast. Check it out on iTunes and at **wdwradio.com.**

At long last, fans of Steven Barrett's *Hidden Mickeys Guide* now have an online destination where they can get updates on the latest tri-circle sightings at **hiddenmickeysguide.com.**

BEST ONLINE TOUR In early 2008, Disney teamed up with Google to present a three-day virtual walk-through of the Orlando theme parks and resorts via Google Earth. While you can't yet go inside the attractions, you do get an unparalleled simulation of the park experience. Visit **disneyworld.com/3dparks** and hope for the day they're able to pipe the smell of the Main Street Bakery to your PC.

BEST INTERNET RADIO STATION We thought our 200-hour collection of theme-park digital audio was complete until we found **mouse worldradio.com.** Several different radio stations are available (some free, others for a small fee), playing everything from attraction ride scores and hotel background music to old sound clips from

Disney-resort TV ads. What makes Mouse World Radio special is that the tracks match what the Disney parks are playing at the time of day you're listening. So every morning at 8 a.m., you'll hear essentially the same music that's currently playing at the Magic Kingdom before it opens.

BEST OFFICIAL MOM'S SITE Who knew? Walt Disney World has a Mom's Panel composed of 26 moms and four red herrings—er, four dads—all chosen from among 10,000-plus applicants. The panelists have a Web site, **disneyworldmoms.com,** where they offer tips, discuss how to plan a Disney World vacation, and answer questions about how those guys got into the henhouse. The moms are unpaid and are free to speak their minds. One mom actually went from fan to cast member when Disney recruited her to head the panel. And the Mom's Panel is now on Facebook. Become a fan at **facebook.com/disney worldmoms.**

There are hundreds of other Disney sites, as well as sites that rate and contrast thrill rides in theme parks in the United States and all over the world. Information about Disney World is also available at public libraries, travel agencies, and AAA.

IMPORTANT WALT DISNEY WORLD TELEPHONE NUMBERS

WHEN YOU CALL THE MAIN INFORMATION NUMBER, you'll be offered a menu of options for recorded information on operating hours, recreation areas, shopping, entertainment, tickets, reservations, and driving directions. If you have a question not covered by recorded information, press 8 at any time to speak to a representative. See page 44 for a list.

 # ALLOCATING TIME

YOU SHOULD ALLOCATE SIX DAYS for a whirlwind tour (seven to ten days if you're old-fashioned and insist on a little relaxation during your vacation). If you don't have six or more days, be prepared to make some hard choices.

A seemingly obvious point lost on many families is that Walt Disney World is not going anywhere. There's no danger that it will be packed up and shipped to Iceland anytime soon. This means that you can come back if you don't see everything this year. Disney has planned it this way, of course, but that doesn't matter. It's infinitely more sane to resign yourself to the reality that seeing everything during one visit is impossible. We recommend, therefore, that you approach Walt Disney World the same way you would an eight-course Italian dinner: leisurely, with plenty of time between courses. The best way not to have fun is to cram too much into too little time.

Important WDW Phone Numbers

General Information	☎ 407-824-4321
General Information for the Hearing Impaired	☎ 407-939-7670
Accommodations/Reservations	☎ 407- W-DISNEY
	or 407-824-8000
Blizzard Beach Information	☎ 407-560-3400
Centracare	☎ 407-200-2273
Formosa Gardens	☎ 407-397-7032
Kissimmee	☎ 407-390-1888
Lake Buena Vista	☎ 407-934-2273
Dr. Phillips	☎ 407-291-9960
Dining Advance Reservations	☎ 407-939-3463
Disabled Guests Special Requests	☎ 407-939-7807
DisneyQuest	☎ 407-828-4600
ESPN Wide World of Sports	☎ 407-939-4263
Golf Reservations and Information	☎ 407-WDW-GOLF
	or 407-939-4653
Guided Tour Information	☎ 407-WDW-TOUR
	or 407-939-8687
Lost and Found:	
Yesterday or before (all Disney parks)	☎ 407-824-4245
Yesterday or before (Downtown Disney)	☎ 407-828-3058
Today at the Magic Kingdom	☎ 407-824-4521
Today at Epcot	☎ 407-560-7500
Today at Disney's Hollywood Studios	☎ 407-560-4668
Today at Animal Kingdom	☎ 407-938-2785
Outdoor Recreation Reservations	☎ 407-WDW-PLAY
and Information	or 407-939-7529
Resort Dining and Recreational	☎ 407-WDW-DINE
Information	or 407-939-3463
Security	☎ 407-560-7959
(routine) or 407-560-1990 (urgent)	
Tennis Reservations/Lessons	☎ 407-621-1991
Ticket Inquiries	☎ 407-566-4985
Typhoon Lagoon Information	☎ 407-560-4141
Walt Disney Travel Company	☎ 407-939-6244
Weather Information	☎ 407-827-4545
Wrecker Service (or call Security after hours; see above)	☎ 407-824-0976

WHEN TO GO TO WALT DISNEY WORLD

LET'S CUT TO THE ESSENCE: Walt Disney World between June 12 and August 18 is rough. You can count on large summer crowds as well as Florida's trademark heat and humidity. Avoid these dates if you can. Ditto for Memorial Day weekend at the beginning of the summer and Labor Day weekend at the end. Other holiday periods (Thanksgiving, Christmas, Easter, Halloween, spring break, and so on) are extremely crowded, but the heat is not as bad.

If you must visit during the busy summer season, cut your visit short by 1 or 2 days so that you will have the weekend or a couple of vacation days remaining to recuperate when you get home.

The best time of year to visit Walt Disney World is in the fall, especially November before Thanksgiving and December before Christmas. Excluding New Year's and other national holidays, January and February are also good, although the weather is generally not as nice as it is in the fall. March and April bring spring break and Easter crowds, though it is sometimes possible (depending on the school and liturgical calendars) to find certain weeks in this period that are not too busy. Late April and May, as well as the beginning of June, are pretty good crowd-wise but are hot and often rainy. Crowds in late August are more tolerable than the heat.

So, parents, what to do? If your children are of preschool age, definitely go during a cooler, less-crowded time. If you have school-age children, look first for an anomaly in your school-year schedule: in other words, a time when your kids will be out of school when most other schools are in session. Anomalies are most often found at the beginning or end of the school year (for example, school starts late or lets out early), at Christmas, or at spring break. In the event that no such anomalies exist, and providing that your kids are good students, our recommendation is to ask permission to take your children out of school either just before or after the Thanksgiving holiday. Teachers can assign lessons that can be made up at home over the Thanksgiving holiday, either before or after your Walt Disney World vacation.

If none of these options are workable for your family, consider visiting Walt Disney World the week immediately before school starts (excluding Labor Day weekend) or the week immediately after school lets out (excluding Memorial Day weekend). This strategy should remove you from the really big mob scenes by about a week or more.

The time that works best for kids is the last week before school ends. Because grades must be finalized earlier, there is often little going on at school during that week. Check far in advance with your child's teacher to determine if any special exams or projects will occur in that last week. If no major assignments are on the child's schedule, then go for it.

Incidentally, taking your kids out of school for more than a few days is problematic. We have received well-considered letters from parents and teachers who don't think taking kids out of school is such a hot idea. A Fairfax, Virginia, dad put it thus:

Annual Attendance Patterns at the Magic Kingdom

visitors per day
(thousands)

100
—
80
—
60
—
40
—
20
—
0

Christmas New Year's

Thanksgiving   Presidents'   Easter

Labor   Day   Memorial
Day   Day

College
Spring
Break

Sept Oct Nov Dec Jan Feb Mar Apr May June July Aug

My wife and I do not encourage families to take their children out of school in order to avoid the crowds at Walt Disney World during the summer months. My wife is an eighth-grade science teacher of chemistry and physics. She has parents pull their children, some honor-roll students, out of school for vacations, only to discover when they return that the students are unable to comprehend the material. Several students have been so thoroughly lost in their assignments that they ask if they can be excused from the tests. Parental suspicions [about] the quality of their children's education should be raised when children go to school for 6 hours a day yet supposedly can complete this same instruction with "less than an hour of homework" each night.

Likewise, a high-school teacher from Louisville, Kentucky, didn't mince words on this subject:

Teachers absolutely hate it when a kid misses school for a week because: (a) parents expect a neat little educational packet to take with them as if every minute can be planned—not practicable; (b) when the kid returns, he is going to be behind, and it is difficult to make up classroom instruction [at the time] when the kid needs it.

If a parent bothers to ask my opinion, I tell them bluntly it's their choice. If the student's grades go down, then they have to accept that as part of their family decision. I have a student out this entire week, skiing in Colorado. There's no way she can make up some of the class activities (and that's exactly what I told her mom).

Though we strongly recommend going to Disney World at less busy times of year, you should know that there are trade-offs. The parks often open late and close early in the off-seasons. When they open as late as 10 a.m., everyone arrives about the same time, making it hard to beat the crowd. A late opening coupled with an early closing drastically reduces the hours available for touring. Even when crowds are small, it's difficult to see a big park like the Magic Kingdom or Epcot between 10 a.m. and 6 p.m. Early closing (before 8 p.m.) may also mean that evening parades or fireworks are eliminated. And, because these are slow times at Disney World, some rides and attractions may be closed for maintenance or renovation. Finally, temperatures there fluctuate wildly during the late fall, winter, and early spring; daytime lows in the 40s are not uncommon.

BE UNCONVENTIONAL The Orange County Convention Center in Orlando hosts some of the largest conventions and trade shows in the world. Rooms anywhere near Walt Disney World are hard to find when there's a big convention, and as this Toronto, Ontario, reader points out, are also expensive:

If saving money on accommodations is an important part of your trip, be sure to check rates on the Net before you settle on a date. Trade shows at the Orange County Convention Center can host over 100,000 attendees, with most of them staying one to a room. This drives rates on even average properties to two or three times [normal] rates. Since all large conventions are scheduled over one year out, these spikes in room rates should be visible up to 12 months prior.

Check the convention schedule for the next seven months at **occc. net/global/calendar.**

DON'T FORGET AUGUST Kids go back to school pretty early in Florida (and in a lot of other places too). This makes mid- to late August a good time to visit Walt Disney World for families who can't vacation during the off-season. A New Jersey mother of two school-age children spells it out:

The end of August is the PERFECT [reader's emphasis] time to go (just watch out for hurricanes; it's the season). There were virtually no wait times, 20 minutes at the most.

JUNE AND THE EARLY BIRD It's not an easy turnaround, but heading for Walt Disney World in late May or early June as soon as school is out will net big rewards. Late May through about June 12 is still considered shoulder season, so the crowds will not have spiked to summer levels. Also the weather is usually cooler than in late August. An exception to the above is the Memorial Day weekend, though the week following the holiday is one of the best crowd-wise of the whole summer.

HOLIDAYS AND SPECIAL EVENTS AT WALT DISNEY WORLD

YOU CAN'T BEAT THE HOLIDAYS FOR live entertainment, special events, parades, fireworks, and elaborate decorations at the theme parks and resort hotels. Unfortunately, you also can't beat holiday periods for crowds. A mom from Ogden, Utah, puts it this way:

> Our family spends part of Christmas week at Walt Disney World every year. We know the lines will be outrageous, but the special shows, parades, and decorations more than make up for it. For first-timers who want to see the rides, Christmas is not ideal, but for us it's the most colorful and exciting time to go.

Here's a look at the larger special events and major holidays at Walt Disney World.

WALT DISNEY WORLD MARATHON Usually held the second weekend after New Year's, the marathon pulls in about 20,000 runners and their families—enough people to affect crowd conditions in the park. The marathon also disrupts vehicular and pedestrian traffic throughout Disney World. The event expanded in 2009 with the addition of kids' races and a health-and-fitness expo.

BLACK HISTORY MONTH It is celebrated throughout Walt Disney World in February. There is no extra charge for the activities (displays, artisans, storytellers, and entertainers), and the celebration's effect on crowd levels is negligible.

ATLANTA BRAVES SPRING TRAINING The Braves hold spring training and play a number of exhibition games at Disney's Wide World of Sports from mid-February through March. You can get the exhibition schedule and purchase tickets by calling TicketMaster at ☎ 800-745-3000 or visiting **ticketmaster.com.** You can watch the training sessions at no charge when you buy general admission to Wide World of Sports ($13.50 for adults, $9 for those under age 13).

EASTER School is out; therefore, all the parks will be crowded. By far the most interesting event of the day is the Easter Parade at the Magic Kingdom. Outstanding floats carry Mickey, Minnie, and the gang, all dressed in their Sunday best, in a special parade. Of course, the appearance of the Easter Bunny is guaranteed. If you're staying in Walt Disney World, ask at the front desk about special activities (such as egg hunts) at your hotel and other Disney resorts.

This is also prime season for all restaurants, and special Easter menus are available. For dinner reservations, call ☎ 407-WDW-DINE. For dining options and actual menus, visit **allearsnet.com/din/dining.htm.**

EPCOT INTERNATIONAL FLOWER & GARDEN FESTIVAL Even if you don't have a green thumb, the 30 million blooms will make your eyes pop. This outstanding event is all yours to enjoy, and best of all, it doesn't affect crowd levels at the parks. The festival is held annually March–May.

STAR WARS WEEKENDS On several weekends, usually from mid-May to mid-June, Disney's Hollywood Studios becomes a mecca for *Star Wars* aficionados. It's characters, trivia games, and merchandise galore during these weekends, and kids can even sign up for a Jedi Training Academy and test their light-saber skills. Celebrities from the film series are available for autographs and appear in the *Star Wars* Celebrity Parade.

GAY DAYS Since 1991, gay, lesbian, bisexual, and transgendered (GLBT) people from around the world have converged on and around the World in June for a long weekend of events centered around the theme parks. Today, Gay Days attracts more than 140,000 GLBT visitors and their families and friends. Universal and Wet 'n Wild also participate, so be prepared: It's going to be crowded. For more information, visit **gaydays.com.**

FOURTH OF JULY AT WALT DISNEY WORLD Keep in mind that this particular holiday at Walt Disney World basically means crowds, crowds, and more crowds. All parks are in a festive and patriotic mood, and the fireworks are incredible. A very special place to visit is The Hall of Presidents at the Magic Kingdom. We recommend leaving the parks prior to the evening fireworks and watching them—from afar—at the Polynesian Resort. Keep in mind that most parks will reach full capacity by 10 a.m., and no advance reservations will get you into a park once it is closed. So pick your park and be prepared to stay there all day. If partying is your thing, consider Downtown Disney, which throws a DJ dance party and a fireworks show of its own.

TOM JOYNER FAMILY REUNION Radio personality Tom Joyner hosts an extremely popular party at Walt Disney World. Usually held during Labor Day weekend, the Reunion typically features live musical performances, comedy acts, and family-oriented discussions. Events take place at the Magic Kingdom, Hollywood Studios, Animal Kingdom, and Pleasure Island. Of special interest to the young crowd are Kids Night Out, a party for kids ages 4–12, and the Tween Dance Party for the 13-and-up set. Past entertainers have included Ashanti, Lionel Richie, Hammer, and Aretha Franklin, to name a few. For more information, visit **blackamericaweb.com.**

NIGHT OF JOY For this Christian-music festival usually held the second weekend of September at the Magic Kingdom, crowds are manageable, but there is an extra fee of about $50 a night and $90 for both nights. The lineup of artists has included MercyMe, Casting Crowns, Kirk Franklin, Rebecca St. James, Jeremy Camp, Todd Agnew, David Crowder Band, Smokie Norful, ZOEgirl, Building 429, Matthew West, and Vicky Beeching. For more information, visit **disneyworld.com/nightofjoy.**

EPCOT INTERNATIONAL FOOD & WINE FESTIVAL From late September to mid-November, about 30 nations trot out their best cuisine, wine, and entertainment. Although many of the activities are included in the park admission fee, the best workshops and tastings are by reservation only. Call ☎ 407-WDW-DINE well in advance for details and reservations. Crowd conditions are affected only slightly.

HALLOWEEN AND MICKEY'S NOT-SO-SCARY HALLOWEEN PARTY Held each year on two dozen or so nights before Halloween until the night after Halloween, the party runs 7 p.m.–midnight at the Magic Kingdom. The event includes trick-or-treating, Mickey's Boo to You Parade (performed twice), several DJ parties throughout the park, storytelling with Merlin, and HalloWishes, a special spooky fireworks show. Several times that evening, Disney villains will put on a great show followed by a Villains' Mix and Mingle in front of Cinderella Castle. Aimed primarily at younger children, the party is happy and upbeat rather than spooky and scary.

The park will be crowded, so arrive early (we recommend getting there an hour before the beginning of the party, as Disney starts letting guests with party tickets inside the park around 6:30 p.m., sometimes much earlier). Proceed directly to the table where the wristbands identifying you as a party guest are obtained. Also, get the special map for the event with details and hours of all the happenings. Go straight to the rides that are on your must-do list, and after that just enjoy the party. If trick-or-treating is a priority, do that first thing after you arrive or toward the end of the night, when crowds thin out and there are no long lines in front of the trick-or-treating stations.

An absolute must-ride is **The Haunted Mansion,** which is especially spooky but only in the sweetest way. Look for the ghost in the garden of the mansion when queuing up. His hilarious tales and interaction with the guests will make you forget you are standing in line. Characters are out in force all over the park, and the Boo to You Parade is pretty amazing. Our two favorite parts of the parade are the Headless Horseman riding at full speed through the park and The Haunted Mansion's groundskeeper, with his dim lantern in one hand and his bloodhound, followed by a large group of ghosts and gravediggers. The many special activities and the costumed kids and adults help you forget the crowds. So don't be shy: Wear a costume—about 50% of all the adults will be wearing a getup of some kind.

Disney's Hollywood Studios has a Halloween party for older kids and adults. Be forewarned that, unlike the Magic Kingdom version, the Studios party will be seriously scary—definitely not for the 10-and-under set. Prices have not been announced, but we expect them to be in line with those of Mickey's Not-So-Scary Halloween Party.

Both parties are by reservation only; admission is about $54 for adults and $48 for ages 3–9 if purchased in advance. Tickets at the gate, if still available, run $60 for adults and $54 for children ages 3–9. Tickets for Halloween night cost a little more. For reservations, call ☎ 407-W-DISNEY.

In addition to activities in the theme parks, Disney's **Fort Wilderness Resort and Campground** offers haunted carriage rides. The carriage rides include a performer who tells the story of Ichabod Crane and the Headless Horseman from Washington Irving's story "The Legend of Sleepy Hollow." The rides leave from Pioneer Hall and cost $60 per carriage. A carriage can accommodate four adults, or two adults with three small children. This excursion can be booked up to 180 days in advance by calling ☎ 407-WDW-PLAY.

Teens and young adults looking for a non-Disney Halloween happening should check out the party at **Universal CityWalk.** And if you'd rather have a monster with a chain saw running after you, consider attending the Universal theme parks' **Halloween Horror Nights.** (*Note:* No costumes are allowed at the parks on these special nights.) For more information, visit **halloweenhorrornights.com.**

THANKSGIVING AT THE PARKS There are no special Thanksgiving events or decorations in the parks, so if you're looking for the equivalent of the Macy's Thanksgiving Parade, you're out of luck, although many of the Christmas decorations are normally in place the day after Thanksgiving. But if you think the lack of festivities translates to smaller crowds, think again—the kids are out of school, and this is the busiest travel weekend of the year. Your best bet for the least-crowded park will be Epcot.

Remember to make your dining arrangements long before your visit, especially if you want a traditional Thanksgiving meal. While there is plenty of food at the World, note that not all restaurants offer turkey with all the trimmings. Some that do include the **Liberty Tree Tavern** at the Magic Kingdom; the **50's Prime Time Cafe** at Disney's Hollywood Studios; **Citrico's** at the Grand Floridian; **Artist Point at the Wilderness Lodge;** and **'Ohana** (which means "family" in Hawaiian) at the Polynesian Resort, which is perfect for families with small children. For information and reservations, call ☎ 407-WDW-DINE.

CELEBRATING CHRISTMAS AT WALT DISNEY WORLD If you're visiting during Christmas week, don't expect to see all the attractions in a single day of touring at any park. All parks, especially the Magic Kingdom, will be filled to capacity, and Disney will stop admitting visitors as early as 10 a.m. (Not to mention that women will have to wait up to 20 minutes to use the restrooms in the Magic Kingdom during Christmas week.) As you might have guessed by now, your only way in is getting there early. Be at the gates with admission passes in hand at least 1 hour before scheduled opening time. Most of all, bring along a humongous dose of patience and humor. The daily tree-lighting ceremonies and the parades are wonderful. Again, most parks will reach full capacity by 10 a.m., and no advance reservations will get you into the park once it is closed. So *pick your park* and be prepared to stay there all day.

Also, be sure to make dinner reservations long before your visit, especially if you are spending Christmas Eve and Christmas Day at the parks. Christmas festivities at Walt Disney World usually run from November 24 through December 30. From the Monday following Thanksgiving weekend until December 20 or so, you can enjoy the decorations and holiday events without the crowds. This between-holidays period is one of our favorite times of year at Walt Disney World.

The **Magic Kingdom** is home to a stunning display of holiday decorations, a **tree-lighting ceremony** on Main Street, and **Mickey's Very Merry Christmas Parade** on select days. Check the *Times Guide* for days and hours. The Magic Kingdom is also the scene of **Mickey's Very Merry Christmas Party,** held from mid-November to mid-December, 7 p.m.–midnight. Separate admission is required, and costs run from $48 to $60; call ☎ 407-W-DISNEY for dates, prices, and reservations. Admission includes holiday-themed stage shows, cookies and hot chocolate, performances of Mickey's Very Merry Christmas Parade, a magical snowfall on Main Street, Christmas carolers, a visit with Santa Claus, and a Holiday Hop DJ Dance Party and fireworks. We do not recommend the party for first-time visitors.

Epcot is a good option on Christmas Day, when the Magic Kingdom is totally mobbed, but this doesn't mean it's a desolate place forgotten by the crowds, just somewhat less crowded than the Magic Kingdom. Again, if your heart is set on touring a park on Christmas Day, you will have to get up early.

At Epcot don't miss the **Candlelight Processional,** featuring a celebrity narrator accompanied by a huge live choir and a full orchestra. The show takes place daily at the America Gardens Theatre and is included with regular Epcot admission. Special lunch and dinner packages are available for an additional charge and include preferred seating for the processional (call ☎ 407-WDW-DINE for reservations). If you don't want to spring for one of the packages, we recommend lining up at least 60 minutes prior to the show of your choice. Guests with preferred seating are well advised not to come at the last minute, either—instead, arrive at the reserved-seating entrance half an hour before the beginning of the show. Seats within this section are available on a first-come, first-served basis and are opened to general admission 15 minutes before the beginning of the show. Check the *Times Guide* for performance hours and information on the day's narrator.

The nightly fireworks, water, and laser show ***Illuminations: Reflections of Earth*** is always worth watching and has an extra-special holiday finale.

Our favorite Epcot holiday event, however, is **Holidays from Around the World.** While strolling from land to land, visitors can enjoy storytellers in each country. In **Canada,** Santa Claus explains how Christmas is celebrated by our neighbor to the north. At the **United Kingdom Pavilion,** Father Christmas tells of his country's holiday customs. **France** is the home of Père Noël, and in **Morocco,** Taariji explains the Feast of Ashoora. In **Japan,** the Daruma

Liliane

A word of advice for families with small children: Reassure the kids that Santa knows where the family is on Christmas Day. You don't want your little ones to suddenly worry that Santa won't find them on Christmas because they're not at home. Consider shipping a small tree and holiday decorations to your hotel. Kids can decorate the window of your hotel room with their drawings.

Seller talks about how Japanese celebrate the New Year. (*Daruma* dolls are symbols of the New Year and are said to bring good luck.)

At the **American Adventure Rotunda,** you can visit Santa's Bakeshop, a life-size Gingerbread House made with real gingerbread, candies, and icing. Santa himself is also on hand to tell Christmas stories. Special programs are held for Kwanzaa and Hanukkah as well. (To learn more about Kwanzaa, an African American celebration of family, community, and culture, visit **officialkwanzaawebsite.org/index.shtml.** Wikipedia offers a nice description of Hanukkah, the Jewish Festival of Lights, at **en.wikipedia.org/wiki/hanukkah.**)

In **Italy,** meet La Befana, the good witch who brings gifts to children on Epiphany. (For more information on La Befana, check out **en.wikipedia.org/wiki/befana.**) **Germany** honors St. Nicholas on December 6, and he welcomes visitors throughout the afternoon. Visitors can also hear the story of the nutcracker's origin. (To find out more about the legend of St. Nicholas, visit **kidsdomain.com/holiday/ xmas/around/stnicholas.html.**)

Visit **China** and listen to the funny stories of the Monkey King. In **Norway,** meet the Christmas elf Julenissen, who represents simplicity and peace. (To learn more about Norway's Santa Claus, visit **julenissen.no.**) In **Mexico,** the Three Sage Kings (Los Tres Reyes Magos) make appearances throughout the afternoon telling the story of Epiphany.

At **Disney's Hollywood Studios,** the park is also dressed for the season, but the big attraction here is the **Osborne Family Spectacle of Lights.** Millions—yes, millions—of lights decorate the buildings on the Streets of America, and snow machines provide the perfect atmosphere. There is no additional fee to see the display, but be prepared for huge crowds. A little background: Jennings Osborne of Little Rock, Arkansas, began putting up Christmas lights on his house about 10 years ago and expanded his display by buying the two houses next to his home. As his collection grew, so did the displeasure of his neighbors. Eventually the matter was brought to court, and in 1994 the Arkansas Supreme Court ruled that his houses, with their 3 million lights, were a public nuisance. The Walt Disney Company brought Osborne's Christmas lights to Disney's Hollywood Studios in 1995 and has a special agreement with him to keep the display.

> Did I mention that it's going to be packed? This is not a good time for first-time visitors, but fun can be had by all at the parks even at peak times. (I actually stayed at Walt Disney World Christmas Eve and Christmas Day and loved it.) If all else fails, go to sleep—tomorrow is another day at Disney, and you should be rolling out of bed early!

At the **Animal Kingdom,** don't miss **Mickey's Jingle Jungle Parade.** The park has festive holiday decorations and a gigantic Christmas tree with carolers performing throughout the day. At Camp Minnie-Mickey, kids can meet "Santa Goofy" and other favorite Disney characters all dressed in their holiday finest. If you don't mind the lines, this is the perfect place for taking holiday photographs.

Downtown Disney features holiday decor and offers photo ops with Santa but is mainly about shopping. The atmosphere is festive, with special window dressings at shops and restaurants.

You thought we were done? No way—there's much more to see outside of the parks.

The holiday decorations at the Walt Disney resorts are attractions in their own right. Generally speaking, each resort incorporates its theme into its holiday finery. At **Port Orleans Resort,** for example, expect Mardi Gras colors in the trees, while the **Yacht Club** has trees adorned with miniature sailboats. At the **Polynesian Resort,** kids will love the gingerbread workshop complete with Santa sleeping in a hammock and elves taking it easy under the sun. For the mother of all Christmas trees, make sure to visit the **Grand Floridian,** where a five-story tree dominates the lobby, flanked by a gingerbread dollhouse and a miniature railroad. At the **Beach Club,** poinsettias, artificial snow, and a gingerbread carousel are the big draw. For a more natural approach, visit the **Wilderness Lodge** and **Animal Kingdom Lodge.**

If you're staying at a Walt Disney resort over Christmas, check with the concierge to see what holiday event your particular resort might be offering. Happenings can range from carolers, brass bands, and country singers to Christmas-cookie decorating, visits with Santa, and readings of *The Night Before Christmas.* Many hotels also offer free cookies and punch in their lobbies.

RINGING IN THE NEW YEAR WITH MICKEY AND FRIENDS If you're in the mood for a night of partying and live entertainment, there's no better place than **Downtown Disney** or **Universal CityWalk.** Both offer a choice of parties and midnight fireworks.

Though all parks, with the exception of the Animal Kingdom, have spectacular fireworks at midnight, here are a few different options for the last night of the year:

- Cirque du Soleil offers a special New Year's production of *La Nouba.* For more information, visit **cirquedusoleil.com.**
- Forget the rides—the lines will be long. Relax at the pool of your hotel and go out for a great dinner that night. If you have little children, get a babysitter. The trick is to arrive a day before New Year's, settle in, go to a water park, and start the touring after January 2, when crowds thin out.
- At Epcot, welcome the New Year several times. Have a drink before 6 p.m. at the Biergarten in Germany. (When the clock strikes 6, it will be midnight in Germany.) Then go over to the Rose & Crown Pub in the United Kingdom and repeat the celebration at 7 p.m., as guests and staff alike will be welcoming the New Year in the United Kingdom. Best of all, you get to start all over again a few hours later when the clock finally strikes midnight at Epcot.

HIGH-LOW, HIGH-LOW, IT'S OFF TO DISNEY WE GO

THOUGH WE RECOMMEND OFF-SEASON TOURING, we realize that it's not possible for many families. We want to make it clear, therefore, that you can have a wonderful experience regardless of when you go. Our advice, irrespective of season, is to arrive early at the parks and avoid the crowds by using one of our touring plans. If attendance is light, kick back and forget the touring plans.

Selecting the Day of the Week for Your Visit

We receive thousands of e-mails and letters from readers each year asking which park is the best bet on a particular day. Because there are now so many variables (about 38) to consider when recommending a specific best park for a given date, we've created a computer program that weighs all the variables and provides the answer. The results are posted in a Crowd Condition Calendar posted on our Web site, **touringplans.com.** Once you've decided the dates of your visit to Walt Disney World, access the Web site and check out your dates on the Crowd Condition Calendar (no charge). The calendar will tell you the park to visit (and to avoid) for each day of your stay. If you don't have regular Internet access, the information is worth a trip to an Internet cafe or to your local library to obtain.

Extra Magic Hours

Extra Magic Hours is a perk for families staying at a Walt Disney World resort, including the Swan, Dolphin, and Shades of Green, and the Hilton in the Downtown Disney resort area. On selected days of the week, Disney resort guests will be able to enter a Disney theme park 1 hour earlier, or stay in a selected theme park up to 3 hours later, than the official park-operating hours. Theme park visitors not staying at a Disney resort may stay in the park for Extra Magic Hour evenings but cannot experience any rides, attractions, or shows. In other words, they can shop and eat.

You'll need to have a Park Hopper option on your theme-park admission to take advantage of Extra Magic Hours at more than one park on the same day.

WHAT'S REQUIRED? A valid admission ticket is required to enter the park, and you must show your Disney Resort ID when entering.

WHEN ARE EXTRA MAGIC HOURS OFFERED? The Extra Magic Hours schedule is subject to constant change, especially during holidays and other periods of peak attendance. Gone are the days when you could be certain which park was running Extra Magic Hours.

You can phone Walt Disney World Information at ☎ 407-824-4321 (press 0 for a live representative), or access **disneyworld.disney.go.com/ wdwi/en_gb/calendar/extramagichour?id=calendarex tramagichourspage&bhcp=1** to check the schedule for the dates of your visit (you can tell by this URL how difficult it is to find the Extra Magic Hours schedule on the official Disney Web site). Scroll down to the question "When are the Extra Magic Hours at each theme park?" The answer will provide the Extra Magic Hours Schedule for the current month. The same information, along with tips for avoiding crowds

Extra Magic Hours draw more Disney resort guests to the host park, which results in longer lines than you would otherwise experience.

during your Disney World vacation, is available at our Web site, **touringplans.com.**

We seriously hope that Disney will adopt a permanent schedule, but if it does not, use the information available from Walt Disney World Information or the Web site listed above to discover any schedule changes that might affect you. To avoid the most crowded park, simply steer clear of the one(s) offering morning Extra Magic Hours, or access **touringplans.com** for guidance.

WHAT DO EXTRA MAGIC HOURS MEAN TO YOU? Crowds are likely to be larger when the theme parks host an Extra Magic Hours session. If you're not staying at a Disney resort, we suggest avoiding the park hosting Extra Magic Hours, if at all possible.

If you're staying at a Disney resort, there are a couple of strategies you can employ to cut down on your wait in lines. One strategy is to avoid the park hosting Extra Magic Hours entirely, if possible. If you can be at the park when it opens, a second strategy would be to visit the park offering a morning Extra Magic Hours session until lunchtime, then visit another, less-crowded park in the afternoon.

PLANNING *Your* WALT DISNEY WORLD VACATION BUDGET

HOW MUCH YOU SPEND DEPENDS on how long you stay at Walt Disney World. But even if you only stop by for an afternoon, be prepared to drop a bundle. Later we'll show you how to save money on lodging. This section will give you some sense of what you can expect to pay for admissions and food. And we'll help you decide which admission option will best meet your needs.

WALT DISNEY WORLD ADMISSION OPTIONS

IN AN EFFORT TO ACCOMMODATE various vacation needs, Disney offers a number of different admission options. These range from the basic "One Day, One Park" ticket, good for a single entry into one Disney theme park, to the top-of-the-line Premium Annual Pass, good for 365 days of admission into every Disney theme or water park, plus DisneyQuest.

The sheer number of ticket options available makes it difficult and, yes, daunting for a family to sort out which option represents the least expensive way to see and do everything they want. An average family staying for a week at an off-World hotel and planning a couple of activities outside the theme parks generally has about a dozen different ticket options to consider. To complicate matters, comparing options requires detailed knowledge of the myriad perks included with specific admissions. Finding the optimum admission, or combination of admissions, however, could save the average family a nice little bundle. Many families, we suspect, become overwhelmed trying to sort out the different options and simply purchase a more expensive ticket with features they will probably never use. Adding to the frustration, Disney's reservation agents are generally trained to avoid answering subjective questions such as which ticket option is "best."

HELP IS ON THE WAY!

TO SIMPLIFY THINGS, we tried to define guidelines to help you choose the best ticket options for your vacation. Eight hours into this project, we sounded like a theme-park version of *Forrest Gump*. Remember that scene where Bubba rattles off 7,000 different ways to prepare shrimp? Well, that was kinda like us, babbling about tickets. Even saying some of the ticket names ("Adult Internet-only Seven-day Base Ticket with Park Hopper Option") made us sound like our local Starbucks barista, only not as perky.

After a day or so, we realized that coming up with a handful of general guidelines was an impossible task, so we built a tool to figure it out. You can use it to determine the best ticket options for you by visiting our Web site, **touringplans.com,** and trying out the Disney Ticket Calculator. The tool aggregates ticket prices from a number of online ticket vendors, including Disney itself. Just answer a few simple questions relating to the size of your party and the theme parks you intend to visit. The tool then identifies your four least expensive ticket options.

The program will also make recommendations for considerations other than price. For example, Annual Passes, although they might cost more, make sense in certain circumstances because Disney often offers substantial resort discounts and other deals to Annual Pass holders. Those resort discounts, especially during off-season times, can more than offset a small incremental charge for the Annual Pass.

MAGIC YOUR WAY

IN 2005, WALT DISNEY WORLD pretty much chucked its entire panoply of admission options and introduced a completely new array of theme-park tickets in a program called Magic Your Way. The new scheme applies to both one-day and multiday passports and begins with a Base Ticket. Features that were previously bundled with certain tickets, such as the ability to visit more than one park per day ("park hopping"), or the inclusion of admission to Disney's minor venues (Typhoon Lagoon, Blizzard Beach, DisneyQuest, and the like), are now available as individual add-ons to the Base Ticket.

As before, there is a volume discount. The more days of admission you purchase, the lower the cost per day. For example, if you buy an adult Five-day Base Ticket for $242.82 (taxes included), each day will cost $48.56, compared with $84.14 a day for a one-day pass. Base Tickets can be purchased from 1 to 10 days and admit you to exactly one theme park per day.

WDW Theme Park Ticket Options

	1-day	2-day	3-day	4-day	5-day
BASE TICKET AGES 3–9					
	$72.42	$141.65	$199.16	$204.48	$207.68
	–	($70.82/day)	($66.39/day)	($51.12/day)	($41.54/day)
BASE TICKET AGE 10 AND UP					
	$84.14	$166.14	$233.24	$239.63	$242.82
	–	($83.07/day)	($77.75/day)	($59.91/day)	($48.56/day)

Base Ticket admits guest to one theme park each day of use. Park choices are Magic Kingdom,

FOR PARK HOPPER, ADD:

	1-day	2-day	3-day	4-day	5-day
	$55.38	$55.38	$55.38	$55.38	$55.38
	–	($27.69/day)	($18.46/day)	($13.85/day)	($11.08/day)

Park Hopper option entitles guest to visit more than one theme park on each day of use.

FOR WATER PARK FUN AND MORE, ADD:

	1-day	2-day	3-day	4-day	5-day
	$55.38	$55.38	$55.38	$55.38	$55.38
	2 visits	2 visits	3 visits	4 visits	5 visits

Water Park Fun and More option entitles guest to a specified number of visits (between 2 and 10)
park, Disney's Typhoon Lagoon water park, DisneyQuest, Oak Trail Golf Course,

FOR NO EXPIRATION, ADD:

	1-day	2-day	3-day	4-day	5-day
	N/A	$19.17	$25.56	$55.38	$77.75
	–	($9.59/day)	($8.52/day)	($13.85/day)	($15.55/day)

No Expiration means unused admissions on a ticket have no expiration date.
All tickets expire 14 days after first use unless No Expiration is purchased.

Under the old system, unused days on multiday passes were good indefinitely. Now passes expire 14 days from the first day of use. If, say, you purchase a Four-day Base Ticket on June 1 and use it that day for admission to the Magic Kingdom, you'll be able to visit a single Disney theme park on any of your three remaining days between June 2 and June 15. After that, the ticket expires and any unused days will be lost. Through another add-on, however, you can avoid the 14-day expiration and make your ticket valid forever. More on that later.

BASE-TICKET ADD-ON OPTIONS

NAVIGATING THE MAGIC YOUR WAY PROGRAM is much like ordering dinner in an upscale restaurant where all menu selections are à la carte: lots of choices, mostly expensive, virtually all of which require some thought.

Three add-on options are offered with the Magic Your Way Base Ticket, each at an additional cost:

(Note: All ticket prices include 6.5% sales tax)

	6-day	7-day	8-day	9-day	10-day
BASE TICKET AGES 3–9					
	$210.87	$214.07	$217.26	$220.46	$223.65
	($35.15/day)	($30.58/day)	($27.16/day)	($24.50/day)	($22.37/day)
BASE TICKET AGE 10 AND UP					
	$246.02	$249.21	$252.41	$255.60	$258.80
	($41.00/day)	($35.60/day)	($31.55/day)	($28.40/day)	($25.88/day)

Epcot, Disney's Hollywood Studios, or Disney's Animal Kingdom.

FOR PARK HOPPER, ADD:

	6-day	7-day	8-day	9-day	10-day
	$55.38	$55.38	$55.38	$55.38	$55.38
	($9.23/day)	($7.91/day)	($6.92/day)	($6.15/day)	($5.54/day)

Park choices are any combination of Magic Kingdom, Epcot, Disney's Hollywood Studios, or Disney's Animal Kingdom on each day of use.

FOR WATER PARK FUN AND MORE, ADD:

	6-day	7-day	8-day	9-day	10-day
	$55.38	$55.38	$55.38	$55.38	$55.38
	6 visits	7 visits	8 visits	9 visits	10 visits

to a choice of entertainment and recreation venues. Choices are Disney's Blizzard Beach water or ESPN Wide World of Sports Complex.

FOR NO EXPIRATION, ADD:

	6-day	7-day	8-day	9-day	10-day
	$89.46	$122.48	$161.88	$189.57	$222.59
	($14.91/day)	($17.50/day)	($20.24/day)	($21.06/day)	($22.26/day)

Note: Check **touringplans.com** for the latest ticket prices, which are subject to change.

PARK HOPPER Adding this feature to your Base Ticket allows you to visit more than one theme park per day. The cost is $55.38 on top of the price of any Base Ticket. It's an exorbitant price for one or two days, but it does become more affordable the longer your stay. As an add-on to a Seven-day Base Ticket, the $55.38 flat fee (including tax) would work out to $7.91 per day for park-hopping privileges. If you want to visit the Magic Kingdom in the morning and dine at Epcot in the evening, this is the feature you should request.

NO EXPIRATION Adding this option to your ticket means that unused admissions to the major theme parks, the swimming parks, and other minor venues, never expire. If you add this option to a Ten-day Base Ticket and used only four days this year, the remaining six days could be used for admission at any date in the future. The No Expiration option ranges from $19.17 with tax for a two-day ticket to $222.59 for a Ten-day Base Ticket. This option is not available on one-day tickets.

WATER PARK FUN AND MORE (WPFAM) This option gives you a single admission to one of Disney's water parks (Blizzard Beach and

Research indicates that less than one in ten admission passes with unused days are ever used. I can report, however, that I have successfully kept track of all the partially used tickets I've taken home over the years. The secret? I keep them in the same place all the time with my passport, insurance papers, and other travel documents. And one more thing: I always keep a copy of my credit card receipt documenting the purchase. I even make a photocopy because receipts fade as time goes by.

Typhoon Lagoon), DisneyQuest, Oak Trail Golf Course, or the ESPN Wide World of Sports Complex. The cost is a flat $55.38 (including tax). Except for the one-day WPFAM ticket, which gives you two admissions, the number of admissions equals the number of days on your base ticket. If you buy an Eight-day Base Ticket, for example, and add the WPFAM option, you get eight WPFAM admissions. What you *can't* do is, say, buy a Ten-day Base Ticket with only three admissions or a Three-day Base Ticket with four admissions. You can, however, skip WPFAM entirely and buy an individual admission to any of these minor parks. This option is almost always the best deal if you want to visit only one of the venues.

The add-ons are available for purchase in any combination (except for the No Expiration add-on on one-day tickets). If you buy a Base Ticket and then decide later on that you want one or more of the options, you can upgrade the Base Ticket to add the feature(s) you desire.

Annual Passes

An Annual Pass provides unlimited use of the major theme parks for one year; a Premium Annual Pass also provides unlimited use of the minor parks. Annual Pass holders also get perks, including free parking and seasonal offers such as room-rate discounts at Disney resorts. The Annual Pass is not valid for special events, such as admission to Mickey's Very Merry Christmas Party. Tax included, Annual Passes run $520.79 for adults and $460.08 for children ages 3–9. A Premium Annual Pass, at $659.24 for adults and $581.49 for children ages 3–9, provides unlimited admission to Blizzard Beach, Typhoon Lagoon, DisneyQuest, and Oak Trail Golf Course, in addition to the four major theme parks. In addition to Annual Passes, Florida residents are eligible for discounts on one-day theme-park Base Tickets (about 10%), as well as on various add-on options.

The new Disney Premier Passport is good for admission to all parks at the Disneyland and Disney World resorts. The Disney Premier Passport grants unlimited admission for one year to Disneyland and Disney California Adventure in Anaheim, California; as well as Magic Kingdom, Epcot, Disney's Hollywood Studios, Disney's Animal Kingdom, Typhoon Lagoon and Blizzard Beach water parks, DisneyQuest indoor interactive theme park, ESPN Wide World of Sports complex, and Disney's Oak Trail golf course in Orlando. Some events may require an additional charge. The pass includes parking at all four theme parks at

Disney World (Magic Kingdom, Epcot, Animal Kingdom, Hollywood Studios), and parking at any pay-on-entry parking lot at Disneyland Resort. Also included are subscriptions to *Mickey Monitor, Backstage Pass,* and *Disney's Family Fun* magazine (one per household).

Those who already hold an annual pass for both resorts will automatically be issued a Disney Premier Passport, with an expiration date based on the later of the two annual passes. Guests can upgrade their annual or seasonal pass for one resort to a Disney Premier Passport for an additional fee. The new pass is available at Disneyland Resort ticket booths, Disney World Guest Relations windows, and at Disney World's Downtown Disney.

This pass may be a good thing, but our estimation is that it is largely a PR move. We estimate that the number of people who would actually benefit from this right now is less than 1,000.

Florida-resident Passes

Disney offers several special admission options to Florida residents. The Florida Resident Annual Pass ($392.99 adults, $346.13 children ages 3–9) and the Florida Resident Premium Annual Pass ($520.79 adults, $459.02 children ages 3–9) both offer unlimited admission and park-hopping privileges to the four major theme parks. The Florida Resident Premium Annual Pass also provides unlimited admission to Blizzard Beach, Typhoon Lagoon, DisneyQuest, and Oak Trail Golf Course, in addition to the four major theme parks. AAA offers some nice discounts on these passes. And the Florida Resident Seasonal Pass ($265.19 adults, $234.30 children ages 3–9) provides unlimited admission to the four major theme parks except on select blackout dates but does not include free parking.

One final note: It doesn't cost as much to renew an Annual Pass as it does to buy it in the first place. When you renew any Annual Pass, you get 8% to 9% savings from the cost of the original pass.

DIZ SPIN

ACCORDING TO DISNEY PRESS RELEASES, Magic Your Way is the hottest thing since barbecue sauce on pig. Former Walt Disney World president Al Weiss announced at the program's debut, "People want things customized to fit their individual needs. And now Walt Disney World guests will have that same ability to customize their dream vacation, creating the ticket that is just right for them." A similar release gushes, "Because Magic Your Way tickets offer savings that increase with the length of stay, a weeklong Walt Disney World vacation becomes even more affordable."

Well, let's see. For starters, Walt Disney World multiday admissions have always incorporated a volume discount: the more days of admission you purchase, the lower the cost per day. So there's nothing new there. And it's always been possible, though confusing, to customize your vacation using one or more of the dizzying 180 different admission options available before Magic Your Way.

In an era of ever-shrinking margins, we understand that Disney needs to continually find ways to increase profits, especially with the theme parks constituting a large share of Disney's operating revenue. When things go south for corporate Disney, it's always the theme parks and we, the guests, who are burdened with making up the shortfall.

To put the increases in perspective, Disney's price hikes have far outpaced those in almost every other sector of the U.S. economy. For example, the price of a One-day, One-park ticket has jumped more than 44%, and the price of a child Four-day Park Hopper has increased 68%. In comparison, the hourly wage of the average American worker has risen only 14%, and consumer prices have increased only 9% during the same period.

Disney seems to be employing an "all the market can bear" pricing strategy that has become substantially more aggressive in the past few years. We think they'll probably continue to boost prices aggressively until there's an angry backlash and attendance starts to decline. If this happens, Disney will lose more in hotel, food-and-beverage, and retail revenue than it will gain from higher admission prices.

Disney is hoping that guests will regard the increases in admission prices as relatively minor compared with the cost of the WDW vacation overall. No matter how you shake it up, however, the runaway price hikes leave a bad taste in your mouth. Walt Disney World was not conceived as an exclusive playground for the rich. However, not all is well in Mouseland, and 2010 saw heavily discounted offers. With the fierce competition of the newly opened Harry Potter attractions at Universal Studios, we see better deals on the horizon.

A CLOUD IS JUST A CLOUD

THIS SECTION WAS FORMERLY TITLED "Every Cloud Has a Polyester Lining." In it we explained the few ways that Magic Your Way could save you money. Well, forget that—almost all good deals have gone the way of the dinosaur. The only exception is for folks who do not intend to park-hop and will require four or more days' admission, all to be used during a single vacation. If this describes your situation, you can realize some significant economies of scale. As you can see from our admissions chart, the more days you buy, the more you save: the cost of an adult Ten-day Base Ticket ($258.80) is only $25.56 more than the cost of an adult Three-day Base Ticket ($233.24). If you buy the ten-day ticket, you can whittle your admission cost per day, tax included, down to $25.88 for adults and $22.37 for children. So what's changed for everybody else?

Consider that most guests only need four or five days' admission; the most cost-effective strategy, then, would seem to be to buy a Ten-day Base Ticket plus the No Expiration option so you could roll over any unused admission days to a subsequent trip. When Disney first rolled out Magic Your Way, the No Expiration option actually was pretty reasonable.

Well, they couldn't let *that* continue, could they?

As of this writing, Disney has increased the cost of the No Expiration option by 86% from the time Magic Their, oops, *Your* Way (a joke any way you look at it) was introduced. If you buy an adult Ten-day Base Ticket for $258.80 plus No Expiration for $222.59, you'll pay $481.39 including tax, or $48.14 a day—a saving of less than $.50 a day compared with simply buying a Five-day Base Ticket each time you visit Walt Disney World. While it is true that admission prices might go up before you visit again, in which case No Expiration would be to your benefit, it's equally true that you might misplace the tickets you bought in the previous scenario, or that you might have some better use for the $222.59 you shelled out on top of your ticket purchase.

BIG BROTHER IS WATCHING

ALL MAGIC YOUR WAY TICKETS are personalized, with the ticket holder's name and biometric information stored on the ticket. This doesn't mean, however, that you have to provide a DNA sample when you plunk down your cash. Recording the biometric information requires a quick and painless measurement of one finger from your right hand, taken the first time you use the ticket. It's been used without incident for a number of years on Disney's Annual Pass.

The advantages of the bio scan are not altogether clear, though it's doubtless intended to prevent the original purchaser of the pass from selling unused days to a third party. If you're purchasing admission for your entire family and are worried about the difficulty in keeping everyone's tickets, we're told that Disney's computer system will link every family member's data to every ticket, allowing anyone to enter with anyone else's ticket. We've confirmed this by having a platoon of *Unofficial Guide* researchers (including men, women, and children) swap passes with each other; all were admitted.

Stay clear of passes bought on the black market or offered on eBay.

Liliane

This new scanning process is so cumbersome, however, that it has taken guests more than 30 minutes to enter some parks during peak periods—and occasionally more than an hour. In response to this, Disney frequently turns off the scanning process entirely (usually at Animal Kingdom).

HOW TO GET THE MOST FROM MAGIC YOUR WAY

FIRST, HAVE A REALISTIC IDEA of what you want out of your vacation. As with anything, it doesn't make sense to pay for options you'll never use. A seven-day theme-park ticket with seven WPFAM admissions might seem like a wonderful idea when you're snowbound and planning your trip in February. But actually trying to visit all those parks in a week in July might end up feeling more like Navy SEAL training. If you're going to make only

Liliane

What do you do with the kid's pass you bought when your now 6-foot teenager was less than 10 years of age? Go to Guest Relations and ask them to change the pass into a regular admission pass for the amount of days left on it. If you are lucky, they will do so without asking you to pay the price difference, but if not, you are still better off paying the difference and using the pass instead of wasting whatever value is left on it.

one visit to a water park, DisneyQuest, or Wide World of Sports, you're almost always better off purchasing that admission separately rather than in the WPFAM option. If you plan to visit two or more WPFAM venues, however, you're better off buying the add-on.

Next, think carefully about paying for the No Expiration option. An inside source reports that fewer than one in ten admission tickets with rollover days are ever reused at a Disney theme park. The rest are misplaced, discarded, or forgotten. Unless you are absolutely certain that you'll be returning to Walt Disney World within the next year or two and have identified a safe place to keep those unused tickets, we don't think that the additional cost is worth the risk. (We've lost a few passes ourselves.)

GOTCHA!

EVIDENTLY AS A MATTER OF PRINCIPLE, Disney increases admission prices each year about a month after the *Unofficial Guide* goes to press. There's very high probability, therefore, that prices will be higher by the time you read this. Generally increases have run about 3% or 4% a year, but as we discussed above, specific categories of tickets are frequently bumped much more. This has been especially true for children's admissions over the past couple of years. In any event, if you're putting a budget together, assume at least a 3% increase.

WHERE TO PURCHASE MAGIC YOUR WAY TICKETS

YOU CAN BUY YOUR ADMISSION PASSES on arrival at Walt Disney World or purchase them in advance. Admission passes are available at Walt Disney World resorts and theme parks. Passes are also available at some non-Disney hotels and Orlando-area shopping centers, as well as through independent ticket brokers. Because Disney admission prices are not discounted in the greater Walt Disney World–Orlando area, the only reason for you to purchase from an independent broker is convenience. Offers of free or heavily discounted tickets abound, but they generally require you to attend a time-share sales presentation.

Magic Your Way tickets are available at Disney Stores and at **disney world.com** for the same prices listed in the chart on pages 58–59.

If you're trying to keep your costs to an absolute minimum, consider using an online ticket wholesaler, such as **Undercover Tourist, Kissimmee Guest Services, Maple Leaf Tickets,** or the **Official Ticket Center,** especially for trips with five or more days in the theme parks. All tickets sold are brand-new, and the savings can range from $7 to more than $25, depending on the ticket and options chosen. We've spoken with representatives from each company, and they're very well versed in the

Undercover Tourist	**undercovertourist.com**
Kissimmee Guest Services	**kgstickets.com**
Maple Leaf Tickets	**mapleleaftickets.com**
The Official Ticket Center	**officialticketcenter.com**

pros and cons of the various tickets and options. If the new options don't make sense for your specific vacation plans, the reps will tell you so.

All four companies offer discounts on tickets for almost all central-Florida attractions, including Disney, Universal, SeaWorld, and Cirque du Soleil. Discounts for the major theme parks are about 6% to 8.5%. Tickets for other attractions are more deeply discounted. **Undercover Tourist** (U.S.: ☎ 800-846-1302, Monday–Friday, 9 a.m.–4 p.m. Eastern Time; U.K.: ☎ 0800 081-1702, Monday–Friday, 2 p.m.–9 p.m. GMT; worldwide: ☎ +1 386 239-8624; fax +1 386 252-3469; **undercover tourist.com**) offers free delivery and has a sweetheart relationship with **mousesavers.com.** If you subscribe to the MouseSavers e-newsletter, you can access Undercover Tourist through a special "secret" link that provides additional savings on top of the normal discount. **Kissimmee Guest Services** (950 Celebration Blvd., Ste. H, in Celebration; ☎ 321-939-2057, Monday–Friday, 8 a.m.–8 p.m., Saturday, 8 a.m.–5 p.m., Sunday, 8 a.m.– noon Eastern Time; U.K.: ☎ 0209 432-4024; **kgstickets.com**) offers a lowest-price guarantee and will ship the tickets to you for $10, or you may pick up the tickets. The **Official Ticket Center** (3148 Vineland Rd., Kissimmee; ☎ 877-406-4836 or 407-396-9029, daily, 8 a.m.–8:30 p.m. Eastern Time; **theofficialticketcenter.com**) offers shipping for a flat $8 fee or $10 for delivery to Orlando-area hotels; it's of course free if you pick up at their office. **Maple Leaf Tickets** (4647 W. Irlo Bronson Hwy. [US 192], Kissimmee; ☎ 407-396-0300 or 800-841-2837, daily, 8 a.m.– 6 p.m. Eastern Time; **mapleleaftickets.com**) offers the same deal on pickup at their store and for $6.95 delivery to Orlando-area hotels; U.S. Priority Mail service is a flat $6.95 per order.

HOW MUCH DOES IT COST PER DAY?

A TYPICAL DAY WOULD COST $569.64, excluding lodging and transportation, for a family of four—Mom, Dad, 12-year-old Tim, and 8-year-old Sandy—driving their own car and staying outside the World. They plan to stay a week, so they buy Five-day Base Tickets with Park Hopper Option. See breakdown on the following page.

While ticket prices account for a big part of any year's price increases, the largest price hikes lately have been at Disney's sit-down restaurants. Our typical dinner at Italy—two shared appetizers, median-priced entrees for the adults, a child's dinner, and two shared desserts—has increased by 47% in the past year and a half.

A Birmingham, Alabama, mom of two begs to differ with our budget recommendation above for souvenirs:

Breakfast for four at Denny's with tax and tip	$30.36
Epcot parking fee (free for passholders and resort guests)	$14.00
One day's admission on a 5-day Base Ticket with Park Hopper Option	
Dad: Adult 5-day with tax = $298.20 divided by five (days)	$59.64
Mom: Adult 5-day with tax = $298.20 divided by five (days)	$59.64
Tim: Adult 5-day with tax = $298.20 divided by five (days)	$59.64
Sandy: Child 5-day with tax = $263.06 divided by five (days)	$52.61
Morning break (soda or coffee)	$11.90
Fast-food lunch (sandwich or burger, fries, soda), no tip	$38.00
Afternoon break (soda and popcorn)	$22.00
Dinner at Italy (no alcoholic beverages) with tax and tip	$182.85
Souvenirs (Mickey T-shirts for Tim and Sandy) with tax*	$39.00
One-day total (without lodging or transportation)	**$569.64**

*Cheer up—you won't have to buy souvenirs every day.

Sorry, but Uncle Bob is totally out of touch when he says "you won't have to buy souvenirs every day." [In my experience,] you'll head home with several sets of character ears; enough dress-up costumes to outfit the neighborhood; and countless pins, toys, and knickknacks.

BABYSITTING

CHILD-CARE CENTERS Child care isn't available inside the theme parks, but three Magic Kingdom resorts connected by monorail or boat (Polynesian, Grand Floridian, and Wilderness Lodge and Villas), four Epcot resorts (the Yacht Club and Beach Club resorts, the Swan, and the Dolphin), and Animal Kingdom Lodge, along with the Hilton at Walt Disney World, have child-care centers for potty-trained children older than age 3 (see chart on page 67). Services vary, but children generally can be left between 4:30 p.m. and midnight. Milk and cookies and blankets and pillows are provided at all centers, and dinner is provided at most. Play is supervised but not organized, and toys, videos, and games are plentiful. Guests at any Disney resort or campground may use the services.

The most elaborate of the child-care centers (variously called "clubs" or "camps") is **Never Land Club** at the Polynesian Resort. The rate for ages 4–12 is $11.50 per hour, per child.

All the clubs accept reservations (some six months in advance!) with a credit-card guarantee. Call the club directly, or reserve through Disney central reservations at ☎ 407-WDW-DINE. Most clubs require a 24-hour cancellation notice and levy a hefty penalty of 2 hours' time or $23 per call for no-shows. A limited number of walk-ins are usually accepted on a first-come, first-served basis.

CHILD-CARE CLUBS*			
HOTEL	NAME OF PROGRAM	AGES	PHONE
Animal Kingdom Lodge	Simba's Cubhouse	4–12	☎ 407-938-4785
Dolphin	Camp Dolphin	4–12	☎ 407-934-4241
Grand Floridian Resort & Spa	Mouseketeer Club	4–12	☎ 407-824-2985
Hilton WDW	All About Kids	4–12	☎ 407-812-9300
Polynesian Resort	Never Land Club	4–12	☎ 407-824-1639
Swan	Camp Dolphin	4–12	☎ 407-934-4241
Yacht and Beach Club Resorts	Sandcastle Club	4–12	☎ 407-934-3750
Wilderness Lodge and Villas	Cub's Den	4–12	☎ 407-824-1083

Child-care clubs operate afternoons and evenings. Before 4 p.m., call the hotels rather than the numbers listed above. All programs require reservations.

If you're staying in a Disney resort that doesn't offer a child-care club and you *don't* have a car, you're better off using in-room babysitting. Trying to take your child to a club in another hotel by Disney bus requires a 50- to 90-minute trip each way. By the time you've deposited your little one, it will almost be time to pick him or her up again.

IN-ROOM BABYSITTING Three companies provide in-room sitting in Walt Disney World and surrounding areas, including the International Drive–Orange County Convention Center area, the Universal Orlando area, and the Lake Buena Vista area. They are **Kid's Nite Out** (run by the KinderCare chain), **All About Kids,** and **Fairy Godmothers** (no kidding). Kid's Nite Out also serves hotels in the greater Orlando area, including downtown. All three provide sitters older than age 18 who are insured, bonded, and trained in CPR. Some sitters have advanced medical and first-aid training and/or education credentials. All sitters are screened, reference checked, and police checked. In addition to caring for your children in your guest room, the sitters will, if you direct (and pay), take your children to the theme parks or other venues. Many sitters arrive loaded with books and games. All three services offer bilingual sitters.

SPECIAL PROGRAMS FOR CHILDREN

SEVERAL PROGRAMS FOR CHILDREN are available, but they are somewhat lacking in educational focus.

DISNEY'S PIRATE ADVENTURE Children don bandannas, hoist the Jolly Roger, and depart on a boat trip to search for buried treasure following a treasure map. At the final port of call, the kids find the treasure (doubloons, beads, and rubber bugs!) and wolf down a PB&J sandwich. The treasure is divided among the kids. For children ages 4–12, the adventure costs $40 per child and is offered at Port Orleans

Babysitting Services

ALL ABOUT KIDS
☎ 407-812-9300 or
800-728-6506
all-about-kids.com

HOTELS SERVED
All WDW hotels and many
outside the WDW area

SITTERS Men and women

MINIMUM CHARGES 4 hours

BASE HOURLY RATES
1 child, $14
2 children, $16
3 children, $18
4 children, $20

EXTRA CHARGES
Transportation fee, $12;
starting before 7 a.m. or after 9
p.m., +$2 per hour

CANCELLATION DEADLINE
More than 24 hours before
service to avoid cancellation
charge

FORM OF PAYMENT
Cash or traveler's checks for
actual payment; gratuity in
cash; credit card to hold
reservation

THINGS SITTERS WON'T DO
Transport children

KID'S NITE OUT
☎ 407-828-0920 or
800-696-8105
kidsniteout.com

HOTELS SERVED
All WDW and Orlando-area
hotels

SITTERS Men and women

MINIMUM CHARGES 4 hours

BASE HOURLY RATES
1 child, $16
2 children, $18.50
3 children, $21
4 children, $23.50

EXTRA CHARGES
Transportation fee, $10;
starting before 6:30 a.m. or
after 9 p.m., +$2 per hour;
additional fee for holidays

CANCELLATION DEADLINE
24 hours before service when
reservation is made

FORM OF PAYMENT
AE, D, MC, V; gratuity in cash

THINGS SITTERS WON'T DO
Transport children in private
vehicle, take children swimming, give baths

FAIRY GODMOTHERS
☎ 407-277-3724

HOTELS SERVED
All WDW hotels and those in
the general WDW area

SITTERS Mothers and grand-
mothers, female college students

MINIMUM CHARGES 4 hours

BASE HOURLY RATES
1 child, $16
2 children, $16
3 children, $16
4 children, $18

EXTRA CHARGES
Transportation fee, $14;
starting after 10 p.m.,
+$2 per hour

CANCELLATION DEADLINE
3 hours before service

FORM OF PAYMENT
Cash or traveler's checks
for actual payment;
gratuity in cash

THINGS SITTERS WON'T DO
Transport children, give
baths. Swimming is at sitter's
discretion.

Liliane

What will Disney think of next? A Bibbidi Bobbidi Boutique for Captain Jack Sparrow's hairdo? If only they had a package that included dinner with Johnny Depp.

(Bayou Pirate Adventure), the Grand Floridian (Pirate Adventure), the Yacht Club (Albatross Cruise), and the Caribbean Resort (Caribbean Pirate Adventure). Though the setting is different at each resort, the program is largely the same. The Grand Floridian runs the excursion every day except Sunday. The other resorts offer the program three days each week. Call ☎ 407-WDW-PLAY for days offered and other information. Kids of both genders really love this outing, many reporting it as the highlight of their vacation. Parents cannot accompany children on the outing.

If you want to go whole hog, check out The Pirate League in Adventureland at the Magic Kingdom, where scoundrels and rogues of all ages can acquire special pirate costumes and accessories, as well as an official pirate name. Two different packages are available:

FIRST MATE PACKAGE: Includes bandanna; choice of facial effects (scars, tattoos, fake teeth, earring, and eye patch); sword and sheath; pirate-coin necklace; one 5-by-7-inch photo; and personalized pirate oath for $30, plus tax.

EMPRESS PACKAGE: Comes with bandanna; shimmering makeup (face gem, tattoos, nail polish, earring, and eye patch); sword and sheath; pirate-coin necklace; one 5-by-7-inch photo; and personalized pirate oath for $30, plus tax.

These packages are available for boys, girls, and adults. Call ☎ 407-WDW-CREW to make an appointment.

WONDERLAND TEA PARTY Although the name of this enchanting event is enough to make most boys break out in hives, it is nevertheless available at the Grand Floridian on Monday–Friday afternoons from 2 p.m.–3 p.m. The program consists of making cupcakes, arranging flower bouquets, and having lunch and tea with characters from *Alice in Wonderland*. Reservations can be made by calling ☎ 407-WDW-DINE up to 180 days in advance.

> I guess I still have to be grateful *Idan* that mom did not make me go to the Princess Tea Party. Believe it or not, it is also available for young princes. She took me at age 17 to the Princess Story-book Dinning at Akerhus, you know. Anything for the research!

MY DISNEY GIRL'S PERFECTLY PRINCESS TEA PARTY If your daughter loves princesses and dressing up, then My Disney Girl's Perfectly Princess Tea Party at the Grand Floridian will give you a boost toward the Parent of the Year Award. Your own little princess can sip tea, listen to stories, and join in sing-alongs led by hostess Rose Petal, all while decked out in her favorite regal attire. Princess Aurora will drop by to visit all the junior royalty. Plus your daughter goes home with a variety of souvenirs, including a special 18-inch My Disney Girl doll dressed in a matching Princess Aurora gown with accessories, her own ribbon tiara, silver link bracelet, fresh rose, scrapbook set, and a Best Friend certificate. To receive the royal treatment, you'd better be prepared to pay a royal bill. The 2010 price for one adult and one child (ages 3–11) was $250. A light lunch is included. Each additional adult costs $85, each additional child an extra $165. Call ☎ 407-939-6397 for reservations or more information.

Important: Disney is tinkering with prices and availability of packages more than ever. Always check for availability and prices prior to promising your kids any activity.

MAGIC KINGDOM FAMILY MAGIC TOUR This is a 2-hour guided tour of the Magic Kingdom for the entire family. Even children in strollers are welcome. The tour combines information about the Magic Kingdom with the gathering of clues that ultimately lead the group to a character greeting at the tour's end. Definitely not for the self-conscious, the tour involves skipping, hopping, and walking sideways as you progress from land to land. There's usually a marginal plot such as saving Wendy from Captain Hook, in which case the character at the end of the tour is Wendy. You get the idea. The tour departs daily at 10 a.m. The cost is $30 per person plus a valid Magic Kingdom admission. The maximum group size is 18 persons. Reservations can be made up to one year in advance by calling ☎ 407-WDW-TOUR.

DISNEY'S THE MAGIC BEHIND OUR STEAM TRAINS You must be age 10 or older for this 3-hour tour, presented every Monday, Thursday, and Saturday. The tour kicks off at 7:30 a.m., when you join the crew of the Walt Disney World Railroad as they prepare their steam locomotives for the day. The cost is $45 per person plus a valid Magic Kingdom admission. Call ☎ 407-WDW-TOUR for additional information and reservations.

BIRTHDAYS AND SPECIAL OCCASIONS

ALL GUESTS WHO CELEBRATE A BIRTHDAY or are visiting Walt Disney World for the first time can pick up a button corresponding to the celebration at Guest Relations when entering any of the parks. Often upon check-in the hotel clerks will ask if any member of your party is celebrating a special event. It is especially fun for birthday kids, as cast members will congratulate your child throughout the day in the hotel, on the bus, in the park, and at restaurants throughout the World. A Lombard, Illinois, mom put the word out and was glad she did:

> My daughter was turning 5 while we were there, and I asked about special things that could be done. Our hotel asked me who her favorite character was and did the rest. We came back to our room on her birthday and there were helium balloons, a card, and a Cinderella 5x7 photo autographed in ink! When we entered the Magic Kingdom, we received an It's My Birthday Today pin (FREE!), and at the restaurant she got a huge cupcake with whipped cream, sprinkles, and a candle. IT PAYS TO ASK!!

Another great and reasonably priced treat is to have your hair cut at the Harmony Barber Shop on Main Street at the Magic Kingdom. Rest assured that you or your kid will walk away with a good haircut, and you may even be treated to a song by the Dapper Dans, Disney's famous barbershop quartet! The best time to go is during a parade. You get a good view and the staff sings along with the parade music. It is a great photo op. An Ohio mom celebrated her child's first haircut at the barber shop:

> The barber shop at the entrance of MK makes a big deal with baby's first haircut—pixie dust, photos, a certificate, and "free" mouse ears hat! ($14 total)

PART THREE

WHERE *to* STAY

WHEN TRAVELING WITH CHILDREN, your hotel is your home away from home, your safe harbor, and your sanctuary. Staying in a hotel, an activity usually reserved for adults, is in itself a great adventure for children. They take in every detail and delight in such things as having a pool at their disposal and obtaining ice from a noisy machine. Of course, it is critical that your children feel safe and secure, but it adds immeasurably to the success of the vacation if they really like the hotel.

In truth, because of their youth and limited experience, kids are far less particular about hotels than adults tend to be. A Spartan room and a small pool at a budget motel will make most kids happier than a beagle with a lamb chop. But kids' memories are like little steel traps, so once you establish a lodging standard, that's pretty much what they'll expect every time. A couple from Gary, Indiana, stayed at the pricey Yacht Club Resort at Walt Disney World because they heard that it offered a knockout swimming area (true). When they returned two years later and stayed at Disney's All-Star Resorts for about a third of the price, their 10-year-old carped all week. If you're on a budget, it's better to begin with more modest accommodations and move up to better digs on subsequent trips as finances permit.

> In our opinion, if you are traveling with a child age 12 or younger, one of your top priorities should be to book a hotel within easy striking distance of the parks.
>
> Bob

"You Can't Roller-skate in a Buffalo Herd"

THIS WAS A SONG TITLE FROM THE 1960s. If we wrote that song today, we'd call it "You Can't Have Fun at Disney World if You're Drop-dead Tired." Believe us, Walt Disney World is an easy place to be penny-wise and pound-foolish. Many families who cut lodging expenses by booking a budget hotel end up so far away from Walt Disney World that it is a major hassle to return to the hotel in the middle of the day for swimming and a nap. By trying to spend the whole day at the theme parks, however, they wear themselves out quickly, and the dream vacation suddenly disintegrates into short tempers and exhaustion. And don't confuse this advice with a sales pitch for Disney hotels. There are, you will find, dozens of hotels outside Walt Disney World that are as close or closer to certain Disney theme parks than some of the resorts inside the World. Our main point—in fact, our only point—is to make it easy on yourself to return to your hotel when the need arises.

SOME BASIC CONSIDERATIONS

COST

A NIGHT IN A HOTEL AT DISNEY WORLD or the surrounding area can run anywhere from $40 to $900. Clearly, if you are willing to sacrifice some luxury and don't mind a 10- to 25-minute commute, you

COSTS PER NIGHT OF DISNEY RESORT HOTEL ROOMS	
All-Star Music Resort Family Suites	$190–$355
All-Star Resorts	$82–$174
Animal Kingdom Lodge	$240–$580
Animal Kingdom Villas (Jambo House and Kidani Village)	$275–$2,260
Bay Lake Tower	$385–$2,475
Beach Club Resort	$340–$815
Beach Club Villas	$340–$1,210
BoardWalk Inn	$340–$860
BoardWalk Villas	$340–$2,260
Caribbean Beach Resort	$149–$304
Contemporary Resort	$250–$880
Coronado Springs Resort	$154–$269
Dolphin (Sheraton)	$235–$540
Fort Wilderness Resort & Campground (cabins)	$270–$435
Grand Floridian Resort & Spa	$410–$1,070
Old Key West Resort	$295–$1,725
Polynesian Resort	$365–$990
Pop Century Resort	$82–$174
Port Orleans Resort	$149–$264
Saratoga Springs Resort & Spa	$295–$1,725
Swan (Westin)	$270–$425
Treehouse Villas	$545–$900
Wilderness Lodge	$240–$815
Wilderness Lodge Villas	$330–$1,205
Yacht Club Resort	$340–$815

can really cut your lodging costs by staying outside Walt Disney World. Hotels in Walt Disney World tend to be the most expensive, but they also offer some of the highest quality, as well as a number of perks not enjoyed by guests who stay outside of the World.

Bay Lake Tower, BoardWalk Villas, Wilderness Lodge Villas, Old Key West Resort, Saratoga Springs Resort, Treehouse Villas, and Beach Club Villas offer condo-type accommodations with one-, two-, and (at Saratoga Springs, BoardWalk Villas, Animal Kingdom Villas, Bay Lake Tower, and Old Key West) three-bedroom units with kitchens, living rooms, DVD players, and washers and dryers. Prices range from about $271 per night for a studio at Animal Kingdom Villas to $2,415 per night for a three-bedroom Grand Villa at Bay Lake Tower. Fully equipped cabins at Fort Wilderness Resort & Campground cost $270 to $410 per night. A limited number of suites are available at the more expensive Disney resorts, but they don't have kitchens.

Also at Disney World are the seven hotels of the Downtown Disney Resort Area (DDRA), also known as the Disney Village Hotel Plaza. Accommodations range from fairly luxurious to Holiday Inn quality. Though not typically good candidates for bargains, these hotels recently surprised us with some great deals. While the DDRA is technically part of Disney World, staying there is like visiting a colony rather than the motherland. Free parking at theme parks isn't offered—nor is early entry, with one exception, the Hilton—and hotels operate their own buses rather than use Disney transportation.

WHAT IT COSTS TO STAY IN THE DOWNTOWN DISNEY RESORT AREA

Best Western Lake Buena Vista Resort Hotel	$104–$250
Buena Vista Palace Hotel & Spa	$179–$1,009
DoubleTree Guest Suites	$82–$505
Hilton Walt Disney World	$95–$329
Holiday Inn at Walt Disney World	$94–$159
Regal Sun Resort	$77–$399
Royal Plaza	$109–$249

LOCATION AND TRANSPORTATION OPTIONS

ONCE YOU HAVE DETERMINED YOUR BUDGET, think about what you want to do at Walt Disney World. Will you go to all four theme parks, or will you concentrate on one or two? If you intend to use your own car, the location of your Disney hotel isn't especially important unless you plan to spend most of your time at the Magic Kingdom. (Disney transportation is always more efficient than your car in this case because it bypasses the Transportation and Ticket Center and deposits you at the theme park entrance.)

Most convenient to the Magic Kingdom are the monorail hotels, which are the Grand Floridian, the Contemporary, Bay Lake Tower,

Liliane

For the record, the resorts within walking distance of the International Gateway (the back door, so to speak, of Epcot) are expensive and are a long, long walk from Future World, the section of Epcot where families tend to spend most of their time.

and the Polynesian resorts. Linked by direct boat to the Magic Kingdom is the Wilderness Lodge.

Most convenient to Epcot and Disney's Hollywood Studios are the BoardWalk Inn and Villas, Yacht and Beach Club Resorts, and the Swan and the Dolphin. Though all are within easy walking distance of Epcot's International Gateway, boat service is also available. Vessels also connect Epcot hotels to Disney's Hollywood Studios. Epcot hotels are best for guests planning to spend most of their time at Epcot and/or the Studios.

If you plan to use Disney transportation and intend to visit all four major parks and one or more of the swimming theme parks, book a centrally located resort with good transportation connections. The Epcot resorts and the Polynesian, Caribbean Beach, and Port Orleans resorts fill the bill.

Though not centrally located, the All-Star, Animal Kingdom Lodge and Villas, and Coronado Springs resorts have very good bus service to all Walt Disney World destinations and are closest to the Animal Kingdom. Independent hotels on US 192 near the entrance to Walt Disney World are also just a few minutes from the Animal Kingdom. Wilderness Lodge and Fort Wilderness Campground have the most convoluted and inconvenient transportation service of the Disney hotels. The Old Key West Resort is also transportation challenged—that is, buses run less frequently than at other Disney resorts. The same is true of the Saratoga Springs Resort and Treehouse Villas.

COMMUTING TO AND FROM THE THEME PARKS

FOR VISITORS LODGING INSIDE WALT DISNEY WORLD With three important exceptions, the fastest way to commute from your hotel to the theme parks and back is in your own car. And although many Walt Disney World guests use the Disney Transportation System and appreciate not having to drive, based on timed comparisons, it is almost always less time-consuming to drive. The exceptions are these: (1) commuting to the Magic Kingdom from the hotels on the monorail (Grand Floridian, Polynesian, Bay Lake Tower, and Contemporary Resorts); (2) commuting to the Magic Kingdom from any Disney hotel by bus or boat; and (3) commuting to Epcot on the monorail from the Polynesian Resort via the Transportation and Ticket Center.

If you stay at the Polynesian Resort, you can catch a direct monorail to the Magic Kingdom, and by walking 100 yards or so to the Transportation and Ticket Center, you can catch a direct monorail to Epcot. Located at the nexus of the monorail system, the Polynesian is certainly the most convenient of all hotels. From either the Magic Kingdom or

DRIVING TIME TO THE THEME PARKS

MINUTES TO: FROM	MAGIC KINGDOM PARKING LOT	EPCOT PARKING LOT	DISNEY'S HOLLYWOOD STUDIOS PARKING LOT	ANIMAL KINGDOM PARKING LOT
Downtown Orlando	35	31	33	37
North International Drive and Universal Studios	24	21	22	26
Central International Drive–Sand Lake Road	26	23	24	27
South International Drive and SeaWorld	18	15	16	20
FL 535	12	9	10	13
US 192, north of I-4	10–15	7–12	5–10	5–10
US 192, south of I-4	10–18	7–15	5–13	5–12

Epcot, you can return to your hotel quickly and easily whenever you desire. Sound good? It is, but it costs $365–$990 per night.

Second to the Polynesian in terms of convenience are the Grand Floridian and Contemporary resorts, also on the Magic Kingdom monorail, but they cost as much as or more than the Polynesian. Less expensive Disney hotels transport you to the Magic Kingdom by bus or boat. For reasons described below, this is more efficient than driving a car.

DRIVING TIME TO THE THEME PARKS FOR VISITORS LODGING OUTSIDE WALT DISNEY WORLD For vacationers staying outside Walt Disney World, we've calculated the approximate commuting time to the major theme parks' parking lots from several off-World lodging areas. Add a few minutes to our times to pay your parking fee and to park. Once parked at the Transportation and Ticket Center (Magic Kingdom parking lot), it takes an average of 20–30 more minutes to reach the Magic Kingdom. To reach Epcot from its parking lot, add 7–10 minutes. At Disney's Hollywood Studios and the Animal Kingdom, the lot-to-gate transit time is 5–10 minutes. If you haven't purchased your theme park admission in advance, tack on another 10–20 minutes.

Our hotel information chart on pages 100–102 shows the commuting time, with no consideration of getting to and from the parking lot to the turnstiles, to the Disney theme parks from each hotel listed. Those commuting times represent an average of several test runs. Your actual time may be shorter or longer depending on many variables.

The commuting times in the Hotel Information Chart show conclusively that distance from the theme parks is not necessarily the dominant factor in determining commuting times. Among those we list, the hotels on Major Boulevard opposite the Kirkman Road entrance to Universal Orlando, for example, are the most distant from the Disney parks. But because they're only one traffic signal from easy access to I-4, commuting time to the parks is significantly less than for many closer hotels.

SHUTTLE SERVICE FROM HOTELS OUTSIDE WALT DISNEY WORLD Many hotels in the Walt Disney World area provide shuttle service to the theme parks. They represent a fairly carefree alternative for getting to and from the parks, letting you off near the entrance (except for the Magic Kingdom), and saving you the cost of parking. The rub is that they might not get you there as early as you desire (a critical point if you take our touring advice) or be available at the time you wish to return to your lodging. Also, be forewarned that most shuttle services do not add vehicles at park opening or closing times. In the morning, your biggest problem is that you might not get a seat. At closing time, however, and sometimes following a hard rain, you can expect a lot of competition for standing space on the bus. If there's not room for everyone, you might have to wait 30 minutes to an hour for the next shuttle.

CONVENIENCE CONVENIENTLY DEFINED Conceptually, it's easy to grasp that a hotel that is closer is more convenient than one that is far away. But nothing is that simple at Walt Disney World, so we'd better tell you exactly what you're in for. If you stay at a Walt Disney World resort and use the Disney transportation system, you'll have a 5- to 10-minute walk to the bus stop, monorail station, or dock (whichever applies). Once there, buses, trains, or boats generally run about every 15–25 minutes, so you might have to wait a short time for your transportation to arrive. Once you're on board, most conveyances make additional stops en route to your destination, and many take a less-than-direct route. Upon arrival, however, they deposit you fairly close to the entrance of the theme park. Returning to your hotel is the same process in reverse and takes about the same amount of time.

Regardless of whether or not you stay in Walt Disney World, if you use your own car, here's how your commute shakes out. After a 1- to 5-minute walk from your room to your car, you drive to the theme park, stopping to pay a parking fee or showing your Disney ID for free parking (if you are a Disney resort guest). Disney cast members then direct you to a parking space. If you arrive early, your space may be close enough to the park entrance (Magic Kingdom excepted) to walk. If you park farther afield, a Disney tram will come along every 5 minutes to collect you and transport you to the entrance.

At the Magic Kingdom, the entrance to the park is away-and-gone, separated from the parking lot by the Transportation and Ticket Center (TTC) and the Seven Seas Lagoon. After parking at the Magic Kingdom lot, you take a tram to the TTC and then board a ferry or monorail (your choice) for the trip across the lagoon to the park. All this is fairly time-consuming and is to be avoided if possible. The only way to avoid it, however, is to lodge in a Disney hotel and commute directly to the Magic Kingdom entrance via Disney bus, boat, or monorail. Happily, all of the other theme parks are situated adjacent to their parking lots.

Because families with children tend to spend more time on average at the Magic Kingdom than at the other parks, and because it's so important to return to your hotel for rest, the business of getting around the lagoon can be a major consideration when choosing a place to stay; the extra hassle of crossing the lagoon (to get back to your car) makes coming and going much more difficult. The half hour it takes to commute to your hotel via car from the Animal Kingdom, Disney's Hollywood Studios, or Epcot takes an hour or longer from the Magic Kingdom. If you stay in a Disney hotel and use the Disney transportation system, you may have to wait 5–25 minutes for your bus, boat, or monorail, but it will take you directly from the Magic Kingdom entrance to your hotel, bypassing the lagoon and the TTC.

DINING

DINING FIGURES INTO THE DISCUSSION of where to stay only if you don't plan to have a car at your disposal. If you have a car, you can go eat wherever you want. Alternatively, if you plan on using the Disney Transportation System (for Disney hotel guests) or the courtesy shuttle of your non-Disney hotel, you will either have to dine at the theme parks or at or near your hotel. If your hotel offers a lot of choices or if other restaurants are within walking distance, then there's no problem. If your hotel is somewhat isolated and offers limited selections, you'll feel like I did on a canoe trip once when we ate northern pike at every meal for a week because that's all we could catch.

At Walt Disney World, although it's relatively quick and efficient to commute from your Disney hotel or campground to the theme parks, it's a long, arduous process requiring transfers to travel from hotel to hotel. Disney hotels that are somewhat isolated and that offer limited dining choices include the Old Key West, Caribbean Beach, All-Star, Pop Century, Animal Kingdom Lodge, Coronado Springs, and Wilderness Lodge resorts, as well as the Fort Wilderness Campground and most of the Saratoga Springs Resort.

If you want a condo-type accommodation so that you have more flexibility for meal preparation than eating out of a cooler, the best deals in Walt Disney World are the Wilderness Cabins (prefab log cabins) at the Fort Wilderness Campground. Other Disney lodgings with kitchens are available at the BoardWalk Villas, Old Key West, Saratoga Springs, Wilderness Lodge Villas, and the Beach Club Villas, but all are much more expensive than the cabins at the campground. Outside Walt Disney World, an ever-increasing number of condos are available, and some are very good deals. See our discussion of lodging outside of Walt Disney World later in this chapter.

THE SIZE OF YOUR GROUP

LARGER FAMILIES AND GROUPS may be interested in how many people can stay in a Disney resort room, but only Lilliputians would be comfortable in a room filled to capacity. Groups requiring two or more

If you share a room with your children, you all need to hit the sack at the same time. Establish a single compromise bedtime, probably a little early for you and a bit later than the children's usual weekend bedtime. Observe any nightly rituals you practice at home, such as reading a book before lights out.

Liliane

rooms should consider condo/suite/villa accommodations, either in or out of Walt Disney World. If there are more than six in your party, you will need either two hotel rooms, a suite (see Wilderness Lodge), or a condo.

STAYING IN OR OUT OF THE WORLD: WEIGHING THE PROS AND CONS

1. COST If cost is your primary consideration, you'll lodge much less expensively outside Walt Disney World.

2. EASE OF ACCESS Even if you stay in Walt Disney World, you're dependent on some mode of transportation. It may be less stressful to use Disney transportation, but with the single exception of commuting to the Magic Kingdom, the fastest, most efficient, and most flexible way to get around usually is a car. If you're at Epcot, for example, and want to take the kids back to Disney's Grand Floridian Beach Resort for a nap, forget the monorail. You'll get back much faster in your own car.

A reader from Raynham, Massachusetts, who stayed at the Caribbean Beach Resort (and liked it very much) writes this:

> Even though the resort is on the Disney bus line, I recommend renting a car if it [fits] one's budget. The buses do not go directly to many destinations, and often you have to switch at the Transportation and Ticket Center. Getting a [bus] seat in the morning is no problem. Getting a bus back to the hotel after a hard day can mean a long wait in line.

The Disney Transportation System is about as efficient as is humanly possible. No matter where you're going, you rarely wait more than 15–20 minutes for a bus, monorail, or boat. It is only for the use and benefit of Disney guests; nevertheless it is public transportation, and users must expect the inconveniences inherent in any transportation system: conveyances that arrive and depart on their schedule, not yours; the occasional need to transfer; multiple stops; time lost loading and unloading large numbers of passengers; and, generally, the challenge of understanding and using a complex transportation network.

3. YOUNG CHILDREN Although the hassle of commuting to most non-World hotels is only slightly (if at all) greater than that of commuting to Disney hotels, a definite peace of mind results from staying in the World. Regardless of where you stay, make sure you get your young children back to the hotel for a nap each day.

4. SPLITTING UP If your party will likely split up to tour (as frequently happens in families with children of widely varying ages), staying in

HOTEL | MAXIMUM OCCUPANCY PER ROOM

All-Star Resorts | 4 people plus child in crib

Animal Kingdom Lodge: Jambo House | *Studio:* 4 people; *2-bedroom:* 8 people; all plus child in crib

Animal Kingdom Lodge: Kidani Village | *Studio:* 4 people; *2-bedroom:* 8 people; *3-bedroom:* 12 people; all plus child in crib

Bay Lake Tower at the Contemporary Resort | *Studio:* 4 people; *2-bedroom:* 8 people; *3-bedroom:* 12 people; all plus child in crib

Beach Club Resort | 5 people plus child in crib

Beach Club Villas | *Studio:* 4 people; *2-bedroom:* 8 people; *Grand Villa:* 12 people; all plus child in crib

BoardWalk Inn | 4 people plus child in crib

BoardWalk Villas | *Studio:* 4 people; *2-bedroom:* 8 people; *Grand Villa:* 12 people; all plus child in crib

Caribbean Beach Resort | 4 people plus child in crib

Contemporary Resort | 5 people plus child in crib

Coronado Springs Resort | 4 people plus child in crib

Dolphin (Sheraton) | 4 people

Fort Wilderness Homes | 6 people plus child in crib

Grand Floridian Beach Resort | 4 or 5 people plus child in crib

Old Key West Resort | *Studio:* 4 people; *2-bedroom:* 8 people; *Grand Villa:* 12 people; all plus child in crib

Polynesian Resort | 5 people plus child in crib

Pop Century Resort | 4 people plus child in crib

Port Orleans French Quarter | 4 people plus child in crib

Port Orleans Riverside | 4 people plus child in crib or trundle bed

Saratoga Springs | *Studio:* 4 people; *2-bedroom:* 8 people; *Grand Villa:* 12 people; all plus child in crib

Swan (Westin) | 4 people

Treehouse Villas | 9 people

Wilderness Lodge | 4 people plus child in crib; junior suites with bunk beds accommodate 6 people

Wilderness Lodge Villas | *Studio:* 4 people; *2-bedroom:* 8 people

Yacht Club Resort | 5 people plus child in crib

the World offers more transportation options, thus more independence. Mom and Dad can take the car and return to the hotel for a relaxed dinner and early bedtime, while the teens can remain in the park for evening parades and fireworks.

5. SLOPPING THE PIGS If you have a large crew that chows down like pigs at the trough, you may do better staying outside the World, where food is far less expensive.

6. VISITING OTHER ORLANDO-AREA ATTRACTIONS If you plan to visit SeaWorld, Kennedy Space Center, the Universal theme parks, or other area attractions, it may be more convenient to stay outside the World. Don't, however, book a hotel halfway to Orlando because you think you might run over to Universal or SeaWorld for a day. Remember the number-one rule: "Stay close enough to Walt Disney World to return to your hotel for rest in the middle of the day."

 # WALT DISNEY WORLD LODGING

BENEFITS OF STAYING IN WALT DISNEY WORLD

IN ADDITION TO PROXIMITY—especially easy access to the Magic Kingdom—Walt Disney World resort hotel and campground guests are accorded other privileges and amenities unavailable to those staying outside the World. Though some of these perks are only advertising gimmicks, others are potentially quite valuable. Here are the benefits and what they mean:

1. EXTRA MAGIC HOURS AT THE THEME PARKS Disney World lodging guests (excluding guests at the independent hotels of Downtown Disney Resort Area, except for the Hilton) are invited to enter a designated park 1 hour earlier than the general public each day or to enjoy a designated theme park for 3 hours after it closes to the general public in the evening. Disney guests are also offered specials on admission, including discount tickets to the water parks. These benefits are subject to change without notice. Early entry can be quite valuable if you know how to use it. It can also land you in gridlock.

2. THEME All of the Disney hotels are themed, in pointed contrast to non-Disney hotels, which are, well, mostly just hotels. Each Disney hotel is designed to make you feel that you're in a special place or period of history. See the next page for a chart depicting the various hotels and their respective themes.

Theming is a huge attraction for children, firing their imaginations and really making the hotel an adventure and a memorable place. Some resorts carry off their themes better than others, and some themes are more exciting. **The Wilderness Lodge,** for example, is extraordinary. The lobby opens eight stories to a timbered ceiling supported by giant columns of bundled logs. One look eases you into the Northwest wilderness theme. The isolated lodge is heaven for kids.

The **Animal Kingdom Lodge and Villas** replicate the grand safari lodges of Kenya and Tanzania and overlooks its own private African game preserve. By far the most exotic of the Disney resorts, it's made to order for families with children.

WALT DISNEY WORLD RESORT HOTEL THEMES

HOTEL	THEME
All-Star Resorts	Sports, movies, and music
Animal Kingdom Lodge and Kidani Village	East African game preserve lodge
Bay Lake Tower at the Contemporary	Ultra-modern high-rise
Beach Club Resort and Villas	New England beach club of the 1870s
BoardWalk Inn	East Coast boardwalk hotel of the early 1900s
BoardWalk Villas	East Coast beach cottage of the early 1900s
Caribbean Beach Resort	Caribbean islands
Contemporary Resort	The future as perceived by past and present generations
Coronado Springs Resort	Northern Mexico and the American Southwest
Dolphin (Sheraton)	Modern Florida resort
Grand Floridian Beach Resort	Turn-of-the-20th-century luxury hotel
Old Key West Resort	Key West
Polynesian Resort	Hawaii/South Sea islands
Pop Century	Icons from various decades of the 20th century
Port Orleans French Quarter	Turn-of-the-19th-century New Orleans and Mardi Gras
Port Orleans Riverside	Antebellum plantation and bayou theme
Saratoga Springs	1880s Victorian lakeside resort
Swan (Westin)	Modern Florida resort
Treehouse Villas	Rustic vacation homes with modern amenities
Wilderness Lodge	National park grand lodge of the early 1900s in the American Northwest
Yacht Club Resort	New England seashore hotel of the 1880s

Another kid's favorite is the exotic Treehouse Villas at Saratoga Springs Resort. Originally introduced in 1975, the tree house accommodations were closed and demolished in 2002. The new tree houses, designed in the adventurous image of their predecessors, are nestled in the woods adjacent to the Lake Buena Vista Golf Course.

The **Polynesian Resort,** also dramatic, conveys the feeling of the Pacific islands. It's great for families. Waterfront rooms in the Moorea building offer a perfect view of Cinderella Castle and the Magic Kingdom fireworks across Seven Seas Lagoon. Kids don't know Polynesia from amnesia, but they like those cool "lodge" buildings and all the torches at night.

Grandeur, nostalgia, and privilege are central to the **Grand Floridian, Yacht and Beach Club resorts, Beach Club Villas, Saratoga Springs Resort,** and the **BoardWalk Inn and Villas.** Although modeled after Eastern Seaboard hotels of different eras, the resorts are amazingly similar. Kids appreciate the creative swimming facilities of these resorts but are relatively neutral toward the themes.

The **Port Orleans Resort** lacks the real mystery and sultriness of the New Orleans French Quarter, but it's hard to replicate the Big Easy in a sanitized Disney version. The Riverside section of Port Orleans, however, hits the mark with its antebellum Mississippi River theme, as does **Old Key West Resort** with its Florida Keys theme. Children like each of these resorts, even though the themes are a bit removed from their frame of reference. The **Caribbean Beach Resort**'s theme is much more effective at night, thanks to creative lighting. By day, the resort looks like a Miami condo development. In 2009 the hotel created pirate-themed suites, which are a big hit with little buccaneers. The playground and swimming pool fit in nicely with the pirate theme, and the shop has a large collection of toys from the trilogy *Pirates of the Caribbean*. All three resorts are more spread out and the buildings built to a more human (two- or three-story) scale.

Coronado Springs Resort offers several styles of Mexican and Southwestern American architecture. Though the lake setting is lovely and the resort is attractive and inviting, the theme (with the exception of the main swimming area) isn't particularly stimulating. Coronado Springs feels more like a Scottsdale, Arizona, country club than a Disney resort.

The **All-Star Resorts** encompass 30 three-story, T-shaped hotels with almost 6,000 guest rooms. There are 15 themed areas: five celebrate sports (surfing, basketball, tennis, football, and baseball), five recall Hollywood movie themes, and five have musical motifs. The resorts' design, with entrances shaped like musical notes, Coke cups, and footballs, is somewhat adolescent, sacrificing grace and beauty for energy and novelty. Guest rooms are small, with décor reminiscent of a teenage boy's bedroom. Despite the themes, the All-Star Resorts lack sports, movies, and music. For children, staying at the All-Star Resorts is like being a permanent resident at a miniature golf course. They can't get enough of the giant footballs, dalmatians, and guitars. On a more subjective level, kids intuit that the All-Star Resorts are pretty close to what you'd get all the time if Disney had 12-year-olds designing their hotels. They're cool, and the kids feel right at home.

Liliane

Pop Century is my favorite Disney resort, and Pepper Market is the best food court in the Mouse empire.

The **Pop Century Resort** is almost a perfect clone of the All-Star Resorts, that is, three-story, motel-style buildings built around a central pool, food court, and registration area. Aside from location, the only differences between the All-Star and Pop Century resorts are the decorative touches. Where the All-Star Resorts are distinguished (if you can call it that) by larger-than-life icons from sports, music, and movies, Pop Century draws its icons from various decades of the 20th century. Look for such oddities as building-size Big Wheel tricycles, hula hoops, and the like.

Pretense aside, the **Contemporary, Bay Lake Tower, Swan,** and **Dolphin** are essentially themeless but architecturally interesting. The Contemporary is a 15-story, A-frame building with monorails running through the middle. Views from guest rooms in the Contemporary are among the best at Walt Disney World. Bay Lake Tower at the Contemporary Resort is a sleek, curvilinear high-rise offering bird's-eye views of Bay Lake. The Swan and Dolphin resorts are massive yet whimsical. Designed by Michael Graves, they're excellent examples of "entertainment architecture." Children are blown away by the giant sea creature and swans atop the Dolphin and Swan and love the idea of the monorail running through the middle of the Contemporary.

3. GREAT SWIMMING AREAS Walt Disney World resorts offer some of the most imaginative swimming facilities that you are likely to encounter anywhere. Exotically themed, beautifully landscaped, and equipped with slides, fountains, and smaller pools for toddlers, Disney resort swimming complexes are a quantum leap removed from the typical, rectangular, hotel swimming pool. Some resorts, such as the Grand Floridian and the Polynesian, even offer a sand beach on the Seven Seas Lagoon in addition to swimming pools. Others, such as the Caribbean

WALT DISNEY WORLD RESORT SWIMMING POOLS: *Rated and Ranked*

Hotel	Pool Rating
1. Yacht and Beach Club Resorts and Villas (shared complex)	★★★★★
2. Animal Kingdom Villas (Kidani Village)	★★★★½
3. Port Orleans Resort	★★★★½
4. Saratoga Springs Resort & Spa—Treehouse Villas	★★★★½
5. Wilderness Lodge and Villas	★★★★½
6. Animal Kingdom Lodge and Villas (Jambo House)	★★★★
7. Bay Lake Tower at the Contemporary Resort	★★★★
8. Coronado Springs Resort	★★★★
9. Dolphin	★★★★
10. Polynesian Resort	★★★★
11. Swan	★★★★
12. BoardWalk Inn and Villas	★★★½
13. Contemporary Resort	★★★½
14. Grand Floridian Resort	★★★½
15. All-Star Resorts	★★★
16. Caribbean Beach Resort	★★★
17. Fort Wilderness Resort and Campground	★★★
18. Old Key West Resort	★★★
19. Pop Century Resort	★★★
20. Shades of Green	★★★

Liliane

Just in case your luggage is delayed or your room isn't ready, always pack a change of clothes and bathing suits for all family members in your carry-on luggage.

Beach and Port Orleans resorts, have provided elaborate themed playgrounds near their swimming areas. Incidentally, lest there be any confusion, we are talking about Disney hotel swimming areas and not the Disney paid-admission water theme parks (Typhoon Lagoon and Blizzard Beach).

4. DISNEY'S MAGICAL EXPRESS SERVICE Checked baggage for those arriving in Orlando by commercial airliner are collected by Disney and sent via bus directly to your Walt Disney World resort, allowing you to bypass baggage claim. There's also a bus waiting to transport you to your hotel. If your flight arrives in Orlando close to or after 10 p.m., you must collect your own bags and bring them with you on the bus. Magical Express Transportation runs 24 hours a day.

If you are flying within the United States or Puerto Rico, when it's time to go home, you can check your baggage and receive your boarding pass at the front desk of your Disney resort. This service is available to all guests at Disney-owned resorts—but not the Swan, Dolphin, Shades of Green, or Downtown Disney resorts—even those who don't use the Magical Express service (folks who have rental cars, for example). Resort check-in counters are open 5 a.m.–1 p.m., and you must check in no later than 3 hours before your flight. At press time the following airlines participated in the program: American, Continental, Delta, JetBlue, TED, US Airways, Air Tran, Alaska Airlines, Northwest, United, and Southwest. Disney's Old Key West and Caribbean Beach resorts should be integrating the program by the end of 2010, after increasing the size of the luggage storage rooms. All participating airlines have restrictions on the number of bags, checking procedures, and various other related items. Consult your carrier before leaving home for specifics.

If your flight departs from Orlando before 8 a.m., Magical Express will pick you up before the Magical Express desk at your resort is open. In this case, because the desk isn't manned until 5 a.m., you cannot use the resort check-in for your bags or get your boarding pass. You'll need to handle your own luggage and get your boarding pass at the airport.

Travel agents report very few complaints about Magical Express. Still, the service is not without its faults. Luggage is transported by truck to Walt Disney World instead of accompanying you on the bus. Readers complain of luggage delivered to their hotel rooms hours late, sometimes in the middle of the night. If you want, you can collect your own luggage at the baggage claim and bring it along with you on the Magical Express bus. It isn't much extra trouble and you will be at peace knowing where your luggage is at all times. If you arrive at your hotel with luggage in hand and your room isn't ready, the hotel will store your luggage and provide a phone number you can call to check the status of your room. Be forewarned that some buses go directly to your resort while others make multiple stops at other resorts. Regarding the return trip to the airport, we've received reports both of readers barely getting to the airport in time for their flight and of others made to depart from their hotel very early. One reader, for example, was picked up at 4:35 a.m. for a 7:40 a.m. flight.

5. BABYSITTING AND CHILD-CARE OPTIONS A number of options for babysitting, child-care, and children's programs are offered to Disney hotel and campground guests. All the resort hotels connected by the monorail, as well as several other Disney hotels, offer "clubs," or themed child-care centers, where potty-trained children ages 4–12 can stay while their adults go out.

Though somewhat expensive, the clubs do a great job and are highly regarded by children and parents. On the negative side, they're open only in the evening, and not all Disney hotels have them. If you're staying at a Disney hotel that doesn't have a child-care club, you're better off using one of the private in-room babysitting services (see page 68). In-room babysitting is also available at hotels outside Disney World.

6. GUARANTEED THEME PARK ADMISSIONS On days of unusually heavy attendance, Disney resort guests are guaranteed admission to the theme parks. In practice, no guest is ever turned away until a theme park's parking lot is full. When this happens, that park most certainly will be packed to the point of absolute gridlock. Under such conditions, you would have to possess the common sense of an amoeba to exercise your guaranteed-admission privilege. The privilege, by the way, doesn't extend to Blizzard Beach and Typhoon Lagoon.

7. CHILDREN SHARING A ROOM WITH THEIR PARENTS There is no extra charge per night for children younger than age 18 sharing a room with their parents. Many hotels outside Walt Disney World also observe this practice.

8. FREE PARKING Disney resort guests with cars don't have to pay for parking in the theme-park lots or at the resorts, which saves about $14 per day.

WALT DISNEY WORLD HOTELS:
Strengths and Weaknesses for Families

FOR THE SAKE OF ORIENTATION, we've grouped the Disney resorts, as well as the Swan and Dolphin resorts, by location. Closest to the Magic Kingdom are the Grand Floridian, the Polynesian, The Bay Lake Tower, and the Contemporary resorts, all on the monorail; the Wilderness Lodge and Villas and Fort Wilderness Campground, which are connected to the Magic Kingdom by boat; and the U.S. military resort, Shades of Green, served exclusively by bus.

Close to Epcot are the Yacht Club and Beach Club resorts, the Beach Club Villas, the BoardWalk Inn and Villas, and the non-Disney-owned Swan and Dolphin resorts. These are the closest hotels to Disney's Hollywood Studios.

Closer to Downtown Disney and Bonnet Creek are the Old Key West, Saratoga Springs, Port Orleans, Caribbean Beach, and Pop Century resorts. Also nearby are the seven independent hotels of the Downtown Disney Resort Area.

The All-Star and the Coronado Springs resorts are located near both Disney's Hollywood Studios and the Animal Kingdom. Closest to the Animal Kingdom is The Animal Kingdom Lodge and Villas.

MAGIC KINGDOM RESORTS

Grand Floridian Resort & Spa

GRAND FLORIDIAN RESORT & SPA

STRENGTHS	WEAKNESSES
On Magic Kingdom monorail	Somewhat formal
Ferry service to Magic Kingdom	Cavernous, impersonal lobby
Excellent guest rooms	Overly large physical layout
Children's programs, character meals	Children don't get theme
Excellent children's pool	Only one on-site restaurant suitable
Beach	for younger children
Recreational options	Imposing, rather formal public areas
Restaurant selection via monorail	Distant guest self-parking
Child-care facility on-site	

The Grand Floridian has a lot to offer: a white sand beach, a spa and fitness center, tennis courts, elaborate theatrical dining from high tea to personal butler service, and so on. But the tone strikes some people as rather hoity-toity; the music in the lobby can be disconcertingly loud, the rooms are not so expansive or good-looking as the public spaces, and the complex is frequently crowded with sightseers and plantation nostalgics waving fat cigars. Also, because the Wedding Chapel is located on the grounds of the Grand Floridian, there are frequently receptions, photo sessions, and tizzies—which, depending on your outlook, add charm or are inconveniences.

Polynesian Resort

The Polynesian is arrayed along the Seven Seas Lagoon facing the Magic Kingdom. It's a huge complex, but the hotel buildings, laid out like a South Sea island village around a ceremonial house, are of a decidedly human scale compared to the hulking Grand Floridian or Contemporary resorts. From the tiki torches at night to the bleached sand beach, kids love the Polynesian. The resort's location at WDW's transportation nexus makes it the most convenient resort for those without a car.

POLYNESIAN RESORT

STRENGTHS

Relaxed and casual

Ferry service to Magic Kingdom

Exotic theme that children love

On Magic Kingdom monorail

Epcot monorail within walking distance

Transportation and Ticket Center
  adjoins resort

Newly redecorated rooms among
  the nicest at WDW

Children's programs, character meals

Beach and marina

Excellent swimming complex

Recreational options

Restaurant selection via monorail

WDW's best child-care facility
  on-site

Easily accessible self-parking

WEAKNESSES

Overly large and confusing layout

Walkways exposed to rain

Noise from nearby motor speedway

Front-desk inefficiency

Contemporary Resort and Bay Lake Tower

The Contemporary Resort has a sleek, almost Asian look, although the pyramid structure itself is a period piece, of course. And it has lots to offer the active family: six lighted tennis courts, three swimming pools, a health club, volleyball courts, a beach, and a marina that rents sailboats of various sizes—you must be at least 18 years old, which helps limit the traffic a little—and offers parasailing and waterskiing. Guest rooms were completely refurbished and are now the nicest to be found at Walt Disney World. There's no compelling theme, but then show me a child who isn't wowed by monorails tearing though the inside of a hotel. With a 2009 debut, the Bay Lake Tower is a high-rise Disney Vacation Club property situated on Bay Lake between the Contemporary Resort and the Magic Kingdom. Like other DVC developments, it offers one-, two-, and three-bedroom suites. Features include a fireworks-viewing deck, a rooftop lounge, a lakeside pool, and a sky bridge linking the tower to the Contemporary Resort's monorail station.

CONTEMPORARY RESORT AND BAY LAKE TOWER

STRENGTHS

On Magic Kingdom monorail

10-minute walk to Magic Kingdom

Interesting architecture

Nicest rooms at WDW

Super views of the Magic Kingdom or
  Bay Lake

Character meals

Excellent children's pool

Marina

Recreational options including super
  games arcade

Restaurant selection via monorail

Child-care facility on-site

Good restaurant on-site

WEAKNESSES

Sterility of theme and decor in public
  areas

Monorail aside, theme leaves children
  cold

Wilderness Lodge Resort

WILDERNESS LODGE RESORT

STRENGTHS

Magnificently rendered theme that children can't get enough of

Good on-site dining

Great views from guest rooms

Extensive recreational options

Romantic setting and interesting architecture

Elaborate swimming complex

Health and fitness center

Child-care facility on-site

Convenient self-parking

WEAKNESSES

Boat service only to Magic Kingdom

No direct bus to many destinations

No character meals

Rooms sleep only four people (plus child in crib)

Must take boat or bus to access off-site dining options

This deluxe resort is inspired by national-park lodges of the early 20th century. The Wilderness Lodge and Villas ranks with Animal Kingdom Lodge as one of the most impressively themed and meticulously detailed Disney resorts. It's also by far the hands-down favorite hotel of children. You won't have any trouble convincing the kids to abandon the theme parks for rest and a swim if you stay at the Wilderness Lodge.

Situated on the shore of Bay Lake, the lodge consists of an eight-story central building flanked by two seven-story guest wings and a wing of studio and one- and two-bedroom condominiums. The hotel features exposed timber columns, log cabin–style facades, and dormer windows. The grounds are landscaped with evergreen pines and pampas grass. The lobby boasts an 82-foot-tall stone fireplace and two 55-foot Pacific Northwest totem poles. Timber pillars, giant tepee chandeliers, and stone- and wood-inlaid floors accentuate the lobby's rustic luxury. Although the resort isn't on vast acreage, it does have a beach and a delightful pool modeled on a mountain stream complete with waterfall and geyser. Adjoining the Wilderness Lodge is the Wilderness Lodge Villas, a Disney Vacation Club property offering condo accommodations.

Shades of Green

This deluxe resort is owned and operated by the U.S. Armed Forces and is available only to U.S. military personnel (including members of the National Guard and reserves, retired military, and employees of the U.S. Public Health Service and the Department of Defense; others may be eligible; call for additional information). Shades of Green consists of one three-story building nestled among three golf courses. Tastefully nondescript, Shades of Green is at the same time pure peace and quiet. There's no beach or lake, but there are several pools, including one shaped like Mickey's head. Surrounding golf courses

SHADES OF GREEN

STRENGTHS

Large guest rooms
Informality
Quiet setting
Views of golf course from guest rooms
Convenient self-parking
Swimming complex
Fitness center

Video arcade
Game rooms with pool
Ice-cream shop

WEAKNESSES

No interesting theme
Limited on-site dining
Limited bus service

are open to all Disney guests. If you qualify to stay here, don't even think about staying anywhere else.

Fort Wilderness Campground

If camping is one of your hobbies, you can rough it in beautiful territory at Fort Wilderness for as little as $44 per campsite. Either set up a tent and use the restrooms, showers, and Laundromat down the lane, or borrow your parents' RV. With the accessibility of two markets on-site, most visitors here choose to do their own cooking; do so and this becomes the absolute rock-bottom priced Disney World vacation.

FORT WILDERNESS CAMPGROUND

784 campsites	$44–$121 per night	boat/bus service
408 wilderness homes and cabins (sleep 4–6)	$270–$435 per night	boat/bus service

Fort Wilderness is ideal for nature lovers. For the less active, electric carts are for rent. Also available are pools, a marina and beach, and a lot

FORT WILDERNESS CAMPGROUND

STRENGTHS

Informality
Children's play areas
Best selection of recreational options at WDW
Special day and evening programs
Campsite amenities
Number of showers and toilets
Limited automobile traffic
Hoop-Dee-Doo Revue musical dinner show
Off-site dining options via boat at Magic Kingdom resorts

Convenient self-parking
Free Wi-Fi

WEAKNESSES

Isolated location
Complicated bus service
Confusing campground layout
Lack of privacy
Very limited on-site dining options
Extreme distance to store and restaurant facilities from many campsites
Crowding at beaches and pools
Small baths in cabins

of outdoor games, such as basketball and volleyball, shuffleboard, fishing and canoeing, biking, even tennis and horseback riding. If you really get into the mood, you can sit around the evening campfire and watch a movie with the other happy campers. The campgrounds are the only accommodations that allow you to have pets (not running loose, of course).

Here's what you cannot do: drive anywhere within the campground, not even from your campsite back to the trading post. You must take the bus, bike, or golf cart (both are for rent), or walk (it's not far). And bus or boat transportation to the theme parks can be laborious.

Obviously, Fort Wilderness draws a lot of families (did we mention the petting farm and the hay rides?), and in hot weather, a lot of bugs and thunderstorms. If you want things a little more comfortable, ask for a full-service hookup and get water, electricity, an outdoor grill, sanitary disposal, and even a cable TV connection. If you want super privacy and even more amenities, rent one of the prefab log cabins, which get you a full kitchen, housekeeping services, air-conditioning, a daily newspaper, voice mail, and, yes, cable TV.

All loops have a comfort station with showers, toilets, Bob phones, an ice machine, and a coin laundry.

For tent and RV campers, there's a fairly stark trade-off between sites convenient to pools, restaurant, trading posts, and other amenities, and those that are most scenic, shady, and quiet. RVers who prefer to be near Guest Services, the marina, the beach, and the restaurant and tavern should go for loops 100, 200, 700, and 400 (in that order). Loops near the campground's secondary facility area with pool, trading post, bike and golf-cart rentals, and campfire program are 1400, 1300, 600, 1000, and 1500, in order of preference. If you're looking for a tranquil, scenic setting among mature trees, we recommend loops 1800, 1900, 1700, and 1600, in that order, and the backside sites on the 700 loop. The best loop of all, and the only one to offer both a lovely setting and proximity to key amenities, is loop 300. The best loops for tents and pop-up campers are loops 1500 and 2000, with 1500 being nearest a pool, convenience store, and the campfire program.

EPCOT RESORTS

Yacht & Beach Club Resorts and Beach Club Villas

Situated on Crescent Lake across from Disney's BoardWalk, the Yacht and Beach Club resorts are connected and share a boardwalk, marina, and swimming complex. The Yacht Club Resort has a breezy Nantucket and Cape Cod atmosphere with its own lighthouse and boardwalks, lots of polished wood, and burnished brass (and boxes of chess or checkers pieces available for your room on request). Its sibling resort, the Beach Club, shares most of the facilities but is a little sportier and more casual in atmosphere. The Disney Vacation Club Villas at the Beach Club are available for rental, have their own small pool, and may offer more privacy. The resorts offer a shared mini–water park, Stormalong Bay, with a white-sand beach and marina, and an unusual number of sports

---

YACHT & BEACH CLUB RESORTS AND BEACH CLUB VILLAS

STRENGTHS

Fun and nautical New England theme

Attractive guest rooms

Good on-site dining

Children's programs, character meals

Excellent selection of nearby off-site dining

Boat service to Disney's Hollywood Studios and Epcot

10-minute walk to rear entrance of Epcot

10-minute walk to BoardWalk

15-minute walk to DHS

Best swimming complex at WDW

Health and fitness center

Convenient self-parking

View from waterside guest rooms

Child-care facility on-site

WEAKNESSES

No transportation to Epcot main entrance, except by taxi

No convenient counter-service food

Poor room-to-hall soundproofing

---

facilities, such as croquet, tennis, and volleyball, plus fitness rooms, and so on. Many of the rooms have balconies with views looking out across the lagoon toward the BoardWalk.

BoardWalk Inn and Villas

On Crescent Lake, the BoardWalk Inn is another of the Walt Disney World deluxe resorts. The complex is a detailed replica of an early-20th-century Atlantic coast boardwalk. Facades of hotels, diners, and shops create an inviting and exciting waterfront skyline. In reality, behind the facades, the BoardWalk Inn and Villas are a single integrated structure. Restaurants and shops occupy the boardwalk level, while accommodations rise up to six stories above. Painted bright red and yellow along with weathered pastel

---

BOARDWALK INN AND VILLAS

STRENGTHS

Lively seaside and amusement pier theme

Newly refurbished guest rooms

10-minute walk to Epcot rear entrance

15-minute walk to DHS

Boat service to Disney's Hollywood Studios and Epcot

Modest but well-themed swimming complex

3-minute walk to BoardWalk midway and nightlife

Selection of off-site dining within walking distance

Health and fitness center

View from waterside guest rooms

Child-care facility on-site

WEAKNESSES

No restaurants in hotel

Limited children's activities and no character meals

No restaurants within easy walking distance suitable for younger children

No transportation to Epcot main entrance

Distant guest self-parking

greens and blues, the BoardWalk resorts are the only Disney hotels that use neon signs as architectural detail. The complex shares one pool having an old-fashioned amusement-park theme and also has two quiet pools.

The BoardWalk Inn and Villas have a lot to offer in terms of entertainment, in that the ESPN Club, the carnival midway, street performers, and for adults, BoardWalk nightspots, are all literally at your feet. But think about what that will mean when you're ready to call it quits; the sound can come right up through the building, and odd lights are glaring at all hours.

Walt Disney World Swan and Dolphin Resorts

THE SWAN AND THE DOLPHIN

STRENGTHS

Exotic architecture

Extremely nice guest rooms

Good on-site and nearby dining

Excellent beach and swimming complex

Health and fitness center

Child-care facilities on-site

Children's programs, character meals

Varied recreational offerings

10-minute walk to BoardWalk nightlife

Boat service to Disney's Hollywood Studios and Epcot

Participates in Extra Magic Hours program

View from guest rooms

WEAKNESSES

Primarily adult convention and business clientele

No transportation to Epcot main entrance

Distant guest self-parking, requires daily fee

Do not qualify for Disney's Magical Express service

Confusing layout

The Walt Disney World Swan and Dolphin resorts were not designed by Disney Imagineers, though you might certainly think they were. They were the playgrounds of postmodern architect Michael Graves; in fact, they are not Disney-owned properties at all, though guests have most of the perks. The Swan and Dolphin are patronized by business types and adult travelers rather than families, and their theme runs more to the surrealistic rather than to the whimsical. That being said, a quick glance at the Swan and Dolphin's strengths will verify that they have as much or more to offer families than the Disney resorts.

BONNET CREEK/DOWNTOWN DISNEY AREA RESORTS

Caribbean Beach Resort

The huge Caribbean Beach Resort occupies 200 acres surrounding a 45-acre lake called Barefoot Bay. This midpriced resort, modeled after resorts in the Caribbean, consists of the registration area (Custom House) and six two-story "villages" named after Caribbean islands. Each

CARIBBEAN BEACH RESORT

STRENGTHS	WEAKNESSES
Attractive Caribbean theme	Lackluster on-site dining
Children's play areas	No easily accessible off-site dining
Convenient self-parking	No character meals
Walking, jogging, biking	Extreme distance of many guest rooms from dining and services
Lakefront setting	Occasionally poor bus service
	Large, confusing layout
	Long lines to check in

village has its own pool, laundry room, and beach. The Caribbean motif is maintained with red-metal roofs, widow's walks, and wooden-railed porches. The atmosphere is cheerful, with buildings painted blue, lime green, and sherbet orange. In addition to the five village pools, the resort's main swimming pool is themed as an old Spanish fort, complete with slides and water cannons.

Port Orleans French Quarter and Riverside Resorts

Port Orleans's Riverside and French Quarter resorts are good-looking, lower-cost hotel alternatives that combine steamboat-era Southern decor and fairly easy access to Downtown Disney, and they're pretty popular among families too.

The 1,008-room French Quarter section is a sanitized Disney version of the New Orleans French Quarter. Consisting of seven three-story buildings next to Bonnet Creek, the resort suggests what New Orleans would look like if its buildings were painted every year and garbage collectors never went on strike. There are prim pink-and-blue guest buildings with wrought-iron filigree, shuttered windows, and old-fashioned iron lampposts. In keeping with the Crescent City theme, the French Quarter is landscaped with magnolia trees and

PORT ORLEANS FRENCH QUARTER AND RIVERSIDE RESORTS

STRENGTHS	WEAKNESSES
Extremely creative swimming areas	No character meals
Nice guest rooms, especially in the French Quarter	Insufficient on-site dining
Pleasant setting along Bonnet Creek	No easily accessible off-site dining
Food courts	Extreme distance of many guest rooms from dining and services
Convenient self-parking	Large, confusing layout
Children's play areas	Congested bus-loading areas
Varied recreational offerings	
Boat service to Downtown Disney	

overgrown vines. The centrally located Mint contains the registration area and food court and is a reproduction of a turn-of-the-19th-century building where Mississippi Delta farmers sold their harvests. The registration desk features a vibrant Mardi Gras mural and old-fashioned bank-teller windows. The section's Doubloon Lagoon swimming complex surrounds a colorful fiberglass creation depicting Neptune riding a sea serpent.

Port Orleans's Riverside Resort draws on the lifestyle and architecture of Mississippi River communities in antebellum Louisiana. Spread along Bonnet Creek, which encircles Ol' Man Island (the section's main swimming area), Riverside is subdivided into two more themed areas: the mansion area, which features plantation-style architecture, and the bayou area, with tin-roofed rustic (imitation) wooden buildings. Mansions are three stories tall, while bayou guesthouses are a story shorter. The river-life theme is augmented by groves of azalea and juniper. Riverside's food court houses a working cotton press powered by a 35-foot waterwheel.

Disney's Old Key West Resort

DISNEY'S OLD KEY WEST RESORT	
STRENGTHS	**WEAKNESSES**
Extremely nice studios and villas	Old Key West theme meaningless to children
Full kitchens in villas	
Quiet, lushly landscaped setting	Large, confusing layout
Convenient self-parking	Substandard bus service
Small, more private swimming pools in each accommodations cluster	Limited on-site dining
	No easily accessible off-site dining
Recreation options	Extreme distance of many guest rooms from dining and services
Boat service to Downtown Disney	
	No character meals

This was the first Disney Vacation Club property. Although the resort is a time-share property, units not being used by owners are rented on a nightly basis. Old Key West is a large aggregation of two- to three-story buildings modeled after Caribbean-style residences and guesthouses of the Florida Keys. Arranged subdivision-style around a golf course and along Bonnet Creek, the buildings are in small neighborhood-like clusters. They feature pastel facades, white trim, and shuttered windows. The registration area is in Conch Flats Community Hall, along with a full-service restaurant, modest fitness center, marina, and sundries shop. Each cluster of accommodations has a quiet pool; a larger pool is at the community hall. A waterslide in the shape of a giant sandcastle is the primary kid pleaser at the main pool.

SARATOGA SPRINGS RESORT & SPA

STRENGTHS	WEAKNESSES
Extremely nice studio rooms and villas	Traffic congestion at resort's southeast exit
Lushly landscaped setting	
Best fitness center at Walt Disney World	Small living areas in villas
Convenient self-parking	Distance of some accommodations from dining and services
Close to Downtown Disney	Limited dining options
Best spa at Walt Disney World	No character meals
Golf on property	Most distant of all Disney resorts from the theme parks
Excellent themed swimming complex	Theme and atmosphere not very kid-friendly
Hiking, jogging, and water recreation	

Saratoga Springs Resort

The main pool is the resort's focal point. Called High Rock Spring, it tumbles over boulders into a clear, free-form heated pool. The area offers a waterslide that winds among the rocks, two whirlpool spas, and an interactive wet-play area for children. The Saratoga Springs complex will eventually be the largest Vacation Club resort, with well over 800 units. It's expanding toward the Downtown Disney shopping area (across the lake) via a path and a pedestrian bridge. There is boat as well as bus service at the facility, although the boats are prohibited from running if lightning threatens. The resort's decor plays on the history and retro-Victorian style of the upstate New York racing resort, with traditional horse-country prints and drawings, stable boy uniforms for the bellhops, and so on. The spa, probably Disney's best, has a fitness center attached. The Downtown Disney fireworks are visible from some areas. Favorites for children are the Treehouse Villas nestled in a pinewood bordering the golf course. With the entire living and sleeping area about 12 feet off the ground, you really feel like you're living in a tree house. Opened in 2009, the rustic Treehouse Villas are among Walt Disney World's most inventive accommodations. There are only 60 three-bedroom units, so if you want a reservation for one of those larger units, book well in advance.

The All-Star, Pop Century, and Caribbean Beach resorts are infamous for long lines at check-in time, which is usually 3 or 4 p.m. To avoid the lines, check in between 11 a.m. and 1 p.m. Your room might not be ready for occupancy, but odds are they'll check you in and issue your room keys. If you have luggage, you can check it with bell services and have it delivered or pick it up later.

Bob

Pop Century Resort

Located on Victory Way near Disney's Wide World of Sports, the Pop Century is the newest Disney value resort. Rather than complete the second phase of Pop Century, Disney elected to use the allocated acreage for a new

POP CENTURY RESORT

STRENGTHS	WEAKNESSES
Kid-friendly theme	Small guest rooms
Low (for Disney) rates	No full-service dining
Large swimming pools	Large, confusing layout
Food court	No character meals
Convenient self-parking	Limited recreation options
Fast check-in	

value resort called Disney's Art of Animation Resort, scheduled to open in late 2012.

Pop Century is an economy resort. In terms of layout, architecture, and facilities, Pop Century is almost a clone of the All-Star Resorts (that is, four-story, motel-style buildings built around a central pool, food court, and registration area). Decorative touches make the difference. Where the All-Star Resorts display larger-than-life icons from sports, music, and movies, Pop Century draws its icons from decades of the 20th century. Look for such oddities as building-size Big Wheels, hula hoops, and the like, punctuated by silhouettes of people dancing the decade's fad dance.

The public areas at Pop Century are marginally more sophisticated than the ones at the All-Star Resorts, with 20th-century period furniture and decor rolled up in a saccharine, those-were-the-days theme. A food court, bar, playground, pools, and so on emulate the All-Star Resorts model in size and location. A Pop Century departure from the All-Star precedent has merchandise retailers thrown in with the fast-food concessions in a combination dining and shopping area. This apparently is what happens when a giant corporation tries to combine selling pizza with hawking Goofy hats. (You just know the word "synergy" was used like cheap cologne in those design meetings.) As at the All-Star Resorts, there is no full-service restaurant. The resort is connected to the rest of Walt Disney World by bus, but because of the limited dining options, we recommend having a car.

If you're considering one of the Disney "value" resorts, this reader from Dublin, Georgia, thinks Pop Century beats the All-Star Resorts hands-down.

Pop Century is now my favorite. 1. It is far superior to the All-Stars but the same price. 2. There is a lake at a value resort and a view of fireworks. 3. The courtyards have Twister games, neat pools, and a Goofy "surprise fountain" for little children. 4. The memorabilia is interesting to us over 18 years old. 5. I love the gift shop, food court, and bar combo. 6. There are frozen Cokes in the refillable-mug section. 7. Bus transportation is better than anywhere else, including Grand Floridian! 8. You can rent surrey bikes. 9. The rooms have real soap instead of the All-Stars' yucky globby stuff. 10. The layout is more convenient to the food court. 11. I never hear construction noise, and the noise from neighbors is not worse than anywhere else. 12. Where else do the [cast members] do the shag to oldies? Also, the shrimp lo mein is the best bargain and among the best food anywhere.

ANIMAL KINGDOM RESORTS

Animal Kingdom Lodge and Villas

The Animal Kingdom Lodge is a snazzy take on safari chic, with balcony views of wildlife that alone may be worth the tabs, but its distance from the other parks may be a drawback for those planning to explore all of Disney World. On the other hand, if you have a car, it's the closest resort to all of the affordable family restaurants lining US 192 (Irlo Bronson Parkway). By far the most exotic Disney resort, it's made for families.

Designed by Peter Dominick of Wilderness Lodge fame, Animal Kingdom Lodge fuses African tribal architecture with the rugged style of grand East African national-park lodges. Five-story, thatched-roof wings fan out from a vast central rotunda housing the lobby and featuring a huge mud fireplace. Public areas and many rooms offer panoramic views of a private 33-acre wildlife preserve punctuated with streams and elevated kopje (rock outcrops) and populated with 100 types of free-roaming animals and 130 birds. Most guest rooms boast hand-carved furnishings and richly colored upholstery. Almost all have full balconies.

Having stayed at Kidani Village shortly after its opening, we think it's a quiet, relaxed resort. The lobby and rooms have a smaller, more personal feel than Jambo House. The building exterior isn't anything special—essentially a set of green rectangles with oversize African-themed decorations attached. Kidani's distance from Jambo House makes it feel even more remote than Jambo. The bus stops are a fair distance from the main building too, and it's easy to head in the wrong direction when you're coming back from the parks at night.

ANIMAL KINGDOM LODGE, JAMBO HOUSE, AND KIDANI VILLAGE

STRENGTHS

Exotic theme

Uniquely appointed guest rooms

Most rooms have private balconies

View of savanna and animals from guest rooms

Themed swimming areas

Excellent on-site dining, including a buffet

On-site nature programs and storytelling

Health and fitness center

Child-care center on-site

Proximity to non-Disney restaurants on US 192

WEAKNESSES

Remote location

Coronado Springs Resort

If you'd like to save a little money without giving up services, consider the Coronado Springs Resort, a rich, Old Mexico–style complex with courtyards, fountains, stucco and terra-cotta buildings, a few Mayan ruins here and there, several swimming pools, a mini water park, a white-sand beach, a fitness center, a walking path circling a 22-acre lake, and so on. Because it is also used as a convention hotel, expect a high percentage of guests to be business travelers. Coronado Springs has particularly good access to the Animal Kingdom and Blizzard Beach.

CORONADO SPRINGS RESORT

STRENGTHS	WEAKNESSES
Nice guest rooms	Insufficient on-site dining
View from waterside guest rooms	*Extreme* distance of many guest rooms from dining and services
Food court	
Mayan-themed swimming area with waterslides	No character meals
Fitness center	Low-flow showerheads make rinsing off take longer
Nightclub on property	
Convenient self-parking	

All-Star Resorts

Disney's version of a budget resort features three distinct themes executed in the same hyperbolic style. Spread over a vast expanse, the resorts comprise almost 35 three-story motel-style guest-room buildings. Although the three resorts are neighbors, each has its own lobby, food court, and registration area. All-Star Sports Resort features huge sports icons: bright football helmets, tennis rackets, and baseball bats—all taller than the buildings they adorn. Similarly,

ALL-STAR RESORTS

STRENGTHS	WEAKNESSES
Super kid-friendly theme	Remote location
Low (for Disney) rates	Small guest rooms (except family suites)
Large swimming pools	
Food courts	No full-service dining
Convenient self-parking	Large, confusing layout
	Congested bus-loading areas
	No character meals
	Limited recreation options
	Close to McDonald's (kidding!)

All-Star Music Resort features 40-foot guitars, maracas, and saxophones, while All-Star Movies Resort showcases giant popcorn boxes and icons from Disney films. Lobbies of all are loud (in both decibels and brightness) and cartoonish, with checkerboard walls and photographs of famous athletes, musicians, and film stars. At 260 square feet, guest rooms at the All-Star Resorts are very small. They're so small that a family of four attempting to stay in one room might redefine family values by week's end. Definitely a family resort, young children exercising their lungs make the All-Stars the noisiest Disney resorts, though guest rooms are well soundproofed and quiet.

To the rejoicing of parents everywhere, Disney opened 192 family suites at its All-Star Music Resort. Located in the Jazz and Calypso buildings, these suites measure roughly 520 square feet, slightly larger than the cabins at Fort Wilderness. Each suite, formed from the combination of two formerly separate rooms, includes a kitchenette with mini-refrigerator, microwave, and coffeemaker. Sleeping accommodations include a queen bed in the bedroom, plus a pullout sleeper sofa and two chairs that convert to beds in the family room.

We get more reader mail about the All-Star Resorts than about all the other Disney hotels combined. The following comments are pretty representative. First from a Baltimore family that had a very positive experience:

We were pleasantly surprised. Yes, the rooms are small. But the overall magic there is amazing. The lobby played Disney movies . . . [and] there are great photo ops everywhere. . . . The food court—let's face it—is crap . . . except for the refrigerator cases where you can buy fresh-tasting (albeit expensive) fruit, water, healthy snacks, and great chicken-salad sandwiches. Further, despite forewarnings of loud children, we were in the Love Bug building and found it very quiet. The express-checkout service was also a godsend.

But a Massachusetts family of four had this to say:

I would never recommend the All-Star for a family. It was like dormitory living. Our room was about one mile from the bus stop, and the food court got old very quickly. Buses were great, but the room was tiny. . . . You needed to step into the bathroom, shut the door, then step around the toilet which blocked half the tub.

Finally, a dad from Rogers, Arkansas, had this to say:

Make sure that people understand how inconvenient the shuttle service becomes when you have to share one bus for all three All-Star resorts. This one issue ruined what was an otherwise very pleasant experience.

continued on page 103

Hotel Information Chart

All-Star Resorts ★ ★ ★
Walt Disney World
1701–1901 W. Buena Vista Dr.
Lake Buena Vista, FL 32830
☎ 407-934-7639
disneyworld.com

LOCATION	WDW
ROOM RATING	73
COST ($ = $50)	$$–

COMMUTING TIMES TO PARKS
(in minutes):

MAGIC KINGDOM	6:15
EPCOT	5:45
ANIMAL KINGDOM	4:15
DHS	5:15

Animal Kingdom Lodge ★ ★ ★ ★
Walt Disney World
2901 Osceola Pkwy.
Lake Buena Vista, FL 32830
☎ 407-938-3000
FAX 407-938-4799
disneyworld.com

LOCATION	WDW
ROOM RATING	89
COST ($ = $50)	$$$$$–

COMMUTING TIMES TO PARKS
(in minutes):

MAGIC KINGDOM	8:15
EPCOT	6:15
ANIMAL KINGDOM	2:15
DHS	6:00

Animal Kingdom Villas (Kidani Village and Jambo House) ★ ★ ★ ★ ½
Walt Disney World
2901 Osceola Pkwy.
Lake Buena Vista, FL 32830
☎ 407-938-3000
FAX 407-938-4799
disneyworld.com

LOCATION	WDW
ROOM RATING	93
COST ($ = $50)	$$$$$$$–

COMMUTING TIMES TO PARKS
(in minutes):

MAGIC KINGDOM	8:15
EPCOT	6:15
ANIMAL KINGDOM	2:15
DHS	6:00

BoardWalk Inn ★ ★ ★ ★
Walt Disney World
2101 Epcot Resorts Blvd.
Lake Buena Vista, FL 32830
☎ 407-939-5100
FAX 407-939-5150
disneyworld.com

LOCATION	WDW
ROOM RATING	89
COST ($ = $50)	$$$$$$–

COMMUTING TIMES TO PARKS
(in minutes):

MAGIC KINGDOM	7:15
EPCOT	5:30
ANIMAL KINGDOM	7:00
DHS	3:00

BoardWalk Villas ★ ★ ★ ★ ½
Walt Disney World
2101 Epcot Resorts Blvd.
Lake Buena Vista, FL 32830
☎ 407-939-5100
FAX 407-939-5150
disneyworld.com

LOCATION	WDW
ROOM RATING	90
COST ($ = $50)	$$$$$$–

COMMUTING TIMES TO PARKS
(in minutes):

MAGIC KINGDOM	7:15
EPCOT	5:30
ANIMAL KINGDOM	7:00
DHS	3:00

Caribbean Beach Resort ★ ★ ★ ½
Walt Disney World
900 Cayman Way
Lake Buena Vista, FL 32830
☎ 407-934-3400
FAX 407-934-3288
disneyworld.com

LOCATION	WDW
ROOM RATING	80
COST ($ = $50)	$$$

COMMUTING TIMES TO PARKS
(in minutes):

MAGIC KINGDOM	8:00
EPCOT	6:00
ANIMAL KINGDOM	7:15
DHS	4:15

Fort Wilderness Resort (cabins) ★ ★ ★ ★
Walt Disney World
4510 N. Fort Wilderness Trl.
Lake Buena Vista, FL 32830
☎ 407-824-2900
FAX 407-824-3508
disneyworld.com

LOCATION	WDW
ROOM RATING	86
COST ($ = $50)	$$$$$+

COMMUTING TIMES TO PARKS
(in minutes):

MAGIC KINGDOM	13:15
EPCOT	8:30
ANIMAL KINGDOM	20:00
DHS	14:00

Grand Floridian Resort & Spa ★ ★ ★ ★ ½
Walt Disney World
4401 Floridian Way
Lake Buena Vista, FL 32830
☎ 407-824-3000
FAX 407-824-3186
disneyworld.com

LOCATION	WDW
ROOM RATING	93
COST ($ = $50)	$$$$$$$$+

COMMUTING TIMES TO PARKS
(in minutes):

MAGIC KINGDOM	on monorail
EPCOT	4:45
ANIMAL KINGDOM	11:45
DHS	6:45

Old Key West Resort ★ ★ ★ ★ ½
Walt Disney World
1510 N. Cove Rd.
Lake Buena Vista, FL 32830
☎ 407-827-7700
FAX 407-827-7710
disneyworld.com

LOCATION	WDW
ROOM RATING	90
COST ($ = $50)	$$$$$

COMMUTING TIMES TO PARKS
(in minutes):

MAGIC KINGDOM	10:45
EPCOT	6:00
ANIMAL KINGDOM	14:30
DHS	10:30

Bay Lake Tower at Contemporary Resort
★★★★½
Walt Disney World
4600 N. World Dr.
Lake Buena Vista, FL 32830
☎ 407-824-1000
FAX 407-824-3539
disneyworld.com

LOCATION	WDW
ROOM RATING	95
COST ($ = $50)	$$$$$$$–

COMMUTING TIMES TO PARKS
(in minutes):

MAGIC KINGDOM	on monorail
EPCOT	11:00
ANIMAL KINGDOM	17:15
DHS	14:15

Beach Club Resort ★★★★½
Walt Disney World
1800 Epcot Resorts Blvd.
Lake Buena Vista, FL 32830
☎ 407-934-8000
FAX 407-934-3850
disneyworld.com

LOCATION	WDW
ROOM RATING	90
COST ($ = $50)	$$$$$$$–

COMMUTING TIMES TO PARKS
(in minutes):

MAGIC KINGDOM	7:15
EPCOT	5:15
ANIMAL KINGDOM	6:45
DHS	4:00

Beach Club Villas
★★★★½
Walt Disney World
1900 Epcot Resorts Blvd.
Lake Buena Vista, FL 32830
☎ 407-934-2175
FAX 407-934-3850
disneyworld.com

LOCATION	WDW
ROOM RATING	90
COST ($ = $50)	$$$$$$$$$$$$$

COMMUTING TIMES TO PARKS
(in minutes):

MAGIC KINGDOM	7:15
EPCOT	5:15
ANIMAL KINGDOM	6:45
DHS	4:00

Contemporary Resort ★★★★½
Walt Disney World
4600 N. World Dr.
Lake Buena Vista, FL 32830
☎ 407-824-1000
FAX 407-824-3539
disneyworld.com

LOCATION	WDW
ROOM RATING	93
COST ($ = $50)	$$$$$$–

COMMUTING TIMES TO PARKS
(in minutes):

MAGIC KINGDOM	on monorail
EPCOT	11:00
ANIMAL KINGDOM	17:15
DHS	14:15

Coronado Springs Resort ★★★★
Walt Disney World
1000 W. Buena Vista Dr.
Lake Buena Vista, FL 32830
☎ 407-939-1000
FAX 407-939-1001
disneyworld.com

LOCATION	WDW
ROOM RATING	83
COST ($ = $50)	$$$

COMMUTING TIMES TO PARKS
(in minutes):

MAGIC KINGDOM	5:30
EPCOT	4:00
ANIMAL KINGDOM	4:45
DHS	4:45

Dolphin ★★★★½
Walt Disney World
1500 Epcot Resorts Blvd.
Lake Buena Vista, FL 32830
☎ 407-934-4000
FAX 407-934-4009
swandolphin.com

LOCATION	WDW
ROOM RATING	90
COST ($ = $50)	$$$$$

COMMUTING TIMES TO PARKS
(in minutes):

MAGIC KINGDOM	6:45
EPCOT	5:00
ANIMAL KINGDOM	6:15
DHS	4:00

Polynesian Resort
★★★★½
Walt Disney World
1600 Seven Seas Dr.
Lake Buena Vista, FL 32830
☎ 407-824-2000
FAX 407-824-3174
disneyworld.com

LOCATION	WDW
ROOM RATING	92
COST ($ = $50)	$$$$$$$+

COMMUTING TIMES TO PARKS
(in minutes):

MAGIC KINGDOM	on monorail
EPCOT	8:00
ANIMAL KINGDOM	16:15
DHS	12:30

Pop Century Resort ★★★
Walt Disney World
1050 Century Dr.
Lake Buena Vista, FL 32830
☎ 407-938-4000
FAX 407-938-4040
disneyworld.com

LOCATION	WDW
ROOM RATING	71
COST ($ = $50)	$$–

COMMUTING TIMES TO PARKS
(in minutes):

MAGIC KINGDOM	8:30
EPCOT	6:30
ANIMAL KINGDOM	6:15
DHS	5:00

Port Orleans Resort (French Quarter) ★★★★
Walt Disney World
2201 Orleans Dr.
Lake Buena Vista, FL 32830
☎ 407-934-5000
FAX 407-934-5353
disneyworld.com

LOCATION	WDW
ROOM RATING	84
COST ($ = $50)	$$$

COMMUTING TIMES TO PARKS
(in minutes):

MAGIC KINGDOM	12:00
EPCOT	8:00
ANIMAL KINGDOM	16:15
DHS	12:30

Hotel Information Chart (continued)

**Port Orleans Resort
(Riverside)** ★★★★
Walt Disney World
1251 Riverside Dr.
Lake Buena Vista, FL 32830
☎ 407-934-6000
FAX 407-934-5777
disneyworld.com

LOCATION	WDW
ROOM RATING	83
COST ($ = $50)	$$$

COMMUTING TIMES TO PARKS
(in minutes):

MAGIC KINGDOM	12:00
EPCOT	8:00
ANIMAL KINGDOM	16:15
DHS	12:30

**Saratoga Springs Resort
& Spa** ★★★★½
Walt Disney World
1960 Broadway
Lake Buena Vista, FL 32830
☎ 407-827-1100
FAX 407-827-4444
disneyworld.com

LOCATION	WDW
ROOM RATING	90
COST ($ = $50)	$$$$$$

COMMUTING TIMES TO PARKS
(in minutes):

MAGIC KINGDOM	14:45
EPCOT	8:45
ANIMAL KINGDOM	18:15
DHS	14:30

Shades of Green ★★★★½
Walt Disney World
1950 W. Magnolia Palm Dr.
Lake Buena Vista, FL 32830
☎ 407-824-3400
FAX 407-824-3665
shadesofgreen.org

LOCATION	WDW
ROOM RATING	91
COST ($ = $50)	$$–

COMMUTING TIMES TO PARKS
(in minutes):

MAGIC KINGDOM	3:30
EPCOT	4:45
ANIMAL KINGDOM	9:30
DHS	6:15

Swan ★★★★½
Walt Disney World
1200 Epcot Resorts Blvd.
Lake Buena Vista, FL 32830
☎ 407-934-3000
FAX 407-934-4499
swandolphin.com

LOCATION	WDW
ROOM RATING	90
COST ($ = $50)	$$$$+

COMMUTING TIMES TO PARKS
(in minutes):

MAGIC KINGDOM	6:30
EPCOT	4:45
ANIMAL KINGDOM	6:15
DHS	4:00

**Treehouse Villas at Disney's
Saratoga Springs Resort
& Spa** ★★★★½
Walt Disney World
1960 Broadway
Lake Buena Vista, FL 32830
☎ 407-827-1100
FAX 407-827-1151
disneyworld.com

LOCATION	WDW
ROOM RATING	90
COST ($ = $50)	$$$$$$$$–

COMMUTING TIMES TO PARKS
(in minutes):

MAGIC KINGDOM	12:45
EPCOT	7:15
ANIMAL KINGDOM	16:45
DHS	12:30

Wilderness Lodge ★★★★
Walt Disney World
901 Timberline Dr.
Lake Buena Vista, FL 32830
☎ 407-824-3200
FAX 407-824-3232
disneyworld.com

LOCATION	WDW
ROOM RATING	86
COST ($ = $50)	$$$$$–

COMMUTING TIMES TO PARKS
(in minutes):

MAGIC KINGDOM	N/A
EPCOT	10:00
ANIMAL KINGDOM	15:15
DHS	13:30

**Wilderness Lodge
Villas** ★★★★½
Walt Disney World
901 Timberline Dr.
Lake Buena Vista, FL 32830
☎ 407-824-3200
FAX 407-824-3232
disneyworld.com

LOCATION	WDW
ROOM RATING	90
COST ($ = $50)	$$$$$$$–

COMMUTING TIMES TO PARKS
(in minutes):

MAGIC KINGDOM	N/A
EPCOT	10:00
ANIMAL KINGDOM	15:15
DHS	13:30

Yacht Club Resort ★★★★
Walt Disney World
1700 Epcot Resorts Blvd.
Lake Buena Vista, FL 32830
☎ 407-934-7000
FAX 407-934-3450
disneyworld.com

LOCATION	WDW
ROOM RATING	89
COST ($ = $50)	$$$$$$–

COMMUTING TIMES TO PARKS
(in minutes):

MAGIC KINGDOM	7:15
EPCOT	5:15
ANIMAL KINGDOM	6:45
DHS	4:00

Amenities at Downtown Disney Resort Area Hotels

RESORT	PROGRAMS	DINING	KID-FRIENDLY	POOLS	RECREATION
Best Western LBV Resort	—	★★½	★★★	★★½	★★
Buena Vista Palace	★★★★	★★★★	★★★½	★★★★	★★★★
DoubleTree Guest Suites	—	★★	★★★	★★½	★★½
Hilton WDW	—	★★★½	★★½	★★★	★★½
Holiday Inn at WDW	—	★★	★★	★★★	★★
Regal Sun Resort	★★½	★★½	★★★	★★★½	★★★
Royal Plaza	★★½	★★	★★½	★★½	★★★

continued from page 99

INDEPENDENT HOTELS OF THE DOWNTOWN DISNEY RESORT AREA

THE SEVEN HOTELS OF THE DOWNTOWN Disney Resort Area (DDRA) were created in the days when Disney had far fewer of its own resorts. The hotels—the Holiday Inn at Walt Disney World, Double-Tree Guest Suites, Regal Sun Resort, Hilton, Royal Plaza, Best Western Lake Buena Vista Resort, and Buena Vista Palace Hotel & Spa—are chain-style hotels with minimal or nonexistent theming, though the Buena Vista Palace especially is pretty upscale. All were hit hard by the tourism slump in recent years, and several of the larger properties shifted their focus to convention and business travelers. Now that Disney has trouble filling its own massive inventory of rooms, DDRA properties are struggling to refurbish or re-create themselves while clinging tenaciously to the Disney World connection.

The main advantage to staying in the DDRA is being in Disney World and proximal to Downtown Disney. Guests at the Hilton, Regal Sun Resort, Buena Vista Palace, and Holiday Inn are an easy 5- to 15-minute walk from Disney Marketplace. Guests at the Royal Plaza, Best Western, or DoubleTree are about 10 minutes farther by foot. Disney transportation can be accessed at Downtown Disney, though the Disney buses take a notoriously long time to leave due to the number of stops throughout the shopping and entertainment complex. Although all DDRA hotels offer shuttle buses to the theme parks, the service is provided by private contractors and is somewhat inferior to Disney Transportation in frequency of service, number of buses, and hours of operation. Get firm details in advance about shuttle service from any DDRA hotel you're considering. All these hotels are easily accessible by car and are only marginally farther from the Disney parks than several of the Disney resorts (and are quite close to Typhoon Lagoon).

All DDRA hotels try to appeal to families, even the business and meeting hotels. Some have pool complexes that rival those at any Disney resort, whereas others offer a food court or all-suite rooms. A few sponsor Disney character meals and organized children's activities; all have counters for buying Disney tickets, and most have Disney gift shops. In addition, we've seen some real room deals in the DDRA, especially in the off-season. To help you decide if the DDRA is right for you, take a peek at the combined Web site for the DDRA hotels at **downtown disneyhotels.com.** Finally, check the comparative chart above.

HOW TO GET DISCOUNTS ON LODGING AT WALT DISNEY WORLD

If all you need is a room, booking through Disney Central Reservation is better than booking online or through the Walt Disney Travel Company because Central Reservation offers better terms for cancellation and payment dates.

THERE ARE SO MANY GUEST ROOMS in and around Walt Disney World that competition is brisk, and everyone, including Disney, wheels and deals to keep them filled. This has led to a more flexible discount policy for Walt Disney World hotels. Here are tips for getting price breaks:

1. SEASONAL SAVINGS You can save $15–$50 or more per night on a Walt Disney World hotel room by scheduling your visit during the slower times of the year.

2. ASK ABOUT SPECIALS When you talk to Disney reservationists, ask specifically about specials. For example, "What special rates or discounts are available at Disney hotels during the time of our visit?" Being specific and assertive paid off for an Illinois reader:

> I called Disney's reservations number and asked for availability and rates. . . . [Because] of the Unofficial Guide warning about Disney reservationists answering only the questions posed, I specifically asked, "Are there any special rates or discounts for that room during the month of October?" She replied, "Yes, we have that room available at a special price. . . ." I saved $440.

3. KNOW THE SECRET CODE The folks at **mousesavers.com** keep an updated list of discounts and reservation codes for Disney resorts. You can sign up for the MouseSavers newsletter and hot deals for discount announcements, Disney news, and exclusive offers not available to the general public. The codes are separated into categories such as "For anyone," "For residents of certain states," and "For Annual Pass holders." For example, the site once listed a code published in an ad in some Spanish-language newspapers and magazines, offering a rate of $65 per night for Disney's All-Star Resorts from April 22 to August 8. Dozens of discounts are usually listed on the site, covering most Disney hotels. Anyone calling the Disney Reservation Center at ☎ 407-WDW-MAGIC can use a current code and get the discounted rate.

You should be aware that Disney is shying away from room-only codes that anyone can use. Instead, Disney is targeting people with pin codes in e-mails and direct mailings. Pin-code discounts are offered to specific individuals and are correlated with that person's name and address. Pin-code offers are nontransferable. When you try to make a reservation using the code, Disney will verify that the street or e-mail address to which the pin code was sent is yours.

To get your name in the Disney system, call the Disney Reservation Center at ☎ 407-824-8000 or 407-WDW-MAGIC and request that written info or the free trip-planning DVD/video be sent to you. If you've been to Walt Disney World previously, your name and address will of course already be on record, but you won't be as likely to receive a pin-code offer as you would by calling and requesting to be sent information. On the Web, go to the official site, **disneyworld.com,** and sign up to automatically be sent offers and news at your e-mail address.

Our blog, **blog.touringplans.com,** often provides advance notice on discount details and their dates of availability. Two other sites, **allears net.com** and **wdwinfo.com,** have discount codes for up to 50% off rack rates at the Swan and Dolphin.

4. INTERNET SELLERS Expedia (**expedia.com**), Travelocity (**travelocity. com**), and One Travel (**onetravel.com**) discount Disney hotels. Most breaks are in the 7% to 25% range but can go as deep as 40%.

5. WALT DISNEY WORLD WEB SITE Particularly with the economic recovery moving slowly, Disney has become more aggressive about offering deals on its Web site. Go to **disneyworld.com** and look for "Special Offers" just below the picture of Cinderella Castle. In the same place also look for seasonal discounts, usually listed as "Summertime Savings," "Fall Savings," or something similar. You can also go to "Tickets and Packages" at the top right of the home page, where you will find a link to Special Offers. You must click on the specific special to get the discounts: If you fill out the information on "Price Your Dream Vacation," you'll be charged the full rack rate with no mention of available discounts.

6. RENTING DISNEY VACATION CLUB POINTS The Disney Vacation Club (DVC) is Disney's time-share condominium program. DVC resorts at Walt Disney World include Old Key West, Saratoga Springs Resort & Spa, the Beach Club Villas, Villas at Wilderness Lodge, and the BoardWalk Villas. Each resort offers studios and one- and two-bedroom villas (the Treehouse Villas only have three bedrooms). All accommodations are roomy and luxurious. The studios are equipped with wet bars and fridges, and the villas come with full kitchens. Most accommodations have patios or balconies.

DVC members receive a number of points annually that they use to pay for their Disney accommodations. Sometimes members elect to "rent" (sell) their points instead of using them in a given year. Though Disney is not involved in the transaction, it allows DVC members to make these points available to the general public. The going rental rate is usually in the range of $12 per point. A studio for a week at the BoardWalk Villas would run you $2,380 plus tax for the regular season if you booked through the Disney Reservation Center. The same studio costs the DVC member 105 points for a week (in peak season). If you rented his points at $12 per point, the BoardWalk Villas studio would cost you $1,260—almost $1,200 less.

When you rent points, you deal with the selling DVC member and pay him or her directly. The DVC member makes a reservation in your name and pays Disney the requisite number of points. Arrangements vary widely, but some trust is required from both parties. Usually your reservation is documented by a confirmation sent from Disney to the owner, and then passed along to you. Though the deal you cut is strictly up to you and the owner, you should always insist on receiving the aforementioned confirmation before making more than a one-night deposit.

Disboards, **disboards.com,** the popular Disney discussion boards site, has a specific board that deals with DVC rentals, and the unofficial discount Web site, **mousesavers.com,** has a page with tips on renting DVC points: see **mousesavers.com/disneyresorts.html#rentpoints.**

6. TRAVEL AGENTS Travel agents are active players and particularly good sources of information on limited-time programs and discounts. We believe a good travel agent is the best friend a traveler can have. And though we at the *Unofficial Guide* know a thing or two about the travel industry, we always give our agent a chance to beat any deal we find. If she can't beat it, we let her book it anyway if it's commissionable. We nurture a relationship that gives her plenty of incentive to roll up her sleeves and work on our behalf.

As you might expect, there are travel agents and agencies that specialize, sometimes exclusively, in selling Walt Disney World. These agents have spent an incredible amount of time at Walt Disney World and have completed extensive Disney education programs. They are usually the most Disney-knowledgeable agents in the travel industry. Most of these specialists and their agencies display the "Earmarked" logo stating that they are an authorized Disney vacation planner.

These Disney specialists are so good we use them ourselves. The needs of our research team are many, and our schedules are complicated. When we work with an authorized Disney vacation planner, we know we're dealing with someone who knows Disney inside and out, including where to find the deals and how to use all the tricks of the trade that keep our research budget under control. Simply stated, they save us time and money, sometimes lots of both.

Each year we ask our readers to rate the travel agent that helped plan their Disney trip. The best of the best include Sue Pisaturo, whom we've used many times and who is a contributor to this guide (**sue@wdw vacations.com**); Sue Ellen Soto-Rios (**disneytravelagent@gmail.com**);

Lynne Amodeo (**lynnetravel@verizon.net**); Kathy McCullock (**kathy mcc@nc.rr.com**); Karen Nunn (**karen.nunn@gmail.com**); and Anne Cook (**anne@smallworldvacations.com**).

Our reader-survey results indicate that for Walt Disney World, you'll be much more satisfied using a travel agent who specializes in Disney and much more likely to recommend those agents to a friend. While the names above are the ones most consistently recommended in our surveys, there are good Disney specialists throughout the country, if you prefer to work with someone close to home.

LODGING *outside*
WALT DISNEY WORLD

AT THIS POINT YOU'RE PROBABLY WONDERING HOW, as mentioned above, a hotel outside Walt Disney World could be as convenient as one inside Walt Disney World. Well, Mabel, Walt Disney World is a *muy largo* place, but like any city or state, it has borders. By way of analogy, let's say you want to stay in a hotel in Cincinnati, Ohio, but can't find one you can afford. Would you rather book a hotel in Toledo or Cleveland, which are both still in Ohio but pretty darn far away, or would you be willing to leave Ohio and stay just across the river from Cincinnati in Covington, Kentucky?

Just west of Walt Disney World on US 192 are a bunch of hotels and condos, some great bargains, that are closer to the Animal Kingdom and Disney's Hollywood Studios than are many hotels in Walt Disney World. Similarly, there are hotels along Disney's east border, FL 535, that are exceptionally convenient if you plan to use your own car.

Lodging costs outside Walt Disney World vary incredibly. If you shop around, you can find a clean motel with a pool within a few minutes of the World for as low as $40 a night. You also can find luxurious, expensive hotels. Because of hot competition, discounts abound.

SELECTING AND BOOKING A HOTEL
OUTSIDE WALT DISNEY WORLD

THERE ARE FOUR PRIMARY out-of-the-World areas to consider:

1. INTERNATIONAL DRIVE AREA This area, about 15–25 minutes northeast of Walt Disney World, parallels I-4 on its eastern side and offers a wide selection of both hotels and restaurants. Accommodations range from $56–$400 per night. The chief drawbacks of the International Drive area are its terribly congested roads, countless traffic signals, and inadequate access to westbound I-4. While the biggest bottleneck is the intersection with Sand Lake Road, the mile of International Drive between Kirkman Road and Sand Lake Road stays in near-continuous gridlock. It's common to lose 25–35 minutes trying to navigate this 1-mile stretch.

Hotels in the International Drive area are listed in the *Orlando Official Vacation Guide,* published by the Orlando/Orange County Convention and Visitors Bureau. For a copy, call ☎ 800-972-3304 or 407-363-5872.

2. LAKE BUENA VISTA AND THE I-4 CORRIDOR   A number of hotels are situated along FL 535 and west of I-4 between Walt Disney World and I-4's intersection with the Florida Turnpike. These properties are easily reached from the interstate and are near a large number of restaurants, including those on International Drive. Most hotels in this area are listed in the *Orlando Official Vacation Guide.*

3. US 192 (IRLO BRONSON MEMORIAL HIGHWAY)   This is the highway to Kissimmee, southeast of Walt Disney World. In addition to a number of large, full-service hotels, there are many small, privately owned motels that are often a good value. Several dozen properties on US 192 are closer to the Disney theme parks than are the more expensive hotels in the Downtown Disney Resort Area. The number and variety of restaurants on US 192 has increased markedly in the past several years, easing the area's primary shortcoming. Hotels on US 192 and in Kissimmee can be found in the *Kissimmee Visitor's Guide;* call ☎ 800-327-9159 or check **floridakiss.com.**

4. UNIVERSAL STUDIOS AREA   In the triangular area bordered by I-4 on the southeast, Vineland Road on the north, and Turkey Lake Road on the west are Universal Orlando and the hotels most convenient to it. Running north-south through the middle of the triangle is Kirkman Road, which connects to I-4. On the east side of Kirkman are a number of independent hotels and restaurants. Universal hotels, theme parks, and CityWalk are west of Kirkman. Traffic in this area is not nearly as congested as on nearby International Drive, and there are good interstate connections in both directions.

THE BEST HOTELS FOR FAMILIES OUTSIDE WALT DISNEY WORLD

WHAT MAKES A SUPER FAMILY HOTEL? Roomy accommodations, in-room fridge, great pool, complimentary breakfast, child-care options, and programs for kids are a few of the things the *Unofficial Guide* hotel team researched in selecting the top hotels for families from among hundreds of properties in the Disney World area. Some of our picks are expensive, others are more reasonable, and some are a bargain. Regardless of price, be assured that these hotels understand a family's needs.

Though all the following hotels offer some type of shuttle to the theme parks, some offer very limited service. Call the hotel before you book and ask what the shuttle schedule will be when you visit. Because families, like individuals, have different wants and needs, we haven't ranked the following properties here. They're listed geographically and then alphabetically.

INTERNATIONAL DRIVE & UNIVERSAL STUDIOS AREAS

DoubleTree Castle Hotel ★★★½

8629 International Dr., Orlando; ☎ 407-345-1511 or 800-952-2785; doubletreecastle.com

Rate per night $100–$230. **Pool** ★★★. **Fridge in room** Available for rent for $15. **Shuttle to parks** Yes (Disney and Universal; additional fee). **Maximum number of occupants per room** 4. **Special comments** For an additional fee ($13.95 adults, $7.95 kids), up to 4 people receive a full breakfast; 2 signature chocolate-chip cookies come with every room. Pets, up to 75 pounds, are welcome for a $75 fee.

YOU CAN'T MISS THIS ONE; it's the only castle on I-Drive. Inside you'll find royal colors (purple dominates), opulent fixtures, European art, Renaissance music, and a mystic Castle Creature at the door. The 216 guest rooms also receive the royal treatment in decor, though some guests may find them gaudy. All, however, are fairly large and well equipped with TV with PlayStation, fridge, three phones, coffeemaker, iron and board, hair dryer, and safe. The Castle Café off the lobby serves full or Continental breakfast. For lunch or dinner, you might walk next door to Vito's Chop House (dinner only) or Café Tu Tu Tango (an *Unofficial* favorite). The heated circular pool is 5 feet deep and features a fountain in the center, a poolside bar, and a whirlpool. There's no separate kiddie pool. Other amenities include a fitness center, gift shop, lounge, valet laundry service and facilities, and guest services desk with park passes for sale and babysitting recommendations. Elevators require an electronic key card.

DoubleTree Resort Orlando–International Drive ★★★★½

10100 International Dr., Orlando; ☎ 407-352-1100 or 800-327-0363; doubletreeorlandoidrive.com

Rate per night $89–$499. **Pools** ★★★½. **Fridge in room** In some rooms; otherwise available for $10 per day. **Shuttle to parks** Yes (Disney, Universal, SeaWorld, Aquatica, and Wet 'n Wild). **Maximum number of occupants per room** 4. **Special comments** A good option if you're visiting SeaWorld.

FORMERLY THE INTERNATIONAL PLAZA RESORT & SPA, this hotel with Balinese decor has undergone a comprehensive $35-million renovation. Situated on 28 lush, tropical acres, the DoubleTree is adjacent to SeaWorld and Aquatica water park. All 1,094 rooms and suites, classified as resort or tower, have been completely refurbished and are equally suitable for business travelers or families. We recommend the tower rooms for good views and the resort rooms for maximum convenience. The Bamboo Grille serves steak and seafood along with breakfast; you can also get a quick bite at the deli, pool bar, or Bangli lounge. Relax and cool off at one of the three pools (there are three more just for kids), or indulge in a special spa treatment. A fitness center, minigolf course, and kids' game area afford even more diversions, and a children's day camp is offered. The resort is about a 15-minute drive to Walt Disney World, a 12-minute drive to Universal, or a short walk to SeaWorld.

Hotel Concentrations around Walt Disney World

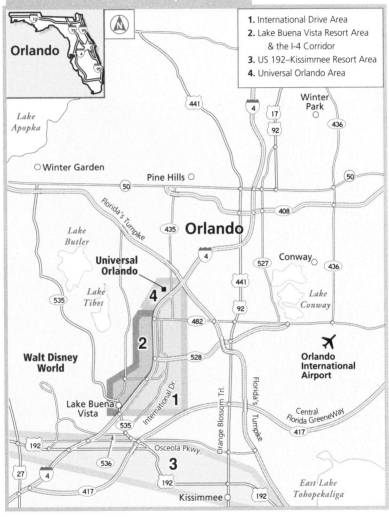

Orlando

1. International Drive Area
2. Lake Buena Vista Resort Area & the I-4 Corridor
3. US 192–Kissimmee Resort Area
4. Universal Orlando Area

Winter Park

Lake Apopka

Winter Garden

Pine Hills

Lake Butler

Orlando

Conway

Universal Orlando **4**

Lake Tibet

Lake Conway

Walt Disney World

2

1

Orlando International Airport

Lake Buena Vista

International Dr.

Orange Blossom Trl.

Florida's Turnpike

Central Florida GreeneWay

Osceola Pkwy.

3

Kissimmee

East Lake Tohopekaliga

Florida's Turnpike

Hard Rock Hotel ★★★★½

5800 Universal Blvd., Orlando; ☎ 407-503-2000; hardrockhotelorlando.com

Rate per night $234–$724. **Pool** ★★★★. **Fridge in room** Minibar; fridge available for $15 per day. **Shuttle to parks** Yes (Universal, SeaWorld, Discovery Cove, Aquatica, and Wet 'n Wild). **Maximum number of occupants per room** 5 for standard double queen rooms; 3 for standard king rooms. **Special comments** Microwaves available for $15 per day.

LOCATED ON UNIVERSAL PROPERTY, the 650-room Hard Rock Hotel is nirvana for any kid older than 8, especially those interested in music. Architecture is California Mission–style, and rock memorabilia is displayed throughout. If you plan to spend at least a few days at Universal parks, this is an excellent upscale option. Guests receive theme park privileges such as |all-day access to the Universal Express line-breaking program, delivery of packages to their rooms, and priority seating at select Universal restaurants. The music-filled pool area has a white-sand beach, a waterslide, a 12,000-square-foot pool, an underwater audio system, and an ultrahip pool bar. You'll also find four restaurants and lounges, a chic lounge, fitness center, and Hard Rock merchandise store. Guest rooms are ultrahip too, with cutting-edge contemporary decor, a CD sound system, TV with pay-per-view movies and video games, coffeemaker, iron and board, robes, hair dryer, and two phones. A supervised activity center, Camp Lil' Rock, serves kids ages 4–14. Pet-friendly rooms available.

Loews Portofino Bay Hotel ★★★★½
5601 Universal Blvd., Orlando; ☎ 407-503-1000 or 888-273-1311; loewshotels.com/en/hotels/portofino-bay-hotel/overview.aspx

Rate per night $274–$809. **Pools** ★★★★. **Fridge in room** Minibar; fridge available for $15 per day. **Shuttle to parks** Yes (Universal, SeaWorld, Discovery Cove, and Wet 'n Wild). **Maximum number of occupants per room** 4. **Special comments** Character dinner on Friday.

LOCATED IN UNIVERSAL ORLANDO, the 750-room Portofino Bay Hotel is themed like an Italian Riviera village. Guests receive theme park privileges such as all-day access to the Universal Express line-breaking program, delivery of packages to their room and priority seating at select Universal restaurants. The rooms are ultraluxurious, with opulent baths, and soothing neutral hues. Standard guest-room amenities include minibar, coffeemaker, iron and board, hair dryer, safe, and TV with pay-per-view movies. Microwaves are available ($15 per day). Campo Portofino offers supervised activities (movies, video games, crafts, and such) for children ages 4–14. The cost is $15 per hour plus $15 per meal, per child; hours vary. Trattoria del Porto restaurant offers a character dinner 6:30–9:30 p.m. on Friday, with characters such as Scooby Doo and Woody Woodpecker in attendance. Portofino has four other Italian restaurants (each with a children's menu), an Italian bakery (also serves gelato), and two bars. Three elaborate pools, gardens, jogging trails, pet-friendly rooms, and a spa and fitness center round out major amenities. If you can pay for it and plan to spend time at Universal, you can't go wrong here.

Nickelodeon Suites Resort Orlando ★★★½
14500 Continental Gateway, Orlando; ☎ 407-387-5437 or 877-NICK-111; nickhotel.com

Rate per night $159–$529. **Pools** ★★★★. **Fridge in room** Yes. **Shuttle to parks**

Yes. **Maximum number of occupants per room** 8 (for three-bedroom suites). **Special comments** Daily character breakfast; resort fee of $25/night.

SPONGEBOB SQUAREPANTS, EAT YOUR HEART OUT. This revamped resort is as kid-friendly as they come. Decked out in all themes Nickelodeon, the hotel is sure to please any fan of TV shows such as *Rugrats, Jimmy Neutron: Boy Genius,* and *The Fairly OddParents,* to name a few. Nickelodeon characters from the channel's many shows hang out in the resort's lobby and mall area, greeting kids while parents check in. Guests can choose from among 777 one-, two-, and three-bedroom suites executed in a number of different themes—all very brightly and creatively decorated. All suites include kitchenettes or full kitchens; also standard are a microwave, fridge, coffeemaker, TV, iron and board, hair dryer, and a safe. KidSuites (two- and three-bedroom units) feature a semiprivate kids' bedroom with bunk or twin beds, pull-out sleeper bed, 32-inch TV, CD player, and activity table. The master bedroom offers ample storage space that the kids' bedroom lacks. Additional amenities include a high-tech video arcade, Studio Nick—a game-show studio that hosts several game shows a night for the entertainment of a live studio audience, a buffet (kids 3 and younger eat free with a paying adult), a food court offering Subway and Uno Express among others, the full-service Nicktoons Cafe (offers character breakfasts), a convenience store, a lounge, a gift shop, a fitness center, a washer and dryer in each courtyard, and a guest-activities desk (buy Disney tickets and get recommendations on babysitting). Not to be missed—don't worry, your kids won't let you—are the resort's two pools, Oasis and Lagoon. Oasis features a water park complete with water cannons, rope ladders, geysers, and dump buckets, as well as a hot tub for adults (with a view of the rest of the pool to keep an eye on little ones) and a smaller play area for younger kids. Kids will love the huge, zero-depth-entry Lagoon Pool, replete with 400-gallon dump bucket, plus nearby basketball court and nine-hole mini-golf course. Pool activities for kids are scheduled several times a day, seasonally; some games feature the infamous green slime. Whatever you do, avoid letting your kids catch you saying the phrase "I don't know" while you're here—trust us.

Rosen Shingle Creek ★★★★

9939 Universal Blvd., Orlando; ☎ 407-996-9939 or 866-996-9939; rosenshinglecreek.com

Rate per night $99–$285. **Pools** ★★★★. **Fridge in room** Yes. **Shuttle to parks** Yes (Universal, Wet 'n Wild, Discovery Cove, Aquatica, and SeaWorld only). **Maximum number of occupants per room** 4.

BEAUTIFUL ROOMS (east-facing ones have great views) and excellent restaurants distinguish this mostly meeting- and convention-oriented resort. The pools are large and lovely and include a lap pool, a family pool, and a kiddie wading pool. There's an 18-hole golf course on-site, as well as a superior spa and an adequate fitness center. On-site babysitting is offered. Though a state-of-the-art video arcade will gobble up your kids' pocket change, the real kicker, especially for the 8 years-and-up crowd, is a natural area encompassing lily ponds, grassy wetlands, Shingle Creek, and an adjacent cypress swamp. Running through the area is a nature trail complete with signs to help you identify wildlife. Great blue herons, wood storks, coots, egrets, mallard ducks, anhingas, and ospreys are common, as are sliders (turtles), chameleons, and skinks (lizards). Oh yeah, there are alligators and snakes too—real ones, but that's part of the fun. If you stay at Shingle Creek and plan to visit the theme parks, you'll want a car. Shuttle service is limited, departing and picking up at rather inconvenient times and stopping at three other hotels before delivering you to your destination.

LAKE BUENA VISTA & I-4 CORRIDOR

Buena Vista Palace Hotel & Spa ★★★½

1900 Buena Vista Dr., Lake Buena Vista; ☎ 407-827-2727 or 888-397-6516; buenavistapalace.com

Rate per night $99–$1,500. **Pools** ★★★½. **Fridge in room** Yes. **Shuttle to parks** Yes (Disney only). **Maximum number of occupants per room** 4. **Special comments** Sunday character breakfast available.

IN THE DOWNTOWN DISNEY RESORT AREA, the Buena Vista Palace is upscale and convenient. Surrounded by a man-made lake and plenty of palms, the spacious pool area contains three heated pools, the largest of which is partially covered; a whirlpool and sauna; a basketball court; and a sand volleyball court. Plus, a pool concierge will fetch your favorite magazine or fruity drink. On Sunday, the Watercress Café hosts a character breakfast ($20 for adults and $10 for children). The 897 guest rooms are posh and spacious; each comes with a desk, coffeemaker, hair dryer, satellite TV with pay-per-view movies, iron and board, and minifridge. There are also 117 suites. In-room babysitting is available through the All about Kids service. One lighted tennis court, a European-style spa offering 60 services, a fitness center, an arcade, a playground, and a beauty salon round out amenities. Two restaurants and a mini-market are on-site. And consider dropping by the Lobby Lounge or the full-menu sports bar for a nightcap. *Note:* These amenities and services come at a price—a $15-per-night resort fee will be added to your bill.

Hilton Walt Disney World ★★★★

1751 Hotel Plaza Blvd., Lake Buena Vista; ☎ 407-827-4000 or 800-782-4414; hilton-wdw.com

Rate per night $99–$309. **Pools** ★★★½. **Fridge in room** Minibar; minifridge available on request. **Shuttle to parks** Yes (Disney theme and water parks only). **Maximum number of occupants per room** 4. **Special comments** Sunday character breakfast and Disney Extra Magic Hours program.

THE HILTON OCCUPIES 23 ACRES in the Downtown Disney Resort Area. Since it's an official Walt Disney World hotel, guests can take advantage of the Disney Extra Magic Hours program, which allows entry to a selected Disney park 1 hour before official opening and late stays to a selected park up to 3 hours after official close. The Hilton's 814 guest rooms and suites are spacious, luxurious, and tasteful. Decorated in earth tones, all standard rooms have granite baths, iron and board, hair dryer, two phones, desk, minibar, coffeemaker, and cable TV with pay-per-view movies and video games. One big plus is the character breakfast, offered 8:30–11 a.m. on Sunday. (Reservations are recommended.) Food is served buffet-style, and five characters attend (only two are present at a time). Other important family amenities include babysitting services; an arcade and pool table; and two beautifully landscaped heated swimming pools, as well as a kiddie pool. Adults and older children can relax in the fitness center after a long day touring. Six restaurants, including Benihana, add to the hotel's convenience.

Holiday Inn SunSpree Resort Lake Buena Vista ★★★½

13351 FL 535, Orlando; ☎ 407-239-4500 or 866-808-8833; hisunspreelbv.com

Rate per night $80–$175. **Pool** ★★★. **Fridge in room** Yes. **Shuttle to parks** Yes (Disney, Universal, and SeaWorld). **Maximum number of occupants per room** 4–6. **Special comments** The first hotel in the world to offer KidSuites; resort fee of $7.95/night entitles guests to numerous perks, including use of fitness center and daily fountain drinks for kids.

THE BIG LURE IS KIDSUITES, rooms with a separate children's area. Themes include a tree house, jail, space capsule, and fort, among others. The kids' area sleeps two to four children in two sets of bunk beds or one bunk bed and a twin. The separate adult area has its own TV, safe, hair dryer, and kitchenette with fridge, microwave, sink, and coffeemaker. Standard guest rooms offer these adult amenities. Other kid-friendly amenities include the tiny Castle Movie Theater, which shows movies all day every day; a playground; an arcade with video games and air hockey, among its many games; Saturday night "dive-in" movies; and a basketball court. Also offered are a large, free-form pool, complete with kiddie pool and two whirlpools, and a fitness center. Maxine's Kitchen serves breakfast and dinner buffets and offers an à la carte menu for dinner. There's also a mini-mart. Another perk: Kids age 12 and younger eat free from a special menu when dining with one paying adult (maximum four kids per adult). Finally, pets weighing 30 pounds or less are welcome (for an additional $40 nonrefundable fee).

Hyatt Regency Grand Cypress ★★★★½

1 Grand Cypress Blvd., Orlando; ☎ 407-239-1234; grandcypress.hyatt.com

Rate per night $215–$355. **Pools** ★★★★★. **Fridge in room** Yes. **Shuttle to parks** Yes (Disney, Universal, and SeaWorld). **Maximum number of occupants per room** 4. **Special comments** Wow, what a pool! Resort fee of $22.50.

THERE ARE MYRIAD REASONS TO STAY at this 1,500-acre resort, but the pool ranks as number one. The 800,000-gallon tropical paradise has two waterslides, waterfalls, grottos, and a bridge. Your kids may never want to leave the pool to visit the theme parks. The Hyatt is also a golfer's paradise. With 45 holes of Jack Nicklaus–designed championship golf, a 9-hole pitch-and-putt course, and a golf academy, there's something for golfers of all abilities. Other recreational perks include a racquet facility with hard and clay courts; a private lake with beach; a fitness center; and miles of trails for biking, walking, and jogging. The 683 standard guest rooms are 360 square feet and have a Florida ambience and private balconies. Amenities include high-speed Internet, iron and board, safe, hair dryer, ceiling fan, and cable TV with pay-per-view movies. Suite accommodations offer even more amenities. Camp Hyatt provides supervised programs for kids ages 3–12; in-room babysitting is available. Five restaurants offer dining options. Three lounges provide nighttime entertainment, while a coffee bar offers a different ambience. If outdoor recreation is high on your family's list, Hyatt is an excellent high-end choice.

Marriott Village at Lake Buena Vista ★★★

8623 Vineland Ave., Orlando; ☎ 407-938-9001 or 877-682-8552; marriottvillage.com

Rate per night $119–$219. **Pools** ★★★. **Fridge in room** Yes. **Shuttle to parks** Yes (Disney only; $7 fee). **Maximum number of occupants per room** 4 (5 at Spring-Hill). **Special comments** Free Continental breakfast at Fairfield and SpringHill.

THIS GATED HOTEL COMMUNITY INCLUDES a 388-room Fairfield Inn, a 400-suite SpringHill Suites, and a 312-room Courtyard. Whatever your budget, you'll find a room here to fit it. If you need a bit more space, book SpringHill Suites; if you're looking for value, try the Fairfield Inn; if you need limited business amenities, reserve at the Courtyard. Amenities at all three properties include fridge, cable TV, iron and board, and hair dryer. Additionally, all SpringHill suites have microwaves. Cribs and rollaway beds are available at no extra charge at all locations. Swimming pools at all three hotels are attractive and medium-size, featuring children's interactive splash zones and whirlpools; in addition, each property has its own fitness center. The incredibly convenient Village Marketplace food court includes Pizza Hut, Village Grill, and Village Coffee House, along with a 24-hour convenience store. The Bahama Breeze, Landry's Seafood House, and Golden Corral full-service restaurants are within walking distance. Other services and amenities include a Disney planning station and ticket sales, an arcade, and a Hertz car-rental desk. Shoppers will find the Orlando Premium Outlets adjacent.

Sheraton Safari Hotel & Suites Lake Buena Vista ★★★★

12205 S. Apopka–Vineland Rd., Orlando; ☎ 407-239-0444 or 800-325-3535; sheratonsafari.com

Rate per night $89–$174. **Pool** ★★★. **Fridge in room** Suites only; available for $10 per night in other rooms. **Shuttle to parks** Yes (Disney free; other parks for a fee). **Maximum number of occupants per room** 4–6. **Special comments** Cool python waterslide. Dogs allowed.

THE SAFARI THEME IS NICELY EXECUTED throughout the property—from the lobby dotted with African artifacts and native decor to the 79-foot python waterslide dominating the pool. The 393 guest rooms, 90 safari suites, and six executive suites sport African-inspired art and tasteful animal-print soft goods in brown, beige, and jewel tones. Amenities include cable TV, coffeemaker, iron and board, hair dryer, and safe. Suites are a good option for families because they provide added space with a separate sitting room and a kitchenette with a fridge, microwave, and sink. The first thing your kids will probably want to do is take a turn on the python waterslide. It's pretty impressive, but as one *Unofficial Guide* researcher pointed out, it's somewhat of a letdown: The python doesn't actually spit you out of its mouth. Instead you're deposited below its chin. Other on-site amenities include a restaurant (children's menu available), lounge, arcade, and fitness center.

Sheraton Vistana Resort Villas ★★★★½

8800 Vistana Centre Dr., Orlando; ☎ 407-239-3100 or 866-208-0003; sheraton.com

Rate per night $139–$279. **Pools** ★★★½. **Fridge in room** Yes. **Shuttle to parks** Yes (Disney only; Universal and SeaWorld for a fee). **Maximum number of occupants per room** 4–8. **Special comments** Though time-shares, the villas are rented nightly as well.

THE SHERATON VISTANA IS DECEPTIVELY LARGE, stretching across both sides of Vistana Centre Drive. Because Sheraton's emphasis is on selling the time-shares, the rental angle is little known. But families should consider it; the Vistana is one of Orlando's best off-Disney properties. If you want a serene retreat from your days in the theme parks, this is an excellent base. The spacious villas come in one-bedroom, two-bedroom, and two-bedroom-with-lock-off (two rooms joined by a door) models. All are decorated in beachy pastels, but the emphasis is on the profusion of amenities. Each villa has a full kitchen (including fridge/freezer, microwave, oven/range, dishwasher, toaster, and coffeemaker, with an option to prestock with groceries), clothes washer and dryer, TVs in the living room and each bedroom (one with DVD player), separate dining area, and private patio or balcony in most. Grounds offer seven swimming pools; four playgrounds; two restaurants; game rooms; fitness centers; a mini-golf course; sports equipment rental; and courts for basketball, volleyball, tennis, and shuffleboard. A mind-boggling array of activities for kids (and adults) ranges from crafts to games and sports tournaments. Of special note: Vistana is highly secure, with locked gates bordering all guest areas, so children can have the run of the place without parents worrying.

US 192 AREA

Comfort Suites Maingate ★★★½

7888 W. Irlo Bronson Memorial Hwy., Kissimmee; ☎ 407-390-9888 or 888-390-9888; comfortsuiteskissimmee.com

Rate per night $80–$170. **Pool** ★★★. **Fridge in room** Yes. **Shuttle to parks**

Yes (Disney, Universal, and SeaWorld). **Maximum number of occupants per room** 4–6. **Special comments** Complimentary Continental breakfast daily.

THIS PROPERTY HAS 150 SPACIOUS one-room suites, each with double sofa bed, microwave, fridge, coffeemaker, TV, hair dryer, and safe. The suites aren't lavish, but they are clean and contemporary, with muted deep-purple and beige tones. Extra bathroom counter space is especially convenient for larger families. The heated pool is large and has plenty of lounge chairs. A kiddie pool, whirlpool, and poolside bar complete the courtyard. But Maingate's big plus is its location next door to a shopping center with about everything a family could need. There, you'll find 10 dining options, including Outback Steakhouse, Cracker Barrel, Subway, T.G.I. Friday's, and Chinese and Italian eateries; a supermarket; a bank; a dry cleaner; a tourist information center with park passes for sale; and a Centra Care walk-in clinic.

Gaylord Palms Hotel & Convention Center ★★★★½

6000 W. Osceola Pkwy., Kissimmee; ☎ 407-586-2000; gaylordpalms.com

Rate per night $129–$279. **Pool** ★★★★. **Fridge in room** Yes. **Shuttle to parks** Yes (Disney). **Maximum number of occupants per room** 4. **Special comments** Probably the closest you'll get off-World to Disney-level extravagance. Resort fee of $15/day.

THIS DECIDEDLY UPSCALE RESORT has a colossal convention facility and strongly caters to business clientele but still is a nice (if pricey) family resort. Hotel wings are defined by the three themed, glass-roofed atriums they overlook. Key West's design is reminiscent of island life in the Florida Keys; Everglades is an overgrown spectacle of shabby swamp chic, complete with piped-in cricket noise and a robotic alligator; and the immense, central St. Augustine harks back to Spanish Colonial Florida. Lagoons, streams, and waterfalls cut through and connect all three, and walkways and bridges abound. Rooms reflect the colors of their respective areas, though there's no particular connection in decor (St. Augustine atrium-view rooms are the most opulent, but they're not Spanish). A fourth wing, Emerald Bay Tower, overlooks the Emerald Plaza shopping and dining area of the St. Augustine atrium. These rooms are the nicest and the most expensive, and they're mostly used by convention-goers. Though rooms have fridges and alarm clocks with CD players (as well as other perks, such as high-speed Internet access), the rooms themselves really work better as retreats for adults rather than kids. However, children will enjoy wandering the themed areas or playing in the family pool (with water-squirting octopus). In-room babysitting is offered.

Orange Lake Resort ★★★★½

8505 W. Irlo Bronson Memorial Hwy., Kissimmee; ☎ 407-239-0000 or 800-877-6522; orangelake.com

Rate per night $126–$270 (2-bedroom summer rate). **Pools** ★★★★. **Fridge in room** Yes. **Shuttle to parks** Yes (fee varies with destination). **Maximum number**

of occupants per room Varies. **Special comments** This is a time-share property, but if you rent directly through the resort, you can avoid time-share sales pitches.

YOU COULD SPEND YOUR ENTIRE VACATION never leaving this property, located about 6–10 minutes from the Disney theme parks. From its 10 pools and 2 mini water parks to its 36 holes of championship golf and 2 nine-hole executive courses, Orange Lake offers an extensive menu of amenities and recreational opportunities. If you tire of lazing by the pool, try waterskiing, wakeboarding, tubing, fishing, or other activities on the 80-acre lake. There's also a live alligator show, exercise programs, organized competitive sports and games, arts-and-crafts sessions, and miniature golf. Activities don't end when the sun goes down. Karaoke, live music, a Hawaiian luau, and movies at the resort cinema are some of the evening options.

The 2,412 units are tastefully decorated and comfortably furnished, ranging from suites and studios to three-bedroom villas, all containing fully equipped kitchens. If you'd rather not cook on vacation, try one of the seven restaurants scattered across the resort: two cafes, three grills, one pizzeria, and a fast-food eatery. If you need help with (or a break from) the kids, babysitters are available to come to your villa, accompany your family on excursions, or take your children to attractions for you.

Radisson Resort Orlando-Celebration ★★★★

2900 Parkway Blvd., Kissimmee; ☎ 407-396-7000 or 800-634-4774; radissonorlandoresort.com

Rate per night $107–$168. **Pool** ★★★★½. **Fridge in room** Yes. **Shuttle to parks** Yes (Disney, Universal, and SeaWorld). **Maximum number of occupants per room** 5. **Special comments** $12.50/day resort fee; kids age 10 and younger eat free with a paying adult at Mandolin's restaurant.

THE POOL ALONE IS WORTH A STAY HERE, but the Radisson Resort gets high marks in all areas. The free-form pool is huge, with a waterfall and water-slide surrounded by palms and flowering plants, plus a smaller heated pool, two whirlpools, and a kiddie pool. Other outdoor amenities include two lighted tennis courts, sand volleyball, a playground, and jogging areas. Rooms are elegant, featuring Italian furnishings and marble baths. They're of above-average size and include a minibar (in some rooms), coffeemaker, TV, iron and board, hair dryer, and safe. Dining options include Mandolin's for breakfast and dinner, and a 1950s-style diner serves burgers, sandwiches, shakes, and Pizza Hut pizza, among other fare. A sports lounge with an 11-by-6-foot TV offers nighttime entertainment. Guest services can help with tours, park passes, car rental, and babysitting. Children can be kept occupied by board games, coloring, a face-painting clown, and juggling classes for starters.

Wyndham Bonnet Creek Resort ★★★★

9560 Via Encinas, Lake Buena Vista; ☎ 407-238-3500; wyndhambonnetcreek.com

Rate per night $179–$359. **Pool** ★★★★. **Fridge in room** Yes. **Shuttle to parks**

Yes (Disney only). **Maximum number of occupants per room** 4 (plus child in crib) to 12 (depending on suite). **Special comments** A non-Disney suite hotel within Walt Disney World.

WYNDHAM BONNET CREEK RESORT is a condo hotel on the south side of Buena Vista Drive, about a quarter mile east of Disney's Caribbean Resort. The property has an interesting history: When Walt Disney began secretly buying up real estate in the 1960s under the names of numerous front companies, the land on which this resort stands was the last holdout and was never sold to Disney, though the company tried repeatedly to acquire it through the years. (The owners reportedly took issue with the way Disney acquired land) The site was ultimately bought by Marriott, which put up a Fairfield Inn time-share development in 2004. The Wyndham is part of a luxury-hotel complex on the same site that includes a 500-room Waldorf Astoria and a 1,000-room Hilton. The development is surrounded on three sides by Disney property and on one side by I-4.

The Bonnet Creek Resort offers upscale, family-friendly accommodations: one- and two-bedroom condos with fully equipped kitchens, washer-dryers, jetted tubs, and balconies. Activities and amenities on-site include two outdoor swimming pools, a "lazy river" float stream, a children's activities program, a game room, a playground, and miniature golf. There is free scheduled transportation to all the Disney parks. One-bedroom units are equipped with a king bed in the bedroom and a sleeper sofa in the living area; two-bedroom condos have two double beds in the second bedroom and an additional bath.

GETTING A GOOD DEAL ON A ROOM OUTSIDE WALT DISNEY WORLD

HOTEL DEVELOPMENT AT WALT DISNEY WORLD has sharpened the competition among lodgings throughout the Orlando/Kissimmee area. Hotels outside Walt Disney World, in particular, struggle to fill their guest rooms. Unable to compete with Disney resorts for convenience or perks, off-World hotels lure patrons with bargain rates. The extent of the bargain depends on the season, day of the week, and local events. Here are tips and strategies for getting a good deal on a room outside Walt Disney World.

1. ORLANDO MAGICARD Orlando MagiCard is a discount program sponsored by the Orlando/Orange County Convention and Visitors Bureau. Cardholders are eligible for discounts of 20–50% at about 50 participating hotels. The MagiCard is also good for discounts at area attractions, including several dinner theaters. Valid for up to six persons, the card isn't available for groups or conventions.

To obtain an Orlando MagiCard and a list of participating hotels and attractions, call ☎ 800-643-9492 or 407-363-5872. Visit **orlando info.com/magicard;** the MagiCard and accompanying brochure can be printed from a personal computer.

Anyone older than 18 is eligible, and the card is free. If you miss getting a card before you leave home, you can get one at the Convention and Visitors Bureau at 8723 International Drive in Orlando. When you call for a MagiCard, also request the *Orlando Official Accommodations Guide.*

2. ROOMSAVER Trader Publishing Company publishes a book of discount coupons for bargain rates at hotels statewide. The book, called *RoomSaver,* is free in many restaurants and motels on main highways leading to Florida. Because most travelers make reservations before leaving home, picking up the coupon book en route doesn't help much. If you call and use a credit card, TPC will send the guide first class for $3 ($5 U.S. for Canadian delivery). Contact:

Trader Publishing Company
☎ 386-418-6800 or 800-332-3948
travelerdiscountguide.com

3. HOTEL SHOPPING ON THE INTERNET Web sites we've found most dependable for Walt Disney Area hotel discounts are shown below.

The secret to shopping on the Internet is . . . shopping. When we're really looking for a deal, we check all the sites below. Flexibility on dates and location are helpful, and we always give our travel agent the opportunity to beat any deal we find.

We recommend choosing a hotel based on location, room quality, price, commuting time to the parks, plus any features important to you. Next, check each of the applicable sites above. You'll be able to ferret out the best Internet deal in about 30 minutes. Then call the hotel to see if you can save more by booking directly. Start by asking the hotel for specials. If their response doesn't beat the Internet deal, tell them what you've found and ask if they can do better.

OUR FAVORITE ONLINE HOTEL RESOURCES

mousesavers.com Best site for hotels in Disney World.

dreamsunlimitedtravel.com Excellent for both Disney and non-Disney hotels.

2000orlando-florida.com Comprehensive hotel site.

valuetrips.com Specializes in budget accommodations.

travelocity.com Multidestination travel superstore.

roomsaver.com Provides discount coupons for hotels.

floridakiss.com Primarily US 192–Kissimmee area hotels.

orlandoinfo.com Good info; not user-friendly for booking.

orlandovacation.com Great rates for condos and home rentals.

expedia.com Largest of the multidestination travel sites.

hotels.com Largest Internet hotel-booking service; many other sites link to this site and its subsidiary, **hoteldiscounts.com.**

Begin your hotel shopping on a search engine such as **kayak.com.** Kayak searches hotel and Internet-seller Web sites to find the cheapest rates for more than 200 Disney-area hotels and provides links to the sellers. Kayak offers search filters such as price, quality rating, and proximity to a specific location (Walt Disney World, Universal Studios, SeaWorld, the convention center, airport, and so on) to help you narrow your search.

4. IF YOU MAKE YOUR OWN RESERVATION Reservationists at the toll-free number are often unaware of local specials. Always phone the hotel directly and ask about specials before you inquire about corporate rates. Don't hesitate to bargain, but do it before you check in. If you're buying a hotel's weekend package, for example, and want to extend your stay, you can often obtain at least the corporate rate for the extra days.

Always call the hotel in question, not the hotel chain's national 800 number.

Bob

CONDOMINIUMS AND VACATION HOMES

VACATION HOMES ARE FREESTANDING, while condominiums are essentially one- to three-bedroom accommodations in a larger building housing a number of similar units. Because condos tend to be part of large developments (frequently time-shares), amenities such as swimming pools, playgrounds, game arcades, and fitness centers often rival those found in the best hotels. Generally speaking, condo developments do not have restaurants, lounges, or spas. In a condo, if something goes wrong, someone will be on hand to fix the problem. Vacation homes rented from a property-management company likewise will have someone to come to the rescue, though responsiveness tends to vary vastly from company to company. If you rent directly from an owner, correcting problems is often more difficult, particularly when the owner doesn't live in the same area as the rental home.

In a vacation home, all the amenities are contained in the home (though in planned developments there may be community amenities available as well). Depending on the specific home, you might find a small swimming pool, hot tub, two-car garage, family room, game room, and even a home theater. Features found in both condos and vacation homes include full kitchens, laundry rooms, TVs, DVD players, and frequently stereos. Interestingly, though almost all freestanding vacation homes have private pools, very few have backyards. This means that, except for swimming, the kids are pretty much relegated to playing in the house or front yard.

Time-share condos are clones when it comes to furniture and decor, but single-owner condos and vacation homes are furnished and decorated in a style that reflects the taste of the owner. Vacation homes, usually one- to two-story houses located in a subdivision, very rarely afford interesting views (though some overlook lakes or natural areas), while condos, especially the high-rise variety, sometimes offer exceptional ones.

The Price Is Nice

The best deals in lodging in the Walt Disney World area are vacation homes and single-owner condos. Prices range from about $65 a night for two-bedroom condos and town homes to $200 to $500 a night for three- to seven-bedroom vacation homes. Forgetting about taxes to keep the comparison simple, let's compare renting a vacation home to staying at one of Disney's Value Resorts. A family of two parents, two teens, and two grandparents would need three hotel rooms at Disney's Pop Century Resort. At the lowest rate obtainable, that would run you $82 per night per room, or $246 total per night. Rooms are 260 square feet each, so you'd have a total of 780 square feet. Each room has a private bath and a television.

Renting at the same time of year from **All Star Vacation Homes** (no relation to Disney's All-Star Resorts), you can rent a 2,053-square-foot, four-bedroom, three-bath vacation home with a private pool three miles from Walt Disney World for $219—a saving of $27 per night over the Disney Value Resort rate. With four bedrooms, each of the teens can have his or her own room. Further, for the dates we checked, All Star Vacation Homes was running a special in which they threw in a free rental car with a one-week home rental.

Location, Location, Location

The best vacation home is one that is within easy commuting distance of the theme parks. If you plan to spend some time at SeaWorld and the Universal parks, you'll want something just to the northeast of Walt Disney World (between the World and Orlando). If you plan to spend most of your time in the World, the best selection of vacation homes is along US 192 to the south of the park.

To get the most from a vacation home, you need to be close enough to commute in 20 minutes or less to your Walt Disney World destination. This will allow for naps, quiet time, swimming, and dollar-saving meals you prepare yourself. Though traffic and road conditions are as important as the distance from a vacation home to your Disney destination, we recommend a home no farther than 5 miles away in areas northeast of Walt Disney World and no farther than 4.5 miles away in areas south of the park.

The only practical way to shop for a rental home is on the Web. This makes it relatively easy to compare different properties and rental companies. On the downside, there are so many owners, rental companies, and individual homes to choose from that you could research yourself into a stupor. There are three main types of Web sites in the home-rental game: those for property-management companies, which showcase a given company's homes and are set up for direct bookings; individual owner sites; and third-party listings sites, which advertise properties through different owners and sometimes management companies as well. Sites in the last category will usually refer prospective renters to an owner's or management company's site for reservations.

The best Web sites provide the following:

- Numerous photos and in-depth descriptions of individual homes to make comparisons quick and easy
- Overview maps or text descriptions that reflect how distant specific homes or developments are from Walt Disney World
- The ability to book the specific individual rental home of your choice on the site
- A prominently displayed phone number for non-Internet bookings and questions

The best sites are also easy to navigate and let you see what you're interested in without logging in or giving personal information.

Recommended Web Sites

After checking out dozens upon dozens of sites, here are the ones we recommend. All of them meet the criteria listed above. If you're stunned that there are so few of them, well, so were we. (For the record, we elected not to list some sites that met our criteria but whose homes are too far away from Walt Disney World.)

All Star Vacation Homes (allstarvacationhomes.com) is easily the best of the management-company sites, with photographs and plenty of details about featured homes. All of the company's rental properties are within either 4 miles of Walt Disney World or 3 miles of Universal Studios.

Orlando's Finest Vacation Homes (orlandosfinest.com) represents both homeowners and vacation-home-management companies. Offering a broad inventory, the Orlando's Finest Web site features photos and information on individual homes. Although the info is not as detailed as that offered by the All Star Vacation Homes site, friendly sales agents can fill in the blanks.

The Web site for the **Orlando–Orange County Convention and Visitors Bureau (orlandoinfo.com)** is the place to go if you're interested in renting a condominium at one of the many time-share developments (click on "Places to Stay" at the site's home page). You can call the developments directly, but going through this Web site allows you to bypass sales departments and escape their high-pressure invitations to sit through sales presentations. The site also lists hotels and vacation homes.

Vacation Rental by Owner (vrbo.com) is a nationwide vacation-homes listings service that puts prospective renters in direct contact with owners of rental homes. The site is straightforward and always lists a large number of rental properties in Celebration, Disney's planned community situated about 8–10 minutes from the theme parks. Two similar listings services with good Web sites are **Vacation Rentals 411 (vacationrentals411.com)** and **Last Minute Villas (last minutevillas.net)**.

We frequently receive letters from readers extolling the virtues of renting a condo or vacation home. This endorsement by a family from St. Joe, Indiana, is typical:

We rented a home in Kissimmee this time, and we'll never stay in a hotel at WDW again. It was by far the nicest, most relaxing time we've ever had down there. Our rental home was within 10–15 minutes of all the Disney parks and 25 minutes from SeaWorld. We had three bedrooms, two baths, and an in-ground pool in a screened enclosure out back. We paid $90 per night for the whole shootin' match. We used AAA Dream Homes Rental Company and . . . [they] provided us with detailed info before we went down so we would know what we needed to bring.

From a New Jersey family of five:

I cannot stress enough how important it is if you have a large family (more than two kids) to rent a house for your stay! . . . We stayed at Windsor Hills Resort, which I booked through **globalresorthomes. com** *. . . It took us about 10 minutes to drive there in the a.m., and we had no traffic issues at all. We had a brand-new four-bedroom, four-bathroom house with our own pool. . . . All for $215 a night! This was in October, but rates never climb above $300, even in the high season. We loved getting away from the hubbub of Disney and relaxing back at the house in "our" pool.*

AAA Dream Homes (floridadreamhomes.com) has a good reputation for customer service and now has photos of and information about the homes in its inventory online.

HOW *to* CHILDPROOF *a* HOTEL ROOM

TODDLERS AND SMALL CHILDREN up to 3 years of age (and sometimes older) can wreak mayhem—if not outright disaster—in a hotel room. They're mobile, curious, and amazingly fast, and they have a penchant for turning the most seemingly innocuous furnishing or decoration into a lethal weapon. Chances are you're pretty experienced when it comes to spotting potential dangers, but just in case you need a refresher course, here's what to look for.

Always begin by checking the room for hazards that you cannot neutralize, like balconies, chipping paint, cracked walls, sharp surfaces, shag carpeting, and windows that can't be secured shut. If you encounter anything that you don't like or is too much of a hassle to fix, ask for another room.

If you use a crib supplied by the hotel, make sure that the mattress is firm and covers the entire bottom of the crib. If there is a mattress cover, it should fit tightly. Slats should be 2.5 inches (about the width of a soda can) or less apart. Test the drop sides to ensure that they work properly and that your child cannot release them accidentally. Examine the crib from all angles (including from underneath) to make sure it has been assembled correctly and that there are no sharp edges. Check for chipping paint and other potentially toxic substances that your child might ingest. Wipe down surfaces your child might touch or mouth to diminish the potential of infection transmitted from a previous occupant. Finally, position the crib away from drape cords, heaters, wall sockets, and air conditioners.

A Monteno, Illinois, mother of a 2-year-old offered this suggestion:

> You can request bed rails [at the Disney resorts]. Our two-and-a-half-year-old is way too big for the pack and play. The bed rails worked perfectly for us.

If your infant can turn over, we recommend changing him or her on a pad on the floor. Likewise, if you have a child seat of any sort, place it where it cannot be knocked over, and always strap your child in.

If your child can roll, crawl, or walk, you should bring about eight electrical outlet covers and some cord to tie cabinets shut and to bind drape cords and the like out of reach. Check for appliances, lamps, ashtrays, ice buckets, and anything else that your child might pull down on him- or herself. Have the hotel remove coffee tables with sharp edges, and both real and artificial plants that are within your child's reach. Round up items from table and countertops such as matchbooks, courtesy toiletries, and drinking glasses, and store them out of reach.

If the bathroom door can be accidentally locked, cover the locking mechanism with duct tape or a doorknob cover. Use the security chain or upper latch on the room's entrance door to ensure that your child doesn't open it without your knowledge.

Inspect the floor and remove pins, coins, and other foreign objects that your child might find. Don't forget to check under beds and furniture. One of the best tips we've heard came from a Fort Lauderdale, Florida, mother who crawls around the room on her hands and knees in order to see possible hazards from her child's perspective.

If you rent a suite or a condo, you'll have more territory to childproof and will have to deal with the possible presence of cleaning supplies, a stove, a refrigerator, cooking utensils, and low cabinet doors, among other things. Sometimes the best option is to seal off the kitchen with a folding safety gate.

PART FOUR

DINING

DINING OPTIONS ABOUND BOTH IN AND OUT of Walt Disney World, and if you're so inclined, there are a lot of ways to save big bucks while keeping your crew nourished and happy.

EATING *outside* WALT DISNEY WORLD

1. **A CAR HELPS** Access to restaurants outside of Walt Disney World can really cut the cost of your overall vacation, but you've got to have wheels. If you eat only your evening meal outside the World, the savings will more than pay for the car.

2. **PLENTY OF CHOICES** Eating outside of Walt Disney World doesn't relegate you to dining in lackluster restaurants. The range of choices is quite broad and includes elegant dining options, as well as familiar chain restaurants and local family eateries.

3. **DISCOUNTS ARE EVERYWHERE** Visitor magazines and booklets containing discount coupons to dozens of out-of-the-World restaurants are available everywhere except in Walt Disney World. The coupons are good at a broad selection of eateries, ranging from burger joints to some of the best restaurants in the area. Though coupon booklets and freebie visitor mags are pretty much everywhere, the mother lode can be found at the Orlando/Orange County Official Visitors Center at 8723 International Dr., Ste. 101, at the corner of Austrian Row, open 8:30 a.m.–6:30 p.m.; ☎ 407-363-5872. Here you'll find copies of every magazine and booklet available. The center also sells slightly discounted tickets to the theme parks. Also see **orlandoinfo.com.**

4. **WHEN YOU DON'T HAVE A CAR** If you're staying in a hotel outside Disney World, Take Out Express (7111 Grand National Dr.; ☎ 407-352-1170; **orlandotakeoutexpress.com**) will deliver a meal from your choice of several area restaurants, including T.G.I. Fridays, TooJay's Gourmet Deli,

Denny's, Kim Wu Chinese, and Cariera's Cucina Italiana. The delivery charge is $5 per restaurant, with a minimum $15 order. Gratuity is added to the bill. Cash, traveler's checks, MasterCard, Visa, American Express, and Discover are accepted. Hours are 4:30 p.m.–11 p.m.

BUFFETS AND MEAL DEALS OUTSIDE WALT DISNEY WORLD

BUFFETS, RESTAURANT SPECIALS, and discount dining abound in the area surrounding Walt Disney World, especially on US 192 (known locally as the Irlo Bronson Memorial Highway) and along International Drive. The local visitor magazines, distributed free at non-Disney hotels among other places, are packed with advertisements and discount coupons for seafood feasts, Chinese buffets, Indian buffets, breakfast buffets, and a host of combination specials for everything from lobster to barbecue. For a family trying to economize, some of the come-ons are mighty appealing. But are these places any good? Is the food fresh, tasty, and appealing? Are the restaurants clean and inviting? Armed with little more than a roll of Tums, the *Unofficial* research team tried all the eateries that advertise heavily in the free tourist magazines. Here's what we discovered.

CHINESE SUPER BUFFETS Whoa! Talk about an oxymoron. If you've ever tried preparing Chinese food, especially a stir-fry, you know that split-second timing is required to avoid overcooking. So it should come as no big surprise that Chinese dishes languishing on a buffet lose their freshness, texture, and flavor in a hurry.

For the past few editions of this guide, we were able to find several Chinese buffets that were better than the rest and that we felt comfortable recommending. Unfortunately, however, our endorsements seem to be the kiss of death: We return the next year to discover that quality has slipped precipitously. We attempted to find a new buffet to replace the ones we deleted from the guide, and we can tell you that wasn't fun work. At the end of the day, **Mei Asian Bistro** (8255 International Dr.; ☎ 407-352-0881) is the only Chinese buffet we've elected to list. To call it a *super* buffet might be stretching things, but aside from a lackluster dessert selection, it's pretty good.

INDIAN BUFFETS Indian food works much better on a buffet than Chinese food; in fact, it actually improves as the flavors marry. In the Walt Disney World area, most Indian restaurants offer a buffet at lunch only—not too convenient if you plan on spending your day at the theme parks. If you're out shopping or taking a day off, here are some Indian buffets worth trying:

Aashirwad Indian Cuisine 5748 International Dr., at the corner of International Drive and Kirkman Road; ☎ 407-370-9830

Punjab Indian Restaurant 7451 International Dr.; ☎ 407-352-7887

continued on page 130

Where to Eat outside Walt Disney World

AMERICAN

J. Alexander's 7335 Sand Lake Rd., Orlando; ☎ 407-345-1039; **jalexanders. com;** moderate. Chic, relaxed ambience; large portions of steak and seafood.

Plantation Room Celebration Hotel, 700 Bloom St., Celebration; ☎ 407-566-6000; **celebrationhotel.com;** moderate–expensive. New Florida cuisine focusing on seafood and locally grown fruits and vegetables.

The Ravenous Pig 1234 N. Orange Ave., Winter Park; ☎ 407-628-2333; **theravenouspig.com;** moderate–expensive. New American cuisine with an award-winning menu that changes frequently, with seasonal ingredients.

Seasons 52 7700 W. Sand Lake Rd., Orlando; ☎ 407-354-5212; **seasons52. com;** moderate–expensive. Delicious, creative New American food (and low in fat and calories). Solid wine list.

BARBECUE

Bubbalou's Bodacious Bar-B-Que 5818 Conroy Rd., Orlando (near Universal Orlando); ☎ 407-423-1212; **bubbalous.com;** inexpensive. Tender, smoky barbecue; tomato-based "killer" sauce.

CHINESE

Ming Court 9188 International Dr., Orlando; ☎ 407-351-9988; **ming-court. com;** moderate to expensive. Wok-fired dishes, sushi.

CUBAN/SPANISH

Columbia 649 Front St., Celebration; ☎ 407-566-1505; **columbiarestaurant. com;** moderate. Cuban/Spanish creations such as paella and the 1905 Salad.

Havana's Cafe 3628 W. Vine St., Kissimmee; ☎ 407-201-7957; **havanascafe. net;** inexpensive. No-frills traditional Cuban eats; excellent seafood.

FRENCH

Le Coq au Vin* 4800 S. Orange Ave., Orlando; ☎ 407-851-6980; **lecoqauvin restaurant.com;** moderate–expensive. Country French cuisine in a relaxed atmosphere. Reservations suggested.

INDIAN

Tabla Bar and Grill 5827 Caravan Ct., Orlando; ☎ 407-248-9400; **tablabar. com;** moderate. Near the entrance to Universal Orlando, this family-owned restaurant offers authentic, innovative dishes.

ITALIAN

Vinito Ristorante 4971 International Dr., Orlando; ☎ 407-354-0404; **vinito usa.com;** moderate. Authentic Italian at the Prime Outlets shopping center.

JAPANESE/SUSHI

Amura 7786 W. Sand Lake Rd., Orlando; ☎ 407-370-0007; **amura.com;** moderate. A favorite sushi bar for locals. The tempura is popular too.

*20 minutes or more from Walt Disney World

Hanamizuki 8255 International Dr., Orlando; ☎ 407-363-7200; **hanamizuki.us;** moderate–expensive. Usually filled with Japanese visitors; pricey but authentic.

Nagoya Sushi 7600 Dr. Phillips Blvd., Suite 66, in the very rear of The Marketplace at Dr. Phillips; ☎ 407-248-8558; **nagoyasushi.com;** moderate. A small, intimate restaurant with great sushi and an extensive menu.

MEXICAN

Cantina Laredo 800 Via Dellagio Way, Orlando; ☎ 407-345-0186; **cantina laredo.com;** moderate–expensive. Authentic Mexican in upscale atmosphere.

Chevys Fresh Mex 12547 State Rd. 535, Lake Buena Vista; ☎ 407-827-1052; **chevys.com;** inexpensive–moderate. Conveniently located across from the FL 535 entrance to WDW.

Don Pablo's 8717 International Dr., Orlando; ☎ 407-354-1345; **donpablos. com;** inexpensive. Good food but can be a bit noisy.

Moe's Southwest Grill 7541-D W. Sand Lake Rd., Orlando; ☎ 407-264-9903; **moesorlando.com;** inexpensive. Dependable southwestern fare.

Vallarta Mexican Grill 12167 S. Apopka–Vineland Rd., Orlando; ☎ 407-238-5300; inexpensive. Family-owned restaurant serving freshly prepared Mexican dishes. Full bar.

SEAFOOD

Bonefish Grill 7830 W. Sand Lake Rd., Orlando; ☎ 407-355-7707; **bonefishgrill. com;** moderate. Casual setting along busy Restaurant Row on Sand Lake Road. Choose your fish; then choose a sauce to accompany. Also steaks and chicken.

STEAK/PRIME RIB

The Capital Grille Pointe Orlando, 9101 International Dr., Orlando; ☎ 407-370-4392; **thecapitalgrille.com;** expensive. Dry-aged steaks, extensive wine list, and classic decor.

Del Frisco's* 729 Lee Rd., Orlando; ☎ 407-645-4443; **delfriscosorlando.com;** Family-owned; rated the top steak house in Central Florida. Prime steaks, lobster, over 6,500 bottles of wine, world-class selection of single-malt scotch.

Texas de Brazil 5259 International Dr., Orlando; ☎ 407-355-0355; **texas debrazil.com;** expensive. All-you-care-to-eat in an upscale Brazilian-style *churrascaria*. Filet mignon, sausage, pork ribs, chicken, lamb, and more. Kids under age 6 free, ages 7–12 half price. Salad bar with more than 40 options.

Vito's Chop House 8633 International Dr., Orlando; ☎ 407-354-2467; **vitos chophouse.com;** moderate. Upscale meat house with a taste of Tuscany.

THAI

Red Bamboo 6803 S. Kirkman Rd. at International Drive, Orlando; ☎ 407-226-8997; **redbamboothai.com;** moderate. Housed in an unassuming strip-mall location and acclaimed by Orlando dining critics for its authentic Thai dishes. Delicious vegetarian options; impressive wine list. The *Unofficial* research team agrees: some of the best Thai food anywhere. Try the fried cheesecake.

continued from page 127

BRAZILIAN BUFFETS A number of Brazilian buffets have sprung up along International Drive. The best of these is **Vittorio's** (5159 International Dr., near the outlet malls at the northern end of International Drive; ☎ 407-352-1255; **vittoriosrestaurant.com**).

SEAFOOD AND LOBSTER BUFFETS These affairs don't exactly fall under the category of inexpensive dining. The main draw (no pun intended) is all the lobster you can eat. The problem is that lobsters, like Chinese food, don't wear well on a steam table. After a few minutes on the buffet line, they make better tennis balls than dinner. If, however, there's someone in the kitchen who knows how to steam a lobster, and if you grab your lobster immediately after a fresh batch has been brought out, it will probably be fine. There are three lobster buffets on US 192 and another two on International Drive. Although all five do a reasonable job, we prefer **Boston Lobster Feast** (6071 West Irlo Bronson Memorial Hwy.; ☎ 407-396-2606; and 8731 International Dr., five blocks north of the Convention Center; ☎ 407-248-8606; **bostonlobsterfeast.com**). Both locations are distinguished by a vast variety of seafood in addition to the lobster. The International Drive location is cavernous and insanely noisy, which is why we prefer the Irlo Bronson location, where you can actually have a conversation over dinner. There's ample parking at the International Drive location, while parking places are in short supply at the Irlo Bronson restaurant. At about $33 for early birds (4–6 p.m.) and $40 after 6 p.m., dining is expensive at both locations.

SALAD BUFFETS The most popular of these in the Walt Disney World area is **Sweet Tomatoes** (6877 S. Kirkman Rd.; ☎ 407-363-1616; 12561 S. Apopka–Vineland Rd.; ☎ 407-938-9461; **sweettomatoes. com**). During lunch and dinner, you can expect a line out the door, but fortunately it moves fast. The buffet features prepared salads and an extensive array of ingredients to build your own. In addition to the rabbit food, Sweet Tomatoes offers a variety of soups, a modest pasta bar, a baked-potato bar, an assortment of fresh fruit, and ice-cream sundaes. Dinner runs $9.79 for adults, $5 for children ages 6–12, and $3.49 for children ages 3–5. Lunch is $8.39 for adults and the same prices as dinner for children (not including tax).

BREAKFAST AND ENTREE BUFFETS Entree buffets are offered by most chain steakhouses in the area, such as **Ponderosa, Sizzler,** and **Golden Corral.** Among them, they have 18 locations in the Walt Disney World area. All serve breakfast, lunch, and dinner. At lunch and dinner, you get the buffet when you buy an entree, usually a steak. Generally speaking, the buffets are less elaborate than a stand-alone buffet but considerably more varied than a salad bar. Breakfast service is a straightforward buffet (that is, you aren't obligated to buy an entree). As for the food, it's chain-restaurant quality but decent all the same. Prices are a bargain, and you can get in and out at lightning speed—important at breakfast when you're trying to get to the theme parks early. Some locations offer lunch and dinner buffets at a set price without your having to buy an entree.

Though you can argue about which chain serves the best steak, Golden Corral wins the buffet contest hands down, with at least twice as many offerings as its three competitors. While buffets at Golden Corral and Ponderosa are pretty consistent from location to location, the buffets at the various Sizzlers vary a good deal. The pick of the Sizzlers is the one at 7602 W. Irlo Bronson Memorial Hwy. (☎ 407-397-0997). In addition to the steakhouses, area **Shoney's** also offer breakfast, lunch, and dinner buffets. Local freebie visitor magazines are full of discount coupons for all of the previous restaurants.

MEAL DEALS Discount coupons are available for a wide range of restaurants, including some wonderful upscale-ethnic places such as **Ming Court** (Chinese; 9188 International Dr.; ☎ 407-351-9988; ming-court.com). Our favorite prime-rib joint is **Wild Jack's Steaks & BBQ** (7364 International Dr.; ☎ 407-352-4407). The decor is strictly cowboy modern, but the beef is some of the best in town, and the price is right.

The best steak deal in the Walt Disney World area is the $11, 10-ounce New York strip at the **Black Angus Steak House.** The beef is served with salad, a choice of vegetables or potato, and bread, and it's available at two locations convenient to Disney: 7516 W. Irlo Bronson Memorial Hwy., ☎ 407-390-4548; and 6231 International Dr., ☎ 407-354-3333. Another meat eater's delight is the Feast for Four at **Sonny's Real Pit Bar-B-Q,** a Florida chain that turns out good barbecue. For $40 per family of four, you get sliced pork and beef, plus chicken, ribs, your choice of three sides (beans, slaw, fries), garlic bread or corn bread, and soft drinks or tea, all served family-style. The closest Sonny's location to the Walt Disney World and Universal tourist areas is at 7423 S. Orange Blossom Trail in Orlando (☎ 407-859-7197); for a listing of other restaurants within a wider radius, visit **sonnysbbq.com.** No coupons are needed or available for Sonny's, but they are available for the other "meateries."

COUPONS Discounts and twofer coupons for many of the restaurants mentioned can be found in freebie visitor guides available at most hotels outside of Walt Disney World. The **Orlando–Orange County Official Visitors Center** (8723 International Dr., Ste. 101; ☎ 407-363-5872; open daily, 8:30 a.m.–6:30 p.m.) offers a treasure trove of coupons and free visitor magazines. On the Internet, check out **couponsalacarte. com** and **orlandocoupons.com** for printable coupons.

DINING *in* WALT DISNEY WORLD

ONCE YOU COULD HAVE JOKED that a chapter about dining in Walt Disney World was an oxymoron. Whatever else it was (and it was many wonderful things), Disney World was no gourmet paradise. For the most part, in fact, the restaurants were as much "entertainment" as the rest of Disney World: The fast-food joints feature character decor, and the international pavilions sport native costumes.

Disney's food and beverage department has vastly expanded, and it has succeeded in launching a remarkable upgrade of the full-service restaurants around the World. Now there are nine or ten first-class restaurants and perhaps an equal number of B+ establishments. The wine lists have been seriously improved and expanded—there is even a full-fledged wine bar at the Yacht and Beach Club, Martha's Vineyard.

Of course, if the average parents roaming the Walt Disney World parks were primarily concerned with pleasing their palates, the hottest dinner ticket at the park would not be the *Hoop-Dee-Doo Musical Revue*. In fact, if you want to know what Disney World visitors really like, look at the numbers: Every year, they consume 1.6 million turkey legs, nearly 10 million hamburgers, 7.7 million hot dogs, 46 million sodas, and 5 million bags of popcorn.

One thing parents should be aware of is that both full- and counter-service restaurants at Walt Disney World serve very substantial portions. You can easily put aside parts of dinners for lunches the next day (if you have a refrigerator in your room), split an entree, or load up at lunch and go light on dinner.

Liliane

So, for many families, food is a secondary consideration, but if you do care more about dining out on your vacation or would like to experiment with different cuisines, *The Unofficial Guide to Walt Disney World*, referred to in the Introduction, includes more detailed reviews not only of the sit-down establishments in Disney World itself but also some of the better restaurants outside the World.

DISNEY DINING 101

It's the Economy, Pluto

As the aftermath of the recession affects the number of travelers visiting the World, Disney scrambled furiously to make up for lost revenue. Unfortunately, this translates to higher and higher prices at Disney restaurants. Main-course prices at some restaurants have risen more than 35%; plus, Disney levies a "dining surcharge" during the summer and other busy times of year. Recently we dined at the new Wave restaurant at the Contemporary Resort and ordered a wine that retails for about $11. It was $9 a glass (!)—about a five-times markup. Believe us, if you rent a car and eat only dinner each day at non-Disney restaurants, you'll save enough to more than pay for the rental cost.

These comments from a Tennessee reader spell it out:

The first time we ate at Liberty Tree Tavern a few years ago, the cost was about $23 per person for each adult. This year, the cost would have been about $33 per person with the increased prices and the "holiday dining surcharge" they add during the summer months. This is a nearly 40% price increase over a period of three years for basically the same experience! We decided that turkey and mashed potatoes weren't worth the $33 and ended up eating elsewhere.

And from a New Orleans mom:

Disney keeps pushing prices up and up. For us, the sky is NOT the limit. We won't be back.

ADVANCE RESERVATIONS: WHAT'S IN A NAME?

DISNEY TINKERS CEASELESSLY with its restaurant-reservations policy. In 1997 reservations were replaced with Priority Seating, a confusing system with a befuddling name that issued reservations that weren't really reservations. In 2005, after eight years, and just when we were beginning to understand what a Priority Seating was, Disney decided to change the name from Priority Seating to the rather redundant Advance Reservations. Indeed, the name is all that changed: When you call, your name and essential information are taken as if you were making an honest-to-goodness reservation. The Disney representative then tells you that you have Advance Reservations for the restaurant on the date and time you requested and usually explains that you'll be seated ahead of walk-ins—that is, those who do not have Advance Reservations.

The no-show rate in January, a slow month, is about 33%, while in July it's less than 10%.

Bob

GETTING YOUR ACT TOGETHER

IF YOU WANT TO PATRONIZE any of the Walt Disney World Resort full-service restaurants, buffets, character meals, or dinner shows, you should make Advance Reservations; page 135 is a listing of how far ahead of time you can make them. Note that you can now make Advance Reservations online (see page 133) as well as by calling ☎ 407-WDW-DINE.

For the busiest full-service restaurants, buffets, and character meals, you should make Advance Reservations 90–180 days ahead of time—although there are exceptions to the rule (see page 134).

If you fail to make Advance Reservations before you leave home, or if you want to make your dining decisions spontaneously, your chances of getting a table at the restaurants of your choice aren't the best, especially during the hours when most folks prefer to eat dinner.

If you visit Walt Disney World during a very busy time of year, it's to your advantage to make Advance Reservations before you leave home, as this Houston couple attests:

Advance Reservations: The Official Line

You can make reservations up to 180 days in advance for:

Afternoon tea and children's programs **at the Grand Floridian Resort & Spa**

All Disney table-service restaurants and character-dining venues

Cirque du Soleil's *La Nouba* **at Downtown Disney**

Fantasmic! dinner package **at Disney's Hollywood Studios**

Hoop-Dee-Doo Musical Revue **at Fort Wilderness Resort**

Mickey's Backyard BBQ **at Fort Wilderness Resort**

Spirit of Aloha Dinner Show **at the Polynesian Resort**

Guests staying at Walt Disney World resorts—these do not include the Swan, the Dolphin, Shades of Green, or the hotels of the Downtown Disney Resort Area—can make Advance Reservations up to 10 additional days ahead, effectively giving them a maximum window of 190 days.

Advance Reservations Go Online

You can also make Advance Reservations at the Walt Disney World Web site. The service is open to everyone, regardless of whether you're lodging inside or outside of Disney World. Go to **disneyworld.disney.go.com/reservations/dining;** if you know which restaurant(s) you're interested in, it's easier to search by alphabetical listing than by location. Click the blue "Sort By" bar just above the restaurant descriptions, and scroll down to the restaurant of your choice. Restaurants that accept Advanced Reservations have a yellow bar just below the restaurant photo that reads "Book a Reservation." Clicking the yellow bar takes you to the reservations page for that restaurant. You can search for reservations on a particular date or within a range of 5 days. If you want to retrieve or review your reservations online, you can register or, if already registered, log in. *Note:* Some readers have reported Disney's online-reservations system opening at 6 a.m. Eastern time—1 hour earlier than the phone-reservations system.

Make reservations if you plan on having table service. Even trying to walk in for full service at off-times was impossible.

Another reader warns of a sea change in Advance Reservations policy that practically eliminates same-day reservations and walk-ins:

While walking around the parks and resorts this weekend, I think literally every sit-down restaurant we passed had a sign out front saying something like, IN ORDER TO SERVE OUR GUESTS WITH DINING RESERVATIONS IN A TIMELY MANNER, WE ARE NOT ACCEPTING WALK-UP DINING REQUESTS AT THIS TIME. *I believe every World Showcase country had this sign, as did the Magic Kingdom, the Yacht and Beach Club, and Animal Kingdom Lodge's two sit-downs, all weekend, so I don't think this is a one-time thing. This may also explain why the World Showcase restaurants are going through refurbishments one by one—must be to add capacity.*

Number of Days in Advance Needed to Book Theme-park Sit-down Restaurants

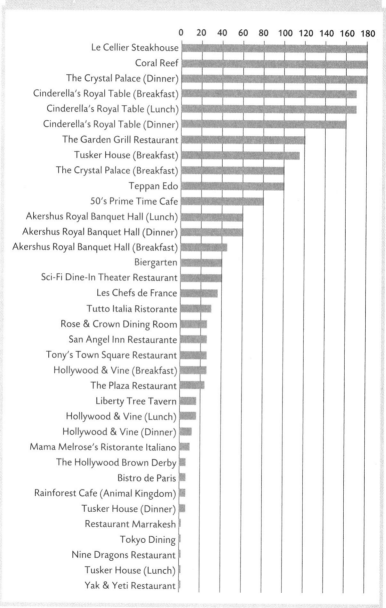

Advance Reservations: The Unofficial Scoop

WHILE WALT DISNEY WORLD VISITOR NUMBERS haven't suffered that much in the current economy, Disney brass has noticed that people are likelier these days to book last-minute trips to Orlando.

Using dozens of volunteers with free long-distance phone plans and access to the online Advance Dining Reservation system used by Disney travel agents, we began building profiles of each theme-park restaurant, showing how many days in advance (on average) that restaurant filled up for various meals. Our results are shown in the chart on page 135. All meals are dinner unless otherwise noted.

Not surprisingly, you'll need to book highly rated restaurants such as Canada's **Le Cellier Steakhouse** and the Magic Kingdom's **Crystal Palace** dinner buffet a full 180 days in advance. Interestingly, however, Epcot's **Coral Reef Restaurant** also requires dining reservations about 180 days in advance—while it's no culinary hot spot, it is one of the few nonethnic sit-down restaurants in Epcot, it has relatively few tables, and it's the only dedicated seafood restaurant in any Walt Disney World park.

Surprisingly, and slightly farther down the list, the Magic Kingdom's three **Cinderella's Royal Table** meals generally need to be booked within one to three weeks of your trip except during the busiest times of year (see page 135). Breakfast here has traditionally been the hottest ticket in the parks, but price increases and additional capacity at lunch and dinner have made tables somewhat easier to get.

It's possible to snag reservations at Germany's **Biergarten** buffet within three weeks of your trip, which is surprising because it's well regarded by both our dining reviewer and our readers. **Tutto Italia Ristorante,** which was exceedingly difficult to get into back when it was L'Originale Alfredo di Roma, now requires less than a month of lead time to reserve.

Bringing up the rear are World Showcase's **Nine Dragons Restaurant** (China) and most of the sit-down restaurants at Animal Kingdom. Nine Dragons' placement is well deserved due to its overpriced, underwhelming food. Regarding Animal Kingdom's eateries, we think that our findings don't have so much to do with these restaurants' quality as they do with the fact that people don't need to hang around until dinner to see the entire park.

A dad from St. Paul, Minnesota, changed course, much to his and his family's satisfaction:

> We had so much difficulty booking the Disney restaurants that we just threw up our hands and reread the part of the guide about places to eat outside of WDW. We ended up eating only one meal (a character breakfast) in a Disney restaurant. The rest of the time we followed your suggestions for non-Disney restaurants in the general area. I'm happy to report that we had some super meals and that the money we saved more than paid for our rental car.

For Advance Reservations, make sure you bring your confirmation number to the restaurant.

Though securing Advance Reservations before you leave home is more important than ever, there's no need, except as stated previously, to call 90 to 180 days in advance. For most restaurants, calling 45 days in advance will get you the restaurants you desire. If you're visiting during an extremely busy time of year, try to call as far in advance as possible.

If you poop out at the theme park and you don't feel like using your Advance Reservations that night, be aware that some restaurants have penalties for being a no-show and will charge you a cancellation fee. Note that you must pay in full at the time of booking for all meals at Cinderella's Royal Table, the *Hoop-Dee-Doo Musical Revue,* the *Spirit of Aloha Dinner Show,* and *Mickey's Backyard BBQ.* If you're a no-show, you lose the entire amount, so be sure to get the exact cancellation policy at the time you book your meal. Incidentally, if you're asked for a credit card to secure a seating, be aware that it's a *real* reservation as opposed to an Advance Reservation. Also be aware that if you're a no-show for a particular reservation, it will not affect any other Advance Reservations you may have made.

If you've lined up many Advance Reservations, it's a good idea to phone ☎ 407-WDW-DINE a few days before you arrive to make sure everything's in order. If you stay at a Disney resort, Guest Relations can print out a summary of all your Advance Reservations.

Disney Kids' Meals are now for ages 3–9; the cutoff used to be age 11.

Liliane

If you have an Advance Reservation for a theme-park restaurant at a time prior to opening, simply proceed to the turnstiles and inform a cast member, who will admit you to the park. If you fail to make Advance Reservations, most full-service theme-park restaurants will take walk-ins 2:30–4:30 p.m.

DRESS

DRESS IS INFORMAL AT MOST THEME-PARK restaurants, but in 2005 Disney instituted a "business casual" dress code for some of its resort restaurants: khakis, dress slacks, jeans, or dress shorts with a collared shirt for men and jeans, skirts, or dress shorts with a blouse or sweater (or a dress) for women. Restaurants with this dress code are **Jiko—The Cooking Place** at Animal Kingdom Lodge and Villas, the **Flying Fish Cafe** at Disney's BoardWalk, the **California Grill** at the Contemporary Resort, **Bistro de Paris** at Epcot's France Pavilion, **Citricos** and **Narcoossee's** at the Grand Floridian Resort & Spa, **Artist Point** at Wilderness Lodge, **Yachtsman Steakhouse** at the Yacht Club Resort, **bluezoo** and **Shula's Steak House** at the Dolphin, and **Il Mulino** at the Swan. **Victoria & Albert's** at the Grand Floridian is the only Disney restaurant that requires men to wear a jacket to dinner.

SMOKING

WALT DISNEY WORLD RESTAURANTS adopted a nonsmoking policy several years ago, after Florida voters passed an amendment to the state's constitution that also prohibits smoking in restaurant lounges. (Free-standing bars—less than 10% of revenues from food sales—are exempt.)

FOOD ALLERGIES AND SPECIAL REQUESTS

IF YOU HAVE FOOD ALLERGIES or observe some specific type of diet like eating kosher, make your needs known when you make your Advance Reservations. Does it work? Well, a Phillipsburg, New Jersey, mom reports her family's experience:

> My 6-year-old has many food allergies, and we often have to bring food with us to restaurants when we go out to eat. I was able to make reservations at the Disney restaurants in advance and indicate these allergies to the reservation clerk. When we arrived at the restaurants, the staff was already aware of my child's allergies and assigned our table a chef who double-checked the list of allergies with us. Each member of the waitstaff was also informed of the allergies. The chefs were very nice and made my son feel very special.

A FEW CAVEATS

BEFORE YOU BEGIN EATING your way through the World, you need to know:

1. Theme-park restaurants rush their customers in order to make room for the next group of diners. Dining at high speed may appeal to families with young children, but to people wanting to relax, it's like eating in a pressure chamber.

   If you want to linger over your expensive meal, don't order your entire dinner at once. Study the menu, then order appetizers. Tell the waiter you need more time to decide among entrees. Order your main course only after appetizers have been served.

2. If you're dining in a theme park and cost is an issue, make lunch your main meal. Entrees are similar to those on the dinner menu but usually are less expensive.

3. Disney adds a surcharge of $4 per adult and $2 per child to certain popular restaurants during weeks of peak attendance, including Presidents' Day, Easter, the third week of April, mid-June to mid-August, Thanksgiving, and Christmas. The following restaurants participate in the gouging: Akershus Royal Banquet Hall (Princess Storybook Meals), Biergarten, Boma (breakfast and dinner), Cape May Café (breakfast and dinner buffet), Chef Mickey's (breakfast and dinner), Cinderella's Royal Table, The Crystal Palace, The Garden Grill Restaurant, Hollywood & Vine (Play 'n Dine character buffets), Liberty Tree Tavern (dinner only) 1900 Park Fare, 'Ohana (breakfast and dinner), Trail's End Restaurant at Fort Wilderness (only a $2 surcharge for adults and $1 for kids), and Tusker House Restaurant. There's no incremental cost to folks on a Disney Dining Plan.

WALT DISNEY WORLD RESTAURANT CATEGORIES

IN GENERAL, FOOD AND BEVERAGE offerings at Walt Disney World are defined by service, price, and convenience.

Walt Disney World Buffets and Family-style Restaurants

ANIMAL KINGDOM

RESTAURANT Tusker House
CUISINE African (L, D)
MEALS SERVED B, L, D
CHARACTERS Yes (B)

ANIMAL KINGDOM LODGE

RESTAURANT
  Boma—Flavors of Africa
CUISINE African (D),
  American (B)
MEALS SERVED B, D
CHARACTERS No

BEACH CLUB RESORT

RESTAURANT Cape May Cafe
CUISINE American
MEALS SERVED B, D
CHARACTERS Yes (B)

CONTEMPORARY RESORT

RESTAURANT Chef Mickey's
CUISINE American
MEALS SERVED B, D
CHARACTERS Yes (B)

CORONADO SPRINGS

RESTAURANT Maya Grill
CUISINE American
MEALS SERVED B*, D
CHARACTERS No

DISNEY'S HOLLYWOOD STUDIOS

RESTAURANT
  Hollywood & Vine
CUISINE American
MEALS SERVED B, L, D
CHARACTERS Yes (B, L)

EPCOT

RESTAURANT Akershus Royal
  Banquet Hall
CUISINE American (B),
  Norwegian (L, D)
MEALS SERVED B, L, D
CHARACTERS Yes (B, L)

EPCOT

RESTAURANT Biergarten
CUISINE German
MEALS SERVED L, D
CHARACTERS No

EPCOT

RESTAURANT The Garden Grill
CUISINE American
MEALS SERVED D
CHARACTERS Yes

FORT WILDERNESS

RESTAURANT
  Hoop-Dee-Doo Musical Revue
CUISINE American
MEALS SERVED D
CHARACTERS No

FORT WILDERNESS

RESTAURANT
  Mickey's Backyard BBQ
CUISINE American
MEALS SERVED D
CHARACTERS Yes

FORT WILDERNESS

RESTAURANT
  Trail's End Restaurant
CUISINE American
MEALS SERVED B, L, D
CHARACTERS No

GRAND FLORIDIAN

RESTAURANT 1900 Park Fare
CUISINE American
MEALS SERVED B, D
CHARACTERS Yes

MAGIC KINGDOM

RESTAURANT Cinderella's Royal
  Table
CUISINE American
MEALS SERVED B*, L, D
CHARACTERS Yes

MAGIC KINGDOM

RESTAURANT The Crystal Palace
CUISINE American
MEALS SERVED B, L, D
CHARACTERS Yes

MAGIC KINGDOM

RESTAURANT
  Liberty Tree Tavern
CUISINE American
MEALS SERVED L, D†
CHARACTERS No

POLYNESIAN RESORT

RESTAURANT 'Ohana
CUISINE Polynesian
MEALS SERVED B, D
CHARACTERS Yes (B)

POLYNESIAN RESORT

RESTAURANT Spirit of Aloha
  Dinner Show
CUISINE American
MEALS SERVED D
CHARACTERS No

SWAN

RESTAURANT Garden Grove
CUISINE American
MEALS SERVED B‡, L‡, D
CHARACTERS Yes (B**, D)

WILDERNESS LODGE

RESTAURANT
  Whispering Canyon Cafe
CUISINE American
MEALS SERVED B, L, D
CHARACTERS No

YACHT CLUB RESORT

RESTAURANT Captain's Grille
CUISINE American
MEALS SERVED B*, L, D
CHARACTERS No

*   Serves family-style meals only at breakfast.   ‡   Serves family-style meals only at breakfast and lunch.
†   Serves family-style meals only at dinner.   **   Character-breakfast buffet served only on weekends.

FULL-SERVICE RESTAURANTS These are found in Disney resorts (except the All-Star complex, Port Orleans French Quarter, and Pop Century) and all major theme parks, Downtown Disney Marketplace, and Disney's West Side. Advance Reservations (see page 134) are recommended for all full-service restaurants except those in the Downtown Disney Resort Area (DDRA). The restaurants accept American Express, Carte Blanche, Diners Club, Japan Credit Bureau, MasterCard, and Visa.

THE COST OF COUNTER-SERVICE FOOD

Bagel or muffin	$2.59
Brownie	$2.39
Cake or pie	$4.00
Cereal with milk	$3.09
Cheeseburger with fries	$6.59–$8.09
Chicken-breast sandwich (grilled)	$7.00 ($8.59 basket)
Children's meals	$5.00
Chips	$1.50–$3.00
Cookies	$2.00
Fish basket (fried) with fries	$7.09–$9.69 (shrimp)
French fries	$2.49
Fried-chicken strips with fries	$7.69
Fruit (whole piece)	$1.00–$2.75
Fruit cup/fruit salad	$3.00–$3.39
Hot dogs	$4.25–$7.50 ($6.59 basket)
Ice cream bars	$2.50–$3.75
Nachos with cheese	$7.95
PB&J sandwich	$5.00
Pizza	$5.59–$8.29
Popcorn	$3.25–$4.50
Pretzel	$3.79–$4.29
Salad (entree)	$7.69–$8.19
Salad (side)	$3.00
Smoked turkey leg	$7.59
Soup/chili	$2.59–$4.49
Sub/deli sandwich	$8.00 (cold), $8.39 (hot)
Taco salad	$7.69
Taco with yellow rice	$5.49 (veggie), $6.00 (beef)
Veggie burger (basket)	$6.79

Drinks	Small	Large
Beer (not available in the Magic Kingdom)	$5.50	$6.25
Bottled water	$1.25	$2.50
Cappuccino/espresso	$2.69/$3.69	$4.25/$5.25 (double)
Coffee	$1.89	$3.75
Floats/milk shakes/sundaes	$3.79	$4.00
Fruit juice	$1.69	$2.59
Hot tea and cocoa	$1.89	$2.09
Milk	$1.29	$2.19
Soft drinks, iced tea, and lemonade	$2.19	$2.49

Refillable souvenir mugs cost $13 (free refills) at Disney resorts and $9.59 at water parks; mugs sold at Animal Kingdom cost $6.79 (refills 93¢).

BUFFETS AND FAMILY-STYLE RESTAURANTS There has been an explosion of buffets at Disney World during recent years. Many have Disney characters in attendance, and most have a separate children's menu featuring dishes such as hot dogs, burgers, chicken nuggets, pizza, macaroni and cheese, and spaghetti and meatballs. In addition to the buffets, several restaurants serve a family-style, all-you-can-eat, fixed-price meal.

Advance Reservations arrangements are required for character buffets and recommended for all other buffets and family-style restaurants. Most major credit cards are accepted.

If you want to eat a lot but don't want to stand in yet another line, then try one of the all-you-can-eat family-style restaurants. These feature platters of food brought to your table in courses by a server. You can sample everything and eat as much as you like. You can even go back to a favorite appetizer after you finish the main course. The food tends to be a little better than what you'll find on a buffet line.

The table on page 139 lists buffets and family-style restaurants (where you can belly up for bulk loading) at Walt Disney World.

FOOD COURTS Featuring a collection of counter-service eateries under one roof, food courts can be found at the moderate (Coronado Springs, Caribbean Beach, Port Orleans) and value (All-Star, Pop Century) Disney resorts. (The closest things to a food court at the theme parks are Sunset Ranch Market at DHS and Sunshine Seasons at Epcot; see below.) Advance Reservations are neither required nor available at these restaurants.

COUNTER SERVICE Counter-service fast food is available in all theme parks and at Downtown Disney Marketplace, Disney's BoardWalk, and Disney's West Side. The food compares in quality with Captain D's, McDonald's, or Taco Bell but is more expensive, though often served in larger portions.

FAST CASUAL Somewhere between burgers and formal dining are the establishments in Disney's "fast casual" category, including three in the theme parks: **Tomorrowland Terrace** in the Magic Kingdom, **Sunshine Seasons** in Epcot, and **Studio Catering Co.** in Disney's Hollywood Studios. Fast-casual restaurants feature menu choices a cut above what you'd normally see at a typical counter-service location. At Sunshine Seasons, for example, chefs will prepare grilled salmon on an open cooking surface while you watch, or you can choose from rotisserie chicken or pork, tasty noodle bowls, or large sandwiches made with artisanal breads. These locations all feature Asian or Mediterranean cuisine, something previously lacking inside the parks. Entrees cost about $2 more on average than traditional counter service, but the variety and food quality more than make up for the difference.

VENDOR FOOD Vendors abound at the theme parks, Downtown Disney Marketplace, Disney's West Side, and Disney's BoardWalk. Offerings include popcorn, ice-cream bars, churros (Mexican pastries), soft drinks, bottled water, and (in theme parks) fresh fruit. Prices include tax, and payment must be in cash.

The Top 10 Snacks at Walt Disney World

Following is a top-10 list of particularly decadent or unusual snacks available at WDW. We've omitted the usual funnel cakes, popcorn, and ice cream available anywhere. Also absent are the truly bizarre snacks, such as the squid treats sold at the Mitsukoshi Department Store in the Japan Pavilion at Epcot's World Showcase. These are the goodies worth scouring the parks and resorts for, in ascending order:

10. Kaki Gori at the Japan Pavilion, Epcot World Showcase A little on the sweet side but lighter than ice cream, the shaved ice at this small stand comes in such unique flavors as honeydew melon, strawberry, and tangerine. And at $3.28, it's a bargain.

9. Turkey legs Available at every theme park, these must come from 85-pound turkeys because they're huge, not to mention extra-juicy and flavorful. Grab some napkins and go primal on one of these bad boys, and don't worry about the stares you might attract—they're all just jealous.

8. Tie-Dyed Cheesecake at Disney's Pop Century Resort This fun and colorful dessert is delicious. Part red-velvet cake and part cheesecake, the dessert is so popular that many discussion boards offer recipes such as this one: **grouprecipes.com/52755/disneys-tie-dyed-cheesecake.html.**

7. Main Street Bakery at the Magic Kingdom Homemade goodies, including some sugar-free offerings. Try the blueberry loaf, hot French-toast loaf, and Mickey Bundt cakes (but probably not all at once). Also check out the assortment of Mickey Mouse Rice Krispie treats, available plain, dipped in chocolate, and with sprinkles.

Liliane

There's another goody that even trumps the Dole Whip, but Bob says we can't tell you. Maybe if you behave, we can slip it in at the end of the chapter.

HARD CHOICES

DINING DECISIONS WILL DEFINITELY affect your Walt Disney World experience. If you're short on time and you want to see the theme parks, avoid full service. Ditto if you're short on funds. If you want to try a Disney full-service restaurant, arrange Advance Reservations—again, they won't actually reserve you a table, but they can minimize your wait.

Integrating Meals into the *Unofficial Guide* Touring Plans

Arrive before the park of your choice opens. Tour expeditiously, using your chosen plan (taking as few breaks as possible), until about 11 or 11:30 a.m. Once the park becomes crowded around midday, meals and other breaks won't affect the plan's efficiency. If you intend to stay in the park for evening parades, fireworks, or other events, eat dinner early enough to be finished in time for the festivities.

6. **Cadbury chocolate bars at the U.K. Pavilion, Epcot World Showcase** If you've never had an English Cadbury bar, you just don't know what you're missing.

5. **Milk shakes from Beaches & Cream at the Beach Club Resort** Hand dipped, thick, and creamy. When was the last time you sported a milk-shake mustache? For large crowds, or large appetites, try the Kitchen Sink: a huge sundae consisting of mountains of ice cream and toppings that is actually served in a kitchen sink.

4. **Selma's cookies at the BoardWalk** Oddly enough, these are available at the candy store, Seashore Sweets, rather than at the BoardWalk Bakery (go figure), but they're worth tracking down for their rich, buttery, homemade taste.

3. **Ghirardelli Soda Fountain and Chocolate Shop at Downtown Disney Marketplace** Everything is good, and the atmosphere has a sophisticated ice-cream-shop–plus–coffee-bar vibe. *Very* San Fran.

2. **Zebra Domes at Animal Kingdom Lodge** Offered as a dessert on the Boma buffet, they're also available at the Mara food court, on the lower level of the resort near the pool. They consist of a layer of sponge cake topped with chocolate mousse, then covered in white- and dark-chocolate ganache stripes. Fun and yum rolled into one!

And the number-one snack at the Walt Disney World Resort is . . .

1. **Two words: Dole Whip!** Available in Adventureland at the Magic Kingdom, a Dole Whip is a soft-serve pineapple–ice-cream dream. Adding to the ecstasy, Dole Whips are also paired with pineapple juice in Dole Floats. Heavenly!

Character Dining

A number of restaurants, primarily those that serve all-you-can-eat buffets and family-style meals, offer character dining. At character meals, you pay a fixed price and dine in the presence of one to five Disney characters who circulate throughout the restaurant, hugging children (and sometimes adults), posing for photos, and signing autographs. Character breakfasts, lunches, and dinners are served at restaurants in and out of the theme parks.

FAST FOOD IN THE THEME PARKS

BECAUSE MOST MEALS DURING a Disney World vacation are consumed on the run while touring, we'll tackle counter-service and vendor foods first. Plentiful in all theme parks are hot dogs, hamburgers, chicken sandwiches, green salads, and pizza. They're augmented by special

items that relate to the park's theme or the part of the park you're touring. In Epcot's Germany, for example, counter-service bratwurst and beer are sold. In Frontierland in the Magic Kingdom, vendors sell smoked turkey legs. Counter-service prices are fairly consistent from park to park. Expect to pay the same for your coffee or hot dog at Animal Kingdom as at Disney's Hollywood Studios.

Getting your act together in regard to counter-service restaurants in the parks is more a matter of courtesy than necessity. Rude guests rank fifth among reader complaints. A mother from Fort Wayne, Indiana, points out that indecision can be as maddening as outright discourtesy, especially when you're hungry:

> *Every fast-food restaurant has menu signs the size of billboards, but do you think anybody reads them? People waiting in line spend enough time in front of these signs to memorize them and still don't have a clue what they want when they finally get to the order taker. If by some miracle they've managed to choose between the hot dog and the hamburger, they then fiddle around another 10 minutes deciding what size Coke to order. Tell your readers PULEEEZ get their orders together ahead of time!*

A North Carolina reader on counter-service food lines:

> *[Many] counter-service registers serve two queues each, one to the left and one to the right of each register. People are not used to this and will instinctively line up in one queue per register, typically on the right side, leaving the left vacant. We had register operators wave us up to the front several times to start a left queue instead of waiting behind others on the right.*

Healthful Food at Walt Disney World

One of the most commendable developments in food service at Walt Disney World has been the introduction of healthier foods and snacks. People who are diabetic, vegetarian, or on a diet, or those who require kosher meals, should have no trouble finding something to eat. The same goes for anyone seeking wholesome, nutritious food. Health-conscious choices are available at most fast-food counters and even from vendors. All the major theme parks, for example, have fruit stands.

Cutting Your Dining Time at the Theme Parks

Even if you confine your meals to vendor and counter-service fast food, you lose a lot of time getting food in the theme parks. At Walt Disney World, everything begins with a line and ends with a cash register. When it comes to fast food, "fast" may apply to the time you spend eating it, not the time invested in obtaining it.

Here are suggestions for minimizing the time you spend hunting and gathering food:

1. **Eat breakfast before arriving.** Don't waste touring time eating breakfast at the parks. Besides, restaurants outside the World offer some outstanding breakfast specials. Some hotels furnish small refrigerators in their guest rooms or offer to rent them. If you can get by on cold cereal, rolls, fruit, and juice, having a fridge in your room will save a ton of time. If you can't get a fridge, bring a cooler.

2. **After a good breakfast,** buy snacks from vendors in the parks as you tour, or stuff some snacks in a hip pack. This is very important if you're on a tight schedule and can't spend a lot of time waiting in line for food.

3. **All theme-park restaurants are busiest** 11:30 a.m.–2:15 p.m. for lunch and 6 p.m.–8:15 p.m. for dinner. For shorter lines and faster service, don't eat during these hours, especially 12:30 p.m.–1:30 p.m.

4. **Many counter-service restaurants sell cold sandwiches.** Buy a cold lunch (except for drinks) before 11:30 a.m. and carry it until you're ready to eat. Ditto for dinner. Bring small plastic bags in which to pack the food. Purchase drinks at the appropriate time from any convenient vendor.

5. **Most fast-food eateries have more than one service window.** Regardless of time of day, check the lines at all windows before queuing. Sometimes a window that's manned but out of the way will have a much shorter line or none at all. Note, however, that some windows may not offer all items.

6. **If you're short on time** and the park closes early, stay until closing and eat dinner outside Disney World before returning to your hotel. If the park stays open late, eat dinner about 4 or 4:30 p.m. at the restaurant of your choice. You should miss the last wave of lunchers and sneak in just ahead of the dinner crowd.

Tips for Saving Money on Food

Every time you buy a soda at the theme parks it's going to set you back about $3, and everything else from hot dogs to salad is comparably high. You can say, "Oh well, we're on vacation," and pay the exorbitant prices, or you can plan ahead and save big bucks. For comparison purposes, let's say that a family of two adults and two young teens arrives at Walt Disney World on Sunday afternoon and departs for home the following Saturday after breakfast. During that period the family eats six breakfasts, five lunches, and six dinners. What those meals cost depends on where and what they eat. It is possible for them to rent a condo and prepare all of their own meals, but they didn't travel all the way to Walt Disney World to cook. So, let's be realistic and assume that they will eat their evening meals out (what most families do, because, among other reasons, they're too tired to think about cooking). It may be just burgers or pizza, but they eat dinner in a restaurant.

That leaves breakfast and lunch to contend with. Here, basically, are the options. Needless to say, there are dozens of other various combinations. They could eat all of their meals in full-service restaurants, for example, but the bottom line is that most people don't, so we'll just keep this relatively simple.

1. Eat breakfast in their room out of their cooler or fridge and prepare sandwiches and snacks to take to the theme parks in their hip packs. Carry water bottles or rely on drinking fountains for water. Cost: $121 for family of four for six days (does not include dinners or food purchased on travel days).

2. Eat breakfast in their room out of their cooler or fridge, carry snacks in their hip packs, and buy lunch at Disney counter-service restaurants. Cost: $298 for family of four for six days (does not include dinners or food purchased on travel days).

3. Eat breakfast at their hotel restaurant, buy snacks from vendors, and eat lunch at Disney counter-service restaurants. Cost: $604 for family of four for six days (does not include dinners or food purchased on travel days).

In case you're wondering, these are the foods on which we've based our grocery costs for those options where breakfast, lunch, and/or snacks are prepared from the cooler:

BREAKFAST Cold cereal (choice of two), breakfast pastries, bananas, orange juice, milk, and coffee.

LUNCH Cold cuts or peanut butter and jelly sandwiches, condiments (mayo, mustard, and such), boxed juice, apples.

SNACKS Packaged cheese or peanut butter crackers, boxed juice, and trail mix (combination of M&Ms, nuts, raisins, and so on).

If you opt to buy groceries, you can stock up on food for your cooler at the Publix Supermarket on the corner of FL 535 and Vineland Avenue. Also, there's a Winn-Dixie about a mile north of the Crossroads Center on FL 535.

Projected costs for snacks purchased at the theme parks are based on drinks (coffee or sodas) twice a day and popcorn once each day. Counter-service meal costs assume basic meals (hot dogs, burgers, fries, and soda or coffee). Hotel breakfast expense assumes eggs, bacon, and toast, or pancakes with bacon, and juice, milk, or coffee to drink.

If you are an Entertainment Club member, don't forget to take your card and coupons for Orlando. Publix currently offers $5 off any purchase over $50.

Liliane

DISNEY DINING SUGGESTIONS

BELOW ARE SUGGESTIONS FOR DINING at each of the major theme parks. If you are interested in trying a theme-park full-service restaurant, be aware that the restaurants continue to serve after the park's official closing time. We showed up at the Hollywood Brown Derby just as Disney's Hollywood Studios closed at 8 p.m. We were seated almost immediately and enjoyed a leisurely dinner while the crowds cleared out. Don't worry if you are depending on Disney transportation: Buses, boats, and monorails run 2–3 hours after the parks close.

The Magic Kingdom

Food at the Magic Kingdom seems to improve a little each year. The **Crystal Palace** at the end of Main Street offers a good (albeit pricey) buffet chaperoned by Disney characters, while the **Liberty Tree Tavern** in Liberty Square features hearty family-style dining. **Cinderella's Royal Table,** a fixed-price full-service restaurant on the second floor of the castle, features characters at all meals.

Authors' Favorite Counter-service Restaurants

Cosmic Ray's Starlight Café (limited kosher items) Tomorrowland
Pecos Bill's Tall Tale Inn & Café Frontierland

Fast food at the Magic Kingdom is, well, fast food. It's more expensive, of course, than what you would pay at McDonald's, but what do you expect? It's like dining at an airport—you're a captive. On the positive side, portions are large, usually large enough for children to share. Overall, the variety of fast food offerings provides a lot of choice, though the number of selections at any specific eatery remains quite limited.

Epcot

From the beginning, dining has been an integral component of Epcot's entertainment product. The importance of dining is reflected in the number of restaurants and in their ability to serve consistently interesting and well-prepared meals. This is in stark contrast to the Magic Kingdom, where food service was once seemingly an afterthought, with quality and selection a distant runner-up to logistical efficiency.

For the most part, Epcot's restaurants have always served decent food, though the World Showcase restaurants have occasionally been timid about delivering an honest representation of the host nation's cuisine. While these eateries have struggled with authenticity and have sometimes shied away from challenging the meat-and-potatoes palate of the average tourist, they are bolder now, encouraged by America's exponentially expanding appreciation of ethnic dining. True, the less adventuresome can still find sanitized and homogenized meals, but the same kitchens will serve up the real thing for anyone with a spark of curiosity and daring.

Authors' Favorite Counter-service Restaurants

Kringla Bakeri og Kafe Norway	Sommerfest Germany
Sunshine Seasons The Land	Yakitori House Japan

Many Epcot restaurants are overpriced, most conspicuously the **Coral Reef** (The Seas). Representing relatively good value through the combination of ambience and well-prepared food are **Biergarten** (Germany) and **Restaurant Marrakesh** (Morocco). Biergarten and Restaurant Marrakesh also have entertainment.

If you want to sample the ethnic foods of World Showcase without eating in restaurants requiring Advance Reservations, we recommend these counter-service specialties:

France Boulangerie Patisserie, for French pastries

Germany Sommerfest, for bratwurst and Beck's beer

Japan Yakitori House, for yakitori (meat or vegetables on skewers)

Morocco Tangierine Café, for hummus, tabbouleh, and lamb

Norway Kringla Bakeri og Kafe, for pastries, open-face sandwiches, and Ringnes beer (our favorite)

United Kingdom Rose & Crown Pub, for Guinness, Harp, and Bass beers and ales

Disney's Hollywood Studios

Dining at Disney's Hollywood Studios is more interesting than in the Magic Kingdom and less ethnic than at Epcot. The Studios has five restaurants where Advance Reservations are recommended: the **Hollywood Brown Derby, 50's Prime Time Café, Sci-Fi Dine-In Theater Restaurant, Mama Melrose's Ristorante Italiano,** and the **Hollywood &**

Liliane

If visiting with small children, the lunch buffet at Hollywood & Vine in Disney's Hollywood Studios by far surpasses the offerings of the Crystal Palace buffet at the Magic Kingdom. We were surprised by the many healthy and tasteful dishes available at the Hollywood & Vine restaurant.

Vine cafeteria. The upscale Brown Derby is by far the best restaurant at the Studios. For simple Italian food, including pizza, Mama Melrose's is fine. Just don't expect anything fancy. At the Sci-Fi Dine-In, you eat in little cars at a simulated drive-in movie of the 1950s. Though you won't find a more entertaining restaurant in Walt Disney World, the food is quite disappointing. Somewhat better is the 50's Prime Time Café, where you sit in Mom's kitchen of the 1950s and scarf down meat loaf while watching clips of vintage TV sitcoms. The 50's Prime Time Café is fun, and the food is a step up. The best way to experience either restaurant is to stop in for dessert or a drink between 2:30 and 4:30 p.m. Hollywood & Vine features singing and dancing characters from Playhouse Disney during lunch and dinner.

Authors' Favorite Counter-service Restaurants

ABC Commissary Commisary Lane		Pizza Planet Streets of America
Backlot Express Echo Lane	Toluca Legs Turkey Co. Sunset Boulevard	

Animal Kingdom

Because touring the Animal Kingdom takes less than a day, crowds are heaviest from 9:30 a.m. until about 3:30 p.m. Expect a mob at lunch and thinner crowds at dinner. We recommend you tour early after a good breakfast, then eat a very late lunch or graze on vendor food. If you tour later in the day, eat lunch before you arrive, then enjoy dinner in or out of the theme park.

The Animal Kingdom offers a lot of counter-service fast food but has converted **Tusker House** to a buffet-style restaurant and added **Yak & Yeti,** a table-service restaurant, in Asia. You will find plenty of traditional Disney theme-park food—hot dogs, hamburgers, deli sandwiches, and the like—in the Animal Kingdom, but even the fast food there is a cut above the average Disney fare. The third restaurant in the Animal Kingdom is the **Rainforest Cafe,** with entrances both inside and outside the theme park (you don't have to purchase theme-park admission, in other words, to eat at the restaurant). Unlike the Rainforest Cafe at the Downtown Disney Marketplace, the Animal Kingdom branch accepts Advance Reservations. Our two favorites: **Flame Tree Barbecue** in Discovery Island, with its waterfront dining pavilions, and **Anandapur Local Foods Cafés,** for casual Asian fare from pot stickers to crispy honey chicken. The sit-down Yak & Yeti also serves above-average dishes from China, Thailand, Vietnam, and Japan.

Although grilled meats are available, don't expect a broad choice of exotic dishes in the Animal Kingdom.

READERS' COMMENTS ABOUT WALT DISNEY WORLD DINING

EATING IS A POPULAR TOPIC AMONG *Unofficial Guide* readers. In addition to participating in our annual restaurant survey, many readers like to share their thoughts with us. The following comments are representative of those we receive.

A reader from Glendale, Illinois, had a positive experience with Disney food, writing:

On the food: In general, we were pleasantly surprised. I expected it to be overpriced, generally bad, and certainly unhealthy. There were a lot of options—and almost all restaurants (including counter service) had generally good food and some healthy options. It is not the place to expect fine cuisine—and is certainly overpriced—but if you understand the parameters, you can eat quite well. One thing I appreciated was having a children's menu that did not consist only of hot dogs and fries. My children ate well, and we were able to get them a good variety of food—with plenty of fruits and vegetables.

We've received consistent raves for Boma:

Boma (the African buffet at the Animal Kingdom Lodge) is terrific!

A Lombard, Illinois, mom underscores the need to make Advance Reservations:

Please stress that if you want a "normal" dining hour at a specific restaurant, call them 90 or 60 days in advance—IT IS WORTH IT! One reservation I wanted to change about two weeks before our arrival date, and I had a choice of dinner times of either 7:45 or 9 p.m. (not feasible with little ones).

A Greenwood, Indiana, family had this to say:

The food was certainly expensive, but contrary to many of the views expressed in the Unofficial Guide, *we all thought the quality was excellent. Everything we had, from chicken strips and hot dogs in the parks to dinner at the Coral Reef, tasted great and seemed very fresh.*

A family from Youngsville, Louisiana, got a leg up on other guests:

The best thing we ate were the smoked turkey legs.

A mom from Aberdeen, South Dakota, writes:

When we want great food, we'll be on a different vacation. Who wants to waste fun time with the kids at a sit-down restaurant when you know the food will be mediocre anyway?

On the topic of saving money, a Seattle woman offered this:

For those wanting to save a few bucks (or in some cases several bucks), we definitely suggest eating outside WDW for as many meals as possible. To keep down our costs, we ate a large breakfast before leaving the hotel, had a fast-food lunch in the park, a snack later to hold us over, and then ate a good dinner outside the park. Several good restaurants in the area have excellent food at reasonable prices, notably Café Tu Tu Tango and Ming [Court], both on International Drive. We also obtained the "Entertainment Book" for Orlando, which offers 50% off meals all over town.

COUNTER-SERVICE RESTAURANT MINI-PROFILES

TO HELP YOU FIND PALATABLE FAST-SERVICE FOOD that suits your taste, we have developed mini-profiles of Walt Disney World theme-park counter-service restaurants. The restaurants are listed alphabetically by theme park.

The restaurants profiled on the following pages are rated for quality and portion size (self-explanatory), as well as for value. The value rating ranges from A to F as follows:

A	=	Exceptional value, a real bargain
B	=	Good value
C	=	Fair value, you get exactly what you pay for
D	=	Somewhat overpriced
F	=	Extremely overpriced

MAGIC KINGDOM

Casey's Corner

QUALITY Good   VALUE B   PORTION Medium   LOCATION Main Street, U.S.A.
READER-SURVEY RESPONSES 82% 👍 18% 👎   DISNEY DINING PLAN Yes

Selections Quarter-pound hot dogs, fries, and brownies.
Comments A little pricey on the dogs and very crowded—keep walking.

Columbia Harbour House

QUALITY Fair   VALUE C+   PORTION Medium   LOCATION Liberty Square
READER-SURVEY RESPONSES 90% 👍 10% 👎   DISNEY DINING PLAN Yes

Selections Fried fish and chicken nuggets; hummus and tuna-salad sandwiches; child's plate with macaroni and cheese or garden chicken salad with grapes and child's beverage; New England clam chowder and vegetarian chili; coleslaw; chips; fries; garden salad; chocolate cake.
Comments No trans fats in the fried items, and the soups and sandwiches are a cut above most fast-food fare. Upstairs seating is usually a little less hectic. It's the quickest service within spitting distance of Fantasyland.

Cosmic Ray's Starlight Café

QUALITY Good   VALUE B   PORTION Large   LOCATION Tomorrowland
READER-SURVEY RESPONSES 87% 👍 13% 👎   DISNEY DINING PLAN Yes

Selections There's something for everyone at this quick-service location: rotisserie chicken and ribs; turkey-bacon and vegetarian wraps; hot dogs; hamburgers, including veggie burgers; Caesar salad with chicken; chili; carrot cake and no-sugar-added brownies for dessert. Kosher choices include a burger, chicken strips, and corned beef on rye.
Comments Big, noisy place. Tables inside usually available. Out-of-this-world entertainment on stage. Kitschy audio-animatronic character Sunny Eclipse. This is the place if everybody in your party is picky—there are plenty of options. Nice burger-fixin's bar. Cosmic Ray's was the first Disney counter-service restaurant to offer kosher food.

El Pirata y el Perico (open seasonally)

QUALITY Fair   VALUE B   PORTION Medium-large   LOCATION Adventureland
READER-SURVEY RESPONSES 83% 👍 17% 👎   DISNEY DINING PLAN Yes

Selections Beef taco salad, vegetarian and beef tacos, quesadillas for kids.
Comments Large, shaded eating area. Open seasonally and sometimes overlooked.

Golden Oak Outpost

QUALITY Good	VALUE B+	PORTION Medium-large	LOCATION Frontierland
READER-SURVEY RESPONSES 100% 🙂 0% 🙁		DISNEY DINING PLAN Yes	

Selections Chicken nuggets, fried-chicken-breast sandwich, vegetable or chicken BLT flatbreads. Chocolate cake, carrot cake, and cookies.
Comments Entrees are served with apple slices or French fries.

The Lunching Pad

QUALITY Good	VALUE B–	PORTION Medium	LOCATION Tomorrowland
READER-SURVEY RESPONSES 81% 🙂 19% 🙁		DISNEY DINING PLAN Yes	

Selections Smoked turkey legs, pretzels, and frozen sodas.
Comments Smack in the middle of Tomorrowland, The Lunching Pad is a good place to grab a smoked turkey leg or cold drink.

Mrs. Potts' Cupboard

QUALITY Good	VALUE B	PORTION Medium	LOCATION Fantasyland
READER-SURVEY RESPONSES 94% 🙂 6% 🙁		DISNEY DINING PLAN No	

Selections Sundaes, including fudge brownie and strawberry shortcake; floats and shakes; cookies; drinks.
Comments An ice-cream stop. Good options and decent value.

Pecos Bill's Tall Tale Inn & Café

QUALITY Good	VALUE B	PORTION Medium-large	LOCATION Frontierland
READER-SURVEY RESPONSES 91% 🙂 9% 🙁		DISNEY DINING PLAN Yes	

Selections Cheeseburgers, veggie burgers, chicken wraps, taco salad, chili, child's plate with hamburger or salad with grilled chicken and child's beverage, fries and chili-cheese fries, strawberry yogurt, carrot cake.
Comments Use the great fixin's station to garnish your burger. Combos come with fries or carrots.

The Pinocchio Village Haus

QUALITY Fair	VALUE C	PORTION Medium	LOCATION Fantasyland
READER-SURVEY RESPONSES 75% 🙂 25% 🙁		DISNEY DINING PLAN Yes	

Selections Personal pizzas, chicken nuggets, Caesar salad with chicken, Mediterranean salad; kids' meals of pizza, mac and cheese, or PB&J.
Comments An easy stop for families in Fantasyland, but it's usually crowded and takes some patience. Consider Columbia Harbour House and Pecos Bill Tall Tale Inn & Café, both only a few minutes' walk away (and with better food).

Tomorrowland Terrace

QUALITY Good	VALUE B	PORTION Medium-large	LOCATION Tomorrowland
READER-SURVEY RESPONSES 68% 🙂 32% 🙁		DISNEY DINING PLAN Yes	

Selections Orange chicken with rice, beef and broccoli, Caesar salad with chicken; child's plate of chicken nuggets, beef and mac, or peanut-butter-and-jelly sandwiches. Chocolate cake, carrot cake, iced green teas, and hot teas.
Comments Only open during busy park times; good if you're looking for something other than dogs and burgers.

EPCOT
Africa Coolpost

QUALITY Good	VALUE B-	PORTION Small	LOCATION Between Germany and China
READER-SURVEY RESPONSES 83%	17%	DISNEY DINING PLAN Yes	

Selections Hot dogs, ice cream (waffle cone), fresh fruit, frozen slushes (frozen soda), coffee or tea, draft Safari Amber beer ($6.25).

Comments Mainly prepackaged food for a quick drink or snack.

Boulangerie Patisserie

QUALITY Good	VALUE B	PORTION Small-medium	LOCATION France
READER-SURVEY RESPONSES 94%	6%	DISNEY DINING PLAN Yes	

Selections Coffee, croissants, pastries, chocolate mousse, sandwiches, baguettes, cheese plate, ham-and-cheese croissant, quiche.

Comments There is always a crowd, savoring the French pastries, at this tucked-away spot. No indoor seating, but a few shaded outside tables provide a place to relax.

La Cantina de San Angel *(reopens fall 2010)*

QUALITY N/A	VALUE N/A	PORTION N/A	LOCATION Mexico
READER-SURVEY RESPONSES Too new to rate	DISNEY DINING PLAN TBD		

Selections Chicken and beef tacos on fresh handmade corn tortillas, nachos, cheese empanada, guacamole and chips, churros.

Comments The Cantina is undergoing a major overhaul with 150 outdoor seats. Also to come: a companion full-service restaurant, La Hacienda de San Angel.

Crêpes des Chefs de France

QUALITY Good	VALUE B+	PORTION Medium	LOCATION France
READER-RESPONSE SURVEYS 88%	12%	DISNEY DINING PLAN No	

Selections Crêpes with chocolate, strawberry, or sugar; vanilla and chocolate ice cream; specialty beer (Kronenbourg 1664); espresso.

Comments These crêpes rate high—even with French guests.

Electric Umbrella Restaurant

QUALITY Fair-good	VALUE B-	PORTION Medium	LOCATION Innoventions East
READER-RESPONSE SURVEYS 80%	20%	DISNEY DINING PLAN Yes	

Selections Burgers and chicken nuggets with fries; toasted turkey sub; Greek salad; child's plate with cheeseburger or turkey-and-cheese pinwheels; fruit cups; cookies; cheesecake.

Comments One of the busiest restaurants in Future World. There's more-interesting fast food in the World Showcase.

Fife & Drum Tavern

QUALITY Fair	VALUE C	PORTION Large	LOCATION United States
READER-RESPONSE SURVEYS 78%	22%	DISNEY DINING PLAN Yes	

Selections Turkey legs, popcorn, pretzels, smoothies, and draft beer.

Comments Better for a cold drink or a quick snack to tide you over than for an actual meal. Seating is available in and around the Liberty Inn, behind the Fife and Drum.

Fountain View Ice Cream

QUALITY Fair   **VALUE** C+   **PORTION** Medium-large   **LOCATION** Future World West
READER-SURVEY RESPONSES 88% 👍 12% 👎   **DISNEY DINING PLAN** Yes

Selections Ice-cream cones, sundaes, floats, ice-cream sandwiches, raspberry smoothies, frozen cappuccinos, soda, coffee, and tea.

Comments Good for a late-morning treat on a hot day. Long lines develop just after lunch and around dinner.

Kringla Bakeri og Kafe

QUALITY Good-excellent   **VALUE** B   **PORTION** Small-medium   **LOCATION** Norway
READER-SURVEY RESPONSES 93% 👍 7% 👎   **DISNEY DINING PLAN** Yes

Selections Cakes and pastries; rice cream; sandwiches (ham and cheese, smoked salmon, turkey); green salad; espresso, cappuccino, imported beers (Carlsberg beer for $7.50).

Comments Delicious and different but pricey. (Try the rice cream.) Shaded outdoor seating.

Liberty Inn

QUALITY Fair   **VALUE** C   **PORTION** Medium   **LOCATION** United States
READER-SURVEY RESPONSE 71% 👍 29% 👎   **DISNEY DINING PLAN** Yes

Selections Bacon double cheeseburger; barbecued pork; veggie burgers; chicken nuggets; Caesar chicken salad; child's plate of grilled chicken over romaine lettuce, chicken nuggets with fries, or PB&J with applesauce.

Comments The menu offers more than dogs and burgers; kosher items also available. Still, World Showcase has more-inspired selections.

Lotus Blossom Café

QUALITY Fair   **VALUE** C   **PORTION** Medium   **LOCATION** China
READER-SURVEY RESPONSE 61% 👍 39% 👎   **DISNEY DINING PLAN** Yes

Selections Egg rolls, pot stickers, veggie stir-fry, sesame chicken salad, shrimp fried rice, orange chicken with steamed rice. For kids, barbecued drumstick.

Comments Middling, overpriced Chinese food.

Promenade Refreshments

QUALITY Fair   **VALUE** C   **PORTION** Large   **LOCATION** Between World Showcase Promenade
READER-SURVEY RESPONSES 85% 👍 15% 👎   **DISNEY DINING PLAN** Yes

Selections Hot dogs, pretzels, popcorn, ice cream, and nonfat yogurt smoothies.

Comments Best for a quick snack, especially if you have a reservation at one of the World Showcase's full-service restaurants. Seating is limited to nonexistent, depending on whether cast members have put out tables and chairs—be prepared to walk and chew.

The Refreshment Port

QUALITY Good   **VALUE** B   **PORTION** Medium   **LOCATION** World Showcase
READER-SURVEY RESPONSES 88% 👍 12% 👎   **DISNEY DINING PLAN** Yes

Selections Crispy fried shrimp or chicken with tostones (green plantains), beef or cheese empanada, frozen Bacardi mojito, iced lattes, *dolce de leche* ice-cream sundae.

Comments Latino-inspired quick service; great tastes for nibbling and sipping as you begin your walk around World Showcase.

Rose & Crown Pub

QUALITY Good	VALUE C	PORTION Medium	LOCATION United Kingdom

READER-SURVEY RESPONSES 90% 👍 10% 👎 DISNEY DINING PLAN Yes

Selections Fish-and-chips; turkey sandwich; Guinness, Harp, and Bass beers, as well as other spirits.

Comments The attractions here are the pub atmosphere and the draft beer—and there's usually a crowd gathered around the bar, as you don't need reservations. Outside the pub is Yorkshire County Fish Shop, which serves food to go. The full-service restaurant Rose & Crown Dining Room requires Advance Reservations.

Sommerfest

QUALITY Good	VALUE B–	PORTION Medium	LOCATION Germany

READER-SURVEY RESPONSES 87% 👍 13% 👎 DISNEY DINING PLAN Yes

Selections Bratwurst and frankfurter sandwiches with kraut; soft pretzels; apple strudel; German wine and beer.

Comments Tucked in the entrance to the Biergarten restaurant, Sommerfest is hard to find from the street. Very limited seating. Not for picky eaters, but a good place to grab a cold brew and bratwurst.

Sunshine Seasons

QUALITY Excellent	VALUE A	PORTION Medium	LOCATION The Land Pavilion

READER-SURVEY RESPONSES 92% 👍 8% 👎 DISNEY-DINING PLAN Yes

Selections Comprises the following four areas: (1) wood-fired grills and rotisseries, with such selections as rotisserie chicken or pork chops and wood-grilled salmon with olive pesto sauce; (2) sandwich shop with made-to-order sandwiches such as oak-grilled flatbread, smoked ham–salami, and turkey and cheese on focaccia; (3) Asian shop, with noodle bowls and various stir-fry combos; (4) soup-and-salad shop, with soups made daily and unusual creations like seared tuna on mixed greens with sesame–rice wine vinaigrette.

Comments No fried food, no pizza, no burgers—everything is prepared fresh as you watch. Diverse choices are perfect for picky eaters.

Tangierine Café

QUALITY Good	VALUE B	PORTION Medium	LOCATION Morocco

READER-SURVEY RESPONSES 93% 👍 7% 👎 DISNEY DINING PLAN Yes

Selections Chicken and lamb *shawarma;* hummus; tabbouleh; lentil salad; chicken and tabbouleh wraps; olives; child's meal of pizza, hamburger, or chicken tenders with carrot sticks and apple slices and small beverage; Moroccan wine and beer; baklava.

Comments You won't get the belly dancers who entertain inside the pavilion at Restaurant Marrakesh, but the food is authentic. The best seating is at the outdoor tables.

Yakitori House

QUALITY Excellent	VALUE B	PORTION Small-medium	LOCATION Japan
READER-SURVEY RESPONSES 85% 👍 15% 👎		DISNEY DINING PLAN Yes	

Selections Shogun combo meal with beef and chicken teriyaki, vegetables, and rice; beef curry; vegetable tempura with shrimp and udon noodles; side salad; sushi; miso soup; green tea; sponge cake with ginger-flavored frosting; Kirin beer, sake, and plum wine.

Comments Great flavors; an easy place to explore new tastes. Nice cultural detailing. Limited seating.

Yorkshire County Fish Shop

QUALITY Good	VALUE B+	PORTION Medium	LOCATION United Kingdom
READER-SURVEY RESPONSE 93% 👍 7% 👎		DISNEY DINING PLAN Yes	

Selections Fish-and-chips, shortbread, Bass Ale draft.

Comments There's usually a line for the crisp, hot fish-and-chips at this convenient fast-food window attached to the Rose & Crown Pub. Outdoor seating overlooks the lagoon.

ANIMAL KINGDOM

Anandapur Local Foods Cafés

QUALITY Fair	VALUE C	PORTION Large	LOCATION Asia
READER-SURVEY RESULTS 88% 👍 12% 👎		DISNEY DINING PLAN Yes	

Selections Crispy honey chicken with steamed rice, kung pao beef, lo mein, Mandarin chicken salad. Kids' menu includes chicken bites, pork egg rolls, or mini-cheeseburgers with applesauce and carrots or chicken-fried rice.

Comments The crispy honey chicken is the best choice—the beef and lo mein simply demonstrate how poorly those dishes fare sitting under a heat lamp until someone orders them. Adjacent to table-service restaurant Yak & Yeti.

Flame Tree Barbecue

QUALITY Good	VALUE B–	PORTION Large	LOCATION Discovery Island
READER-SURVEY RESPONSES 93% 👍 7% 👎		DISNEY DINING PLAN Yes	

Selections Half slab St. Louis–style ribs; smoked half chicken; smoked beef and pork sandwiches; crisp green salad with barbecued chicken; child's plate of baked chicken drumsticks or hot dog; French fries, coleslaw, onion rings; chocolate cake; Safari Amber beer, Bud Light, and wine.

Comments Queues very long at lunch time, but seating is ample and well shaded. One of our favorites for lunch. Try the covered gazebo overlooking the water.

Kusafiri Coffee Shop

QUALITY Good	VALUE B	PORTION Medium	LOCATION Africa
READER-SURVEY RESPONSES 82% 👍 18% 👎		DISNEY DINING PLAN No	

Selections Fruit turnovers, Danish and other pastries, muffins, croissants, bagel with cream cheese, cookies, brownies, cake, fruit cup, yogurt, coffee, cocoa, juice.

Comments A good early-morning sugar rush on the way to Kilimanjaro Safaris. Shares space with Tusker House; easy walk-up window.

Pizzafari

QUALITY Fair	VALUE B	PORTION Medium	LOCATION Discovery Island
READER-SURVEY RESULTS 84% 16%	DISNEY DINING PLAN Yes		

Selections Cheese and pepperoni personal pizzas, grilled-chicken Caesar salad, breadsticks, hot Italian-style sandwich, child's cheese pizza or mac and cheese, chocolate mousse, no-sugar-added strawberry parfait, Safari Amber beer, and wine.

Comments A favorite with children. Hectic at peak mealtimes. The pizza is pretty unimpressive. Kosher menu is available.

Restaurantosaurus

QUALITY Good	VALUE B+	PORTION Medium-large	LOCATION DinoLand U.S.A.
READER-SURVEY RESPONSES 69% 31%	DISNEY DINING PLAN Yes		

Selections Cheeseburgers; hot dogs; chicken nuggets; Mandarin chicken salad; veggie burger; fries; chocolate cake and carrot cake; coffee, tea, and cocoa; apple and orange juice; beer.

Comments Fast food with a good toppings bar for the burgers.

Royal Anandapur Tea Company

QUALITY Good	VALUE B	PORTION Medium	LOCATION Asia
READER-SURVEY RESPONSES 97% 3%	DISNEY DINING PLAN No		

Selections Wide variety of hot and iced teas; lattes; coffee, espresso, and cappuccino; fruit and cheese Danishes; cookies.

Comments Located halfway between Expedition Everest and Kali River Rapids, this is the kind of small, eclectic food stand unique to the Animal Kingdom that you wish could be found at other parks. Offers loose-leaf teas from Asia and Africa, many of which can be made either hot or iced.

Tamu Tamu

QUALITY Good	VALUE C	PORTION Large	LOCATION Africa
READER-SURVEY RESPONSES 83% 17%	DISNEY DINING PLAN No		

Selections Milk shakes, turkey and Swiss on focaccia, tuna-salad on pita, and cheeseburgers on multigrain buns are on the menu at Tamu Tamu and neighboring Drinkwallah.

Comments Seating is behind building and could easily be overlooked.

DISNEY'S HOLLYWOOD STUDIOS

ABC Commissary

QUALITY Fair	VALUE B-	PORTION Medium-large	LOCATION Backlot
READER-SURVEY RESPONSES 63% 37%	DISNEY DINING PLAN Yes		

Selections Asian salad; chicken bleu sandwich; chicken curry; cheeseburgers with apple slices or fries; fried fish with apple slices or fries; child's chicken nuggets, cheeseburger, or turkey sandwich; chocolate mousse; no-sugar-added strawberry parfait; wine and beer.

Comments Indoors, centrally located, air-conditioned, and usually not too crowded. Also offers limited breakfast food: egg-and-cheese bagel, oatmeal, fresh fruit. Hard to find. Offers kosher food.

Backlot Express

QUALITY Fair	VALUE C	PORTION Medium-large	LOCATION Backlot
READER-SURVEY RESPONSES 80% 👍 20% 👎		DISNEY DINING PLAN Yes	

Selections Burgers with fries or carrot sticks, Southwest salad with chicken, grilled turkey and cheese, chicken nuggets, hot dogs, grilled-vegetable sandwich, desserts. For children, chicken nuggets or chicken with vegetables. Soft drinks and beer.

Comments A big dining space that's often overlooked. Great burger-fixin's bar. Indoor and outdoor seating.

Min and Bill's Dockside Diner

QUALITY Fair	VALUE C	PORTION Small-medium	LOCATION Echo Lake
READER-SURVEY RESPONSE 80% 👍 20% 👎		DISNEY DINING PLAN No	

Selections Italian sausage, chicken Caesar sandwich, frankfurter on a pretzel roll, shakes and soft drinks, beer, chips and cookies.

Comments Walk-up window with limited outdoor seating.

Pizza Planet

QUALITY Good	VALUE B+	PORTION Medium	LOCATION Backlot
READER-SURVEY RESPONSE 75% 👍 25% 👎		DISNEY DINING PLAN Yes	

Selections Cheese, pepperoni, and vegetarian pizzas; salads; cookies and crisped-rice treats.

Comments The place for pizza at the Studios. Fresh ingredients. Gets good marks from readers.

Starring Rolls Cafe

QUALITY Good	VALUE B	PORTION Small-medium	LOCATION Sunset Boulevard
READER-SURVEY RESPONSES 88% 👍 12% 👎		DISNEY DINING PLAN Yes	

Selections Giant deli sandwiches, salads, oversize pastries and desserts, coffee.

Comments Open for breakfast on some mornings. Slowest service of any counter-service eatery.

Studio Catering Co.

QUALITY Good	VALUE B	PORTION Small-medium	LOCATION Backlot
READER-SURVEY RESPONSES 84% 👍 16% 👎		DISNEY DINING PLAN Yes	

Selections Veggie sandwich, grilled turkey club, buffalo chicken sandwich. Peanut butter and jelly for kids.

Comments Good place for a break while your kids enjoy the *Honey, I Shrunk the Kids* playground. Shady outside seating.

Sunset Ranch Market

QUALITY Good	VALUE B	PORTION Medium-large	LOCATION Boulevard
READER-SURVEY RESPONSES 77% 👍 23% 👎		DISNEY DINING PLAN Yes	

Selections Five restaurants in one location offering everything from smoked turkey legs, hot dogs, and beer at Toluca Legs; pizzas, hot Italian deli sandwiches, salads, and apple pie at Catalina Eddie's; and veggie burgers, soups, and child's cheeseburger or chicken nuggets with grapes, carrot sticks, or applesauce at Rosie's.

Comments Seldom crowded; nearby picnic tables. Backlot Express is a better option than Rosie's for the same fare.

DISNEY'S FULL-SERVICE RESTAURANTS: A QUICK ROMP AROUND THE WORLD

DISNEY RESTAURANTS OFFER AN EXCELLENT (though expensive) opportunity to introduce young children to the variety and excitement of ethnic food. No matter how formal a restaurant appears, the staff is accustomed to wiggling, impatient, and often boisterous children. **Les Chefs de France** at Epcot, for example, may be the nation's only French restaurant where most patrons wear shorts and T-shirts and at least two dozen young diners are attired in basic black . . . mouse ears.

Almost all Disney restaurants offer children's menus, and all have booster seats and high chairs. They understand how tough it may be for children to sit for an extended period of time, and waiters will supply little ones with crackers and rolls and serve your dinner much faster than in comparable restaurants elsewhere. Letters from readers suggest that being served too quickly is much more common than having a long wait.

In **Epcot,** preschoolers most enjoy the **Biergarten** in Germany, **San Angel Inn** in Mexico, and **Coral Reef** in the Seas Pavilion in Future World. The Biergarten combines a rollicking and noisy atmosphere with good basic food, including roast chicken and German sausages; a German oompah band entertains. Children often have the opportunity to participate in Bavarian dancing. San Angel Inn is in the Mexican village marketplace. From the table, children can watch boats on Gran Fiesta Tour drift beneath a smoking volcano. With a choice of chips, tacos, and other familiar items, picky children usually have no difficulty finding something to eat. Be aware that the service is sometimes glacially slow. The Coral Reef, with tables beside windows looking into The Seas' aquarium, offers a colorful mealtime diversion for all ages. If your kids don't eat fish, Coral Reef also serves beef and chicken. The downside is that the food is extremely expensive. For a more affordable splurge, forget lunch or dinner and drop in during off-hours for one of the Coral Reef's decadent desserts. The San Angel Inn is likewise overpriced but not in the same league as Coral Reef. The Biergarten offers reasonable value, plus good food.

Cinderella's Royal Table in Cinderella Castle is the big draw in the **Magic Kingdom.** Interestingly, other Magic Kingdom full-service restaurants hold little appeal for children. For the best combination of food and entertainment, book a character meal at the **Liberty Tree Tavern** or **The Crystal Palace.**

At **Disney's Hollywood Studios,** all ages enjoy the atmosphere and entertainment at the **Sci-Fi Dine-In Theater Restaurant** and the **50's**

Prime Time Café. Unfortunately, the Sci-Fi's food is close to dismal except for dessert, and the Prime Time's is uneven. Theme aside, children enjoy the character meals at **Hollywood & Vine,** and the pizza at **Mama Melrose's** never fails to please.

There are three full-service restaurant at the **Animal Kingdom.** The **Rainforest Cafe,** which is a great favorite of children, **Yak & Yeti,** a 300-seat table-service restaurant near Expedition Everest, and **Tusker House,** a buffet-style restaurant.

As you've undoubtedly noticed by now, Disney World is a trend-savvy place, and every market share has its niche. But Disney World is also about stars, about fantasies, and about meeting characters. So if you've become habituated to wood-fired pizza, the **California Grill** atop the Contemporary Resort will oblige. Great sushi can be had at **Teppan Edo** at Japan in Epcot and at **Kimonos** in the Swan. The best and biggest steaks are at **Shula's** in the Dolphin, **Le Cellier Steakhouse** of Canada, or the **Yachtsman Steakhouse** at the Yacht Club, albeit way overpriced. Spoodles at Disney's Boardwalk closed and has been replaced by **Kouzzina,** a family-style eatery featuring celebrity chef Cat Cora's Mediterranean-style recipes. Epcot saw two additions as of fall 2010: In Italy **Via Napoli,** an authentic Neapolitan pizzeria, features wood-burning ovens and imports water from a source that most resembles the water in Naples, Italy, home of some of the world's best pizza dough. The 300-seat pizzeria is inspired by the Naples 45 pizzeria on East 45th Street in New York City and has both indoor and outdoor dining. In Mexico, popular **La Cantina de San Angel** is expanding, adding a new full-service restaurant, **La Hacienda de San Angel** (dinner only), which together will feature 400 seats with alfresco seating for lunch and a perfect place for viewing *IllumiNations,* the nightly Epcot fireworks spectacular.

Bottom line: Young children are the rule, not the exception, at Disney restaurants.

The **Planet Hollywood** at Downtown Disney (teens love it) famously belongs to and has memorabilia from the likes of Demi Moore, Bruce Willis, and Sylvester Stallone (and because this branch of the chain really looks like a planet, it becomes the "globe" entrance that matches Epcot's Spaceship Earth, which just goes to show you how big an attraction it is). The West Side has two other celebrity-connected restaurant-nightclubs: the **House of Blues,** a New Orleans–style night-spot partly owned by surviving Blues Brother Dan Aykroyd and James Belushi; and **Bongos,** a Cuban-flavored cafe created by Gloria Estefan and her husband, Emilio.

Not only film and sports stars but also Food Network and food-magazine stars have been enlisted in the Disney World parade. Paul Bocuse was one of the eponymous **Chefs de France** who designed the menu for that restaurant and the **Bistro de Paris** in Epcot (and now that the building actually has a kitchen rather than hauling in food from outside commissaries, it does them much more credit). Boston star chef

Todd English created **bluezoo** for the Dolphin. California's Wolfgang Puck is so celebrity-kitchen conscious that the TV monitors at his cafe-plex in the West Side show not sports or movies but the cooks at work (a fad English has also adopted).

Celebrity status notwithstanding, neither Wolfgang Puck's Café nor the Estefans' Bongos have drawn much praise from diners, though bluezoo is very good (but also quite adult). The House of Blues, surprisingly enough, has done much better with its New Orleans–style jambalayas and gospel brunch.

If your kids haven't had their fill of robotic crocodiles, Abraham Lincolns, singing parrots, and the like, **T-REX** and Rainforest Cafe will serve up all they can handle. T-REX features animatronic dinosaurs and an occasional woolly mammoth, while Rainforest Cafe is stuffed with jungle critters. Both of course have gift shops. There are not one but two super-trendy Rainforest Cafe branches, one at the renovated Disney Village Marketplace and a super-theatrical version at the entrance to Animal Kingdom, where the decor and audio-animatronic elephants make it fit right into the scenery there. Not surprisingly in a place where the sky "rains" and the stars flicker overhead, more thought went into naming the dishes than perfecting the recipes.

If your kids prefer dinosaurs to pachyderms, try T-REX, which is located within spitting distance of the Rainforest Cafe and operated by the same folks. The food is better than Rainforest, and children go nuts about being surrounded by a life-size animatronic brontosaurus, triceratops, and such.

In fact, although Disney's "official" guides to Walt Disney World describe various restaurants as "delicious," "delectable," or "delightful"—George Gershwin, call your agent—the truth is that only perhaps a dozen of the nearly 100 full-service establishments are first-rate. And some of the most disappointing restaurants, in general, are the often attractive but commissary-bland ethnic kitchens.

Though a blessing in disguise to many children and picky eaters of all ages, most of the "ethnic" food at Walt Disney World is Americanized, or rather homogenized, especially at Epcot, where visitors from so many countries, as well as the United States, tend to have preconceived notions of egg rolls and enchiladas. **Teppan Edo** in the Japan Pavilion happens to be one of the better restaurants in the World, with pretty good teppanyaki (and good tempura next door)—but it specializes in a particularly Westernized form of Japanese cuisine, first produced in New York only about 30 years ago. The **Nine Dragons** restaurant in the China Pavilion has been seriously reconceived and now features not only quite satisfying dim sum but handmade noodles (taffy-pulled out in the dining room), a respectable five-spiced fish, and really crisp vegetables. The **San Angel Inn** in the Mexico Pavilion is associated with the famous Debler family of Mexico City. And **Les Chefs de France/Bistro de Paris,** with executive chefs Paul Bocuse, Gaston LeNotre, and Roger Verge, is now a fairly serious destination—one with an old-world view.

The buffet at Norway's **Akershus** isn't bad, but it's stodgy, smoky, and cheese- and mayonnaise-heavy. (Frankly, if smoked meats are your thing, the smoked turkey legs from the carts, which are enough for at least two people and only $4, are far better.)

Among the places the culinary staff actually recommends (off the record) are the classic-continental prix-fixe **Victoria & Albert's** at the Grand Floridian, where you pay $125 a head to have every waitress introduce herself as Vicky and all the waiters as Al; the **Flying Fish Café; Artist Point; Jiko; Sanaa; Citricos;** and the **California Grill,** which has one of only seven ultra-chic Tom Shandley soufflé ovens in the United States. All of the above are best reserved for a parents' night out.

And yes, OK, because you've been good, I'll tell you the one junk food to blow your calorie budget on: As you cross the bridge between Future World and the World Showcase in Epcot, there's a little wagon just to the right, toward Canada, that sells cones of glazed pecans called "sticky beavers." Don't say we never spoiled you.

Another thing: A lot of the food at Disney World, particularly the fast food, is not what you'd describe as healthy. (Funnel cakes? Happy Meals?) But this is an area that the parks have started to address. **Artist's Palette** at Saratoga Springs Resort and **Sunshine Seasons** in The Land Pavilion at Epcot have been reconceived as "fast casual" spots, where the food is prepared fresh, often when you order it, but can be carried out or taken to nearby tables. At Sunshine Seasons, there are four different fully staffed kitchens, one preparing entree salads with seared tuna, roasted beets with goat cheese, and soups du jour; another stir-frying veggies and preparing Asian noodle soup; a third wood-grilling chicken and beef to be wrapped in grilled flatbread or salmon with pesto; and a fourth preparing deluxe focaccia sandwiches. Artist's Palette offers everything from French toast to individual wood-grilled pizzas to gourmet-prepared entrees for carryout. See the nice **Turf Club Bar & Grill** next door for roasted and grilled specialties.

Beyond that, there are fruit stands and juice bars scattered around, veggie sandwiches and chili, wraps, rotisserie chicken, soft pretzels as well as the deceptively simple popcorn, baked potatoes (not, frankly, prepared with the apparent care of the turkey legs but about one-tenth the calories and salt), as well as the frozen fruit bars in the ice-cream freezers, and frozen yogurt or smoothies at the ice-cream shops. Yes, it's hard, especially with all those fudge and cookie stands blasting chocolate at you, but stick to your guns. Look for the fruit markets in Liberty Square in the Magic Kingdom, on Sunset Boulevard in Disney's Hollywood Studios, and in the Harambe marketplace at Animal Kingdom.

MAGIC YOUR WAY DINING PLAN

INTRODUCED IN 2005, this dining plan provides, for each member of your group, for each night of your stay, one counter-service meal, one full-service meal, and one snack at participating Disney dining locations and restaurants, including room service at some Disney resorts (type "Disney Dining Plan Locations 2010 [or 2011]" into your favorite Internet search engine to find sites with the entire list). For guests age 10 and up, the price is $42–$47 per night (varies seasonally); for guests ages 3–9, the price is $12–$13 per night, tax included. Children younger than age 3 eat free from an adult's plate.

The counter-service meal includes a main course (sandwich, dinner salad, pizza, or the like), dessert, and nonalcoholic drink, or a complete combo meal (a main course and a side dish—think burger and fries), dessert, and nonalcoholic drink, including tax. The full-service sit-down meals include a main course, dessert, a nonalcoholic drink, and tax. If you're dining at a buffet, the full-service meal includes the buffet, a nonalcoholic drink, and tax. The snack includes items normally sold from carts or small stands throughout the parks and resorts: ice cream, popcorn, soft drinks, fruit, chips, apple juice, and the like.

For instance, if you're staying for three nights, each member of your party will be credited with three counter-service meals, three full-service meals, and three snacks. All those meals will be put into an individual "meal account" for each person in your group. Meals in your account can be used on any combination of days, so you're not required to eat every meal every day. Thus, you can skip a full-service meal one day and have two on another day.

Disney's top-of-the-line restaurants (dubbed "Disney Signature" restaurants in the plan), along with all the dinner shows, count as two full-service meals. If you dine at one of these locations, two full-service meals will be deducted from your account for each person dining.

In addition to the preceding, the dining plan comes with several other important rules:

- Everyone staying in the same resort room must participate in the plan.
- Children ages 3–9 must order from the kids' menu, if one is available. This rule is occasionally not enforced at Disney's counter-service restaurants, enabling older children to order from the regular (adult) menu.
- In-room minibars are not included in the plan.
- Refillable mugs are only included in some of the dining plans, such as the Magic Your Way Quick Service Dining Plan.
- A full-service meal can be breakfast, lunch, or dinner. The greatest savings occur when you use your full-service meal allocations for dinner.
- The meal plan expires at midnight **on the day you check out** of the Disney resort. **Unused meals are nonrefundable.**
- The dining plan is occasionally unavailable when using certain room-only discounts.

QUICK SERVICE DINING PLAN This plan includes meals, snacks, and non-alcoholic drinks at most counter-service eateries in Walt Disney World. The cost is $32 per day for guests age 10 and up, $10 per day for kids ages 3–9. The plan includes two counter-service meals and two snacks per day, plus one refillable drink mug per person, per package (eligible for refills only at counter-service locations only in your Disney resort), and 30 minutes of play at a Disney-resort arcade. The economics of the plan are difficult to justify unless you're drinking gallons of soda or coffee to offset Disney's inflated prices.

MAGIC YOUR WAY DELUXE DINING PLAN This one offers a choice of full-service or counter-service meals for three meals a day at any participating restaurant. In addition to the three meals a day, the plan also includes two snacks per day and a refillable drink mug. The Deluxe Plan costs $72 for adults and $21 for children for each night of your stay. Cranking it up another notch, there are even more extravagant dining plans associated with Magic Your Way Premium and Platinum packages, both described a little later.

In addition to food, all the plans include deal sweeteners such as a free round of miniature golf, a certificate for a 5-by-10-inch print from Disney's PhotoPass, a sort of two-for-one certificate for use of Sea Raycers watercraft, a "commemorative" luggage tag, and such.

Disney ceaselessly tinkers with the dining plans' rules, meal definitions, and participating restaurants. For example, it's possible (though not documented) to exchange a sit-down-meal credit for a counter-service meal, although doing this even once can negate any savings you get from using a plan in the first place. Any Magic Your Way package that includes table-service dining can be upgraded—for a fee—to a Wine and Dine Plan, which includes one wine entitlement per night, per room.

THINGS TO CONSIDER WHEN EVALUATING THE PLUS DINING PLAN If you prefer to always eat at counter-service restaurants, you'll be better off with the Quick Service plan. Other poor candidates for the Plus plan include finicky eaters, light eaters, families who can't agree on restaurants, and those who can't get reservations at their first- or second-choice sit-down restaurants. It's usually not cost-effective during the holidays or summer either. In addition, if you have children age 10 and up, be sure they can eat an adult-size dinner at a sit-down restaurant every night; if not, you'd probably come out ahead just paying for everyone's meals without the plan.

When the dining plan was first introduced, it included an appetizer and gratuity for each full-service meal, making it a pretty good deal; by our estimate, savings of up to 13% per person per day were possible in some of Disney's best restaurants. As a result, the dining plan was one of the most requested of Disney's package add-ons.

Alas, with the initial success of the plan, Disney saw an opportunity to make more money. In 2008, Disney eliminated the appetizer and gratuity from the plan, increasing the cost of a full-service meal by at least 15% to 18% for the gratuity alone, and an additional 15% to 20% per appetizer per person. (To be fair, many appetizers are large enough to share.) Some of the pricier entrees were modified or eliminated from menus.

If you decide to opt for the plan, keep in mind that skipping a single full-service meal during a visit of five or fewer days can mean the difference between saving and losing money. In our experience, having a scheduled sit-down meal for every day of a weeklong vacation can be mentally exhausting, especially for kids and teens. One option might be to schedule a meal at a Disney Signature restaurant, which requires two full-service credits. Because you have a full dinner credit for the day you check out, and because it's not likely that you'll still be around for dinner, you have an extra credit to use during your stay to dine in a signature restaurant without skipping a full-service meal one night.

Many of the most popular restaurants are fully booked as soon as their reservation window opens, so book your restaurants as soon as possible. Then decide whether the dining plan makes economic sense.

If you're making reservations at restaurants in Disney hotels other than your own, a car allows you to easily access all the participating restaurants. When you use the Disney transportation system, dining at the various Disney-resort restaurants can be a logistical nightmare. Those without a car may want to weigh the immediate services of a taxi (typically at $10–$12 each way across Disney property) versus a 45- to 60-minute trip on Disney transportation each way.

For an in-depth discussion of the various plans, including number-crunching (and even algebra!), visit **touringplans.com** (click "Dining" on the home page, then "Disney Dining Plan").

Readers who tried the Disney dining plan had varying experiences. A mother of two from Marshalltown, Iowa, volunteered this:

The dining plan is great in theory, but it had way too much food and used too much valuable park time for the table-service meals. We won't use it again.

From a Minnesota family of three:

We purchased the basic Disney Dining Plan, and my wife and I were almost overwhelmed by the amount of food we received. I skipped a counter-service meal one day, which allowed my son to use [the meal credit] for breakfast from the resort food court the next day.

A St. Louis family of three comments:

We purchased the dining plan and would never do it again. Far too expensive, far too much food, and then you have to tip on top of the expense. Additionally, table-service meals were hard to use for us, reservations hard to obtain. Much easier to purchase what you want, where and when you want. (Intended to use a counter-service meal at McDonald's at Epcot for 12-year-old. Found out you had to get the large [nine-piece] nuggets, the large fries, a large drink, and a McFlurry in order to use the counter-service meal. Most adults I know wouldn't eat that much food, let alone a 12-year-old!) Food is a "gotcha" at Disney, but the dining plan proved to be a poor choice for us.

A Toronto family says gratuities add up:

Families should be warned that tips in Disney table-service restaurants can add up quickly in a week. The tip for our party of five at Le Cellier alone was $45.

A Belmont, Massachusetts, dad likes the Quick Service Dining Plan:

If you intend to eat Disney food, the counter-service meal plan is a good option. We didn't want the full plan because the restaurants seemed overpriced, and the necessity of reservations months in advance seemed crazy and a bar to flexibility. You get two counter-service meals (entree/combo, dessert, drink) and two snacks (food item or drink) per person as part of the plan, and even though kids' meals are cheaper, there is no distinction when you order—kids can order (more-expensive) adult meals.

But a reader from The Woodlands, Texas, laments that the plan has altered the focus of her vacation:

For me, the Disney Dining Plan has taken a lot of the fun out of going to Disney World. No longer are we free to enjoy the parks and fit in meals as a secondary matter. Now, dining for each day must be planned months in advance, unless one is to eat just hot dogs, pizza, and other walk-up items. As heretical as it may sound, I'm actually less inclined to go to WDW now. I want to have fun. I don't want to be locked into a tight schedule, always worrying about where we need to be when it's time to eat. I don't want to eat when I'm not hungry just because I have a reservation somewhere. Eating has become the primary consideration at WDW, not the parks and entertainment.

Along similar lines, a Bethany, Connecticut, dad adds this:

We took the dining plan and were disappointed. It was a lot of work to coordinate. We made travel plans six weeks prior to departure and were unable to procure reservations in our favorite restaurants (or they were at inconvenient times—9:50 p.m. at Boma).

A Midland Park, New Jersey, family of four says ditto:

With so many people now using the dining plan, it seems that if you were to book a last-minute trip or miss one of your reservations, you might not be able to get a table-service meal at all—reservations were hard to come by, even though I called two months before our trip!

A mom from Orland Park, Illinois, comments on the difficulty of getting Advance Reservations:

I purchased the dining plan for this trip and must say I will never do that again. It's impossible to get table reservations anywhere good— the [restaurants] that are available are available for a reason. We

*found ourselves taking whatever was open and were unhappy with
every sit-down meal we had, except for lunch at Liberty Tree Tavern.
I do not enjoy planning my day exclusively around eating at a certain
restaurant at a certain time, but that is what you must do six months
in advance if you want to eat at a good sit-down restaurant in
Disney. That is ridiculous.*

As this reader from San Jose, California, explains, guests who are
not on the dining plan need to know how the plan has affected
obtaining Advance Reservations:

*The Disney Dining Plan has almost eliminated any chance of sponta-
neity when visiting any of the sit-down restaurants. When planning
90 days out for the off-season, I was told by the Disney rep to make
all my priority-seating reservations then because the restaurants are
booked by people on the dining plan. In fact, I was told that most of
the sit-down restaurants don't even take walk-ins anymore. Sure
enough, even though I was well over 90 days away from my vacation,
a lot of my restaurant choices were unavailable. I had to rearrange
my entire schedule to fit the open slots at the restaurants I didn't
want to miss.*

We should add to this discussion that during the recession and
now in its aftermath, Disney lures guests to Walt Disney World by
including the Dining Plan free with certain vacation packages. This
vastly increases the number of people on the dining plan and makes
getting advance reservations much more difficult.

Pesky Technicalities and Administrative Problems

Readers report experiencing a host of problems with both understanding and using the Disney Dining Plan. A dad from Tonawanda,
New York, opines:

*The dining plan is great, but unfortunately, not enough guests actu-
ally read the literature about it and become confused, leading to
long, slow lines at some counter-service locations.*

A family of four from Mount Pleasant, South Carolina, observes:

*The impact of the Disney Dining Plan was amazing. It created longer
lines at the registers because they were programmed to ring up each
thing individually, or so it seemed. For instance, for a Mickey Meal,
the checkout guy had to push buttons for chicken nuggets, applesauce,
milk, and fries—not just one button for the entire meal. It took the guy
about 7 minutes to figure it and process us.*

A woman from Atco, New Jersey, warns:

*The Disney Dining Plan does not always work for snacks, even though
vendors have signs posted stating they accept the card. We were told
many times, "Oh, the machine isn't working today."*

An Atlanta reader has this to say:

The downside to our stay was [using credits] at the fast-food counter at Coronado Springs. I thought I was prepared. . . . not! Servers didn't seem to know what was included as a snack or what comprised a meal with the dining plan. It was a very frustrating experience. We spent the majority of our [credits] at the parks or other resorts.

Many families purchase the dining plan without understanding how limited the menu choices are for kids age 9 and under. First from a Westchester, Ohio, mom:

We had only one complaint in our six days there, and that was with the Disney Dining Plan. All three of our girls are under 9 and had to choose "Kid's Picks" wherever offered. We did not come across any offerings like hamburgers, hot dogs, or pizza the whole time we were there. My kids couldn't even get pizza at Pizzafari in Animal Kingdom! They were so sick of mac and cheese and chicken nuggets after day two that going out to eat wasn't that exciting for them. We were given a hard time by food-service workers when we asked about substituting something different, and we were turned down 50% of the time. On our last day, a sympathetic employee told us we could get any counter-service food we wanted and just not tell the cashier that it was for a child (apparently, for counter service, Disney doesn't keep track of whether it is for an adult or child). It did work for us on that last day, but I wish we would have known that sooner. Hope this info will help some families with young kids.

A Pittsburgh mother of three recounts a similar experience:

My two kids were actually sick of eating macaroni and cheese and chicken fingers. The amount of food they get is also very small—OK for my 4-year-old but not for my 9-year-old, who ended up eating off my plate; otherwise, I would have had to buy something extra to fill him up. Plus, we went to a pizza place in Animal Kingdom park, and there was NO pizza on the [dining plan's] kids' menu. No pizza at a pizza place?

From a Midwestern reader:

We could almost relate our dining experience to that of a person who receives food stamps—very restricted and always at the mercy of someone else for food selection. We spent close to $1,000 on food and were extremely frustrated with the entire experience. I would prefer to be able to eat whatever I want rather than be restricted to certain food items at certain places.

From a Wisconsin father of two:

On the last day of our visit, we were still learning about acceptable substitutions. For example, at breakfast you can have two drinks (coffee and OJ). You can also do this for lunch, but you have to give up your dessert. In the 90-degree heat, I would have gladly given up my fattening dessert to have a bottle of cold water to bring along.

The dining plan left a family of five from Nashville, Tennessee, similarly dazed and confused:

What was annoying was the inconsistency. You can get a 16-ounce chocolate milk on the kids' plan but only 8 ounces of white milk at many places. At the Earl of Sandwich, you can get 16 ounces of either kind. A pint of milk would count as a snack (price $1.52), but they wouldn't count a quart of milk (price $1.79) because it wasn't a single serving. However, in Animal Kingdom, my husband bought a water-bottle holder (price $3.75) and used a snack credit. The kids choices' were limited as well, maybe one or two per restaurant.

Readers also report difficulties in keeping their accounts straight. A Saskatoon, Saskatchewan, father of three says you have to watch vendors like a hawk:

We had a problem with a vendor who charged us meal service for each of the ice-cream bars we purchased. This became evident at our final sit-down meal, when we didn't have any meal vouchers left. Check the receipts after every purchase!

A Havre de Grace, Maryland, mom had a similar experience:

I did want to tell you that we used the dining plan and found it to be not at all user-friendly. There was a lot of confusion on how many meals were on which card, and each place charged differently. It was very frustrating to use. Anyone else using this plan should make sure they put the correct number of meals on the correct cards.

A mom from Shawnee, Kansas, found the dining plan too complex on the restaurants' end:

A comment on Disney Dining—a great savings for us, but it seems like it was tough on the servers at the restaurants. It always took FOREVER for everything to be settled. They just seemed to really dislike dealing with the plan.

Reader Tips for Getting the Most Out of the Plan

A mom from Radford, Virginia, shares this tip:

If you eat a late lunch (where, by the way, they feed you the same ungodly amount of food), you WILL NOT be hungry for dinner. Also, depending on where you go, different Disney employees give you different answers on what counts as a snack. One employee told us anything under $5, and another one said anything under $3. Hint: Use the snacks as your breakfast once you get in the park—we did this the last two days and it worked out great!

A mom from Overland Park, Kansas, who has children with dietary restrictions submitted this comment:

Our children are allergic to dairy products, and I found the staff were pretty willing to provide a nondairy dessert option so the kids didn't feel left out.

Magic Your Way Premium Package

With the Magic Your Way Premium Package you get lodging; Magic Your Way Premium tickets with Park Hopping and Plus Pack features; breakfast, lunch, and dinner, including character meals and dinner shows; unlimited golf, tennis, fishing excursions, and water sports; select theme-park tours; **Cirque du Soleil** show tickets; unlimited use of child-care facilities—everything you can think of except for alcoholic beverages. (*Note:* The length of the Magic Your Way Premium Package must equal the total number of nights you stay at a Disney resort, plus one day. Package length cannot be customized to fit your touring plans.)

Disney, needless to say, has built a nice profit into every component of the Magic Your Way Premium Package. If you don't use all features of the plan and did not purchase the No Expiration option on your tickets, Disney makes out even better.

PLATINUM PACKAGE REPRISE The favorite of high rollers who want to prepay for everything they might desire while at Walt Disney World, the Platinum Package gets you lodging; tickets; breakfast, lunch, and dinner in full-service restaurants; unlimited golf, tennis, boating, and recreation; unlimited dinner shows and character breakfasts; primo Cirque du Soleil seats; private in-room child care; unlimited use of child-care facilities; personalized itinerary planning; dinner at Victoria & Albert's restaurant; a spa treatment; a fireworks cruise; admission to select tours; reserved seating for *Fantasmic!*; and (here's the kicker) nightly turndown service! Everything you can think of, in other words, except alcoholic beverages. Per diem prices for the Platinum Package are $220 for adults and $155 for kids in addition to the cost of a standard Magic Your Way package—but anyone who buys this package doesn't really care what the prices are anyway.

NUMBER CRUNCHING

COMPARING A MAGIC YOUR WAY PACKAGE with purchasing the package components separately is a breeze.

1. Pick a Disney resort and decide how many nights you want to stay.
2. Next, work out a rough plan of what you want to do and see, so you can determine the admission passes you'll require.
3. When you're ready, call the Disney Reservations Center (DRC) at ☎ 407-934-7639 and price a Magic Your Way package with tax for your selected resort and dates. The package will include both admissions and lodging. It's also a good idea to get a quote from a Disney-savvy travel agent.

4. Now, to calculate the costs of buying your accommodations and admission passes separately, call the DRC a second time. This time, price a room-only rate for the same resort and dates. Be sure to ask about the availability of any special deals. While you're still on the line, obtain the prices, with tax, for the admissions you require. If you're not sure which of the various admission options will best serve you, consult our free Admissions Option analyzer at **touringplans.com.**

5. Add the room-only rates and the admission prices. Compare this sum to the DRC quote for the Magic Your Way package.

6. Check for deals and discounts for packages, room-only rates, and admission.

When you upgrade to a Magic Your Way Premium Package, you load the plan with so many features that it's extremely difficult to price them individually. For a rough comparison, price the plan of your choice using the previous steps. To complete the picture, work up a dining budget, excluding alcohol. Add your estimated dining costs to the room-only quote and admissions quote, and compare this to the price of the plan.

THROW ME A LINE!

IF YOU BUY A VACATION PACKAGE FROM DISNEY, don't expect reservationists to offer suggestions or to help you sort out your options. Generally, they respond only to your specific questions, ducking queries that require an opinion. A reader from North Riverside, Illinois, complains:

> I have received various pieces of literature from WDW, and it is very confusing to figure out everything. My wife made two telephone calls, and the representatives from WDW were very courteous. However, they only answered the questions posed and were not eager to give advice on what might be most cost-effective. [The] WDW reps would not say if we would be better off doing one thing over the other. I feel a person could spend 8 hours on the phone with WDW reps and not have any more input than you get from reading the literature.

If you can't get the information that you need from Disney, contact a good travel agent. Chances are that the agent can help you weigh all of your options.

PURCHASING ROOM-ONLY PLUS PASSES VERSUS A PACKAGE

*Sue Pisaturo of Small World Vacations (**smallworldvacations.com**), a travel agency that specializes in Disney, also thinks there is more involved in a package-purchase decision than money. Her suggestions follow.*

Should you purchase a Walt Disney World package or buy all the components of the package separately? There's no single answer to this confusing question.

A Walt Disney World package can be compared to a store-bought prepackaged kids' meal, the kind with the little compartments filled with meat, cheese, crackers, drink, and dessert: You just grab the package and go. It's easy, and if it's on sale, why bother doing it yourself? If it's not on sale, it still may be worth the extra money for convenience.

Purchasing the components of your vacation separately is like buying each of the meal's ingredients, cutting them up into neat piles and packaging the lunch yourself. Is it worth the extra time and effort to do it this way? Will you save money if you do it this way?

You have two budgets to balance when you plan your Disney World vacation: time and money. Satisfying both is your ultimate goal. Research and planning are paramount to realizing your Disney vacation dreams. Create your theme-park touring plan prior to making a final decision with regard to the number of days and options on your theme-park passes. Create your dining itinerary (along with advance dining reservations, if possible) to determine if Disney's dining plan can save you some money.

CHARACTER DINING

ALL THE RAGE AT WALT DISNEY WORLD for more than a decade, character dining combines a meal with meeting the characters. The characters circulate throughout the meal, stopping at each table to sign autographs, pose for photos, and lavish attention on mostly adoring (but sometimes stupefied) children. For a detailed description of this Disney ritual, see pages 244–251.

WALT DISNEY WORLD RESTAURANTS: RATED AND RANKED

STAR RATING The star rating represents the entire dining experience: style, service, and ambience, in addition to taste, presentation, and quality of food. Five stars is the highest rating and indicates that the restaurant offers the best of everything. Four-star restaurants are above average, and three-star restaurants offer good, though not necessarily memorable, meals. Two-star restaurants serve mediocre fare, and one-star restaurants are below average. Our star ratings don't correspond to ratings awarded by AAA, Mobil, Zagat, or other restaurant reviewers.

COST RANGE The next rating tells how much a complete meal will cost. We include a main dish with vegetable or side dish, and a choice of soup or salad. Appetizers, desserts, drinks, and tips aren't included. We've rated the cost as inexpensive, moderate, or expensive.

Inexpensive	$12 or less per person
Moderate	$13–$23 per person
Expensive	More than $23 per person

QUALITY RATING The food quality is rated on a scale of one to five stars, five being the best rating attainable. The quality rating is based on the taste, freshness of ingredients, preparation, presentation, and creativity of food served. There is no consideration of price. If you are a person who wants the best food available and cost is not an issue, you need look no further than the quality ratings.

VALUE RATING If, on the other hand, you are looking for both quality and value, then you should check the value rating, expressed as stars.

★★★★★	Exceptional value, a real bargain
★★★★	Good value
★★★	Fair value, you get exactly what you pay for
★★	Somewhat overpriced
★	Significantly overpriced

Walt Disney World Restaurants by Cuisine

CUISINE	LOCATION	OVERALL RATING	COST	QUALITY RATING	VALUE RATING
AFRICAN					
Jiko—The Cooking Place	Animal Kingdom Lodge	★★★★½	Exp	★★★★ ½	★★★½
Boma—Flavors of Africa	Animal Kingdom Lodge	★★★★	Exp	★★★★	★★★★½
Tusker House Restaurant	Animal Kingdom	★½	Mod	★	★★
AMERICAN					
California Grill	Contemporary	★★★★½	Exp	★★★★½	★★★
The Hollywood Brown Derby	DHS	★★★★	Exp	★★★★	★★★
Artist Point	Wilderness Lodge	★★★½	Exp	★★★★	★★★
Cape May Café	Beach Club	★★★½	Mod	★★★½	★★★★
Whispering Canyon Café	Wilderness Lodge	★★★	Mod	★★★½	★★★★
Captain's Grille	Yacht Club	★★★	Mod	★★★½	★★★
The Crystal Palace	Magic Kingdom	★★★	Mod	★★★½	★★★
House of Blues	West Side	★★★	Mod	★★★½	★★★
50's Prime Time Café	DHS	★★★	Mod	★★★	★★★
The Garden Grill Restaurant	Epcot	★★★	Exp	★★★	★★★
Liberty Tree Tavern	Magic Kingdom	★★★	Mod	★★★	★★★
Cinderella's Royal Table	Magic Kingdom	★★★	Exp	★★★	★★
Planet Hollywood	West Side	★★★	Mod	★★	★★
T-REX	Downtown Disney	★★★	Mod	★★	★★
The Wave . . . of American Flavors	Contemporary	★★★	Mod	★★	★★
Chef Mickey's	Contemporary	★★½	Exp	★★★	★★★
ESPN Club	BoardWalk	★★½	Mod	★★★	★★★
ESPN Wide World of Sports Grill	ESPN Wide World of Sports Complex	★★½	Mod	★★★	★★★
Hollywood & Vine	DHS	★★½	Mod	★★★	★★★
1900 Park Fare	Grand Floridian	★★½	Mod	★★★	★★★
Beaches & Cream Soda Shop	Beach Club	★★½	Inexp	★★½	★★½
Boatwrights Dining Hall	Port Orleans	★★½	Mod	★★★	★★
Grand Floridian Café	Grand Floridian	★★½	Mod	★★★	★★
Sand Trap Bar & Grill	Osprey Ridge Golf Course	★★½	Mod	★★½	★★½

CUISINE	LOCATION	OVERALL RATING	COST	QUALITY RATING	VALUE RATING
AMERICAN (CONTINUED)					
Rainforest Cafe	Downtown Disney and Animal Kingdom	★★½	Mod	★★	★★
Garden Grove	Swan	★★	Mod	★★★	★★
Olivia's Cafe	Old Key West	★★	Mod	★★½	★★
Sci-Fi Dine-In Theater Restaurant	DHS	★★	Mod	★★½	★★
Big River Grille & Brewing Works	BoardWalk	★★	Mod	★★	★★
The Fountain	Dolphin	★★	Mod	★★	★★
The Plaza Restaurant	Magic Kingdom	★★	Mod	★★	★★
Trail's End Restaurant	Fort Wilderness Resort	★★	Mod	★★	★★
Turf Club Bar & Grill	Saratoga Springs	★★	Mod	★★	★★
Wolfgang Puck Café	West Side	★★	Exp	★½	★½
LakeView Restaurant	Regal Sun Resort	★★	Mod	★	★★★
Tusker House Restaurant	Animal Kingdom	★½	Mod	★	★★
Maya Grill	Coronado Springs	★	Mod	★	★
BUFFET					
Boma—Flavors of Africa	Animal Kingdom Lodge	★★★★	Exp	★★★★	★★★★½
Cape May Café	Beach Club	★★★½	Mod	★★★½	★★★★
Akershus Royal Banquet Hall	Epcot	★★★½	Exp	★★★	★★★★
Biergarten	Epcot	★★★½	Exp	★★★	★★★★
The Crystal Palace	Magic Kingdom	★★★	Mod	★★★½	★★★
Chef Mickey's	Contemporary	★★½	Exp	★★★	★★★
Hollywood & Vine	DHS	★★½	Mod	★★★	★★★
1900 Park Fare	Grand Floridian	★★½	Mod	★★★	★★★
Garden Grove	Swan	★★	Mod	★★★	★★
Trail's End Restaurant	Fort Wilderness Resort	★★	Mod	★★	★★
Tusker House Restaurant	Animal Kingdom	★½	Mod	★	★★
CHINESE					
Nine Dragons Restaurant	Epcot	★★★	Mod	★★★	★★

WDW Restaurants by Cuisine (continued)

CUISINE	LOCATION	OVERALL RATING	COST	QUALITY RATING	VALUE RATING
CUBAN					
Bongos Cuban Café	West Side	★★	Mod	★★	★★
ENGLISH					
Rose & Crown Dining Room	Epcot	★★★	Mod	★★★½	★★
FRENCH					
Bistro de Paris	Epcot	★★★	Exp	★★★½	★★
Les Chefs de France	Epcot	★★★	Exp	★★★	★★★
GERMAN					
Biergarten	Epcot	★★★½	Exp	★★★	★★★★
GLOBAL					
Paradiso 37	Downtown Disney	★★★	Inexp	★★★	★★★
GOURMET					
Victoria & Albert's	Grand Floridian	★★★★★	Exp	★★★★★	★★★★
INDIAN/AFRICAN					
Sanaa	Animal Kingdom Villas	★★★★	Exp	★★★★	★★★★
IRISH					
Raglan Road Irish Pub & Restaurant	Downtown Disney	★★★★	Mod	★★★½	★★★
ITALIAN					
Andiamo Italian Bistro & Grille	Hilton	★★★	Exp	★★★	★★★
Il Mulino New York Trattoria	Swan	★★★	Exp	★★★	★★
Portobello	Downtown Disney	★★★	Exp	★★★	★★
Mama Melrose's Ristorante Italiano	DHS	★★½	Mod	★★★	★★
Tony's Town Square Restaurant	Magic Kingdom	★★½	Mod	★★★	★★
Tutto Italia Ristorante	Epcot	★★½	Exp	★★½	★★½
JAPANESE					
Kimonos	Swan	★★★★	Mod	★★★★½	★★★
Teppan Edo	Epcot	★★★½	Exp	★★★★	★★★
Tokyo Dining	Epcot	★★★	Mod	★★★★	★★★
Benihana	Hilton	★★★	Mod	★★★½	★★★

CUISINE	LOCATION	OVERALL RATING	COST	QUALITY RATING	VALUE RATING
MEDITERRANEAN					
Kouzzina by Cat Cora	BoardWalk	★★★★	Mod	★★★★	★★★★
Citricos	Grand Floridian	★★★½	Exp	★★★★½	★★★
Fresh Mediterranean Market	Dolphin	★★½	Mod	★★½	★★
MEXICAN					
San Angel Inn	Epcot	★★★	Exp	★★	★★
MOROCCAN					
Restaurant Marrakesh	Epcot	★★	Mod	★★½	★★
NORWEGIAN					
Akershus Royal Banquet Hall	Epcot	★★★½	Exp	★★★	★★★★
POLYNESIAN/PAN-ASIAN					
'Ohana	Polynesian	★★★	Mod	★★★½	★★★
Yak & Yeti Restaurant	Animal Kingdom	★★★	Exp	★★★½	★★★
Kona Café	Polynesian	★★★	Mod	★★★	★★★★
SEAFOOD					
Flying Fish Café	BoardWalk	★★★★	Exp	★★★★	★★★
Artist Point	Wilderness Lodge	★★★½	Exp	★★★★	★★★
Narcoossee's	Grand Floridian	★★★½	Exp	★★★½	★★
bluezoo	Dolphin	★★★	Exp	★★★	★★
Fulton's Crab House	Downtown Disney	★★½	Exp	★★★½	★★
Cap'n Jack's Restaurant	Downtown Disney	★★½	Mod	★★	★★
Coral Reef Restaurant	Epcot	★★½	Exp	★★	★★
Shutters at Old Port Royale	Caribbean Beach	★★	Mod	★★½	★★
STEAK					
Shula's Steak House	Dolphin	★★★★	Exp	★★★★	★★
Le Cellier Steakhouse	Epcot	★★★½	Exp	★★★½	★★★
Yachtsman Steakhouse	Yacht Club	★★★	Exp	★★★½	★★
The Outback	Buena Vista Palace	★★	Exp	★★★	★★
Shutters at Old Port Royale	Caribbean Beach	★★	Mod	★★½	★★

PART FIVE

DISNEY BOOT CAMP:
Basic Training for World-bound Families

The **BRUTAL TRUTH** *about* **FAMILY VACATIONS**

IT HAS BEEN SUGGESTED THAT THE PHRASE *family vacation* is a bit of an oxymoron. This is because you can never take a vacation from the responsibilities of parenting if your children are traveling with you. Though you leave your work and normal routine far behind, your children require as much attention, if not more, when traveling as they do at home.

Parenting on the road is an art. It requires imagination and organization. Think about it: You have to do all the usual stuff (feed, dress, bathe, supervise, teach, comfort, discipline, put to bed, and so on) in an atmosphere where your children are hyperstimulated, without the familiarity of place and the resources you take for granted at home. Although it's not impossible—and can even be fun—parenting on the road is not something you want to learn on the fly, particularly at Walt Disney World.

The point we want to drive home is that preparation, or the lack thereof, can make or break your Walt Disney World vacation. Believe us, you do *not* want to leave the success of your expensive Disney vacation to chance. But don't confuse chance with good luck. Chance is what happens when you fail to prepare. Good luck is when preparation meets opportunity.

Your preparation can be organized into several categories, all of which we will help you undertake. Broadly speaking, you need to prepare yourself and your children mentally, emotionally, physically, organizationally, and logistically. You also need a basic understanding of Walt Disney World and a well-considered plan for how to go about seeing it.

MENTAL *and* EMOTIONAL PREPARATION

THIS IS A SUBJECT THAT WE WILL TOUCH on here and return to many times in this book. Mental preparation begins with realistic expectations about your Disney vacation and consideration of what each adult and child in your party most wants and needs from their Walt Disney World experience. Getting in touch with this aspect of planning requires a lot of introspection and good, open family communication.

DIVISION OF LABOR

TALK ABOUT WHAT YOU AND YOUR PARTNER NEED and what you expect to happen on the vacation. This discussion alone can preempt some unpleasant surprises midtrip. If you are a two-parent (or two-adult) family, do you have a clear understanding of how the parenting workload is to be distributed? We have seen some distinctly disruptive misunderstandings in two-parent households where one parent is (pardon the legalese) the primary caregiver. Often, the other parent expects the primary caregiver to function on vacation as she (or he) does at home. The primary caregiver, on the other hand, is ready for a break. She expects her partner to either shoulder the load equally or perhaps even assume the lion's share so she can have a *real* vacation. However you divide the responsibility, of course, is up to you. Just make sure you negotiate a clear understanding *before* you leave home.

TOGETHERNESS

ANOTHER DIMENSION TO CONSIDER is how much "togetherness" seems appropriate to you. For some parents, a vacation represents a rare opportunity to really connect with their children, to talk, exchange ideas, and get reacquainted. For others, a vacation affords the time to get a little distance, to enjoy a round of golf while the kids are participating in a program organized by the resort.

At Walt Disney World you can orchestrate your vacation to spend as much or as little time with your children as you desire, but more about that later. The point here is to think about your and your children's preferences and needs concerning your time together. A typical day at a Disney theme park provides the structure of experiencing attractions together, punctuated by periods of waiting in line, eating, and so on, which facilitate conversation and sharing. Most attractions can be enjoyed together by the whole family, regardless of age ranges. This allows for more consensus and less dissent when it comes to deciding what to see and do. For many parents and children, however, the rhythms of a Walt Disney World day seem to consist of passive entertainment experiences alternated with endless discussions of where to go and what to do next. As a mother from Winston-Salem, North Carolina, reported:

*Our family mostly talked about what to do next with very little shar-
ing or discussion about what we had seen. [The conversation] was
pretty task oriented.*

Two observations: First, fighting the crowds and keeping the family moving along can easily escalate into a pressure-driven outing.
Having an advance plan or itinerary eliminates moment-to-moment
guesswork and decision making, thus creating more time for savoring
and connecting. Second, external variables such as crowd size, noise,
and heat, among others, can be so distracting as to preclude any
meaningful togetherness. These negative impacts can be moderated,
as previously discussed, by your being selective concerning the time
of year, day of the week, and time of day you visit the theme parks.
The bottom line is that you can achieve the degree of connection and
togetherness you desire with a little advance planning and a realistic
awareness of the distractions you will encounter.

LIGHTEN UP

PREPARE YOURSELF MENTALLY to be a little less compulsive on vacation about correcting small behavioral deviations and pounding home
the lessons of life. Certainly, little Mildred will have to learn eventually
that it's very un-Disney-like to take off her top at the pool. But there's
plenty of time for that later. So what if Matt eats hamburgers for
breakfast, lunch, and dinner every day? You can make him eat peas and
broccoli when you get home and are in charge of meal preparation
again. Roll with the little stuff, and remember when your children act
out that they are wired to the max. At least some of that adrenaline is
bound to spill out in undesirable ways. Coming down hard will send an
already frayed little nervous system into orbit.

SOMETHING FOR EVERYONE

IF YOU TRAVEL WITH AN INFANT, TODDLER, or any child who
requires a lot of special attention, make sure that you have some energy
and time remaining for your other children. In the
course of your planning, invite each child to name
something special to do or see at Walt Disney World
with mom or dad alone. Work these special activities
into your trip itinerary. Whatever else, if you commit,
write it down so that you don't forget. Remember, a
casually expressed willingness to do this or that may
be perceived as a promise by your children.

Try to schedule some
time alone with each of
your children, if
not each day,
then at least a
couple of times
during the trip.
Liliane

WHOSE IDEA WAS THIS, ANYWAY?

THE DISCORD THAT MANY VACATIONING FAMILIES experience
arises from the kids being on a completely different wavelength from
mom and dad. Parents and grandparents are often worse than children
when it comes to conjuring up fantasy scenarios of what a Walt Disney
World vacation will be like. A Disney vacation can be many things, but

believe us when we tell you that there's a lot more to it than just riding Dumbo and seeing Mickey.

In our experience, most parents and nearly all grandparents expect children to enter a state of rapture at Walt Disney World, bouncing from attraction to attraction in wide-eyed wonder, appreciative beyond words of their adult benefactors. What they get, more often than not, is not even in the same ballpark. Preschoolers will, without a doubt, be wide-eyed, often with delight but also with a general sense of being overwhelmed by noise, crowds, and Disney characters as big as tool sheds. We have substantiated through thousands of interviews and surveys that the best part of a Disney vacation for a preschooler is the hotel swimming pool. With some grade-schoolers and pre-driving-age teens you get near-manic hyperactivity coupled with periods of studied non-chalance. This last, which relates to the importance of being "cool at all costs," translates into a maddening display of boredom and a "been there, done that" attitude. Older teens are frequently the exponential version of the younger teens and grade-schoolers, except without the manic behavior.

As a function of probability, you may escape many—but most likely not all—of the above behaviors. Even in the event that they are all visited on you, however, take heart, there are antidotes.

For preschoolers you can keep things light and happy by limiting the time you spend in the theme parks. The most critical point is that the overstimulation of the parks must be balanced by adequate rest and more mellow activities. For grade-schoolers and early teens, you can moderate the hyperactivity and false apathy by enlisting their help in planning the vacation, especially by allowing them to take a leading role in determining the itinerary for days at the theme parks. Being in charge of specific responsibilities that focus on the happiness of other family members also works well. One reader, for example, turned a 12-year-old liability into an asset by asking him to help guard against attractions that might frighten his 5-year-old sister.

Knowledge enhances anticipation and at the same time affords a level of comfort and control that helps kids understand the big picture. The more they feel in control, the less they will act out of control.

Short forays to the parks interspersed with naps, swimming, and quiet activities such as reading to your children will go a long way toward keeping things on an even keel.

Liliane

The more information your children have before arriving at Walt Disney World, the less likely they will be to act out.

Liliane

DISNEY, KIDS, AND SCARY STUFF

DISNEY ATTRACTIONS, BOTH RIDES AND SHOWS, are adventures. They focus on themes common to adventures: good and evil, life and death, beauty and the grotesque, fellowship and enmity. As you sample

continued on page 186

Small-child Fright-potential Chart

This is a quick reference to identify attractions to be wary of, and why. The chart represents a generalization, and all kids are different. It relates specifically to kids ages 3–7. On average, children at the younger end of the range are more likely to be frightened than children in their sixth or seventh year.

Magic Kingdom

MAIN STREET, U.S.A.

Main Street Vehicles Not frightening in any respect.

Walt Disney World Railroad Not frightening in any respect.

ADVENTURELAND

Enchanted Tiki Room A thunderstorm, loud volume level, and simulated explosions frighten some preschoolers.

Jungle Cruise Moderately intense, some macabre sights. A good test attraction for little ones.

Pirates of the Caribbean Slightly intimidating queuing area; intense boat ride with gruesome (though humorously presented) sights and a short, unexpected slide down a flume.

The Magic Carpets of Aladdin Much like Dumbo. A favorite of young children.

Swiss Family Treehouse May not be suitable for kids who are afraid of heights.

FRONTIERLAND

Big Thunder Mountain Railroad Visually intimidating from outside, with moderately intense visual effects. The roller coaster is wild enough to frighten many adults, particularly seniors. Switching-off option (see page 238).

Country Bear Jamboree Not frightening in any respect.

Frontierland Shootin' Arcade Not frightening in any respect.

Splash Mountain Visually intimidating from outside, with moderately intense visual effects. The ride, culminating in a 52-foot plunge down a steep chute, is somewhat hair-raising for all ages. Switching-off option (see page 238).

Tom Sawyer Island Some very young children are intimidated by dark walk-through tunnels that can be easily avoided.

LIBERTY SQUARE

The Hall of Presidents Not frightening, but boring for young ones.

The Haunted Mansion Name raises anxiety, as do sounds and sights of waiting area. Intense attraction with humorously presented macabre sights. The ride itself is gentle.

Liberty Belle Riverboat Not frightening in any respect.

FANTASYLAND

Dumbo the Flying Elephant A tame midway ride; a great favorite of most young children.

It's a Small World Not frightening in any respect.

Mad Tea Party Midway-type ride can induce motion sickness in all ages.

The Many Adventures of Winnie the Pooh Frightens a small percentage of preschoolers.

Peter Pan's Flight Not frightening in any respect.

Prince Charming Regal Carrousel Not frightening in any respect.

Snow White's Scary Adventures Moderately intense spook-house-genre attraction with some grim characters. Absolutely terrifies many preschoolers.

TOMORROWLAND

Astro Orbiter Visually intimidating from the waiting area, but the ride is relatively tame.

Buzz Lightyear's Space Ranger Spin Dark ride with cartoonlike aliens may frighten some preschoolers.

Monsters, Inc. Laugh Floor May frighten a small percentage of preschoolers.

Space Mountain Very intense roller coaster in the dark; the Magic Kingdom's wildest ride and a scary roller coaster by any standard. Switching-off option (see page 238).

Stitch's Great Escape! Very intense. May frighten children age 9 and younger. Switching-off option (see page 238).

Tomorrowland Speedway Noise of waiting area slightly intimidates preschoolers; otherwise, not frightening.

Tomorrowland Transit Authority Not frightening in any respect.

Walt Disney's Carousel of Progress Not frightening in any respect.

Epcot

FUTURE WORLD

Innoventions East and West Not frightening in any respect.

Journey into Imagination—*Honey, I Shrunk the Audience* or *Captain Eo* Extremely intense visual effects and loudness frighten many young children.

Journey into Imagination with Figment Loud noises and unexpected flashing lights startle younger children.

The Land—*Circle of Life* Theater Not frightening in any respect.

The Land—*Living with the Land* Not frightening in any respect.

The Land—*Soarin'* May frighten children age 7 and younger. Really a very mellow ride.

Mission: SPACE Extremely intense space-simulation ride that has been known to frighten guests of all ages. Preshow may also frighten some children. Switching-off option (see page 238).

The Seas—**The Seas with Nemo & Friends** Very sweet but may frighten some toddlers.

The Seas—**The Main Tank and Exhibits** Not frightening in any respect.

The Seas—*Turtle Talk with Crush* Not frightening in any respect.

Small-child Fright-potential Chart (cont'd)

Epcot (continued)

FUTURE WORLD (CONTINUED)

Spaceship Earth Dark, imposing presentation intimidates a few preschoolers.

Test Track Intense thrill ride may frighten any age. Switching-off option (see page 238).

Universe of Energy Dinosaur segment frightens some preschoolers; visually intense, with some intimidating effects.

WORLD SHOWCASE

The American Adventure Not frightening in any respect.

Canada—O Canada! Not frightening in any respect, but audience must stand.

China—Reflections of China Not frightening in any respect.

France—Impressions de France Not frightening in any respect.

Germany Not frightening in any respect.

Italy Not frightening in any respect.

Japan Not frightening in any respect.

Mexico—Gran Fiesta Tour Not frightening in any respect.

Morocco Not frightening in any respect.

Norway—Maelstrom Visually intense in parts; features trolls. Ride ends with a plunge down a 20-foot flume. A few preschoolers are frightened.

United Kingdom Not frightening in any respect.

Disney's Hollywood Studios

The American Idol Experience At times, the singing may frighten anyone.

Backstage Walking Tours Not frightening in any respect.

Disney's Hollywood Studios Backlot Tour Sedate and nonintimidating except for Catastrophe Canyon, where an earthquake and a flash flood are simulated. Prepare younger children for this part of the tour.

Fantasmic! Terrifies some preschoolers.

The Great Movie Ride Intense in parts, with very realistic special effects and some visually intimidating sights. Frightens many preschoolers.

Honey, I Shrunk the Kids **Movie Set Adventure** Not scary (though oversize).

Indiana Jones Epic Stunt Spectacular An intense show with powerful special effects, including explosions, but young children generally handle it well.

Jim Henson's Muppet-Vision 3-D Intense and loud, but not frightening.

Lights, Motors, Action! Extreme Stunt Show Super stunt spectacular; intense with loud noises and explosions, but not threatening in any way.

The Magic of Disney Animation Not frightening in any respect.

Playhouse Disney—Live on Stage!   Not frightening in any respect.

Rock 'n' Roller Coaster   The wildest coaster at Walt Disney World. May frighten guests of any age. Switching-off option (see page 238).

Sounds Dangerous   Noises in the dark frighten children as old as 8.

Star Tours   Extremely intense visually for all ages. Switching-off option (see page 238).

Toy Story Mania!   Dark ride may frighten some preschoolers.

The Twilight Zone Tower of Terror   Visually intimidating to young children; contains intense and realistic special effects. The plummeting elevator at the ride's end frightens many adults as well as kids. Switching-off option (see page 238).

Voyage of the Little Mermaid   Not frightening in any respect.

Walt Disney: One Man's Dream   Not frightening in any respect.

Animal Kingdom

The Boneyard   Not frightening in any respect.

DINOSAUR   High-tech thrill ride rattles riders of all ages. Switching-off option (see page 238).

Expedition Everest   Frightening to guests of all ages. Switching-off option (see page 238).

Festival of the Lion King   A bit loud, but otherwise not frightening in any respect.

Finding Nemo: The Musical   Not frightening in any respect, but loud.

Flights of Wonder   Swooping birds alarm a few small children.

It's Tough to Be a Bug!   Very intense and loud with special effects that startle viewers of all ages and potentially terrify young children.

Kali River Rapids   Potentially frightening and certainly wet for guests of all ages. Switching-off option (see page 238).

Kilimanjaro Safaris   A "collapsing" bridge and the proximity of real animals make a few young children anxious.

Maharajah Jungle Trek   Some children may balk at the bat exhibit.

The Oasis   Not frightening in any respect.

Pangani Forest Exploration Trail   Not frightening in any respect.

Primeval Whirl   A beginner roller coaster. Most children age 7 and older will take it in stride. Switching-off option (see page 238).

Rafiki's Planet Watch   Not frightening in any respect.

TriceraTop Spin   A midway-type ride that will frighten only a small percentage of younger children.

Wildlife Express Train   Not frightening in any respect.

My first roller coaster experience was with my mom. We rode The Barnstormer at Goofy's Wiseacre Farm [a coaster for the under-7 crowd]—and she screamed my ears off. Next she took a ride with you know who: Bob. He somehow managed to get her on The Incredible Hulk Coaster at Universal's Islands of Adventure. I can't begin to imagine what she must have said to him. [Editor's Note: Bob is still deaf in one ear.]

continued from page 181

continued from page 181

the attractions at Walt Disney World, you transcend the spinning and bouncing of midway rides to thought-provoking and emotionally powerful entertainment. All of the endings are happy, but the adventures' impact, given Disney's gift for special effects, often intimidates and occasionally frightens young children.

There are rides with menacing witches, burning towns, and ghouls popping out of their graves, all done with a sense of humor, provided you're old enough to understand the joke. And bones. There are bones everywhere: human bones, cattle bones, dinosaur bones, even whole skeletons. There's a stack of skulls at the headhunter's camp on the Jungle Cruise, a platoon of skeletons sailing ghost ships in Pirates of the Caribbean, and a haunting assemblage of skulls and skeletons in The Haunted Mansion. Skulls, skeletons, and bones punctuate Snow White's Scary Adventures, Peter Pan's Flight, and Big Thunder Mountain Railroad. In the Animal Kingdom, there's an entire children's playground made up exclusively of giant bones and skeletons.

Monsters and special effects at Disney's Hollywood Studios are more real and sinister than those in the other theme parks. If your child has difficulty coping with the witch in Snow White's Scary Adventures, think twice about exposing him or her to machine-gun battles, earthquakes, and the creature from *Alien* at the Studios.

One reader tells of taking his preschool children on Star Tours:

We took a 4-year-old and a 5-year-old, and they had the *^%#! scared out of them at Star Tours. We did this first thing in the morning, and it took hours of Tom Sawyer Island and Small World to get back to normal.

Our kids were the youngest by far in Star Tours. I assume that other adults had more sense or were not such avid readers of your book. Preschoolers should start with Dumbo and work up to the Jungle Cruise in late morning, after being revved up and before getting hungry, thirsty, or tired. Pirates of the Caribbean is out for preschoolers. You get the idea.

Before lining up for any attraction, be it a ride or a theater presentation, check out our description of it and see our Small-child Fright-potential Chart on page 182.

At Walt Disney World, anticipate the almost inevitable emotional overload of your young children. Be sensitive, alert, and prepared for practically anything, even behavior that is out of character for your child at home. Most young children take Disney's macabre trappings in stride, and others are easily comforted by an arm around the shoulder or a squeeze of the hand. Parents who know that their children tend to become upset should take it slow and easy, sampling more benign adventures, gauging reactions, and discussing with the children how they felt about what they saw.

Some Tips

1. START SLOW AND WARM UP Although each major theme park offers several fairly unintimidating attractions that you can sample to determine your child's relative sensitivity, the Magic Kingdom is probably the best testing ground. At the Magic Kingdom, try Buzz Lightyear's Space Ranger Spin in Tomorrowland, Peter Pan's Flight in Fantasyland, and the Jungle Cruise in Adventureland to measure your child's reaction to unfamiliar sights and

> You know I scream a lot on roller coasters, but did you know — Liliane
> that I don't leave my feet on the floor during the *It's Tough to Be a Bug!* 3-D show at the Animal Kingdom? Well, now you know I do not like bugs, and they sting too; they do, they do.

sounds. If your child takes these in stride, try Pirates of the Caribbean. Try the Astro Orbiter in Tomorrowland, the Mad Tea Party in Fantasyland, or The Barnstormer at Goofy's Wiseacres Farm in Mickey's Toontown Fair to observe how your child tolerates certain ride speeds and motions.

Do not assume that because an attraction is a theater presentation it will not frighten your child. Trust us on this one. An attraction does not have to be moving to trigger unmitigated, panic-induced hysteria. Rides such as the Big Thunder Mountain Railroad and Splash Mountain may look scary, but they do not have even one-fiftieth the potential for terrorizing children as do theater attractions such as *Stitch's Great Escape!*

2. BE ATTUNED TO PEER AND PARENT PRESSURE Sometimes young children will rise above their anxiety in an effort to please parents or siblings. This doesn't necessarily indicate a mastery of fear, much less enjoyment. If children leave a ride in apparently good shape, ask if they would like to go on it again (not necessarily now, but sometime). The response usually will indicate how much they actually enjoyed the experience. There's a big difference between having a good time and just mustering the courage to get through.

3. ENCOURAGE AND EMPATHIZE Evaluating a child's capacity to handle the visual and tactile effects of Walt Disney World requires patience, understanding, and experimentation. Each of us, after all, has our own demons. If a child balks at or is frightened by a ride, respond constructively. Let your children know that lots of people, adults and children, are scared by what they see and feel. Help them understand that it's OK if they get frightened and that their fear doesn't lessen your love or respect. Take pains not to compound the discomfort by making a child feel inadequate; try not to undermine self-esteem, impugn courage, or ridicule. Most of all, don't induce guilt by suggesting the child's trepidation might be ruining the family's fun. It is also sometimes necessary to restrain older siblings' taunting or teasing.

A visit to Walt Disney World is more than just an outing or an adventure for a young child. It's a testing experience, a sort of controlled rite of passage. If you help your little one work through the challenges, the time can be immeasurably rewarding and a bonding experience for you both.

The Fright Factor

Of course, each youngster is different, but there are eight attraction elements that alone or combined can push a child's buttons:

While there is no certain way to know what will scare your kids or what will garner a big smile, many rides are so intense that they can even eat Liliane adults. I make a huge detour around The Twilight Zone Tower of Terror or Space Mountain, but I can't get enough of Star Tours, Mission: SPACE, and the Kali River Rapids—and I have survived the Mad Tea Party and Expedition Everest. Parents know their children best. I do remember braving The Twilight Zone Tower of Terror once because I felt that I could not deprive my 10-year-old just because I was a chicken. I didn't let on that this was not my cup of tea. My prayers to exit the attraction were answered when he asked me shyly if we could ask a cast member to get out. The request was granted instantly by both me and the cast member.

1. NAME OF THE ATTRACTION Young children will naturally be apprehensive about something called "The Haunted Mansion" or "The Twilight Zone Tower of Terror."

2. VISUAL IMPACT OF THE ATTRACTION FROM OUTSIDE Big Thunder Mountain Railroad and Splash Mountain look scary enough to give even adults second thoughts, and they visually terrify many young children.

3. VISUAL IMPACT OF THE INDOOR QUEUING AREA Pirates of the Caribbean's caves and dungeons and The Haunted Mansion's "stretch rooms" can frighten kids even before they board the ride.

4. INTENSITY OF THE ATTRACTION Some attractions are overwhelming, inundating the senses with sights, sounds, movement, and even smell. *It's Tough to Be a Bug!* in the Animal Kingdom (no pun intended), for example, combines loud sounds, lasers, lights, and 3-D cinematography to create a total sensory experience. For some preschoolers, this is two or three senses too many.

5. VISUAL IMPACT OF THE ATTRACTION ITSELF Sights in various attractions range from falling boulders to lurking buzzards, from grazing dinosaurs to attacking white blood cells. What one child calmly absorbs may scare the bejeebers out of another.

6. DARK Many Disney World attractions operate indoors in the dark. For some children, darkness alone triggers fear. A child who is frightened on one dark ride (Snow White's Scary Adventures, for example) may be unwilling to try other indoor rides.

7. THE RIDE ITSELF; THE TACTILE EXPERIENCE Some rides are wild enough to cause motion sickness, to wrench backs, and to discombobulate patrons of any age.

8. LOUD The sound levels in some attractions and live shows are so loud that younger children flip out even though the general content of the presentation is quite benign. For toddlers and preschoolers especially, it's good to have a pair of earplugs handy.

Disney Orientation Course

We receive many tips from parents telling how they prepared their young children for the Disney experience. A common strategy is to acquaint children with the characters and stories behind the attractions by reading Disney books and watching Disney DVDs at home. A more direct approach is to watch Walt Disney World travel DVDs that show the attractions. You can order the free Disney Parks Vacation Planning Kit and DVD by calling Disney reservations at ☎ 407-824-8000, or log on to **disneyworld.disney.go.com** and click on "FREE Vacation Planning DVD" at the top of the page to order. Ignore all prompts, and the phone system will assume that you're on a rotary phone and patch you through to a live person (though you may be on hold a couple minutes). This DVD isn't as comprehensive as travelogues you might rent, but it's adequate for giving your kids a sense of what they'll see. Also, as discussed in a previous chapter, you can find a video of every Disney attraction on **youtube.com.**

A MAGICAL TIME FOR MOM AND DAD

OK, LILIANE WRITING HERE. Because Bob's idea of a romantic evening is watching ESPN's Monday Night Football on the sofa with his honey instead of sitting in his La-Z-Boy, I'm going to tackle this subject solo. Let's face it: We all know that moms and dads deserve some special time. But the reality on the ground is that the kids come first. And when the day is over, mom and dad are way too tired to think about having a special evening alone. It is difficult enough to catch a movie or go out for a romantic dinner in our hometowns, so how realistic is a romantic parents' night out while on vacation at Walt Disney World?

The answer is: No planning, no romance! With a little magic and some advance preparation, you can make it happen. Here we offer a few suggestions.

Staying at a hotel that offers great kids' programs is a big plus. Consider signing up small children for a half-day program with lunch or dinner while you enjoy your resort. Go to the pool and read a book, and then have a meal in calm and peace. Rent a bike, a boat, or just take off outside the World. This is also a great opportunity to enjoy the thrill rides you passed up when you were busy worshipping at the altar of Dumbo.

PREPARING YOUR CHILDREN TO MEET THE CHARACTERS

ALMOST ALL DISNEY CHARACTERS ARE QUITE LARGE; several, like Br'er Bear, are huge! Young children don't expect this and can be intimidated if not terrified. Discuss the characters with your children before you go. If there is a high school or college with a costumed mascot nearby, arrange to let your kids check it out. If not, then Santa Claus or the Easter Bunny will do.

On the first encounter at Walt Disney World, don't thrust your child at the character. Allow the little one to deal with this big thing from whatever distance feels safe to him or her. If two adults are present, one should stay near the youngster while the other approaches the character and demonstrates that it's safe and friendly. Some kids warm to the characters immediately; some never do. Most take a little time and several encounters.

At Walt Disney World there are two kinds of characters: those whose costume includes a face-covering headpiece (animal characters and such humanlike characters as Captain Hook) and "face characters," those who resemble the characters so no mask or headpiece is necessary. Face characters include Mary Poppins, Ariel, Belle, Jasmine, Aladdin, Cinderella, Snow White, Tarzan, Esmerelda, and Prince Charming.

Tell children in advance that headpiece characters don't talk.

Ian

Only face characters speak. Headpiece characters don't make noises of any kind. Because cast members couldn't possibly imitate the distinctive cinema voice of the character, Disney has determined that it's more effective to keep them silent. Lack of speech notwithstanding, headpiece characters are very warm and responsive, and communicate very effectively with gestures. Disney is currently testing new technology that will allow headpiece characters to speak. It is assumed that the technology is a portable version of that used in *Turtle Talk With Crush* at Epcot, where an animated turtle converses in real time with audience members. A less advanced option is a menu-driven selection of recorded phrases such as, "Hi, I'm Mickey," or "What's your name?"

Some character costumes are cumbersome and give cast members very poor visibility. (Eye holes frequently are in the mouth of the costume or even on the neck or chest.) This means characters are somewhat clumsy and have limited sight. Children who approach the character from the back or side may not be noticed, even if the child touches the character. It's possible in this situation for the character to accidentally step on the child or knock him or her down. It's best for a child to approach a character from the front, but occasionally not even this works. Duck characters (such as Donald, Daisy, and Uncle Scrooge), for example, have to peer around their bills.

Liliane

If a character appears to be ignoring your child, pick up your child and hold him or her in front of the character until the character responds.

It's OK for your child to touch, pat, or hug the character. Understanding the unpredictability of children, the character will keep his feet very still, particularly refraining from moving backward or sideways. Most characters will sign autographs or pose for pictures.

Another great way to show young kids how the characters appear in the parks is to rent or buy a Disney SingAlong Songs DVD. Not unlike similar Barney videos, they are children's sing-along programs showing the costumed Disney characters interacting with real kids. At a minimum the shows will give your kids a sense of how big the Disney characters are. The best two are *Flik's Musical Adventure* SingAlong Songs at Disney's Animal Kingdom and *Campout* SingAlong Songs at Walt Disney World. *It's a Small World* SingAlong Songs—Disneyland Fun is a third offering, but then there's THAT SONG. No sense turning your brain to mush before even leaving home.

If your child wants to collect character autographs, it's a good idea to carry a pen the width of a magic marker. Costumes make it exceedingly difficult for characters to wield a pen, so the bigger the writing instrument, the better.

Bob

ROLE-PLAYING

ESPECIALLY FOR YOUNGER CHILDREN, role-playing is a great way to inculcate vital lessons concerning safety, contingency situations, and potential danger. Play "what would you do if" for a variety of scenarios, including getting lost, being approached by strangers, getting help if mommy is sick, and so on. Children have incredible recall when it comes to role-playing with siblings and parents, and are much more likely to respond appropriately in an actual situation than they will if the same information is presented in a lecture.

PHYSICAL PREPARATION

YOU'LL FIND THAT SOME PHYSICAL CONDITIONING, coupled with a realistic sense of the toll that Walt Disney World takes on your body, will preclude falling apart in the middle of your vacation. As one of our readers put it, "If you pay attention to eat, heat, feet, and sleep, you'll be OK."

As you contemplate the stamina of your family, it's important to understand that somebody is going to run out of steam first, and when they do, the whole family will be affected. Sometimes a cold drink or a snack will revive the flagging member. Sometimes, however, no amount of cajoling or treats will work. In this situation it's crucial that you recognize that the child, grandparent, or spouse is at the end of his or her rope. The correct decision is to get them back to the hotel. Pushing the exhausted beyond their capacity will spoil the day for them—and you. Accept that stamina and energy levels vary and be prepared to administer to members of your family who poop out. One more thing: no guilt trips. "We've driven a thousand miles to take you to Disney World and now you're going to ruin everything!" is not an appropriate response.

THE AGONY OF THE FEET

HERE'S A LITTLE FACTOID TO CHEW ON: If you spend a day at Epcot and visit both sections of the park, you will walk 5–9 miles! The walking, however, will be nothing like a 5-mile hike in the woods. At Epcot (and the other Disney parks as well) you will be in direct sunlight most of the time, will have to navigate through huge jostling crowds, will be walking on hot pavement, and will have to endure waits in line between bursts of walking. The bottom line, if you haven't figured it out, is that Disney theme parks (especially in the summer) are not for wimps!

Though most children are active, their normal play usually doesn't condition them for the exertion of touring a Disney theme park. We recommend starting a program of family walks six weeks or more before your trip. A Pennsylvania mom who did just that offers the following:

If your children (or you, for that matter) do not consider it cool to wear socks, get over it! Bare feet, whether encased in Nikes, Weejuns, Docksides, or Birkenstocks, will turn into lumps of throbbing red meat if you tackle a Disney park without socks.

We had our 6-year-old begin walking with us a bit every day one month before leaving—when we arrived [at Walt Disney World], her little legs could carry her and she had a lot of stamina.

The first thing you need to do, immediately after making your hotel reservation, is to get thee to a footery. Take the whole family to a shoe store and buy each member the best pair of walking, hiking, or running shoes you can afford. Wear exactly the kind of socks to try on the shoes that you will wear when using them to hike. Do not under any circumstances attempt to tour Walt Disney World shod in sandals, flip-flops, loafers, or any kind of high heel or platform shoe.

Good socks are as important as good shoes. When you walk, your feet sweat like a mule in a peat bog, and moisture increases friction. To minimize friction, wear a pair of SmartWool or Coolmax hiking socks, available at most outdoor retail (camping equipment) stores. To further combat moisture, dust your feet with some antifungal powder.

All right, now you've got some good shoes and socks. The next thing to do is to break the shoes in. You can accomplish this painlessly by wearing the shoes in the course of normal activities for about three weeks.

Once the shoes are broken in, it's time to start walking. The whole family will need to toughen up their feet and build endurance. As you begin, remember that little people have little strides, and though your 6-year-old may create the appearance of running circles around you, consider that (1) he won't have the stamina to go at that pace very long, and (2) more to the point, he probably has to take two strides or so to every one of yours to keep up when you walk together.

Be sure to give your kids adequate recovery time between training walks
Liliane
(48 hours will usually be enough), however, or you'll make the problem worse.

Start by taking short walks around the neighborhood, walking on pavement, and increasing the distance about a quarter of a mile on each outing. Older children will shape up quickly. Younger children should build endurance more slowly and incrementally. Increase distance until you can manage a 6- or 7-mile hike without requiring CPR. And remember, you're not training to be able to walk 6 or 7 miles just once; at Walt Disney World you will be hiking 5–9 miles or more almost *every* day. So unless you plan to crash after the first day, you've got to prepare your feet to walk long distances for three to five consecutive days.

Let's be honest and admit up front that not all feet are created equal. Some folks are blessed with really tough feet, whereas the feet of others sprout blisters if you look at them sideways. Assuming that there's nothing wrong with either shoes or socks, a few brisk walks will clue you in to what kind of feet your family have. If you have a tenderfoot in your family, walks of incrementally increased distances will usually toughen up his or her feet to some extent. For those whose feet refuse to toughen, your only alternative is preventive care. After several walks, you will know where your tenderfoot tends to develop blisters. If you can anticipate where blisters will develop, you can cover sensitive spots in advance with moleskin, a friction-resistant adhesive dressing.

If your child is age 8 or younger, we recommend regular feet
Bob
inspections whether he or she understands the hot spot idea or not. Even the brightest and most well-intentioned child will fail to sound off when distracted.

When you initiate your walking program, teach your children to tell you if they feel a "hot spot" on their feet. This is the warning that a blister is developing. If your kids are too young, too oblivious, too preoccupied, or don't understand the concept, your best bet is to make regular foot checks. Have your children remove their shoes and socks and present their feet for inspection. Look for red spots and blisters, and ask if they have any places on their feet that hurt.

During your conditioning, and also at Walt Disney World, carry a foot emergency kit in your day pack or hip pack. The kit should contain gauze, Betadine antibiotic ointment, moleskin, an assortment of Band-Aid Advance Healing Blister Cushions, scissors, a sewing needle or some such to drain blisters, as well as matches to sterilize the needle. An extra pair of dry socks and foot powder are optional.

If you discover a hot spot, dry the foot and cover the spot immediately with moleskin. Cut the covering large enough to cover the skin surrounding the hot spot. If you find that a blister has fully or partially developed, first air out and dry the foot. Next, using your sterile needle, drain the fluid, but do not remove the top skin. Clean the area with antiseptic cleaner, and place a blister bandage over the blister. If you do not have moleskin or blister bandages, do not try to cover the hot spot or blister with regular Band-Aid bandages. Regular ones slip and wad up.

If you have a child who will physically fit in a stroller, rent one, no matter how well conditioned your family is.

Liliane

A stroller will provide the child the option of walking or riding, and, if he collapses, you won't have to carry him. Even if your child hardly uses the stroller at all, it serves as a convenient rolling depository for water bottles and other stuff you may not feel like carrying. Strollers at Walt Disney World are covered in detail on pages 255–258.

SLEEP, REST, AND RELAXATION

OK, WE KNOW THAT THIS SECTION is about physical preparation *before you go*, but this concept is so absolutely critical that we need to tattoo it on your brain right now.

Physical conditioning is important but is *not* a substitute for adequate rest. Even marathon runners need recovery time. If you push too hard and try to do too much, you'll either crash or, at a minimum, turn what should be fun into an ordeal. Rest means plenty of sleep at night, naps during the afternoon on most days, and planned breaks in your vacation itinerary. And don't forget that the brain needs rest and relaxation as well as the body. The stimulation inherent in touring a Disney theme park is enough to put many children and some adults into system overload. It is imperative that you remove your family from this unremitting assault on the senses, preferably for part of each day, and do something relaxing and quiet like swimming or reading.

The theme parks are huge; don't try to see everything in one day. Tour in early morning and return to your hotel around 11:30 a.m. for

lunch, a swim, and a nap. Even during off-season, when the crowds are smaller and the temperature more pleasant, the size of the major theme parks will exhaust most children under age 8 by lunchtime. Return to the park in late afternoon or early evening and continue touring. A family from Texas underlines the importance of naps and rest:

> *Despite not following any of your "tours," we did follow the theme of visiting a specific park in the morning, leaving midafternoon for either a nap back at the room or a trip to the pool, and then returning to one of the parks in the evening. On the few occasions when we skipped your advice, I was muttering to myself by dinner. I can't tell you what I was muttering . . .*

When it comes to naps, this mom does not mince words:

> *One last thing for parents of small kids—take the book's advice and get out of the park and take the nap, take the nap, TAKE THE NAP! Never in my life have I seen so many parents screaming at, ridiculing, or slapping their kids. (What a vacation!) Walt Disney World is overwhelming for kids and adults. Even though the rental strollers recline for sleeping, we noticed that most of the toddlers and preschoolers*

If your kids are little and don't mind a hairdo change, consider getting them a short haircut before Liliane you leave home. Not only will they be cooler and more comfortable, but—especially with your girls—you'll save them (and yourselves) the hassle of tangles and about 20 minutes of foo-fooing a day. Don't try this with your confident teen or preteen, though. Braids will do the trick for girls, and your Mick Jagger in the party will be grateful for the bandanna or sports headband, unless of course the hair is meant to keep the monsters and dinosaurs out of sight!

didn't give up and sleep until 5 p.m., several hours after the fun had worn off, and right about the time their parents wanted them to be awake and polite in a restaurant.

A mom from Rochester, New York, was equally adamant:

[You] absolutely must rest during the day. Kids went 8 a.m.–9 p.m. in the Magic Kingdom. Kids did great that day, but we were all completely worthless the next day. Definitely must pace yourself. Don't ever try to do two full days of park sightseeing in a row. Rest during the day. Go to a water park or sleep in every other day.

If you plan to return to your hotel in midday and would like your room made up, let housekeeping know.

DEVELOPING *a* GOOD PLAN

ALLOW YOUR CHILDREN TO PARTICIPATE in the planning of your time at Walt Disney World. Guide them diplomatically through the options, establishing advance decisions about what to do each day and how the day will be structured. Begin with your trip *to* Walt Disney World, deciding what time to depart, who sits by the window, whether to stop for meals or eat in the car, and so on. For the Walt Disney World part of your vacation, build consensus for wake-up call, bedtime, and building naps into the itinerary, and establish ground rules for eating, buying refreshments, and shopping. Determine the order for visiting the different theme parks and make a list of "must-see" attractions. To help you with filling in the blanks of your days, and especially to prevent you from spending most of your time standing in line, we offer a number of field-tested touring plans. The plans are designed to minimize your waiting time at each park by providing step-by-step itineraries that route you counter to the flow of traffic. The plans are explained in detail on pages 224–230.

To keep your thinking fresh and to adequately cover all bases, develop your plan in a series of family meetings no longer than 30 minutes each. You'll discover that all members of the family will devote a lot of thought to the plan both in and between meetings. Don't try to anticipate every conceivable contingency, or you'll end up with something as detailed and unworkable as the tax code.

Generally it's better to just sketch in the broad strokes on the master plan. The detail of what to do when you actually arrive at the park can be decided the night before you go or with the help of one of our touring plans once you get there. Above all, be flexible. One important caveat, however: Make sure you keep any promises or agreements that you make when planning. They may not seem important to you, but they will to your children, who will remember for a long, long time that you let them down.

The more that you can agree to and nail down in advance, the less potential you'll have for disagreement and confrontation once you arrive. Because children are more comfortable with the tangible than the conceptual, and also because they sometimes have short memories, we recommend typing up all of your decisions and agreements and providing a copy to each child. Create a fun document, not a legalistic one. You'll find that your children will review it in anticipation of all the things they will see and do, will consult it often, and will even read it to their younger siblings.

By now you're probably wondering what one of these documents looks like, so here's a sample. Incidentally, this itinerary reflects the preferences of its creators, the Langston family, and is not meant to be offered as an example of an ideal itinerary. It does, however, incorporate many of our most basic and strongly held recommendations, such as setting limits and guidelines in advance, getting enough rest, getting to the theme parks early, touring the theme parks in shorter visits with naps and swimming in between, and saving time and money by having a cooler full of food for breakfast. As you will see, the Langstons go pretty much full-tilt without much unstructured time and will probably be exhausted by the time they get home, but that's their choice. One more thing—the Langstons visited Walt Disney World in late June, when all of the theme parks stay open late.

THE GREAT WALT DISNEY WORLD EXPEDITION

CO-CAPTAINS Mary and Jack Langston

TEAM MEMBERS Lynn and Jimmy Langston

EXPEDITION FUNDING The main Expedition Fund will cover everything except personal purchases. Each team member will receive $40 for souvenirs and personal purchases. Anything above $40 will be paid for by team members with their own money.

EXPEDITION GEAR Each team member will wear an official expedition T-shirt and carry a hip pack.

PREDEPARTURE Jack makes priority seating arrangements at Walt Disney World restaurants. Mary, Lynn, and Jimmy make up trail mix and other snacks for the hip packs.

Notice that the Langstons' itinerary on pages 198–201 provides minimal structure and maximum flexibility. It specifies which park the family will tour each day without attempting to nail down exactly what the family will do there. No matter how detailed your itinerary is, be prepared for surprises at Walt Disney World, both good and bad. If an unforeseen event renders part of the plan useless or impractical, just roll with it. And always remember that it's your itinerary; you created it, and you can change it. Just try to make any changes the result of family discussion, and be especially careful not to scrap an element of the plan that your children perceive as something you promised them.

Langston Family Itinerary

DAY 1: FRIDAY

6:30 p.m. . . . . Dinner

After dinner . . . . Pack car

10 p.m. . . . . Lights out

DAY 2: SATURDAY

7 a.m. . . . . Wake up!

7:15 a.m. . . . . Breakfast

8 a.m. Depart Chicago for Hampton Inn, Chattanooga;
Confirmation # DE56432; Lynn rides shotgun

About noon . . . . Stop for lunch; Jimmy picks restaurant

7 p.m. . . . . Dinner

9:30 p.m. . . . . Lights out

DAY 3: SUNDAY

7 a.m. . . . . Wake up!

7:30 a.m. . . . . Breakfast

8:15 a.m. . Depart Chattanooga for Walt Disney World, Port Orleans Resort–
Riverside; Confirmation # L124532; Jimmy rides shotgun

About noon . . . . Stop for lunch; Lynn picks restaurant

5 p.m. . . . . Check in, buy park admissions, and unpack

6–7 p.m. . . . . Mary and Jimmy shop for breakfast food for cooler

7:15 p.m. . . . . Dinner at Boatwright's at Port Orleans Riverside

After dinner . . . . Walk along Bonnet Creek

10 p.m. . . . . Lights out

Routines That Travel

If when at home you observe certain routines—for example, reading a book before bed or having a bath first thing in the morning—try to incorporate these familiar activities into your vacation schedule. They will provide your children with a sense of security and normalcy.

Maintaining a normal routine is especially important with toddlers, as a mother of two from Lawrenceville, Georgia, relates:

> *The first day, we tried an early start, so we woke the children (ages 2 and 4) and hurried them to get going. BAD IDEA with toddlers. This put them off schedule for naps and meals the rest of the day. It is best to let young ones stay on their regular schedule and see Disney at their own pace, and you'll have much more fun.*

DAY 4: MONDAY

7 a.m. . . . . .Wake up! Cold breakfast from cooler in room

8 a.m. . . . . Depart room to catch bus for Epcot

Noon. . . . . Lunch at Epcot

1 p.m. . . . . Return to hotel for swimming and a nap

5 p.m. . . . . Return to Epcot for touring, dinner, and *IllumiNations*

9:30 p.m. . . . . .Return to hotel

10:30 p.m. . . . . Lights out

DAY 5: TUESDAY

7 a.m. . . . . .Wake up! Cold breakfast from cooler in room

7:45 a.m. . . . . Depart room to catch bus for Disney's Hollywood Studios

Noon. . . . . .Lunch at Studios

2:30 p.m. . . . . Return to hotel for swimming and a nap

6 p.m. . . . . .Drive to dinner at cafe at Wilderness Lodge

7:30 p.m. . . . . Return to Studios via car for touring and *Fantasmic!*

10 p.m. . . . . .Return to hotel

11 p.m. . . . . Lights out

DAY 6: WEDNESDAY

ZZZZZZ! . . . . Lazy morning—sleep in!

10:30 a.m. . . . . Late-morning swim

Noon. . . . . Lunch at Riverside Mill Food Court at Port Orleans

1 p.m. . . . . Depart room to catch bus for Animal Kingdom;
tour until Animal Kingdom closes

We offer a Sleepyhead Touring Plan for each park, perfect for families like this reader's.

LOGISTIC PREPARATION

WHEN WE RECENTLY LAUNCHED into our spiel about good logistic preparation for a Walt Disney World vacation, a friend from Indianapolis said, "Wait, what's the big deal? You pack clothes, a few games for the car, then go!" So OK, we confess, that will work, but life can be sweeter and the vacation smoother (as well as less expensive) with the right gear.

Langston Family Itinerary (continued)

DAY 6: WEDNESDAY (CONTINUED)

8 p.m. . . . . Dinner at Rainforest Cafe at Animal Kingdom

9:15 p.m. . . . . Return to hotel via bus

10:30 p.m. . . . . Lights out

DAY 7: THURSDAY

6 a.m. . . . . Wake up! Cold breakfast from cooler in room

6:45 a.m. . . . . Depart via bus for early entry at Magic Kingdom

11:30 a.m. . . . . Return to hotel for lunch, swimming, and a nap

4:45 p.m. . . . . Drive to Contemporary for dinner at Chef Mickey's

6:15 p.m. . . . . Walk from the Contemporary to the Magic Kingdom
for more touring, fireworks, and parade

11 p.m. . . . . Return to Contemporary via walkway or monorail;
get car, and return to hotel

11:45 p.m. . . . . Lights out

DAY 8: FRIDAY

8 a.m. . . . . Wake up! Cold breakfast from cooler in room

8:40 a.m. . . . . Drive to Blizzard Beach water park

Noon. . . . . Lunch at Blizzard Beach

CLOTHING

LET'S START WITH CLOTHES. We recommend springing for vacation uniforms. Buy for each child several sets of jeans (or shorts) and T-shirts, all matching, and all the same. For a one-week trip, as an example, get each child three or so pairs of khaki shorts, three or so light yellow T-shirts, three pairs of SmartWool or Coolmax hiking socks. What's the point? First, you don't have to play fashion designer, coordinating a week's worth of stylish combos. Each morning the kids put on their uniform. It's simple, it's time-saving, and there are no decisions to make or arguments about what to wear. Second, uniforms make your children easier to spot and keep together in the theme parks. Third, the uniforms give your family, as well as the vacation itself, some added identity. If you're like the Langston family who created the sample itinerary in the section on organizational planning, you might go so far as to create a logo for the trip to be printed on the shirts.

Give your teens the job of coming up with the logo for your shirts. They will love being the family designers.

Liliane

When it comes to buying your uniforms, we have a few suggestions. Purchase well-made, durable shorts or jeans that will serve your children well beyond the vacation. Active children can never have too many pairs

1:30 p.m. . . . . Return to hotel for nap and packing

4 p.m. . . . . .Revisit favorite park or do whatever we want

Dinner . . . . .When and where we decide

10 p.m. . . . . .Return to hotel

10:30 p.m. . . . . Lights out

DAY 9: SATURDAY

7:30 a.m. . . . . Wake up!

8:30 a.m. . . . . After fast-food breakfast, depart for Executive Inn,
Nashville; Confirmation # SD234; Lynn rides shotgun

About noon . . . . .Stop for lunch; Jimmy picks restaurant

7 p.m. . . . . .Dinner

10 p.m. . . . . Lights out

DAY 10: SUNDAY

7 a.m. . . . . Wake up!

7:45 a.m. . . . . Depart for home after fast-food breakfast;
Jimmy rides shotgun

About noon . . . . Stop for lunch; Lynn picks restaurant

4:30 p.m. . . . . .Home sweet home!

of shorts or jeans. As far as the T-shirts go, buy short-sleeve shirts in light colors for warm weather or long-sleeve, darker-colored T-shirts for cooler weather. We suggest that you purchase your colored shirts from a local T-shirt printing company. Cleverly listed under "T-shirts" (sometimes under "Screen Printing") in the Yellow Pages, these firms will be happy to sell you either printed T-shirts or unprinted T-shirts (called "blanks") with long or short sleeves. You can select from a wide choice of colors not generally available in retail clothing stores and will not have to worry about finding the sizes you need. Plus, the shirts will cost a fraction of what a clothing retailer would charge. Most shirts come in the more durable 100% cotton or in the more wrinkle-resistant 50% cotton and 50% polyester (50/50s). The cotton shirts are a little cooler and more comfortable in hot, humid weather. The 50/50s dry a bit faster if they get wet.

Consider affixing labels to the clothing of young children to help in the event that they become separated from the family.

LABELS A great idea, especially for younger children, is to attach labels with your family name, hometown, the name of your hotel, the dates of your stay, and your cell phone number inside the shirt. For example:

Carlton Family of Frankfort, KY; Port Orleans Riverside
May 5–12; 502-662-2108

Instruct your smaller children to show the label to an adult if they get separated from you. Elimination of the child's first name (which most children of talking age can articulate in any event) allows you to order labels that are all the same, that can be used by anyone in the family, and that can also be affixed to such easily lost items as caps, hats, jackets, hip packs, ponchos, and umbrellas. If fooling with labels sounds like too much of a hassle, check out "When Kids Get Lost" (pages 258–260) for some alternatives.

DRESSING FOR COOLER WEATHER Central Florida experiences temperatures all over the scale from November through March, so it could be a bit chilly if you visit during those months. Our suggestion is to layer: For example, a breathable, waterproof or water-resistant Windbreaker over a light, long-sleeved polypropylene shirt over a long-sleeved T-shirt. As with the baffles of a sleeping bag or down coat, it is the air trapped between the layers that keeps you warm. If all the layers are thin, you won't be left with something bulky to cart around if you want to pull one or more off. Later in this section, we'll advocate wearing a hip pack. Each layer should be sufficiently compatible to fit easily in that hip pack, along with whatever else is in it.

ACCESSORIES

I (BOB) WANTED TO CALL THIS PART "Belts and Stuff," but Liliane (who obviously spends a lot of time at Macy's) thought "Accessories" put a finer point on it. In any event, we recommend pants for your children with reinforced elastic waistbands that eliminate the need to wear a belt (one less thing to find when you're trying to leave). If your children like belts or want to carry an item suspended from their belts, buy them military-style 1-inch-wide web belts at any Army/ Navy surplus or camping equipment store. The belts weigh less than half as much as leather, are cooler, and are washable.

SUNGLASSES The Florida sun is so bright and the glare so blinding that we recommend sunglasses for each family member. For children and adults of all ages, a good accessory item is a polypropylene eyeglass strap for spectacles or sunglasses. The best models have a little device for adjusting the amount of slack in the strap. This allows your child to comfortably hang sunglasses from his or her neck when indoors or, alternately, to secure them fast to his or her head while experiencing a fast ride outdoors.

HIP PACKS AND WALLETS Unless you are touring with an infant or toddler, the largest thing anyone in your family should carry is a hip pack, or fanny pack. Each adult and child should have one. They should be large enough to carry at least a half-day's worth of snacks, as well as other items deemed necessary (lip balm, bandanna, antibacterial hand

gel, and so on), and still have enough room left to stash a hat, poncho, or light Windbreaker. We recommend buying full-size hip packs as opposed to small, child-size hip packs at outdoor retailers. The packs are light; can be made to fit any child large enough to tote a hip pack; have slip-resistant, comfortable, wide belting; and will last for years.

Do not carry billfolds or wallets, car keys, Disney Resort IDs, or room keys in your hip packs. We usually give this advice because hip packs are vulnerable to thieves (who snip them off and run), but pickpocketing and theft are not all that common at Walt Disney World. In this instance, the advice stems from a tendency of children to inadvertently drop their wallet in the process of rummaging around in their hip packs for snacks and other items.

You should weed through your billfold and remove to a safe place anything that you will not need on your vacation (family photos, local library card, department store credit

Unless you advise the front desk to the contrary, all Disney resort room keys can be used for park admission and as credit cards. They are definitely something you don't want to lose. Our advice is to void the charge privileges on your preteen children's cards, and then collect them and put them together someplace safe when not in use.

cards, business cards, movie rental ID cards, and so on). In addition to having a lighter wallet to lug around, you will decrease your exposure in the event that your wallet is lost or stolen. When we are working at Walt Disney World, we carry a small profile billfold with a driver's license, a credit card, our Disney Resort room key, and a small amount of cash. Think about it: You don't need anything else.

DAY PACKS We see a lot of folks at Walt Disney World carrying day packs (that is, small, frameless backpacks) and/or water bottle belts that strap around the waist. Day packs might be a good choice if you plan to carry a lot of camera equipment or if you need to carry baby supplies on your person. Otherwise, try to travel as light as possible. Packs are hot, cumbersome, not very secure, and must be removed every time you get on a ride or sit down for a show. Hip packs, by way of contrast, can simply be rotated around the waist from your back to your abdomen if you need to sit down. Additionally, our observation has been that the contents of one day pack can usually be redistributed to two or so hip packs (except in the case of camera equipment).

CAPS Caps protect young eyes from damaging ultraviolet rays, but the lifespan of a child's hat is usually pretty short. Simply put, kids pull caps on and off as they enter and exit attractions, restrooms, and restaurants, and . . . big surprise, they lose them. In fact, they lose them by the thousands. You could provide a ball cap for every Little Leaguer in America from the caps that are lost at Walt Disney World each summer.

Equip each child with a big bandanna. Although bandannas come in handy for wiping noses, scouring ice cream from chins and mouths, and dabbing sweat from the forehead, they can also be tied around the neck to protect from sunburn.

If your children are partial to caps, there is a device sold at ski and camping supply stores that might increase the likelihood of the cap returning home with the child. Essentially, it's a short, light cord with little alligator clips on both ends. Hook one clip to the shirt collar and the other to the hat. It's a great little invention. Bob uses one when he skis in case his ball cap blows off.

RAINGEAR Rain in central Florida is a fact of life, although persistent rain day after day is unusual (it is the Sunshine State, after all!). Our suggestion is to check out The Weather Channel or weather forecasts on the Internet for three or so days before you leave home to see if there are any major storm systems heading for central Florida. Weather forecasting has improved to the extent that predictions concerning systems and fronts four to seven days out are now pretty reliable. If it appears that you might see some rough weather during your visit, you're better off bringing rain gear from home. If, however, nothing big is on the horizon weatherwise, you can take your chances.

We at the *Unofficial Guide* usually do not bring rain gear. First, scattered thundershowers are more the norm than are prolonged periods of rain. Second, raingear is pretty cheap at Walt Disney World, especially the ponchos that sell for about $8 per adult, $7 per child, available in seemingly every retail shop. Third, in the theme parks, a surprising number of attractions and queuing areas are under cover. Fourth, we prefer to travel light.

If you do find yourself in a big storm, however, you'll want to have both a poncho and an umbrella. As one *Unofficial* reader put it, "Umbrellas make the rain much more bearable. When rain isn't beating down on your ponchoed head, it's easier to ignore."

An advantage of buying ponchos before you leave home is that you can choose the color. At Walt Disney World all the ponchos are clear, and it's quite a sight when 30,000 differently clad individuals suddenly transform themselves into what looks like an army of really big larvae. If your family is wearing blue ponchos, they'll be easier to spot.

And consider this tip from a Memphis, Tennessee, mom:

Scotchgard your shoes. The difference is unbelievable.

MISCELLANEOUS ITEMS

MEDICATION Some parents of hyperactive children on medication discontinue or decrease the child's normal dosage at the end of the school year. If you have such a child, be aware that Walt Disney World might overly stimulate him or her. Consult your physician before altering your child's medication regimen. Also, if your child has attention deficit disorder, remember that especially loud sounds can drive him or her right up the wall. Unfortunately, some Disney theater attractions are almost unbearably loud.

SUNSCREEN Overheating and sunburn are among the most common problems of younger children at Walt Disney World. Carry and use sunscreen of SPF 15 or higher. Be sure to put some on children in strollers, even if the stroller has a canopy. Some of the worst cases of sunburn we've seen were on the exposed foreheads and feet of toddlers and infants in strollers. Protect skin from overexposure. To avoid overheating, rest regularly in the shade or in an air-conditioned restaurant or show.

Often little ones fall asleep in their strollers (hallelujah!). Bring a large lightweight cloth to drape over the stroller to cover your child from the sun. A few clothespins will keep it in place.

— Liliane

WATER BOTTLES Don't count on keeping young children hydrated with soft drinks and stops at water fountains. Long lines may hamper buying refreshments, and fountains may not be handy. Furthermore, excited children may not realize or tell you that they're thirsty or hot. We recommend renting a stroller for children age 6 and younger and carrying plastic bottles of water. Plastic squeeze bottles with caps run about $3 in all major parks.

COOLERS AND MINI-FRIDGES If you drive to Walt Disney World, bring two coolers: a small one for drinks in the car and a large one for the hotel room. If you fly and rent a car, stop and purchase a large Styrofoam

Don't Let the Sun See You Frying

Health-and-science writer Avery Hurt sheds some light on the variety of products and often confusing methods for avoiding sunburn.

No matter what time of year you travel to Walt Disney World, don't make the mistake of underestimating the Florida sun. Even in the winter, it can be a problem. And in the summer, old Sol can be wicked indeed.

The most obvious precaution is to slather on the sunscreen. But when you get to the drugstore or discount shop to load up, you may discover that choosing a product is anything but simple. Cream? Lotion? Spray? Waterproof or not? And what's this SPF number all about, anyway?

Making sense of sunscreen is so complex that the dilemma has precipitated lawsuits, required the amendment (and revision of amendments) of Food and Drug Administration (FDA) regulations, and confused officials almost as much as consumers. The sunscreen manufacturers, the FDA, and all of the lawyers involved may have plenty of time to duke it out, but you've got a trip planned! Don't worry. It's not as complicated as it seems. Following is some basic advice from the medical experts:

Choose a sunscreen that is convenient for you to use. Some people prefer sprays, others lotions. The form of the sunscreen doesn't matter as much as the amount of it you use and the technique of its application. Apply sunscreen a half hour before going out, and be sure to get enough on you. One ounce per application is recommended, which means that you should apply the equivalent of a full shot glass each time. The one-ounce amount is the recommendation for average adults in swimsuits; very large adults will need proportionately more. For a 1-year-old child wearing a bathing suit, figure about one-third of an ounce (10 cc) per application. An average 7-year-old child will probably take two-thirds of an ounce (20 cc). It's a good idea to measure that ounce in your hands (at home, when an ounce measure—shot glass or whatever—is handy), so that you will be familiar with what an ounce looks like in your palms. It is far more sunscreen than you tend to think.

Liliane

About two weeks before I arrive at WDW, I always ship a box to my hotel containing food, plastic cutlery, and toiletries, plus pretty much any other consumables that might come in handy during my stay. If you fly, this helps avoid overweight fees and problems with liquid restrictions for carry-on luggage.

cooler, which can be discarded at the end of the trip. If you will be without a car, rent a mini-fridge from your hotel. At Disney Value resorts, mini-refrigerators cost about $15 a day. Make sure you reserve one when you book your room. Refrigerators in all Disney Deluxe and Moderate resort rooms are free of charge. If you arrive at your room and there is no refrigerator, call housekeeping and request one. Along with free fridges, coffeemakers have also been added in the rooms.

Coolers and mini-fridges allow you to have

Be sure not to miss any spots. A few years ago, a group of researchers from Berlin journeyed to the beach to measure how well covered the beachgoers really were. It turned out that even the most dedicated sunscreen users did an abysmal job of applying their chosen brand. Most areas of skin were only sparsely covered, and areas such as the ears and the tops of feet were hardly covered at all. Be sure to get a generous covering on all exposed skin. Then re-apply (another full shot glass) every 2 hours, or after swimming or sweating. No matter what it says on the label, no sunscreen is waterproof, and water resistance is limited. And none of them last all day.

SPF stands for "sun protection factor" and is a measure of how long the protection will last. Geniuses in lab coats come up with this number by calculating how long it will take a person to burn without sunscreen (please don't volunteer me for that study) and comparing that information with how long the same person takes to burn with sunscreen. Theoretically a sunscreen with an SPF of 15 will protect you 15 times longer than if you wear no sunscreen at all.

This might make it sound like the higher the SPF the better, but studies have not borne that out. The effectiveness of the sunscreen diminishes as the number gets higher, and the initial estimate doesn't take into account the fact that during the day your sunscreen rubs off, washes off, and sweats off. In actual practice, there is very little difference in protection between an SPF of 15 or so and an SPF of 45 or 50 or greater. There is no need to spend more for higher SPF numbers. In fact, it is much safer to choose a lower (and typically less expensive) SPF (as long as it is at least 15) and apply it more often. The American Academy of Dermatology (AAD) and the American Academy of Pediatrics (AAP) both recommend an SPF of at least 15. Paying more for a higher SPF will give you very little more protection, and the false sense of security that comes with an SPF of 45 or 50 may do more harm than the (very) slight increase in protection. However, do be sure to choose a product that has "broad-spectrum coverage," meaning that it filters out both UVA and UVB rays.

breakfast in your hotel room, store snacks and lunch supplies to take to the theme parks, and supplant expensive vending machines for snacks and beverages at the hotel. To keep the contents of your cooler cold, we suggest freezing a 2-gallon milk jug full of water before you head out. In a good cooler, it will take the jug five or more days to thaw. If you buy a Styrofoam cooler in Florida, you can use bagged ice and ice from the ice machine at your hotel. Even if you have to rent a mini-fridge, you will save a bundle of cash, as well as significant time, by reducing dependence on restaurant meals and expensive snacks and drinks purchased from vendors.

FOOD PREP KIT If you plan to make sandwiches, bring along your favorite condiments and seasonings from home. A good travel kit will

Don't Let the Sun See You Frying (cont'd)

It is best to keep babies under 6 months old covered and out of the sun. However, the AAP condones a small amount of sunscreen on vulnerable areas, such as the nose and chin, when you have the baby out. Be very careful to monitor your baby, even if he or she is wearing a hat and sitting under an umbrella. The sun moves. A spot that was shady when you ordered your funnel cake might be baking by the time you've finished eating it. If your child develops a rash while using sunscreen, get the baby out of the sun, stop using the sunscreen, and call your doctor.

With older children, slather sunscreen liberally and often. Don't make the mistake of thinking that because you've coated your children in a "bazillion-SPF-water-resistant-all-day-protection-top-of-the-line-surfers-use-it-so-should-you" brand of sunscreen that you don't have to worry until dinnertime. Reapply and check for redness often. Sunburn can be sneaky. Children aren't likely to notice the mild discomfort of impending sunburn, especially when they are having fun. Check them often and get them out of the sun as soon as you see even slight redness. You don't have to pay extra for special formulas made for children. As long as the SPF is at least 15 and offers broad-spectrum protection, one brand can serve the whole family.

NOT JUST SKIN DEEP

It is just as important to protect the eyes and lips as the skin. Using a lip balm with an SPF of 15 is pretty easy to do but also easy to forget. Be sure to keep several tubes in your bag or pocket, and reapply often to your own lips and

include mayonnaise, ketchup, mustard, salt and pepper, and packets of sugar or artificial sweetener. Also bring some plastic knives and spoons, paper napkins, plastic cups, and a box of zip-top plastic bags. For breakfast you will need some plastic bowls for cereal. Of course, you can buy this stuff in Florida, but you probably won't consume it all, so why waste the money? If you drink bottled beer or wine, bring a bottle opener and corkscrew.

ENERGY BOOSTERS Kids get cranky when they're hungry, and when that happens, your entire group has a problem. Like many parents you might, for nutritional reasons, keep a tight rein on snacks available to your children at home. At Walt Disney World, however, maintaining energy and equanimity trumps between-meal snack discipline. For maximum zip and contentedness, give your kids snacks containing complex carbohydrates (fruits, crackers, nonfat energy bars, and the like) *before* they get hungry or show signs of exhaustion. You should avoid snacks that are high in fats and proteins because these foods take a long time to digest and will tend to unsettle your stomach if it's a hot day.

those of your kids. Again, the brand is less important than choosing something that you will use and remembering to use it.

Sunglasses are also a must. Too much sun exposure can contribute to age-related macular degeneration, among other things. This may not seem to be much of an issue when you are young and healthy, but when you get old and go blind you'll wish you had remembered to put on some shades. Not all sunglasses filter out damaging rays. Be sure to choose shades (for both the adults and the kids) that have 99-percent-UV protection. Large lenses and wraparound styles might not look as cool, but they offer much better protection. This is one case where you may have to spend a little more to be sure you are getting adequate protection, but you don't want to skimp on this. Much of the damage to the eyes from too much sun is irreversible and, like sun damage to the skin, it starts accumulating in childhood.

If you do slip up and get a burn, cool baths, aloe gels, and ibuprofen (or for the adults, aspirin) usually help ease the suffering. But occasionally sunburns can be as dangerous in the short term as they are in the long term. If you or your child experiences nausea, vomiting, high fever, severe pain, confusion, or fainting, seek medical care immediately.

All of the above is important—and sunscreen is a must if you are headed to Florida after a nice, cushy winter indoors in less sun-drenched climes—but don't let that little bottle with its inscrutable numbers take you off guard. You still need to wear a hat, stay out of the sun during the hottest part of the day (between 10 a.m. and 3 p.m.), and stay well-hydrated.

ELECTRONICS Regardless of your children's ages, always bring a night-light. Flashlights are also handy for finding stuff in a dark hotel room after the kids are asleep. If you are big coffee drinkers and if you drive, bring along a coffeemaker if it's not included in your room.

Portable CD players and iPods with headphones, as well as some electronic games, are often controversial gear for a family outing. We recommend compromise. Headphones allow kids to create their own space even when they're with others, and that can be a safety valve. That said, try to agree before the trip on some headphone parameters, so you don't begin to feel as if they're being used to keep other family members and the trip itself at a distance. If you're traveling by car, take turns choosing the radio station or CD for part of the trip.

DON'T FORGET THE TENT This is not a joke and has nothing to do with camping. When Bob's daughter was preschool age, he about went crazy trying to get her to sleep in a shared hotel room. She was accustomed to having her own room at home and was hyperstimulated whenever she traveled. Bob tried makeshift curtains and room dividers and even rearranged the furniture in a few hotel rooms to create the illusion of a more private, separate space for her. It was all for naught. It wasn't until she was around 4 years old and Bob took her camping that he seized on an idea that had some promise. She liked the cozy, secure, womblike feel of a backpacking tent and quieted down much more readily than she ever had in hotel rooms. So the next time the family stayed in a hotel, he pitched his backpacking tent in the corner of the room. In she went, nested for a bit, and fell asleep.

Since the time of Bob's daughter's childhood, there has been an astounding evolution in tent design. Responding to the needs of climbers and paddlers who often have to pitch tents on rocks (where it's impossible to drive stakes), tent manufacturers developed a broad range of tents with self-supporting frames that can be erected virtually anywhere without ropes or stakes. Affordable and sturdy, many are as simple to put up as opening an umbrella. So, if your child is too young for a room of his or her own, or you can't afford a second hotel room, try pitching a small tent. Modern tents are self-contained, with floors and an entrance that can be zipped up (or not) for privacy but cannot be locked. Kids appreciate having their own space and enjoy the adventure of being in a tent, even one set up in the corner of a hotel room. Sizes range from children's "play tents" with a 2- to 3-foot base to models large enough to sleep two or three husky teens. Light and compact when stored, a two-adult-size tent in its own storage bag (called a "stuff sack") will take up about one-tenth or less of a standard overhead bin on a commercial airliner. Another option for infants and toddlers is to drape a sheet over a portable crib or playpen to make a tent.

THE BOX Bob writing: On one memorable Walt Disney World excursion when my children were younger, we started each morning with an immensely annoying, involuntary scavenger hunt. Invariably, seconds before our scheduled departure to the theme park, we discovered that some combination of shoes, billfolds, sunglasses, hip packs, or other necessities were unaccountably missing. For the next 15 minutes we would root through the room like pigs hunting truffles in an attempt to locate the absent items. Now I don't know about your kids, but when my kids lost a shoe or something, they always searched where it was easiest to look, as opposed to where the lost article was most likely to be. I would be jammed under a bed feeling around, while my children stood in the middle of the room intently inspecting the ceiling. As my friends will tell you, I'm as open to a novel theory as the next guy, but we never did find any shoes on the ceiling. Not once. Anyway, here's what I finally did: I swung by a liquor store and mooched a big empty box. From then on, every time we returned to the room, I had the kids deposit shoes, hip packs, and other potentially wayward items in the box. After that the box was off-limits until the next morning, when I doled out the contents.

PLASTIC GARBAGE BAGS There are two attractions, the Kali River Rapids raft ride in the Animal Kingdom and Splash Mountain in the

Magic Kingdom, where you are certain to get wet and possibly soaked. If it's really hot and you don't care, then fine. But if it's cool or you're just not up for a soaking, bring a large plastic trash bag to the park. By cutting holes in the top and on the sides, you can fashion a sack poncho that will keep your clothes from getting wet. On the raft ride, you will also get your feet wet. If you're not up for walking around in squishing, soaked shoes, bring a second, smaller plastic bag to wear over your feet while riding.

SUPPLIES FOR INFANTS AND TODDLERS

BASED ON RECOMMENDATIONS FROM HUNDREDS of *Unofficial Guide* readers, here's what we suggest you carry with you when touring with infants and toddlers:

- A disposable diaper for every hour you plan to be away from your hotel room
- A plastic (or vinyl) diaper wrap with Velcro closures
- A cloth diaper or kitchen towel to put over your shoulder for burping
- Two receiving blankets: one to wrap the baby, one to lay the baby on or to drape over you when you nurse
- Ointment for diaper rash
- Moistened towelettes such as Wet Ones
- Prepared formula in bottles if you are not breast-feeding
- A washable bib, baby spoon, and baby food if your infant is eating solids
- For toddlers, a small toy for comfort and to keep them occupied during attractions

Baby Care Centers at the theme parks will sell you just about anything that you forget or run out of. Like all things Disney, prices will be higher than elsewhere, but at least you won't need to detour to a drug store in the middle of your touring day.

TIPS FOR PREGNANT MOTHERS

LET'S FACE IT: A visit to Walt Disney World is not the ideal vacation for an expecting mom, but we also know that quite a lot of pregnant moms visit the World every year. The most important advice for pregnant moms is to take it easy. If you travel by car or plane, make sure you prepare your schedule in such a manner that you have plenty of rest. Don't stay on your feet all day; stick to a healthy, balanced diet; but most of all don't skip meals; and drink plenty of fluids. Keep the dining options flexible; morning sickness or sudden aversions or preferences to food can be dealt with easily if you don't make reservations and go for whatever you feel like eating. Always carry some snacks and bottled water with you. A plastic bag folded in your pocket in case you feel unwell takes no space but gives peace of mind. You also should discuss your upcoming Walt Disney World visit with your physician. He or she will certainly have valuable tips.

Comfortable clothes are a must and so are well-worn-in supporting shoes. You may consider getting a maternity support belt to keep your back from hurting. If you are using a special pillow to support your belly, this is not the time to leave it at home. If you do not have enough space for it in your suitcase, consider shipping one ahead in a care box. Of course the hotel will provide you with extra pillows if needed.

Maternity bathing suit: If you don't own one, purchase a maternity bathing suit; you will be glad you did. A relaxing afternoon at the pool or a float down the lazy river in the water parks is wonderful.

At the parks take frequent breaks; put your legs up! The Baby Care Centers also welcome expectant moms, and you can sit and relax in a pleasant atmosphere. Go back to the hotel for a nap during the day, and plan a day away from the parks. Go splurge and have a massage; your back and feet will be grateful. Sleep is precious, so don't overdo it; a good night of sleep is better than all the fireworks in the sky.

Heed the warnings! Here is a short list of rides that are absolutely not suitable for expecting moms: The Barnstormer at Goofy's Wiseacre Farm; Big Thunder Mountain Railroad; DINOSAUR; Expedition Everest; Kali River Rapids; Kilimanjaro Safaris; Mission: SPACE; Rock 'n' Roller Coaster; Star Tours; Space Mountain; Splash Mountain; Test Track; Tomorrowland Speedway; and The Twilight Zone Tower of Terror. Remember, this is just a short list; use your own better judgment.

A word about the water parks: Obviously this is not the time to experience the offerings of Crush 'n' Gusher at Typhoon Lagoon or the moment to come down Summit Plummet at Blizzard Beach, but the water parks offer great lazy rivers and pools, as well as shady beaches where you can relax and let the rest of your family enjoy the wild things.

Tips for Nursing Mothers

Baby Care Centers are available at all Walt Disney World parks, and nursing mothers will not have difficulty finding a comfortable, clean, and pleasant place to take care of their infants. In addition to breast-feeding rooms equipped with rocking chairs and love seats, the child-care facilities have sinks for washing, and a room with toys and videos for your older children. Should you need diapers, baby clothes, children's medicines, and other small necessities, Disney has those items available right there for a fee.

Here are some tips to remember when visiting:

- Getting there by plane: Remember to nurse your child at takeoff and landing. It helps to open the baby's ears and so eliminates discomfort due to pressure changes.
- Nurse your infant at the first sign of hunger. You and the baby will be calmer, and you will attract much less attention if you feed the baby before he or she gets fussy and screams at the top of his or her lungs.
- Wear comfortable clothes. While you can access the Baby Care Centers at any time, there is nothing wrong with nursing your infant in a calm, shady spot anywhere at Walt Disney World or at the pool of your hotel. A dress with buttons in the front and a small baby blanket to put over your shoulder will do the trick. A large T-shirt that allows the baby to nurse "from under" is another option. Besides, breast-feeding is completely legal in Florida. As a matter of fact, Florida was the first state to protect breast-feeding in public by law in 1993.
- Pick a quiet place to nurse your baby.
- Adequate rest is another must. Schedule several breaks into your day, and go back to the hotel for a nap.
- Make sure you plan regular healthy meals. A nursing mom, much like an expecting mother, has increased nutritional needs. In addition to eating a well-balanced diet and drinking plenty of fluids, it is always a good idea to take along some snacks.
- It is hot in Florida, and while it is important for all visitors to drink lots of water, it is crucial for nursing moms, so stay hydrated!
- Schedule a down day into your trip. If you have older children, let dad take them to the park while you stay behind with the baby. A day of rest works wonders.
- If you plan on a parent's evening out, consider pumping milk for later use or supplementing breast milk with a bottle of formula.
- Nursing is exhausting, and so is touring Walt Disney World. Fatigue can reduce milk flow. Get enough rest and don't stay up past your bedtime. The night of a nursing mom is already short. Leave the park whenever you feel tired and get enough sleep.
- A bath and a massage calm most fussy babies and are good for mom too.

Enjoy your visit. If you take it easy, Walt Disney World is certainly a magical place to be for expecting and nursing mothers alike. And did we mention the shopping? Of course you will fall for the cute baby clothes, the crib decorations, babies' first Christmas ornament and keepsake, and for at least one of the millions of toys Disney thinks you absolutely need.

Other suggested reading:

- PassPorter's *Open Mouse for Walt Disney World and the Disney Cruise Line: Easy Access Vacations for Travelers With Extra Challenges* has a good section for expectant moms, nursing your baby, and infant travel.
- *Baby Massage: A Practical Guide to Massage and Movement for Babies and Infants* by Peter Walker.

REMEMBERING *Your* TRIP

1. Purchase a notebook for each child, and spend some time each evening recording the events of the day. If your children have trouble getting motivated or don't know what to write about, start a discussion; otherwise, let them write or draw whatever they want to remember from the day's events.

2. Collect mementos along the way, and create a treasure box in a small tin or cigar box. Months or years later, it's fun to look at postcards, pins, seashells, or ticket stubs to jump-start a memory.

3. Add inexpensive postcards to your photographs to create an album; then write a few words on each page to accompany the images.

4. Give each child a disposable camera to record his or her version of the trip. One 5-year-old snapped an entire series of photos that never showed anyone above the waist—his view of the world (and the photos were priceless).

5. Nowadays, many families travel with a camcorder, though we recommend using one sparingly—parents end up viewing the trip through the lens rather than being in the moment. If you must, take it along, but only record a few moments of major sights (too much is boring anyway). And let the kids tape and narrate. On the topic of narration, speak loudly so as to be heard over the not insignificant background noise of the parks. Make use of lockers at all of the parks when the camcorder becomes a burden or when you're going to experience an attraction that might damage it or get it wet. Unless you've got a camcorder designed for underwater shots, leave it behind on Splash Mountain, the Kali River Rapids, and any other ride where water is involved.

6. Another inexpensive way to record memories is a palm-size tape recorder. Let all family members describe their experiences. Hearing a small child's voice years later is so endearing, and those recorded descriptions will trigger an album's worth of memories, far more focused than what many novices capture with a camcorder.

Finally, when it comes to taking photos and collecting mementos, don't let the tail wag the dog. You are not going to Walt Disney

World to build the biggest scrapbook in history. Or as this Houston mom put it:

Tell your readers to get a grip on the photography thing. We were so busy shooting pictures that we kind of lost the thread. We had to get our pictures developed when we got home to see what all we did (while on vacation).

HOW TO HAVE FUN BEFORE AND AFTER YOU VISIT—OR THE THINGS BOB WOULD NEVER DO

Don't forget to send Bob an invitation.

Liliane

PREPARING FOR YOUR Walt Disney World vacation is important, but it is equally important to have a good time. Doing so before you leave is yet another way to get the whole family involved.

The weekend before your departure, plan a party for all who are going to Walt Disney World. Pick a Disney movie the entire family will enjoy, and plan a meal in front of the TV. A chocolate cake or cookies shaped like the famous mouse head will be a guaranteed success and add to the fun. This is the perfect time to go over the must-see list and reiterate the dos and dont's.

A similar event can be planned upon your return, when it is time to share the pictures and maybe even the movie you made during your visit to Walt Disney World.

Liliane will throw a party with the least provocation— Groundhog Day, National Tulip Day, Bless the Reptiles Day, you name it. But scheduling a wingding the weekend before you go to Disney World is to me like holding an Easter egg hunt in a cattle stampede—just a little too much going on to add one more thing.

Bob

Great Web sites:

Arts and crafts and party tips: **disney.go.com/ magicartist**

For some serious cooking check out: **wdisneyw.co.uk/recipes.html**

Recommended Books:

The Disney Party Handbook by Alison Boteler

The Disney Bakery by Adrienne Berofsky

TRIAL RUN

IF YOU GIVE THOUGHTFUL CONSIDERATION to all areas of mental, physical, organizational, and logistical preparation discussed in this chapter, what remains is to familiarize yourself with Walt Disney World itself, and of course, to conduct your field test. Yep, that's right, we want you to take the whole platoon on the road for a day to see if you are combat ready. No joke, this is important. You'll learn who poops out first, who is prone to developing blisters, who has to

"No, no, really, it's OK. It's just not what I was expecting."

pee every 11 seconds, and given the proper forum, how compatible your family is in terms of what you like to see and do.

For the most informative trial run, choose a local venue that requires lots of walking, dealing with crowds, and making decisions on how to spend your time. Regional theme parks and state fairs are your best bets, followed by large zoos and museums. Devote the whole day. Kick off the morning with an early start, just like you will at Walt Disney World, paying attention to who's organized and ready to go and who's dragging his or her butt and holding up the group. If you have to drive an hour or two to get to your test venue, no big deal. You'll have to do some commuting at Walt Disney World too. Spend the whole day, eat a couple meals, and stay late.

Don't bias the sample (that is, mess with the outcome) by telling everyone you are practicing for Walt Disney World. Everyone behaves differently when they know they are being tested or evaluated. Your objective is not to run a perfect drill but to find out as much as you can about how the individuals in your family, as well as the family as a group, respond to and deal with everything they experience during the day. Pay attention to who moves quickly and who is slow; to who is adventuresome and who is reticent; to who keeps going and who needs frequent rest breaks; to who sets the agenda and who is content to follow; to who is easily agitated and who stays cool; to who tends to dawdle or wander off; to who is curious and who is bored; to who is demanding and who is accepting. You get the idea.

Discuss the findings of the test run with your spouse the next day. Don't be discouraged if your test day wasn't perfect; few (if any) are. Distinguish between problems that are remediable and problems that are intrinsic to your family's emotional or physical makeup (no amount of hiking, for example, will toughen up some people's feet).

Establish a plan for addressing remediable problems (further conditioning, setting limits before you go, trying harder to achieve family consensus, whatever) and develop strategies for minimizing or working around problems that are a fact of life (waking sleepyheads 15 minutes early, placing moleskin on likely blister sites before setting out, packing familiar food for the toddler who balks at restaurant fare). If you are an attentive observer, a fair diagnostician, and a creative problem solver, you'll be able to work out a significant percentage of the problems you're likely to encounter at Walt Disney World before you ever leave home.

PART SIX

GET *in the* BOAT, MEN!

THE ABOVE IS NOT A *JEOPARDY!* ANSWER, but if it were, the question would be this: "What did George Washington say to his soldiers before they crossed the Delaware?" We share this interesting historic aside as our way of sounding the alarm, blowing the bugle, or whatever. It's time to move beyond preparation and practice and to leap into action. Walt Disney World, here we come! Get in the boat, men!

READY, SET, TOUR!
Some Touring Considerations

HOW MUCH TIME IS REQUIRED TO SEE EACH PARK?

THE MAGIC KINGDOM AND EPCOT offer such a large number of attractions and special live entertainment options that it is impossible to see everything in a single day, with or without a midday break. For a reasonably thorough tour of each, allocate a minimum of one and a half days and preferably two days. The Animal Kingdom and Disney's Hollywood Studios can each be seen in a day, although planning on a day and a half allows for a more relaxed visit.

WHICH PARK TO SEE FIRST?

THIS QUESTION IS LESS ACADEMIC than it appears. Children who see the Magic Kingdom first expect more of the same type of entertainment at the other parks. At Epcot, children are often disappointed by the educational orientation and more serious tone (as are many adults). Disney's Hollywood Studios offers some pretty wild action, but the general presentation is educational and more mature. Though most children enjoy zoos, live animals can't be programmed to entertain. Thus, children may not find the Animal Kingdom as exciting as the Magic Kingdom or the Studios.

First-time visitors should see Epcot first; you will be able to enjoy it fully without having been preconditioned to think of Disney entertainment as solely fantasy or adventure. Children will be more likely to enjoy Epcot on its own merits if they see it first, and they will be more relaxed and patient in their touring.

See the Animal Kingdom second. Like Epcot, it has an educational thrust, but it provides a change of pace because it features live animals. Next, see Disney's Hollywood Studios, which helps all ages make a fluid transition from the educational Epcot and Disney's Animal Kingdom to the fanciful Magic Kingdom. Also, because Disney's Hollywood Studios is smaller, you won't walk as much or stay as long. Save the Magic Kingdom for last.

If you can't postpone the Magic Kingdom without a major revolt, at least see Epcot first. Adult orientation notwithstanding, there's lots that children 7 and up will love, younger children not so much. Be sure to participate in the Kim Possible and Kidcot programs, both described in Part 8. They will be the highlight of your child's day. If seeing Mickey is your kid's top priority, be advised that you can see him in each of the four major theme parks. Any cast member can tell you where to find him.

OPERATING HOURS

DISNEY CAN'T BE ACCUSED of being inflexible regarding operating hours at the parks. They run a dozen or more schedules each year, making it advisable to call ☎ 407-824-4321 for the exact hours before you arrive. In the off-season, parks may be open for as few as 8 hours (10 a.m.–6 p.m.). By contrast, at busy times (particularly holidays), they may be open 8 a.m.–2 a.m. the next morning.

Usually, hours approximate the following: September through mid-March, excluding holiday periods, the Magic Kingdom is open from 9 a.m. to 7, 8, or 9 p.m. During the same period, Epcot is open 9 a.m.–9 p.m., and Hollywood Studios is open from 9 a.m. to 7 or 8 p.m. The Animal Kingdom is open from 9 a.m. until 6 or 7 p.m. During summer, expect the Animal Kingdom to remain open until 8 p.m. Epcot and Hollywood Studios are normally open until 9 or 10 p.m., with the Magic Kingdom sometimes open as late as 1 a.m.

We also maintain more easily readable park hours, as well as entertainment and Extra Magic Hour schedules, on our Web site, **touringplans.com,** and conveniently through our mobile application, Lines (**touringplans.com/lines**).

OFFICIAL OPENING VERSUS REAL OPENING

THE OPERATING HOURS YOU'RE QUOTED when you call are "official hours." The parks sometimes open earlier. Many visitors, relying on information disseminated by Disney Guest Relations, arrive at the official opening time and find the park packed with people. If the official hours are 9 a.m.–9 p.m., for example, Main Street in the Magic

Kingdom opens at 8 or 8:30 a.m., with the remainder of the park opening at 8:30 or 9 a.m. If the official opening for the Magic Kingdom is 8 a.m. and you're eligible for early entry (if you are staying in a Disney resort), you sometimes are able to enter the park as early as 6:30 a.m.

Disney publishes hours of operation well in advance but reserves the flexibility to react daily to gate conditions. Disney traffic controllers survey local hotel reservations, estimate how many visitors they should expect on a given day, and open the theme parks early to avoid bottlenecks at parking facilities and ticket windows and to absorb the crowds as they arrive.

If you're a Disney resort guest and want to take advantage of Extra Magic Hours early entry, arrive 1 hour and 20 minutes before the early-entry park is scheduled to open to the general public. Buses, boats, and monorails will initiate service to the early-entry park about 2 hours before it opens to the general public.

At day's end, rides and attractions shut down at approximately the official closing time. Main Street remains open 30 minutes to an hour after the rest of the Magic Kingdom has closed.

THE RULES

SUCCESSFUL TOURING OF THE MAGIC KINGDOM, Disney's Animal Kingdom, Epcot, or Disney's Hollywood Studios hinges on five rules:

1. Determine in Advance What You Really Want To See

What rides and attractions appeal most to you? Which additional rides and attractions would you like to experience if you have some time left? What are you willing to forgo?

To help you set your touring priorities, we describe each theme park and its attractions later in this book. In each description, we include the author's evaluation of the attraction and the opinions of Walt Disney World guests expressed as star ratings. Five stars is the best possible rating.

Finally, because attractions range from midway-type rides and horse-drawn trolleys to colossal, high-tech extravaganzas, we have developed a hierarchy of categories to pinpoint an attraction's magnitude:

SUPER HEADLINERS The best attractions the theme park has to offer. Mind-boggling in size, scope, and imagination. Represents the cutting edge of modern attraction technology and design.

HEADLINERS Full-blown, multimillion-dollar, full-scale themed adventures and theater presentations. Modern in technology and design and employing a complete range of special effects.

MAJOR ATTRACTIONS Themed adventures on a more modest scale but incorporating state-of-the-art technologies. Or, larger-scale attractions of older design.

MINOR ATTRACTIONS Midway-type rides, small "dark" rides (cars on

a track, zigzagging through the dark), small theater presentations, transportation rides, and elaborate walk-through attractions.

DIVERSIONS Exhibits, both passive and interactive. Includes playgrounds, video arcades, and street theater.

Though not every Walt Disney World attraction fits neatly into these descriptions, the categories provide a comparison of attractions' size and scope. Remember that bigger and more elaborate doesn't always mean better. Peter Pan's Flight, a minor attraction in the Magic Kingdom, continues to be one of the park's most beloved rides. Likewise, for many young children, no attraction, regardless of size, surpasses Dumbo.

2. Arrive Early! Arrive Early! Arrive Early!

This is the single most important key to efficient touring and avoiding long lines. There are no lines and fewer people first thing in the morning. The same four rides you can experience in one hour in early morning can take as long as 3 hours to see after 10:30 a.m. Have breakfast before you arrive, so you won't waste prime touring time sitting in a restaurant.

The earlier a park opens, the greater the potential advantage. This is because most vacationers won't make the sacrifice to rise early and get to a theme park before it opens. Fewer people are willing to be on hand for an 8 a.m. opening than for a 9 a.m. opening. On those rare occasions when a park opens at 10 a.m., almost everyone arrives at the same time, so it's almost impossible to get a jump on the crowd. If you're a Disney resort guest and have early-entry privileges, arrive as early as early entry allows (6:30 a.m. if the park opens to the public at 8 a.m. or 7:30 a.m. if the park opens to the public at 9 a.m.). If you are visiting during midsummer, arrive at non-early-entry parks 30 minutes before the official opening time. During holiday periods, arrive at non-early-entry parks 40 minutes before the official opening.

3. Avoid Bottlenecks

Crowd concentrations and/or faulty crowd management cause bottlenecks. Avoiding bottlenecks involves being able to predict where, when, and why they occur. Concentrations of hungry people create bottlenecks at restaurants during lunch and dinner. Concentrations of people moving toward the exit at closing time create bottlenecks in gift shops en route to the gate. Concentrations of visitors at new and popular rides and at rides slow to load and unload create bottlenecks and long lines. To help you get a grip on which attractions cause bottlenecks, we have developed a Bottleneck Scale with a range of one to ten. If an attraction ranks high on the Bottleneck Scale, try to experience it during the first 2 hours the park is open. The scale is included in each attraction profile in Parts Seven through Eleven.

The best way to avoid bottlenecks, however, is to use one of our field-tested touring plans available in clip-out form complete with a map on pages 445–468. The plans will save you as much as 4½ hours of standing in line in a single day.

4. Go Back to Your Hotel for a Rest in the Middle of the Day

You may think we're beating the dead horse with this midday nap thing, but if you plug away all day at the theme parks, you'll understand how the dead horse feels. No joke; resign yourself to going back to the hotel in the middle of the day for swimming, reading, and a snooze.

If you can't calm them— dunk them. Whenever my son was too wound up to nap or go to bed at night, I took him to the pool— water works wonders.

— Liliane

5. Let Off Steam

Time at a Disney theme park is extremely regimented for younger children. Often held close for fear of losing them, they are ushered from line to line and attraction to attraction throughout the day. After a couple of hours of being on such a short leash, it's not surprising that they're in need of some physical freedom and an opportunity to discharge that pent-up energy. As it happens, all of the major theme parks except Epcot offer some sort of elaborate, creative playground perfect for such a release. Be advised that each playground (or plaza) is fairly large, and it's pretty easy to misplace a child while they're exploring. All children's playgrounds, however, have only one exit, so although your kids might get lost within the playground, they cannot wander off into the rest of the park without passing through the single exit (usually staffed by a Disney cast member).

YOUR DAILY ITINERARY

PLAN EACH DAY IN THREE BLOCKS:

1. Early morning theme-park touring
2. Midday break
3. Late afternoon and evening theme-park touring

Choose the attractions that interest you most, and check their bottleneck ratings along with what time of day we recommend you visit. If your children are 8 years old or younger, review the attraction's fright potential rating. Use one of our touring plans or work out a step-by-step plan of your own and write it down. Experience attractions with a high bottleneck rating as early as possible, transitioning to attractions with bottleneck ratings of six to eight around midmorning. Plan on departing the park for your midday break by 11:30 a.m. or so.

For your late afternoon and evening touring block, you do not necessarily have to return to the same theme park. If you have purchased one of the Disney admission options that allow you to "park hop," that is, visit more than one theme park on a given day, you may opt to spend

We strongly recommend deferring special parades, stage shows, and other productions until the afternoon/evening block.

— Bob

the afternoon/evening block somewhere different. In any event, as you start your afternoon/evening block, see attractions with low bottleneck ratings until about 5 p.m. After 5 p.m., any attraction with a rating of one to seven is fair game. If you stay into the evening, try attractions with ratings of eight to ten during the hour just before closing.

In addition to attractions, each theme park offers a broad range of special live entertainment events. In the morning block, concentrate on the attractions. For the record, we regard live shows that offer five or more daily performances a day (except for street entertainment) as attractions. Thus, *Indiana Jones* at Disney's Hollywood Studios is an attraction, as is *Festival of the Lion King* at the Animal Kingdom. *IllumiNations* at Epcot or the parades at the Magic Kingdom, on the other hand, are live entertainment events. A schedule of live performances is listed in the *Times Guide* available at the entrance of each park. When planning your day, also be aware that major live events draw large numbers of guests from the attraction lines. Thus, a good time to see an especially popular attraction is during a parade or other similar event.

TOURING PLANS

OUR TOURING PLANS ARE STEP-BY-STEP GUIDES for seeing as much as possible with a minimum of standing in line. They're designed to help you avoid crowds and bottlenecks on days of moderate-to-heavy attendance. On days of lighter attendance (see "When To Go to Walt Disney World," page 45), the plans will still save time, but they won't be as critical to successful touring.

Don't get obsessed with the touring plans. It's your vacation, after all. You can amend or even scrap the plans if you want.

— Liliane

What You Can Realistically Expect from the Touring Plans

The best way to see as much as possible with the least amount of waiting is to arrive early. Several of our touring plans require that you be on hand when the park opens. Because this is often difficult and sometimes impossible for families with young children or nocturnal teens, we've developed additional touring plans for families who get a late start. You won't see as much as with the early-morning plans, but you'll see significantly more than visitors without a plan.

Variables That Will Affect the Success of the Touring Plans

The plans' success will be affected by how quickly you move from ride to ride; when and how many refreshment and restroom breaks you take; when, where, and how you eat meals; and your ability (or lack thereof) to find your way around. Smaller groups almost always move faster than larger groups, and parties of adults generally cover more ground than families with young children. Switching off (page 238), also known as baby swapping or child swapping, among other things, inhibits families with little ones from moving expeditiously among attractions.

Character meals are another way to collect autographs and might be something you could promise your avid collector in exchange for a full day of touring when the signature hunt is off.

— Liliane

If you have young children in your party, be prepared for character encounters. The appearance of a Disney character usually stops a touring plan in its tracks. While some characters stroll the parks, it's equally common that they assemble in a specific venue (such as character trails at the Animal Kingdom) where families queue up for photos and autographs. Meeting characters, posing for photos, and collecting autographs can burn hours of touring time. If your kids collect character autographs, you need to anticipate these interruptions and negotiate some understanding with your children about when you will follow the plan and when you will collect autographs. Our advice is to go with the flow or set aside a specific morning or afternoon for photos and autographs. Note that queues for autographs, especially in the Magic Kingdom and Camp Minnie-Mickey at the Animal Kingdom, are sometimes as long as the queues for major attractions. The only time-efficient way to collect autographs is to line up at the character-greeting areas first thing in the morning. Because this is also the best time to experience the popular attractions, you may have tough choices to make.

While we realize that following the plans isn't always easy, we nevertheless recommend continuous, expeditious touring until around noon. After noon, breaks and diversions won't affect the plans significantly.

A multigenerational family from Aurora, Ohio, wonders how to know if you are on track or not, writing:

It seems like the touring plans were very time dependent, yet there were no specific times attached to the plan outside of the early morning. On more than one day, I often had to guess as to whether we were "on track." Having small children and a grandparent in our group, we couldn't move at a fast pace.

There is no objective measurement for being on track. Each family's or touring group's experience will differ to some degree. Regardless of whether your group is large or small, fast or slow, the sequence of attractions in the touring plans will allow you to enjoy the greatest number of attractions in the least possible amount of time. Two quickly moving adults will probably take in more attractions in a specific time period than will a large group made up of children, parents, and grandparents. However, given the characteristics of the respective groups, each will maximize their touring time and experience as many attractions as possible.

What To Do if You Lose the Thread

Anything from a blister to a broken attraction can throw off a touring plan. If unforeseen events interrupt a plan:

1. Skip one step on the plan for every 15 minutes' delay. If, for example, you lose your billfold and spend an hour finding it, skip three steps and pick up from there.

2. Forget the plan and organize the remainder of your day using the bottleneck ratings in conjunction with the best-times-to-go suggestions in each attraction profile.

What To Expect When You Arrive at the Parks

Because most touring plans are based on being present when the theme park opens, you need to know about opening procedures. Disney transportation to the parks begins 1½–2 hours before official opening. The parking lots open at around the same time.

Each park has an entrance plaza outside the turnstiles. Usually, you're held there until 30 minutes before the official opening time, when you're admitted. What happens next depends on the season and the day's crowds.

1. **LOW SEASON** At slower times, you will usually be confined outside the turnstiles or in a small section of the park until the official opening time. At the Magic Kingdom you might be admitted to Main Street, U.S.A.; at Animal Kingdom, to The Oasis and sometimes to Discovery Island; at Epcot, to the fountain area around Spaceship Earth; and at Disney's Hollywood Studios, to Hollywood Boulevard. Rope barriers supervised by Disney cast members keep you there until the "rope drop," when the barrier is removed and the park and its attractions begin operating at the official opening time.

2. **HIGH-ATTENDANCE DAYS** When large crowds are expected, you will be admitted through the turnstiles 30 minutes before official opening, and the entire park will be operating.

3. **VARIATIONS** Sometimes Disney will run a variation of those two procedures. In this, you'll be permitted through the turnstiles and find that one or several specific attractions are open early. At Epcot, Spaceship Earth and sometimes Test Track or Soarin' will be operating. At Animal Kingdom, you may find Kilimanjaro Safaris and *It's Tough to Be a Bug!* running early. At Disney's Hollywood Studios, look for Tower of Terror and/or Rock 'n' Roller Coaster. The Magic Kingdom almost never runs a variation. Instead, you'll usually encounter plan number one described above or occasionally plan two.

HOW TO FIND THE TOURING PLAN THAT'S BEST FOR YOU

THE DIFFERENT TOURING PLANS FOR EACH PARK are described in the chapter pertaining to that park. The descriptions will tell you for whom (for example, teens, parents with preschoolers, grandparents, and so on) or for what situation (such as sleeping late or enjoying the park at night) the plans are designed. The actual touring plans are located on pages 445–468 at the back of the book. Each plan includes a numbered map of the park in question to help you find your way around. Clip the plan of your choice out of the book by cutting along the line indicated, and take it with you to the park.

Will the Plans Continue to Work Once the Secret Is Out?

Yes! First, some of the plans require that a patron be there when a park opens. Many Disney World patrons simply won't get up early while on vacation. Second, less than 1% of any day's attendance has been exposed to the plans—too few to affect results. Last, most groups tailor the plans, skipping rides or shows according to taste.

How Frequently Are the Touring Plans Revised?

Because Disney is always adding new attractions and changing operations, we revise the plans every year, and updates are always available at **touringplans.com.** Most complaints we receive come from readers using out-of-date editions of the *Unofficial Guide.* Be prepared, however, for surprises. Opening procedures and show times may change, for example, and you can't predict when an attraction might break down.

"Bouncing Around"

Many readers object to crisscrossing a theme park, as our touring plans sometimes require. A lady from Decatur, Georgia, said she "got dizzy from all the bouncing around." We empathize, but here's the rub, park by park.

We've revised the Epcot plans to eliminate most of the "bouncing around" and have added instructions to further minimize walking.

Bob

In the Magic Kingdom, the most popular attractions are positioned across the park from one another. This is no accident. It's a method of more equally distributing guests throughout the park. If you want to experience the most popular attractions in one day without long waits, you can arrive before the park fills and see those attractions first (which requires crisscrossing the park), or you can enjoy the main attractions on one side of the park first, then try the most popular attractions on the other side during the hour or so before closing, when crowds presumably have thinned. Using Fastpass lessens the time you wait in line but tends to increase the bouncing around because you must visit the same attraction twice: once to obtain your Fastpass and again to use it.

The best way to minimize "bouncing around" at the Magic Kingdom is to do half the touring plan on one day and the other half on another. This makes for much more relaxing touring and facilitates returning to your hotel for rest and a swim. Disney's Hollywood Studios is configured in a way that precludes an orderly approach to touring or to a clockwise or counterclockwise rotation. Orderly touring is further confounded by live entertainment that prompts guests to interrupt their touring to head for whichever theater is about to crank up. At the Studios, therefore, you're stuck with "bouncing around," whether you use our plan or not. In our opinion, when it comes to Disney parks, it's best to have a plan.

The Animal Kingdom is arranged in a spoke-and-hub configuration like the Magic Kingdom, simplifying crisscrossing the park. Even so, the only way to catch various shows is to stop what you're doing and troop across the park to the next performance.

Touring Plans and the Obsessive-compulsive Reader

We suggest you follow the touring plans religiously, especially in the mornings, if you're visiting during busy times. The consequence of touring spontaneity in peak season is hours of standing in line. During quieter times, there's no need to be compulsive about following the plans.

A mom in Atlanta suggests:

Emphasize perhaps not following [the touring plans] in off-season. There is no reason to crisscross the park when there are no lines.

A mother in Minneapolis advises:

Please let your readers know to stop along the way to various attractions to appreciate what else may be going on around them. We encountered many families using the Unofficial Guide *[who] became too serious about getting from one place to the next, missing the fun in between.*

What can we say? It's a lesser-of-two-evils situation. If you visit Walt Disney World at a busy time, you can either rise early and hustle around, or you can sleep in and see less.

When using the plans, however, relax and always be prepared for surprises and setbacks. When your type-A brain does cartwheels, reflect on the advice of a woman from Trappe, Pennsylvania:

You cannot emphasize enough the dangers of using your touring plans that were printed in the back of the book, especially if the person using them has a compulsive personality. I have a compulsive personality. I planned for this trip for two years and researched it by use of guidebooks, computer programs, and information received from WDW. I had a two-page itinerary for our one-week trip in addition to your touring plans of the theme parks. On night three of our trip, I ended up taking an unscheduled trip to the hospital emergency room in Lake Buena Vista. When the doctor asked what seemed to be the problem, I responded with, "I don't know, but I can't stop shaking, and I can't stay here very long because I have to get up in a couple hours to go to the Studios according to my itinerary." Diagnosis: an anxiety attack caused by my excessive itinerary. He gave me a shot of something, and I slept through the first four attractions the next morning. This was our third trip to WDW (not including one trip to Disneyland); on all previous trips I used only the Steve Birnbaum book, and I suffered no ill effects. I am not saying your book was not good. It was excellent! However, it should come with a warning label for people with compulsive personalities.

Touring Plan Rejection

Some folks don't respond well to the regimentation of a touring plan. If you encounter this problem with someone in your party, roll with the punches, as this Maryland couple did:

The rest of the group was not receptive to the use of the touring plans. I think they all thought I was being a little too regimented about planning this vacation. Rather than argue, I left the touring plans behind as we ventured off for the parks. You can guess the outcome. We took our camcorder with us and watched the movies when we returned home. About every 5 minutes or so there is a shot of us all gathered around a park map trying to decide what to do next.

As a Connecticut woman alleges, the plans are incompatible with some readers' bladders and personalities:

I want to know if next year when you write those "day" schedules you could schedule bathroom breaks in there too. You expect us to be at a certain ride at a certain time and with no stops in between. In one of the letters in your book, a guy writes, "You expect everyone to be theme-park commandos." When I read that, I thought there is a man who really knows what a problem the schedules are if you are a laid-back, slow-moving, careful detail noticer. What were you thinking when you made these schedules?

Finally, note that our mobile app Lines can be used to find attractions with low wait times, even if you're not using a structured touring plan.

Touring Plans for Low-attendance Days

We receive a number of letters each year similar to this one from Lebanon, New Jersey:

The guide always assumed there would be large crowds. We had no lines. An alternate tour for low-traffic days would be helpful.

If attendance is low, you don't need a touring plan. Just go where your taste and instinct direct, and glory in the hassle-free touring. Having said that, however, there are attractions in each park that bottleneck even if attendance is low. These are Space Mountain, Splash Mountain, Dumbo, The Many Adventures of Winnie the Pooh, and Peter Pan's Flight in the Magic Kingdom; Test Track and Soarin' at Epcot; Kilimanjaro Safaris and Expedition Everest at Animal Kingdom; and Tower of Terror and Rock 'n' Roller Coaster at Disney's Hollywood

Studios. Most are Fastpass attractions. Experience them immediately after the parks open, or use Fastpass. Remember that crowd size is relative and that large crowds can gather at certain attractions even during less-busy times. We recommend following a touring plan through the first five or six steps. If you're pretty much walking onto every attraction, feel free to scrap the remainder of the plan.

Extra Magic Hours and the Touring Plans

If you're a Disney resort guest and use your morning Extra Magic Hours privileges, complete your early-entry touring before the general public is admitted and position yourself to follow the touring plan. When the public is admitted, the park will suddenly be aswarm. A Wilmington, Delaware, mother advises:

> *The early-entry times went like clockwork. We were finishing up The Great Movie Ride when Disney's Hollywood Studios opened [to the public], and [we] had to wait in line quite a while for* Voyage of the Little Mermaid, *which sort of screwed up everything thereafter. Early-opening attractions should be finished up well before regular opening time so you can be at the plan's first stop as early as possible.*

In the Magic Kingdom, the early-entry attractions are in Fantasy-land and Tomorrowland. At Epcot, they're in the Future World section. At Disney's Hollywood Studios, they're dispersed. Practically speaking, see any attractions on the touring plan that are open for early entry, crossing them off as you do. If you finish all early-entry attractions on the touring plan and have time left before the general public is admitted, sample early-entry attractions not included in the plan. Stop touring about 10 minutes before the public is admitted, and position yourself for the first attraction on the plan that wasn't open for early entry. During early entry in the Magic Kingdom, for example, you can usually experience Peter Pan's Flight and It's a Small World in Fantasyland, plus Space Mountain and *Stitch's Great Escape!* in Tomorrowland. As official opening nears, go to the boundary between Fantasyland and Liberty Square, and be ready to blitz to Splash Mountain and Big Thunder Mountain Railroad, according to the touring plan, when the rest of the park opens.

Evening Extra Magic Hours, when a designated park remains open for Disney resort guests 3 hours beyond normal closing time, have less effect on the touring plans than early entry in the morning. Parks are almost never scheduled for both early entry and evening Extra Magic Hours on the same day. Thus a park offering evening Extra Magic Hours will enjoy a fairly normal morning and early afternoon. It's not until late afternoon, when park hoppers coming from the other theme parks descend, that the late-closing park will become especially crowded. By that time, you'll be well toward the end of your touring plan.

FASTPASS

IN 1999 DISNEY LAUNCHED A SYSTEM for moderating the wait at many popular attractions. Called Fastpass, it was originally tried at Animal Kingdom and then expanded to attractions at the other parks.

Fastpass works remarkably well, mainly because Fastpass holders get amazingly preferential treatment.

Bob

Here's how it works. Your handout park map and signage at attractions will tell you which attractions are included. Attractions operating Fastpass will have both a regular line and a Fastpass line. A sign at the entrance will say how long the wait is in the regular line. If the wait is acceptable to you, hop in line. If it seems too long, insert your park admission pass into a Fastpass machine and receive an appointment time (for later in the day) to return and ride. When you return at the designated time, you enter the Fastpass line and proceed directly to the attraction's preshow or boarding area. Interestingly, this procedure was pioneered by Universal Studios Hollywood years ago and had been virtually ignored by theme parks since (Universal now has a reworked variation called Universal Express). The system works well and can save a lot of waiting time. There's no extra charge to use Fastpass.

Fastpass is evolving, and attractions continue to be added and deleted from the lineup. Changes aside, here's an example of how to use Fastpass. Say you have only one day to tour the Magic Kingdom. You arrive early and ride Space Mountain and Buzz Lightyear with minimal waits. Then you cross the park to Splash Mountain and find a substantial line. Because Splash Mountain is a Fastpass attraction, you can insert your admission pass into the machine and receive an appointment to come back and ride, thus avoiding a long wait.

The effort to accommodate Fastpass holders makes anyone in the regular line feel second class. And a telling indication of their status is that they're called "standby guests." Indeed, we watched people in regular lines despondently stand by and stand by, while dozens and sometimes hundreds of Fastpass holders were ushered into the boarding area ahead of them. Disney is sending a message here: Fastpass is heaven; anything else is limbo at best and probably purgatory. In any event, you'll think you've been in hell if you're stuck in the regular line during the hot, crowded part of the day.

Readers regularly send standby-line horror stories. Here's one from a Pequea, Pennsylvania, family:

We, a group of four 12-year-olds and five adults, decided to ride Test Track when we arrived at Epcot at 11 a.m. Fastpasses were being issued for [late that night] and the singles line was not open yet, so we decided to brave the 120-minute wait (at MK and the Studios many waits ended up being less than the posted time). What a disaster! Once inside the building, the Fastpass and singles line (which opened when we were very near the building) sped ahead while the standby line barely moved. After 3 hours and 20 minutes, we finally made it to the car! One man who was in the Fastpass line said that he counted a 12:1 ratio between Fastpassers and standby people being let into the [boarding] area. Disney needs to seriously reconsider their boarding policy!

Each person in your party must have his or her own Fastpass.

Bob

Fastpass doesn't eliminate the need to arrive early at a theme park. Because each park offers a limited number of Fastpass attractions, you still need an early start if you want to see as much as possible in one day. Plus, there's a limited supply of Fastpasses available for each attraction on any day. If you don't arrive until midafternoon, you might find that no more Fastpasses are available. Fastpass does make it possible to see more with less waiting, and it's a great benefit to those who like to sleep late or who choose an afternoon or evening at the parks on their arrival day. It also allows you to postpone wet rides, such as Kali River Rapids at Animal Kingdom or Splash Mountain at the Magic Kingdom, until a warmer time of day.

Understanding the Fastpass System

The purpose of Fastpass is to reduce the wait for designated attractions by distributing guests at those attractions throughout the day. This is accomplished by providing an incentive (a shorter wait) for guests willing to postpone experiencing the attraction until later in the day. The system also, in effect, imposes a penalty (standby status) on those who don't use it. However, spreading out guest arrivals sometimes also decreases the wait for standby guests.

When you insert your admission pass into a Fastpass time clock, the machine spits out a slip of paper about two-thirds the size of a credit card—small enough to fit in your wallet but also small enough to lose easily. Printed on it is the attraction's name and a time window, for example 1:15–2:15 p.m., during which you can return to ride.

Returning to Ride

In practice, cast members are not very strict about enforcing the return window. They won't let you in before your window begins, but they'll usually admit you after your return window expires.

As a rule of thumb, the earlier in the day you secure a Fastpass, the shorter the interval between time of issue and your 1-hour return window.

Liliane

We've used Fastpasses more than three years old, and the worst we got was a snarky comment from the cast member minding the line. We'd estimate the probability of being denied entry at 10% or less—it's only happened a couple of times in many dozens of attempts. We don't know why, but Soarin' at Epcot is the only attraction in all four parks that sometimes rejects expired Fastpasses.

At Disneyland in Anaheim, California, the return window expiration time is ignored as a matter of policy, though Disneyland keeps this somewhat of a secret. In other words, a Fastpass is good from the beginning of the return window until closing time. This is shaping up to be the actuality at Walt Disney World, even if not a matter of policy.

When you report back, you'll enter a line marked "Fastpass Return" that routes you more or less directly to the boarding or preshow area. Each person in your party must have his own Fastpass and be ready to show it at the entrance of the Fastpass return line. Before you enter the boarding area or theater, another cast member will collect your Fastpass.

Cast members are instructed to minimize waits for Fastpass holders. Thus, if the Fastpass return line is suddenly inundated (something that occurs by chance), cast members intervene to reduce the Fastpass line. As many as 25 Fastpass holders will be admitted for each standby guest until the Fastpass line is reduced to an acceptable length. Although Fastpass usually eliminates 80% or more of the wait you would experience in the regular line, you can still expect a short wait, usually less than 15 minutes and frequently under 10 minutes.

Obtaining a Fastpass

You can ordinarily obtain a Fastpass anytime after a park opens (some attractions are a little tardy getting their Fastpass system up), but the Fastpass return lines don't usually begin operating until 45–90 minutes after opening.

Whenever you obtain a Fastpass, you can be assured of a period of time between when you receive your Fastpass and when you report back. The interval can be as short as 15 minutes or as long as 7 hours, depending on park attendance and the attraction's popularity and hourly capacity. Generally, the earlier in the day you obtain a Fastpass, the shorter the interval before your return window. If the park opens at 9 a.m. and you obtain a Fastpass for Splash Mountain at 9:25 a.m., your appointment for returning to ride would be 10–11 a.m. or 10:10–11:10 a.m. The exact time will be determined by how many other guests have obtained Fastpasses before you.

The fewer guests who obtain Fastpasses for an attraction, the shorter the interval between receipt of your pass and the return window. Conversely, the more guests issued Fastpasses, the longer the interval. If an attraction is exceptionally popular and/or its hourly capacity is relatively small, the return window might be pushed back almost to park closing time. When this happens, the Fastpass machines shut down and a sign is posted saying all Fastpasses are gone for the day. It's not unusual, for example, for Test Track at Epcot or The Many Adventures of Winnie the Pooh at the Magic Kingdom to have distributed all available Fastpasses by 1 p.m.

Rides routinely exhaust their daily Fastpass supply, but shows almost never do. Fastpass machines at theaters try to balance attendance at each show so that the audience for any given performance is

Bob

Regardless of the time of day, if the wait in the regular line at a Fastpass attraction is 25–30 minutes or less, join the regular line.

divided about evenly between standby and Fastpass guests. Consequently, standby guests for shows aren't discriminated against to the degree that standby guests for rides are. In practice, Fastpass for shows also diminishes the wait for standby guests. With few exceptions, the standby line at theater attractions requires less waiting than using Fastpass.

If you have a Fastpass for an attraction and it breaks down or is closed due to inclement weather, take the Fastpass to Guest Relations. They will issue you Fastpasses for the next day for any park in the World that you plan to visit.

When To Use Fastpass

Except as discussed below, there's no reason to use Fastpass during the first 30–40 minutes a park is open. Lines for most attractions are manageable during this period, and this is the only time of day when Fastpass attractions exclusively serve those in the regular line.

Using Fastpass requires two trips to the same attraction: one to obtain the pass and another to use it. You must invest time to obtain the pass (sometimes Fastpass machines have lines!), then interrupt your touring later to backtrack to use your Fastpass. The additional time, effort, and touring modification are justified only if you can save more than 30 minutes. Don't forget: Even the Fastpass line requires some waiting.

Nine attractions build lines so quickly in the morning that failing to queue up within the first 6 or so minutes of operation will mean a long wait: Test Track, Soarin', and Mission: SPACE (Epcot); Kilimanjaro Safaris and Expedition Everest (Animal Kingdom); Space Mountain (Magic Kingdom); and Tower of Terror, Toy Story Mania, and Rock 'n' Roller Coaster (Disney's Hollywood Studios). With these, you should race directly to the attractions when the park opens or obtain a Fastpass.

Another four Fastpass attractions—Splash Mountain, The Many Adventures of Winnie the Pooh, Peter Pan's Flight, and Jungle Cruise in the Magic Kingdom—develop long lines within 30–50 minutes of park opening. If you can get to them before the wait becomes intolerable, great. Otherwise, your options are Fastpass or a long wait.

You can obtain a second Fastpass at a time printed on the bottom of your most recent Fastpass, usually 2 hours or less from the time the first was issued. Always check the posted return time before obtaining a Fastpass. If the return time is hours away, forgo Fastpass. Especially in the Magic Kingdom, there will be other Fastpass attractions where the return time is only an hour or so away.

When obtaining Fastpasses, it's quicker and more considerate if one person obtains passes for your entire party. This means entrusting one individual with your valuable park-admission passes and your Fastpasses, so choose wisely.

Obtain Fastpasses for all members of your party, including those who are too short, too young, or simply not interested in riding, as this family of four recommends:

Utilize the Fastpasses of people in your group who don't want to ride. Our 6-year-old didn't want to ride anything rough. All four of us got Fastpasses for each ride. [When] the 6-year-old didn't want to ride, my husband and I took turns riding with the 12-year-old. It was our version of the Fastpass child swap, and the 12-year-old got double rides.

Fastpass Guidelines

- Don't mess with Fastpass unless it can save you 30 minutes or more.
- If you arrive after a park opens, obtain a Fastpass for your preferred Fastpass attraction first thing.
- Do not obtain a Fastpass for a theater attraction until you have experienced all the Fastpass rides on your itinerary. (Using Fastpass at theater attractions usually requires more time than using the standby line.)
- Check the Fastpass return time before obtaining a Fastpass.
- Obtain Fastpasses for Rock 'n' Roller Coaster and Toy Story Mania! at Disney's Hollywood Studios; Mission: SPACE, Soarin', and Test Track at Epcot; Expedition Everest at the Animal Kingdom; and The Many Adventures of Winnie the Pooh, Peter Pan's Flight, Space Mountain, and Splash Mountain at the Magic Kingdom as early in the day as possible.
- Try to obtain Fastpasses for rides not mentioned by 1 p.m.
- Don't depend on Fastpasses being available after 2 p.m. during busier times.
- Make sure everyone in your party has his or her own Fastpass.
- You can obtain a second Fastpass at the time printed at the bottom of your first Fastpass.
- Note your Fastpass return slot, and plan activities accordingly.

A WORD ABOUT DISNEY THRILL RIDES

READERS OF ALL AGES SHOULD ATTEMPT to be open-minded about the so-called Disney "thrill rides." In comparison with rides at other theme parks, most Disney thrill attractions are quite tame, with more emphasis on sights, atmosphere, and special effects than on the motion, speed, or feel of the ride itself. While we suggest you take Disney's preride warnings seriously, we can tell you that guests of all ages report enjoying rides such as Tower of Terror, Big Thunder Mountain Railroad, and Splash Mountain.

A reader from Washington sums up the situation well:

Our boys and I are used to imagining typical amusement park rides when it comes to roller coasters. So, when we thought of Big Thunder Mountain [Railroad] and Space Mountain, what came to mind was gigantic hills, upside-down loops, huge vertical drops, etc. I actually hate roller coasters, especially the unpleasant sensation of a long drop, and I have never taken a ride that loops you upside down.

In fact, the Disney [rides] are tame in comparison. There are never any long and steep hills (except Splash Mountain, and it is there for anyone to see, so you have informed consent going on the ride). I was able to build up courage to go on all of them, and the more I rode them the more I enjoyed them—the less you tense up expecting a big long drop, the more you enjoy the special effects and even swinging around curves. Swinging around curves is really the primary motion challenge of Disney roller coasters.

Disney, recognizing that it needs more attractions that appeal to the youth and young adult markets, has added some roller coasters to its parks. The Rock 'n' Roller Coaster at Disney's Hollywood Studios and Expedition Everest at the Animal Kingdom, for example, incorporate at least some of the features our Washington reader seeks to avoid.

A WORD ABOUT HEIGHT REQUIREMENTS

A NUMBER OF ATTRACTIONS REQUIRE children to meet minimum height and age requirements. If you have children too short or too young to ride, you have several options, including switching off (described on page 238). Although the alternatives may resolve some practical and logistical issues, be forewarned that your smaller children might nonetheless be resentful of their older (or taller) siblings who qualify to ride. A mom from Virginia bumped into just such a situation, writing:

You mention height requirements for rides but not the intense sibling jealousy this can generate. Frontierland was a real problem in that respect. Our very petite 5-year-old, to her outrage, was stuck hanging around while our 8-year-old went on Splash Mountain and [Big] Thunder Mountain [Railroad] with Grandma and Granddad, and the nearby alternatives weren't helpful (too long a line for rafts to Tom Sawyer Island, etc.). If we had thought ahead, we would have left the younger kid . . . with one of the grown-ups for another roller-coaster ride or two and then met up later at a designated point. The best areas had a playground or other quick attractions for short people near the rides with height requirements, like The Boneyard near the Dinosaur ride at the Animal Kingdom.

The reader makes a valid point, though in practical terms splitting the group and meeting later can be more complicated than she might imagine. If you choose to split up, ask the Disney greeter at the entrance to the attraction(s) with height requirements how long the wait is. Tack 5 minutes for riding onto the anticipated wait, and then add 5 or so minutes to exit and reach the meeting point for an approximate sense of how long the younger kids (and their supervising adult) will have to do other stuff. Our guess is that even with a long line for the rafts, the reader would have had more than sufficient time to take her daughter to Tom Sawyer Island while the sibs rode Splash Mountain and Big Thunder Mountain Railroad with the grandparents. For sure she had time to tour the Swiss Family Treehouse in adjacent Adventureland.

WAITING-LINE STRATEGIES FOR ADULTS WITH YOUNG CHILDREN

CHILDREN HOLD UP BETTER THROUGH THE DAY if you minimize the time they spend in lines. Arriving early and using our touring plans immensely reduces waiting. Here are additional ways to reduce stress for children:

1. LINE GAMES Wise parents anticipate restlessness in line and plan activities to reduce the stress and boredom. In the morning, have waiting children discuss what they want to see and do during the day. Later, watch for and count Disney characters or play simple guessing games such as 20 Questions. Lines move continuously, so games requiring pen and paper are impractical. The holding area of a theater attraction, however, is a different story. Here, tic-tac-toe, hangman, drawing, and coloring make the time fly by. As an alternative we've provided a trivia game for each park, developed by Walt Disney World trivia guru Lou Mongello, author of *The Walt Disney World Trivia Book, Volumes 1 and 2*; see **intrepidtraveler.com.**

2. LAST-MINUTE ENTRY If an attraction can accommodate an unusually large number of people at once, it's often unnecessary to stand in line. The Magic Kingdom's *Liberty Belle* Riverboat is a good example. The boat holds about 450 people, usually more than are waiting in line. Instead of standing uncomfortably in a crowd, grab a snack and sit in the shade until the boat arrives and loading is under way. After the line is almost gone, join it.

ATTRACTIONS YOU CAN USUALLY ENTER AT THE LAST MINUTE

Magic Kingdom

Liberty Square	The Hall of Presidents
	Liberty Belle Riverboat

Epcot

Future World	The Circle of Life (except during mealtimes)
World Showcase	Reflections of China
The American Adventure	O Canada!

Disney's Hollywood Studios

Sounds Dangerous	Backlot Tour

Animal Kingdom

Flights of Wonder

At large-capacity theaters like that for Epcot's *The American Adventure,* ask the entrance greeter how long it will be until guests are admitted for the next show. If it's 15 minutes or more, take a restroom break or get a snack, returning a few minutes before the show starts. You aren't allowed to carry food or drink into the attraction, so make sure you have time to finish your snack.

3. THE HAIL MARY PASS Certain lines are configured to allow you and your smaller children to pass under the rail to join your partner just before actual boarding or entry. This technique allows children and one adult to rest, snack, or go to the potty while another adult or older sibling stands in line. Other guests are very understanding about this strategy when used for young children. You're likely to meet hostile opposition, however, if you try to pass older children or more than one adult under the rail. To preempt hostility, tell the folks behind you in line what you are doing and why.

ATTRACTIONS WHERE YOU CAN USUALLY COMPLETE A HAIL MARY PASS

Magic Kingdom

Adventureland

Frontierland

Fantasyland

    Snow White's Scary Adventures   *Country Bear Jamboree*

    Prince Charming Regal Carrousel   Mad Tea Party

     Swiss Family Treehouse

     Dumbo the Flying Elephant

     Peter Pan's Flight

Epcot Future World

    Spaceship Earth   Living with the Land

Disney's Hollywood Studios

    Sounds Dangerous

Animal Kingdom

    DinoLand U.S.A.   TriceraTop Spin

---

4. SWITCHING OFF (also known as the Baby Swap) Several attractions have minimum height and/or age requirements, usually 40–48 inches tall to ride with an adult, or age 7 *and* 40 inches to ride alone. Some

---

ATTRACTIONS WHERE SWITCHING OFF IS COMMON

Magic Kingdom	**Epcot**
Big Thunder Mountain Railroad	Mission: SPACE
Space Mountain	Test Track
Splash Mountain	**Animal Kingdom**
Stitch's Great Escape!	DINOSAUR
Disney's Hollywood Studios	Expedition Everest
Rock 'n' Roller Coaster	Kali River Rapids
The Twilight Zone Tower of Terror	Primeval Whirl
Star Tours	

couples with children too small or too young forgo these attractions, while others take turns to ride. Missing some of Disney's best rides is an unnecessary sacrifice, and waiting in line twice for the same ride is a tremendous waste of time.

Instead, take advantage of the "switching-off" option, also called "the baby swap." To switch off, there must be at least two adults. Everybody waits in line together, adults and children. When you

Attractions and Ride Restrictions

MAGIC KINGDOM

The Barnstormer at Goofy's Wiseacre Farm	35" minimum height
Big Thunder Mountain Railroad	40" minimum height
Mickey's Toontown Fair Toon Park	40" maximum height
Space Mountain	44" minimum height
Splash Mountain	40" minimum height
Stitch's Great Escape!	40" minimum height
Tomorrowland Speedway	32" minimum height (54" to drive unassisted)

EPCOT

Maelstrom	3 years minimum age
Mission: SPACE	44" minimum height
Soarin'	40" minimum height
Test Track	40" minimum height

DISNEY'S HOLLYWOOD STUDIOS

Honey, I Shrunk the Kids Movie Set Adventure	4 years minimum age
Rock 'n' Roller Coaster	48" minimum height
Star Tours	40" minimum height
The Twilight Zone Tower of Terror	40" minimum height

ANIMAL KINGDOM

DINOSAUR	40" minimum height
Expedition Everest	44" minimum height

reach an attendant (called a "greeter"), tell him or her that you want to switch off. The greeter will allow everyone, including the young children, to enter the attraction. When you reach the loading area, one adult rides while the other stays with the kids. Then the riding adult disembarks and takes charge of the children while the other adult rides. A third adult in the party can ride twice, once with each of the switching-off adults, so that the switching-off adults don't have to experience the attraction alone.

On many Fastpass attractions, Disney handles switching off somewhat differently. When you tell the cast member that you want to switch off, he or she will issue you a special "rider exchange" Fastpass good for three people. One parent and the nonriding child (or children) will at that point be asked to leave the line. When those riding reunite with the waiting adult, the waiting adult and two other persons from the party can ride using the special Fastpass. This system eliminates confusion and congestion at the boarding area, while sparing the nonriding adult and child the tedium and physical exertion of waiting in line.

Kali River Rapids. . . . . 38" minimum height
Primeval Whirl . . . . 48" minimum height

BLIZZARD BEACH WATER PARK
Chair Lift . . . . 32" minimum height
Downhill Double Dipper slide . . . . 48" minimum height
Slush Gusher slide . . . . 48" minimum height
Summit Plummet slide . . . . 48" minimum height
T-Bar (in Ski Patrol Training Camp) . . . . 60" maximum height
Tike's Peak children's area . . . . 48" maximum height

TYPHOON LAGOON WATER PARK
Bay Slides . . . . 60" minimum height
Crush 'n' Gusher. . . . . 48" minimum height
Humunga Kowabunga slide . . . . 48" minimum height
Ketchakiddee Creek children's area . . . . 48" maximum height
Shark Reef saltwater reef swim . . . . .10 years minimum age
                                              unless accompanied by an adult
Wave Pool . . . . .Adult supervision required

DISNEY QUEST
Buzz Lightyear's AstroBlasters . . . . 51" minimum height
CyberSpace Mountain . . . . 51" minimum height
Mighty Ducks Pinball Slam . . . . 48" minimum height
Pirates of the Caribbean: Battle for Buccaneer Gold . . . . 35" minimum height

Attractions at which switching off is practiced are oriented to more mature guests. Sometimes it takes a lot of courage for a child just to move through the queue holding dad's hand. In the boarding area, many children suddenly fear abandonment as one parent leaves to experience the attraction. Unless your children are prepared for switching off, you might have an emotional crisis on your hands. A mom from Edison, New Jersey, advises:

> Once my son came to understand that the switch-off would not leave him abandoned, he did not seem to mind. I would recommend to your readers that they practice the switch-off on some dry runs at home so that their child is not concerned that he will be left behind. At the very least, the procedure could be explained in advance so that the little ones know what to expect.

Finally, a mother from Ada, Michigan, who discovered that the procedure for switching off varies from attraction to attraction, offered this suggestion:

Parents need to tell the very first attendant they come to that they would like to switch off. Each attraction has a different procedure for this. Tell every other attendant too because they forget quickly.

5. LAST-MINUTE COLD FEET If your young child gets cold feet just before boarding a ride where there is no age or height requirement, you usually can arrange with the loading attendant for a switch off. This is common at Pirates of the Caribbean, where children lose their courage while winding through the dungeon-like waiting area. Additionally, no law says you *have* to ride. If you reach the boarding area and someone is unhappy, tell an attendant you've changed your mind and you'll be shown the way out.

6. CATCH-22 AT TOMORROWLAND SPEEDWAY Though Tomorrowland Speedway is a great treat for young children, they're required to be 52 inches tall in order to drive unassisted. Few children age 6 and younger measure up, so the ride is essentially withheld from the very age group that would most enjoy it. To resolve this catch-22, go on the ride with your small child. The attendants will assume that you will drive. After getting into the car, shift your child over behind the steering wheel. From your position, you will still be able to control the foot pedals. Children will feel like they're really driving, and because the car travels on a self-guiding track, there's no way they can make a mistake while steering.

CHARACTER ANALYSIS

THE LARGE, FRIENDLY COSTUMED VERSIONS of Mickey, Minnie, Donald, Goofy, and others—known as "Disney characters"—provide a link between Disney animated films and the theme parks. To people emotionally invested, the characters in Disney films are as real as next-door neighbors, never mind that they're just drawings on plastic. In recent years, theme park personifications of the characters also have become real to us. It's not just a person in a mouse costume we see; it is Mickey himself. Similarly, meeting Goofy or Snow White in Fantasyland is an encounter with a celebrity, a memory to be treasured.

If your children can't enjoy things until they see Mickey, ask a cast member where to find him. If the cast member doesn't know right away, he or she can find out quickly. Cast members have a number they can call to learn exactly where the characters are at any time.

While there are hundreds of Disney animated film characters, only about 250 have been brought to life in costume. Of these, a relatively small number (less than a fifth) are "greeters" (characters who mix with guests). The remaining characters perform in shows or parades. Originally confined to the Magic Kingdom, characters are now found in all the major theme parks and Disney hotels.

CHARACTER WATCHING

CHARACTER WATCHING has become a pastime. Families once were content to meet characters only occasionally and by chance. They now pursue them relentlessly, armed with autograph books and cameras. Because some characters are only rarely seen, character watching has become character collecting. (To cash in on character collecting, Disney sells autograph books throughout the World.) Mickey, Minnie, and Goofy are a snap to bag; they seem to be everywhere. But Jiminy Cricket seldom comes out. Other characters appear regularly but only in a location consistent with their starring roles. Cinderella, predictably, reigns at Cinderella Castle in Fantasyland, while Br'er Fox and Br'er Bear frolic in Frontierland near Splash Mountain.

A Brooklyn, New York, dad thinks the character autograph–hunting craze has gotten out of hand, complaining:

> *Whoever started the practice of collecting autographs from the characters should be subjected to Chinese water torture! We went to Walt Disney World 11 years ago, with an 8-year-old and an 11-year-old. We would bump into characters, take pictures, and that was it. After a while, our children noticed that some of the other children were getting autographs. We managed to avoid joining in during our first day at the Magic Kingdom and our first day at Epcot, but by day three our children were collecting autographs. However, it did not get too out of hand, since it was limited to accidental character meeting.*
>
> *This year when we took our youngest child (who is now age 8), he had already seen his siblings' collection and was determined to outdo them. However, rather than random meetings, the characters are now available practically all day long at different locations, according to a printed schedule, which our son was old enough to read. We spent more time standing in line for autographs than we did for the most popular rides!*

A family from Birmingham, Alabama, found some benefit in their children's relentless pursuit of characters, writing:

> *We had no idea we would be caught up in this madness, but after my daughters grabbed your guidebook to get Pocahontas to sign it (we had no blank paper), we quickly bought a Disney autograph book and gave in. It was actually the highlight of their trip, and my son even got into the act by helping get places in line for his sisters. They LOVED looking for characters. . . . The possibility of seeing a new character revived my 7-year-old's energy on many occasions. It was an amazing, totally unexpected part of our visit.*

Our advice for parents with pre-schoolers is to stay with the kids when they meet characters, stepping back only to take a quick picture.

Bob

"THEN SOME CONFUSION HAPPENED" Young children sometimes become lost at character encounters. Usually, there's a lot of activity around a character, with both adults and children touching it or posing for pictures. Most commonly, mom and dad stay in the crowd while Junior approaches to meet the character. In the excitement and with people milling and the character moving around, Junior heads off in the wrong direction to look for mom and dad. In the words of a Salt Lake City mom: "Milo was shaking hands with Dopey one minute, then some confusion happened and [Milo] was gone." Families with several young children and parents who are busy with cameras can lose track of a youngster in a heartbeat.

CHARACTER DINING: WHAT TO EXPECT

CHARACTER DINING HAS BECOME SO POPULAR that Disney offers character breakfasts, brunches, lunches, and dinners where families can dine in the presence of Mickey, Minnie, Goofy, and other costumed versions of animated celebrities. Besides grabbing customers from Denny's and Hardee's, character meals provide a controlled setting in which young children can warm to the characters. All meals are attended by several characters. Adult prices apply to persons age 10 or older, children's prices to kids ages 3–9. Children younger than 3 years eat free. For more information on character dining, call ☎ 407-WDW-DINE (407-939-3463).

Because character dining is very popular, arrange Advance Reservations as early as possible by calling ☎ 407-WDW-DINE. Advance

"Casting? There's been a mistake. We were supposed to get the Assorted Character Package with one Mickey, one Goofy, one Donald . . . "

Reservations aren't reservations, per se—only a commitment to seat you ahead of walk-in patrons at the scheduled date and time. At character meals that very popular, such as breakfast at Cinderella's Royal Table, you are required to make a for-real reservation and to guarantee it with a for-real deposit.

Character meals are bustling affairs held in hotels' or theme parks' largest full-service restaurants. Character breakfasts offer a fixed menu served individually, family-style, or on a buffet. The typical breakfast includes scrambled eggs; bacon, sausage, and ham; hash browns; waffles or French toast; biscuits, rolls, or pastries; and fruit. With family-style service, the meal is served in large skillets or on platters at your table. Seconds (or thirds) are free at both family-service and fixed-menu character meals. Buffets offer much the same fare, but you fetch it yourself.

Character dinners range from a set menu served family-style to buffets or ordering off the menu. Character dinner buffets offer separate adults' and children's serving lines. Typically, the children's buffet includes hamburgers, hot dogs, pizza, fish sticks, fried chicken nuggets, macaroni and cheese, and peanut-butter-and-jelly sandwiches. Selections at the adult buffet usually include prime rib or other carved meat, baked or broiled Florida seafood, pasta, chicken, an ethnic dish or two, vegetables, potatoes, and salad.

At all meals characters circulate around the room. During your meal, each of the three to five characters present will visit your table, arriving one at a time to cuddle the kids (and sometimes the adults), pose for photos, and sign autographs. Keep autograph books (with pens) and loaded cameras handy. For the best photos, adults should sit across the table from their children. Seat the children where characters can easily reach them. If a table is against a wall, for example, adults should sit with their backs to the wall and children on the aisle.

At some larger restaurants, including 'Ohana at the Polynesian Resort and Chef Mickey's at the Contemporary, character meals involve impromptu parades of characters and children around the room, group singing, napkin waving, and other organized mayhem.

Servers don't rush you to leave after you've eaten—you can stay as long as you wish to enjoy the characters. Remember, however, that lots of eager kids and adults are waiting not so patiently to be admitted.

When my son was 3 years old, he was nuts to meet Cinderella. Like *Liliane* so many moms before me, I stood in line at Cinderella Castle to meet her (this was before you had to buy a meal to meet Cinderella). The wait was long, and when it was finally our turn, my boy had fallen asleep. Oh, the agony! Should I wake him? Should I leave the mission unaccomplished? Well, in the end Cinderella came to the rescue. She smiled and asked me to sit down for a chat. She signed my son's autograph book and said, "Tell him to look for me waving at him tonight at the evening parade." And wave she did. I am not even sure it was the same Cinderella, but my son was convinced she was and believed that he had met Cinderella, albeit in his dreams.

When To Go

Attending a character breakfast usually prevents you from arriving at the theme parks in time for opening. Because early morning is best for touring and you don't want to burn daylight lingering over breakfast, we suggest the following:

1. Go to a character dinner or lunch instead of breakfast; it won't conflict with your touring schedule.

2. Substitute a late character breakfast for lunch. Have a light breakfast early from room service or your cooler to tide you over. Then tour the theme park for an hour or two before breaking off around 10:15 a.m. to go to the character breakfast. Make a big brunch of your character breakfast and skip lunch. You should be fueled until dinner.

3. Go on your arrival or departure day. The day you arrive and check in is usually good for a character dinner. Settle at your hotel, swim, then dine with the characters. This strategy has the added benefit of exposing your children to the characters before chance encounters at the parks. Some children, moreover, won't settle down to enjoy the parks until they have seen Mickey. Departure day also is good for a character meal. Schedule a character breakfast on your check-out day before you head for the airport or begin your drive home.

4. Go on a rest day. If you plan to stay five or more days, you'll probably take a day or half day from touring to rest or do something else. These are perfect days for a character meal.

How To Choose a Character Meal

Many readers ask for advice about character meals. This question from a Waterloo, Iowa, mom is typical:

Are all character breakfasts pretty much the same, or are some better than others? How should I go about choosing one?

In fact, some are better, sometimes much better. When we evaluate character meals, we look for these things:

1. **THE CHARACTERS** The meals offer a diverse assortment of characters. Select a meal that features your kids' favorites. Check out our Character Meal Hit Parade chart (pages 248–249) to see which characters are assigned to each meal. Most restaurants stick with the same characters. Even so, check the lineup when you call to make Advance Reservations.

A mom from Michigan offers this report:

Our character meal at 1900 Park Fare was a DISASTER!!! Please warn other readers with younger children that if they make Advance Reservations and the characters are villains, they may want to rethink their options. We went for my daughter's fifth birthday, and she was scared to death. The Queen of Hearts chased her sobbing and screaming down the hallway. Most young children we saw at the dinner were very frightened. Captain Hook and Prince John were laid-back, but Governor Ratcliff [from Pocahontas*] and the Queen were amazingly rude and intimidating.*

The villains have abdicated 1900 Park Fare in favor of more benign characters, but you never know where the baddies might show up next. Moral? Call before making Advance Reservations and ask with which characters you'll be dining.

2. **ATTENTION FROM THE CHARACTERS** At all character meals, characters circulate among guests, hugging children, posing for pictures, and signing autographs. How much time a character spends with you and your children depends primarily on the ratio of characters to guests. The more characters and fewer guests, the better. Because many character meals never fill to capacity, the character-to-guest ratios found in our Character Meal Hit Parade chart (pages 248–249) have been adjusted to reflect an average attendance. Even so, there's quite a range. The best ratio is at Cinderella's Royal Table, where there's approximately one character to every 26 guests.

The worst ratio is theoretically at the Swan Resort's Garden Grove, where there could be as few as 1 character for every 198 guests. We say "theoretically," however, because in practice there are far fewer guests at the Garden Grove than at character meals in Disney-owned resorts, and often more characters. During one recent meal, friends of ours were literally the only guests in the restaurant for breakfast and had to ask the characters to leave them alone to eat.

3. **THE SETTING** Some character meals are in exotic settings. For others, moving the event to an elementary-school cafeteria would be an improvement. Our chart rates each meal's setting with the familiar scale of zero (worst) to five (best) stars. Two restaurants, Cinderella's Royal Table in the Magic Kingdom and The Garden Grill Restaurant in the Land Pavilion at Epcot, deserve special mention. Cinderella's Royal Table is on the first and second floors of Cinderella Castle in Fantasyland, offering guests a look inside the castle. The Garden Grill is a revolving restaurant overlooking several scenes from the Living with The Land boat ride. Also at Epcot, the popular Princesses Character Breakfast is held in the castlelike Akershus Royal Banquet Hall. Though Chef Mickey's at the Contemporary Resort is rather sterile in appearance, it affords a great view of the monorail running through the hotel. Themes and settings of the remaining character-meal venues, while apparent to adults, will be lost on most children.

4. **THE FOOD** Although some food served at character meals is quite good, most is average (palatable but nothing to get excited about). In variety, consistency, and quality, restaurants generally do a better job with breakfast than with lunch or dinner (if served). Some restaurants offer a buffet, while others opt for "one-skillet" family-style service, in which all hot items are served from the same pot or skillet. To help you sort it

Many kids take special delight in meeting the "face characters," such as Jasmine, Aladdin, and Cinderella, who can speak to them and engage them in a way that the mute animal characters can't.

Character Meal Hit Parade

1. CINDERELLA'S ROYAL TABLE

LOCATION: Magic Kingdom
MEALS SERVED: Breakfast/lunch/ dinner
CHARACTERS: Cinderella, Snow White, Belle,
Jasmine, the Fairy Godmother
SERVED: Daily
SETTING: ★★★★★
TYPE OF SERVICE: Fixed menu
FOOD VARIETY AND QUALITY: ★★★
NOISE LEVEL: Quiet
CHARACTER-TO-GUEST RATIO: 1:26

2. AKERSHUS ROYAL BANQUET HALL

LOCATION: Epcot
MEALS SERVED: Breakfast/lunch/ dinner
CHARACTERS: 4–6 characters chosen from Belle,
Mulan, Snow White, Sleeping Beauty,
Ariel, Alice, Mary Poppins, Jasmine
SERVED: Daily
SETTING: ★★★★
TYPE OF SERVICE: Family-style and menu
  (all you care to eat)
FOOD VARIETY AND QUALITY: ★★★½
NOISE LEVEL: Quiet
CHARACTER-TO-GUEST RATIO: 1:54

3. CHEF MICKEY'S

LOCATION: Contemporary
MEALS SERVED: Breakfast/dinner
CHARACTERS: *Breakfast:* Minnie, Mickey, Chip, Pluto,
Goofy;   *Dinner:* Mickey, Minnie, Donald, Pluto, Goofy
SERVED: Daily
SETTING: ★★★
TYPE OF SERVICE: Buffet
FOOD VARIETY AND QUALITY: ★★★ *(breakfast);*
  ★★★½ *(dinner)*
NOISE LEVEL: Loud
CHARACTER-TO-GUEST RATIO: 1:56

4. CRYSTAL PALACE

LOCATION: Magic Kingdom
MEALS SERVED: Breakfast/lunch/ dinner
CHARACTERS: Pooh, Tigger, Eeyore, Piglet
SERVED: Daily
SETTING: ★★★
TYPE OF SERVICE: Buffet
FOOD VARIETY AND QUALITY: ★★½ *(breakfast);*
  ★★★½ *(lunch and dinner)*
NOISE LEVEL: Very loud
CHARACTER-TO-GUEST RATIO: 1:67 *(breakfast);*
  1:89 *(lunch and dinner)*

5. 1900 PARK FARE

LOCATION: Grand Floridian
MEALS SERVED: Breakfast/dinner
CHARACTERS: *Breakfast:* Mary Poppins, Alice,
Mad Hatter, Pooh;   *Dinner:* Cinderella,
Prince Charming, Lady Tremaine, the two stepsisters
SERVED: Daily
SETTING: ★★★
TYPE OF SERVICE: Buffet
FOOD VARIETY AND QUALITY: ★★★ *(breakfast);*
  ★★★½ *(dinner)*
NOISE LEVEL: Moderate
CHARACTER-TO-GUEST RATIO: 1:54 *(breakfast);*
  1:44 *(dinner)*

6. THE GARDEN GRILL RESTAURANT

LOCATION: Epcot
MEALS SERVED: Dinner
CHARACTERS: Mickey, Chip 'n Dale, Pluto
SERVED: Daily
SETTING: ★★★★½
TYPE OF SERVICE: Family-style
FOOD VARIETY AND QUALITY: ★★★½
NOISE LEVEL: Very quiet
CHARACTER-TO-GUEST RATIO: 1:46

7. TUSKER HOUSE RESTAURANT

LOCATION: Animal Kingdom
MEALS SERVED: Breakfast
CHARACTERS: Donald, Daisy, Mickey, Goofy
SERVED: Daily
SETTING: ★★★
TYPE OF SERVICE: buffet
FOOD VARIETY AND QUALITY: ★★★
NOISE LEVEL: Very loud
CHARACTER-TO-GUEST RATIO: 1:112

8. CAPE MAY CAFE

LOCATION: Beach Club
MEALS SERVED: Breakfast
CHARACTERS: Goofy, Donald, minnie
SERVED: Daily
SETTING: ★★★
TYPE OF SERVICE: Buffet
FOOD VARIETY AND QUALITY: ★★½
NOISE LEVEL: moderate
CHARACTER-TO-GUEST RATIO: 1:67

Character Meal Hit Parade (continued)

9. 'OHANA

LOCATION: Polynesian Resort
MEALS SERVED: Breakfast
CHARACTERS: Mickey, Pluto, Lilo, Stitch
SERVED: Daily
SETTING: ★★
TYPE OF SERVICE: Family-style
FOOD VARIETY AND QUALITY: ★★½
NOISE LEVEL: Moderate
CHARACTER-TO-GUEST RATIO: 1:57

10. HOLLYWOOD & VINE

LOCATION: Disney's Hollywood Studios
MEALS SERVED: Breakfast/lunch
CHARACTERS: JoJo, Goliath, June, Leo
SERVED: Daily
SETTING: ★★½
TYPE OF SERVICE: Buffet
FOOD VARIETY AND QUALITY: ★★★
NOISE LEVEL: Moderate
CHARACTER-TO-GUEST RATIO: 1:71

11. GARDEN GROVE

LOCATION: Swan
MEALS SERVED: Breakfast/dinner
CHARACTERS: Rafiki and Timon *(Mon. and Fri.)*; Goofy and Pluto other nights
SERVED: daily
SETTING: ★★★
TYPE OF SERVICE: Buffet
FOOD VARIETY AND QUALITY: ★★★½
NOISE LEVEL: Moderate
CHARACTER-TO-GUEST RATIO: 1:198, but often much better

out, we rate the food at each character meal in our chart using the five-star scale.

5. **THE PROGRAM** Some larger restaurants stage modest performances where the characters dance, head a parade around the room, or lead songs and cheers. For some guests, these activities give the meal a celebratory air; for others, they turn what was already mayhem into absolute chaos. Either way, the antics consume time the characters could spend with families at their table.

6. **NOISE** If you want to eat in peace, character meals are a bad choice. That said, some are much noisier than others. Our chart gives you an idea of what to expect.

7. **WHICH MEAL** Although breakfasts seem to be most popular, character lunches and dinners are usually more practical because they don't interfere with early-morning touring. During hot weather, a character lunch can be heavenly.

8. **COST** Dinners cost more than lunches, and lunches are more than breakfasts. Prices for meals (except those at Cinderella Castle) vary only about $4 from the least expensive to the most expensive restaurant. Breakfasts run $21–$45 for adults and $12–$23 for ages 3–9. For character lunches, expect to pay $23–$48 for adults and $13–$31 for kids. Dinners are $27–$55 for adults and $18–$34 for children. Little ones age 2 and younger eat free. The meals at the high end of the price range are at Cinderella's Royal Table in the Magic Kingdom and Akershus Royal Banquet Hall at Epcot. The reasons for the sky-high prices are (1) Cinderella's Royal Table is small but in

great demand, and (2) the prices at Cinderella's and Akershus include a set of photos of your group taken by a Disney photographer. Whereas photos at other venues are optional, at Cindy's and Akershus, you don't have a say in the matter.

9. **ADVANCE RESERVATIONS** The Disney dining reservations system makes Advance Reservations for character meals up to 180 days before you wish to dine. Advance Reservations for most character meals are easy to obtain, even if you call only a couple of weeks before you leave home. Breakfast and lunch at Cinderella's Royal Table are another story. To eat at Cinderella's, you'll need our strategy as well as help from Congress and the Pope.

10. **HOMELESS CHARACTERS** Disney periodically pulls the plug on one or another of the character meals. Reconfirm all character-meal Advance Reservations three weeks or so before you leave home by calling ☎ 407-WDW-DINE. In the past year things have been changing more often, so if it must be Pooh and Piglet, double-check before you go to the character meal. And as recommended earlier, it is better to not promise something over which you do not have control.

11. **FRIENDS AND PALS** For some venues, Disney has stopped specifying characters scheduled for a particular meal. Instead, they say it's a certain character "and friends (or pals)." For example, "Pooh and friends," meaning Eeyore, Piglet, and Tigger, or some combination thereof, or "Mickey's pals" with some assortment chosen among Minnie, Goofy, Pluto, Donald, and Daisy. Most are self-evident, but others such as "Mary Poppins and friends" are unclear. Who knows whom Mary Poppins hangs out with? (Don't expect Dick van Dyke.)

12. **THE BUM'S RUSH** Most character meals are leisurely affairs, and you can usually stay as long as you want. An exception is Cinderella's Royal Table in the Magic Kingdom. Because Cindy's is in such high demand, the restaurant does everything short of pre-chewing your food to move you through, as this European mother of a 5-year-old can attest:

We dined a lot, did three character meals and a few signature restaurants, and every meal was awesome except for lunch with Cinderella in the castle. While I'd often read it wouldn't be a rushed affair, it was exactly that. We had barely sat down when the appetizers were thrown on our table, the princesses each spent just a few seconds with our daughter—almost no interaction—and the side dishes were cold. We were out of there within 40 minutes and felt very stressed. Considering the price for the meal, I cannot recommend it.

Boosting Sales of Mementos and Souvenirs

Usually when Disney sees a horse carrying moneybags, it rides it until it drops. Disney's latest scheme of bundling photos and souvenirs in the price of character meals at Cinderella's Royal Table and Akershus Royal Banquet Hall is probably something we'll see again at other venues. Adding photos of your group taken by a Disney photographer is Disney's justification for raising the price of the character meals by about 60%. Disney insists that you're getting the photos at a bargain price. This is well and good if you're in the market, but if buying photos was not in your plans, well, they've gotcha. It's a matter of some conjecture how far Disney will run with this idea. Maybe next year the price will be $200 and include fanciful medieval costumes for your entire party (charges for the changing room and locker to store your street clothes not included).

GETTING AN ADVANCE RESERVATION AT CINDERELLA'S ROYAL TABLE

CINDERELLA'S ROYAL TABLE, in Cinderella Castle in the Magic Kingdom, hosts the immensely popular character breakfast starring Cinderella and various and sundry other Disney princesses. Admittedly, the toughest ticket at Disney World is an Advance Reservation for this character meal. Why? Cinderella's Royal Table is Disney's tiniest

If you've secured Advance Reservations for a character meal, I say roll out the costume chest. Dress up your little tyke—from princess to pirate, anything goes. As a matter of fact, if your little princess wants to wear her princess dress when visiting the Magic Kingdom for the first time, indulge her. And don't worry about the unavoidable food landing on the precious dress; that is what stain removers are for. Besides, if not today, when?

Liliane

character-meal restaurant, accommodating only about 130 diners at a time. Demand so outdistances supply for this event that Walt Disney World visitors go to unbelievable lengths to secure an Advance Reservation. After decades of guests complaining and beating their chests over their inability to get a table, Disney also offers a noon–2 p.m. character lunch with the same cast of characters and a fixed-price evening meal presided over solo by the Fairy Godmother.

This frustrated reader from Golden, Colorado, complains:

I don't know what you have to do to get an Advance Reservation for Cinderella's Royal Table in the castle. I called Disney Dining every morning at 7 a.m., which was 5 a.m. where I live! It was like calling in to one of those radio shows where the first person to call wins a prize. Every time I finally got through, all the tables were gone. I am soooo frustrated and mad I could spit. What do you have to do to get a table for Cinderella's breakfast?

The only way to get a table is to obtain an Advance Reservation through Disney reservations. You must call ☎ 407-WDW-DINE at 7 a.m. EST exactly 180 days before the day you want to eat at Cinderella's. If you live in California and have to get up at 4 a.m. Pacific time to call, Disney couldn't care less. There's no limit to the number of hoops they can make their patrons jump through if demand exceeds supply.

Here's how it works. It's 6:50 a.m. EST and all the Disney dining reservationists are warming up their computers to begin filling available seats at 7 a.m. As the clock strikes 7, Disney dining is blasted with an avalanche of calls, all trying to make Advance Reservations for the character meals at Cinderella's Royal Table. There are more than 100 reservationists on duty, and most Advance Reservations can be assigned in 2 minutes or less. Thus, the coveted seats go quickly, selling out as early as 7:02 a.m. on many days.

To be among the fortunate few who score an Advance Reservation, try the following. First, call on the correct morning. Use a calendar and count backward exactly 180 days from (but not including) the day you wish to dine. (The computer doesn't understand months, so you can't, for example, call on January 1 to make an Advance Reservation for July 1 because that's more than 180 days.) If you want to eat on May 1, for example, begin your 180-day backward count on April 30. If you count correctly, you'll find that the correct morning to call is October 31. If you don't feel like counting days, call ☎ 407-WDW-DINE and the Disney folks will calculate it for you. Call them during the afternoon, when they're less busy, about 185 days before your trip. Let them know when you'd like your Advance Reservation, and they'll tell you the morning to call.

To get a table, you must dial at almost exactly 7 a.m. EST. Disney does not calibrate its clock with the correct time as determined by the U.S. Naval Observatory or the National Institute of Standards and Technology, but we conducted synchronizing tests and determined that Disney reservation-system clocks are accurate to within 1–3 seconds. Several Internet sites will give you the exact time. Our favorite is **atomictime.net,** which offers the exact time in displays that show hours, minutes, and seconds. Once the Atomic Time home page is up, click on "HTML multizone continuous" and look for the Eastern Time Zone. Using this site or your local Time of Day number from the phone directory, synchronize your watch TO THE SECOND. About 18–20 seconds before 7 a.m., dial ☎ 407-WDW-DINE, waiting to dial the final E in DINE until 7 seconds before the hour.

Hang up and redial until your call is answered. When it is, you will hear one of two recorded messages:

1. "Thank you for calling the Disney Reservation Center. Our office is closed. . . ." If you get this message, hang up the instant you hear the words "Our office," and hit redial.

OR

2. You'll get a recording with a number of prompts. The prompts change periodically. Call a few mornings before the day you actually make your reservation to learn what prompts are being used. Once you know the prompts, you can determine which numbers on your touch-tone phone to press in order to work through the prompts at warp speed. Some prompts begin with "If," others may request info such as your phone number or resort reservation number. Do not listen to the entire prompt. Immediately press the appropriate numbered key(s) as determined by your previous trial run.

Your call will be answered momentarily by a Disney Reservation

Center (DRC) agent. Don't get nervous if you're on hold for a bit. The worst thing you can do now is hang up and try again.

As soon as a live DRC agent comes on the line, interrupt immediately and say, "I need Cindy's breakfast [lunch], for May 1, for four people, any available time" (substituting your own breakfast or lunch dates, of course). Don't engage in "good mornings" or other pleasantries. Time is of the essence. You can apologize later to the DRC agent for your momentary rudeness if you feel the need to do so, but she already knows what's going on. Don't try to pick a specific time. Even 2 seconds to ask for a specific time will seriously diminish your chances of getting an Advance Reservation.

If the atomic-clock thing seems too complicated (not to mention anal), start dialing ☎ 407-WDW-DINE about 50 seconds before 7 a.m. If the reservation center isn't open yet, you'll get a recorded message saying so. When this happens, hang up and call back immediately. If you have a redial button on your phone, use it to speed the dialing process. Continue hanging up and redialing as fast as you can until you get the recording with the prompts. This recording verifies that your call has been placed in the service queue in the order in which it was received. If you were among the first to get through, a reservationist will normally pick up in 3–20 seconds. What happens next depends on how many others got through ahead of you, but chances are good that you'll be able to get an Advance Reservation. Bear in mind that while you're talking, other agents are confirming Advance Reservations for other guests, so you want the transaction to go down as fast as possible. Flexibility on your part counts. It's much harder to get a seating for a large group; give some thought to breaking your group into numbers that can be accommodated at tables for four.

All Advance Reservations for Cinderella's Royal Table character meals require complete prepayment with a credit card at the time of the booking. The name on the booking can't be changed after the Advance Reservation is made. Advance Reservations may be canceled with the deposit refunded in full by calling ☎ 407-WDW-DINE at least 24 hours before the seating time.

While many readers have been successful using our strategies, some have not:

> [Regarding] reservations for breakfast at Cinderella Castle, I did exactly what you suggested, five days in a row, and was unable to get through to an actual person until after 7:15 each day (although I was connected and put on hold at exactly 7 a.m. each time). Of course, by then, all reservations were gone (this was for the first week in May, not a peak time).

On most days, a couple of hundred calls slam Disney's automated call-queuing system within milliseconds of one another. With this call volume, a 20th of a second or less can make the difference between getting a table and not getting one. As it happens, there are variables beyond your control. When you hit the first digit of a long-distance number, your phone system leaps into action. As you continue entering digits, your phone system is already searching for the best path to the number you're calling. According to federal regulation, a phone system must connect the call to the target number within 20 seconds of your entering the last digit. In practice, most systems make the connection much faster, but your system could be pokey. How fast your call is connected, therefore, depends on your local phone system's connection speed, and even this varies according to traffic volume and available routing paths for individual calls. Distance counts too, though we're talking milliseconds. Thus, it takes just a bit longer for a call to reach Disney World from Chicago than from Atlanta, and longer yet if you're calling from San Francisco.

So, if you're having trouble getting an Advance Reservation at Cinderella's Royal Table using the strategies outlined earlier, here are our suggestions. Make a test call to ☎ 407-WDW-DINE at 7 a.m. EST a couple of days before you call in earnest. Using a stopwatch or the stopwatch function on your watch, time the interval between entering the last digit of the number and when the phone starts to ring. This exercise will provide a rough approximation of the call connection speed at that time from your area, taking into account both speed of service and distance. For most of you, the connection interval will be very short. Some of you, however, might discover that your problem in getting through is because of slow service. Either way, factor in the connection interval in timing your call to Disney. Phone traffic is heavier on weekdays than weekends, so if you plan to call reservations on a weekday, conduct your test on a weekday. Finally, don't use a cell phone to make the call. The connection time will usually be slower and certainly less predictable.

This is one of the most widely used sections in this guidebook, but we're amazed that anyone would go to this much trouble to eat with Cinderella . . . atomic clocks, split-second timing, test calls . . . egad!

As a postscript, we've found it's often easier to get through to reservations if you call on Saturday or Sunday. Presumably, folks don't mind calling at the break of dawn if they're up getting ready for work but object to interrupting their beauty rest on weekends.

If You Can't Get an Advance Reservation

If you insist on a meal at Cinderella's but can't get an Advance Reservation, go to the restaurant on the day you wish to dine and try for a table as a walk-in. This is a long shot, though it's possible during the least busy times of year. There's also a fair shot at success on cold or rainy days when there's an above-average probability of no-shows. If you try to walk in, your chances are best during the last hour of serving.

Landing an Advance Reservation for dinner is somewhat easier, but only the Fairy Godmother is present, and the price is a whopping $55 for adults and $34 for children ages 3–9. As at breakfast and lunch, five photos of your group and a photo of the castle, along with a Cinderella-themed photo holder, are included in the price (like it or not). If you're unable to lock up a table for breakfast or lunch, a dinner reservation will at least get your children inside the castle. Even without characters, a meal in the castle costs a bundle, as this Snellville, Georgia, mom points out:

> We ate [dinner] at Cinderella Castle to fulfill my longtime dream. The menu was very limited and expensive. For three people, no appetizers or dessert, the bill was $100.

And no alcoholic beverages, either. Alcohol isn't served in the Magic Kingdom.

THE CINDERELLA ALTERNATIVE A Rochester, Michigan, mother of two toddlers suggests a less stressful way to dine with Cinderella:

> We went to the Cinderella character dinner at 1900 Park Fare. Once we did this, I stopped trying to get a last-minute reservation at Cinderella's Royal Table. My daughter loved the dinner. The decor of the restaurant was elegant and befitting Cinderella. I think you should emphasize that this is a more easily obtained alternative to Cinderella's Royal Table. It wasn't easy to get, but I was able to get a reservation only about two months in advance instead of the 180-days-and-atomic-clock routine that the Royal Table requires. Maybe someday we'll do the Royal Table, but this time my daughter was delighted with the dinner at 1900 Park Fare.

OTHER CHARACTER EVENTS

CHIP 'N' DALE'S CAMPFIRE, SING-A-LONG, AND MOVIE are held nightly (times vary with the season) near the Meadow Trading Post and Bike Barn at Fort Wilderness Resort & Campground. Chip 'n' Dale lead the songs, and two Disney films are shown. The program is free and open to resort guests (☎ 407-824-2900).

Another character encounter at Fort Wilderness is Mickey's Backyard BBQ, held seasonally on Thursday and Saturday. Prices range $27–$45.

WONDERLAND TEA PARTY Although the name of this enchanting soiree is enough to give most boys hives, it's nevertheless available at the Grand Floridian's 1900 Park Fare restaurant, Monday through Friday, at 1:30 p.m. for about $40 per child (ages 4–12). The program consists of decorating cupcakes and having lunch and tea with characters from *Alice in Wonderland*. Reserve up to 180 days in advance by calling ☎ 407-WDW-DINE.

STROLLERS

STROLLERS ARE AVAILABLE FOR RENT at all four theme parks and the Downtown Disney area (single stroller, $15 per day, no deposit,

Liliane

I strongly recommend bringing your own stroller. In addition to the parks there is the walk from and to the parking lot or the bus/monorail/boat station to the park entrance, not to mention many other occasions at your hotel or during shopping when you will be happy to have a stroller handy.

or $13 per day for the entire stay; double stroller, $31 per day, no deposit, or $27 per day for the entire stay; stroller rentals at Downtown Disney require a $100 credit-card deposit; double strollers are not available at Downtown Disney). Strollers are welcome at Blizzard Beach and Typhoon Lagoon, but no rentals are available. We recommend that you pay in advance for your stroller rentals—this allows you to bypass the "paying" line and head straight for the "pickup" line. Make sure that you keep the receipt in a safe place. If you rent a stroller at the Magic Kingdom and decide to go to Epcot, the Animal Kingdom, or Disney's Hollywood Studios, turn in your Magic Kingdom stroller and present your receipt at the next park. You will be issued another stroller without additional charge. Rental at all parks is fast and efficient, and returning the stroller is a breeze.

Readers inform us that there is a lively "gray market" for strollers at the parks. Families who arrive late look for families who are heading for the exit and "buy" their stroller at a bargain price.

If you do not want to bring your own stroller, you may consider buying one of the umbrella-style collapsible strollers. Walmart retails a very basic collapsible stroller for about $15–$20. You may even consider ordering online at places such as **walmart.com, toysrus.com,** or **sears.com** and shipping it right to your hotel in Orlando. Make sure you leave enough time between your order and arrival dates. When you are ready to go home, keep it or donate it to Goodwill or some other worthy charity.

Liliane

Rental strollers are too large for all infants and many toddlers. If you plan to rent a stroller for your infant or toddler, bring pillows, cushions, or rolled towels to buttress him in.

Another important matter is protection against the sun. Liliane always used a stroller with an adjustable canopy and also had lightweight pieces of cloth handy to protect her child from the sun. You can use anything for that purpose; a receiving blanket works well. Liliane used clothespins and security pins to attach the pieces to the canopy.

Strollers are a must for infants and toddlers, but we have observed many sharp parents renting strollers for somewhat older children (up to age 5 or so). The stroller prevents parents from having to carry children when they sag and provides a convenient place to carry water and snacks.

A family from Tulsa, Oklahoma, recommends springing for a double stroller:

We rent a double for baggage room or in case the older child gets tired of walking.

If you go to your hotel for a break and intend to return to the park, leave your rental stroller by an attraction near the park entrance, marking it with something personal, such as a bandanna. When you return, your stroller will be waiting.

Bringing your own stroller is permitted. However, only collapsible strollers are allowed on monorails, parking-lot trams, and buses. Your stroller is unlikely to be stolen, but mark it with your name.

Having her own stroller was indispensable to a Mechanicsville, Virginia, mother of two toddlers:

How I was going to manage to get the kids from the parking lot to the park was a big worry for me before I made the trip. I didn't read anywhere that it was possible to walk to the entrance of the parks instead of taking the tram, so I wasn't sure I could do it.

I found that for me personally, since I have two kids aged 1 and 2, it was easier to walk to the entrance of the park from the parking lot with the kids in (my own) stroller than to take the kids out of the stroller, fold the stroller (while trying to control the two kids and associated gear), load the stroller and the kids onto the tram, etc. . . No matter where I was parked I could always just walk to the entrance . . . it sometimes took awhile, but it was easier for me.

An Oklahoma mom, however, reports a bad experience with bringing her own stroller:

The first time we took our kids, we had a large stroller (big mistake). It is so much easier to rent one in the park. The large (personally owned) strollers are nearly impossible to get on the buses and are a hassle at the airport. I remember feeling dread when a bus pulled up that was even semifull of people. People look at you like you have a cage full of live chickens when you drag heavy strollers onto the bus.

When you enter a show or board a ride, you must park your stroller, usually in an open area. Bring a cloth or towel to dry it if it rains before you return.

Bob

STROLLER WARS Sometimes strollers disappear while you're enjoying a ride or show. Disney staff will often rearrange strollers parked outside an attraction. This may be done to tidy up or to clear a walkway. Don't assume that your stroller is stolen because it isn't where you left it. It may be neatly arranged a few feet away.

Sometimes, however, strollers are taken by mistake or ripped off by people not wanting to spend time replacing one that's missing. Don't be alarmed if yours disappears. You won't have to buy it, and you'll be issued a new one.

Keep in mind that it is very hard to navigate a stroller in a huge crowd, especially when in a hurry and when trying to exit after the fireworks and shows at closing time. Sometimes guests without strollers may try to get ahead of you, making you wish to use the stroller as a lethal weapon. Don't. Given the number of strollers, pedestrians, and tight spaces, mishaps are inevitable on both sides. A simple apology and a smile are usually the best remediation.

WHEN KIDS GET LOST

IF ONE OF YOUR CHILDREN gets separated from you, don't panic. All things considered, Walt Disney World is about the safest place to get lost we can think of. Disney cast members are trained to watch for seemingly lost kids, and because children become detached from parents so frequently in the theme parks, cast members know exactly what to do.

If you lose a child in the Magic Kingdom, report it to a Disney employee, then check at the Baby Care Center and at City Hall, where lost-children logs are kept. At Epcot, report the loss, then check at the Baby Care Center in the Odyssey Center. At Disney's Hollywood Studios, report the situation at the Guest Relations building at the entrance end of Hollywood Boulevard. At Animal Kingdom, go to the Baby Care Center in Discovery Island. Paging isn't used, but in an emergency an all points bulletin can be issued throughout the park(s) via internal communications. If a Disney employee encounters a lost child, he or she will immediately take the child to the park's Baby Care Center.

As comforting as this knowledge is, however, it's nevertheless scary when a child turns up missing. Fortunately, circumstances surrounding a child becoming lost are fairly predictable and, for the most part, preventable.

We suggest that children younger than age 8 be color-coded by dressing them in "vacation uniforms" with distinctively colored T-shirts or equally eye-catching apparel. For starters, consider how much alike children dress, especially in warm climates where shorts and T-shirts are the norm. Throw your children in with 10,000 other kids the same size and suddenly that "cute little outfit" turns into theme-park camouflage. It's also smart to sew a label into each child's shirt that states your family name, your hometown, your cell phone number, and the name of your hotel. The same thing can be accomplished by writing the information on a strip of masking tape. Hotel security professionals suggest the information be printed in small letters and the tape be affixed to the outside of the child's shirt, 5 inches below the armpit or, alternatively, on the tongue of the child's shoe. Another way to skin the cat is to attach a luggage tag to a belt loop. Finally, special name tags can be obtained at the major theme parks.

Other than just blending in, children tend to become separated from their parents under remarkably similar circumstances:

1. PREOCCUPIED SOLO PARENT In this situation, the party's only adult is preoccupied with something like buying refreshments, loading the camera, or using the restroom. Junior is there one second and gone the next.

2. THE HIDDEN EXIT Sometimes parents wait on the sidelines while two or more young children experience a ride together. Parents expect the kids to exit in one place and, lo and behold, the youngsters pop out somewhere else. Exits from some attractions are distant from the entrances. Make sure you know exactly where your children will emerge before letting them ride by themselves. If in doubt, ask a cast member.

3. AFTER THE SHOW At the end of many shows and rides, a Disney staffer will announce, "Check for personal belongings and take small children by the hand." When dozens, if not hundreds, of people leave an attraction simultaneously, it's surprisingly easy for parents to lose contact with their children unless they have them directly in tow.

4. RESTROOM PROBLEMS Mom tells 6-year-old Tommy, "I'll be sitting on this bench when you come out of the restroom." Three possibilities: One, Tommy exits through a different door and becomes disoriented (Mom may not know there is another door). Two, Mom decides she also will use the restroom, and Tommy emerges to find her gone. Three, Mom pokes around in a shop while keeping an eye on the bench but misses Tommy when he comes out.

If you can't be with your child in the restroom, make sure there's only one exit. The restroom on a passageway between Frontierland and Adventureland in the Magic Kingdom is the all-time worst for disorienting visitors. Children and adults alike have walked in from the Adventureland side and walked out on the Frontierland side (and vice versa). Adults realize quickly that something is wrong. Young children, however, sometimes fail to recognize the problem. Designate a meeting spot more distinctive than a bench, and be thorough in your instructions: "I'll meet you by this flagpole. If you get out first, stay right here." Have your child repeat the directions back to you.

5. PARADES There are many parades and shows at which the audience stands. Children tend to jockey for a better view. By moving a little this way and that, the child quickly puts distance between you before either of you notices.

6. MASS MOVEMENTS Be on guard when huge crowds disperse after fireworks or a parade, or at park closing. With 20,000–40,000 people at once in an area, it's very easy to get separated from a child or others in your party. Use extra caution after the evening parade and fireworks in the Magic Kingdom, *Fantasmic!* at Disney's Hollywood Studios, or *IllumiNations* at Epcot. Families should have specific plans for where to meet if they get separated.

7. CHARACTER GREETINGS Activity and confusion are common when the Disney characters appear, and children can slip out of sight. See "Then Some Confusion Happened" (page 243).

8. GETTING LOST AT THE ANIMAL KINGDOM It's especially easy to lose a child at the Animal Kingdom, particularly in the Oasis entryway, on the Maharajah Jungle Trek, and on the Pangani Forest Exploration Trail. Mom and dad will stop to observe an animal. Junior stays close for a minute or so, and then, losing patience, wanders to the other side of the exhibit or to a different exhibit.

9. LOST . . . IN THE OZONE More often than you'd think, kids don't realize they're lost. They are so distracted that they sometimes wander around for quite a while before they notice that their whole family has mysteriously disappeared. Fortunately, Disney cast members are trained to look out for kids who have zoned out and will either help them find their family or deposit them at the Baby Care Center. There are times, however, when parents panic during the interval in which these scenarios play out. If you lose a child and he doesn't turn up at the Baby Care Center right away, take a deep breath. He's probably lost in the ozone.

10. TEACH YOUR KIDS WHO THE GOOD GUYS ARE On your very first day in the parks, teach your kids how to recognize a Disney cast member by pointing out the Disney name tags that they all wear. Instruct your children to find someone with such a name tag if they get separated from you.

LILIANE'S TIPS FOR KEEPING TRACK OF YOUR BROOD

ON A GOOD DAY, it's possible for Liliane to lose a cantaloupe in her purse. Being thus challenged, she works overtime developing ways to hang on to her possessions, including her child. Here's what she has to say:

I've seen parents write their cell phone numbers on a child's leg with a felt-tip marker . . . effective but crude. Before you resort to a brand or tattoo, consider some of the tips I've busted my brain dreaming up. My friends (some much ditzier than I) have used them with great success.

- Same-colored T-shirts for the whole family will help you gather your troops in an easy and fun way. You can opt for just a uniform color or go the extra mile and have the T-shirts printed with a logo such as "The Brown Family's Assault on the Mouse." You might also include the date or the year of your visit. Your imagination is the limit. Light-colored T-shirts can even be autographed by the Disney characters.
- Clothing labels are great, of course. If you don't sew, buy labels that you can iron on the garment. If you own a cell phone, be sure to include the number on the label. If you do not own a cell phone, put in the phone number of the hotel where you'll be staying.
- In pet stores you can have name tags printed for a very reasonable price. These are great to add to necklaces and bracelets, or attach to your child's shoelace or belt loop.

- When you check into the hotel, take a business card of the hotel for each member in your party, especially those old enough to carry wallets and purses.
- Always agree on a meeting point before you see a parade, fireworks, and nighttime spectacles such as *IllumiNations* and *Fantasmic!* Make sure the meeting place is in the park (as opposed to the car or someplace outside the front gate).
- If you have a digital camera or cell-phone camera, you may elect to take a picture of your kids every morning. If they get lost, the picture will show what they look like and what they are wearing.
- If all the members of your party have cell phones, it's easy to locate each other. Be aware, however, that the ambient noise in the parks is so loud that you probably won't hear your cell phone ring. Your best bet is to carry your phone in a front pants pocket and to program the phone to vibrate. If any of your younger kids carry cell phones, secure the phones with a strap. Even better, send text messages.
- Save key tags and luggage tags for use on items you bring to the parks, including your stroller, diaper bag, and backpack or hip pack.
- Don't underestimate the power of the permanent marker, such as a Sharpie. They are great for labeling pretty much anything. Mini Sharpies are sold as clip-ons and are great for collecting character autographs. The Sharpie will also serve well for writing down (Bob suggests on my son's forehead) the location of your car in the parking lot.

A word about keeping track of your park-admission passes. One minute you have them, the next you don't. The passes (which for Disney hotel guests also serve as a credit card and room key) are precious. They are also your key to obtaining Fastpasses and this, typically, is how they get lost. I have tried many ways of keeping track of my passes, but my all-time favorite is a clear badge case that you wear around your neck. It is perfect for holding admission passes, room keys, and some cash; best of all it is completely waterproof, and you can wear the case in the pool or at the water parks.

PART SEVEN

The *MAGIC* KINGDOM

AT THE MAGIC KINGDOM, stroller and wheelchair rentals are to the right of the train station, and lockers are on the station's ground floor. On your left as you enter Main Street is City Hall, the center for information, lost and found, guided tours, and entertainment schedules. Automated tellers (ATMs) are underneath the Main Street railroad station, near the Transportation and Ticket Center (TTC), near City Hall, near the Frontierland shooting gallery, near Pinocchio Village Haus in Fantasyland, and inside the Tomorrowland Arcade. Down Main Street and left around the central hub (toward Adventureland) are the Baby Care Center and a first-aid post. Disney no longer has pet care facilities adjacent to the park, but the new Best Friends Pet Resort across from Disney's Port Orleans Resort will provide a comfortable home-away-from-home for Fido, Frisky, and all their pet pals.

If you don't already have a handout park map, get one at City Hall. The handout lists all attractions, shops, and eateries; provides helpful information about first aid, baby care, and assistance for the disabled; and gives tips for good photos. It also lists times for the day's special events, live entertainment, Disney character parades, concerts, and other activities. Additionally, it tells when and where to find Disney characters.

Often the guide map is supplemented by a daily entertainment schedule known as a *Times Guide,* which provides info on special Disney character appearances and what Disney calls Extra Magic Hours. This term refers to attractions that open late or close early and to the operating hours of park restaurants. If you are lodging at a Walt Disney World resort hotel and the park is operating on an Extra Magic Hour evening schedule, make sure you also pick up the Extra Magic Hours "Evenings" flyer, which will list which attractions are open late. All members of your party need to present a resort ID and theme-park ticket to participate.

Main Street ends at a central hub from which branch the entrances to five other sections of the Magic Kingdom: Adventureland, Frontierland, Liberty Square, Fantasyland, and Tomorrowland. Mickey's Toontown Fair doesn't connect to the central hub—for now it is wedged like a dimple between the cheeks of Fantasyland and Tomorrowland.

In this and the following three chapters, we rate the individual attractions at each of the four major Disney theme parks. The authors' ratings, as well as ratings according to age group, are given on a scale of zero to five stars—the more stars, the better the attraction. The authors' rating is from the perspective of an adult. The authors, for example, might rate a ride such as Dumbo much lower than the age group for which the ride is intended, in this case, children. This rating, therefore, will more closely approximate how another adult will experience the attraction than how your children will like it. The bottleneck rating ranges from 1 to 10; the higher the rating, the more congested the attraction. In general, try to experience attractions with a high bottleneck rating early in the morning (that is, 8–10:30 a.m.) before the park gets crowded or late in the day when the crowd has diminished.

MAIN STREET, U.S.A.

BEGIN AND END YOUR VISIT ON MAIN STREET, which may open a half hour before and closes a half hour to an hour after the rest of the park. It is easy to get sidetracked when entering Main Street, as this Disney-fied turn-of-the-19th-century small town street is lovely, with exceptional attention to detail. But remember: Time is of the essence, and the rest of the park is waiting to be discovered. The same goes for the one and only Cinderella Castle. Stick with your touring plan and return to Cinderella Castle and Main Street after you've experienced the "Must-Do's" on your list.

Walt Disney World Railroad ★★½

APPEAL BY AGE	PRESCHOOL ★★★★	GRADE SCHOOL ★★½	TEENS ★★★
YOUNG ADULTS ★★★		OVER 30 ★★	SENIORS ★★★

What it is Scenic railroad ride around perimeter of the Magic Kingdom, and transportation to Frontierland and Mickey's Toontown Fair. **Scope and scale** Minor attraction. **Fright potential** Not frightening in any respect. **Bottleneck rating** 6. **When to go** Anytime. **Special comments** Main Street is usually the least congested station. **Authors' rating** Plenty to see; ★★½. **Duration of ride** About 20 minutes for a complete circuit. **Average wait in line per 100 people ahead of you** 8 minutes. **Assumes** 2 or more trains operating. **Loading speed** Moderate.

Later in the day when you need a break, this full-circuit ride will give you and your feet 20 minutes

Thumbs Up for the Whole Family

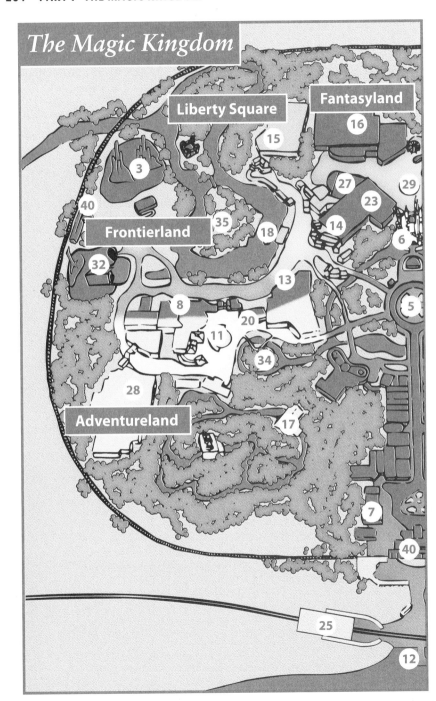

The Magic Kingdom

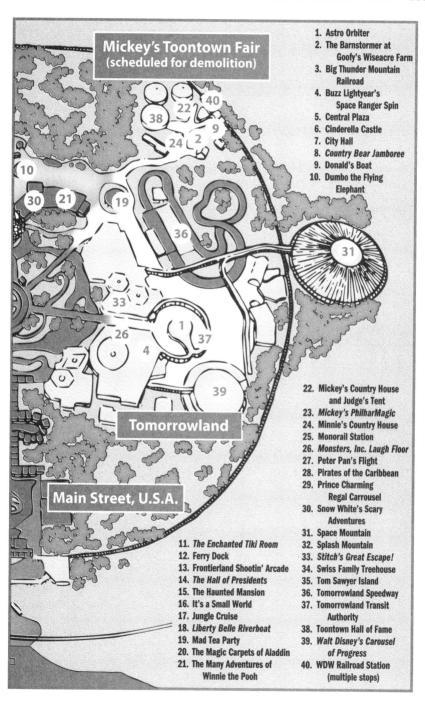

Mickey's Toontown Fair
(scheduled for demolition)

Tomorrowland

Main Street, U.S.A.

1. Astro Orbiter
2. The Barnstormer at Goofy's Wiseacre Farm
3. Big Thunder Mountain Railroad
4. Buzz Lightyear's Space Ranger Spin
5. Central Plaza
6. Cinderella Castle
7. City Hall
8. *Country Bear Jamboree*
9. Donald's Boat
10. Dumbo the Flying Elephant

11. *The Enchanted Tiki Room*
12. Ferry Dock
13. Frontierland Shootin' Arcade
14. *The Hall of Presidents*
15. The Haunted Mansion
16. It's a Small World
17. Jungle Cruise
18. *Liberty Belle Riverboat*
19. Mad Tea Party
20. The Magic Carpets of Aladdin
21. The Many Adventures of Winnie the Pooh

22. Mickey's Country House and Judge's Tent
23. *Mickey's PhilharMagic*
24. Minnie's Country House
25. Monorail Station
26. *Monsters, Inc. Laugh Floor*
27. Peter Pan's Flight
28. Pirates of the Caribbean
29. Prince Charming Regal Carrousel
30. Snow White's Scary Adventures
31. Space Mountain
32. Splash Mountain
33. *Stitch's Great Escape!*
34. Swiss Family Treehouse
35. Tom Sawyer Island
36. Tomorrowland Speedway
37. Tomorrowland Transit Authority
38. Toontown Hall of Fame
39. *Walt Disney's Carousel of Progress*
40. WDW Railroad Station (multiple stops)

of rest. You cannot take your rental stroller on the train; but if you get off short of a complete circuit, you can get a free replacement. Be advised that the railroad shuts down immediately preceding and during parades.

ADVENTURELAND

THE FIRST LAND TO THE LEFT OF MAIN STREET, Adventureland combines an African safari theme with an old New Orleans/ Caribbean atmosphere.

Enchanted Tiki Room—Under New Management ★★★½

APPEAL BY AGE	PRESCHOOL ★★★	GRADE SCHOOL ★★★	TEENS ★★★
YOUNG ADULTS ★★★		OVER 30 ★★★	SENIORS ★★★

What it is Audio-animatronic Pacific Island musical theater show. **Scope and scale** Minor attraction. **Fright potential** Young children might be frightened by the thunder and lightning storm, plus the theater is at times plunged into utter darkness. **Bottleneck rating** 4. **When to go** Before 11 a.m. or after 3:30 p.m. **Special comments** Frightens some preschoolers. **Authors' rating** Very, very unusual; ★★★½. **Duration of presentation** 15½ minutes. **Preshow entertainment** Talking birds. **Probable waiting time** 15 minutes.

Dark   Loud

The Tiki birds are a great favorite of the 8-and-under set. The sarcasm of Iago from *Aladdin* and Zazu from *The Lion King* save the show for older patrons. If you can look beyond the cheese, it is actually hilariously funny. The air-conditioned theater is a great place to cool off and rest your feet.

Jungle Cruise (Fastpass) ★★★

APPEAL BY AGE	PRESCHOOL ★★★★	GRADE SCHOOL ★★★★	TEENS ★★★½
YOUNG ADULTS ★★★½		OVER 30 ★★★★	SENIORS ★★★★

What it is Outdoor safari-themed boat ride adventure. **Scope and scale** Major attraction. **Fright potential** Moderately intense, some macabre sights; a good test attraction for little ones. **Bottleneck rating** 10. **When to go** Before 10 a.m., 2 hours before closing, or use Fastpass. **Authors' rating** An enduring Disney masterpiece; ★★★. **Duration of ride** 8–9 minutes. **Average wait in line per 100**

A PEEK BEHIND THE SCENES WITH JIM HILL

"BUT MILLI VANILLI STARTED THIS WAY!"
During an aborted *George of the Jungle* retheming of Jungle Cruise, Imagineers installed a sound system for a silly taped narration. George was booted in the end, but clever JC captains took advantage of the boat's audio upgrade by inserting homemade sound effects such as comical boos, applause, and the occasional rimshot to punctuate their jokes. This creative touch was ill-received by management. The captains' handiwork was thrown out and the set script restored—but that's what happens when you ruffle the People Who Sit on Sticks.

Thumbs Up for the Whole Family

people ahead of you 3½ minutes. **Assumes** 10 boats operating. **Loading speed** Moderate.

You have to put things into perspective to truly enjoy this ride and realize that it once was a super-headliner attraction at the Magic Kingdom. It still is a relaxing and enjoyable boat ride, but it won't capture the fascination of the high-tech savvy youngsters of the new millennium.

Magic Carpets of Aladdin ★★★

APPEAL BY AGE	PRESCHOOL ★★★★½		GRADE SCHOOL ★★★★
TEENS ★★★	YOUNG ADULTS ★★½	OVER 30 ★★★	SENIORS ★★½

What it is Elaborate midway ride. **Scope and scale** Minor attraction. **Fright potential** Much like Dumbo; a favorite of most younger children. **Bottleneck rating** 10. **When to go** Before 10 a.m. or in the hour before park closing. **Authors' rating** An eye-appealing children's ride; ★★★. **Duration of ride** 1½ minutes. **Average wait in line per 100 people ahead of you** 16 minutes. **Loading speed** Slow.

For parents with preschoolers there's no way out—like Dumbo, it is a must. Try to get your kids to ride in the first 30 minutes the park is open or just before park closing. Beware, the ride has a spitting camel positioned to spray jets of water on riders. The magic-carpet vehicles are rider-controlled, so you can fly your magic carpet up, down, or pitch forward or backward. The front-seat control is for up and down, while the backseat control pitches the carpet forward or backward. Sweet, but oh-so-slow loading. One more tip: Jasmine and Aladdin are often on hand for greeting and meeting.

Movie Tip

Of course the ride is inspired by the 1992 Disney movie *Aladdin*. Did you know that Robin Williams is the voice of the Genie?

Pirates of the Caribbean ★★★★★

APPEAL BY AGE	PRESCHOOL ★★★½	GRADE SCHOOL ★★★★	TEENS ★★★★
YOUNG ADULTS ★★★★½		OVER 30 ★★★★½	SENIORS ★★★★½

What it is Indoor pirate-themed adventure boat ride. **Scope and scale** Headliner. **Fright potential** Slightly intimidating queuing area; intense boat ride with gruesome (though humorously presented) sights and a short, unexpected slide down a flume. **Bottleneck rating** 7. **When to go** Before noon or after 5 p.m. **Special comments** Frightens some young children. **Authors' rating** Disney audio-animatronics at its best; not to be missed; ★★★★★. **Duration of ride** About 7½ minutes. **Average wait in line per 100 people ahead of you** 1½ minutes. **Assumes** Both waiting lines operating. **Loading speed** Fast.

Dark

Loud

Scary

Yo ho, yo ho, a pirate's life for me! This indoor cruise through a series of sets depicting a pirate raid on an island settlement has been a favorite for decades, but with the release of *Pirates of the Caribbean: The Curse of the Black Pearl* (2003), *Pirates of the Caribbean: Dead Man's Chest* (2006), and *Pirates of the Caribbean: At World's End* (2007), the popularity of the ride has soared to new heights. Oh yeah, the films' protagonist, Captain Jack Sparrow, has joined the attraction's animatronic cast. A must for all young pirates is Captain Jack Sparrow's Pirate Tutorial, which takes place several times a day next to the Pirates of the Caribbean ride. Check the daily entertainment schedule (*Times Guide*) and arrive 15 minutes in advance if you want your little buccaneer to have a chance of joining the ranks of Captain Jack Sparrow and his faithful companion Mack.

Chances of being picked as an apprentice pirate are good at most shows, so don't push your kid in front of Jack and Mack. Dressing up for the part helps, however.

Liliane

When you're entering the ride's line, you can look through the bars in the jail cells and see guns, barrels, and skeletons. The scariest part is when there's a cannon fight between the pirate's boat and the town. And Davy Jones looks kind of creepy.

Hannah

For all fans of the *Pirates of the Caribbean* movies, rent the movies before you go to Walt Disney World. They're a blast.

Swiss Family Treehouse ★★★

APPEAL BY AGE	PRESCHOOL ★★★	GRADE SCHOOL ★★★	TEENS ★★★
YOUNG ADULTS ★★½		OVER 30 ★★★	SENIORS ★★½

What it is Outdoor walk-through tree house. **Scope and scale** Minor attraction. **Fright potential** Not frightening in any respect. **Bottleneck rating 6. When to go** Before 11:30 a.m. or after 5 p.m. **Special comments** Requires climbing a lot of stairs. **Authors' rating** A visual delight; ★★★. **Duration of tour** 10–15 minutes. **Average wait in line per 100 people ahead of you** 7 minutes. **Loading speed** Doesn't apply.

This king of all tree houses is perfect for the 10-and-under crowd. Though a minor attraction, it's a great place to expend pent-up energy. Parents might be inclined to sit across the walkway and watch their aspiring Tarzans, but in truth the tree house is fun for adults too.

Thumbs Up for the Whole Family

It's pretty fun to look at, but my sister and I thought it was expendable. However, if you're over 30 years old, it's a good thing to take a look at because you'll really appreciate it.

Shelton

Swiss Family Robinson is a 1960 film adaptation of the Johann David Wyss novel and was the inspiration for the Swiss Family Treehouse.

FRONTIERLAND

FRONTIERLAND ADJOINS ADVENTURELAND as you move clockwise

around the Magic Kingdom. The focus is on the Old West, with stockade-type structures and pioneer trappings.

Big Thunder Mountain Railroad ★★★★ (Fastpass)

APPEAL BY AGE   PRESCHOOL ★★★½   GRADE SCHOOL ★★★★½   TEENS ★★★★½
YOUNG ADULTS ★★★★   OVER 30 ★★★★½   SENIORS ★★★★

What it is Tame, Western-mining-themed roller coaster. **Scope and scale** Headliner. **Fright potential** Visually intimidating from outside, with moderately intense visual effects; the roller coaster is wild enough to frighten many adults, particularly seniors. **Bottleneck rating** 9. **When to go** Before 10 a.m., in the hour before closing, or use Fastpass. **Special comments** Must be 40" tall to ride; children younger than age 7 must ride with an adult. Switching-off option provided (page 238). **Authors' rating** Great effects; relatively tame roller coaster; not to be missed; ★★★★. **Duration of ride** Almost 3½ minutes. **Average wait in line per 100 people ahead of you** 2½ minutes. **Assumes** 5 trains operating. **Loading speed** Moderate to fast.

Scary   Rough   Lose Things

Zooming on a runaway train around a mountain and through a deserted mining town is Disney at its best (if only one could concentrate on the scenery). The ride is rough, and if you do not like roller coasters, this one is going to remind you why. If you are a fan, however, the scenery deserves three rides in a row and an extra one for atmosphere after dark.

Big Thunder Mountain Railroad. Watch out on this one. Sitting in the back jerks me around too much. If you go in the front or the middle, you'll have a smoother ride. It has a lot of dips but no flips because it is more like a wooden roller coaster.

Ian

I was not "feeling the love" the first time I went on this. You always feel like you're going to hit your head on one rock or another, and there are a lot of twists and turns. Eventually, I liked the bumps and how high the ride went, so I went on it again with my dad.

Hannah

My whole family loved the falling rocks and earthquakes. DO NOT duck right near the end. There is a very low rock, which looks like it will hit your head. I ducked, and I got whiplash because there is then a sudden 5-foot drop. It's very small but very quick.

Shelton

Country Bear Jamboree ★★★

APPEAL BY AGE   PRESCHOOL ★★★½   GRADE SCHOOL ★★★   TEENS ★★
YOUNG ADULTS ★★½   OVER 30 ★★★   SENIORS ★★★½

What it is Audio-animatronic country hoedown theater show. **Scope and scale** Major attraction. **Fright potential** Not frightening in any respect. **Bottleneck rating** 8. **When to go** Before 11:30 a.m., before a parade, or during the 2 hours before closing. **Authors' rating** A Disney classic; ★★★. **Duration of**

presentation 15 minutes. **Preshow entertainment** None. **Probable waiting time** This attraction is moderately popular but has a comparatively small capacity. Probable waiting time between noon and 5:30 p.m. on a busy day will average 15–45 minutes.

Kids up to age 10 especially will enjoy this funny country music show. The show is a little dusty, but Teddi Bara, Big Al, Trixie, and the rest of the gang are Disney classics.

 Kids will love watching *The Country Bears,* a live-action film produced by Walt Disney Pictures based loosely on the *Country Bear Jamboree* show. It was Disney's first movie based on a ride or attraction, released in 2002, almost a year before *Pirates of the Caribbean: The Curse of the Black Pearl.*

Frontierland Shootin' Arcade ★½

APPEAL BY AGE	PRESCHOOL ★★½	GRADE SCHOOL ★★★½	TEENS ★★★
YOUNG ADULTS ★★½		OVER 30 ★★½	SENIORS ★½

What it is Electronic shooting gallery. **Scope and scale** Diversion. **When to go** Whenever convenient. **Special comments** Costs $1 per play. **Authors' rating** Very nifty shooting gallery; ★½.

Bring quarters. It is big-time fun.

Idan

Splash Mountain (Fastpass) ★★★★★

APPEAL BY AGE	PRESCHOOL ★★★★	GRADE SCHOOL ★★★★½	TEENS★★★★★
YOUNG ADULTS ★★★★★		OVER 30 ★★★★½	SENIORS ★★★★

† *Many preschoolers are too short to meet the height requirement. Among preschoolers who actually ride, most give the attraction high marks.*

What it is Indoor/outdoor water-flume adventure ride. **Scope and scale** Super headliner. **Fright potential** Visually intimidating from outside, with moderately intense visual effects. The ride, culminating in a 52-foot plunge down a steep chute, is somewhat hair-raising for all ages. **Bottleneck rating** 10. **When to go** As soon as the park opens, during afternoon or evening parades, just before closing, or use Fastpass. **Special comments** Must be 40" tall to ride; children younger than 7 must ride with an adult. Switching-off option provided (page 238). **Authors' rating** A wet winner; not to be missed; ★★★★★. **Duration of ride** About 10 minutes. **Average wait in line per 100 people ahead of you** 3½ minutes. **Assumes** Operating at full capacity. **Loading speed** Moderate.

  Zip-a-dee-doo-dah, are we having fun yet, my-o-my, did we get wet! The half-mile ride through swamps, caves, and backwoods bayous is wonderful. Based on the 1946 Disney film

Scary Wet Lose Things

Song of the South, you travel in a log through Uncle Remus's tales of Br'er Rabbit. Three small drops lead up to the big one, a five-story drop at 40 mph.

 Splash Mountain. Way too cool! If you want to feel what it's like to go over a waterfall, sit in the front, but I prefer the

Ian

back. I think you get wetter. Get as many big people sitting in front of you as you can. They weigh down the boat and make the biggest splash.

Unavailable in the United States, *Song of the South* will become public domain in 2039, and Disney might re-release the movie before they lose the rights to it. If you are interested in the history of this controversial movie, check out **songofthesouth.net/home.html.**

 You get really wet on this ride, and there are a lot of surprises! When you get in, the seats are going to be really wet.

Hannah

I don't know why people complain about getting wet. You really don't get all that wet. My sister and I were in the front row, and it really is not much. My sister even complained that she didn't get wet enough!

Shelton

Tom Sawyer Island and Fort Langhorn ★★★

| APPEAL BY AGE | PRESCHOOL ★★★★ | GRADE SCHOOL ★★★★ |
| TEENS ★★★ | YOUNG ADULTS ★★★ | OVER 30 ★★★ | SENIORS ★★★ |

What it is Outdoor walk-through exhibit/rustic playground. **Scope and scale** Minor attraction. **Fright potential** Not frightening in any respect. **Bottleneck rating** 4. **When to go** Midmorning through late afternoon. **Special comments** Closes at dusk. **Authors' rating** The place for rambunctious kids; ★★★.

Thumbs Up for the Whole Family

This is a great place for kids age 5 and up to unwind. The wildest and most uncooperative youngster will relax after exploring caves and climbing around in an old fort. While it is also a great place for a picnic, there is no food, so bring your own. Access to the island is by raft with a (usually short) wait both coming and going. Plan to give your kids at least 20 minutes on the island. Left to their own devices, they would likely stay all day.

Each morning, Disney cast members hide about a half-dozen colored paintbrushes around the island for guests to find. (Look for colored handles with white paint on the bristles, on display shelves and in buildings. They'll all be within arm's reach.) Notify a cast member if you find one; you'll be rewarded with a small prize ranging from a front-of-line pass on any Magic Kingdom attraction to free sodas for your entire group. One of each prize is available each day on a first-come basis, so this is a great activity to do early on the second day in the park.

 The caves were interesting. It may sound like a little kid's playground, but I think it's worth a look for all ages.

Shelton

I thought this was really cool because I like adventurous stuff like the rope bridges. There's also a playground. You take a boat across the lake to get there.

Hannah

LIBERTY SQUARE

LIBERTY SQUARE RE-CREATES COLONIAL AMERICA at the time of the American Revolution. The architecture is Federal or Colonial. The Liberty Tree, a real live oak that's more than 130 years old, lends dignity and grace to the setting.

The Hall of Presidents ★★★

APPEAL BY AGE	PRESCHOOL ★★	GRADE SCHOOL ★★★	TEENS ★★★
YOUNG ADULTS ★★★		OVER 30 ★★★★	SENIORS ★★★★

What it is Audio-animatronic historical theater presentation. **Scope and scale** Major attraction. **Fright potential** Not frightening in any respect. **Bottleneck rating** 4. **When to go** Anytime. **Authors' rating** Impressive and moving; ★★★. **Duration of presentation** Almost 23 minutes. **Preshow entertainment** None. **Probable waiting time** Lines for this attraction look awesome but are usually swallowed up as the theater exchanges audiences. Your wait will probably be the remaining time of the show that's in progress when you arrive. Even during the busiest times, waits rarely exceed 40 minutes.

Thumbs Up for the Whole Family

Disney immortalizes the presidents of the United States with their own audio-animatronic counterparts. In 2009 Disney added Barack Obama and revamped the entire show, which includes a new narration by Morgan Freeman and a new speech by George Washington. The Father of Our Country joins Presidents Lincoln and Obama as the only chief executives with speaking parts. Although the show is revamped roughly every decade, the presentation remains strongly inspirational and patriotic and highlights milestones in American history. *The Hall of Presidents* is a very moving show for Americans and features one of Disney's best and most ambitious audio-animatronic efforts. The show is definitely a must-see for adults. Kids will fidget or fall asleep.

Shelton

Not very interesting, but I thought the presidents were real actors. Very realistic and kind of creepy is what we thought.

If you want to know more about Valerie Edwards, who sculpts the presidents, check out **mouse treasures.com/wdcc/valerie.** Her dad was a Disney animator and worked on *Sleeping Beauty*.

Liliane

The Haunted Mansion ★★★★

APPEAL BY AGE	PRESCHOOL ★★★	GRADE SCHOOL ★★★★	TEENS ★★★★½
YOUNG ADULTS ★★★★½		OVER 30 ★★★★½	SENIORS ★★★★½

What it is Haunted-house dark ride. **Scope and scale** Major attraction. **Fright potential** The name raises anxiety, as do the sounds and sights of the waiting area. An intense attraction with humorously presented macabre sights, the ride itself is gentle. **Bottleneck rating** 8. **When to go** Before 11:30 a.m. or after 8 p.m. **Special comments** Frightens some very young children. **Authors' rating**

Some of Walt Disney World's best special effects; not to be missed; ★★★★. **Duration of ride** 7-minute ride plus a 1½-minute preshow. **Average wait in line per 100 people ahead of you** 2½ minutes. **Assumes** Both "stretch rooms" operating. **Loading speed** Fast.

Scary   Dark

Don't let the apparent spookiness of the old-fashioned Haunted Mansion put you off. This is one of the best attractions in the Magic Kingdom (and, in fact, one that seems to get a few new twists each year). It's not scary, except in the sweetest of ways, but it will remind you of the days before ghost stories gave way to slasher flicks. The Haunted Mansion takes less than 10 minutes to ride, preshow included, but you may have to do it more than once—it's jam-packed with visual puns, special effects, Hidden Mickeys, and really lovely Victorian-spooky sets.

Ian

It's freaky, man. One time I almost chickened out. Real people in costumes stare you down. There's lots of weird stuff going on, like eyes in paintings on the wall following you and a lady's face inside a crystal ball. At the end, a ghost rides in the car with you. Read the funny tombstones before you go in.

Liberty Belle Riverboat ★★½

APPEAL BY AGE	PRESCHOOL ★★★	GRADE SCHOOL ★★★	TEENS ★★½
YOUNG ADULTS ★★★	OVER 30 ★★★		SENIORS ★★★★

What it is Outdoor scenic boat ride. **Scope and scale** Major attraction. **Fright potential** Not frightening in any respect. **Bottleneck rating** 4. **When to go** Anytime. **Authors' rating** Slow, relaxing, and scenic; ★★½. **Duration of ride** About 16 minutes. **Average wait to board** 10–14 minutes.

Thumbs Up for the Whole Family

This fully narrated 16-minute trip is relaxing and offers great photo ops. It's a good choice also at night when the boat and the attractions along the waterfront are lighted. Did you know that the *Liberty Belle* Riverboat runs on a track hidden just below the water?

FANTASYLAND

FANTASYLAND IS THE HEART of the Magic Kingdom, a truly en-chanting place spread gracefully like a miniature Alpine village beneath the lofty towers of the Cinderella Castle. Over the next three years Disney will redesign Fantasyland in the largest expansion in Magic Kingdom history. The focus will be on immersive encounters with Disney princesses Cinderella, Aurora (Sleeping Beauty), Belle, and Ariel, allowing guests to step into their favorite Disney fairy tales. Fantasyland Forest will feature a themed village for each princess.

In the new Journey of the Little Mermaid attraction, Ariel and friends will entertain in an enclosed ride carrying guests through an underwater world. An Omnimover ride system similar to the one used in The Haunted Mansion will move visitors through adventures featuring favorite songs from the movie. At Dreams Come True with Cinderella, guests can meet Cinderella face to face in her castle, and little tykes will be able to dance with Cinderella. Inside the Briar Rose Cottage, children will be able to celebrate Princess Aurora's birthday. Guests will be transported from Belle's father's cottage to the Beast's castle for a storytelling performance. This section of the park will also feature a three-room themed restaurant called Be Our Guest. Another addition will be Pixie Hollow, a character-greeting area dedicated to Tinker Bell and her fairy friends.

Dumbo the Flying Elephant ride will double in size—all our prayers have been heard—and the two identical rides will be relocated inside new circus grounds with an interactive queue under a big-top tent.

To accommodate the expansion, most of Mickey's Toontown Fair, with the exception of The Barnstormer at Goofy's Wiseacre Farm roller coaster, will be torn down. Will Goofy be Goofy after all the remodeling? We're not sure; a circus-themed makeover is likely. Mickey and Minnie will get new homes near the front entrance of the park.

The first phase of the Fantasyland expansion, which will include the mermaid ride and the new home for the princesses, is scheduled to open in 2012. Tinker Bell fans will have to be patient, as the Pixie Hollow opening is scheduled for 2013.

Dumbo the Flying Elephant ★★★

APPEAL BY AGE	PRESCHOOL ★★★★★	GRADE SCHOOL ★★★★	TEENS ★★
YOUNG ADULTS ★★½	OVER 30 ★★★		SENIORS ★★½

What it is Disney-fied midway ride. **Scope and scale** Minor attraction. **Fright potential** A tame midway ride; a great favorite of most young children. **Bottleneck rating** 10. **When to go** Before 10 a.m. or after 9 p.m. **Authors' rating** An attractive children's ride; ★★★. **Duration of ride** 1½ minutes. **Average wait in line per 100 people ahead of you** 20 minutes. **Loading speed** Slow.

Making sure your child gets his fill of this tame, happy children's ride is what mother love is all about. The 90-second ride is hardly worth the long lines, unless, of course, you're under 7 years old. If Dumbo's on your must-see list, try to get the kids on board during the first half hour the park is open.

A PEEK BEHIND THE SCENES WITH JIM HILL

DUMBO LIKE A FOX

As part of Fantasyland's expansion, Disney is placing its new Double Dumbo attraction at the very back of the Magic Kingdom. To reach it, families will have to walk by lots of shops and restaurants on their way in. After these families finish riding Dumbo, they're going to have to retrace their steps past those retail and dining opportunities on their way out. Double Dumbo will virtually double Disney's chances of getting into your wallet.

If you have not seen *Dumbo* (first released in 1941 and winner of an Academy Award for original music score), you have an elephant-size gap in your Disney education. Fun for all ages, rent the movie when you get home.

It's a Small World ★★★

APPEAL BY AGE	PRESCHOOL ★★★★½	GRADE SCHOOL ★★★★	TEENS ★★★
YOUNG ADULTS ★★★		OVER 30 ★★★½	SENIORS ★★★★

What it is World brotherhood–themed indoor boat ride. **Scope and scale** Major attraction. **Fright potential** Not frightening in any respect. **Bottleneck rating** 6. **When to go** Anytime. **Authors' rating** Exponentially "cute"; ★★★. **Duration of ride** Approximately 11 minutes. **Average wait in line per 100 people ahead of you** 11 minutes. **Assumes** Busy conditions with 30 or more boats operating. **Loading speed** Fast.

Thumbs Up for the Whole Family

Small boats carry visitors on a tour around the world, with singing and dancing dolls showcasing the dress and culture of each nation. Totally rehabbed in 2005, Small World is one of Disney's oldest entertainments. Did you know that the ride originated at the 1964 New York World's Fair? If you listen closely, you will realize that the theme song is actually sung in numerous languages as your boat is carried from one continent to the next. Of course, there's no escaping the brain-numbing little tune. You'll go home with it lodged in your brain like a bullet, and just when you think you've repressed it, the song will resurface without warning to torture you some more.

Ian

This ride is why MP3 players were invented. Just put on your headphones and listen to Velvet Revolver all the way through the ride. The Small World song won't bother you a bit. Promise.

I must be immune to the tune. I love the ride and would not miss riding It's a Small World anytime I visit.

Idan

Mad Tea Party ★★

APPEAL BY AGE	PRESCHOOL ★★★★	GRADE SCHOOL ★★★★	TEENS ★★★★
YOUNG ADULTS ★★★		OVER 30 ★★★	SENIORS ★★

What it is Midway-type spinning ride. **Scope and scale** Minor attraction. **Fright potential** Low, but this type of ride can induce motion sickness in all ages. **Bottleneck rating** 9. **When to go** Before 11 a.m. or after 5 p.m. **Special comments** You can make the teacups spin faster by turning the wheel in the center of the cup. **Authors' rating** Fun, but not worth the wait; ★★. **Duration of ride** 1½ minutes. **Average wait in line per 100 people ahead of you** 7½ minutes. **Loading speed** Slow.

Motion Sickness

It's a party, and a mad one at that. Prepare yourself for a whirling adventure inside a giant teacup (also known as the human centrifuge). Teenagers love to lure adults into the spinning teacups, then turn the wheel in the middle (making the cup spin faster) until the adults are plastered against the sides and on the verge of throwing up. The only sane way to experience this ride with teenagers is, paradoxically, to put them in straight jackets so they can't spin the wheel. We're dying to try this. Volunteers, anyone?

My son loves this ride, but then again he is a teenager. As for me, I love the ride too. I'll take the Mad Tea Party over Big Thunder Mountain any day. Plus, it's good training for experiencing Mission: SPACE at Epcot.

Liliane

The Mad Tea Party is inspired by the unusual tea party scene in the 1951 Disney adaptation of Lewis Carroll's *Alice in Wonderland.* Did you know that the voice of Alice, British voice actress and schoolteacher Kathryn Beaumont, is also the voice of Wendy in Disney's *Peter Pan*?

Researchers at NASA determined that you're less likely to experience motion sickness if you don't ride on an empty stomach.

Bob

The Many Adventures of Winnie the Pooh ★★★½ (Fastpass)

APPEAL BY AGE	PRESCHOOL ★★★★	GRADE SCHOOL ★★★★	TEENS ★★★
YOUNG ADULTS ★★★		OVER 30 ★★★½	SENIORS ★★★½

What it is Indoor track ride. **Scope and scale** Minor attraction. **Fright potential** Not frightening in any respect. **Bottleneck rating** 8. **When to go** Before 10 a.m., in the 2 hours before closing, or use Fastpass. **Authors' rating** Cute as the Pooh-bear himself; ★★★½. **Duration of ride** About 4 minutes. **Average wait in line per 100 people ahead of you** 4 minutes. **Loading speed** Moderate.

Thumbs Up for the Whole Family

This ride is a romp through the Hundred-Acre Wood on a blustery day. The visuals are gentle and charming without being saccharine. The Many Adventures of Winnie the Pooh is a perfect test to assess how your very young children will react to the indoor, so-called dark rides.

The ride is based on a 1977 Disney animated feature, *The Many Adventures of Winnie the Pooh.* The movie and Winnie the Pooh books are perfect for very young children. Did you know that Paul Winchell won a Grammy for his voicing of Tigger? Other Disney roles of Paul Winchell include parts in *The Aristocats* as a Chinese cat and *The Fox and the Hound* as Boomer the woodpecker. He also lends his voice to evil Gargamel in the Smurfs.

Mickey's PhilharMagic (Fastpass seasonally) ★★★★

APPEAL BY AGE	PRESCHOOL ★★★★	GRADE SCHOOL ★★★★½	TEENS ★★★★
YOUNG ADULTS ★★★★½		OVER 30 ★★★★½	SENIORS ★★★★★

What it is 3-D movie. **Scope and scale** Major attraction. **Special comments** Not to be missed. **When to go** Before 11 a.m., during parades, or use Fastpass if available. **Authors' rating ★★★★**. A masterpiece. **Duration of presentation** About 12 minutes. **Probable waiting time** 12–30 minutes.

A real stunner, *Mickey's PhilharMagic* combines three fabulous ideas: Mickey and Donald mix and meet with latter-day Disney stars such as Aladdin, Jasmine, Ariel, the Beast's pantry servants (such as Lumiere and Mrs. Potts), and Simba; it employs a form of computer-enhanced 3-D video technology that is truly impressive (it's the first time most of these characters have been digitally animated, which will make them more "flexible," so to speak, in the future); and the whole shebang is projected on a 150-foot-wide, 180-degree screen. *Mickey's PhilharMagic* even employs some of those famous Disney scent effects and turns the old *Sorcerer's Apprentice* trick back on Mickey. Some preschoolers might be a little scared at first, but taking off the 3-D glasses tones down the effect.

You want to duck when corks and other things come flying out at you. I loved the part with Aladdin, when they were flying on their magic carpet. It felt very real!
Shelton

Peter Pan's Flight (Fastpass) ★★★★

APPEAL BY AGE   PRESCHOOL ★★★★   GRADE SCHOOL ★★★★   TEENS ★★★½   YOUNG ADULTS ★★★★   OVER 30 ★★★★   SENIORS ★★★★

What it is Indoor track ride. **Scope and scale** Minor attraction. **Fright potential** Not frightening in any respect. **Bottleneck rating** 8. **When to go** Before 10 a.m., or use Fastpass after 6 p.m. **Authors' rating** Happy, mellow, and well done; ★★★★. **Duration of ride** A little more than 3 minutes. **Average wait in line per 100 people ahead of you** 5½ minutes. **Loading speed** Moderate to slow.

Thumbs Up for the Whole Family

Take a snort of pixie dust and off you go soaring over London and on to Never Land.

Disney's animated film version of 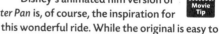 *Peter Pan* is, of course, the inspiration for this wonderful ride. While the original is easy to find, the sequel, *Return to Never Land,* is not. Try to get a copy at a library or find a used one at **amazon.com** and reunite with Peter, Wendy, Tinker Bell, Mr. Smee, the Lost Boys, and Captain Hook. But most of all: Don't grow up.

Prince Charming Regal Carrousel ★★★

APPEAL BY AGE   PRESCHOOL ★★★★   GRADE SCHOOL ★★★½   TEENS ★★   YOUNG ADULTS ★★★   OVER 30 ★★★   SENIORS ★★★

What it is Merry-go-round. **Scope and scale** Minor attraction. **Fright potential** Not frightening in any respect. **Bottleneck rating** 9. **When to go** Before 11 a.m. or after 8 p.m. **Special comments** Adults enjoy the beauty and nostalgia of this ride. **Authors' rating** A beautiful children's ride; ★★★. **Duration of ride** About 2 minutes. **Average wait in line per 100 people ahead of you** 5 minutes. **Loading speed** Slow.

It is a long wait, but the beauty of the carousel (formerly known as Cinderella's Golden Carrousel) captures everyone. The carousel (built in 1917) was discovered in New Jersey, where it was once part of an amusement park. It is beautifully maintained and especially magical at night when all the lights are on. Check out your children's delighted expressions as the painted ponies go up and down.

Snow White's Scary Adventures ★★½

APPEAL BY AGE	PRESCHOOL ★★★	GRADE SCHOOL ★★★	TEENS ★★★
YOUNG ADULTS ★★★		OVER 30 ★★★	SENIORS ★★★

What it is Indoor track ride. **Scope and scale** Minor attraction. **Fright potential** Moderately intense spook-house-genre attraction with some grim characters. Terrifies many preschoolers. **Bottleneck rating** 8. **When to go** Before 11 a.m. or after 6 p.m. **Authors' rating** Worth seeing if the wait isn't long; ★★½. **Duration of ride** Almost 2½ minutes. **Average wait in line per 100 people ahead of you** 6¼ minutes. **Loading speed** Moderate to slow.

Dark Scary

"I'm Wishing" is one of the most beloved songs from Disney's first animated feature, but experiencing Snow White's Scary Adventures gives this song a new twist. You end up wishing not for the Prince to come but for the wicked witch to GO AWAY. The ride is intimidating to many young children because Snow White's Scary Adventures is more about the witch, who's more persistent than a time-share salesman, than about Snow White.

Movie Tip

The movie, a classic of course, is scary for preschoolers but a timeless must-see for older children. Walt Disney won an honorary Academy Award for significant screen innovation with this film and received a full-size Oscar statuette with seven miniature ones. The honorary award was presented in 1938 to Walt Disney by Shirley Temple; the seven miniatures represented Doc, Grumpy, Happy, Sneezy, Bashful, Sleepy, and Dopey.

MICKEY'S TOONTOWN FAIR

MICKEY'S TOONTOWN FAIR IS THE ONLY LAND that doesn't connect to the central hub of Magic Kingdom. For children ages 2–8, Mickey's Toontown Fair will be a highlight of their day. However, with the possible exception of The Barnstormer, we think all of Mickey's Toontown is slated for demolition as part of the Fantasyland expansion described on page 273. (We don't expect the rest of Toontown's attractions to survive into 2011.) But because construction plans can change, we're including the attraction descriptions for all of Toontown until we're sure they're gone. The touring plans, however, reflect the closing of all Toontown attractions. Check this book's Web site, **touringplans.com,** for the latest developments.

The Barnstormer at Goofy's Wiseacre Farm ★★

| APPEAL BY AGE | PRESCHOOL ★★★★ | GRADE SCHOOL ★★★★ | TEENS ★★½ |
| YOUNG ADULTS ★★½ | | OVER 30 ★★★ | SENIORS ★★ |

What it is Small roller coaster. **Scope and scale** Minor attraction. **Fright potential** A children's coaster; frightens some preschoolers. **Bottleneck rating** 9. **When to go** Before 10:30 a.m., during parades, or in the evening just before the park closes. **Special comments** Must be 35" tall to ride. **Authors' rating** Great for little ones but not worth the wait for adults; ★★. **Duration of ride** About 53 seconds. **Average wait in line per 100 people ahead of you** 7 minutes. **Loading speed** Slow.

Rough   Scary

Remember that the height requirement for this ride is 35 inches. If you want to see how your child handles riding coasters, Goofy's Barnstormer is the perfect testing ground.

Liliane

Yours truly screamed big-time from start to end (thankfully it only lasted a minute and a half), and no way would I let the apple of my eye ride alone unless he or she is 6 years or older.

Liliane is a gentle and sensitive soul. Most kids experience rides wilder than Goofy's Barnstormer on their tricycles. When I heard Liliane wailing like a banshee on this little coaster, I thought her appendix must have ruptured.

Bob

Donald's Boat ★★½

| APPEAL BY AGE | PRESCHOOL ★★★★ | GRADE SCHOOL ★★★ | TEENS ★½ |
| YOUNG ADULTS ★ | | OVER 30 ★ | SENIORS ★ |

What it is Playground and (when the water is running) interactive fountain. **Scope and scale** Diversion. **Fright potential** Not frightening in any respect. **Bottleneck rating** 3. **When to go** Anytime. **Authors' rating** A favorite of the 5-and-under set; ★★½.

Donald's Boat is an interactive playground themed as a fat, cartoon-style tugboat. It affords a great opportunity for easing regimentation and allowing young children to expend pent-up energy.

Mickey's Country House and Judge's Tent ★★★

| APPEAL BY AGE | PRESCHOOL ★★★★ | GRADE SCHOOL ★★★★ | TEENS ★★½ |
| YOUNG ADULTS ★★½ | | OVER 30 ★★★ | SENIORS ★★★ |

What it is Walk-through tour of Mickey's house and meeting with Mickey. **Scope and scale** Minor attraction. **Fright potential** Not frightening in any respect. **Bottleneck rating** 9. **When to go** Before 11:30 a.m. or after 4:30 p.m. **Authors' rating** Well done; ★★★. **Duration of tour** 15–30 minutes (depending on the crowd). **Average wait in line per 100 people ahead of you** 20 minutes. **Touring speed** Slow.

Mickey's Country House is perfect for preschoolers who want to see how Mickey lives. If your child actually insists on seeing Mickey, you'll find the famous mouse on duty in the Judge's Tent next door all day. His friends, including all the princesses you can count, can be found nearby at the Toontown Hall of Fame.

Minnie's Country House ★★

APPEAL BY AGE	PRESCHOOL ★★★★		GRADE SCHOOL ★★★★
TEENS ★★½	YOUNG ADULTS ★★½	OVER 30 ★★★	SENIORS ★★★

What it is Walk-through exhibit. **Scope and scale** Minor attraction. **Fright potential** Not frightening in any respect. **Bottleneck rating** 9. **When to go** Before 11:30 a.m. or after 4:30 p.m. **Authors' rating** Great detail; ★★. **Duration of tour** About 10 minutes. **Average wait in line per 100 people ahead of you** 12 minutes. **Touring speed** Slow.

I see color! I see pink! Minnie's kitchen looks like a cartoon version of a set for *Martha Stewart Living*. The kitchen is filled with recipes, magazines, and awards Minnie has won for canning and baking. The attention to detail throughout gives the house a real lived-in feel. Occasionally Minnie appears in her backyard, but usually she's in Scrooge McDuck's vault reviewing stock options with Martha.

Toontown Hall of Fame ★★

APPEAL BY AGE	PRESCHOOL ★★★★		GRADE SCHOOL ★★★★
TEENS ★★★	YOUNG ADULTS ★★½	OVER 30 ★★★	SENIORS ★★½

What it is Character-greeting venue. **Scope and scale** Minor attraction. **Fright potential** Not frightening in any respect. **Bottleneck rating** 10. **When to go** Before 10:30 a.m. or after 5:30 p.m. **Authors' rating** You want characters? We got 'em! ★★. **Duration of greeting** About 7–10 minutes. **Average wait in line per 100 people ahead of you** 35 minutes. **Touring speed** Slow.

If your child's heart is set on meeting as many characters as possible, you've come to the right place. Of course, the wait can be a long one. Make sure—especially when it comes to the Princess Room—to know which characters are present. Many adults would rather skip this time-consuming attraction, but a parent has to do what a parent has to do. Watching your children meet their favorite Disney characters one-on-one is, as the credit card commercial puts it, priceless.

TOMORROWLAND

TOMORROWLAND IS A MIX OF RIDES and experiences relating to the technological development of humankind and what life will be like in the future. When Disney overhauled Tomorrowland a few years back, it bailed on trying to predict how the future might appear, opting instead for a timeless, retro Buck Rogers look.

Keep an eye out for PUSH, the talking trash can of Tomorrowland. Kids love PUSH and delight in the opportunity to talk trash with the real thing.

Astro Orbiter ★★

APPEAL BY AGE	PRESCHOOL ★★★½		GRADE SCHOOL ★★★½
TEENS ★★★	YOUNG ADULTS ★★	OVER 30 ★★½	SENIORS ★★

What it is Buck Rogers–style rockets revolving around a central axis. **Scope and scale** Minor attraction. **Fright potential** Visually intimidating waiting area for a relatively tame ride. **Bottleneck rating** 10. **When to go** Before 11 a.m. or after 5 p.m. **Special comments** This attraction, formerly StarJets, is not as innocuous as it appears. **Authors' rating** Not worth the wait; ★★. **Duration of ride** 1½ minutes. **Average wait in line per 100 people ahead of you** 13½ minutes. **Loading speed** Slow.

Parents beware! If you are prone to motion sickness, this ride (a) spins round and round; (b) is faster than Dumbo; and (c) for added "fun," there's a joystick that lets you raise and lower the rocket throughout your 1½-minute journey. We like to ride the Astro Orbiter at night. The combination of lighting and the view are spectacular.

I don't have a fear of heights, but I get scared when something that's moving up and down is leaning outwards like it's going to dump you out. It's very scary for me.

Shelton

Buzz Lightyear's Space Ranger Spin (Fastpass) ★★★★

APPEAL BY AGE	PRESCHOOL ★★★★	GRADE SCHOOL ★★★★½	TEENS ★★★★
YOUNG ADULTS ★★★★		OVER 30 ★★★★	SENIORS ★★★★

What it is Combination space travel–themed indoor ride and shooting gallery. **Scope and scale** Minor attraction. **Fright potential** Dark ride with cartoonlike aliens may frighten some preschoolers. **Bottleneck rating** 8. **When to go** Before 10:30 a.m., after 6 p.m., or use Fastpass. **Authors' rating** A real winner! ★★★★. **Duration of ride** About 4½ minutes. **Average wait in line per 100 people ahead of you** 3 minutes. **Loading speed** Fast.

Once you get the hang of it, you will come back for more, to infinity and beyond.

Totally awesome! I earned my Space Ranger Wings on my first ride. Use the joystick to spin and set up your shots, but don't spin too much because that uses up time and energy. Always aim and never stop shooting, especially at the big alien targets. Those are the ones with lots of arms and legs, and four eyes. They get you the most points.

Ian

Movie Tip The ride is based on the space-commando character Buzz Lightyear from the 1995 Disney/Pixar feature *Toy Story.* Did you know that Tom Hanks and Tim Allen are the voices of Woody and Buzz?

You'll see Zurg in jail at the end of the ride. Little kids can squeeze through the bars and pretend they're in jail too.

Hannah

Monsters, Inc. Laugh Floor ★★★½

APPEAL BY AGE	PRESCHOOL ★★★½	GRADE SCHOOL ★★★★	TEENS ★★★★
YOUNG ADULTS ★★★★		OVER 30 ★★★★	SENIORS ★★★★

What it is Interactive animated comedy routines. **Scope and scale** Major attraction. **Fright potential** Not much is frightening, but they are monsters, after all. **Bottleneck rating** 8. **When to go** Before 11 a.m. or after 4 p.m. **Special comments** Audience members may be asked to participate in skits. **Author's rating** Good concept; jokes are hit-and-miss; ★★★½ **Duration of presentation** About 15 minutes. **Preshow entertainment** Yes. **Probable waiting time** 25 minutes.

We learned in Disney/Pixar's *Monsters, Inc.* that children's screams could be converted into electricity, which was used to power a town inhabited by monsters. During the film, the monsters discovered that children's laughter was an even better source of energy. In this attraction, the monsters have set up a comedy club to capture as many laughs as possible. Mike Wazowski, the one-eyed character from the film, emcees the club's three comedy acts. Each consists of an animated monster (most not seen in the film) trying out various bad puns, knock-knock jokes, and Abbott and Costello–like routines. Using the same cutting-edge technology as Epcot's popular *Turtle Talk with Crush*, behind-the-scenes Disney employees voice the characters and often interact with audience members during the skits. As with any comedy club, some performers are funny and some are not. A good thing about this attraction is that Disney has shown a willingness to try new routines and jokes, so the show should remain fresh to repeat visitors. A Sioux Falls, South Dakota, mom is a big fan:

> The Laugh Floor *was great. It's amazing how the on-screen characters interact with the audience—I got picked on twice without trying. This should definitely be seen; plus, kids are able to text jokes to Roz.*

 The show is based on the 2001 Pixar film *Monsters, Inc.,* which starred Billy Crystal (voice) in the role of Mike Wazowski and won an Oscar for Best Song.

Space Mountain (Fastpass) ★★★★

APPEAL BY AGE†	PRESCHOOL ★★½	GRADE SCHOOL ★★★★½	TEENS ★★★★½
YOUNG ADULTS ★★★★½		OVER 30 ★★★★½	SENIORS ★★★

† Some preschoolers love Space Mountain; others are frightened. The sample size of senior citizens who experienced this ride was too small to develop an accurate rating.

What it is Roller coaster in the dark. **Scope and scale** Super headliner. **Fright potential** Very intense roller coaster in the dark; the Magic Kingdom's wildest ride and a scary roller coaster by any standard. **Bottleneck rating** 10. **When to go** When the park opens, between 6 and 7 p.m., during the hour before closing, or use Fastpass. **Special comments** Great fun and action; much wilder than Big Thunder Mountain Railroad. Must be 44" tall to ride; children younger than age 7 must be accompanied by an adult. Switching-off option provided (page 238). **Authors' rating** An unusual roller coaster with excellent special effects; not to be missed; ★★★★. **Duration of ride** Almost 3 minutes.

A PEEK BEHIND THE SCENES WITH JIM HILL

LOST HORIZON

As you exit Space Mountain, keep an eye out for a warm tribute to a long-gone Epcot attraction. In a pile of luggage alongside the speed ramp that whisks you out, the Imagineers placed a sticker reading MESA VERDE on the side of one suitcase. Mesa Verde was one of three destinations that you were able to choose at the end of Horizons, a classic Future World attraction that closed in January 1999 to make way for Mission: SPACE.

Average wait in line per 100 people ahead of you 3 minutes. **Assumes** Two tracks, one dedicated to Fastpass riders, dispatching at 21-second intervals. **Loading speed** Moderate to fast.

Dark

Scary

Rough

Motion Sickness

Space Mountain is one of the zippiest (and darkest) rides in Walt Disney World, lasting just under 3 minutes and including several abrupt turns and plummets. So, those with neck or back problems or vertigo should probably skip it. However, this ride achieves "only" about 28 mph, a leisurely pace by 21st-century standards.

Space Mountain also involves sudden blackouts, as do many thrill rides at Disney World. Those who suffer from claustrophobia (Liliane), tend to panic in the dark (Liliane), or have vision problems with extremes of light and darkness (Liliane) should avoid this attraction. Plunged into darkness and bouncing around like a marble in a spittoon, many warmly recall Space Mountain as the longest 3 minutes of their lives. Your kids will love it, of course.

Refurbished in 2009, Space Mountain got a smoother track and larger ride vehicles, as well as interactive video games to pass time in the standby line. We think the new ride is quieter and slightly faster than the old.

Ian

If you're not sure that you are brave enough to ride Space Mountain, you can always take the Tomorrowland Transit Authority and watch the actual ride in action before you get in line.

I dream of riding Space Mountain at the pace of Spaceship Earth in Epcot. At last, I would be able to enjoy the twinkling lights.

Liliane

Hannah

All of the people screaming sort of scared me at first. I did like all the flashing lights and the astronaut stuff. Look for the giant chocolate-chip cookies flying by on the ceiling when you're in line.

Stitch's Great Escape! ★ ★

APPEAL BY AGE	PRESCHOOL ★½	GRADE SCHOOL ★★½	TEENS ★★
YOUNG ADULTS ★★		OVER 30 ★★	SENIORS ★★

What it is Theater-in-the-round sci-fi adventure show. **Scope and scale** Major attraction. **Fright potential** Frightens children of all ages; must be 40" tall.

A PEEK BEHIND THE SCENES WITH JIM HILL

SOUNDS KIND OF FAMILIAR The voice of Sarge, the animatronic figure featured in the *Stitch* preshow, should ring a bell for most of you. The actor behind the character is Richard Kind, best known for playing nerdy Paul Lassiter on the long-running 1990s sitcom *Spin City*. The kids in your family will know this Second City vet as the voice of grasshopper Molt in *A Bug's Life* and, more recently, the Bookworm in *Toy Story 3*.

Bottleneck rating 6. **When to go** Before 11 a.m. or after 6 p.m.; try during parades. **Authors' rating** A cheap coat of paint on a broken car; ★★. **Duration of presentation** About 12 minutes. **Preshow entertainment** About 6 minutes. **Probable waiting time** 12–35 minutes.

Dark   Loud   Scary

Disney's press release touting *Stitch* as a child-friendly attraction was about as accurate as Lehman Brothers bookkeeping. You are held in your seat by overhead restraints and subjected to something weird clambering around you and whispering to you in a theater darker than a stack of black cats. Enough to scare the pants off many kids age 10 and younger.

Liliane

Not fair! I love *Stitch* but agree with parents of young children who have complained about how scary the show is, especially because the overhead restraint prevents you from leaving your seat to comfort your child if need arises. Preteens and up, however, will enjoy the wicked fun of the show. All I could think of was the Pink Floyd song "Comfortably Numb": "Is there anybody in there?"

Movie Tip

Skip the show, but do not discount the movie. *Lilo & Stitch* (released in 2002) is a great family movie. The Hawaiian culture of 'Ohana, which in Hawaiian means extended family including friends, is the cornerstone philosophy of this wonderful flick. The movie reminds children about the importance of good behavior and points out to adults that there is good inside every child, no matter how rotten he or she may behave at times.

This should be scrapped. My dad thought it was mediocre, but everyone else hated it.

Shelton

Tomorrowland Speedway ★★

APPEAL BY AGE	PRESCHOOL ★★★★		GRADE SCHOOL ★★★★
TEENS ★★★	YOUNG ADULTS ★★½	OVER 30 ★★★	SENIORS ★★½

What it is Drive-'em-yourself miniature cars. **Scope and scale** Major attraction. **Fright potential** Not frightening in any respect. **Bottleneck rating** 9. **When to go** Before 11 a.m. or after 5 p.m. **Special comments** Must be 54" tall to drive unassisted. **Authors' rating** Boring for adults (★★); great for preschoolers. **Duration**

of ride About 4¼ minutes. **Average wait in line per 100 people ahead of you** 4½ minutes. **Assumes** 285-car turnover every 20 minutes. **Loading speed** Slow.

The sleek cars and racetrack noise will get your younger kids hopped up to ride this extremely prosaic attraction. The minimum height requirement of 54 inches means that the younger (or shorter) set will have to ride with an adult. We suggest you work the accelerator and brakes and let your future Kasey Kahne steer the car. Resist the urge to dispatch your little one with a taller sibling, unless the sibling is willing to hand over the steering wheel. The loading and unloading speed is excruciatingly slow, and the attraction offers hardly any protection from the sun.

Ian

What I like about this ride is you don't have to be 16 years old to drive! Dude, you've got total control . . . well, almost. Pretend you're an Indy car driver like Sam Hornish Jr. Turn the steering wheel, put your foot on the gas, and even hit the brakes . . . just like a go-cart. Sweet!

Tomorrowland Transit Authority ★★★

APPEAL BY AGE	PRESCHOOL ★★★★	GRADE SCHOOL ★★★½	TEENS ★★★½
YOUNG ADULTS ★★★★		OVER 30 ★★★★	SENIORS ★★★★

What it is Scenic tour of Tomorrowland. **Scope and scale** Minor attraction. **Fright potential** Not frightening in any respect. **Bottleneck rating** 3. **When to go** During hot, crowded times of day (11:30 a.m.–4:30 p.m.). **Special comments** A good way to check out the Fastpass line at Space Mountain. **Authors' rating** Scenic, relaxing, informative; ★★★. **Duration of ride** 10 minutes. **Average wait in line per 100 people ahead of you** 1½ minutes. **Assumes** 39 trains operating. **Loading speed** Fast.

Thumbs Up for the Whole Family

There is never a line, and the ride is ideal for taking a break. It's also a great way to see Tomorrowland all aglow at night. The route gives a sneak preview of Buzz Lightyear's Space Ranger Spin, and you can check on those screams emanating from Space Mountain. Most of the time cast members will let you ride several times in a row without having to get off. This last thing, according to many moms, makes the ride a great option for nursing.

It's good because you don't have to scream at anything, and there are no hills.

Hannah

Walt Disney's Carousel of Progress ★★★

APPEAL BY AGE	PRESCHOOL ★★★	GRADE SCHOOL ★★★	TEENS ★★★
YOUNG ADULTS ★★★½		OVER 30 ★★★½	SENIORS ★★★★

What it is Audio-animatronic theater production. **Scope and scale** Major attraction. **Fright potential** Not frightening in any respect. **Bottleneck rating** 4. **When to go** Anytime. **Authors' rating** Nostalgic, warm, and happy; ★★★. **Duration of presentation** 21 minutes. **Preshow entertainment** Documentary on the attraction's long history. **Probable waiting time** Less than 10 minutes.

A piece of Disney history not to be missed. The attraction offers a nostalgic look at how technology and electricity have changed the lives of an audio-animatronic family over several generations.

> My dad forced us all to see it, and we're glad he did.
> It was very good!

Shelton

LIVE ENTERTAINMENT *and* **PARADES** *in the* MAGIC KINGDOM

IT'S IMPOSSIBLE TO TAKE IN ALL THE MANY live entertainment offerings at the Magic Kingdom in a single day. To experience both the attractions and the live entertainment, we recommend you allocate at least two days to this park. In addition to parades, stage shows, and fireworks, check the daily entertainment schedule (*Times Guide*) or ask a cast member about concerts in Fantasyland, square dancing in front of the *Country Bear Jamboree,* the Flag Retreat at Town Square, and the appearances of the various bands, singers, and street performers that roam the park daily. WDW live-entertainment guru Steve Soares usually posts the Magic Kingdom's performance schedule about a week in advance at **pages.prodigy.net/stevesoares.**

Following is a short list of daily events with special appeal for families with children:

CASTLE FORECOURT STAGE "DREAM-ALONG WITH MICKEY" A daytime stage show in front of Cinderella Castle featuring a veritable pantheon of Disney characters and music.

STORYTIME WITH BELLE AT THE FAIRYTALE GARDEN Belle and several helpers select children from the small amphitheater audience and dress them up as characters from *Beauty and the Beast*. As Belle tells the story, the children act out the roles. There is a 3- to 5-minute meet-and-greet with photo and autograph opportunities afterward. Storytime takes place six to eight times a day; check the daily entertainment schedule (*Times Guide*) for showtimes. The Fairytale Garden is located next to the Enchanted Grove refreshment stand in Fantasyland, across from Cosmic Ray's in Tomorrowland.

Storytime with Belle reminds me of the movie *The Secret Garden*. It's possibly the only entertainment offering that can make you forget for a moment that you're in a bustling theme park with 50,000 other people. Don't forget to load your camera; the performance is a top photo op. Priceless!

— Liliane

MOVE IT! SHAKE IT! CELEBRATE IT! PARADE Starting at the train station end of Main Street, U.S.A., and working toward the central hub, this short walk incorporates about a dozen guests with a handful of floats, Disney characters, and entertainers. Music is provided by one of Disney's latest artists (Miley Cyrus currently), and there's a good amount of interaction between the entertainers and the crowd.

FLAG RETREAT At 4:45 p.m. daily at Town Square (railroad-station end of Main Street). Sometimes performed with great fanfare and college marching bands, sometimes with a smaller Disney band.

MAGIC KINGDOM BANDS Banjo, Dixieland, steel drum, marching, and fife-and-drum bands play daily throughout the park.

CAPTAIN JACK SPARROW'S PIRATE TUTORIAL Sign up with Captain Jack Sparrow and his crewman Mack for a hilarious pirate one-on-one. Check your *Times Guide* for the scheduled daily encounters and meet the Johnny Depp lookalike right next to the Pirates of the Caribbean ride. The lucky chosen buccaneers are taught how to be pirates and receive an honorary pirate certificate at the end of the show.

The show is wonderful for little wannabe pirates and grown-ups alike and draws quite a crowd, especially ladies. I signed up for the pirate's life in a jiffy.

— Liliane

PARADES Parades at the Magic Kingdom are full-fledged spectaculars with dozens of Disney characters and amazing special effects. An outstanding new afternoon parade is introduced every year or two; while some elements such as the Disney characters remain constant, the theme, music, and float design change. The evening parade is a high-tech affair and not to be missed. Always check your entertainment schedule (*Times Guide*) to make sure what parade is happening when,

A PEEK BEHIND THE SCENES WITH JIM HILL

CHANNEL YOUR INNER GOOD FAIRY

In *Sleeping Beauty*, Flora and Merryweather spar with their wands over whether Briar Rose's dress should be pink or blue. If the Imagineers have their way, you'll soon be able to wave a high-tech wand (look for it in Magic Kingdom shops within two years) to change the color of new props and costumes in the Main Street Electrical Parade and SpectroMagic.

as well as the guide map for the parade route.

Remember, parades disrupt traffic, and it is nearly impossible to move around the park when one is going on. Parades also draw thousands of guests away from the attractions, making parade time the perfect moment to catch your favorite attraction with a shorter line. Finally, be advised that the Walt Disney World Railroad shuts down during parades.

The best place to view a parade is the upper platform of the Walt Disney Railroad station, but you will have to stake out your position 30–45 minutes before the event. Try also, especially on rainy days, the covered walkway between Liberty Tree Tavern and The Diamond Horseshoe Saloon on the border of Liberty Square and Frontierland.

TINKER BELL'S FLIGHT This nice special effect in the sky above Cinderella Castle heralds the beginning of the fireworks show (when the park is open late).

FIREWORKS The nightly fireworks show starts just after Tinker Bell's flight in the sky above Cinderella Castle. The fireworks are synchronized to music from beloved Disney films.

View the fireworks from the upper platform of the railroad station. This vantage point also provides an easy path to the park exit when the fireworks are over. Our favorite spot, if we intend to remain in the park after the fireworks, is the roofless patio of the Tomorrowland Terrace Noodle Station, located in Tomorrowland on the border with Main Street, U.S.A.

A very special spot to view the fireworks is atop the nearby Contemporary Resort at the California Grill. Once the fireworks begin, the restaurant dims its lights and broadcasts the music from the show.

Liliane

If all you want is a serene spot to watch the fireworks or the Bay Lake and Seven Seas Floating Electrical Pageant, you do not need to spend big bucks. The gardens of the Grand Floridian are perfect for the fireworks, and the beach of the Polynesian Resort does the trick for the electrical pageant.

FIREWORKS CRUISE For a different view you can watch the fireworks from the Seven Seas Lagoon aboard a chartered pontoon boat. The charter comes with a price (about $350 for up to 10 people and includes chips and drinks), of course. Your Disney captain will take you for a little cruise and then position the boat in a perfect place to watch the fireworks. For an additional cost, you can arrange for more substantial food items through the catering department. Life jackets are provided, but wearing them is at your discretion. To reserve, call 407-WDW-PLAY 90 days prior to your visit. Similar charters are available for viewing *IllumiNations* at Epcot.

BAY LAKE AND SEVEN SEAS LAGOON FLOATING ELECTRICAL PAGEANT Performed at nightfall at about 9 p.m. most of the year on Seven Seas Lagoon and Bay Lake, this pageant is the perfect culmination of a wonderful day. You have to leave the Magic Kingdom to see this floating electric light show. Take the monorail to the Polynesian Resort, get the kids a snack and yourself a drink, and walk to the end of the pier to watch the show. Pure magic, less the crowds. You can also watch the show at the Grand Floridian at 9:15 p.m. and at the Contemporary at 10:05 p.m.

EXIT STRATEGIES

LEAVING THE PARK AFTER EVENING PARADES and fireworks is no small matter. Huge throngs depart the Magic Kingdom after parades, fireworks, and at closing. Trust us, with small children, you don't want to be among them. The best strategy for avoiding the mass exodus is to view both fireworks and parades from the upper platform of the railroad station at the Town Square end of Main Street. As soon as the performance concludes, beat feet to the park exits. If you remain in the park after the fireworks and parades, don't wait until closing time to leave. On a busy day give yourself a 30- to 40-minute cushion.

Another strategy for beating the masses out of the park (if your car is in the TTC lot) is to watch the early parade and then leave before the fireworks begin. Line up for the ferry instead of the monorail. A ferry departs about every 8–10 minutes. Try to catch the ferry that will be crossing Seven Seas Lagoon while the fireworks are in progress. The best vantage point is on the top deck to the right of the pilothouse. Your chances are about 50/50 of catching it just right. If you are in front of the line for the ferry and you don't want to board the boat that's loading, stop at the gate and let people pass you. You'll be the first to board the next boat.

MAGIC KINGDOM TOURING PLANS

OUR STEP-BY-STEP TOURING PLANS are field-tested, independently verified itineraries that will keep you moving counter to the crowd flow and allow you to see as much as possible in a single day with minimum time wasted in line.

Don't worry that other people will be following the plans and render them useless. Fewer

than 1 in every 350 people in the park will have been exposed to this information.

Bob

We developed many of these plans when preparing to visit the Magic Kingdom with our own children (ages 2–8). Some plans offer a midday break of at least 3 hours back at your hotel. It's debatable whether the kids will need the nap more than you, but you'll thank us later, we promise. Our kids are picky eaters too: One went through a phase where she ate nothing but beige food (chicken fingers, pasta, macaroni and cheese, and the like). The restaurants we recommend in these plans are all kid-friendly and should work for almost everyone.

If you've got just one day to spend in the Magic Kingdom, our single-day plans will allow you to see the best attractions for kids while avoiding crowds and long waits in line. If you're looking for a more relaxed, less structured tour of the park, try the one-and-a-half, two-day, or Sleepy-head plans. These alternatives have less backtracking, the same midday breaks, and a much more casual feel. The Sleepyhead plans assume you'll get to the park around 11 a.m., so they're great for mornings when you don't feel like getting out of bed early.

The different touring plans for each park are described below. The descriptions will tell you for whom (for example, tweens, parents with preschoolers, grandparents, and so on) or for what situation (such as sleeping late) the plans are designed. The actual touring plans are located on pages 445–453 at the back of the book. Each plan includes a numbered map of the park in question to help you find your way around. Clip the plan of your choice out of the book by cutting along the line indicated, and take it with you to the park.

Switching off allows adults to enjoy the more adventuresome

attractions while keeping the group together.

Liliane

MAGIC KINGDOM HAPPY FAMILY ONE-DAY TOURING PLAN This is a one-day touring plan of the Magic Kingdom that includes something for everyone in the family: small children, tweens (children ages 8–12), teenagers, parents, and seniors. The plan keeps the entire family together for most of the day, plus lunch and dinner. A midday break is integrated into the day's touring.

The plan includes attractions very popular with small children, such as Dumbo in Fantasyland and the Magic Carpets of Aladdin in Adventureland. For older kids and teenagers, we recommend thrill rides such as Space Mountain and Big Thunder Mountain, with both groups getting back together when each is done.

MAGIC KINGDOM ONE-DAY TOURING PLAN FOR GRANDPARENTS WITH SMALL CHILDREN The attractions in this touring plan are generally those rated at least three stars (out of five) by both seniors and small children, plus a handful of senior-friendly attractions that children just love. Specifically designed to minimize walking, this plan also includes a midday break of at least 3 hours and dining recommendations for lunch and dinner. We don't try to cover the entire park, either: Most of Tomorrowland is left as an option if everyone's feeling up for it.

To convert this itinerary into a two-day plan, one option is to do steps 1 through 14 on Day One. If you're returning in the morning of Day Two, do steps 25 and 26 first, then steps 16 through 24. An alternate strategy for a morning and afternoon is to do steps 1 through 14 on the morning of Day One and steps 15 through 28 on the afternoon of Day Two.

MAGIC KINGDOM ONE-DAY TOURING PLAN FOR TWEENS AND THEIR PARENTS A one-day plan for parents with children ages 8–12. It includes every attraction rated three stars and higher by this age group and sets aside ample time for lunch and dinner.

MAGIC KINGDOM TWO-DAY TOURING PLAN FOR PARENTS WITH SMALL CHILDREN This is a two-day touring plan designed specifically to eliminate extra walking and backtracking. It is a comprehensive touring plan of the Magic Kingdom and includes every child-friendly attraction in the park. The plan features long midday breaks for rest and naps outside the park, as well as recommendations for good dining choices inside the park.

MAGIC KINGDOM TWO-DAY SLEEPYHEAD TOURING PLAN FOR PARENTS WITH SMALL CHILDREN Another version of the two-day touring plan described above, this plan allows families with young children to sleep in, arrive at the park in the late morning, and still see the very best attractions in the Magic Kingdom over two days. Each day also contains a one-hour break inside the park, and we've made specific recommendations on the best spots to rest and cool off. The plan includes lunch and dinner suggestions for both days, with plenty of time to explore the park on either day.

PARENTS' MAGIC KINGDOM TOURING PLANS FOR AN AFTERNOON AND ONE FULL DAY This day-and-a-half plan works perfectly if you're arriving in Orlando late in the morning of your first vacation day and can't wait to start touring. It also works great for families who want to sleep in one morning after spending a full day in the Magic Kingdom the day before.

The attractions in these plans are the same as those found in the standard one-day plans for parents with small children, so these day-and-a-half itineraries also work as relaxed versions of those plans. Both plans employ Fastpass and some version of a "wait 'em out" crowd strategy, whereby you'll take advantage of lower evening crowds to visit the more popular attractions. The plans should work well during the more crowded times of the year, and we've provided Fastpass alternatives for the more popular attractions in case they're out of passes by the time you arrive.

PRELIMINARY INSTRUCTIONS FOR ALL MAGIC KINGDOM TOURING PLANS

ON DAYS OF MODERATE-TO-HEAVY ATTENDANCE, follow your chosen touring plan exactly, deviating only:

1. When you aren't interested in an attraction it lists. For example, the plan may tell you to go to Tomorrowland and ride Space Mountain, a roller coaster. If you don't enjoy roller coasters, skip this step and proceed to the next.

2. When you encounter a very long line at an attraction the touring plan calls for. Crowds ebb and flow at the park, and an unusually long line may have gathered at an attraction to which you're directed. For example, you arrive at The Haunted Mansion and find extremely long lines. It's possible that this is a temporary situation caused by several hundred people arriving en masse from a recently concluded performance of *The Hall of Presidents* nearby. If this is the case, skip The Haunted Mansion and go to the next step, returning later to retry.

WHAT TO DO IF YOU GET OFF TRACK

IF AN UNEXPECTED INTERRUPTION or problem throws the touring plan off, consult the recommended attraction visitation times in the attraction profile for the preferred times of day to visit.

BEFORE YOU GO

1. Call ☎ 407-824-4321 the day before you go to check the official opening time.

2. Purchase admission before you arrive.

3. Familiarize yourself with park-opening procedures (described on page 226) and reread the touring plan you've chosen so that you know what you're likely to encounter.

MAGIC KINGDOM TRIVIA QUIZ

By Lou Mongello

1. What is the name of Sonny Eclipse's (unseen) backup group at Cosmic Ray's Starlight Café?
   a. The Space Cadets
   b. The Sun Bonnets
   c. Space Angels
   d. Cranium Commandos

2. What is the name of the riverboat at Liberty Square?
   a. *Joe Fowler*
   b. *Mark Twain*

    c. *Liberty Belle*

    d. *Lily Belle*

3. What is the name of Mike Wazowski's nephew in *Monsters, Inc. Laugh Floor*?

    a. Roz

    b. Henry

    c. Bob

    d. Marty

4. Where in the Magic Kingdom can you find a dog named Nana?

    a. *The Hall of Presidents*

    b. The Haunted Mansion

    c. *Walt Disney's Carousel of Progress*

    d. Peter Pan's Flight

5. In what scene can you find a bride in The Haunted Mansion?

    a. The ballroom

    b. The séance room

    c. The attic

    d. The graveyard

6. The number on the front of *The Hall of Presidents* building represents:
- **a.** The year Walt Disney World opened
- **b.** The current year
- **c.** The year America gained its independence
- **d.** The year the Constitution was ratified

7. The narrator on the Liberty Square riverboat is:
- **a.** Mark Twain
- **b.** Ben Franklin
- **c.** Prince Naveen
- **d.** Paul Revere

8. About how many leaves can you find on the Swiss Family Treehouse?
- **a.** 3,000
- **b.** 30,000
- **c.** 300,000
- **d.** 3,000,000

9. At the end of *Mickey's PhilharMagic,* how does Mickey wake up Donald?
- **a.** Blowing a trumpet in his face
- **b.** Grabbing his feet
- **c.** Tickling him
- **d.** Banging a drum

10. What is Pete's Garage in Mickey's Toontown Fair?
- **a.** A snack stand
- **b.** Restrooms
- **c.** A character meet-and-greet location
- **d.** A souvenir shop

11. The Main Street Electrical Parade features a float based on a character from which of these movies:
- **a.** *Pete's Dragon*
- **b.** *The Sword in the Stone*
- **c.** *The Incredibles*
- **d.** *101 Dalmations*

Answers can be found on page 426.

Trivia content courtesy of Lou Mongello, author of Walt Disney World Trivia Books *(Volumes I and II), as well as the Audio Guides to WDW. Lou is also the host and producer of WDW Radio (wdwradio.com) and is the publisher of* Celebrations *magazine (celebrations press.com). Dream Team Project (dreamteamproject.org), which Mongello founded, helps raise money for the Make-A-Wish Foundation of America to send seriously ill children and their families to Walt Disney World.*

PART EIGHT

EPCOT

EDUCATION, INSPIRATION, AND CORPORATE IMAGERY are the focus at Epcot, the most adult of the Walt Disney World theme parks. What it gains in taking a futuristic, visionary, and technological look at the world, it loses, just a bit, in warmth, happiness, and charm. Some people find the attempts at education to be superficial; others want more entertainment and less education. Most visitors, however, are in between, finding plenty of amusement *and* information alike.

Epcot's theme areas are distinctly different. Future World combines Disney creativity and major corporations' technological resources to examine where humankind has come from and where we're going. World Showcase features landmarks, cuisine, and culture from almost a dozen nations and is meant to be a sort of permanent World's Fair.

So you thought the Magic Kingdom was big? Epcot is more than twice as large as the Magic Kingdom; so unless one day is all you have, plan on spending two days at Epcot to savor all it has to offer. While Epcot, unlike the Magic Kingdom, does not stand out as a "natural" for kids, rest assured that families can have as much fun at Epcot as at any of the other theme parks.

Now for the practical stuff: Future World always opens first; that is where you start your day. The World Showcase opens later at 11 a.m. But first things first: Call ☎ 407-824-4321 for exact park hours. If you are lodging at a Disney hotel, consider visiting when the park offers morning or evening Extra Magic Hours. Once you arrive, pick up a park map and the daily entertainment schedule (*Times Guide*). If you are a Disney hotel guest and the park offers Extra Magic (morning or evening) Hours, grab the extra flyer that lists all the attractions open during the additional hours. If you intend to stay for Extra Magic Hours in the evening, each member of your party will need to have his or her resort ID.

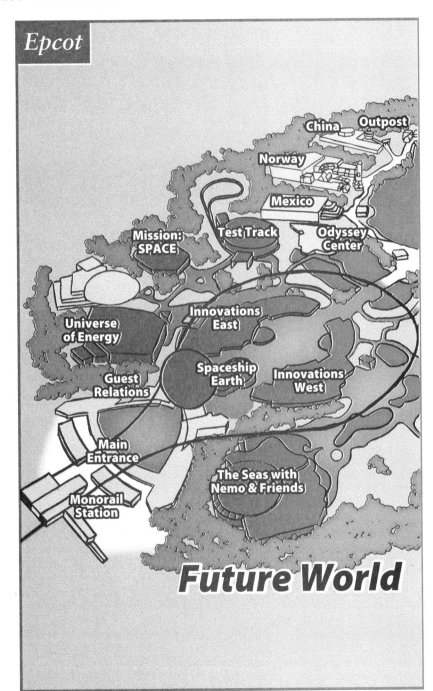

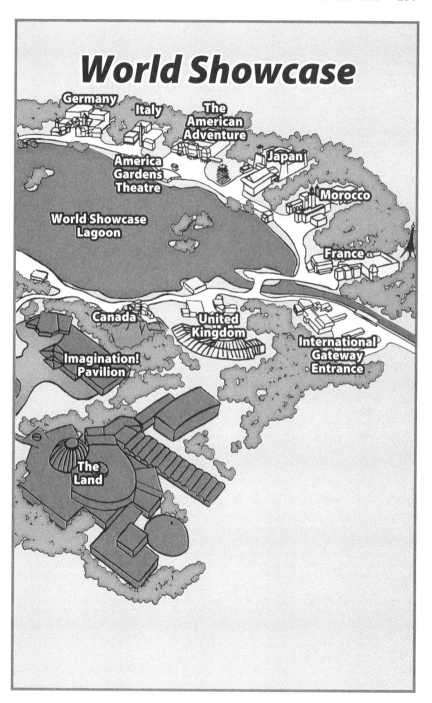

World Showcase

Germany

Italy

The American Adventure

America Gardens Theatre

Japan

Morocco

World Showcase Lagoon

France

Canada

United Kingdom

International Gateway Entrance

Imagination! Pavilion

The Land

Stroller and wheelchair rentals are available inside the main entrance to the left, toward the rear of the Entrance Plaza. For storage lockers, turn right at Spaceship Earth. The Baby Care Center is on the World Showcase side of the Odyssey Center complex, to the rear of Test Track. At the same location are first-aid and lost-persons services. For a live entertainment schedule and dining reservations, stop at Guest Relations to the left of Spaceship Earth. Lost and Found is located at the main entrance. Banking services (ATMs) are available outside the main entrance, on the Future World Bridge, and in World Showcase at the Germany Pavilion. Disney no longer has pet care facilities adjacent to the park, but the new Best Friends Pet Resort across from Disney's Port Orleans Resort will provide a comfortable home-away-from-home for Fido, Frisky, and all their pet pals.

KIDCOT FUN STOPS

THIS PROGRAM, DESIGNED TO MAKE EPCOT more interesting for younger visitors, is basically a movable feast of simple arts and crafts projects. Tables are set up at some locations in Future World and at each pavilion in World Showcase. The tables are staffed by cast members who discuss their native country with the children and engage them in a craft project. Look for the brightly colored Kidcot signs. Participation is free. For a memento and to augment the experience, you can purchase a World Showcase Passport for your children. The passports are sold for $10 at most stores throughout Epcot. As you visit the different lands, cast members at the Kidcot stations will stamp the passport. If your child is really interested in different lands, Guest Relations offers free fact sheets for each country.

Children as young as age 3 will enjoy the Kidcot Fun Stops. If you do not want to spring for the Passport, the Disney folks will be happy to stamp an autograph book or just about anything else, including your child's forehead.

FUTURE WORLD

Innoventions ★★★½

APPEAL BY AGE	PRESCHOOL ★★★½	GRADE SCHOOL ★★★★	TEENS ★★★½
YOUNG ADULTS ★★★		OVER 30 ★★★	SENIORS ★★★

What it is Static and hands-on exhibits relating to products and technologies of the near future. **Scope and scale** Major diversion. **Fright potential** Not frightening in any respect. **Bottleneck rating** 8. **When to go** On your second day at Epcot or after seeing all major attractions. **Special comments** Most exhibits demand time and participation to be rewarding; not much gained here by a quick walk-through. **Authors' rating** Vastly improved; ★★★½.

A PEEK BEHIND THE SCENES WITH JIM HILL

A FAREWELL TO ARMS

The Kuka arms that drive Sum of All Thrills are incredibly cool, but this attraction isn't the one the Imagineers originally had in mind for this technology. They had an *Incredibles*-themed headliner mapped out, featuring a battle with the menacing Omnidroids from the 2004 Pixar film. But then Kuka cut a deal with Universal Studios to use its robotics wizardry to power another film-based blockbuster: Harry Potter and the Forbidden Journey at Islands of Adventure (see pages 398–400).

Innoventions—a huge, busy collection of walk-through, hands-on exhibits—consists of two huge, crescent-shaped, glass-walled structures separated by a central plaza. Exhibits, many of which are changed each year, demonstrate such products as virtual-reality games, high definition TV, voice-activated appliances, future cars, medical diagnostic equipment, and Internet applications. Each of the major exhibit areas is sponsored by a different manufacturer or research lab, emphasizing the effect of the products or technology on daily living. The most popular Innoventions attraction is an arcade of video and simulator games. One of the coolest exhibits, however, is the demonstration area for the Segway Human Transporter, the much-publicized two-wheeled vehicle that makes riders look as if they're standing on top of a push lawn mower. A limited number of brief test rides are also offered to the general public. The latest addition to Innoventions is The Sum of All Thrills, a virtual roller coaster.

The newer exhibits are certainly more compelling, but they require waiting in line to be admitted. Because the theater at each exhibit is quite small, you often wait as long for an Innoventions infomercial as for a real attraction elsewhere in the park. We observed a wide range of reactions by visitors to the exhibits and can suggest only that you form your own opinion. We suggest skipping exhibits with waits of more than 10 minutes or experiencing them first thing in the morning when there are no lines.

This is a great place for parents to abandon their teenagers—at least for a while—to enjoy a meal of escargot at Bistro de Paris in France.

Liliane

Whoa! You gotta check out the e-mail postcards. Star in your own cartoon and e-mail it to all your friends. The best is in Innoventions. I put myself in an alien movie and landed on Mars! On the way home, we couldn't wait to get there to see it on our computer. A very cool souvenir—and it's free.

Ian

Spaceship Earth ★★★★

APPEAL BY AGE	PRESCHOOL ★★★★	GRADE SCHOOL ★★★★	TEENS ★★★★
YOUNG ADULTS ★★★★		OVER 30 ★★★★	SENIORS ★★★★½

What it is Educational dark ride through past, present, and future. **Scope and scale** Headliner. **Fright potential** Dark and imposing presentation intimidates a few preschoolers. **Bottleneck rating** 7. **When to go** Before 10 a.m. or after 4 p.m. **Special comments** If lines are long when you arrive, try again after 4 p.m. **Authors' rating** One of Epcot's best; not to be missed; ★★★★. **Duration of ride** About 16 minutes. **Average wait in line per 100 people ahead of you** 3 minutes. **Loading speed** Fast.

Thumbs Up for the Whole Family

This ride spirals through the 18-story interior of Epcot's premier landmark, taking guests through audio-animatronic scenes depicting mankind's development in communications from cave painting to the Internet. It's actually more fun than it sounds and is carried off with a lot of humor. Spaceship Earth draws crowds like a magnet first thing in the morning because it is so close to the park entrance.

I hate this ride because it's boring. Most of these people didn't have cars or TV or anything we have today. — Hannah

CLUB COOL

ATTACHED TO THE FOUNTAIN SIDE OF INNOVENTIONS WEST is a sort of international soda fountain called Club Cool. The exhibit provides free unlimited samples of soft drinks from around the world. Kids will love to fill their own tasting cups and move from one sampling station to the next. Mix lemon, water, and honey and you get Kinley, popular in Israel. In Mozambique Krest Ginger Ale is in; in China a drink based on watermelon is highly popular. The Japanese recommend the nutrition and health benefits of a vitamin drink, and the Italians are in love with a beverage that could chalk up great sales as an emetic in the U.S. VegitaBeta, anyone?

Club Cool also lives up to its name; it is cool inside and makes for a good meeting place.

Ian

Club Cool is my favorite place to go when I'm thirsty, and the drinks are FREE. You can have as much as you want, soft drinks that is, from all over the world. Some are pretty yucky, but some are pretty good. Give it a try and see what you think. Coke from China is not bad.

THE SEAS WITH NEMO AND FRIENDS PAVILION

THE SEAS IS HOME TO ONE OF AMERICA'S top marine aquariums, a ride, an interactive animated film, and a number of first-class educational exhibits. A comprehensive makeover featuring characters from the animated feature *Finding Nemo* brings some whimsy and much-needed levity to what was heretofore educationally brilliant but somewhat staid. Before the makeover, The Seas (or The Living Seas, as it was previously known) was a snoozer for children. In its new incarnation, it ranks near the top of the kids' hit parade.

The Seas Main Tank and Exhibits ★★★½

APPEAL BY AGE   PRESCHOOL ★★★★   GRADE SCHOOL ★★★★   TEENS ★★★★
YOUNG ADULTS ★★★★   OVER 30 ★★★★   SENIORS ★★★★

What it is A huge saltwater aquarium, plus exhibits on oceanography, ocean ecology, and sea life. **Scope and scale** Major attraction. **Fright potential** Not frightening in any respect. **Bottleneck rating** 7. **When to go** Before 11:30 a.m. or after 5 p.m. **Authors' rating** An excellent marine exhibit; ★★★½. **Average wait in line per 100 people ahead of you** 3½ minutes. **Loading speed** Fast.

Thumbs Up for the Whole Family

Take a *Finding Nemo*–themed ride to Sea Base to start your discovery of The Seas' main tank and exhibits. Watch scientists and divers conduct actual marine experiments in the main tank containing fish, mammals, and crustaceans in a simulation of an ocean ecosystem. Visitors can observe the activity through windows below the surface (including inside the Coral Reef restaurant). Children will be enchanted to discover the substantial fish population and the many exhibits offered. With the addition of *Turtle Talk with Crush* and The Seas with Nemo & Friends, The Seas has been transformed from a Future World backwater into one of Epcot's most popular venues. We recommend experiencing the ride and *Turtle Talk* in the morning before the park gets crowded, saving the excellent exhibits for later.

The Seas with Nemo & Friends ★★★

APPEAL BY AGE   PRESCHOOL ★★★★½   GRADE SCHOOL ★★★★   TEENS ★★★
YOUNG ADULTS ★★★½   OVER 30 ★★★½   SENIORS ★★★★

What it is Ride through a tunnel in The Seas' main tank. **Scope and scale** Major attraction. **Fright potential** Not frightening in any respect. **Bottleneck rating** 7. **When to go** Before 11 a.m. or after 5 p.m. **Special comments** Ride features characters from the animated hit *Finding Nemo*. **Authors' rating** Educational *and* fun; ★★★½. **Duration of ride** 4 minutes. **Average wait in line per 100 people ahead of you** 3½ minutes. **Loading speed** Fast.

Upon entering The Seas, you proceed to the loading area, where you'll be made comfortable in a "clamobile" for your journey through the aquarium. The technology used makes it seem as if the animated characters are swimming with the live fish. Meet Mr. Ray and help Dory, Bruce, Marlin, Squirt, and Crush find Nemo. This cool ride attracts lots of the lovable clown fish's fans, so ride early.

Hannah

Clamobiles! This ride is fun because it shows real fish and real dolphins, and sometimes real scuba divers! I still get really cautious when I see real sharks, but they can't break the glass and attack you.

If you have not seen *Finding Nemo*, rent it prior to your visit. You will not soon forget this superb family movie that won the 2004 Oscar for best animated feature. Did you know that Alexander Gould, who gives his voice to little Nemo, is also the voice behind Bambi in the Disney animated sequel *Bambi II*?

Movie Tip

Turtle Talk with Crush ★★★★

APPEAL BY AGE	PRESCHOOL ★★★★½	GRADE SCHOOL ★★★★½	TEENS ★★★★
YOUNG ADULTS ★★★★		OVER 30 ★★★★	SENIORS ★★★★

What it is An interactive animated film. **Scope and scale** Minor attraction. **Fright potential** Not frightening in any respect. **Bottleneck rating** 9. **When to go** Before 11 a.m. or after 5 p.m. **Special comments** Get there early to avoid long lines; a real spirit lifter. **Authors' rating** Amazing technology; ★★★★. **Duration of the presentation** 17 minutes. **Preshow entertainment** None. **Probable waiting time** 10–20 minutes before 11 a.m. and after 5 p.m.; as much as 40–60 minutes during the more crowded part of the day.

Thumbs Up for the Whole Family

This interactive theater show starring the 153-year-old surfer-turtle from the film *Finding Nemo* starts like a typical Disney theme-park movie but quickly turns into an interactive encounter, as Crush begins conversations with guests in the audience. Not to be missed! The capacity of the attraction is relatively small, and the show is a big hit, so you'll want to get here as early as you can to avoid long lines.

Ian

Turtle Talk with Crush? I like this show a lot. Don't miss it. You actually feel like you're in the movie Finding Nemo. Turtle Talk comes alive when Crush swims up on the movie screen and talks to people. I mean really talks to people. He saw me raise my hand and—Dude!—he said my name and we had a conversation. I don't know how they do it, but it was great.

THE LAND PAVILION

THE LAND IS A HUGE PAVILION containing three attractions and several restaurants. When the pavilion was originally built, its emphasis was on farming, but now it focuses on environmental concerns. Dry as that sounds, kids really enjoy The Land's attractions, especially Soarin', a thrill ride where the operative word is "thrill," not terror. The Land Pavilion is a great place to grab a fast-food lunch. If you're here to see the attractions, however, stay away during mealtimes, as the place is super crowded.

The Circle of Life ★★★½

APPEAL BY AGE	PRESCHOOL ★★★	GRADE SCHOOL ★★★	TEENS ★★★
YOUNG ADULTS ★★★		OVER 30 ★★★	SENIORS ★★★

What it is Film exploring man's relationship with his environment. **Scope and scale** Minor attraction. **Fright potential** Not frightening in any respect. **Bottleneck rating** 5. **When to go** Before 11 a.m. or after 2 p.m. **Authors' rating** Highly interesting and enlightening; ★★★½. **Duration of presentation** About 20 minutes. **Preshow entertainment** None. **Probable waiting time** 10–15 minutes.

The Swahili saying *hakuna matata* (don't worry) does not apply to this movie. On the contrary, Simba, Pumbaa, and Timon from Disney's animated feature *The Lion King* offer a sugar-coated lesson on how to protect and care for the environment.

 Did you know that Elton John wrote the music to the song "Hakuna Matata"?

Living with the Land (Fastpass seasonally) ★★★★

APPEAL BY AGE PRESCHOOL ★★★½ GRADE SCHOOL ★★★★ TEENS ★★★½
YOUNG ADULTS ★★★★   OVER 30 ★★★★   SENIORS ★★★★

What it is Indoor boat-ride adventure through the past, present, and future of U.S. farming and agriculture. **Scope and scale** Major attraction. **Fright potential** Not frightening in any respect, but loud. **Bottleneck rating** 9. **When to go** Before 10:30 a.m., after 5 p.m., or use Fastpass if available. **Authors' rating** Interesting and fun; not to be missed; ★★★★. **Duration of ride** About 14 minutes. **Average wait in line per 100 people ahead of you** 3 minutes. **Assumes** 15 boats operating. **Loading speed** Moderate.

Thumbs Up for the Whole Family

This boat ride through four experimental growing areas is inspiring and educational. Kids like seeing the giant pumpkins and hearing about the tomato tree that has produced 20,000 tomatoes. Teens will be fascinated by the imaginative ways to grow crops—without soil, hanging in the air, even on a space station. A lot of the fruits and vegetables grown here are served to guests in the restaurants at Epcot, such as the Garden Grill and the Coral Reef.

I like the gardening part and looking at the fruits and vegetables. They need to make Living with the Land into a rock song.

Hannah

Soarin' (Fastpass) ★★★★½

APPEAL BY AGE PRESCHOOL ★★★★ GRADE SCHOOL ★★★★★ TEENS ★★★★★
YOUNG ADULTS ★★★★★   OVER 30 ★★★★★   SENIORS ★★★★★

What it is Flight simulation ride. **Scope and scale** Super headliner. **Fright potential** Frightens almost no one who meets the minimum height requirements. **Bottleneck rating** 10. **When to go** First 30 minutes the park is open or use Fastpass. **Special comments** Entrance on the lower level of The Land Pavilion. May induce motion sickness; must be 40" tall to ride; switching-off option provided (see page 238). **Authors' rating** Exciting and mellow at the same time; ★★★★½. Not to be missed. **Duration of ride** 5½ minutes. **Average wait in line per 100 people ahead of you** 4 minutes. **Assumes** 2 concourses operating. **Loading speed** Moderate.

This is the closest to hang gliding you will come without trying the real thing. Once airborne, you are flying over California with IMAX-quality images projected all around you, while a flight simulator moves your hang glider in sync with the movie. The experience is extremely mellow and nonthreatening. Any child (or adult) who meets the 40-inch minimum height requirement will love Soarin'. If you opt for Fastpass, make sure to get one before lunch, as there may not be any passes left after 12:30 p.m.

or so. As a matter of fact, Liliane had to be rescued by her son during her last visit, as a mob of gone-wild guests nearly ran her over on her way to the Fastpass machine.

Now I know what it feels like to be a kite. Fly high into the clouds and soar like a bird! It's like you have a front row seat to see the world. You feel the wind in your face and smell the oranges as you fly over the trees. I'll never forget flying through the golf course when all of a sudden—oh, dude!—a golf ball whooshed by my head.

It's a ride, but you don't really move that much. There's a huge movie screen in front of you. You go past an orange farm in the ride, and it starts to smell like oranges. It's a good thing you don't go near any wet dogs!

IMAGINATION! PAVILION

THIS MULTIATTRACTION PAVILION is situated on the west side of Innoventions West and down the walk from The Land. Outside is an "upside-down waterfall" and one of our favorite Future World landmarks, the "jumping water," a fountain that hops over the heads of unsuspecting passersby.

When it's hot, all I want to do is wear my swim trunks and get wet. One of the best places is outside of the Imagination! Pavilion. They have dancing waters skipping through the air. I like to follow where the water is flying and let it splash my face. Another place to get wet is near Test Track. Water shoots up from the ground. It's fun!

Honey, I Shrunk the Audience ★★★★½
Captain EO   ★★★★

| APPEAL BY AGE | PRESCHOOL ★★★★½ | GRADE SCHOOL ★★★★ | TEENS ★★★ |
| YOUNG ADULTS ★★ | | OVER 30 ★★½ | SENIORS ★★ |

What they are 3-D films with special effects. **Scope and scale** Headliners. **Fright potential** Extremely intense visual effects and loudness frighten young children. **Bottleneck rating** 8. **When to go** Before noon or after 4 p.m. **Special comments** Adults should not be put off by the sci-fi theme (or rock music, for *Captain EO*). The high decibels and *Honey's* tactile effects frighten some young children. **Authors' rating** *Honey:* An absolute hoot! Not to be missed; ★★★★½. *EO:* ★★★★. **Duration of presentation** About 17 minutes. **Preshow entertainment** 8 minutes. **Probable waiting time** 15 minutes (at suggested times).

In response to Michael Jackson's death in 2009, Disney has brought back his 3-D space-themed musical film presentation *Captain EO* for a "limited engagement" in its theme parks; at Epcot, it's temporarily supplanted *Honey, I Shrunk the Audience*. *Captain EO*

originally ran here from 1986 to 1994; there's no telling how long it'll last on its second run, but we've heard Disney will yank the film as soon as its audience numbers begin to drop. Both films share exceptionally loud soundtracks and a propensity to frighten small kids.

HONEY, I SHRUNK THE AUDIENCE A 3-D offshoot of Disney's feature film *Honey, I Shrunk the Kids, Honey, I Shrunk the Audience* features an array of special effects, including simulated explosions, smoke, fiber optics, lights, water spray, and moving seats. This attraction is played strictly for laughs—a commodity that's in short supply when it comes to Epcot entertainment.

CAPTAIN EO The ultimate music video. Starring the late Michael Jackson and directed by Francis Ford Coppola, this 3-D space fantasy is more than a film; it's a happening. Action on the screen is augmented by lasers, fiber optics, cannons, and a host of other special effects in the theater, as well as by some audience participation. There's not much of a story, but there's plenty of music and dancing performed by some of the most unlikely creatures ever to shake a tail feather. If nothing else, *Captain EO* reminds us that music videos once contained more than young urbanites dancing in clubs or five ill-dressed, unshaven guys whining onstage.

Young children will be frightened at times. If, however, they want to see the show, I recommend letting them watch first without the 3-D glasses and with earplugs.

Liliane

Yikes, Liliane, you could cover them up with a blanket too! About those mice in *Honey*: If the thought of several thousand (simulated) mice loose in the theater gives you the willies, sit with your feet crossed in yoga position. You'll never know the mice are there (except for the screaming of everyone around you, of course).

Bob

Journey into Imagination with Figment ★★½

| APPEAL BY AGE | PRESCHOOL ★★★½ | GRADE SCHOOL ★★★½ | TEENS ★★★ |
| YOUNG ADULTS ★★★ | | OVER 30 ★★★ | SENIORS ★★★ |

What it is Dark fantasy-adventure ride. **Scope and scale** Major attraction wannabe. **Fright potential** Frightens a small percentage of preschoolers. **Bottleneck rating** 6. **When to go** Anytime. **Authors' rating** Vacuous; ★★½. **Duration of ride** About 6 minutes. **Average wait in line per 100 people ahead of you** 2 minutes. **Loading speed** Fast.

"One little spark of inspiration is at the heart of all creation," croons the ever-popular Figment, as he takes you on a tour of the zany Imagination Institute with the help of your five senses. Young children will love the little purple dragon, but grown-ups and teens will be mildly amused at best.

Mission: SPACE (Fastpass) ★★★★

| APPEAL BY AGE | PRESCHOOL ★★★ | GRADE SCHOOL ★★★★ | TEENS ★★★★½ |
| YOUNG ADULTS ★★★★ | | OVER 30 ★★★★ | SENIORS ★★★ |

What it is Space flight simulation ride. **Scope and scale** Super headliner. **Fright potential** Intense thrill ride may frighten guests of any age. Switching-off option

A PEEK BEHIND THE SCENES WITH JIM HILL

AND IT'S $25 PER BAG, ONE-WAY

Mission: SPACE is supposed to simulate what an astronaut might experience during a trip to Mars. But once you're stuck on the Red Planet, how do you get back home? Simple. Just head for the attraction's postshow area, where you can play the Mission: SPACE Race game. You and your friends compete against another team to see who'll be first to get their rocket from Mars back to Earth.

provided (see page 238). **Bottleneck rating** 9. **When to go** First 30 minutes the park is open, or use Fastpass. **Special comments** Not recommended for pregnant women or people prone to motion sickness; must be 44" tall to ride; a gentler, nonspinning version is also available. **Authors' rating** Impressive; ★★★★. **Duration of ride** About 5 minutes plus preshow. **Average wait in line per 100 people ahead of you** 4 minutes.

Rough

Motion Sickness

In this attraction, you join three other guests in a four-man crew to fly a space mission. Each guest plays a role (commander, pilot, navigator, or engineer) and is required to perform certain functions during the flight. A cleverly conceived, technological marvel, Mission: SPACE made national news when, in separate incidents, two guests died after riding it. While neither of the deaths were linked to the attraction (the victims had unknown preexisting conditions), the negative publicity caused many guests to skip it entirely. In response, Disney has added a less stressful nonspinning version of Mission: SPACE. If you want to experience the spinning version of the ride, join the "orange" team, and if you prefer to check it out without those pesky g-forces, join the "green" team.

Liliane

Follow the orange brick road because it's much more fun. The ride is too intense for little ones and anybody prone to motion sickness, but grade-schoolers, teens, and brave moms and dadstronauts will love it! And don't worry about the job assignments—do you really think Disney is going to let you meddle around with their multimillion-dollar high-tech toys?

The host during your expedition is Gary Sinise, known for his roles in the space flicks *Apollo 13* and *Mission to Mars*.
Movie Tip

The "Mom, I Can't Believe It's Disney!" Fountain ★★★★

APPEAL BY AGE	PRESCHOOL ★★★★★	GRADE SCHOOL ★★★★★
TEENS ★★★★	YOUNG ADULTS ★★★★	OVER 30 ★★★★ SENIORS ★★★★★

What it is Combo fountain/shower. **Scope and scale** Diversion. **Fright potential** Not frightening in any respect. **Bottleneck rating** 2. **When to go** When it's hot. **Special comments** Secretly installed by Martians during *IllumiNations*. **Authors' rating** Yes! ★★★★★. **Duration of experience** Indefinite. **Probable waiting time** None.

Thumbs Up for the Whole Family

On a broiling Florida day, when you think you might suddenly combust, fling yourself into the fountain and do decidedly un-Disney things. Dance, skip, sing, jump, splash, stick your toes down the spouts, or catch the water in your mouth! Toddlers and preschoolers, along with hippies, especially love the fountain. We know that your kids will be right in the middle of this thing before your brain sounds the alert. Our advice: Pack a pair of dry shorts and turn the kids loose. Make sure they do not go into the fountain with sneakers, as wet sneakers are a recipe for blisters.

Test Track (Fastpass) ★★★½

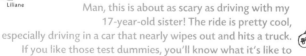

**APPEAL BY AGE   PRESCHOOL ★★★★   GRADE SCHOOL ★★★★½   TEENS ★★★★★
YOUNG ADULTS ★★★★½   OVER 30 ★★★★½   SENIORS ★★★★**

What it is Automobile test-track simulator ride. **Scope and scale** Super headliner. **Fright potential** Intense thrill ride may frighten guests of any age. Switching-off option provided (see page 238). **Bottleneck rating** 10. **When to go** First 30 minutes the park is open, just before closing, or use Fastpass. **Special comments** Must be 40" tall to ride. **Authors' rating** Good but not worth a 40-minute or longer wait; ★★★½. **Duration of ride** About 4 minutes. **Average wait in line per 100 people ahead of you** 4½ minutes. **Loading speed** Moderate to fast.

Scary   Rough

Visitors test a future model car at high speeds through hairpin turns, up and down steep hills, and over rough terrain. The six-guest vehicle is a motion simulator that rocks and pitches. The grand finale is a spin around a steep-banked loop at 65 mph! It is much fun if you meet the height requirements. Test Track is a favorite attraction of teens.

Liliane

There is a Kidcot Fun Stop at Test Track where those too short to ride can occupy themselves with arts and crafts. When the temperature's boiling, try the neighboring Cool Wash misting station.

Idan

Man, this is about as scary as driving with my 17-year-old sister! The ride is pretty cool, especially driving in a car that nearly wipes out and hits a truck. If you like those test dummies, you'll know what it's like to be one. The best time is when you hit the speed track outside and rip around an oval like you're a NASCAR driver.

Ian

If nobody in your family wants to join you on the ride and you don't have a Fastpass, join the singles line. It moves much faster.

Hannah

I love fast things, and this was more than fast! You ride in a really cool car on what looks like a real road. There's no radio, but it's a convertible, and I like convertibles!

Shelton

It was pretty fun but not as exciting as I thought it would be. The thought of going 65 miles an hour was amazing, but you might as well get in a convertible and go down the highway.

Universe of Energy: *Ellen's Energy Adventure* ★★★★

APPEAL BY AGE	PRESCHOOL ★★★	GRADE SCHOOL ★★★½	TEENS ★★★
YOUNG ADULTS ★★★		OVER 30 ★★★½	SENIORS ★★★½

What it is Combination ride/theater presentation about energy. **Scope and scale** Major attraction. **Fright potential** Dinosaur segment frightens some preschoolers; visually intense, with some intimidating effects. **Bottleneck rating** 7. **When to go** Before 11:15 a.m. or after 4:30 p.m. **Special comments** Don't be dismayed by long lines; 580 people enter the pavilion each time the theater changes audiences. **Authors' rating** The most unique theater in Walt Disney World; ★★★★. **Duration of presentation** About 26½ minutes. **Preshow entertainment** 8 minutes. **Probable waiting time** 20–40 minutes.

Join Ellen DeGeneres and Bill Nye, the science guy, who star in this 26-minute presentation about energy. Visitors are seated in what appears to be an ordinary theater. After a short film, the theater seats divide into six 97-passenger traveling cars that glide among swamps and through a prehistoric forest full of animatronic dinosaurs. The ride itself is smooth and not scary at all, though some children are frightened by the dinosaurs.

Scary

Ellen DeGeneres lent her voice to the role of Dory, a fish with short-term memory loss, in the animated Disney/Pixar film *Finding Nemo*.

Movie
Tip

WORLD SHOWCASE

WORLD SHOWCASE, EPCOT'S SECOND THEME AREA, is an ongoing World's Fair encircling a picturesque, 40-acre lagoon. The cuisine, culture, history, and architecture of almost a dozen countries are permanently displayed in individual national pavilions spaced along a 1.2-mile promenade. Pavilions replicate familiar landmarks and street scenes from the host countries. Now moving clockwise around the World Showcase promenade, here are the nations represented and their attractions.

Kim Possible World Showcase Adventure ★★★★

APPEAL BY AGE	PRESCHOOL ★★★½	GRADE SCHOOL ★★★★½	TEENS ★★★
YOUNG ADULTS ★★★★		OVER 30 ★★★½	SENIORS ★★

What it is Interactive scavenger hunt in select World Showcase pavilions. **Scope and scale** Minor attraction. **When to go** Anytime. **Authors' rating** One of our favorite additions to the parks; ★★★★. **Duration of experience** Allow 30 minutes per adventure. **Preshow entertainment** None. **Probable waiting time** None.

Disney Channel's *Kim Possible* show follows the teen heroine as she battles the forces of evil in exotic locations while trying to navigate typical teen challenges like proms, parents, and homework. In the *Kim Possible* World Showcase Adventure, you play the part of Kim and are given a cell-phone-like "Kimmunicator" before being dispatched on a mission to your choice of seven World Showcase pavilions. Once you arrive at the pavilion, the Kimmunicator's video screen and audio provide various clues about the adventure. As you discover each clue, you'll find special effects such as talking statues and flaming lanterns, plus live "secret agents" stationed in the pavilions just for this game.

Kim Possible is Disney's attempt at making static World Showcase pavilions more interactive and kid-friendly. It succeeds wildly, even as Disney is still ironing out all the technological kinks. The adventures have relatively simple clues, fast pacing, and neat rewards for solving the puzzles. Disney clearly put a lot of thought into game play and substantial investment into the effects. Since the experience debuted, reader reviews have been uniformly positive, with the Japan adventure being the most popular.

Playing the game is free, and no deposit is required for the Kimmunicator. You'll need a valid theme-park ticket to sign up before you play, and you can choose both the time and location of your adventure. Register at either Future World's Innovations East or Innoventions West buildings, along the main walkway from Future World to World Showcase, or on the Odyssey Bridge. You'll report to the Italy, Norway, or United Kingdom Pavilion to pick up your Kimmunicator before heading off to your chosen country.

Each group can have up to three Kimmunicators for the same adventure. Because you're working with a device about the size of a cell phone, it's best if you have one Kimmunicator for every two people in your group.

Kim Possible opens up a world of adventure for little ones and ones who are young at heart. It's most fun if you are at least in two pairs. Split up in teams and see who can solve the most missions first!

Idan

MEXICO PAVILION

PRE-COLUMBIAN PYRAMIDS dominate the architecture of this exhibit. Inside you will find authentic and valuable artifacts, a village scene complete with restaurant, and the boat ride.

SPANISH 101

Hello: *Hola*	Pronunciation: *Oh-la*
Goodbye: *Adios*	Pronunciation: *Ah-dee-ohs*
Thank you: *Gracias*	Pronunciation: *Grah-see-ahs*
Mickey Mouse: *El Ratón Miguelito*	Pronunciation: *El Rah-tone Mee-gell-lee-toe*

Gran Fiesta Tour Starring the Three Caballeros ★★½

APPEAL BY AGE	PRESCHOOL ★★★★	GRADE SCHOOL ★★★½	TEENS ★★★
YOUNG ADULTS ★★★		OVER 30 ★★★	SENIORS ★★★

What it is Indoor scenic boat ride. **Scope and scale** Minor attraction. **Fright potential** Not frightening in any respect. **Bottleneck rating** 5. **When to go** Before noon or after 5 p.m. **Authors' rating** New role for classic Disney characters; ★★½. **Duration of ride** About 7 minutes (plus 1½-minute wait to disembark). **Average wait in line per 100 people ahead of you** 4½ minutes. **Assumes** 16 boats in operation. **Loading speed** Moderate.

Thumbs Up for the Whole Family

Gran Fiesta Tour replaces El Río del Tiempo, which had run since Epcot's opening in 1982. The story line features Donald Duck, José Carioca (a parrot), and Panchito (a Mexican charro rooster) from the 1944 Disney film *The Three Caballeros;* the story has our heroes racing to Mexico City for a gala reunion performance. The sets were refurbished to enhance the new film.

NORWAY PAVILION

SURROUNDING A COURTYARD is an assortment of traditional Scandinavian buildings, including a replica of the 14th-century Akershus Castle, now home to Princesses-hosted character meals. Other attractions include Maelstrom, a ride, and a Viking ship playground (the only dedicated playground at Epcot).

NORWEGIAN 101

Hello: *God dag*	**Pronunciation:** *Good dagh*
Goodbye: *Ha det*	**Pronunciation:** *Hah deh*
Thank you: *Takk*	**Pronunciation:** *Tahk*
Mickey Mouse: *Mikke Mus*	**Pronunciation:** *Mikeh Moose*

It is hard to say no to the mouth-watering pastries at Kringla Bakeri og Kafe.

Liliane

Maelstrom (Fastpass) ★★★

APPEAL BY AGE	PRESCHOOL ★★★	GRADE SCHOOL ★★★½	TEENS ★★★½
YOUNG ADULTS ★★★½		OVER 30 ★★★½	SENIORS ★★★★

What it is Indoor adventure boat ride. **Scope and scale** Major attraction. **Fright potential** Dark, visually intense in parts. Ride ends with a plunge down a 20-foot flume. **Bottleneck rating** 9. **When to go** Before noon, after 4:30 p.m., or use Fastpass. **Authors' rating** Too short, but has its moments; ★★★. **Duration of ride** 4½ minutes, followed by a 5-minute film with a short wait in between; about 14 minutes for the ride and show combo. **Average wait in line per 100 people ahead of you** 4 minutes. **Assumes** 12 or 13 boats operating. **Loading speed** Fast.

Dark

Scary

Board a dragon-headed ship for a voyage through the fabled seas of Viking history and legends with brave trolls, rocky gorges, and a storm at sea. Sounds dangerous? The ride can be intense at times, but the only hold-your-breath moment is when your boat descends a 20-foot slide. The rather short ride is followed by a 5-minute film on Norway, but if you don't want to see the film, you will be given the opportunity to exit before it begins.

CHINA PAVILION

THERE IS NO RIDE AT THE CHINA PAVILION, but the majestic half-size replica of the Temple of Heaven in Beijing will surely make it into your photo album. Inside the pavilion see *Reflections of China,* an impressive film about the people and natural beauty of China. Children will enjoy the regularly scheduled performances of Chinese acrobats. Check your entertainment schedule (*Times Guide*) for showtimes.

CHINESE (MANDARIN) 101

Hello: *Ni hao*	Pronunciation: *Knee how*
Goodbye: *Zai jian*	Pronunciation: *Zy jehn*
Thank you: *Xiè xie*	Pronunciation: *Chi-eh chi-eh*
Mickey Mouse: *Mi Lao Shu*	Pronunciation: *Me Lah-oh Su*

Reflections of China ★★★½

APPEAL BY AGE	PRESCHOOL ★★	GRADE SCHOOL ★★★	TEENS ★★★
YOUNG ADULTS ★★★½		OVER 30 ★★★★	SENIORS ★★★½

What it is Film about the Chinese people and country. **Scope and scale** Major attraction. **Fright potential** Not frightening in any respect. **Bottleneck rating** 4. **When to go** Anytime. **Special comments** Audience stands throughout performance. **Authors' rating** This beautifully produced film was introduced in 2003; ★★★½. **Duration of presentation** About 14 minutes. **Preshow entertainment** None. **Probable waiting time** 10 minutes.

GERMANY PAVILION

THE GERMANY PAVILION DOES NOT HAVE RIDES. The main focus is the Biergarten, a full-service (reservations suggested) restaurant serving German food and beer. Yodeling, folk dancing, and oompah-band music are regularly performed during mealtimes. Be sure to check out the large, elaborate model railroad located just beyond the restrooms as you walk from Germany toward Italy.

GERMAN 101

Hello: *Hallo*	Pronunciation: *Hall-o*
Goodbye: *Auf wiedersehen*	Pronunciation: *Ow-f veeh-der-zain*
Thank you: *Danke*	Pronunciation: *Dan-keh*
Mickey Mouse: *Micky Maus*	Pronunciation: *Me-key Mouse*

Biergarten German restaurant: The best party I ever went to. Good chicken fingers, lots of salads, yummy desserts. My dad liked the beer band, and so did I. They shouted, "Ticky tocky, ticky tocky!" and we yelled back, "Oy, oy, oy!" (whatever that means). Everybody raised their beer glasses, sang songs, and did goofy dances. I think I had one too many root beers.

Ian

The Germany Pavilion is the perfect place to introduce your kids to a great snack: *Gummibaerchen* (gummy bears), my favorite childhood candy.

Liliane

ITALY PAVILION

THE ENTRANCE TO ITALY IS MARKED by an 83-foot-tall campanile (bell tower) intended to mirror the tower in St. Mark's Square in Venice. Left of the campanile is a replica of the 14th-century Doge's Palace.

Streets and courtyards in the Italy Pavilion are among the most realistic in the World Showcase. You really feel as if you're in Italy. Because there's no film or ride, tour any time.

ITALIAN 101	
Hello: *Buon giorno*	Pronunciation: *Bon jor-no*
Goodbye: *Ciao* (informal)	Pronunciation: *Chow*
Thank you: *Grazie*	Pronunciation: *Grah-zee-eh*
Mickey Mouse: *Topolino*	Pronunciation: *To-po-lee-no*

Ian

I don't know how they do this, but I couldn't stop watching. A lady statue comes alive and messes with people. She stands perfectly still in front of Italy. When people have their pictures taken next to her, she moves and does crazy things to them. My family laughed a lot, but I was too chicken to go up to her.

UNITED STATES PAVILION

THE UNITED STATES PAVILION is an imposing brick structure reminiscent of colonial Philadelphia and is home to a very moving and patriotic, albeit sanitized, retrospective of U.S. history. Street entertainment outside includes the Voices of Liberty choral ensemble and the Spirit of America Fife & Drum Corps, among others. Across the plaza is the America Gardens Theatre, Epcot's premier venue for concerts and stage shows.

The American Adventure ★★★★

APPEAL BY AGE	PRESCHOOL ★★½	GRADE SCHOOL ★★★	TEENS ★★★
YOUNG ADULTS ★★★½		OVER 30 ★★★★	SENIORS ★★★★

What it is Patriotic mixed-media and audio-animatronic theater presentation on U.S. history. **Scope and scale** Headliner. **Fright potential** Not frightening in any respect. **Bottleneck rating** 6. **When to go** Anytime. **Authors' rating** Disney's best historic/patriotic attraction; not to be missed; ★★★★. **Duration of presentation** About 29 minutes. **Preshow entertainment** Voices of Liberty chorale singing. **Probable waiting time** 25 minutes.

The 29-minute multimedia show is narrated by animatronic Mark Twain and Ben Franklin. *The American Adventure* reminds you of a contest: Tell us everything you love about America in 30

Thumbs Up for the Whole Family

minutes or less. Only four female figures are among the 12 personified ideals around the theater, one of them representing the rather ambiguous "tomorrow" by virtue of holding a baby. The North American continent seemingly does not exist prior to the landing of the *Mayflower.*

JAPAN PAVILION

THE FIVE-STORY, BLUE-ROOFED PAGODA, inspired by a 17th-century shrine in Nara, sets this pavilion apart. A hill garden behind it encompasses waterfalls, rocks, flowers, lanterns, paths, and rustic bridges. There are no attractions unless you count the huge Japanese retail venue. Not to be missed, though, are the Matsuriza Taiko drummers. The drums can often be heard throughout the World Showcase, but you need to be up-close to see the graceful way the drums are played. Check the *Times Guide* for scheduled performances.

JAPANESE 101

Hello: *Konnichiwa*	Pronunciation: *Ko-nee-chee wah*
Goodbye: *Sayonara*	Pronunciation: *Sigh-yo-nah-ra*
Thank you: *Arigato*	Pronunciation: *Ah-ree-gah-to*
Mickey Mouse: *Mikki Mausu*	Pronunciation: *Mikkee Mou-su*

MOROCCO PAVILION

THE BUSTLING MARKET, WINDING STREETS, lofty minarets, and stuccoed archways re-create the romance and intrigue of Marrakesh and Casablanca. Attention to detail makes Morocco one of the most exciting World Showcase pavilions, but there are no attractions.

ARABIC 101

Hello: *Salaam alekoum*	Pronunciation: *Sah-lahm ah-leh-koom*
Goodbye: *Ma'salama*	Pronunciation: *Mah sah-lah-mah*
Thank you: *Shoukran*	Pronunciation: *Shoe-krah-n*
Mickey Mouse: *Mujallad Miki*	Pronunciation: *Muh-jahl-lahd Me-key*

I love Middle Eastern food and enjoy the music and belly dancing at Restaurant Marrakesh. Try the falafel; it's delicious. In the courtyard Aladdin and Jasmine come to greet kids several times a day. I wish Disney would bring out Jaffar, my favorite character from *Aladdin,* more often.

FRANCE PAVILION

WELCOME AND BIENVENUE to Paris, Eiffel Tower, and all. There is not much to do for the kids here, but you won't have any trouble luring them into Boulangerie Patisserie for a scrumptious French pastry. Givenchy, the famed French perfume empire, opened a shop at the

France Pavilion and is the only retail location in the United States offering the full line of Givenchy make-up and skin-care products, as well as a large selection of Givenchy fragrances.

Here is something for mom. . . . Seriously, do they really think that this is why we go to Epcot?

Liliane

Impressions de France ★★★½

APPEAL BY AGE	PRESCHOOL ★★	GRADE SCHOOL ★★★	TEENS ★★★
YOUNG ADULTS ★★★½	OVER 30 ★★★½		SENIORS ★★★★

What it is Film essay on the French people and country. **Scope and scale** Major attraction. **Fright potential** Not frightening in any respect. **Bottleneck rating** 7. **When to go** Anytime. **Authors' rating** Exceedingly beautiful film; not to be missed; ★★★½. **Duration of presentation** About 18 minutes. **Preshow entertainment** None. **Probable waiting time** 15 minutes (at suggested times).

France, here I come! This truly lovely 18-minute movie will make you want to pack your suitcase. An added bonus is that the showing is "très civilizé," as you get to sit down and rest your weary feet.

UNITED KINGDOM PAVILION

A BLEND OF ARCHITECTURE ATTEMPTS to capture Britain's city, town, and rural atmospheres. One street alone has a thatched-roof cottage, four-story timber-and-plaster building, pre-Georgian plaster building, formal Palladian exterior of dressed stone, and a city square with a Hyde Park bandstand (whew!). There are no attractions.

If your child loves Mary Poppins, your best chance to meet her is here. Teens and yours truly have a good time with the Beatles impersonation band. Check your entertainment schedule (*Times Guide*) for a trip down Abbey Road.

Liliane

CANADA PAVILION

CANADA'S CULTURAL, NATURAL, AND architectural diversity is reflected in this large and impressive pavilion. Older kids will be interested in the 30-foot-tall totem poles that embellish a Native American village. Canada is also home to a sort of punk-Celtic-country band called Off Kilter—yes, the lead singer wears a kilt—that performs in front of the showcase entrance. Check your entertainment schedule (*Times Guide*) for performance times.

O Canada! ★★★½

| APPEAL BY AGE | PRESCHOOL ★★ | GRADE SCHOOL ★★★ | TEENS ★★★ |
| YOUNG ADULTS ★★★½ | | OVER 30 ★★★★ | SENIORS ★★★★ |

What it is Film essay on the Canadian people and their country. **Scope and scale** Major attraction. **Fright potential** Not frightening in any respect. **Bottleneck rating** 5. **When to go** Anytime. **Special comments** Audience stands during performance. **Authors' rating** Makes you want to catch the first plane to Canada! ★★★½. **Duration of presentation** About 18 minutes. **Preshow entertainment** None. **Probable waiting time** 10 minutes.

O Canada! showcases Canada's natural beauty and population diversity and demonstrates the immense pride Canadians have in their country. A new film has replaced the decades-old original. Starring Martin Short, it features clips and dialogue interspersed with some of the original film's

FAVORITE EATS AT EPCOT

LAND	SERVICE LOCATION	FOOD ITEM
JAPAN	Yakitori House	Beef & chicken teriyaki
FRANCE	Boulangerie Patisserie	Croissants, chocolate mousse, yummy sandwiches on baguettes
	Crepes des Chefs de France	Crêpes & espresso
MEXICO	La Cantina de San Angel	Children's plate with burrito, chips, and beverage
NORWAY	Kringla Bakeri og Kafe	Salmon sandwiches & pastries
GERMANY	Sommerfest	Bratwurst and frankfurter with kraut and apple strudel
MOROCCO	Tangierine Café	Shawarma, hummus, couscous, and kids' meals; outdoor seating
UNITED KINGDOM	UK Shop	You must have an English Cadbury bar once in your life
CHINA	Lotus Blossom Cafe	Beef and chicken rice bowls, vegetable lo mein, and egg rolls
ITALY	Tutto Italia*	Reasonable pasta, kids' menu
UNITED STATES	Liberty Inn	If you are craving all-American food
CANADA	Le Cellier Steakhouse*	The Northern Lights dessert for kids; great steaks for mom and dad
INNOVENTIONS EAST	Electric Umbrella Restaurant	French toast, bagels, and talking trash can
THE LAND PAVILION	Sunshine Seasons	Healthy choices—our all-time favorite
THE SEAS PAVILION	Coral Reef Restaurant*	Food with a view—fish menu The aquarium will keep the kids happy for quite some time

* table service only—Advance Reservations highly recommended

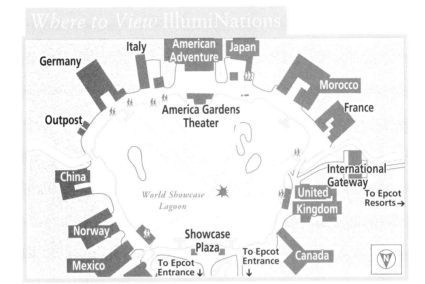

Where to View IllumiNations

scenes. Visitors leave the theater through Victoria Gardens, which was inspired by the famed Butchart Gardens of British Columbia.

Cast members often run a preshow quiz on Canadian trivia outside the theater before the show. Here are some helpful tips: Canada's capital is Ottawa; its $1 coin is nicknamed the Loonie, after the bird engraved on it; and the $2 coin is the Toonie—not, unfortunately, the Doubloonie.

This large-capacity attraction (guests must stand) gets fairly heavy late-morning attendance, as Canada is the first pavilion encountered as one travels counterclockwise around World Showcase Lagoon.

LIVE ENTERTAINMENT
at EPCOT

IN FUTURE WORLD

KIDS WILL LOVE THE CREW OF DRUMMING JANITORS (The JAMMitors), as well as the Krystos gymnasts in alien attire and the dancing fountains show in the plaza between the Innoventions East and West buildings.

Combine a rest break with a little fun. Let your kids experience one of the special talking water fountains at Epcot (located outside the Mouse Works shop, behind Innoventions West; between Innoventions and *Honey, I Shrunk the Audience* or *Captain EO* in the Imagination Pavilion; and next to the play fountain between Future

Liliane

World and World Showcase). For a hilarious chat, seek out PUSH the talking
trash can at the Electric Umbrella Restaurant in Innoventions East.

AROUND THE WORLD SHOWCASE

STREET PERFORMANCES IN AND AROUND the World Showcase are
what set live entertainment at Epcot apart from the other Disney
parks. A strolling mariachi group can be found in Mexico; street
actors in Italy; a fife-and-drum corps or The Voices of Liberty at The
American Adventure; traditional songs, drums, and dances in Japan;
street comedy and a Beatles impersonation band in the United Kingdom; white-faced mimes in France; bagpipes and Celtic bands in
Canada, among other performances. Check your entertainment
schedule *(Times Guide)* for performance times. Some restaurants get
in on the act too. You can dine among singing waiters in Italy, enjoy
Oktoberfest entertainment in Germany, and see belly dancing in
Morocco. WDW live-entertainment guru Steve Soares usually posts
the Epcot performance schedule about a week in advance at **pages.
prodigy.net/stevesoares.**

AMERICA GARDENS THEATRE

THE AMERICA GARDENS THEATRE, a pleasant amphitheater on the
lagoon across from the U.S. Pavilion, showcases stage shows featuring
Disney characters, international dance troupes, acrobatic companies,
choruses, musical groups, dinosaur rock bands (particularly appropriate), comedians who book engagements of several weeks, and even
cheerleading competitions. Some of these are very good indeed,
although whether you're interested in a particular show may depend
on how tired you are and what else you have scheduled. Showtimes
(all free, of course) are listed on a board outside the exits and in the
daily *Times Guide*.

ILLUMINATIONS

A NIGHTLY CAPSTONE EVENT AT EPCOT called *IllumiNations*
features a program of music, fireworks, erupting fountains, special
lightning, and laser technology performed on World Showcase
Lagoon. This enchanting and ambitious show (it tells the history of
the universe starting with the Big Bang) is well worth keeping the kids
up late. The best place to view the show is from the lakeside veranda
of the Cantina de San Angel Inn at the Mexico Pavilion. Come early
and relax with a drink or snack. The drawback is, you guessed it, that
you will have to claim this spot at least 90 minutes before *Illumi-
Nations*. Also consider dinner on the patio of the Rose & Crown Pub
in the U.K. Pavilion (Advance Reservations recommended).

For other great viewing spots, check out our "Where to View
IllumiNations" map. Note that the boat dock opposite Germany may
be exposed to a lot of smoke from the fireworks because of Epcot's
prevailing winds.

IllumiNations is the climax of every day at Epcot, so keep in mind that once the show is over you will be leaving the park, and so will almost everybody else. For suggested exit strategies, see below.

For a really good view of the show, you can charter a pontoon boat for about $350. Captained by a Disney cast member, the boat holds up to 10 guests. Your captain will take you for a little cruise and then position the boat in a perfect place to watch *IllumiNations*. For more information, call ☎ 407-WDW-PLAY.

IllumiNations ★★★½

APPEAL BY AGE	PRESCHOOL ★★★½	GRADE SCHOOL ★★★★	TEENS ★★★★½
YOUNG ADULTS ★★★★½		OVER 30 ★★★★½	SENIORS ★★★★½

What it is Nighttime fireworks and laser show at World Showcase Lagoon. **Scope and scale** Super headliner. **Fright potential** Not frightening in any respect. **When to go** Stake out viewing position 20–40 minutes before showtime. **Special comments** Showtime is listed in the daily entertainment schedule on the handout park map. Audience stands during performance. **Authors' rating** Epcot's most impressive entertainment event; ★★★★½. **Duration of presentation** About 18 minutes.

EXIT STRATEGIES

MORE GROUPS GET SEPARATED and more children lost after *IllumiNations* than at any other time. Make sure that you have preselected a meeting point in the Epcot entrance area. Warn your group not to leave through the exit turnstiles until everyone is reunited.

Suggested meeting point: the fountain just inside the main entrance.

- If you are staying at the Swan, Dolphin, Yacht and Beach Club Resorts, or BoardWalk Inn and Villas, watch *IllumiNations* from somewhere between Italy and the United Kingdom, and exit the park through the International Gateway between France and the United Kingdom. You can walk or take a boat back to your hotel.

- If you have a car in the Epcot lot, find a viewing spot at the Future World end of World Showcase Lagoon (Showcase Plaza) and leave immediately as soon as *IllumiNations* ends. The problem is not the traffic in the parking lot—it actually moves pretty well—it's making your way to, and finding, your car. Make sure you write down where you are parked—this is not the time to rely on your memory. If you are parked near the entrance, skip the tram and walk. If you walk, watch your children closely and hang on to them for all you're worth. The parking lot is pretty wild at this time of night.

EPCOT TOURING PLANS

OUR STEP-BY-STEP TOURING PLANS ARE FIELD-TESTED, independently verified itineraries that will keep you moving counter to the crowd flow and allow you to see as much as possible in a single day with minimum time wasted in line. We present three Epcot one-day touring plans specifically geared toward visiting with children. We also offer, and recommend, a two-day touring plan that is much more relaxing and far less tiring.

Touring Epcot is much more strenuous and demanding than touring the other theme parks. Epcot requires about twice as much walking. And, unlike the Magic Kingdom, Epcot has no effective in-park transportation—wherever you want to go, it's always quicker to walk. Our plans will help you avoid crowds and bottlenecks on days of moderate to heavy attendance, but they can't shorten the distance you have to walk. (Wear comfortable shoes.) On days of lighter attendance, when crowd conditions aren't a critical factor, the plans will help you organize your tour.

As a group, the *Unofficial Guide* research staff loves Epcot. Because we spend so much time there, we really wanted our small children to enjoy it too. The challenge was figuring out how to get the kids connected to the theme or presentation at each pavilion, especially in Future World. Let's face it—a 7-year-old is only going to take so much talk about hydroponic vegetables, nuclear fission, or communication systems before tuning out.

The key for us was to brief our children on what they were likely to see in each attraction and then tie it back to something they could relate to in their everyday lives. During the tour of the greenhouse in Living with the Land, for example, we made a game of finding foods they like. (They've got cocoa beans—chocolate—so we think that covers almost everyone.) While riding Test Track, we asked our daughter to figure out which parent's driving was most like the ride's. (To avoid further sleeping in the garage, we'll not disclose who "won" that contest.) Our point here is that Epcot's Future World attractions can be a lot more palatable to young children if they're engaged and prepared going in. It's all about presentation.

The different touring plans are described below. The descriptions will tell you for whom (for example, tweens, parents with preschoolers, and so on) or for what situation (such as sleeping late) the plans are designed. The actual touring plans are located on pages 454–458 at the back of the book. Each plan includes a numbered map of the park in question to help you find your way around. Clip the plan of your choice out of the book by cutting along the line indicated, and take it with you to the park.

EPCOT ONE-DAY TOURING PLAN FOR PARENTS WITH SMALL CHILDREN This plan is designed for parents of children ages 3–8 who wish to see the very best age-appropriate attractions in Epcot. Every attraction has a rating of at least three stars (out of five) from preschool and grade-school children surveyed by the *Unofficial Guide*. Special advice is provided for touring the park with small children, including restaurant recommendations. The plan keeps walking and backtracking to a minimum.

EPCOT ONE-DAY SLEEPYHEAD TOURING PLAN FOR PARENTS WITH SMALL CHILDREN A relaxed plan that allows families with small children to sleep late and still see the highlights of Epcot. The plan begins around 11 a.m., sets aside ample time for lunch, and includes the very best child-friendly attractions in the park. The plan also points out where Fastpass can best be used.

EPCOT ONE-DAY TOURING PLAN FOR TWEENS AND THEIR PARENTS A one-day touring plan for parents with children ages 8–12. It includes every attraction rated three stars and higher by this age group, and it sets aside ample time for lunch and dinner.

PARENTS' EPCOT TOURING PLANS FOR AN AFTERNOON AND ONE FULL DAY This touring plan is for families who want to tour Epcot comprehensively over two days. Day One uses early-morning touring opportunities. Day Two begins in the afternoon and continues until closing.

BEFORE YOU GO

1. Call ☎ 407-824-4321 in advance for the hours of operation on the day of your visit.
2. Make reservations at the Epcot full-service restaurant(s) of your choice in advance of your visit.

EPCOT TRIVIA QUIZ

By Lou Mongello

1. In what World Showcase pavilion can you meet Donald Duck?
   a. United States
   b. Germany
   c. United Kingdom
   d. Mexico

2. In Soarin', what U.S. state do you soar over?
   a. Florida
   b. California
   c. Texas
   d. The entire nation

3. Captain EO is played by which of these famous stars?
   a. Michael Jordan
   b. Michael Jackson
   c. Robin Williams
   d. Joe Jonas

4. In World Showcase what country is found between Germany and the United States?
   a. France
   b. Morocco
   c. Japan
   d. Italy

5. What is the largest pavilion at Epcot?
   a. The Seas with Nemo & Friends
   b. Mission: SPACE
   c. Universe of Energy
   d. The Land

6. How many different international pavilions can be found in World Showcase?
   a. 7
   b. 9
   c. 11
   d. 13

7. What is unique about the waterfalls outside the Imagination! Pavilion?
   a. They flow upwards
   b. The water is purple
   c. They are holograms
   d. They only flow at night

8. What does EPCOT stand for?
   a. Employee Paychecks Come On Tuesday
   b. Every Person Comes Out Tired
   c. Experimental Prototype Community of Tomorrow
   d. Economic Private City of Orlando Taxation

9. Kids of all ages can participate in an adventure through World Showcase based on which Disney Channel show?
   a. *Phineas and Ferb*
   b. *Wizards of Waverly Place*
   c. *Kim Possible*
   d. *The Replacements*

10. The Gran Fiesta Tour starring the Three Caballeros features Donald and:
   a. Daisy and Goofy
   b. José Carioca and Panchito
   c. Pepe and Pancho
   d. José Carioca and Marco

11. What color are Figment's eyes?
   a. Red
   b. Orange
   c. Yellow
   d. Green

12. In the Universe of Energy, what does Ellen nickname her college roommate?
   a. Jumpin' Judy
   b. Stupid Judy
   c. Smarty Pants
   d. Einstein

Answers can be found on page 426.

PART NINE

ANIMAL KINGDOM

WITH ITS LUSH FLORA, WINDING STREAMS, meandering paths, and exotic setting, the Animal Kingdom is a stunningly beautiful theme park. The landscaping alone conjures images of a rain forest, veld, and even formal gardens. Add to this loveliness a population of more than 1,700 animals, replicas of Africa's and Asia's most intriguing architecture, and a diverse array of singularly original attractions, and you have the most unique of all Walt Disney World theme parks. The Animal Kingdom's seven sections, or "lands," are Oasis, Discovery Island, DinoLand U.S.A., Camp Minnie-Mickey, Africa, Asia, and Rafiki's Planet Watch.

On Discovery Island, behind the Creature Comforts Shop, is the Baby Care Center with supplies, changing tables, and a quiet place to nurse, as well as a first-aid center. Garden Gate Gifts at the main entrance and Duka La Filimu in Africa will save the day if you run out of film.

At the entrance plaza, ticket kiosks front the main entrance. To your right before the turnstiles, you'll find an ATM. Passing through the turnstiles, wheelchair and stroller rentals (at Garden Gate Gifts) are to your right. Guest Relations—the park headquarters for information, handout park maps, entertainment schedules, missing persons, and lost and found— is to the left. Disney no longer has pet care facilities adjacent to the park, but the new Best Friends Pet Resort across from Disney's Port Orleans Resort will provide a comfortable home away from home for Fido, Frisky, and all their pet pals.

The park is arranged somewhat like the Magic Kingdom. The lush, tropical Oasis serves as Main Street, funneling visitors to Discovery Island at the center of the park. Discovery Island is the park's retail and dining center. From Discovery Island, guests can access the respective theme areas: Africa, Camp Minnie-Mickey, Asia, and DinoLand U.S.A. Rafiki's Planet Watch is accessed from Africa.

Extra Magic Hours are offered to guests lodging at the Disney hotels. Should you take advantage of these hours, keep in mind that you will see very little of the animals after 5 p.m. Most animal exhibits and all of Rafiki's Planet Watch, including the Wildlife Express Train and Conservation Station, close at the same time that is posted for day guests. Exceptions to this are Kilimanjaro Safaris and Pangani Forest Exploration Trail. These vary by sunset and stay open during Extra Magic Hours until 7:30 p.m. on days when regular closing hours are 5, 6, or 8 p.m. In the fall, Disney closes all animal exhibits as early as 4:45 p.m. Extra Magic Hours do, however, space Animal Kingdom theater productions over a longer time period, making it possible to see them all at a more leisurely pace. Keep in mind that the evening hours are also cooler.

Kali River Rapids in Asia, as well as the Boneyard playground, the Wildlife Express Train, and Conservation Station are sometimes not opened until 30 minutes or longer after the rest of Animal Kingdom opens. It is not clear if these delayed openings are temporary, permanent, seasonal, or year-round. Check before you run to ride Kali River Rapids!

The OASIS

THOUGH THE FUNCTIONAL PURPOSE OF THE OASIS is to funnel guests to the center of the park, it also sets the stage and gets you into the right mood to enjoy Animal Kingdom. The Oasis immediately envelops you in an environment that is replete with choices. There is not one broad thoroughfare but rather multiple paths. Each will deliver you to Discovery Island at the center of the park, but which path you choose and what you see along the way is up to you. The natural-habitat zoological exhibits are primarily designed for the comfort and well-being of the animals. A sign will identify the animal(s) in each exhibit, but there's no guarantee the animals will be immediately visible. Because most habitats are large and provide ample terrain for the occupants to hide, you must linger and concentrate, looking for small movements in the vegetation. The Oasis is a place to linger and appreciate, and although this is exactly what the designers intended, it will be largely lost on Disney-conditioned guests who blitz through at warp speed to queue up for the big attractions. If you are a blitzer in the morning, plan to spend some time in The Oasis on your way out of the park. The Oasis usually closes 30–60 minutes after the rest of the park.

DISCOVERY ISLAND

DISCOVERY ISLAND IS AN ISLAND OF TROPICAL GREENERY and whimsical equatorial African architecture, executed in vibrant hues of teal, yellow, red, and blue. Connected to the other lands by bridges, the island is the hub from which guests can access the park's

Disney's Animal Kingdom

Africa

Discovery Island

Camp Minnie-Mickey

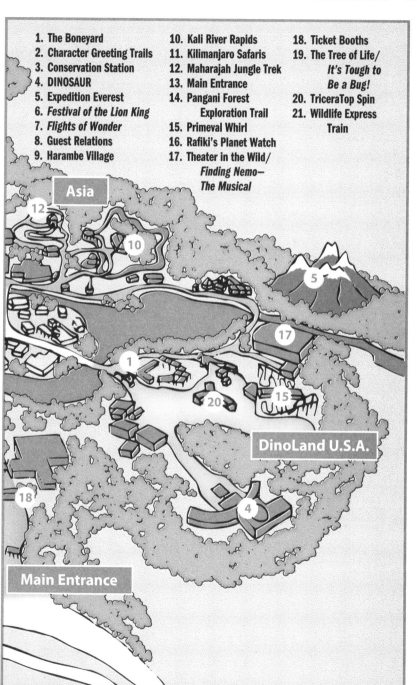

1. The Boneyard
2. Character Greeting Trails
3. Conservation Station
4. DINOSAUR
5. Expedition Everest
6. *Festival of the Lion King*
7. *Flights of Wonder*
8. Guest Relations
9. Harambe Village
10. Kali River Rapids
11. Kilimanjaro Safaris
12. Maharajah Jungle Trek
13. Main Entrance
14. Pangani Forest
    Exploration Trail
15. Primeval Whirl
16. Rafiki's Planet Watch
17. Theater in the Wild/
    *Finding Nemo—
    The Musical*
18. Ticket Booths
19. The Tree of Life/
    *It's Tough to
    Be a Bug!*
20. TriceraTop Spin
21. Wildlife Express
    Train

Asia

DinoLand U.S.A.

Main Entrance

various theme areas. Discovery Island is the park's central shopping, dining, and services headquarters. It is here that you will find the First Aid and Baby Care centers. For the best selection of Disney trademark merchandise, try the Island Mercantile shop. Counter-service food and snacks are available but no full-service restaurants. In addition to several wildlife exhibits, Discovery Island's Tree of Life hosts the film *It's Tough to Be a Bug!*

The Tree of Life/*It's Tough to Be a Bug!* ★★★★

APPEAL BY AGE **PRESCHOOL** ★★★	**GRADE SCHOOL** ★★★★	**TEENS** ★★★★
YOUNG ADULTS ★★★★	**OVER 30** ★★★★	**SENIORS** ★★★★

What it is 3-D theater show. **Scope and scale** Major attraction. **Fright potential** Very intense and loud, with special effects that startle viewers of all ages and potentially terrify young children. **Bottleneck rating** 9. **When to go** Before 10:30 a.m. or after 4 p.m.. **Special comments** The theater is inside the tree. **Authors' rating** Zany and frenetic; ★★★★. **Duration of presentation** Approximately 8 minutes. **Preshow entertainment** None. **Probable waiting time** 12–30 minutes.

Dark Loud Scary

Before entering the show, take a close look at the Tree of Life, the remarkable home of this 3-D movie. The primary icon and focal point of the Animal Kingdom, the tree features a trunk with high-relief carvings depicting 325 animals.

It's Tough to Be a Bug! is a zany, cleverly conceived, but very intense 3-D show housed below the Tree of Life. For starters, the show is about bugs and bugs always rank high on the ick-factor scale. That coupled with some startling special effects and a very loud soundtrack make *It's Tough to Be a Bug!* a potential horror show for the age-7-and-under crowd. Tread cautiously, but don't write off the attraction. You can prepare by watching the animated feature *A Bug's Life* before you leave home—many of the characters are the same.

We thought the animals were very cool. But don't get too close to the spoonbills. One squawked at me!

Shelton

 The closing lines of the show tipped me off when it was announced that "honorary bugs (read: audience members) remain seated while all the lice, bed bugs, maggots, and cockroaches exit first." In plain English, this means if you

Liliane

don't like bugs crawling on you, even simulated ones, keep your feet off the floor. And thanks to Disney ingenuity, the bugs sting too—they do, they do.

On the Tree of Life I saw different things each time I looked. It was great!

Shelton

CAMP MINNIE-MICKEY

THIS LAND IS DESIGNED TO BE THE DISNEY characters' Animal Kingdom headquarters. A small land, Camp Minnie-Mickey has a rustic and woodsy theme like a summer camp. In addition to a character meeting and greeting area, Camp Minnie-Mickey is home to two live stage productions featuring Disney characters.

Character Trails

Characters can be found at the end of each of several "character trails." Each trail has its own private reception area and, of course, its own queue. Unless your child is really into character autograph and photo-op sessions, skip this part of Camp Minnie-Mickey and experience the real gem, the *Festival of the Lion King* stage show.

Festival of the Lion King ★★★★

APPEAL BY AGE	PRESCHOOL ★★★★½		GRADE SCHOOL ★★★★½
TEENS ★★★★½	YOUNG ADULTS ★★★★½	OVER 30 ★★★★½	SENIORS ★★★★★

What it is Theater-in-the-round stage show. **Scope and scale** Major attraction. **Fright potential** A bit loud, but otherwise not frightening in any respect. **Bottleneck rating** 9. **When to go** Before 11 a.m. or after 4 p.m. **Special comments** Performance times are listed in the handout park map or *Times Guide*. **Authors' rating** Upbeat and spectacular, not to be missed; ★★★★. **Duration of presentation** 30 minutes. **Preshow entertainment** None. **Probable waiting time** 20–35 minutes.

Thumbs Up for the Whole Family

Great pageantry, dazzling costumes, a mini–Broadway show, and air-conditioning too. *Festival of the Lion King* at the Animal Kingdom was the precursor of the Broadway production of *The Lion King*.

This was one of my favorite things I did on the whole trip. It was cool how they put us on teams.
Shelton

 The show is based on the animated feature *The Lion King*, a must-see movie. Did you know that James Earl Jones, the voice behind Mufasa (father of Simba), is also the voice behind Darth Vader in *Star Wars*?

Try to score front-row seats. Kids are invited to play musical instruments and join the performance.
Liliane

AFRICA

AFRICA IS THE LARGEST OF THE ANIMAL KINGDOM'S lands, and guests enter through Harambe, Disney's idealized and immensely sanitized version of a modern, rural African town. There is a market (with modern cash registers), and a sit-down buffet, limited counter service, and snack stands are available.

Kilimanjaro Safaris (Fastpass) ★★★★★

APPEAL BY AGE **PRESCHOOL ★★★★½**	**GRADE SCHOOL ★★★★½**	**TEENS ★★★★½**
YOUNG ADULTS ★★★★	**OVER 30 ★★★★½**	**SENIORS ★★★★**

What it is Truck ride through an African wildlife reservation. **Scope and scale** Super headliner. **Fright potential** A "collapsing" bridge and the proximity of real animals make a few young children anxious. **Bottleneck rating** 10. **When to go** As soon as the park opens, in the 2 hours before closing, or use Fastpass. **Authors' rating** Truly exceptional; ★★★★. **Duration of ride** About 20 minutes. **Average wait in line per 100 people ahead of you** 4 minutes. **Assumes** Full-capacity operation with 18-second dispatch interval. **Loading speed** Fast.

A PEEK BEHIND THE SCENES WITH JIM HILL

YOU'RE GONNA 'GUANA SEE THIS

As you walk up to the entrance of Kilimanjaro Safaris, look up into that baobab tree just outside of the queue. See the small green thing high in the tree? It's a fake rubber iguana that one of the Imagineers sneaked in as they were finishing dressing Harambe for the park's grand opening back in May 1998. He never dreamed that his gag would still live on some 13 years later.

Thumbs Up for the Whole Family

Off you go in an open safari vehicle through a simulated African savanna. Preschoolers will enjoy looking for hippos, zebras, giraffes, lions, and rhinos, while the older kids will get a kick out of the story line about poachers. Many readers have asked us whether fewer animals are visible from Kilimanjaro Safaris around lunchtime than at park opening, out of concern that the animals might be less active in the midday heat. To help answer that question, we sent a team of researchers to ride continuously during one week in the summer and had them count the number of animals visible at different times of day. We subdivided our counting into large animals (elephants, hippos, and lions, for example), small (deer and other ungulates), and birds. Our results indicate that you'll probably see the same number of animals regardless of when you visit. This finding is almost certainly due to Disney's deliberate placement of water, food, and shade near the safari vehicles.

Feast your eyes on the habitat and the animals and forget the story (which can really get to you if you ride more than once). The experience would be infinitely more educational if Disney ditched the hokey poacher plot and replaced it with interesting facts about the animals.

Liliane

Hannah

There are animals here that I've never heard of. It was cool to discover new animals, learn about them, and see what they look like. I didn't know how big a baby giraffe really is!

Pangani Forest Exploration Trail ★★★★

APPEAL BY AGE   PRESCHOOL ★★★★   GRADE SCHOOL ★★★★   TEENS ★★★½
YOUNG ADULTS ★★★★   OVER 30 ★★★★   SENIORS ★★★★

What it is Walk-through zoological exhibit. **Scope and scale** Major attraction. **Fright potential** Not frightening in any respect. **Bottleneck rating** 9. **When to go** Before 10 a.m. and after 2:30 p.m. **Authors' rating** ★★★. **Duration of tour** About 20–25 minutes.

The Pangani Forest Exploration Trail is lush, beautiful, and jammed to the gills with people much of the time. This is particularly unpleasant if you have to wiggle your way through with a stroller. Walk the trail before 11 a.m. or after 2:30 p.m.

If you are more into the wildlife than the thrill rides, head to Kilimanjaro Safaris as soon as the park opens and get a Fastpass. Early in the morning, the return window will be short—just long enough, in fact, for an uncrowded, leisurely tour of the Pangani Forest Exploration Trail before you go on safari.

Rafiki's Planet Watch

Rafiki's Planet Watch is not a "land" and not really an attraction either. Our best guess is that Disney is using the name as an umbrella for Conservation Station, the petting zoo, and the environmental exhibits accessible from Harambe via the Wildlife Express train. Presumably, Disney hopes that invoking Rafiki (a beloved character from *The Lion King*) will stimulate guests to make the effort to check out things in this far-flung corner of the park. As for your kids seeing Rafiki, don't bet on it. The closest likeness we've seen here is a two-dimensional wooden cutout.

> I think we went to this, but I'm not sure.
> It wasn't very memorable.
> Shelton

Conservation Station and Affection Section ★★★

APPEAL BY AGE   PRESCHOOL ★★★½   GRADE SCHOOL ★★★½   TEENS ★★★
YOUNG ADULTS ★★★   OVER 30 ★★★   SENIORS ★★★

What it is Behind-the-scenes walk-through educational exhibit and petting zoo. **Scope and scale** Minor attraction. **Fright potential** Not frightening in any respect. **Bottleneck rating** 6. **When to go** Anytime. **Special comments** Opens 30 minutes after rest of park. **Authors' rating** Evolving; ★★★. **Probable waiting time** None.

This is the Animal Kingdom's veterinary and conservation headquarters. Guests can meet wildlife experts, observe some of the ongoing projects, and learn about the operations of the park. A rehabilitation area for injured animals and a nursery for recently born or hatched critters and a petting zoo are included. Conservation Station is interesting, but you have to invest a little effort, and it helps to be inquisitive. What you see at Conservation Station will largely depend on what happens to be going on when you arrive. Because it's so removed from the rest of the park, you'll never bump into Conservation Station unless you take the train round-trip from Harambe.

Habitat Habit!

Located on the pedestrian path between the train station and Conservation Station, and listed on the park maps as an attraction, Habitat Habit! consists of a tiny collection of signs (about coexistence with wildlife) and a few cotton-top tamarins. To call it an attraction is absurd.

Wildlife Express Train ★★

APPEAL BY AGE	PRESCHOOL ★★★½	GRADE SCHOOL ★★★	TEENS ★★★
YOUNG ADULTS ★★½		OVER 30 ★★★	SENIORS ★★★

What it is Scenic railroad ride to Rafiki's Planet Watch and Conservation Station. **Scope and scale** Minor attraction. **Fright potential** Not frightening in any respect. **Bottleneck rating** 7. **When to go** Anytime. **Special comments** Opens 30 minutes after the rest of the park. **Authors' rating** Ho hum; ★★. **Duration of ride** About 5–7 minutes one way. **Average wait in line per 100 people ahead of you** 9 minutes. **Loading speed** Moderate.

Take the train only if you have small kids who would really enjoy the Affection Section petting zoo at Rafiki's Planet Watch. If you have a future veterinarian in your family, it is also well worth checking out the behind-the-scenes exhibits at Conservation Station.

ASIA

CROSSING THE ASIA BRIDGE FROM DISCOVERY ISLAND, you enter Asia through the village of Anandapur, a veritable collage of Asian themes inspired by the architecture and ruins of India, Thailand, Indonesia, and Nepal.

Expedition Everest (Fastpass) ★★★★½

APPEAL BY AGE	PRESCHOOL ★★★	GRADE SCHOOL ★★★★½	TEENS ★★★★★
YOUNG ADULTS ★★★★★		OVER 30 ★★★★★	SENIORS ★★★★

What it is High-speed roller coaster through Mount Everest. **Scope and scale** Super headliner. **Fright potential** Frightens guests of all ages. **Bottleneck rating** 8. **When to go** Before 9:30 a.m., after 3 p.m., or use Fastpass. **Special comments** Contains some of the park's most stunning visual elements. Must be 44" tall to ride. **Authors' rating** ★★★★½. **Duration of ride** 4 minutes. **Average wait in line per 100 people ahead of you** Just under 4 minutes. **Assumes** 2 tracks operating. **Loading speed** Moderate to fast.

Scary   Lose Things

As you enjoy one of the most spectacular panoramas in Walt Disney World, you wish this expedition would never end. But you get over that in a hurry as the train starts whirring through the guts of Disney's largest man-made mountain (not only the largest in Florida, but it also beats out Mount Petty Poot Poot in Kansas by 2 feet). After a high-speed encounter with a large, smelly Yeti and a dead stop at the top of the mountain, the 50-mile-per-hour chase continues backward. The ride is very smooth and rich both in visuals and special effects. The backward segment is one of the most creative and exciting 20 seconds in roller coaster annals.

I think it's cool because there are a lot of big hills. There's a Yeti, and he tries to eat you. If you're a big screamer like me, you'll probably just close your eyes and open your mouth.

Hannah

Flights of Wonder ★★★★

APPEAL BY AGE   PRESCHOOL ★★★★   GRADE SCHOOL ★★★★   TEENS ★★★★
YOUNG ADULTS ★★★★   OVER 30 ★★★★   SENIORS ★★★★

What it is Stadium show about birds. Scope and scale Major attraction. Fright potential Swooping birds startle some younger children. Bottleneck rating 6. When to go Anytime. Special comments Performance times are listed in the hand-out park map or *Times Guide*. Authors' rating Unique; ★★★★. Duration of presentation 30 minutes. Preshow entertainment None. Probable waiting time 20–30 minutes.

Thumbs Up for the Whole Family

Humorously presented, the show is ideal for kids. Don't expect parrots riding unicycles though. *Flights of Wonder* is about the natural talents and characteristics of various bird species. If your child is comfortable with you sitting a few rows behind, encourage him or her to take a seat in the up-front "for kids only" section. When the show is over, stick around and talk to the bird trainers and meet the feathery cast of the show up close and personal. It is a great opportunity to ask questions and take pictures. *Flights of Wonder* plays at the stadium located near the Asia Bridge on the walkway between Asia and Africa. Though the stadium is covered, it's not air-conditioned; thus, early-morning and late-afternoon performances are more comfortable. To ensure finding a seat, arrive about 10–15 minutes before showtime.

Kali River Rapids (Fastpass) ★★★½

APPEAL BY AGE   PRESCHOOL ★★★★   GRADE SCHOOL ★★★★½   TEENS ★★★★½
YOUNG ADULTS ★★★★   OVER 30 ★★★★   SENIORS ★★★★

What it is White-water raft ride. Scope and scale Headliner. Fright potential Potentially frightening and certainly wet for guests of all ages; must be 38" tall to ride. Bottleneck rating 9. When to go Before 10:30 a.m., after 4:30 p.m., or use Fastpass. Special comments You are guaranteed to get wet. Opens 30 minutes after the rest of the park. Switching-off option provided (see page 238). Authors' rating Short but scenic; ★★★½. Duration of ride About 5 minutes. Average wait in line per 100 people ahead of you 5 minutes. Loading speed Moderate.

Scary   Wet

The ride itself is tame and allows you to take in the outstanding scenery as you drift through a dense rain forest, past waterfalls and temple ruins. There are neither big drops nor terrifying rapids waiting to swallow the raft and all inside. The foregoing information notwithstanding, Disney still manages to drench you. Nonriding park guests will take great pleasure squirting water at the rafters from above. The water-squirting elephant stations are a great consolation prize for young ones who do not meet the 38-inch height requirement.

Don't wear anything fancy because you're going to get soaked.

Hannah

On a hot summer day, the Kali River Rapids are just what the doctor ordered. However, if you ride early in the morning or on a cool day, use rain gear to protect yourself and make sure your shoes stay dry. Touring in wet clothes is unpleasant, and walking all day in soaked sneakers is a recipe for blisters.

Liliane

Maharajah Jungle Trek ★★★★

APPEAL BY AGE	PRESCHOOL ★★★★	GRADE SCHOOL ★★★★	TEENS ★★★★
YOUNG ADULTS ★★★★		OVER 30 ★★★★	SENIORS ★★★★

What it is Walk-through zoological exhibit. **Scope and scale** Headliner. **Fright potential** Some children may balk at the bat exhibit. **Bottleneck rating** 5. **When to go** Anytime. **Special comments** Opens 30 minutes after the rest of the park. **Authors' rating** A standard-setter for natural habitat design; ★★★★. **Duration of tour** About 20–30 minutes.

The Jungle Trek is less congested than the Pangani Forest Exploration Trail and is a good choice for midday touring. Tigers, gibbons, bats, and birds are waiting to be discovered along a path winding through the fabulous ruins of the maharajah's palace.

The bat enclosure is outstanding and my favorite section of the trek. From Batman to Dracula, this is the opportunity to increase your knowledge of these mysterious mammals.

Liliane

DINOLAND U.S.A.

THIS MOST TYPICALLY DISNEY of the Animal Kingdom's lands is a cross between an anthropological dig and a quirky roadside attraction. Accessible via the bridge from Discovery Island, DinoLand U.S.A. is home to a children's play area, a nature trail, a 1,500-seat amphitheater, and DINOSAUR, one of the Animal Kingdom's three thrill rides.

Children ages 4–12 will feel right at home at DinoLand U.S.A. Speaking of home, DinoLand U.S.A. is the residence of *Finding Nemo—The Musical*, replacing *Tarzan Rocks!* at the Theater in the Wild.

The Boneyard ★★★½

APPEAL BY AGE	PRESCHOOL ★★★★½	GRADE SCHOOL ★★★★
TEENS ★★	YOUNG ADULTS ★★	OVER 30 ★★½	SENIORS ★★

What it is Elaborate playground. **Scope and scale** Diversion. **Fright potential** Not frightening in any respect. **Bottleneck rating** 5. **When to go** Anytime. **Special**

comments Opens 30 minutes after the rest of the park. **Authors' rating** Stimulating fun for children; ★★★½. **Duration of visit** Varies. **Probable waiting time** None.

It's playtime! The Boneyard is an elaborate playground for the 12-and-younger crowd and a great place for kids to let off steam and get dirty (or at least sandy). The playground equipment consists of skeletal replicas of triceratops, Tyrannosaurus rex, Brachiosaurus, and the like. In addition, there are climbing mazes, as well as sand pits where little ones can scrounge around for bones and fossils.

The Boneyard can get very hot in the scorching Florida sun, so make sure your kids are properly hydrated and protected against sunburn. The playground is huge and parents might lose sight of a small child. Fortunately, however, there's only one entrance and exit. Your little ones are going to love the Boneyard, so resign yourself to staying awhile.

DINOSAUR (Fastpass) ★★★★½

| APPEAL BY AGE | PRESCHOOL ★★½ | GRADE SCHOOL ★★★½ | TEENS ★★★★ |
| YOUNG ADULTS ★★★★ | | OVER 30 ★★★★ | SENIORS ★★★½ |

† Sample size too small for an accurate rating.

What it is Motion-simulator dark ride. **Scope and scale** Super headliner. **Fright potential** High-tech thrill ride rattles riders of all ages. **Bottleneck rating** 8. **When to go** Before 10:30 a.m., in the hour before closing, or use Fastpass. **Special comments** Must be 40" tall to ride. Switching-off option provided (see page 238). **Authors' rating** Really improved; ★★★★½. **Duration of ride** 3½ minutes. **Average wait in line per 100 people ahead of you** 3 minutes. **Assumes** Full-capacity operation with 18-second dispatch interval. **Loading speed** Fast.

Dark   Scary   Rough

Here you board a time capsule to return to the Jurassic age in an effort to bring back a live dinosaur before a meteor hits the Earth and wipes them out. The bad guy in this epic is the little-known carnotaurus, an evil-eyed, long in the tooth, Tyrannosaurus rex–type fellow. A combination track ride and motion simulator, the DINOSAUR ride is not for the faint-hearted. You get tossed and pitched around in the dark with pesky dinosaurs jumping out at you. DINOSAUR has left many an adult weak-kneed. Most kids under age 9 find it terrifying.

Liliane

DINOSAUR is an absolute no-no for preschoolers and any child easily frightened. The carnotaurus, unlike Barney and Figment, did not make my favorite dino list.

It doesn't really go up any hills, and it didn't make me scream, but it scared my cousin half to death when she was 4. Even if you're 5 or 6, the dinosaurs might scare you.

Hannah

Shelton

I love the story line, which is thick and detailed and not thin like the stories for some other rides. I love the part where you just barely escape and you go under a carnotaurus's belly!

Primeval Whirl ★★★

APPEAL BY AGE	PRESCHOOL ★★	GRADE SCHOOL ★★★★	TEENS ★★★★
YOUNG ADULTS ★★★½		OVER 30 ★★★	SENIORS ★★½

What it is Small coaster. **Scope and scale** Minor attraction. **Fright potential** Scarier than it looks. **Bottleneck rating** 9. **When to go** During the first 2 hours the park is open or in the hour before park closing. **Special comments** Must be 48" tall to ride. Switching-off option provided (see page 238). **Authors' rating** "Wild Mouse" on steroids; ★★★. **Duration of ride** Almost 2½ minutes. **Average wait in line per 100 people ahead of you** 4½ minutes. **Loading speed** Slow.

Scary Rough Motion Sickness

This is a tricky little coaster with short drops, curves, and tight loops. As if that's not enough, the coaster cars also spin. The problem is, unlike with the evil teacups, guests cannot control the spinning. Complete spins are fun, but watch out for the screeching-stop half-spins.

Theater in the Wild/*Finding Nemo–The Musical* ★★★★

APPEAL BY AGE	PRESCHOOL ★★★★	GRADE SCHOOL ★★★★	TEENS ★★★★
YOUNG ADULTS ★★★★		OVER 30 ★★★★	SENIORS ★★★★

What it is Open-air venue for live stage shows. **Scope and scale** Major attraction. **Fright potential** Not frightening in any respect. **Bottleneck rating** 6. **When to go** Anytime. **Special comments** Performance times are listed in the handout park map or *Times Guide*. **Authors' rating** ★★★★. **Duration of presentation** 30 minutes. **Preshow entertainment** None. **Probable waiting time** About 30 minutes.

Thumbs Up for the Whole Family

Based on the Disney/Pixar animated feature, *Finding Nemo–The Musical* is an elaborate stage show headlining puppets, dancing, acrobats, and special effects. *Finding Nemo* is arguably the most elaborate live show in any Disney World theme park. A few scenes, such as one in which Nemo's mom is eaten (!!!), may be too intense for some very small children. Some of the mid-show musical numbers slow the pace, so the main concern for parents is whether the kids can sit still for an entire show. With that in mind, we advise parents to catch an afternoon performance—around 3 p.m. would be great—after seeing the rest of Animal Kingdom.

To get a seat, show up 20–25 minutes in advance for morning and late-afternoon shows, and 30–35 minutes in advance for shows scheduled between noon and 4:30 p.m. Access to the theater is via a relatively narrow pedestrian path; if you arrive as the previous show is letting out, you will feel like a salmon swimming upstream.

When the line is very long, don't assume that you will get into the next show just by queuing up. Disney cast members monitor the line; ask them if you are likely to get into the next show.

Liliane

TriceraTop Spin ★★

APPEAL BY AGE	PRESCHOOL ★★★★½	GRADE SCHOOL ★★★★	TEENS ★★★
YOUNG ADULTS ★★		OVER 30 ★★½	SENIORS ★★

What it is Hub-and-spoke midway ride. **Scope and scale** Minor attraction. **Fright potential** May frighten preschoolers. **Bottleneck rating** 9. **When to go** First 90 minutes the park is open and in the hour before park closing. **Authors' rating** Dumbo's prehistoric forebear; ★★. **Duration of ride** 1½ minutes. **Average wait in line per 100 people ahead of you** 10 minutes. **Loading speed** Slow.

Motion Sickness

Instead of Dumbo you get Dino spinning around a central axis. The ride is fun for young children, but this slow loader is infamous for inefficiency and long waits.

Tusker House is my favorite. It has a lot of choices, and there are always a lot of people there because the food is good. You can get cinnamon rolls here as big as a stuffed animal!

Hannah

FAVORITE EATS AT ANIMAL KINGDOM

LAND | SERVICE LOCATION | FOOD ITEM

DISCOVERY ISLAND   Flame Tree Barbecue | Ribs, chicken with beans, and corn on the cob

Pizzafari | Pizza and chicken Caesar salad, breadsticks

DINOLAND U.S.A.   Restaurantosaurus | Cheeseburger comes with choice of two sides (grapes, carrot sticks, or applesauce) and choice of 1% milk, bottled water, or apple juice

ASIA   Royal Anandapur Tea Company | Teas & specialty coffees
Yak & Yeti | Shaoxing steak and shrimp

AFRICA   Tamu Tamu | Smoothies
Tusker House Restaurant | Marrakesh couscous with roasted veggies Donald's Safari Breakfast at Tusker House is a character breakfast including Donald, Daisy, Goofy, and Mickey. All-you-can-eat buffet, 8 a.m.–10:30 a.m.

OUTSIDE ENTRANCE   Rainforest Cafe | Breakfast, lunch, and dinner in a tropical rain forest setting with a huge saltwater aquarium, gorillas going wild once in a while, and simulated thunderstorms. The place to take the kids if you want to sit down! They'll love you for it, cross my heart, hope to die. *(table service only)*

LIVE ENTERTAINMENT
at ANIMAL KINGDOM

STAGE SHOWS ARE PERFORMED DAILY at the Animal Kingdom; check your entertainment schedule (*Times Guide*) for showtimes. Street performers can be found most of the time at Discovery Island;

in Harambe, Africa; Anandapur, Asia; and in DinoLand U.S.A. For an updated listing of live entertainment at Animal Kingdom, check out Steve Soares' Web site **pages.prodigy.net/stevesoares.**

LOOK WHO'S TALKING At The Oasis, don't miss introducing your kids to **Wes Palm,** the talking palm tree who loves to poke fun at unsuspecting guests. At Conservation Station have a silly-dilly (Liliane's term) chat with **Pipa,** the recycling trash can.

Though Wes Palm and Pipa will have you roaring with laughter, **DiVine** will leave you speechless. A perfect fusion between fantasy and reality, DiVine is an artist in a garb half-vine and half-creeping plant. She blends perfectly with the foliage at the Animal Kingdom and is only noticeable when she moves (which can be quite startling if you're not aware of her presence). DiVine travels around the park but seems to love the vicinity of the Rainforest Cafe entrance. The silent gracefulness of her movements and the serenity of her demeanor are totally captivating. If you don't encounter her, ask a cast member where she can be found. There is a video of DiVine on YouTube; go to **youtube.com.**

ANIMAL ENCOUNTERS Throughout the day, Disney staff conduct impromptu short lectures on specific animals at the park. Look for a cast member in safari garb holding a bird, reptile, or small mammal. If you see a cast member being strangled or eaten by a reptile or large animal, keep walking.

GOODWILL AMBASSADORS A number of Asian and African natives are on hand throughout the park. Both gracious and knowledgeable, they are delighted to discuss their countries. Look for them in Harambe and along the Maharajah Jungle Trek in Asia. They can also be found near the main entrance and at The Oasis.

KIDS' DISCOVERY CLUB Activity stations offer kids ages 4–8 a structured learning experience as they tour Animal Kingdom. Set up along walkways in six themed areas, Discovery Club stations are manned by cast members who supervise a different activity at each station. A souvenir logbook is available at no charge and will be stamped at each station when the child completes a craft or exercise. Kids enjoy collecting the stamps and completing logbook puzzles while in attraction lines.

AFTERNOON PARADE Mickey's Jammin' Jungle Parade features characters from *The Lion King* and other Disney stories. The parade starts in Africa, crosses the bridge to Discovery Island, proceeds counterclockwise around the island, and then crosses the bridge to Asia. In Asia, the parade turns left and follows the walkway paralleling the river back to Africa.

The walking path between Africa and Asia has small cutouts that offer good views of the parade and excellent sun protection. Most guests scramble to Harambe, the starting point of the parade, and leave this area as soon as the parade crosses over the bridge to Discovery Island. Because guests don't realize that the parade cycles back through Harambe, there is never much of a crowd when the parade rumbles through the second time en route to going offstage. Therefore, if you make your way to Harambe about 20 minutes after the parade time listed in the *Times Guide,* you'll be able to score a super vantage point at the last minute.

ANIMAL KINGDOM TOURING PLANS

OUR STEP-BY-STEP TOURING PLANS ARE FIELD-TESTED, independently verified itineraries that will keep you moving counter to the crowd flow and allow you to see as much as possible in a single day with minimum time wasted in line.

You can take in all the attractions at the Animal Kingdom in a single day even when traveling with young children.

If you are not interested in an attraction listed on the touring plan, just skip that step and proceed to the next one. Should you encounter a very long line at an attraction the touring plan calls for, skip the attraction and go to the next step, returning later to retry. The use of Fastpass is factored into the touring plans.

The different touring plans are described below. The descriptions will tell you for whom (for example, tweens, parents with preschoolers, and so on) or for what situation (such as sleeping late) the plans are designed. The actual touring plans are located on pages 459–462 at the back of the book. Each plan includes a numbered map of the park in question to help you find your way around. Clip the plan of your choice out of the book by cutting along the line indicated, and take it with you to the park.

ANIMAL KINGDOM ONE-DAY TOURING PLAN FOR PARENTS WITH SMALL CHILDREN This plan is designed for parents of children ages 3–8 who wish to see the very best age-appropriate attractions in the Animal Kingdom. Every attraction has a rating of at least three stars (out of five) from preschool and grade-school children surveyed by the *Unofficial Guide.* Special advice is provided for touring the park with small children, including restaurant recommendations. The plan keeps walking and backtracking to a minimum, with no criss-crossing of the park.

ANIMAL KINGDOM ONE-DAY SLEEPYHEAD TOURING PLAN FOR PARENTS WITH SMALL CHILDREN A relaxed plan that allows families with small children to sleep late and still see the highlights of the Animal Kingdom. The plan begins around 11 a.m., sets aside ample time for lunch, and includes the very best child-friendly attractions in the park.

ANIMAL KINGDOM ONE-DAY TOURING PLAN FOR TWEENS AND THEIR PARENTS A one-day plan for parents with children ages 8–12. It includes every attraction rated three stars and higher by this age group and sets aside ample time for lunch and dinner.

ANIMAL KINGDOM ONE-DAY HAPPY FAMILY TOURING PLAN A plan for families of all ages. Includes time-saving tips for teens and adults visiting the Animal Kingdom's thrill rides, as well as age-appropriate attractions for parents with small children. The entire family stays together as much as possible (including lunch), but this plan allows groups with different interests to explore their favorite attractions without having everyone wait around.

BEFORE YOU GO

1. Call ☎ 407-824-4321 before you go for the park's operating hours.
2. Purchase your admission prior to arrival.

DISNEY'S ANIMAL KINGDOM TRIVIA QUIZ

By Lou Mongello

1. Who are the proprietors of DinoRama?
   a. Mickey and Minnie
   b. Wes Palm and Dr. Seeker
   c. Chester and Hester
   d. Freddy the Yeti

2. Disney spends more than $1,700,000 yearly on what for Disney's Animal Kingdom?
   a. Worms
   b. Manure
   c. Transportation costs to import new animals from overseas
   d. Plant food

3. About how many branches are on The Tree of Life?
   a. 500
   b. 1,000
   c. 3,000
   d. 8,000

4. What are the ride vehicles in DINOSAUR called?
   a. Jurassic Jeeps
   b. Time Rovers
   c. XP-37s
   d. Omnimovers

5. What land in Disney's Animal Kingdom has the greatest number of attractions?
   a. Discovery Island
   b. Asia
   c. Africa
   d. DinoLand U.S.A.

6. Which of these attractions is the largest in all of Walt Disney World?
   a. Maharajah Jungle Trek
   b. Kilimanjaro Safaris
   c. Pangani Forest Exploration Trail
   d. Primeval Whirl

7. What attraction's ride vehicles are known as Steam Donkeys?
   a. Wildlife Express Train to Rafiki's Planet Watch
   b. Expedition Everest
   c. Kali River Rapids
   d. Kilimanjaro Safaris

8. Where can you find Guano Joe?
   a. Pangani Forest Exploration Trail
   b. Rafiki's Planet Watch
   c. Maharajah Jungle Trek
   d. *Flights of Wonder*

9. As you enter Disney's Animal Kingdom, what is the first land that you reach?
   a. Africa
   b. Discovery Island
   c. The Oasis
   d. Harambe Village

10. About how many different food items are available in Walt Disney World?
   a. 400
   b. 1,600
   c. 3,000
   d. 6,000

Answers can be found on page 426.

PART TEN

DISNEY'S HOLLYWOOD STUDIOS

ABOUT HALF OF DISNEY'S HOLLYWOOD STUDIOS is set up as a theme park. The other half is off-limits except by guided tour. Though modest in size, the Studios' open-access areas are confusingly arranged (a product of the park's hurried expansion in the early 1990s). As at the Magic Kingdom, you enter the park and pass down a main street, only this time it's Hollywood Boulevard of the 1920s and 1930s. Though the park is largely organized by street names rather than by "lands," the easiest way to navigate it is by landmarks and attractions using the park map.

After Disney severed its relationship with MGM in 2008, the park formerly known as Disney-MGM Studios was renamed Disney's Hollywood Studios. Though the attraction lineup is essentially unchanged, the vision for the park going forward is to develop themes and attractions based on Pixar films and characters. The use of "Hollywood" in the park's name represents a more generic reference to moviemaking. In popular usage, however, many folks drop the "Hollywood" entirely, referring to the park simply as "Disney Studios" or "The Studios."

While it is true that Disney's Hollywood Studios educates and entertains, what it does best is promote. Self-promotion of Disney films and products was once subtle and in context but is now blatant, inescapable, and distracting. Although most visitors are willing to forgive Disney its excesses, Studios veterans will lament the changes and remember how good it was when education was the park's goal instead of the medium.

Guest Relations, on your left as you enter, serves as the park headquarters and information center, similar to City Hall in the Magic Kingdom. Go there for a schedule of live performances, lost persons, package pickup, lost and found (on the right side of the entrance), general information, or in an emergency. If you haven't received a map of the Studios, get one here. To the right of the entrance are locker, stroller, and wheelchair rentals.

A Baby Care Center is located at Guest Relations, and Oscar's sells baby food and other necessities. More film for those precious moments can be purchased at The Darkroom on the right side of Hollywood Boulevard, just past Oscar's. Oddly enough the closest ATM is located outside the park to the right of the turnstiles. Disney no longer has pet care facilities adjacent to the park, but the new Best Friends Pet Resort across from Disney's Port Orleans Resort will provide a comfortable home-away-from-home for Fido, Frisky, and all their pet pals.

Guests enter the park on Hollywood Boulevard, a palm-lined street reminiscent of the famous Hollywood main avenue of the 1930s. The best way to navigate is to decide what you really want to see and go for it! If you want the whole enchilada, it can be done in one day. But, as with the other parks, this is best accomplished by using one of our touring plans.

Architecture on Hollywood Boulevard is streamlined modern with Art Deco embellishments. Most service facilities are here, interspersed with eateries and shops. Merchandise includes Disney trademark items, Hollywood and movie-related souvenirs, and one-of-a-kind collectibles obtained from studio auctions and estate sales. Hollywood characters and roving performers entertain on the boulevard, and daily parades and other happenings pass this way.

Sunset Boulevard, evoking the 1940s, is a major component of DHS. The first right off Hollywood Boulevard, Sunset Boulevard provides another venue for dining, shopping, and street entertainment.

The American Idol Experience ★★★★

APPEAL BY AGE	PRESCHOOL ★★★	GRADE SCHOOL ★★★★	TEENS ★★★★½
YOUNG ADULTS ★★★★		OVER 30 ★★★★	SENIORS ★★★

What it is Theme-park version of the popular TV show, with guests doing the singing. Scope and scale Major attraction. Fright potential Some of the singing would frighten Frankenstein. Bottleneck rating 5. When to go Anytime. Special comments All shows except the finale last 20 minutes; the finale can last around 40. Authors' rating Even if you don't watch the show, you'll find someone to cheer for; ★★★★. Duration of presentation About 20–30 minutes.

Based on the successful *American Idol* television show, *The American Idol Experience* is your chance to showcase your karaoke abilities to the world. Your path to stardom goes something like this: Potential singers of all ages will select a song and audition in front of a live judge. Most singers will receive a "thanks for auditioning" message from the judge, but a handful will be selected to perform in the attraction's next stage show, held several times per day. During the show, contestants repeat their songs in front of a live audience of theme-park guests. As with *American Idol,* three judges (Disney cast members here) provide feedback. Don't worry that your operatic rendition of "Achy Breaky Heart" will meet with critical disdain. For the most part, the Disney panel uses humor to tell you not to quit your day job. Audience members vote to decide the winner. During the last

Disney's Hollywood Studios

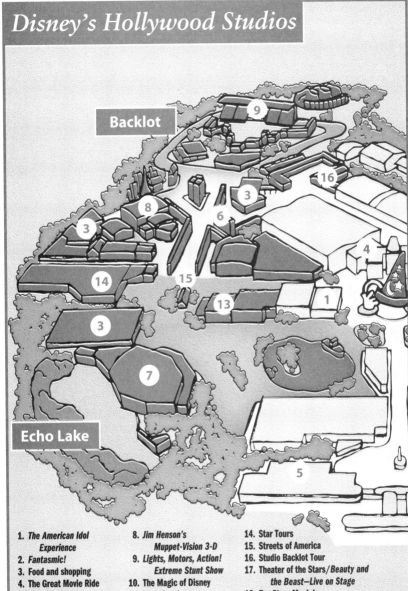

Backlot

Echo Lake

1. *The American Idol Experience*
2. *Fantasmic!*
3. Food and shopping
4. The Great Movie Ride
5. Guest Relations
6. Honey, I Shrunk the Kids Movie Set Adventure
7. *Indiana Jones Epic Stunt Spectacular!*
8. *Jim Henson's Muppet-Vision 3-D*
9. *Lights, Motors, Action! Extreme Stunt Show*
10. The Magic of Disney Animation
11. *Playhouse Disney— Live on Stage!*
12. Rock 'n' Roller Coaster
13. *Sounds Dangerous with Drew Carey*
14. Star Tours
15. *Streets of America*
16. Studio Backlot Tour
17. Theater of the Stars/*Beauty and the Beast—Live on Stage*
18. Toy Story Mania!
19. *The Twilight Zone Tower of Terror*
20. *Voyage of the Little Mermaid*
21. *Walt Disney: One Man's Dream*
22. Oscar's Super Service

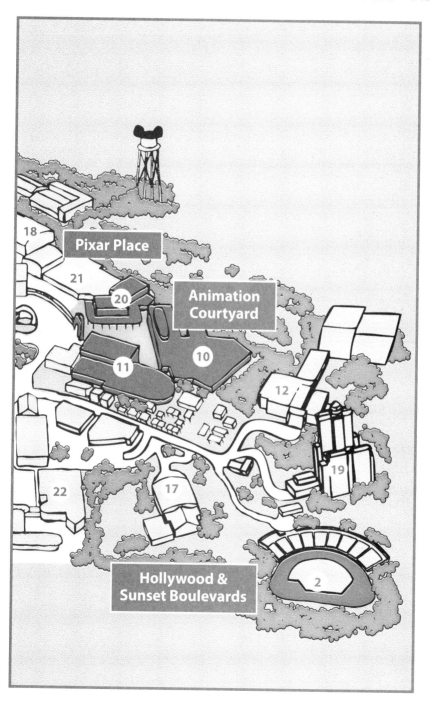

show of the night, all of the winners from throughout the day meet for one final competition. The winner of that show receives a "front-of-the-line" pass for the next season's audition of *American Idol* in their local city. The last show of the day offers (ostensibly) the best talent but is twice the length of the daytime shows. If you've got dinner reservations or are lining up early for *Fantasmic!,* see one of the daytime shows. The finale show is broadcast live on the Jumbotron outside the theater.

Beauty and the Beast—Live on Stage / Theater of the Stars ★★★★

APPEAL BY AGE	PRESCHOOL ★★★★	GRADE SCHOOL ★★★★	TEENS ★★★★
YOUNG ADULTS ★★★★		OVER 30 ★★★★	SENIORS ★★★★

What it is Live musical, featuring Disney characters; performed in an open-air theater. **Scope and scale** Major attraction. **Fright potential** Not frightening in any respect. **Bottleneck rating** 5. **When to go** Anytime; evenings are cooler. **Special comments** Performances are listed in the daily *Times Guide.* **Authors' rating** Excellent; ★★★★. **Duration of presentation** 25 minutes. **Preshow entertainment** Sometimes. **Probable waiting time** 20–30 minutes.

Join Cogsworth, Lumiere, Chip, and Mrs. Potts as they help Belle to break the spell. This 25-minute musical stage show of Disney's *Beauty and the Beast* feature will charm everybody. The show is popular, so show up half an hour early to get a seat.

The decor and the costumes, the actors and the music: Everything is in perfect harmony. Little girls fond of Belle will want to have that ball gown, and young boys will be eager to teach that mean Gaston a lesson!

Liliane

The Great Movie Ride ★★★½

APPEAL BY AGE	PRESCHOOL ★★★	GRADE SCHOOL ★★★½	TEENS ★★★½
YOUNG ADULTS ★★★½		OVER 30 ★★★½	SENIORS ★★★★

What it is Movie-history indoor adventure ride. **Scope and scale** Headliner. **Fright potential** Intense in parts, with very realistic special effects and some visually intimidating sights. **Bottleneck rating** 8. **When to go** Before 11 a.m. or after 4:30 p.m. **Special comments** Elaborate, with several surprises. **Authors' rating** Unique; ★★★½. **Duration of ride** About 19 minutes. **Average wait in**

A PEEK BEHIND THE SCENES WITH JIM HILL

DREAMS AND SECRETS Ever wonder how those huge theater cars in The Great Movie Ride operate? Or how the Imagineers created the sets and props for this affectionate tribute to the Golden Age of Hollywood? You'll find some of the answers in the *Walt Disney: One Man's Dream* exhibit, where recently installed models and schematics reveal TGMR's inner workings. So if you really wanna know how the gangster sequence works, you should get your mug over to *One Man's Dream,* see?

line per 100 people ahead of you 2 minutes. **Assumes** All trains operating. **Loading speed** Fast.

  Inside the re-creation of Hollywood's Chinese Theater awaits a trip down memory lane. From *Casablanca* to *Raiders of the Lost Ark,* classic movies are showcased in this ride through some of the movies' most memorable sets. Young movie buffs might be flipped out along the way (*Alien* is one of the movies represented), but the wonderful Munchkins from *The Wizard of Oz* scene will make up for it—the Wicked Witch of the North notwithstanding.

 I've only seen some of these movies, so I like how it's not just a ride, but a hostess that tells you about the movies, like if it's a western or something. There's the yellow-brick road from *The Wizard of Oz,* and the Munchkins sing "Follow the Yellow Brick Road."

Honey, I Shrunk the Kids **Movie Set Adventure** ★★½

APPEAL BY AGE	PRESCHOOL ★★★★½	GRADE SCHOOL ★★★★	TEENS ★★½
YOUNG ADULTS ★★		OVER 30 ★★½	SENIORS ★★★

What it is Small but elaborate playground. **Scope and scale** Diversion. **Fright potential** Everything is oversize, but nothing is scary. **Bottleneck rating** 8. **When to go** Before 11 a.m. or after dark. **Special comments** Opens an hour later than the rest of the park. **Authors' rating** Great for young children, more of a curiosity for adults; ★★½. **Average wait in line per 100 people ahead of you** 20 minutes.

This elaborate playground appeals particularly to kids age 11 and younger. Tunnels, slides, rope ladders, and a variety of oversize props offer lots of playtime fun. There are a few problems with the attraction, though. The place is too small to accommodate all the children who would like to play, and supervision inside the jam-packed and poorly ventilated playground can be trying. Last but not least, kids play as long as parents allow, so be prepared for this stop to take a big chunk of time out of your touring day. If you visit during the warmer months and want your children to experience the playground, get them in and out before 11 a.m. By late morning, this attraction is way too hot and crowded for anyone to enjoy. A mom from Tolland, Connecticut, found the playground exasperating:

> We let the kids hang out at [Honey, I Shrunk the Kids] because we thought it would be relaxing. NOT! You have three choices here: (1) Let your kids go anywhere and hope that if they try to get out without your permission, someone will stop them. Also hope that someone else will help your kids if they get caught up in the exhibit. (2) Go everywhere with your kids—this takes a lot of stamina and some athleticism. If you care about appearances, this could be a problem because you look pretty stupid coming down those slides. (3) Try to visually keep track of your kids. This is impossible, so you will be either on the edge of or in the middle of an anxiety attack the whole time you are there.

Indiana Jones Epic Stunt Spectacular! ★★★★

APPEAL BY AGE	PRESCHOOL ★★★½	GRADE SCHOOL ★★★★		TEENS ★★★★
YOUNG ADULTS ★★★★		OVER 30 ★★★★		SENIORS ★★★★

What it is Movie-stunt demonstration and action show. **Scope and scale** Headliner. **Fright potential** An intense show with powerful special effects, including explosions. Presented in an educational context that young children generally handle well. **Bottleneck rating 8. When to go** First 3 morning shows or last evening show. **Special comments** Performance times posted on a sign at the entrance to the theater. **Authors' rating** Done on a grand scale; ★★★★. **Duration of presentation** 30 minutes. **Preshow entertainment** Selection of "extras" from audience. **Probable waiting time** None.

A PEEK BEHIND THE SCENES WITH JIM HILL

THIS ATTRACTION HAS RUN NEARLY FOUR TIMES AS LONG AS WWII With George Lucas and Steven Spielberg reportedly hard at work developing the fifth Indiana Jones film, you'd think the *Indiana Jones Epic Stunt Spectacular* would be safe for a few more years. But because of licensing fees that The Walt Disney Company has to pay to Lucasfilm, plus the cost of keeping two huge stunt shows running at the Studios (the other being *Lights, Motors, Action!*), Disney has been considering closing the *Stunt Spectacular* to make a sizable chunk of real estate available for development. Will Dr. Jones once again escape certain death? Stay tuned.

Professional stunt men and women demonstrate dangerous stunts with a behind-the-scenes look at how it is done. Most kids handle the show well. The show always needs a few "extras." To be chosen from the audience, arrive early, sit down front, and display unmitigated enthusiasm. Unfortunately "victims" must be 18 years old and up.

An amazing show with fiery explosions and nonstop action. Did you know that the folks at Disney have a vault filled with sound-effects CDs ranging from gunshots to magical twinkles? When a show is created, they pick and choose from this treasure chest and upload the sounds into their state-of-the-art computerized mixing table.

Idan

Huh? What's a "magical twinkle" sound like? But now that I think about it, I sure remember the noise my innards made after eating about a dozen magical twinkles.

Bob

Liliane   Those were Twinkies, Mr. Tiki-Birdbrain!

Jim Henson's Muppet-Vision 3-D ★★★★½

APPEAL BY AGE	PRESCHOOL ★★★★	GRADE SCHOOL ★★★★	TEENS ★★★★
YOUNG ADULTS ★★★★		OVER 30 ★★★★	SENIORS ★★★★

What it is 3-D movie starring the Muppets. **Scope and scale** Major attraction. **Fright potential** Intense and loud but not frightening. **Bottleneck rating** 8.

When to go Before 11 a.m. or after 3 p.m. **Authors' rating** Uproarious; not to be missed; ★★★★½. **Duration of presentation** 17 minutes. **Preshow entertainment** Muppets on television. **Probable waiting time** 12 minutes.

Thumbs Up for the Whole Family

Kermit, Miss Piggy, and the rest of the gang will lift your spirits as they unleash their hilarious mayhem. Because adults tend to associate Muppet characters with the children's show *Sesame Street,* many bypass this attraction. Big mistake. *Muppet-Vision 3-D* operates on several planes, and there's as much here for oldsters as for youngsters. The presentation is intense and sometimes loud, but most preschoolers handle it well. If your child is a little scared, encourage him to watch without the 3-D glasses at first.

Lights, Motors, Action! Extreme Stunt Show ★★★½

APPEAL BY AGE	PRESCHOOL ★★★½	GRADE SCHOOL ★★★★½	TEENS ★★★★½
YOUNG ADULTS ★★★★		OVER 30 ★★★★	SENIORS ★★★★

What it is Auto stunt show. **Scope and scale** Headliner. **Fright potential** Loud with explosions but not scary. **When to go** First show of the day or after 4 p.m. **Authors' rating** Good stunt work, slow pace; ★★★½. **Duration of presentation** 33 minutes. **Preshow entertainment** Selection of audience "volunteers."

Loud

This show features cars and motorcycles in a blur of chases, crashes, jumps, and explosions. The secrets behind the special effects are explained after each stunt sequence. The show runs about 30 minutes, and small children may become restless. Teens, however, will be gobsmacked.

Idan

The show left me speechless. This is one of the most amazing, unbelievable shows of all. You won't believe your eyes.

Maybe it's an age thing, but I'm less impressed than Idan. The stunts are super, but there's too much dead time and redundancy in this show.

Bob

The Magic of Disney Animation ★★½

APPEAL BY AGE	PRESCHOOL ★★★	GRADE SCHOOL ★★★½	TEENS ★★★★
YOUNG ADULTS ★★★½		OVER 30 ★★★½	SENIORS ★★★½

What it is Overview of Disney Animation process with limited hands-on demonstrations. **Scope and scale** Minor attraction. **Fright potential** Not frightening in any respect. **Bottleneck rating** 7. **When to go** Before 11 a.m. or after 5 p.m. **Special comment** Opens an hour later than the rest of the park. **Authors' rating** Not as good as previous renditions; ★★½. **Duration of presentation** 20 minutes. **Preshow entertainment** Gallery of animation art in waiting area. **Average wait in line per 100 people ahead of you** 7 minutes.

The consolidation of Disney Animation at the Burbank, California, studio has left this attraction without a story to tell. A shadow of its former self, the attraction doesn't warrant waiting in line. Guests learn very little about animation. The only interesting part, especially for children, is Animation

Academy, an optional stop after the presentation. Here, kids and grown-ups alike can draw their own cartoon with the help of an animator. (Space is limited and on a first-come, first-serve basis.) The compelling presentation provides a good idea of how difficult hand-drawn animation is. Children who need more time or assistance with their drawing may become frustrated.

Movie Promo Soundstage

Disney uses this soundstage to promote its latest films. Disney's biggest effort went into building the set's doors in the shape of the wardrobe described in *The Chronicles of Narnia*. To call this anemic offering an attraction would be a stretch. If you are a C. S. Lewis fan, see the attraction; it has some behind-the-scenes footage and concept art from the films, new props and costumes, and a Prince Caspian greeting area. Otherwise, skip it.

Playhouse Disney—Live on Stage! ★★★★

APPEAL BY AGE	PRESCHOOL ★★★★½	GRADE SCHOOL ★★★★	TEENS ★½
YOUNG ADULTS ★★	OVER 30 ★★½		SENIORS ★★½

What it is Live show for children. **Scope and scale** Minor attraction. **Fright potential** Not frightening in any respect. **Bottleneck rating** 8. **When to go** Per the daily entertainment schedule. **Authors' rating** A must for families with preschoolers; ★★★★. **Duration of presentation** 20 minutes. **Special comments** Audience sits on the floor. **Probable waiting time** 30 minutes.

The show features characters from the Disney Channel's *Little Einsteins, Mickey Mouse Clubhouse,* and *Handy Manny,* as well as Mickey, Minnie, Donald, Daisy, and Goofy. Reengineered in 2007, *Playhouse Disney* replaced live Disney characters with elaborate puppets. A simple plot serves as the platform for singing, dancing, some great puppetry, and a great deal of audience participation. The characters, who ooze love and goodness, rally throngs of tots and preschoolers to sing and dance along with them. All the jumping, squirming, and high-stepping is facilitated by having the audience sit on the floor so that kids can spontaneously erupt into motion when the mood strikes. Even for adults without children, it's a treat to watch the tykes rev up. If you have a younger child in your party, all the better: Just stand back and let the video roll. For preschoolers, *Playhouse Disney* will be the highlight of their day, as a Thomasville, North Carolina, mom attests:

> Playhouse Disney *was fantastic! My 3-year-old loved it. The children danced, sang, and had a great time.*

Many readers are less than enthralled with the new version of *Playhouse Disney!* These comments from a Virginia Beach, Virginia, couple are typical:

> We were disappointed with the newly updated Playhouse Disney. *This did not consist of "live" characters, and I think the level of excitement from the kids was lower because of this. I mean, the kids enjoyed it, but you would think they would be more excited when it's a show with some of their favorite characters.*

The show is headquartered in what was formerly the Soundstage Restaurant, located to the right of the Animation Tour. Because the tykes just can't get enough, it has become the toughest ticket at the Studios. Show up at least 30 minutes before showtime. Once inside, pick a spot on the floor and take a breather until the performance begins.

Rock 'n' Roller Coaster (Fastpass) ★★★★

APPEAL BY AGE	PRESCHOOL ★	GRADE SCHOOL ★★★½	TEENS ★★★★★
YOUNG ADULTS ★★★★★		OVER 30 ★★★★★	SENIORS ★★★

What it is Rock music–themed roller coaster. **Scope and scale** Headliner. **Fright potential** Extremely intense for all ages; the ride is one of Disney's wildest. **Bottleneck rating** 10. **When to go** Before 10 a.m., in the hour before closing, or use Fastpass. **Special comments** Must be 48" tall to ride; children younger than age 7 must ride with an adult. Switching-off option provided (page 238). **Authors' rating** Disney's wildest American coaster; not to be missed; ★★★★. **Duration of ride** Almost 1½ minutes. **Average wait in line per 100 people ahead of you** 2½ minutes. **Assumes** All trains operating. **Loading speed** Moderate to fast.

Dark   Scary   Rough   Lose Things   Motion Sickness

Aerosmith once did a tour called Route of All Evil, and the notorious ride at the Studios will make good on fans' expectations. Loops, corkscrews, and drops that make Space Mountain seem like the Jungle Cruise is what to expect and what is delivered—pronto. You will be launched from 0 to 57 miles per hour in less than 3 seconds, and by the time you enter the first loop, you'll be pulling five Gs. By comparison, that is two more Gs than astronauts experience at liftoff on a space shuttle.

Aerosmith describes this ride best in one of their songs: "Living on the Edge."

Liliane

Sounds Dangerous with Drew Carey (open seasonally) ★★★

APPEAL BY AGE	PRESCHOOL ★	GRADE SCHOOL ★★	TEENS ★★★
YOUNG ADULTS ★★		OVER 30 ★★	SENIORS ★★½

What it is Show demonstrating sound effects. **Scope and scale** Minor attraction. **Fright potential** Sounds in darkened theater frighten some preschoolers. **Bottleneck rating** 6. **When to go** Before 11 a.m. or after 4 p.m. **Authors' rating** Funny and informative; ★★★. **Duration of presentation** 12 minutes. **Preshow entertainment** Video introduction to sound effects. **Probable waiting time** 15–30 minutes.

Dark

Put on your headphones, turn off the lights, and join Drew Carey in a hilarious presentation about sound effects. The show is not geared toward preschoolers. The theater is completely dark during much of the presentation, and the sound effects are very realistic and not a little disconcerting.

Star Tours (Fastpass) † ★★★★

APPEAL BY AGE	PRESCHOOL ★★★★	GRADE SCHOOL ★★★★	TEENS ★★★★
YOUNG ADULTS ★★★★		OVER 30 ★★★★	SENIORS ★★★★

† Scheduled for renovation from September 2010 until 2011.

What it is Indoor space flight–simulation ride. **Scope and scale** Headliner. **Fright potential** Extremely intense visually for all ages; the ride is one of Disney's wildest. Likely to cause motion sickness. Switching-off option provided (see page 238). **Bottleneck rating** 8. **When to go** Before 11 a.m., after 4:30 p.m., or use Fastpass **Special comments** Expectant mothers and anyone prone to motion sickness are advised against riding. Too intense for many children younger than age 8. Must be 40" tall to ride. **Authors' rating** Not to be missed; ★★★★. **Duration of ride** About 7 minutes. **Average wait in line per 100 people ahead of you** 5 minutes. **Assumes** All simulators operating. **Loading speed** Moderate to fast.

Scary   Rough   Motion Sickness

Based on the *Star Wars* movie series, this attraction takes guests on a flight-simulator ride to Endor. You could swear you are moving at light speed and somehow when all hell breaks loose you are confident that, total mayhem aside, the Force will be with you. This ride is wonderful for all *Star Wars* fans and a living nightmare for guests prone to motion sickness.

Star Tours II will be coming to a galaxy near you in 2011. (The attraction is scheduled to close in September 2010 for the renovation.) The ride will be given new 3-D special effects and interactive elements as guests take a tour of the planets of the *Star Wars* galaxy. Characters from the prequel films released from 1999 to 2005 will be included in the makeover. Does that mean that Jar Jar Binks will be making an appearance? May the Force be with us!

Oh, no! We're caught in a tractor beam!

Liliane

Star Wars weekends are a must for any and all *Star Wars* fans. Shame on Disney for keeping Darth Vader away from his fans. While he appears in Jedi Training Academy, he is no longer part of the parade.

Idan

My whole family thought it reeked of geekiness.

Shelton

Every year (usually mid-May to mid-June) Walt Disney World hosts four *Star Wars* weekends. Celebrities from the saga and fans converge at the park in celebration of George Lucas's epic series. Even Mickey turns into a Jedi and joins Ewoks, Jawas, and Wookies for a ride to a galaxy far, far away.

Disney, I am watching you—you better get this one right. And I am still demanding that you put *Star Wars* characters back on the streets of DHS now!

Idan

Streets of America ★★★

APPEAL BY AGE	PRESCHOOL ★★½	GRADE SCHOOL ★★★	TEENS ★★★
YOUNG ADULTS ★★★		OVER 30 ★★★½	SENIORS ★★★½

What it is Walk-through backlot movie set. **Scope and scale** Diversion. **Fright potential** Not frightening in any respect. **Bottleneck rating** 1. **When to go** Anytime. **Authors' rating** Interesting, with great detail; ★★★. **Duration of presentation** Varies. **Average wait in line per 100 people ahead of you** None.

There is never a wait to enjoy the Streets of America; save your visit here until you have seen those attractions that develop long lines. During the Christmas season, Streets of America are decorated with millions of Christmas lights and serve as a backdrop for the Osborne Family Spectacle of Lights.

Studio Backlot Tour ★★★★

APPEAL BY AGE	PRESCHOOL ★★★	GRADE SCHOOL ★★★½	TEENS ★★★½
YOUNG ADULTS ★★★		OVER 30 ★★★½	SENIORS ★★★½

What it is Combination tram and walking tour of modern film and video production. **Scope and scale** Headliner. **Fright potential** Sedate and nonintimidating except for Catastrophe Canyon, where an earthquake and flash flood are simulated. Prepare younger children for this part of the tour. **Bottleneck rating** 6. **When to go** Anytime. **Special comments** Use the restroom before getting in line. **Authors' rating** Educational and fun; not to be missed; ★★★★. **Duration of tour** About 35 minutes. **Preshow entertainment** A video before the special effects segment and another video in the tram boarding area.

About two-thirds of Disney's Hollywood Studios is a film and television facility. The tour is an absolute must. Special effects are explained with demonstrations of rain and a naval battle. Next, visitors board a tram that takes them through wardrobe and craft shops where costumes, sets, and props are designed. The tour continues through the backlot, where western canyons exist side-by-side with New York City brownstones. The tour's highlight is Catastrophe Canyon, an elaborate special-effects movie set where a thunderstorm, earthquake, oil-field fire, and a flash flood are simulated. Prepare young children for Catastrophe Canyon, as the rattling earthquake and the sudden flood shake the tram and yes, if you are sitting on the left side facing the canyon, you will get wet.

I took the tour first at age 3 and was very scared. Now, of course, Catastrophe Canyon is my favorite part of the ride. I also love to see the costumes and props and wish I could pack all of it up to take home with me.

Toy Story Mania! (Fastpass) ★★★★ ½

APPEAL BY AGE	PRESCHOOL ★★★★	GRADE SCHOOL ★★★★	TEENS ★★★★★
YOUNG ADULTS ★★★★★		OVER 30 ★★★★★	SENIORS ★★★★½

What it is 3-D ride through indoor shooting gallery. **Scope and scale** Headliner. **Fright potential** Not frightening in any respect. **Bottleneck rating** 10. **When to go** Before 10:30 a.m., after 6 p.m., or use Fastpass (if available). **Authors' rating** ★★★★½. **Duration of ride** About 6½ minutes. **Average wait in line per 100 people ahead of you** 4½ minutes. **Loading Speed** Fast.

This is an interactive shooting gallery much like Buzz Lightyear's Space Ranger Spin, but in Toy Story Mania! your vehicle passes through a totally virtual midway, with booths offering such games as the ring toss and ball throw. You use a cannon on your ride vehicle to play as you move along from booth to booth. The pull-string cannon takes advantage of computer-graphic image technology to toss rings, shoot balls, and even throw eggs and pies. Each game booth is manned by a *Toy Story* character who is right beside you in 3-D glory cheering you on. In addition to 3-D imagery, you experience various smells, vehicle motion, wind, and water spray. The ride begins with a training round to familiarize you with the nature of the games, and then continues through a number of games that count for score, in which you compete against your riding mate. The technology has the ability to self-adjust the level of difficulty, and there are plenty of easy targets for small children to reach. Tip: Let the pull-string retract all the way back into the cannon before pulling it again.

Toy Story Mania! is the hottest ticket in the park and stays packed all day. Ride first thing after the park opens or use Fastpass. Regarding the latter, pick up your Fastpasses before 11 a.m. or they will likely be exhausted for the day. Following are reports from readers. First from a Cold Spring, New York, mom:

> There was a 20-minute wait just for Fastpasses as soon as the park opened, and by 11 [a.m.] Fastpasses were gone for the day. Thanks to the DIS forums I was aware of how popular the ride was though, so I got Fastpasses for it first, then followed the touring plan, and everything fell into place nicely.

A Nashville, Tennessee, mom shared this:

> Toy Story Mania! was swamped by the time we got to it, still fairly early in the day. We had to resort to getting some of the last Fastpasses, and it elongated our day to wait until our [return] time came up. But, oh my gosh, what fun! It was worth the wait!

An Ontario, Canada, mom observed :

> By 10 a.m. the line was 50 minutes long and we got Fastpasses for 2 in the afternoon. At 2 p.m. the line was 80 minutes and there were no more Fastpasses left.

From an Evansville, Indiana, mom:

> We immediately went to Toy Story Mania! and found a HUGE line for the ride. We figured we'd be smart and get a Fastpass. Turns out the HUGE line WAS the Fastpass line! The FP return time was already at 12:45. Unfortunately we had to skip this ride due to the long wait.

Toy Story Mania! has become the biggest bottleneck in Walt Disney World, surpassing even Test Track at Epcot. The only way to get aboard without a horrendous wait is to be one of the first through the turnstiles when the park opens and zoom to the attraction. Another alternative is to obtain Fastpasses for Toy Story Mania! as soon as the park opens, and then backtrack to ride the Rock 'n' Roller Coaster and Tower of Terror. Expect long queues at the Fastpass kiosks. If you decide to get Fastpasses, spare your family the extra legwork and dispatch the fittest member to get Fastpasses for all while you get in line to ride Tower of Terror or Rock 'n' Roller Coaster. If you have a cell phone, text your location in line to the brave warrior getting the Fastpasses and reunite to ride together.

The Twilight Zone Tower of Terror (Fastpass) ★★★★

APPEAL BY AGE **PRESCHOOL** ★★½ **GRADE SCHOOL** ★★★★ **TEENS** ★★★★★
YOUNG ADULTS ★★★★ **OVER 30** ★★★★★ **SENIORS** ★★★★

What it is Sci-fi-theme indoor thrill ride. **Scope and scale** Super headliner.
Fright potential Visually intimidating to young children; contains intense and
realistic special effects. The plummeting elevator at the ride's end frightens many
adults. Switching-off option provided (see page 238). **Bottleneck rating** 10.
When to go Before 9:30 a.m., after 6 p.m., or use Fastpass. **Special comments**
Must be 40" tall to ride. **Authors' rating** Walt Disney World's best attraction;
not to be missed; ★★★★★. **Duration of ride** About 4 minutes plus preshow.
Average wait in line per 100 people ahead of you 4 minutes. **Assumes** All
elevators operating. **Loading speed** Moderate.

Dark   Scary   Rough

And suddenly the cable went *snap*. If riding a
capricious elevator in a haunted hotel sounds
like fun to you, this is your ride. Erratic yet
thrilling, the Tower of Terror is an experi-
ence to savor. The Tower has great potential for terrifying young children
and rattling more mature visitors. Random ride-and-drop sequences make
the attraction wilder and keep you guessing about when, how far, and how
many times the elevator drops. We suggest you use teenagers in your
party as experimental probes. If they report back that they really, really
liked the Tower of Terror, run as fast as you can in the opposite direction.
Tower of Terror is one of the hottest tickets in the park. If you're up to it,
experience the ride first thing in the morning or use Fastpass.

Another ride that gives you surprises. I like it when you go up and
think you're going to stay up but end up zooming down. There's
a part of the ride where it looks like you're in outer space, then it
turns back into the hotel.

Hannah

The part where you get up and then you
suddenly start moving through the floor is cool. I did not see
that coming. I consider it a thrill ride for people who don't like
thrill rides. You can easily trick someone into going on it.

Shelton

Voyage of the Little Mermaid ★★★★

APPEAL BY AGE **PRESCHOOL** ★★★★ **GRADE SCHOOL** ★★★★ **TEENS** ★★★
YOUNG ADULTS ★★★★ **OVER 30** ★★★★ **SENIORS** ★★★★

Thumbs Up for the Whole Family

What it is Musical stage show featuring characters
from the Disney movie *The Little Mermaid*. **Scope
and scale** Major attraction. **Fright potential** Ursula
the sea witch may frighten preschoolers. **Bottleneck
rating** 10. **When to go** Before 9:45 a.m. or just
before closing. **Authors' rating** Romantic, lovable,
and humorous in the best Disney tradition; not to be missed; ★★★★. **Duration of presentation** 15 minutes. **Preshow entertainment** Taped ramblings

about the decor in the preshow holding area. **Probable waiting time** Before 9:30 a.m., 10–30 minutes; after 9:30 a.m., 35–70 minutes.

This most tender and romantic stage show is a winner, appealing to every age. Once inside the theater, the audience is transported into the wonderful underwater world of Ariel and her friends. Very young children might be frightened by Ursula the sea witch (she is actually a puppet standing 12 feet tall).

> The scary characters like the eels just show up on the side—they don't come out at you. Ariel's hair is really, really bright red.
>
> Hannah

Because it's well done and located at a busy pedestrian intersection, *Voyage of the Little Mermaid* plays to capacity crowds all day. When the theater doors open, pick a row of seats, and let 6–10 people enter the row ahead of you. The strategy is twofold: to obtain a good seat and be near the exit.

Walt Disney: One Man's Dream ★★★

APPEAL BY AGE	PRESCHOOL ★★	GRADE SCHOOL ★★★	TEENS ★★★½
YOUNG ADULTS ★★★★		OVER 30 ★★★★	SENIORS ★★★★

What it is Tribute to Walt Disney. **Scope and scale** Minor attraction. **Fright potential** Not frightening in any respect. **Bottleneck rating** 2. **When to go** Anytime. **Authors' rating** Excellent! ★★★ and about time. **Duration of presentation** 25 minutes. **Preshow entertainment** Disney memorabilia. **Probable waiting time** For film, 10 minutes.

One Man's Dream is a long-overdue tribute to Walt Disney. The attraction consists of an exhibit area showcasing Disney memorabilia, followed by a film documenting Disney's life. Teens and adults, especially those old enough to remember Walt Disney, will enjoy this homage to the man behind the mouse.

> Hands off! Don't even think of packing this gem of. I pay tribute every time I visit and discover something I had not noticed before.
>
> Idan

LIVE ENTERTAINMENT *at* DISNEY'S HOLLYWOOD STUDIOS

WHEN THE STUDIOS OPENED, live entertainment, parades, and special events weren't as fully developed or impressive as those at the Magic Kingdom or Epcot. With the introduction of an afternoon parade and elaborate shows at **Theater of the Stars,** the Studios joined the big leagues. In 1998 DHS launched a new edition of *Fantasmic!* (see

A PEEK BEHIND THE SCENES WITH JIM HILL

BLOCK PARTY TO PARTY ON

Just as Block Party Bash was imported from Disney's California parks, it's been assumed that the Florida parks would inherit the Pixar Play Parade from the West Coast. But with the debut of Toy Story Playland at Disneyland Paris's Walt Disney Studios, it's looking far more likely that the Pixar Play Parade will bypass the World and head straight for France. What will be replacing Block Party Bash? Disney has expressed interest in creating an all-new parade, but it could be quite a while before we see it because the Bash is still such a crowd-pleaser.

page 356), a water, fireworks, and laser show that draws rave reviews. Staged in its own specially designed 10,000-person amphitheater, *Fantasmic!* makes the Studios the park of choice for spectacular nighttime entertainment. WDW live-entertainment guru Steve Soares usually posts the DHS performance schedule about a week in advance at **pages.prodigy.net/stevesoares.**

AFTERNOON PARADE Staged once a day, the parade begins near the park's entrance, continues down Hollywood Boulevard, and circles in front of the giant hat. From there, it passes in front of *Sounds Dangerous* and ends by Star Tours. An alternate route begins at the far end of Sunset Boulevard and turns right onto Hollywood Boulevard.

Block Party Bash features floats and characters based on Disney's animated features, including *Toy Story; Monsters, Inc.;* and *A Bug's Life*. It's a colorful, high-energy affair with plenty of acrobatics, singing, and dancing. It's also loud beyond belief. *Unofficial Guide* coauthor Len Testa, who considers most Disney afternoon parades to be clichéridden mobile musicals affording a high chance of heatstroke, grudgingly concedes that this may be the best of the lot.

HIGH SCHOOL MUSICAL PEP RALLY We can't fault Disney for trying to cash in on the phenomenal success of the 2006 TV movie *High School Musical,* and the kids who sing and dance their way through this 20-minute recap of the film's major musical numbers do an admirable job. With little dialogue and stage scenery that consists of nothing more than a few blow-up basketball-shaped balloons and cheesy "Go Wildcats!" banners, Disney's not given them much to work with. Children will be disappointed at not seeing the actual stars from the movie. Adults will spend more time wondering what the school's feeding these kids to eliminate all traces of teen angst and raging hormones.

DISNEY CHARACTERS Find characters at the Theater of the Stars, in parades, at Al's Toy Barn (near Mama Melrose's on Streets of America), in the Animation Courtyard, on the Backstage Plaza, and along Pixar Place. Mickey sometimes appears for autographs and photos on

Sunset Boulevard. Times and locations for character appearances are listed in the complimentary *Times Guide*.

JEDI TRAINING ACADEMY This interactive show is staged several times daily to the left of the Star Tours building entrance, opposite Backlot Express. Young Skywalkers-in-training are selected from the audience to train in the ways of the Force and do battle against Darth Vader. If all this sounds too intense, it's not—Storm Troopers provide comic relief, and just as in the movies, the Jedi always win. Check the daily entertainment schedule for showtimes. Let your little Jedi wear his costume. It might help him get selected.

STREET ENTERTAINMENT With the possible exception of Epcot's World Showcase Players, the Studios has the best collection of roving street performers in all of Walt Disney World. Appearing primarily on Hollywood and Sunset boulevards, the cast of characters includes Hollywood stars and wannabes, their agents, film directors, and gossip columnists, as well as various police officers and Hollywood public-works crews.

The performers are not shy about asking you to join in their skits, and you may be asked anything from explaining why you came to "Hollywood" all the way to reciting a couple of lines in one of the directors' new films. If you're looking for a spot to rest and a bit of entertainment, grab a drink and seek out these performers.

THEATER OF THE STARS This covered amphitheater on Sunset Boulevard is the stage for production revues, usually featuring music from Disney movies and starring Disney characters. Performances are posted in front of the theater and are listed in the daily entertainment schedule in the handout *Times Guide*.

Fantasmic! ★★★★★

APPEAL BY AGE	PRESCHOOL ★★★★	GRADE SCHOOL ★★★★½	TEENS ★★★★½
YOUNG ADULTS ★★★★★		OVER 30 ★★★★½	SENIORS ★★★★½

What it is Mixed-media nighttime spectacular. **Scope and scale** Super headliner. **Fright potential** Loud and intense with fireworks and some scary villains, but most young children like it. **Bottleneck rating** 9. **When to go** Only staged in the evening. **Special comments** Disney's best nighttime event. **Authors' rating** Not to be missed; ★★★★★. **Duration of presentation** 25 minutes. **Probable waiting time** 50–90 minutes for a seat; 35–40 minutes for standing room.

  Until recently, *Fantasmic!* was staged nightly and always played to a full house. Presumably as a cost-containment measure, Disney has cut performances to two evenings a week, or three nights a week during busier times. As you might imagine, trying to cram seven nights of capacity crowds into two nights is not working very well, as a reader from Sandwich, Illinois, reports:

Loud   Scary

The reduction in Fantasmic! *shows per week is ridiculous to me. The Studios is an absolute ghost town on nights it doesn't show and packed to capacity on nights when it does! There has to be a happy medium.*

Nonetheless, *Fantasmic!* is far and away the most unique outdoor spectacle ever attempted in any theme park and a must-see for the whole family. Starring Mickey Mouse in his role as the Sorcerer's apprentice from *Fantasia,* the production uses lasers, images projected on a shroud of mist, dazzling fireworks, lightning effects, and powerful music. *Fantasmic!* has the potential to frighten young children. Prepare your children for the show, and make sure that they know that in addition to all the favorite Disney characters, the maleficent dragon and the evil Jafar will make appearances. To give you an idea, just picture this: The evil Jafar turns into a cobra 100 feet long and 16 feet high. Rest assured, however, that during the final parade your kids will cheer on Cinderella and Prince Charming, Belle, Snow White, Ariel and Prince Eric, Jasmine and Aladdin, Donald Duck, Minnie, and Mickey.

You can alleviate the fright factor somewhat by sitting back a bit. Also, if you are seated in the first 12 rows, you will get sprayed with water at times.

The theater is huge, but so is the popularity of the show. If there are two performances, the second show will almost always be less crowded. If you attend the first (or only) scheduled performance, show up at least 60–80 minutes in advance. Plan to use that time for a picnic. Bring food and drinks and something to entertain the younger kids. If you forget to bring munchies, not to worry, there are food concessions in the theater. In 2009, as a cost-cutting measure, Disney staged *Fantasmic!* on only two nights a week. This made it almost impossible to see the show without lining up 90 minutes to 2 hours in advance. Yes, *Fantasmic!* is a great show, but is it worth a 2-hour wait?

Unless you buy a *Fantasmic!* dinner package, you will not have assigned seats, so arrive early for best choice. Try to sit in the middle three or four sections, a bit off center. Finally, understand that you are out of luck if *Fantasmic!* is cancelled due to weather or other circumstances.

FAVORITE EATS AT DISNEY'S HOLLYWOOD STUDIOS

LAND | SERVICE LOCATION | FOOD ITEM

BACKLOT   ABC Commissary | Great traditional breakfast; chicken nuggets and strips with veggies
                Backlot Express | Great burgers and fixin's; gyro-style steak and lamb kefta on flatbread
                Pizza Planet | THE place for pizza
                Studios Catering Co. | Good place for a break while your kids check out *Honey, I Shrunk the Kids* playground

COMMISSARY LANE   Sci-Fi Dine-In Theater | It's not about the food (dismal) but about eating in a vintage convertible car watching old sci-fi movie previews. Teens love it! Great place to cool off. *(table service only)*

Fantasmic! Dinner Packages

Three restaurants offer a ticket-voucher for the members of your dining party to enter *Fantasmic!* via a special entrance and sit in a reserved section of seats. The package consists of a buffet at Hollywood & Vine, or a fixed-price dinner at Mama Melrose's Ristorante Italiano or The Hollywood Brown Derby (full-service restaurants). You can call ☎ 407-WDW-DINE up to 90 days in advance and request the *Fantasmic!* Dinner Package. This is a real reservation and must be guaranteed by a credit card at the time of booking. There's a 48-hour cancellation policy.

	HOLLYWOOD BROWN DERBY	MAMA MELROSE'S RISTORANTE ITALIANO	HOLLYWOOD & VINE BUFFET
Adult	$50.05	$35.14	$28.75
Child (3-9)	$12.77	$12.77	$14.90

Nonalcoholic drinks and tax are included; park admission and gratuity are not. Please note that prices fluctuate according to season, so call ☎ 407-WDW-DINE if you want to know exactly what the dinner charge will be for a particular date.

Allow yourselves a minimum of 2 hours to eat. You will receive the vouchers (tickets for the show) at the restaurants. After dinner, report to the *Fantasmic!* sign on Hollywood Boulevard next to Oscar's Super Service filling station (just inside the front entrance to the park) no later than 35 minutes prior to showtime. A cast member will collect the vouchers and escort you to the reserved section. If *Fantasmic!* is cancelled for any reason, such as weather, technical problems, and the like, you'll not receive a refund or even a voucher for another performance.

EXIT STRATEGIES

EXITING THE STUDIOS at the end of the day following *Fantasmic!* is not nearly as difficult as leaving Epcot after *IllumiNations*. We recommend you take it easy and make your way out of the park after the first wave of guests has departed. Pick a spot inside the park and give instructions that nobody is to go through the turnstiles before the group is reunited. Most important, latch on to your kids.

DISNEY'S HOLLYWOOD STUDIOS TOURING PLANS

OUR STEP-BY-STEP TOURING PLANS ARE FIELD-TESTED, independently verified itineraries that will keep you moving counter to the crowd flow and allow you to see as much as possible in a single day with a minimum of time wasted in line.

The different touring plans are described below. The descriptions will tell you for whom (for example, tweens, parents with preschoolers, and so on) or for what situation (such as sleeping late) the plans are designed. The actual touring plans are located on pages 463–466 at the back of the book. Each plan includes a numbered map of the park in question to help you find your way around. Clip the plan of your choice out of the book by cutting along the line indicated, and take it with you to the park.

You can take in all the attractions at the Disney's Hollywood Studios in one day, even when traveling with young children. If you are not interested in an attraction listed on the touring plan, just skip that attraction and proceed to the next step. Likewise, should you encounter a very long line at an attraction, skip it. Use of Fastpass is factored into the touring plans.

DISNEY'S HOLLYWOOD STUDIOS ONE-DAY TOURING PLAN FOR PARENTS WITH SMALL CHILDREN This plan is designed for parents of children ages 3–8 who wish to see the very best age-appropriate attractions and shows in Disney's Hollywood Studios. Every attraction has a rating of at least three stars (out of five) from preschool and grade-school children surveyed by the *Unofficial Guide*. The plan includes a midday break inside the park so families can rest, relax, and regroup. The plan keeps walking and backtracking to a minimum, with no crisscrossing of the park.

DISNEY'S HOLLYWOOD STUDIOS ONE-DAY SLEEPYHEAD TOURING PLAN FOR PARENTS WITH SMALL CHILDREN A relaxed plan that allows families with small children to sleep late and still see the highlights of Disney's Hollywood Studios. The plan begins around 11 a.m., sets aside ample time for lunch, and includes the very best child-friendly attractions and shows in the park. Special advice is provided for touring the park with small children. The plan points out where Fastpass can best be used.

DISNEY'S HOLLYWOOD STUDIOS ONE-DAY TOURING PLAN FOR TWEENS AND THEIR PARENTS A one-day plan for parents with children ages 8–12. It includes every attraction rated three stars and higher by this age group and sets aside ample time for lunch and dinner.

DISNEY'S HOLLYWOOD STUDIOS ONE-DAY HAPPY FAMILY TOURING PLAN A one-day itinerary for multigenerational families, this plan allows teens and older children to experience the Studios' thrill rides while parents and small children visit more age-appropriate attractions. The family stays together most of the day, including lunch and dinner, and each attraction in the plan is rated three stars or higher.

BEFORE YOU GO

1. Call ☎ 407-824-4321 to verify the park's hours.
2. Buy your admission before arriving.
3. Make lunch and dinner advance reservations or reserve the *Fantasmic!* dinner package (if desired) before you arrive by calling ☎ 407-WDW-DINE.

4. The schedule of live entertainment changes from month to month and even from day to day. Review the handout daily *Times Guide* to get a fairly clear picture of your options.

DISNEY'S HOLLYWOOD STUDIOS TRIVIA QUIZ

By Lou Mongello

1. In *Muppet-Vision 3-D,* Sam the Eagle states that the finale will be "A Salute to All Nations but Mostly . . . ":

  a. America

  b. Muppets

  c. Florida

  d. Walt Disney World

2. What is the name of the hotel featuring The Twilight Zone Tower of Terror?

  a. Hollywood Tower Hotel

  b. Hollywood Hills Hotel

  c. Hightower Hotel

  d. The Sunset Hotel

3. At the end of *Muppet-Vision 3-D,* what "crashes" through the screen?

  a. A monorail

  b. An animal

  c. A fire engine

  d. Dumbo

4. What color are your 3-D glasses in Toy Story Mania!?

  a. Yellow

  b. Black

  c. Blue

  d. Purple

5. What band is featured in Rock 'n' Roller Coaster?

  a. Jonas Brothers

  b. Aerosmith

  c. U2

  d. Guns 'n Roses

6. The Mr. Potato Head figure in the queue for Toy Story Mania! is able to:

  a. Remove his ear

  b. Tip his hat

  c. Walk up stairs

  d. Moonwalk

7. How many people disappear in the elevator of The Twilight Zone Tower of Terror?

   a. 0

   b. 1

   c. 5

   d. 7

8. The Block Party Bash parade features characters from all of these movies, EXCEPT:

   a. *Cars*

   b. *Toy Story 2*

   c. *The Incredibles*

   d. *A Bug's Life*

9. Many Walt Disney World attractions are based on movies, but which of these attractions had a movie made about it *after* it opened at Disney's Hollywood Studios?

   a. *Muppet-Vision 3-D*

   b. The Twilight Zone Tower Of Terror

   c. The Great Movie Ride

   d. *Sounds Dangerous*

10. The giant replica of a *Star Wars* vehicle outside the Star Tours attraction is:

   a. A landspeeder

   b. A Star Destroyer

   c. An AT-AT walker

   d. A probe droid

11. What is the name of the dinosaur that is also an ice cream stand?

   a. Deeno

   b. Gertie

   c. Diner-Saur

   d. Hector

12. What animals make up the orchestra in *Muppet-Vision 3-D*?

   a. Penguins

   b. Rats

   c. Frogs

   d. Bunnies

Answers can be found on page 426.

PART ELEVEN

UNIVERSAL ORLANDO *and* SEAWORLD

UNIVERSAL ORLANDO

UNIVERSAL ORLANDO HAS TRANSFORMED into a complete destination resort, with two theme parks, three hotels, and a shopping, dining, and entertainment complex. The second theme park, Islands of Adventure, opened in 1999 with five themed areas.

A system of roads and two multistory parking facilities are connected by moving sidewalks to **CityWalk,** a shopping, dining, and nighttime-entertainment complex that also serves as a gateway to the **Universal Studios Florida** and **Islands of Adventure** theme parks.

LODGING AT UNIVERSAL ORLANDO

UNIVERSAL CURRENTLY HAS THREE OPERATING resort hotels. The 750-room **Portofino Bay Hotel** is a gorgeous property set on an artificial bay with an Italian coastal town theme. The 650-room **Hard Rock Hotel** is an ultracool "Hotel California" replica, with slick contemporary design and a hip, friendly attitude. The 1,000-room, Polynesian-themed **Loews Royal Pacific Resort** is sumptuously decorated and richly appointed. All three are excellent hotels; the Portofino and the Hard Rock are on the pricey side, and the Royal Pacific ain't exactly cheap.

ARRIVING AT UNIVERSAL ORLANDO

THE UNIVERSAL ORLANDO COMPLEX can be accessed directly from I-4. Once on site, you will be directed to park in one of two multitiered parking garages. Parking runs $14 to $18 for cars and $20 for RVs. Be sure to write down the location of your car before heading for the parks. From the garages, moving sidewalks deliver you to the Universal CityWalk dining, shopping, and entertainment venue described above. From CityWalk, you can access the main entrances of both Universal Studios Florida and Islands of Adventure theme parks.

Universal offers One-day, Two-day, Three-day, Four-day, and Seven-day Passes for one park or two parks, as well as Annual Passes for both parks.

Passes can be obtained in advance on the phone with your credit card at ☎ 800-711-0080 or **universalorlando.com.** Prices do not include tax or applicable fees.

	ADULTS	CHILDREN (3–9)
One-day, One-park Pass	$79	$69
One-day, Two-park Pass	$109	$99
Two-day, Two-park Pass	$134.99	$121.99
Seven-day, Two-park Pass	$169.99	$149.99

Be sure to check Universal's Web site for seasonal deals and specials. You can save as much as 25% by buying your tickets in advance on Universal's Web site. Combination passes are available by phone only: A five-park, 14-day pass called the Orlando Flex Ticket allows unlimited entry to Universal Studios, Islands of Adventure, SeaWorld, Aquatica, and Wet 'n Wild and costs about $279 for adults and $259 for children (ages 3–9). A six-park, 14-day pass called the Orlando Flex Ticket Plus provides unlimited entry to Universal Studios, Islands of Adventure, SeaWorld, Aquatica, Wet 'n Wild, and Busch Gardens for about $320 for adults and $299 for children. The six-park ticket includes a free shuttle to Busch Gardens.

Multiday passes allow you to visit both Universal theme parks on the same day, and unused days are good indefinitely. Multiday passes also allow for early entry on select days.

The main Universal Orlando information number is ☎ 407-363-8000. Reach Guest Services at ☎ 407-224-4233, schedule a character lunch at **universalorlando.com,** and order tickets by mail at ☎ 877-247-5561. The numbers for Lost and Found are ☎ 407-224-4244 (Universal Studios) and 407-224-4245 (Islands of Adventure).

UNIVERSAL EXPRESS

DISNEY'S FASTPASS AND UNIVERSAL EXPRESS were once roughly comparable. They both offered a system whereby a guest could schedule an appointment to experience an attraction later in the day with little or no waiting. The Universal Express program is actually two programs: one for Universal hotel guests, called Universal Express, and one available to everyone for an additional fee, called Universal Express Plus. There is no longer a basic program similar to Disney's Fastpass.

If you're willing to drop the extra cash, you can upgrade your regular ticket to Universal Express Plus, which allows you to use the Express entrance one time only at each designated Universal Express attraction (although we have found that the one-time use policy is loosely enforced, except for major attractions on crowded days). Universal Express Plus is good only for the date of purchase *at one park* (though there's a more expensive two-park option) and can be used only by one person.

Universal Express Plus prices vary $20–$50, plus tax, cheaper in the off-seasons and more expensive during peak seasons and holidays. You can purchase Universal Express Plus online or at the theme park's ticket windows, just outside the front gates. Once in the Universal Studios theme park, Universal Express Plus is available at NickStuff or Sahara Traders. Inside Islands of Adventure, you can buy Universal Express Plus at Jurassic Outfitters, Toon Extra, and the Marvel Alterniverse Store. Universal Express Plus is available on the Internet up to eight months in advance. You must know what date you plan on using Universal Express Plus because different dates have different prices.

The Universal Express program for Universal resort guests allows guests to bypass the regular line anytime and as often as desired by simply showing their room keys. This perk far surpasses any perk accorded to guests of Disney resorts.

In 2010 Universal initiated a new early-entry program in conjunction with its Wizarding World of Harry Potter Exclusive Vacation Package. Purchasers of the package can enter The Wizarding World section of Islands of Adventure theme park 1 hour before the general public. As it stands the vacation package will be available until December 31, 2010, but may be extended.

IS UNIVERSAL EXPRESS PLUS WORTH IT?

THE ANSWER DEPENDS ON THE SEASON you visit, hours of park operation, and crowd levels. For the first 12–18 months The Wizarding World of Harry Potter is open, crowd levels are expected to increase dramatically at Islands of Adventure and remain steady or decline slightly at the Universal Studios Park. In the Studios, there's only one attraction—Hollywood Rip Ride Rockit, a roller coaster (not a Universal Express attraction)—that might be difficult to ride without waiting an unacceptable length of time. However, if you arrive 30 minutes before park opening and use our touring plan (see page 468), you should experience it with a minimal wait. For the Studios, therefore, you shouldn't need Universal Express Plus.

Islands of Adventure is a different story because of the hoopla surrounding Harry Potter and the lack of high-capacity theater shows at IOA to siphon off crowds (one show at IOA compared to six shows at the Studios). Using our touring plan will cut your waiting to a minimum, so our advice is to try it first. The beauty of Universal Express Plus is that you can purchase it in the park if waits for the rides become intolerable.

UNIVERSAL MEAL DEALS

AT UNIVERSAL'S ISLANDS OF ADVENTURE try the character breakfast at Confisco Grille. For $18 for those age 10 and older (age 9 and under pay $12), you can enjoy a buffet breakfast in the presence of Universal characters. A character breakfast is offered each Thursday and Sunday 9 a.m.–10:30 a.m. Character breakfast prices do not include theme-park admission. Call ☎ 407-224-4012 for reservations after purchasing your ticket. Reservations must be made at least one day prior to your visit. Tickets are nonrefundable.

ONE-PARK MEAL DEAL With your Universal Meal Deal ticket, enjoy as much food as you would like all day long at participating Meal Deal locations in one park only. Meal includes one entree platter and one dessert. Food service ends 30 minutes before theme-park closing time; children under age 9 must eat from a kid's menu. Guests will receive a wristband in exchange for the Meal Deal coupon at the first participating restaurant they visit in the park. Costs (before tax) for adults are $20, $10 for children.

TWO-PARK MEAL DEAL With your Universal Meal Deal ticket, enjoy as much food as you would like all day long at participating Meal Deal locations in both parks. Meal includes one entree platter and one dessert. Food service ends 30 minutes before theme park closing time; children under age 9 must eat from a kid's menu. Guests must order from a limited menu. Guests will receive a wristband in exchange for the Meal Deal coupon at the first participating restaurant they visit that day in either park. Costs for adults are $24 and $12 for children.

ONE-DAY MEAL DEAL SOUVENIR CUP This ticket entitles you to one day of unlimited soft-drink fountain beverages at all participating Meal Deal locations at either Universal Studios Florida OR Islands of Adventure. Cost is $8.99 for all ages.

DINNER AND A MOVIE DEAL This deal includes a ticket to any movie playing at the Universal Cineplex and a meal from a limited menu at participating CityWalk restaurants. The meal includes one entree and a coffee, tea, or soft drink. This combination costs $21.95 for all ages. Buy your Meal and Movie Deal tickets at the CityWalk Guest Services ticket window, at all Destination Universal locations, or call a CityWalk sales coordinator at ☎ 407-224-2691.

UNIVERSAL, KIDS, AND SCARY STUFF

ALTHOUGH THERE'S PLENTY for younger children to enjoy at the Universal parks, the majority of their attractions have the potential for wigging out kids less than 8 years of age. At Universal Studios Florida, forget Hollywood Rip Ride Rockit, Revenge of the Mummy, *TWISTER . . . Ride It Out, Disaster!*, JAWS, Men in Black Alien Attack, and *Terminator 2: 3-D*. The Simpsons Ride is not too scary but very intense and rough. At Universal's Islands of Adventure, watch out for The Incredible Hulk Coaster, Doctor Doom's Fearfall, The Amazing Adventures of Spider-Man, the Jurassic Park River Adventure, Harry Potter and the Forbidden Journey, Dragon

Challenge, and *Poseidon's Fury*. Popeye & Bluto's Bilge-Rat Barges is wet and wild, but younger children handle it well. Dudley Do-Right's Ripsaw Falls is a toss-up, to be considered only if your kids like water-flume rides. *The Eighth Voyage of Sindbad* stunt show includes some explosions and startling special effects, but once again, children tolerate it well. Nothing else should pose a problem.

TNA IMPACT! AND BLUE MAN GROUP

UNIVERSAL ORLANDO OFFERS theater productions that do not require theme-park admission. At Soundstage 21, guests can sit in on the taping of Spike TV's TNA iMPACT! professional-wrestling program. There is no admission for the rasslin'; a taping calendar and directions to Soundstage 21 can be found at **universalorlando.com/shows/tna-wrestling.aspx.** The minimum age required for audience members is 14 years.

Universal Studio's Sharp Aquos Theater, near CityWalk, is home to the Blue Man Group. Tickets for shows start at $64 for adults and $25 for children ages 3–9 and can be purchased online or at the Universal box office; tickets purchased at the box office are $10 higher. Upon presenting a valid International Student Identity Card, students can purchase tickets for $30. The show can be accessed from inside or outside the Universal Studios theme park. We recommend seats at least 15 rows back from the stage.

UNIVERSAL STUDIOS FLORIDA

UNIVERSAL STUDIOS FLORIDA OPENED IN JUNE 1990. At that time, it was almost four times the size of Disney's Hollywood Studios (The Studios has since expanded somewhat), with much more of the facility accessible to visitors. Like its sister facility in Hollywood, Universal Studios Florida is spacious, beautifully landscaped, meticulously clean, and delightfully varied in its entertainment. Rides are exciting and innovative and, as with many Disney rides, focus on familiar and/or beloved movie characters or situations.

Universal Studios Florida is laid out in an upside-down-L configuration. Beyond the main entrance, a wide boulevard stretches past several shows and rides to Streets of America. Branching off this pedestrian thoroughfare to the right are five streets that access other areas of the studios and intersect a promenade circling a large lake.

The park is divided into six sections: Production Central, New York, Hollywood, San Francisco–Amity, Woody Woodpecker's Kid-Zone, and World Expo. Where one section begins and another ends is blurry, but no matter. Guests orient themselves by the major rides, sets, and landmarks and refer, for instance, to New York, the waterfront, over by E.T., or by Mel's Diner. The area of Universal Studios Florida open to visitors is about the size of Epcot.

The park offers all standard services and amenities, including stroller and wheelchair rentals, lockers, diaper-changing and infant-nursing facilities, car assistance, and foreign-language assistance. Most of the park is accessible to disabled guests, and TDDs are available for the hearing impaired. Almost all services are in the Front Lot, just inside the main entrance.

DISNEY'S HOLLYWOOD STUDIOS *versus* UNIVERSAL STUDIOS FLORIDA

DISNEY'S HOLLYWOOD STUDIOS and Universal Studios Florida are direct competitors. Because both are large and expensive and they take at least one day to see, some guests must choose one park over the other. In the summer of 1999, Universal launched its second major theme park, Universal's Islands of Adventure, which competes directly with Disney's Magic

Half of Disney's Hollywood Studios is off-limits to guests—except by guided tour—while most of Universal Studios Florida is open to exploration.

Bob

Kingdom. (Universal Studios Florida theme park, Islands of Adventure theme park, the three Universal hotels, and the CityWalk complex are collectively known as Universal Orlando.)

Both Disney's Hollywood Studios and Universal Studios Florida draw their themes and inspiration from film and television. Both offer movie- and TV-themed rides and shows, some of which are just for fun, while others provide an educational, behind-the-scenes introduction to the cinematic arts.

Unlike Disney's Hollywood Studios, Universal Studios Florida's open area includes the entire back lot, where guests can walk at leisure among movie sets. Universal Studios Florida is about twice as large as the Studios, and because almost all of it is open to the public, the crowding and congestion so familiar at Disney's Hollywood Studios are largely mitigated. Universal Studios has plenty of elbowroom.

Both parks include working film and television-production studios. Guests are more likely, however, to see a movie, commercial, or television production in progress at Universal Studios than at Disney's Hollywood Studios. On most days, production crews will be shooting on the Universal back lot in full view of guests who care to watch.

Attractions are excellent at both parks, though Disney's Hollywood Studios attractions are on average engineered to move people

continued on page 372

Universal Orlando

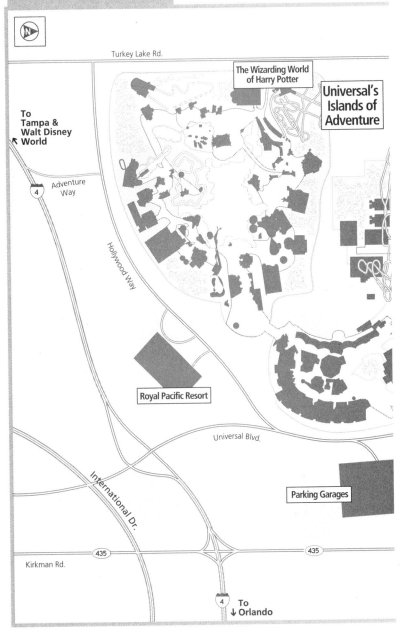

Turkey Lake Rd.

The Wizarding World
of Harry Potter

Universal's
Islands of
Adventure

To
Tampa &
Walt Disney
World

Adventure
Way

Hollywood Way

Royal Pacific Resort

Universal Blvd.

International Dr.

Parking Garages

Kirkman Rd.

To
↓ Orlando

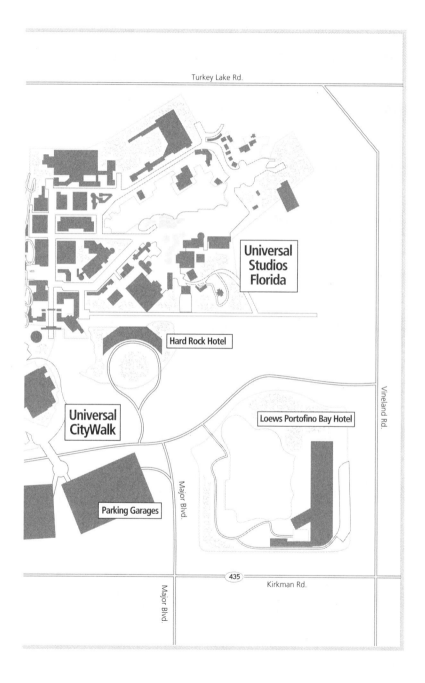

Universal Studios Florida

1. *Animal Actors on Location*
2. *Beetlejuice's Graveyard Revue*
3. *A Day in the Park with Barney*
4. *Disaster!*
5. E.T. Adventure
6. *Fear Factor Live* (open seasonally)
7. *Fievel's Playland*
8. Hollywood Rip Ride Rockit
9. JAWS
10. Jimmy Neutron's Nicktoon Blast
11. *Lucy—A Tribute*
12. Men in Black Alien Attack
13. Revenge of the Mummy
14. *Shrek 4-D*
15. The Simpsons Ride
16. *Terminator 2: 3-D*
17. *TWISTER . . . Ride It Out*
18. *Universal 360: A Cinesphere Spectacular* (summer only)
19. *Universal Orlando's Horror Make-Up Show*
20. Woody Woodpecker's Nuthouse Coaster, Curious George Goes to Town

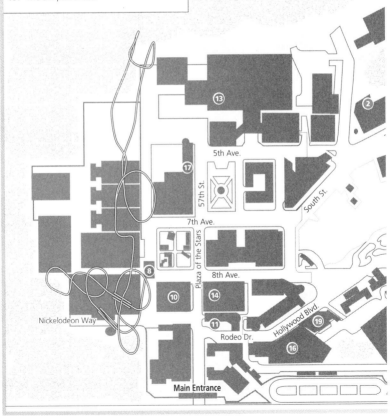

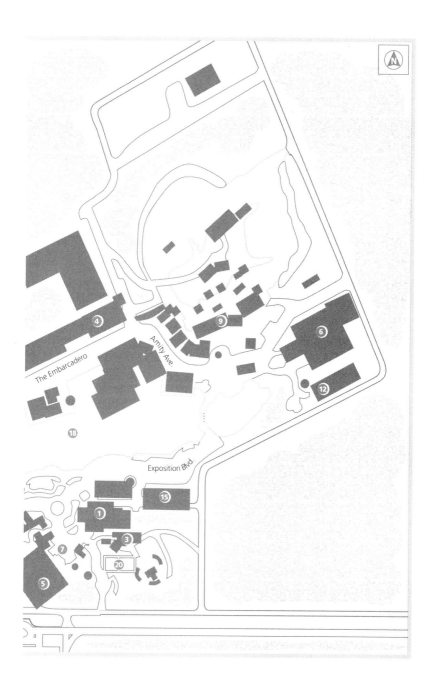

continued from page 367

more efficiently. Each park offers stellar attractions that break new ground, transcending in power, originality, and technology any prior standard for theme-park entertainment. Universal offers Revenge of the Mummy, an indoor roller coaster that combines space-age robotics with live effects and pyrotechnics; *Terminator 2: 3-D,* which we consider the most extraordinary theater attraction in any American theme park; and Men in Black Alien Attack, an interactive high-tech ride where guests' actions determine the ending of the story. The Studios features The Twilight Zone Tower of Terror, Disney's best attraction to date in our book; Rock 'n' Roller Coaster, an indoor coaster that's launched like a jet off an aircraft carrier; and Jim Henson's *Muppet-Vision 3-D,* a zany theater attraction.

Amazingly, and to the visitor's advantage, each park offers a completely different product mix, so there is little or no redundancy for a person who visits both. Disney's Hollywood Studios and Universal Studios Florida each provide good exposure to the cinematic arts. Disney's Hollywood Studios over the years has turned several of its better tours into infomercials for Disney films. At Universal, you can still learn about postproduction, soundstages, set creation, and special effects without being bludgeoned by promotional hype.

Finally the muggles completed the long-awaited Wizarding World of Harry Potter at Islands of Adventure, which opened its doors in June 2010. It will be crowded, it will be packed, and no magic will save you from the long lines unless you stay in one of the three Universal resort hotels, as the Universal Express program allows you to bypass the regular lines any time and as often as you like. Another solution, though pricier and less satisfactory, is to buy a Universal Express Plus pass, which allows you to bypass the lines, but only once per Universal Express attraction.

We recommend trying one of the studios. If you enjoy one, you'll probably enjoy the other. If you have to choose, consider the following:

1. TOURING TIME If you tour efficiently, it takes about 8–10 hours to see Disney's Hollywood Studios (including a lunch break). Because Universal Studios Florida is larger and contains more rides and shows, touring, including one meal, takes about 9–11 hours.

2. CONVENIENCE If you're lodging along International Drive, Interstate 4's northeast corridor, the Orange Blossom Trail (US 441), or in Orlando, Universal Studios Florida is closer. If you're lodging along US 27 or FL 192 or in Kissimmee or Walt Disney World, Disney's Hollywood Studios is more convenient.

3. ENDURANCE Universal Studios Florida is larger and requires more walking than Disney's Hollywood Studios, but it is also much less congested, so the walking is easier. Both parks offer wheelchairs and disabled access.

4. COST Both parks cost about the same for one-day admission, food, and incidentals, though Universal admission can be purchased in combo packages that include discounted passes to SeaWorld, Busch Gardens, and/or Wet 'n Wild. When Disney instituted the multiday Magic Your Way admission system in which you pay extra for park-hopping privileges, admissions to the minor parks, and the nonexpiring-pass option, Universal was quick to move in the opposite direction. With Universal multiday passports, all these extras are included at no extra charge. Also consider that Universal discounts its admission tickets more deeply on its Web site than does Disney.

5. BEST DAYS TO GO In order, Tuesdays, Mondays, Thursdays, and Wednesdays are best to visit Universal Studios Florida. For Disney's Hollywood Studios, see the crowd-level calendar at **touringplans.com.**

6. WHEN TO ARRIVE For Disney's Hollywood Studios, arrive with your ticket in hand 30–40 minutes before official opening time. For Universal Studios, arrive with your admission already purchased about 30 minutes before official opening time.

7. YOUNG CHILDREN Both Disney's Hollywood Studios and Universal Studios Florida are relatively adult entertainment offerings. By our reckoning, half the rides and shows at Disney's Hollywood Studios and about two-thirds at Universal Studios have a significant potential for frightening young children.

8. FOOD For counter-service food, Universal Studios has a decided edge. Disney's Hollywood Studios full-service restaurants are marginally better.

9. LOCKERS Universal has instituted a mandatory locker system at its big thrill rides. Bags and other items must be placed in lockers outside the attractions. Lockers are free for the first 45 minutes. Then, you can either pay $8 for the entire day or $2 per hour with a $14 maximum.

The locker banks are easy to find; each bank has a small computer in the center. When the sun is bright, the screen is almost impossible to read, so have someone block the sun or use a different computer. After selecting your language, press your thumb onto the keypad and have your fingerprints scanned. We've seen people walk off cursing at this step, having repeated it over and over with no success. Most patrons press their thumb down too hard. The computer cannot read your thumbprint if it's squished onto the scanner, so take a deep breath and just lightly place your thumb on the designated spot.

After your thumb scans, you will receive a locker number. Write it down! When you return from your ride, go to the same kiosk machine, enter your locker number, and scan your thumb again. At Guest Services, family-size lockers are available for $10 for the entire day, but remember that only the person who scanned his thumb can open it.

UNIVERSAL STUDIOS FLORIDA ATTRACTIONS

Animal Actors on Location (Universal Express) ★★★

APPEAL BY AGE	PRESCHOOL ★★★★	GRADE SCHOOL ★★★★	TEENS ★★★
YOUNG ADULTS ★★★		OVER 30 ★★★	SENIORS ★★★★

What it is Animal-tricks and comedy show. **Scope and scale** Major attraction. **Fright potential** Not frightening in any respect. **Bottleneck rating** 4. **When to go** After you have experienced all rides. **Authors' rating** Cute li'l critters; ★★★. **Duration of presentation** 20 minutes. **Probable waiting time** 25 minutes.

This show integrates video segments with live sketches, jokes, and animal tricks performed onstage. Live animals, some of which are veterans of television and movies, take part, and kids are invited to participate. Where else can you get the chance to hold an 8-foot albino reticulated python in your lap? Check the daily entertainment schedule for showtimes.

Successful touring of Universal Studios with young children is absolutely possible, and this show is a must-see!

Liliane

Beetlejuice's Graveyard Revue (Universal Express) ★★★½

APPEAL BY AGE	PRESCHOOL ★★★★	GRADE SCHOOL ★★★★	TEENS ★★★★
YOUNG ADULTS ★★★★		OVER 30 ★★★★	SENIORS ★★★★

What it is Rock-and-roll stage show. **Scope and scale** Almost major attraction. **Fright potential** Costumes and loud noises scare the under-7 crowd. **Bottleneck rating** 2. **When to go** At your convenience. **Authors' rating** Outrageous; ★★★½. **Duration of presentation** 18 minutes. **Probable waiting time** None.

This high-powered rock-and-roll stage show stars Beetlejuice, Frankenstein, the Bride of Frankenstein, Wolfman, and Dracula. Mercifully, this attraction is under cover. If you have small children, tell them beforehand that it is a live show with "monsters," but that they are all really very funny and totally nice, albeit a little loud. Rock on!

The show is based on the popular movie *Beetlejuice*, which won an Oscar in 1989 for Best Makeup.

Movie Tip

The Blues Brothers ★★★½

APPEAL BY AGE	PRESCHOOL ★★★	GRADE SCHOOL ★★★½	TEENS ★★★½
YOUNG ADULTS ★★★½		OVER 30 ★★★★	SENIORS ★★★★

What it is Blues concert. **Scope and scale** Diversion. **Fright potential** Not frightening in any respect. **Bottleneck rating** 1. **When to go** Scheduled show times. **Authors' rating** ★★★½. **Special comments** A party in the street. **Duration of presentation** 15 minutes.

An impromptu concert featuring live singing and saxophone playing with a background track. The concert is a great pick-me-up, and the short run-time keeps the energy high.

A Day in the Park with Barney (Universal Express) ★★★★

| APPEAL BY AGE | PRESCHOOL ★★★★★ | GRADE SCHOOL ★★★ | TEENS ★★ |
| YOUNG ADULTS ★★★ | | OVER 30 ★★★ | SENIORS ★★★ |

What it is Live character stage show. **Scope and scale** Major children's attraction. **Fright potential** Toddlers may balk at Barney's size. **Bottleneck rating** 4. **When to go** Anytime. **Authors' rating** A great hit with preschoolers; ★★★★. **Duration of presentation** 20 minutes plus preshow and character greeting. **Probable waiting time** 15 minutes.

> I love you, and you love me. This show should be a top priority if you have little ones.
>
> Liliane

Barney, the purple dinosaur of public-television fame, leads a sing-along with the help of the audience and sidekicks Baby Bop and BJ. A short preshow gets the kids lathered up before they enter Barney's Park (the theater). Interesting theatrical effects include wind, falling leaves, clouds and stars in the simulated sky, and snow. After the show, Barney exits momentarily to allow parents and children to gather along the stage. He then returns and moves from child to child, hugging each and posing for photos. If your child likes Barney, this show is a must. It's happy and upbeat, and the character greeting that follows is the best organized we've seen in any theme park. There's no line and no fighting for Barney's attention. Just relax by the rail and await your hug.

Disaster! (Universal Express) ★★★★

| APPEAL BY AGE | PRESCHOOL ★★★ | GRADE SCHOOL ★★★★ | TEENS ★★★★ |
| YOUNG ADULTS ★★★★ | | OVER 30 ★★★★ | SENIORS ★★★★ |

What it is Combination theater presentation and adventure ride. **Scope and scale** Major attraction. **Fright potential** Special effects frighten those age 8 and under. **Bottleneck rating** 7. **When to go** In the morning or late afternoon. **Special comments** May frighten young children. **Authors' rating** Shaken, not stirred; ★★★★. **Duration of ride** 20 minutes. **Loading speed** Moderate.

Scary Loud

Disaster! is a updated version of *Earthquake: The Big One.* Guests are recruited for roles in a film called *Mutha Nature,* directed by an overbearing and conceited director. After the recruiting, the audience enters a soundstage where a number of scenes are filmed starring the guests/volunteers. If you ever wondered about special effects, this is the show to see. Next, guests board a faux subway where they experience a simulated earthquake. For younger children the earthquake is pretty intense. Older kids will love it! Following the quake, while the subway returns to the station, guests view a finished cut of *Mutha Nature* that incorporates all the soundstage shots.

> Yours truly was recruited for a part in *Mutha Nature.* I am so happy that the movie is shown only once!
>
> Liliane

> Yep, I saw that movie. Liliane starred as the earthquake.
>
> Bob

E.T. Adventure (Universal Express) ★★★½

APPEAL BY AGE	PRESCHOOL ★★★★	GRADE SCHOOL ★★★★	TEENS ★★★
YOUNG ADULTS ★★★		OVER 30 ★★★★	SENIORS ★★★★

What it is Indoor adventure ride based on the *E.T.* movie. **Scope and scale** Major attraction. **Fright potential** Too intense for some preschoolers. **Bottleneck rating** 8. **When to go** Before noon; before 10 a.m. if you have small children. **Authors' rating** A happy reunion; ★★★½. **Duration of ride** 4½ minutes. **Loading speed** Moderate.

Thumbs Up for the Whole Family

Guests aboard a bicycle-like conveyance escape with E.T. from earthly law enforcement officials and then journey to E.T.'s home planet. The attraction is similar to Peter Pan's Flight at the Magic Kingdom but is longer and has more elaborate special effects. Make sure you give the attendant your name—we recommend you just state your name, don't try to spell it—and relish the end of the ride as E.T. will personalize his goodbye message. Lines build quickly after 10 a.m., and waits can be more than two hours on busy days. Ride in the morning or late afternoon.

Liliane

Very cute. Liliane wants to phone home . . .

Movie Tip

E.T. is based on Steven Spielberg's film *E.T.: The Extra-Terrestrial*—a great family movie that won four Oscars in 1982.

Fear Factor Live (Universal Express) ★★★★ (open seasonally)

APPEAL BY AGE	PRESCHOOL ½	GRADE SCHOOL ★★	TEENS ★★★★
YOUNG ADULTS ★★★		OVER 30 ★★★	SENIORS ★½

What it is Live version of the gross-out-stunt television show on NBC. **Scope and scale** Headliner. **Fright potential** Stuff of nightmares. **Bottleneck rating** 6. **When to go** 6–8 shows daily; crowds are smallest at the first and second-to-last shows. **Authors' rating** Great fun if you love the TV show; ★★★★. **Duration of presentation** 30 minutes.

Fear Factor Live is a live stage show in which up to six volunteers compete for one prize by doing dumb and yucky things like swimming with eels and eating bugs. The show is really payback for adults; adolescents will enjoy watching mom squirm during the icky parts. For children age 8 and under, *Fear Factor Live* is nightmare material. Whether you participate or simply watch, this show will keep your innards in an uproar.

Fievel's Playland ★★★★

APPEAL BY AGE	PRESCHOOL ★★★★	GRADE SCHOOL ★★★★
TEENS —	YOUNG ADULTS —	OVER 30 —	SENIORS —

What it is Children's play area with waterslide. **Scope and scale** Minor attraction. **Fright potential** Not frightening in any respect. **Bottleneck rating** 1. **When to go** Anytime. **Authors' rating** A much-needed attraction for preschoolers;

★★★★. **Probable waiting time** 20–30 minutes for the waterslide; otherwise, no waiting.

This is a great playground that features ordinary household items reproduced on a giant scale, seen as a mouse would experience them. Preschoolers and grade-schoolers can climb nets, walk through a huge boot, splash in a sardine-can fountain, seesaw on huge spoons, and climb onto a cow skull. Most of the playground is reserved for preschoolers, but a waterslide/raft ride is open to all ages. There's almost no waiting in queue here, and you can stay as long as you want. Younger children love the oversize items, and there's enough to keep teens and adults busy while little ones let off steam. The waterslide/raft ride is open to everyone but is extremely slow loading and carries only 300 riders per hour. With an average wait of 20–30 minutes, we don't think the 16-second ride is worth the trouble and, yes, you will get soaked.

Fievel's Playland is another must for a successful visit to Universal Studios with small children. The playground is themed after the 1991 Spielberg movie *Fievel Goes West*. Young children will love to identify with the tales of Fievel Mousekewitz.

Liliane

Hollywood Rip Ride Rockit ★★★★

APPEAL BY AGE	PRESCHOOL —	GRADE SCHOOL ★★★★	TEENS ★★★★½
YOUNG ADULTS ★★★★½		OVER 30 ★★★★	SENIORS ★★★½

What it is Super-high-tech roller coaster. **Scope and scale** Headliner. **Fright potential** Frightening for all ages. **Bottleneck rating** 9. **When to go** Immediately after park opening. **Special comments** Expect long waits in line; must be 51" tall to ride. **Authors' rating** ★★★★. **Duration of ride** 2½ minutes. **Average waiting time per 100 people ahead of you** 6-8 minutes. **Loading speed** Fast.

Opened in the summer of 2009, Hollywood Rip Ride Rockit has some features we've never seen before. Let's start with the basics: Rip Ride Rockit is a sit-down X-Car coaster that runs on a 3,800-foot steel track, with a maximum height of 167 feet and a top speed of 65 miles an hour. X-Car vehicles are more maneuverable than most other kinds and use less restrictive restraints, making for an exhilarating ride.

Motion Sickness   Rough

You ascend—vertically—at 11 feet per second to crest the 17-story-tall first hill, the highest point reached by any roller coaster in Orlando. The drop is almost vertical, too, and launches you into Double Take, a loop inversion in which you begin on the inside of the loop, twist to the outside at the top (so you're upright), and then twist back inside the loop for the descent. Double Take stands 136 feet tall, and its loop is 103 feet in diameter at its widest point. You next hurl (not that hurl—it comes later) into a stretch of track shaped like a musical treble clef. As on Double Take, the track configuration on Treble Clef is a first. Another innovation is Jump Cut, a spiraling negative-gravity maneuver. Usually on coasters, you experience negative gravity on long, steep vertical drops; with Jump Cut you feel like you're in a corkscrew inversion, but you never actually go upside down. Other high points include a 95-degree turn, a downhill into an "underground chasm" (gotta love those Universal PR wordsmiths!), and a final incline loop banked at 150 degrees.

The ride starts in the Production Central area; weaves into the New York area near *TWISTER*, popping out over the heads of guests in the square below; and then storms out and over the lagoon separating Universal Studios from Islands of Adventure. Each row is outfitted with color-changing LEDs and high-end audio and video technology for each seat. Like the Rock 'n' Roller Coaster at Disney's Hollywood Studios, this coaster features a musical soundtrack. With Rip Ride Rockit, however, you can choose the genre of music you want to hear as you ride: classic rock, country, disco, pop, or rap. After the ride, Universal flogs a digital-video "rip" of your ride, complete with the soundtrack you chose, that you can upload to Web sites such as YouTube.

No, Liliane, don't even ask. I'm still half-deaf from the last roller coaster I rode with you.

Bob

The incentive to try out this thingy has not been invented. Therefore, Bob, stop asking me to ride the monster. The answer is NO.

Liliane

JAWS (Universal Express) ★★★★

| APPEAL BY AGE | PRESCHOOL ★★★ | GRADE SCHOOL ★★★★ | TEENS ★★★★ |
| YOUNG ADULTS ★★★★ | | OVER 30 ★★★★ | SENIORS ★★★★ |

What it is Adventure boat ride. **Scope and scale** Headliner. **Fright potential** Frightening for all ages. **Bottleneck rating** 8. **When to go** Before 11 a.m. or after 5 p.m. **Special comments** Will frighten young children; must be 42" tall to ride. **Authors' rating** Not to be missed; ★★★★. **Duration of ride** 5 minutes. **Average waiting time per 100 people ahead of you** 3 minutes. **Assumes** All 8 boats are running. **Loading speed** Fast.

Scary   Wet

JAWS delivers 5 minutes of nonstop action, with the huge shark repeatedly attacking. The attraction builds an amazing degree of suspense. It isn't just a cruise into the middle of a pond with a scary rubber fish. People on the boat's left side tend to get splashed more. If you have young children, consider switching off (see page 238). If you want to add a little extra suspense, go for a ride after dark.

The ride is based on the 1975 Spielberg film *Jaws*.
All that panic earned him *three* Oscars!

Movie Tip

Jimmy Neutron's Nicktoon Blast ★★★ (Universal Express)

| APPEAL BY AGE | PRESCHOOL ★★★ | GRADE SCHOOL ★★★★ | TEENS ★★★ |
| YOUNG ADULTS ★★★ | | OVER 30 ★★★ | SENIORS ★★ |

What it is Cartoon science demonstration and simulation ride. **Scope and scale** Major attraction. **Fright potential** Ride is wild and jerky but not frightening.

Bottleneck rating 9. **When to go** The first hour after park opening or after 5 p.m. **Authors' rating** Incomprehensible but fun; ★★★. **Duration of ride** A little more than 4 minutes. **Average waiting time per 100 people ahead of you** 5 minutes. **Assumes** All 8 simulators in use. **Loading speed** Moderate to slow.

Motion Sickness   Rough

This ride, based on the Nickelodeon movie *Jimmy Neutron: Boy Genius,* features motion simulators that move and react in sync with a cartoon projected onto a huge screen. The attraction draws sizable crowds primarily because it's just inside the entrance and is next door to *Shrek 4-D.* Be aware that a very small percentage of riders suffer motion sickness. Stationary seating is available and is mandated for persons less than 40 inches tall.

I want Barney! The ride is OK, but if you have choices to make, this is an easy one: Skip it.

Liliane

Lucy—A Tribute ★★★

APPEAL BY AGE	PRESCHOOL ★	GRADE SCHOOL ★★	TEENS ★★
YOUNG ADULTS ★★★		OVER 30 ★★★	SENIORS ★★★

What it is Walk-through tribute to Lucille Ball. **Scope and scale** Diversion. **Fright potential** Not frightening in any respect. **Bottleneck rating** 0. **When to go** Anytime. **Authors' rating** A touching remembrance; ★★★. **Probable waiting time** None.

This museumlike exhibit spotlights the life and career of comedienne Lucille Ball. See Lucy during the hot, crowded midafternoon or on your way out of the park.

The well-deserved tribute is not for young children, and most teenagers will lack a frame of reference. As for me: "I love Lucy."

Liliane

Men in Black Alien Attack (Universal Express) ★★★★½

APPEAL BY AGE	PRESCHOOL †	GRADE SCHOOL ★★★★★	TEENS ★★★★★
YOUNG ADULTS ★★★★★		OVER 30 ★★★★★	SENIORS ★★★★

† Due to height requirement, sample size too small for an accurate rating.

What it is Interactive dark thrill ride. **Scope and scale** Super headliner. **Fright potential** Dark and intense; frightens many children age 10 and under. **Bottleneck rating** 9. **When to go** In the morning after Revenge of the Mummy. **Special comments** May induce motion sickness. Must be 42" tall to ride. Switching-off option provided (page 238). **Authors' rating** Buzz Lightyear on steroids; not to be missed; ★★★★½. **Duration of ride** 2½ minutes. **Loading speed** Moderate to fast.

Dark   Scary

Based on the movie of the same name, the story line has you volunteering as a Men in Black (MIB) trainee. After an introduction warning that aliens "live among us" and articulating MIB's mission to round them up, Zed expands on the finer points of alien spotting and familiarizes you with your training vehicle and your weapon, an alien "zapper." Following this, you load up and are dispatched on an innocuous training mission that immediately deteriorates into a situation where only you are in a position to prevent aliens from taking over the universe. Now, if you saw the movie, you understand that the aliens are mostly giant exotic bugs and cockroaches and that zapping the aliens involves exploding them into myriad, gooey body parts. Thus, the meat of the ride (no pun intended) consists of careening around Manhattan in your MIB vehicle and shooting aliens. Each of the 120 or so alien figures has sensors that activate special effects and respond to your zapper. Aim for the eyes and keep shooting until the aliens' eyes turn red. To avoid a long wait, hotfoot it to MIB immediately after riding Mummy in the first 30 minutes the park is open.

Bugs are everywhere. The ride is really fun, especially if you have seen the movie. Can't wait to go back and shoot some aliens.

Ian

Revenge of the Mummy (Universal Express) ★★★★½

APPEAL BY AGE	PRESCHOOL ★★	GRADE SCHOOL ★★★★	TEENS ★★★★★
YOUNG ADULTS ★★★★½		OVER 30 ★★★★	SENIORS ★★★½

What it is Combination dark ride and roller coaster. **Scope and scale** Super headliner. **Fright potential** Scary for all ages. **Bottleneck rating** 8. **When to go** The first hour the park is open or after 6 p.m. **Special comments** Must be 48" tall to ride. **Authors' rating** Killer! ★★★★½. **Duration of ride** 4 minutes. **Average waiting time per 100 people ahead of you** 7 minutes. **Loading speed** Moderate.

Dark Scary Motion Sickness

Revenge of the Mummy is an indoor dark ride based on the *Mummy* flicks, where guests fight off "deadly curses and vengeful creatures" while flying through Egyptian tombs and other spooky places on a high-tech roller coaster. The special effects are cutting edge, integrating the best technology from such attractions as *Terminator 2: 3-D* and Spider-Man (the ride). The ride begins slowly, passing through various chambers, including one where flesh-eating scarab beetles descend on you. Suddenly your vehicle stops, then drops backward and rotates. Next thing you know, you're shot at high speed up the first hill of the roller coaster. Though it's a wild ride by anyone's definition, the emphasis remains as much on the visuals, robotics, and special effects as on the ride itself.

The mummy scared the willies out of me. This one is definitely not for young children.

Liliane

Shrek 4-D (Universal Express) ★★★★½

APPEAL BY AGE	PRESCHOOL ★★★★	GRADE SCHOOL ★★★★★	TEENS ★★★★★
YOUNG ADULTS ★★★★★		OVER 30 ★★★★★	SENIORS ★★★★★

What it is 3-D movie. **Scope and scale** Headliner. **Fright potential** Loud but not frightening. Preshow area is a little macabre. **Bottleneck rating** 7. **When to go** The first hour the park is open or after 4 p.m. **Authors' rating** Warm, fuzzy mayhem; ★★★★½. **Duration of presentation** 20 minutes.

This attraction is a real winner. It's irreverent, frantic, laugh-out-loud funny, and iconoclastic. In contrast to Disney's *It's Tough to Be a Bug!*, *Shrek 4-D* doesn't generally frighten children under age 7.

Children under age 7 might be frightened at times. Take off the 3-D glasses if it is all too scary, and consider earplugs. Did you know that Shrek in German means "the scare"?

Liliane

The Simpsons Ride (Universal Express) ★★★★

APPEAL BY AGE	PRESCHOOL —	GRADE SCHOOL ★★★★	TEENS ★★★★
YOUNG ADULTS ★★★★		OVER 30 ★★★★	SENIORS ★★★½

What it is Mega-simulator ride. **Scope and scale** Super headliner. **Fright potential** Visuals not scary but very wild ride. **Bottleneck rating** 9. **When to go** First thing after park opening. **Special comments** Must be 40" tall to ride; not recommended for pregnant women or people prone to motion sickness. Switching-off option provided (page 238). **Authors' rating** Jimmy Neutron with attitude; ★★★★. **Duration of ride** 4⅓ minutes. **Probable waiting time** 5 minutes. **Loading speed** Moderate.

Motion Sickness

Rough

Two preshows involve Simpsons characters speaking sequentially on different video screens around the line area. Their comments help define the characters for guests who are unfamiliar with the TV show. The attraction is a simulator ride, similar to Star Tours at Disney's Hollywood Studios and Jimmy Neutron's Nicktoon Blast at Universal, but with a larger screen more like that of Soarin' at Epcot. The attraction takes a wild and humorous poke at thrill rides, dark rides, and live shows. Like the show on which it's based, The Simpsons Ride definitely has an edge— and more than a few wild hairs. Like *Shrek 4-D*, it operates on several levels. There will be jokes and visuals that you'll get but will fly over your children's heads—and most assuredly vice versa. You can expect large crowds all day.

The ride is a long way from being tame. Skip it if you're an expectant mom or prone to motion sickness. Several families we interviewed found the humor a little too adult for their younger children.

Bob

Street Scenes ★★★★★

APPEAL BY AGE	PRESCHOOL ★★★	GRADE SCHOOL ★★★★★	TEENS ★★★★★
YOUNG ADULTS ★★★★★		OVER 30 ★★★★★	SENIORS ★★★★★

What it is Elaborate outdoor sets for making films. **Scope and scale** Diversion. **Fright potential** Not frightening in any respect. **Bottleneck rating** 0. **When to go** Anytime. **Special comments** You'll see most sets without special effort as you tour the park. **Authors' rating** One of the park's great assets; ★★★★★. **Probable waiting time** No waiting.

Unlike at Disney's Hollywood Studios, all Universal Studios Florida's backlot sets are accessible for guest inspection. You'll see most as you walk through the park. Enjoy a New York City street, San Francisco's waterfront, a New England coastal town, Rodeo Drive, and Hollywood Boulevard. The sets make for great photo ops!

Terminator 2: 3-D (Universal Express) ★★★★

APPEAL BY AGE	PRESCHOOL ★★★	GRADE SCHOOL ★★★★	TEENS ★★★★
YOUNG ADULTS ★★★★★		OVER 30 ★★★★★	SENIORS ★★★★

What it is 3-D thriller mixed-media presentation. **Scope and scale** Super headliner. **Fright potential** Intense; will frighten children age 7 and under. **Bottleneck rating** 7. **When to go** After 3:30 p.m. **Special comments** The nation's best theme-park theater attraction; very intense for some preschoolers and grade-schoolers. **Authors' rating** Furiously paced high-tech experience; not to be missed; ★★★★. **Duration of presentation** 20 minutes, including an 8-minute preshow. **Probable waiting time** 20–40 minutes.

Dark   Scary   Loud

The attraction, like the films, is all action, and you really don't need to understand much. What's interesting is that it uses 3-D film and a theater full of sophisticated technology to integrate the real with the imaginary. Images seem to move in and out of the film, not only in the manner of traditional 3-D but also in actuality. Remove your 3-D glasses momentarily and you'll see that the guy on the motorcycle is actually onstage. *Terminator 2: 3-D* has been eclipsed a bit by newer attractions like Revenge of the Mummy, Hollywood Rip Ride Rockit, and The Simpsons Ride. We suggest that you save *Terminator* and other theater presentations until you have experienced all of the rides. Families with young children should know that the violence characteristic of the *Terminator* movies is largely absent from the attraction. There's suspense and action but not much blood and guts.

Idan

Greatest show ever! Saw it twice on the same day and will go back for more next time I visit. Of all the shows I've seen, this one is the most impressive ever.

TWISTER . . . Ride It Out (Universal Express) ★★★½

APPEAL BY AGE	PRESCHOOL ★★	GRADE SCHOOL ★★★★	TEENS ★★★★
YOUNG ADULTS ★★★★		OVER 30 ★★★★	SENIORS ★★★

What it is Theater presentation featuring special effects from the movie *Twister*. **Scope and scale** Major attraction. **Fright potential** Will frighten children age 7 and under. **Bottleneck rating** 7. **When to go** Should be your first show after experiencing all rides. **Special comments** High potential for frightening young children. **Authors' rating** Gusty; ★★★½. **Duration of presentation** 15 minutes. **Probable waiting time** 26 minutes.

Dark   Scary   Loud

Twister combines an elaborate set and special effects, climaxing with a five-story-tall simulated tornado created by circulating more than 2 million cubic feet of air per minute. The wind, pounding rain, and freight-train sound of the tornado are deafening, and the entire presentation is exceptionally intense. Schoolchildren are mightily impressed, while younger children are terrified and overwhelmed. Unless you want the kids hopping in your bed whenever they hear thunder, try this attraction yourself before taking your kids.

Universal Orlando's Horror Make-Up Show ★★★½ (Universal Express)

APPEAL BY AGE	PRESCHOOL ★★★	GRADE SCHOOL ★★★★	TEENS ★★★★
YOUNG ADULTS ★★★★		OVER 30 ★★★★	SENIORS ★★★★

What it is Theater presentation on the art of makeup. **Scope and scale** Major attraction. **Fright potential** Gory but not frightening. **Bottleneck rating** 6. **When to go** After you have experienced all rides. **Special comments** May upset young children. **Authors' rating** A gory knee-slapper; ★★★½. **Duration of presentation** 25 minutes. **Probable waiting time** 20 minutes.

Thumbs Up for the Whole Family

Lively, well-paced look at how makeup artists create film monsters, realistic wounds, severed limbs, and other unmentionables. Exceeding most guests' expectations, the *Horror Make-Up Show* is the sleeper attraction at Universal. Its humor and tongue-in-cheek style transcend the gruesome effects, and most folks (including preschoolers) take the blood and guts in stride. It usually isn't too hard to get into.

Universal 360: A Cinesphere Spectacular (open seasonally) ★★★½

APPEAL BY AGE	PRESCHOOL ★★★	GRADE SCHOOL ★★★★	TEENS ★★★½
YOUNG ADULTS ★★★★		OVER 30 ★★★★	SENIORS ★★★★

What it is Fireworks, lasers, and movies. **Scope and scale** Major attraction. **Fright potential** Fireworks and scary movie footage frighten preschoolers. **Bottleneck rating** 7. **When to go** 1 show a day, usually 10 minutes before park closes. **Special comments** Movie trailers galore. **Authors' rating** Good effort; ★★★½. **Duration of presentation** 10 minutes.

A nighttime spectacular presented at the Universal Studios lagoon, the presentation is a celebration of hit movies and is built around four 360-degree projection cinespheres, each 36 feet tall and 30 feet wide. The cinespheres project images relating to the chosen films, augmented by lasers and fireworks. Realize that not all of the movie clips may be suitable for young viewers. During the horror movie montage, parents may want to cover some eyes. The action movie montage is also stuffed with gunplay and gore. The ends of the lagoon are not recommended for viewing. The best spot is directly across the lagoon from Richter's Burger Co. in the San Francisco area, where the sidewalk juts out over the water. This side of the lagoon also offers the best view of the projections on the buildings and cinespheres. Scoring a viewing spot here can be very difficult. We recommend arriving at least 45 minutes ahead of time and taking turns holding the spot while the rest of your crew rides JAWS at night! *Universal 360* is presented during the summer and holiday periods.

If you want to beat the crowds out of the park after *Universal 360,* watch the show from the Mel's Diner end of the lagoon.

Bob

Woody Woodpecker's Nuthouse Coaster and Curious George Goes to Town ★★★

APPEAL BY AGE	PRESCHOOL ★★★★	GRADE SCHOOL —	TEENS —
YOUNG ADULTS —	OVER 30 —		SENIORS —

What it is Interactive playground and kid's roller coaster. **Scope and scale** Minor attraction. **Fright potential** Not frightening in any respect. **Bottleneck rating** 5. **When to go** Anytime. **Special comments** Must be 36" tall to ride coaster. **Authors' rating** A good place to turn the kids loose; ★★★.

The KidZone consists of Woody Woodpecker's Nuthouse Coaster and an interactive playground called Curious George Goes to Town. The child-size roller coaster is small enough for kids, though its moderate speed might unnerve some smaller children. The Curious George playground exemplifies the Universal obsession with wet stuff; in addition to innumerable spigots, pipes, and spray guns, two giant roof-mounted buckets periodically dump *a thousand gallons* of water on unsuspecting visitors below. Kids who want to stay dry can mess around in the foam-ball playground, also equipped with chutes, tubes, and ball-blasters. The playground is creatively designed and a great place for kids to cut loose after being in tow all day.

Have the kids wear a bathing suit under their clothes so they can enjoy the water features. Simpler still, let the 4-and-unders frolic in their underwear (bring an extra pair).

Liliane

LIVE ENTERTAINMENT *at* UNIVERSAL STUDIOS

IN ADDITION TO THE SHOWS profiled above, Universal offers a wide range of street entertainment. Costumed comic-book and cartoon characters (Shrek, Donkey, SpongeBob SquarePants, Woody Woodpecker) roam the park for photo ops, along with movie star look-alikes, plus the Frankenstein monster, who can be said to be neither. The handout park map has a section called "Character Zones" that provides times and places for character appearances and shows.

Musical acts include Blues Brothers impersonators dancing and singing in the New York section of the park.

UNIVERSAL STUDIOS FLORIDA TOURING PLAN

UNIVERSAL STUDIOS FLORIDA ONE-DAY TOURING PLAN FOR FAMILIES

THIS PLAN IS FOR FAMILIES. If a ride or show is listed that you don't want to experience, skip that step and proceed to the next. Move quickly from attraction to attraction and, if possible, don't stop for lunch until after Step 9. Minor street shows occur at various times and places throughout the day; check the daily schedule for details. The actual touring plan in clip-out version with a map is on page 467. The touring plan is geared toward the whole family. Because there are so many attractions with the potential to frighten young children, be prepared to skip a few things and to practice switching off (works the same way as at Walt Disney World). For the most part, attractions designed especially for young children, such as playgrounds, can be enjoyed anytime. Work them into the plan at your convenience.

UNIVERSAL'S ISLANDS
of ADVENTURE

WHEN UNIVERSAL'S ISLANDS OF ADVENTURE theme park opened in 1999, it provided Universal with enough critical mass to actually compete with Disney. Universal finally has on-site hotels, a shopping and entertainment complex, and two major theme parks. Doubly interesting is that Islands of Adventure is pretty much just for fun—in other words, a direct competitor to Disney's Magic Kingdom, the most visited theme park in the world.

Disney and Universal officially downplay their fierce competition, pointing out that any new theme park or attraction makes central Florida a more marketable destination. Behind closed doors, however, it's a Pepsi versus Coke–type rivalry that will keep both companies working hard to gain a competitive edge. The good news, of course, is that all this translates into better and better attractions for you to enjoy.

The year 2010 is Islands of Adventure's year. In one of the greatest seismic shifts in theme-park history, Universal secured the rights to build a Harry Potter theme area within the park. This is proving to be a competitive game changer. Harry Potter is possibly the only character extant capable of trumping Mickey Mouse, and Universal has gone all out (under author J. K. Rowling's watchful and very particular eye) to create a setting and attractions designed to be the envy of the industry.

If you're having trouble sizing up how big a deal The Wizarding World is, you need only to check the discussion boards of any Web site associated with Orlando, theme parks, Harry Potter, Daniel Radcliffe, J. K. Rowling, or dozens of other tenuously related topics. What you're likely to see is a billion or so postings like this:

> OMG!!!!!!!!!!!! I CAN'T WAIT!!!!!!!!!! I LOVE Harry Potter SOOOOOOOO much you wouldn't BELIEVE!!!!!!!!!!!!!!!!!! I was just looking for Harry Potter stuff and I saw a link to this!! I am so EXCITED!!!!

CHOICES

WHEN IT COMES TO TOURING IOA efficiently, you have two basic choices, and as you might expect, there are trade-offs. The Wizarding World of Harry Potter sucks up guests like a Hoover vacuum. If you're intent on experiencing the Harry Potter and the Forbidden Journey ride without suffering 1–2 hours in line, you need to be at the turnstiles waiting to be admitted at least 1 hour before the park opens. Once admitted, move as swiftly as possible to Wizarding World and ride Forbidden Journey and Dragon Challenge in that order. If you can knock off these two attractions in about an hour or so, you'll find much of the remainder of the park sparsely populated. If you take this route, finish up the two attractions and then head for the other less crowded parts of the park. Come back to Wizarding World later in the day to explore Hogsmeade.

A second option is to blow off Potterville and enjoy the attractions in the other theme areas. You'll still be able to visit The Wizarding World later in the day but probably won't be able to experience the attractions there without exceedingly long waits. If you can't be on hand at park opening, the second option is recommended.

BEWARE OF THE WET AND WILD

ALTHOUGH WE HAVE DESCRIBED Universal's Islands of Adventure as a direct competitor to the Magic Kingdom, there is one major qualification you should be aware of. Whereas most Magic Kingdom attractions are designed to be enjoyed by guests of any age, attractions at Islands of Adventure are largely created for an under-40 population. The roller coasters at Universal are serious with a capital S, making Space Mountain and Big Thunder Mountain look about as tough as Dumbo. In fact, seven out of the nine top attractions at Islands are thrill rides, and of these, there are three that not only scare the bejeebers out of you but also drench you with water.

Consider yourself warned: Several attractions at Islands of Adventure will drench you to the bone.

Liliane

For families, there are three interactive playgrounds, as well as six rides that young children will enjoy. Of the thrill rides, only the two in Toon Lagoon (described later) are marginally appropriate for young children, and even on these rides your child needs to be fairly stalwart.

Roller coasters at Islands of Adventure are the real deal— not for the timid or for little ones.

Bob

GETTING ORIENTED AT ISLANDS OF ADVENTURE

BOTH UNIVERSAL THEME PARKS are accessed via the Universal CityWalk entertainment complex. Crossing CityWalk from the parking garages, you can bear right to Universal Studios Florida or left to Universal's Islands of Adventure.

Islands of Adventure is arranged much like Epcot's World Showcase is—in a large circle surrounding a lake. Unlike Epcot, however, the Islands of Adventure areas evidence the sort of thematic continuity pioneered by Disneyland and the Magic Kingdom. Each land, or island in this case, is self-contained and visually consistent in its theme, although you can see parts of the other islands across the lake.

You first encounter the Moroccan-style Port of Entry, where you'll find Guest Services, lockers, stroller and wheelchair rentals, ATM banking, lost and found, and shopping. From the Port of Entry, moving clockwise around the lake, you can access Marvel Super Hero Island, Toon Lagoon, Jurassic Park, The Wizarding World of Harry Potter, the Lost Continent, and Seuss Landing.

ISLANDS *of* ADVENTURE ATTRACTIONS

MARVEL SUPER HERO ISLAND

THIS ISLAND, WITH ITS FUTURISTIC AND RETRO-FUTURE design and comic-book signage, offers shopping and attractions based on Marvel Comics characters.

The Amazing Adventures of Spider-Man ★★★★★ (Universal Express)

APPEAL BY AGE	PRESCHOOL ★★★	GRADE SCHOOL ★★★★★	TEENS ★★★★★
YOUNG ADULTS ★★★★★		OVER 30 ★★★★★	SENIORS ★★★★

What it is Indoor adventure simulator ride based on Spider-Man. **Scope and scale** Super headliner. **Fright potential** Intense; kids tall enough to ride usually take it in stride. **Bottleneck rating** 9. **When to go** Before 10 a.m. **Special comments** Must be 40" tall to ride. **Authors' rating** One of the best attractions anywhere; ★★★★★. **Duration of ride** 4½ minutes. **Loading speed** Fast.

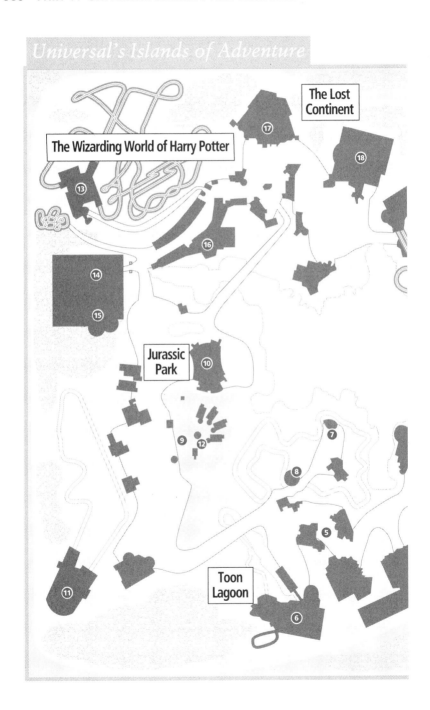

Universal's Islands of Adventure

The Lost Continent

The Wizarding World of Harry Potter

Jurassic Park

Toon Lagoon

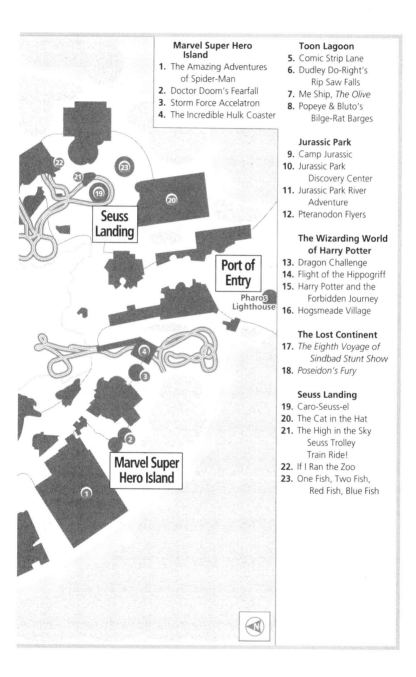

Marvel Super Hero Island
1. The Amazing Adventures of Spider-Man
2. Doctor Doom's Fearfall
3. Storm Force Accelatron
4. The Incredible Hulk Coaster

Toon Lagoon
5. Comic Strip Lane
6. Dudley Do-Right's Rip Saw Falls
7. Me Ship, *The Olive*
8. Popeye & Bluto's Bilge-Rat Barges

Jurassic Park
9. Camp Jurassic
10. Jurassic Park Discovery Center
11. Jurassic Park River Adventure
12. Pteranodon Flyers

The Wizarding World of Harry Potter
13. Dragon Challenge
14. Flight of the Hippogriff
15. Harry Potter and the Forbidden Journey
16. Hogsmeade Village

The Lost Continent
17. *The Eighth Voyage of Sindbad Stunt Show*
18. *Poseidon's Fury*

Seuss Landing
19. Caro-Seuss-el
20. The Cat in the Hat
21. The High in the Sky Seuss Trolley Train Ride!
22. If I Ran the Zoo
23. One Fish, Two Fish, Red Fish, Blue Fish

Dark   Scary   Rough

Covering one-and-a-half acres and combining moving ride vehicles, 3-D film, and live action, Spider-Man is frenetic, fluid, and astounding. The visuals are rich, and the ride is wild but not jerky. Spider-Man is technologically on a par with Disney's Hollywood Studios' Tower of Terror, which is to say that it will leave you in awe. Ride as early in the morning as possible or in the hour before closing.

Idan

An absolute must. Soar above buildings without ever leaving the ground! Kudos to Universal, this is the ultimate deception, and I loved every turn. Must ride several times to take in all the details. And do hold on to your personal belongings, as I managed to lose my room key (still wondering how I did it).

Doctor Doom's Fearfall (Universal Express) ★★★

APPEAL BY AGE	PRESCHOOL —	GRADE SCHOOL ★★★	TEENS ★★★★
YOUNG ADULTS ★★★★		OVER 30 ★★★	SENIORS —

What it is Lunch liberator. **Scope and scale** Headliner. **Fright potential** Frightening for all ages. **Bottleneck rating** 10. **When to go** Before 9:15 a.m. **Special comments** Must be 52" tall to ride. **Authors' rating** More bark than bite; ★★★. **Duration of ride** 40 seconds. **Loading speed** Slow.

Scary   Lose Things

Here you are strapped into a seat with your feet dangling, blasted 200 feet up in the air, and then allowed to partially free-fall back down. We've seen glaciers that move faster than the line to Doctor Doom. If you want to ride without investing half a day, be one of the first in the park to ride.

This attraction is best experienced with your mother right next to you. Hold her hand for personal comfort (it makes you look good too) and brace for her expression of absolute terror.

Ian

The Incredible Hulk Coaster (Universal Express) ★★★★½

APPEAL BY AGE	PRESCHOOL ★	GRADE SCHOOL ★★★★★	TEENS ★★★★★
YOUNG ADULTS ★★★★		OVER 30 ★★★★	SENIORS ★★★

What it is Roller coaster. **Scope and scale** Super headliner. **Fright potential** Frightening for all ages. **Bottleneck rating** 10. **When to go** Before 9:30 a.m. **Special comments** Must be 54" tall to ride. **Authors' rating** A coaster-lover's coaster; ★★★★½. **Duration of ride** 2¼ minutes. **Loading speed** Moderate.

Scary   Motion Sickness   Lose Things

The Hulk is a great roller coaster, one of the best in Florida, providing a ride comparable to Montu (Busch Gardens) with the added thrill of an accelerated launch (instead of the more typical uphill crank). Plus, like Montu, this coaster has a smooth ride. The Hulk gives Dragon Challenge a run as the park's most popular coaster. Ride first thing in the morning.

Unfortunately, Liliane lost her very polite European ways at about 100 decibels. My ears hurt for days

You know who made me ride it, and for the duration of the ride I did lose my very polite European ways. .

Liliane

Storm Force Accelatron (Universal Express) ★★★

What it is Indoor spinning ride. **Scope and scale** Minor attraction. **Fright potential** Nauseating but not frightening. **Bottleneck rating** 9. **When to go** Before 10:30 a.m. **Special comments** May induce motion sickness. **Authors' rating** Teacups in the dark; ★★★. **Duration of ride** 1½ minutes. **Loading speed** Slow.

Storm Force is a spiffed-up indoor version of Disney's nausea-inducing Mad Tea Party. Ride early or late to avoid long lines. Skip it if you're prone to motion sickness.

Dark   Motion Sickness

TOON LAGOON

TOON LAGOON IS CARTOON ART TRANSLATED into real buildings and settings. Whimsical and gaily colored, with rounded and exaggerated lines, Toon Lagoon is Universal's answer to Mickey's Toontown Fair in the Magic Kingdom. The main difference between the two toon lands is that (as you will see) you have about a 60% chance of drowning at Universal's version.

Comic Strip Lane

What it is Walk-through exhibit and shopping and dining venue. **Scope and scale** Diversion. **Fright potential** Not frightening in any respect. **Bottleneck rating** 0. **When to go** Anytime.

This is the main street of Toon Lagoon. Here you can visit the domains of Beetle Bailey, Hagar the Horrible, Krazy Kat, the Family Circus, and Blondie and Dagwood, among others of whom your kids have never heard. Shops and eateries tie into the cartoon strip theme. This is a great place for photo ops with cartoon characters.

Dudley Do-Right's Ripsaw Falls ★★★½ (Universal Express)

What it is Flume ride. **Scope and scale** Major attraction. **Fright potential** The big drop frightens guests of all ages. **Bottleneck rating** 8. **When to go** Before 11 a.m. **Special comments** Must be 44" tall to ride. **Authors' rating** A minimalist Splash Mountain; ★★★½. **Duration of ride** 5 minutes. **Loading speed** Moderate.

Scary Wet

Inspired by the *Rocky and Bullwinkle* cartoons, this ride features Canadian Mountie Dudley Do-Right as he attempts to save Nell from evil Snidely Whiplash. Story line aside, it's a flume ride, with the inevitable big drop at the end. Universal claims this is the first flume ride to "send riders plummeting 15 feet below the surface of the water." In reality, though, you're just plummeting into a tunnel. This ride will get you wet, but on average not as wet as you might expect (it looks worse than it is). If you want to stay dry, however, arrive prepared with a poncho or at least a big garbage bag with holes cut out for your head and arms. While younger children are often intimidated by the big drop, those who ride generally enjoy themselves. Ride first thing in the morning after experiencing the Marvel Super Hero rides.

Liliane

Small children will be intimidated by the big drop. Try Popeye & Bluto's Bilge-Rat Barges first.

Bob

Right, Liliane. Popeye & Bluto's Bilge-Rat Barges is perfect for small children . . . as long as they have wet suits and life jackets.

Me Ship, *The Olive* ★★★

APPEAL BY AGE	PRESCHOOL ★★★★		GRADE SCHOOL ★★★★
TEENS ½	YOUNG ADULTS ½	OVER 30 ½	SENIORS —

What it is Interactive playground. **Scope and scale** Minor attraction. **Fright potential** Not frightening in any respect. **Bottleneck rating** 4. **When to go** Anytime. **Authors' rating** Colorful and appealing for kids; ★★★.

The Olive is Popeye's three-story boat come to life as an interactive playground. Younger children can scramble around in Swee'Pea's Playpen, while older sibs shoot water cannons at riders trying to survive the adjacent Bilge-Rat raft ride. If you're into the big rides, save this for later in the day.

Popeye & Bluto's Bilge-Rat Barges ★★★★ (Universal Express)

APPEAL BY AGE	PRESCHOOL ★★★	GRADE SCHOOL ★★★★★	TEENS ★★★★
YOUNG ADULTS ★★★★		OVER 30 ★★★★	SENIORS ★★★

What it is White-water raft ride. **Scope and scale** Major attraction. **Fright potential** Ride is wild and wet but not frightening. **Bottleneck rating** 8. **When to go** Before 10:30 a.m. **Special comments** Must be 42" tall to ride. **Authors' rating** Bring your own soap; ★★★★. **Duration of ride** 4½ minutes. **Loading speed** Moderate.

Rough Wet

This white-water raft ride for the whole family is engineered to ensure that everyone gets drenched; the ride even provides water cannons for highly intelligent nonparticipants ashore to fire at those aboard. The rapids are rougher and more interesting, and the ride longer, than the Animal Kingdom's Kali River Rapids. If you didn't drown on Dudley Do-Right, here's a second chance.

Remember you will get wet. It is OK on a hot summer day, unless it's first thing in the morning. Now is the time to use the rain gear or plastic bags to protect yourselves. Most important, keep your footwear dry. Put your shoes in a locker and ride barefoot.

Liliane

JURASSIC PARK

JURASSIC PARK (FOR ANYONE WHO'S BEEN ASLEEP for 20 years) is a Steven Spielberg film franchise about a fictitious theme park with real dinosaurs. Jurassic Park at Universal's Islands of Adventure is a real theme park (or at least a section of one) with fictitious dinosaurs.

Camp Jurassic ★★★

APPEAL BY AGE	PRESCHOOL ★★★		GRADE SCHOOL ★★★
TEENS —	YOUNG ADULTS —	OVER 30 —	SENIORS —

What it is Interactive play area. **Scope and scale** Minor attraction. **Fright potential** Not frightening in any respect. **Bottleneck rating** 3. **When to go** Anytime. **Authors' rating** Creative playground, confusing layout; ★★★.

Camp Jurassic is a great place for children to run and explore. Sort of a Jurassic version of Tom Sawyer Island, kids can explore lava pits, caves, mines, and a rain forest.

Very small children should not be left to explore this place alone, as they will get lost inside the playground and might get very scared. Kids over age 8 are guaranteed an adventure and lots of fun. I loved the playground and regret that due to my height I was not allowed on the pteranodon whatchamacallit.

Ian

Jurassic Park Discovery Center ★★★

APPEAL BY AGE	PRESCHOOL ★★★	GRADE SCHOOL ★★★★	TEENS ★★★
YOUNG ADULTS ★★★		OVER 30 ★★★	SENIORS ★★★

What it is Interactive natural history exhibit. **Scope and scale** Minor attraction. **Fright potential** Not frightening in any respect. **Bottleneck rating** 3. **When to go** Anytime. **Authors' rating** ★★★.

The Discovery Center is an interactive, educational exhibit that mixes fiction from the movie *Jurassic Park,* such as using fossil DNA to bring dinosaurs to life, with various skeletal remains and other paleontological displays. Cycle back after experiencing all the rides or on a second day. Most folks can digest this exhibit in 10–15 minutes.

Don't skip the Discovery Center. On a hot summer day, it is a great place to cool off. The best exhibit of all is the one where an animatronic raptor hatches from an egg. Young children will delight in the hatching and are afforded an opportunity to name the baby dino.

Liliane

Jurassic Park River Adventure ★★★★ (Universal Express)

APPEAL BY AGE	PRESCHOOL ★★★	GRADE SCHOOL ★★★★★	TEENS ★★★★★
YOUNG ADULTS ★★★★		OVER 30 ★★★★	SENIORS ★★★★

What it is Indoor-outdoor adventure river-raft ride based on the *Jurassic Park* movies. **Scope and scale** Super headliner. **Fright potential** Visuals and big drop frighten guests of all ages. **Bottleneck rating** 9. **When to go** Before 11 a.m. **Special comments** Must be 42" tall to ride. **Authors' rating** Better than its Hollywood cousin; ★★★★. **Duration of ride** 6½ minutes. **Loading speed** Fast.

Scary

Guests board boats for a water tour of Jurassic Park. Everything is tranquil as the tour begins, then, as word is received that some of the carnivores have escaped their enclosure, the tour boat is accidentally diverted into Jurassic Park's maintenance facilities. Here, the boat and its riders are menaced by an assortment of hungry meat-eaters. At the climactic moment, the boat and its passengers escape by plummeting over an 85-foot drop. Young children must endure a double whammy on this ride. First, they are stalked by giant, salivating (sometimes spitting) reptiles, and then they're sent catapulting over the falls. Unless your children are fairly stalwart, wait a year or two before you spring the River Adventure on them.

Pteranodon Flyers ½

APPEAL BY AGE	PRESCHOOL ★★★	GRADE SCHOOL ★★★	TEENS ★
YOUNG ADULTS ★★		OVER 30 ★	SENIORS ★★

What it is Slow as Christmas. **Scope and scale** Minor attraction. **Fright potential** Not frightening in any respect. **Bottleneck rating** 10. **When to go** When there's no line. **Authors' rating** All sizzle, no steak; ½. **Duration of ride** 1 minute and 25 seconds. **Loading speed** Slower than a hog in quicksand.

This ride swings you along a track that passes over a small part of Jurassic Park. We recommend that you skip this one. Why? Because the Jurassic period will probably end before you reach the front of the line! And your reward for all that waiting? A 1-minute-and-15-second ride. Plus, the attraction has a name that nobody over 12 years old can pronounce.

THE LOST CONTINENT

THIS AREA IS AN EXOTIC MIX of Silk Road bazaar and ancient ruins, with Greco-Moroccan accents. (And you thought your decorator was nuts.) This is the land of mythical gods, fabled beasts, and expensive souvenirs.

The Eighth Voyage of Sindbad (Universal Express) ★★

APPEAL BY AGE	PRESCHOOL ★★★	GRADE SCHOOL ★★★★	TEENS ★★★
YOUNG ADULTS ★★★		OVER 30 ★★★	SENIORS ★★★

What it is Theater stunt show. **Scope and scale** Major attraction. **Fright potential** Special effects startle preschoolers. **Bottleneck rating** 4. **When to go** Anytime as per the daily entertainment schedule. **Authors' rating** Not inspiring; ★★. **Duration of presentation** 17 minutes. **Probable waiting time** 15 minutes.

A story about Sindbad the Sailor is the glue that (loosely) binds this stunt show featuring water explosions, 10-foot-tall circles of flame, and various other daunting eruptions and perturbations. It's billed as a stunt show, but the production is so vacuous and redundant that it's hard to get into the action. See *Sindbad* after you've experienced the rides and the better-rated shows. The theater seats 1,700.

Not to be missed is the Mystic Fountain at the entrance to the theater. The fountain may not grant you wishes, but it will talk to you. But watch out, it's a fountain with attitude. Keep your umbrella handy.

Liliane

Poseidon's Fury (Universal Express) ★★★★

APPEAL BY AGE	PRESCHOOL ★★	GRADE SCHOOL ★★★★	TEENS ★★★★
YOUNG ADULTS ★★★★		OVER 30 ★★★★	SENIORS ★★★★

What it is High-tech theater attraction. **Scope and scale** Headliner. **Fright potential** Intense visuals and special effects frighten some preschoolers. **Bottleneck rating** 7. **When to go** After experiencing all the rides. **Special comments** Audience stands throughout. **Authors' rating** Much improved; ★★★★. **Duration of presentation** 17 minutes, including preshow. **Probable waiting time** 25 minutes.

The Greek god Poseidon tussles with an evil wizardish guy using fire, water, lasers, smoke machines, and angry lemurs (*Note:* Lemurs are not actually used—just seeing if you're paying attention). The plot unravels in installments as you pass from room to room and finally into the main theater preshow. There's some great technology at work here. *Poseidon* is by far and away the best of the Islands of Adventure theater attractions. Frequent explosions and noise may frighten younger children, so exercise caution with preschoolers. We recommend catching *Poseidon* after experiencing your fill of the rides.

THE WIZARDING WORLD OF HARRY POTTER

IN WHAT MAY PROVE TO BE the competitive coup of all time between archrivals Disney and Universal, the latter inked a deal with Warner Brothers Entertainment to create a fully immersive Harry Potter–themed environment based on the best-selling children's books by J. K. Rowling and the companion blockbuster movies from Warner Brothers. The project was blessed by Rowling, who is known for tenaciously protecting the integrity of her work. In the case of the films, she demanded that Warner Brothers be true, almost to an unprecedented degree, to the books on which the films were based. She had many suitors over the years vie for the rights to translate her novels into a theme park, but she never consented until now.

The 20-acre Wizarding World draws its inspiration from all the Harry Potter movies and books, creating an amalgamation of landmarks, sights, creatures, and themes that are faithful to the films. The Wizarding World is situated in the northwest corner of the park between The Lost Continent and Jurassic Park. Let's begin our exploration at Wizarding World's main entrance on the Lost Continent side of the theme area.

Bob

The Wizarding World will suck up guests like a vacuum on steroids. This means, among other things, that crowds will be considerably lighter in other sections of Islands of Adventure, especially in the morning.

Passing beneath a stone archway, you enter the village of **Hogsmeade.** The **Hogwarts Express** locomotive sits belching steam on your right, and the village, depicted in winter, stretches before you, following the contours of a gently curving street. While decidedly different and visually rich, the winter thing seems like a stretch in the dog days of August. On your left opposite the locomotive and train station is **Zonko's,** a joke and novelty shop specializing in such necessities as shrunken heads, extendable ears, and screaming yo-yos. If your sweet tooth is on a rampage, the shop also sells sweets such as Fever Fudge, Nosebleed Nougat, and our personal favorite, Puking Pastilles. Connected to Zonko's through an interior passage is **HoneyDukes**. For those whose appetite has recovered from disgorging their Puking Pastilles, HoneyDukes—specializing in Acid Pops, Exploding Bonbons, and Fizzing Whizbees—offers another opportunity to expand your midriff.

Across the street from HoneyDukes next to the train station is the entrance to the Dragon Challenge dueling roller coasters. Next door to HoneyDukes and set back from the main street is the **Three Broomsticks,** a rustic tavern serving English staples such as fish and chips, shepherd's pie, Cornish pastry, and turkey legs. A children's menu includes standards such as mac and cheese and the obligatory chicken fingers. The Three Broomsticks is also a good, albeit expensive, venue for ice cream and dessert treats. Adjacent to the restaurant is the **Hog's Head** pub with a nice selection of beer, as well as The Wizarding World's signature nonalcoholic beverage, butterbeer. Except for some meager snacks from vendor carts, no other hot food or sandwiches are available in The Wizarding World. In the summer of 2010 Universal would not let you back in if you exited Wizarding World, informing you that to reenter you'd have to go to the end of the queue waiting to enter Wizarding World through Jurassic Park. This policy left most guests without a practical alternative for getting something to eat. Also the Three Broomsticks doesn't participate in any of Universal's meal plans.

Down the street from the Hog's Head are restrooms. Roughly across the street from the pub, you'll find benches in the shade at the **Owlery,** where animatronic owls (complete with owl poop) ruffle and hoot from the rafters.

Next to the Owlery is the **Owl Post,** a functioning post office where any postcards you mail will be delivered with a Hogsmeade postmark. The Owl Post also sells stationery, toy owls, and the like. To access the Owl Post enter through an interior door following the wand-choosing demonstration at **Ollivanders** (see below) or through **Dervish and Banges,** a magical supplies and equipment shop, which is interconnected with the Owl Post. The Owl Post front door is used exclusively as an exit. Because it's so difficult to get into the Owl Post, Universal sometimes stations a team member outside to stamp your postcards with The Wizarding World postmark.

Next to the Owl Post is the above-mentioned Ollivanders magic wand shop. Here, following a script from the Potter books, you can buy a wand. You can pick it out yourself, or in an interactive experience, a wand will choose you. This is one of the most truly imaginative elements of The Wizarding World. The store is musty and stacked to the ceiling with boxes of wands. A wand keeper sizes you up and presents a wand, inviting you to try it out. Naturally your attempted spells produce unintended, unwanted, and very amusing consequences. The experience is delightful, but the tiny shop can accommodate only about 24 guests at a time. Usually only one person in each group goes through the process of being chosen by a wand, and then the whole group is dispatched to the Owl Post and Dervish and Banges to actually make purchases. Wands run upwards of $19 with most in the $28–$38 range. If Ollivanders is a priority, experience it first thing in the morning or after 7:30 p.m. Average wait time during summer and other busy periods is 45–85 minutes 9:30 a.m.–7:30 p.m.

At the far end of the village is the massive **Hogwarts Castle,** set atop a rock face and towering over Hogsmeade and the entire Wizarding World. Follow the path through the gates of Hogwarts to the Harry Potter and the Forbidden Journey attraction. To the right of the castle and at the base of the cliff are the Forbidden Forest, Hagrid's Hut, and the Flying Hippogriff children's roller coaster. Located in the village near the gate to Hogwarts Castle is **Filch's Emporium of Confiscated Goods.** The shop offers all manner of Potter-themed gifts and apparel, including Quidditch clothing, magical creature toys, film-based chess sets, and of course, Death Eater masks (breath mints extra). Because the shops are so jammed, Universal sells some merchandise, including wands, through street vendors. Wizarding World items are also for sale in Port of Entry shops.

Dragon Challenge (Universal Express) ★★★★½

APPEAL BY AGE	PRESCHOOL —	GRADE SCHOOL ★★★★	TEENS ★★★★
YOUNG ADULTS ★★★★		OVER 30 ★★★★	SENIORS ★★

What it is Roller coaster. **Scope and scale** Headliner. **Fright potential** Frightening to guests of all ages. **Bottleneck rating** 4. **When to go** After Harry Potter and the Forbidden Journey. **Special comments** Must be 54" tall to ride. **Authors' rating** As good as the Hulk coaster; ★★★★½. **Duration of ride** 2½ minutes. **Loading speed** Moderate.

This high-tech coaster launches two trains, the Chinese Fireball and the Hungarian Horntail, at the same time on tracks that are closely intertwined. Each track is configured differently so that you get a different experience on each. A collision with the other train sometimes seems imminent—a catastrophe that seems all the more real because the coasters are suspended from above so that you sit with your feet dangling. At times the two trains and their passengers are separated by a mere 12 inches. Because this is an inverted coaster, your view of the action is limited unless you're sitting in the front row. This means that most passengers miss seeing all these near collisions. Dragon Challenge is the highest coaster in the park and also claims the longest drop at 115 feet, not to mention five inversions.

Dragon Challenge, formerly Dueling Dragons, was renamed and incorporated into the new Wizarding World of Harry Potter in 2010. The story line is that you are preparing to compete in the Tri-Wizard Tournament (from *Harry Potter and the Goblet of Fire*). As you wind through the long, long queue, you pass through tournament tents and dark passages. You'll see the Goblet of Fire on display and hear the distant roar of the crowd in the supposed stadium above you.

We prefer the front row on either train, but coaster loonies hype the front row of Chinese Fireball and the last row of Hungarian Horntail. If you don't have time to ride both coasters, the *Unofficial* crew unanimously prefers the Hungarian Horntail.

Flight of the Hippogriff (Universal Express) ★★½

APPEAL BY AGE	PRESCHOOL ★★★★		GRADE SCHOOL ★★★★
TEENS ★★	YOUNG ADULTS ★★	OVER 30 ★	SENIORS ★

What it is Children's roller coaster. **Scope and scale** Minor attraction. **Fright potential** Frightens a small percentage of preschool riders. **Bottleneck rating** 5. **When to go** First 90 minutes the park is open. **Special comments** Must be 36" tall to ride. **Authors' rating** A good beginner coaster; ★★½. **Duration of ride** 1 minute. **Loading speed** Slow.

Previously called the Flying Unicorn, the coaster underwent a name and theme change when it was incorporated into The Wizarding World. Located below and to the right of Hogwarts Castle next to Hagrid's Hut, the Hippogriff is short and sweet but not worth much of a wait. Fortunately, waits usually don't exceed 20 minutes, even in the non-Express line. Have your children ride soon after the park opens, while older sibs enjoy Dragon Challenge. Even if you don't ride, it's worth a stroll down to see Hogwarts Castle from the cliff bottom and to check out Hagrid's Hut situated above the path for the regular line.

Harry Potter and the Forbidden Journey ★★★★½

APPEAL BY AGE	PRESCHOOL −	GRADE SCHOOL ★★★★	TEENS ★★★★★
YOUNG ADULTS ★★★★	OVER 30 ★★★★★	SENIORS ★★★★★	

What it is Motion simulator dark ride. **Scope and scale** Super headliner. **Fright potential** Intense special effects and wild ride. **Bottleneck rating** Off the chart. **When to go** Immediately after park opening or after 8 p.m. The ride has a Universal Express line, but for the time being, it is not being used. **Special comments** Expect *long* waits in line; must be 48" tall to ride. The seats are designed for certain body types. Sample seats are at the beginning of the queue, and just before the boarding area is a bench with four fully functional seats. To ride, the overhead restraint has to click three times. If you don't pass muster, you'll be escorted to a place where you can wait for the rest of your party. **Authors' rating** ★★★½. **Duration of ride** 4⅓ minutes. **Loading speed** Moderate.

This attraction is the big banana of The Wizarding World and provides the only opportunity to actually come in contact with the Harry Potter characters. Half of the attraction is a series of preshows that sets the stage for the main event, a dark ride. To understand the story line and get the most out of the attraction, it's critical to see and hear the entire presentation in each of the queue's preshow rooms. You can get on the ride in only 10–20 minutes using the single-riders line, but everyone should go through the main queue at least once. If you see a complete iteration of each of the preshows in the queue and then experience the 4⅓-minute ride, you'll invest 25–35 minutes even if you don't have to wait.

From Hogsmeade you reach the attraction through the imposing Winged Boar gate and progress along a winding path. Entering the castle on a lower level, you walk through a sort of dungeon with various icons and prop replicas from the Potter flicks, including the Mirror of Erised from *Harry Potter and the Sorcerer's Stone* (*Harry Potter and the Philosopher's Stone* outside the United States). Later you emerge outside and into the Hogwarts' greenhouses, which comprise the larger part of the Forbidden Journey's queuing area. The greenhouses are not air-conditioned, but fans move the (hot) air around. Also, blessedly, drinking fountains are in the greenhouse, but no restrooms—take care of that before getting in line for the attraction.

Once through horticulture purgatory, you reenter the castle, moving along its halls and passageways. One chamber you'll probably remember from the films is a multistory gallery of portraits, many of whose subjects come alive when they take a notion. The four founders of Hogwarts—Rowena Ravenclaw, Helga Hufflepuff holding her famous cup, Godric Gryffindor nearby, and the tall, moving portrait of Salazar Slytherin straight ahead—argue about Quidditch and Dumbledore's controversial decision to host an open house for muggles (garden-variety humans who are neither wizards nor witches) at Hogwarts. Don't rush through the gallery—the effects are very cool and the conversation among the portraits is essential to understanding the rest of the attraction.

After navigating some more passages, you reach Dumbledore's office, where Dumbledore appears on a balcony and welcomes you to Hogwarts. The headmaster's appearance is your introduction to Musion Eyeliner® technology, a high-definition video projection system that produces breathtakingly realistic, three-dimensional, moving, life-size holograms. After his welcoming remarks, Dumbledore dispatches you to the Defence Against the Dark Arts classroom to hear a presentation on the history of Hogwarts.

As you await the lecturer, Harry, Ron Weasley, and Hermione Granger pop out from under an invisibility cloak. They suggest that you ditch the lecture in favor of joining them for a proper tour of Hogwarts, including a Quidditch match. After some repartee between the characters and a couple of special effects surprises, it's off to the Hogwarts Official Attraction Safety Briefing and Boarding Instructions Chamber—OK, we made up the name of the room, but that's what goes on there. The briefing and instructions are presented by talking portraits including an etiquette

FAVORITE EATS AT UNIVERSAL'S ISLANDS OF ADVENTURE		
LAND	SERVICE LOCATION	FOOD ITEM
SEUSS LANDING	Circus McGurkus Cafe Stoo-pendous	Fried chicken & mashed potatoes with gravy
	Green Eggs and Ham Cafe	Green eggs & ham sandwich platter *(Green herbs are the reason for the green eggs, not food coloring.)*
LOST CONTINENT	Fire Eater's Grill	Gyro	Mythos	Risotto & pizza
WIZARDING WORLD	Three Broomsticks	Fish and chips
PORT OF ENTRY	Croissant Moon Bakery	Croissant & soups
TOON LAGOON	Ale to the Chief	Nathan's hot dogs
	Blondie's Home of the Dagwood	Sandwiches
JURASSIC PARK	Pizza Predatorria	Pizza

teacher. Later on, even the famed Sorting Hat gets into the act. All this leads to the Requirement Room with hundreds of candles floating overhead. This is where you board the ride.

After all the high-tech stuff in your queuing odyssey, you will naturally expect to be wowed by your ride vehicle. Surely it's a Nimbus 3000 turbobroom, a Phoenix, a Hippogriff, or at least the Weasleys' flying car. But no, what you will ride in the most technologically advanced theme-park attraction in America is, ta-daa . . . a bench!?! Yes, you heard right, a bench. Not that there's anything wrong with a bench. We're just saying that maybe the well ran a little dry in the imagination department.

But as benches go, it's a doozy, mounted to a Kuka robotic arm that can be programmed to replicate all the sensations of flying, including broad swoops, steep dives, sharp turns, sudden stops, and fast acceleration. The ride vehicle moves you through a series of alternating sets and domes where scenes are projected all around you. The movement of the Kuka arm is synchronized to create the motion that corresponds to what is happening in the set or film. When everything works correctly, it's mind blowing. You'll soar over Hogwarts Castle, get tossed into a Quidditch match, spar with the Whomping Willow, narrowly evade an attacking dragon, and fight off Dementers.

Many riders experience various degrees of motion sickness on Forbidden Journey. The best defense against motion sickness is not to ride on an empty stomach. If you have a child who doesn't meet the minimum-height requirement of 48 inches, a child-swapping option is provided at the loading area. Be advised that the seats on each bench are compartmentalized, so your child will not be able to see you or hold your hand.

SEUSS LANDING

A 10-ACRE THEMED AREA BASED ON Dr. Seuss's famous children's books. As at the old Mickey's Toontown in the Magic Kingdom, all of the buildings and attractions replicate a whimsical, brightly colored cartoon style with exaggerated features and rounded lines. There are four rides at Seuss Landing (described below) and an interactive play area, **If I Ran the Zoo,** populated by Seuss creatures.

If you have only young children in your party, Seuss Landing is the place to spend lots of happy time. A great stop in Seuss Landing is Dr. Seuss's All the Books You Can Read bookstore. Last but not least, if your kids cannot get enough of Dr. Seuss, check out **seussville.com.**

Liliane

Caro-Seuss-El (Universal Express) ★★★½

APPEAL BY AGE   PRESCHOOL ★★★★   GRADE SCHOOL ★★★★
TEENS —   YOUNG ADULTS —   OVER 30 —   SENIORS —

What it is Merry-go-round. **Scope and scale** Minor attraction. **Fright potential** Not frightening in any respect. **Bottleneck rating** 8. **When to go** Before 11 a.m. **Authors' rating** Wonderfully unique; ★★★½. **Duration of ride** 2 minutes. **Loading speed** Slow.

Totally outrageous, the Caro-Seuss-El is a full-scale, 56-mount merry-go-round made up exclusively of Dr. Seuss characters. If you are touring with young children, try to get them on early in the morning.

The Cat in the Hat (Universal Express) ★★★½

APPEAL BY AGE   PRESCHOOL ★★★★   GRADE SCHOOL ★★★★   TEENS ★★★
YOUNG ADULTS ★★★★   OVER 30 ★★★★   SENIORS ★★★★

What it is Indoor adventure ride. **Scope and scale** Major attraction. **Fright potential** Not frightening in any respect. **Bottleneck rating** 8. **When to go** Before 11:30 a.m. **Authors' rating** Seuss would be proud; ★★★½. **Duration of ride** 3½ minutes. **Loading speed** Moderate.

A must for preschoolers, guests ride on "couches" through 18 different sets inhabited by animatronic Seuss characters, including The Cat in the Hat, Thing 1, Thing 2, and the beleaguered goldfish who tries to maintain order in the midst of bedlam. Well done overall, with nothing that should frighten younger children. This is fun for all ages. Try to ride early.

The High in the Sky Seuss Trolley Train Ride! ★★★½
(Universal Express)

APPEAL BY AGE   PRESCHOOL ★★★★   GRADE SCHOOL ★★★½   TEENS ★
YOUNG ADULTS ★★½   OVER 30 ★★½   SENIORS ★★★

What it is Elevated train. **Scope and scale** Major attraction. **Fright potential** Not frightening in any respect. **Bottleneck rating** 8. **When to go** Before 11:30 a.m. **Authors' rating** ★★★½. **Special comments** Relaxed tour of Seuss Landing; must be 34" tall to ride. **Duration of ride** 3½ minutes. **Average wait in line per 100 people ahead of you** 11 minutes. **Loading speed** Molasses.

Trains putter along elevated tracks, while a voice reads one of four Dr. Seuss stories over the train's speakers. As each train makes its way through Seuss Landing, it passes a series of animatronic characters in scenes that are part of the story being told. The trains are small, fitting about 20 people, and the loading speed is glacial. Save the train ride for the end of the day or ride first thing in the morning.

If I Ran the Zoo ★★★ (Universal Express)

APPEAL BY AGE	PRESCHOOL ★★★★★	GRADE SCHOOL ★★★	TEENS —
YOUNG ADULTS —		OVER 30 —	SENIORS —

What it is Interactive playground. **Scope and scale** Minor attraction. **Fright potential** Not frightening in any respect. **Bottleneck rating** 2. **When to go** Any time. **Authors' rating** Whimsical and funny; ★★★★; great for preschoolers.

A playground with 19 different interactive elements, this area is great silly-dilly fun for little tykes. How silly? The sign at the entrance of this crazy zoo should give you a clue: "Keep track of adults, they get lost all the time." And yes, you should know by now that there is no way the kids will stay dry.

One Fish, Two Fish, Red Fish, Blue Fish ★★★½ (Universal Express)

APPEAL BY AGE	PRESCHOOL ★★★★	GRADE SCHOOL ★★★★	TEENS ★★★
YOUNG ADULTS ★★★		OVER 30 ★★★	SENIORS ★★★

What it is Wet version of Dumbo the Flying Elephant. **Scope and scale** Minor attraction. **Fright potential** Not frightening in any respect. **Bottleneck rating** 8. **When to go** Before 10 a.m. **Authors' rating** Who says you can't teach an old ride new tricks? ★★★½. **Duration of ride** 2 minutes. **Loading speed** Slow.

Wet

Imagine Dumbo with Seuss-style fish instead of elephants and you've got half the story. Guests steer their fish up or down 15 feet in the air while traveling in circles trying to avoid streams of water projected from "squirt posts."

I followed Dr. Seuss's advice: If you never did. You should. These things are fun. These things are good. And all wet there I stood! My favorite ride in Seuss Landing!

Liliane

FAVORITE EATS AT CITYWALK

WHAT | WHERE | COMMENTS

JAMAICAN AND CARIBBEAN CUISINE | Bob Marley—A Tribute to Freedom | *Food and reggae, yeah!*

MEXICAN AND SOUTH AMERICAN FARE | Latin Quarter | *Salsa and merengue—a perfect match.*

SHRIMP, SHRIMP, DID WE SAY SHRIMP? | The Bubba Gump Shrimp Co. Restaurant and Market | *All you need is shrimp.*

ITALIAN CUISINE | Pastamoré | *Great for the entire family.*

CAJUN CUISINE, GREAT JAMBALAYAS | Pat O'Brien's Orlando | *Pleasant outside dining and, of course, the one and only dueling pianos.*

SOPHISTICATED DINING, CREOLE-INSPIRED DISHES | Emeril's Restaurant Orlando | *Perfect for a romantic evening without the kids.*

AMERICAN CUISINE | Hard Rock Cafe Orlando | *A great place for your musical teen to discover clothes and guitars from rock legends such as KISS, Elvis, and The Beatles.*

Note: All restaurants offer table service.

ISLANDS *of* ADVENTURE TOURING PLAN

ISLANDS OF ADVENTURE ONE-DAY TOURING PLAN FOR FAMILIES

WE PRESENT ONE ISLANDS OF ADVENTURE TOURING PLAN geared toward the whole family. Because there are so many attractions with the potential to frighten young children, be prepared to skip a few things and to practice switching off (works the same way as at Walt Disney World). For the most part, attractions designed especially for young children, such as playgrounds, can be enjoyed anytime. Work them into the plan at your convenience.

Be aware that in this park there are an inordinate number of attractions that will get you wet. If you want to experience them, come armed with ponchos, large plastic garbage bags, or some other protective covering. Failure to follow this prescription will make for a squishy, sodden day.

This plan is for families of all sizes and ages and includes thrill rides. If the plan calls for you to experience an attraction that does not interest you, simply bypass that attraction and proceed to the next step. Be aware that the plan calls for some backtracking. The plan can be found in clip-out form with a map on page 468.

ROLLING THE DICE WITH HARRY POTTER

THE WIZARDING WORLD, AND PARTICULARLY the Harry Potter and the Forbidden Journey attraction, create some real challenges when trying to develop an optimal touring plan for IOA. Some of this will sort itself out over time, but for The Wizarding World's first year:

- The 20-acre section of the park will be completely overrun by crowds.
- The science and innovation behind Forbidden Journey is remarkable, but the ride is subject to malfunctions both large and small.
- Because of Forbidden Journey's several preshows, it takes about 30–35 minutes to experience the attraction, even if there's no wait.

Next year, after Forbidden Journey works out the bugs, we'll probably recommend unequivocally that you experience it first thing. This year, however, you're really rolling the dice. If you try to enjoy Forbidden Journey first thing after the park opens, and if the ride operates as designed, you're golden. You'll be off to other must-see attraction before the park gets crowded. On the other hand, if the ride suffers technical difficulties, you may be stuck in there a long while, during which time the crowds will spread out to other areas of IOA. Depending on the time you exit Forbidden Journey, there could be long lines for all of the park's other popular attractions. Even if everything goes perfectly, experiencing Forbidden Journey will consume more prime morning touring time than Dragon Challenge, the Incredible Hulk, and Spider-Man put together.

If, like many, your top priority is Wizarding World, your best bet is to experience it early in the morning and take your chances with crowds in the other parts of the parks later on. If you're an IOA first-timer, or if Wizarding World is not such a hot button, skip Forbidden Journey and enjoy short waits at the park's other top attractions. Or, as a third alternative, spring for Universal Express Plus if The Wizarding World attractions are included. For its first year, Universal is likely to exclude Forbidden Journey from Universal Express Plus.

Following are what the first two alternatives look like in the first five steps of a touring plan:

PLAN A: HARRY POTTER OR DIE	PLAN B: EASY TOURING
1. Harry Potter and the Forbidden Journey	1. Dragon Challenge
2. Dragon Challenge	2. The Incredible Hulk Coaster
3. The Incredible Hulk Coaster	3. The Amazing Adventures of Spider-Man
4. The Amazing Adventures of Spider-Man	4. Doctor Doom's Fearfall
5. Popeye and Bluto's Bilge-Rat Barges	5. Popeye and Bluto's Bilge-Rat Barges

UNIVERSAL CITYWALK

AT CITYWALK you will find a number of great restaurants, clubs, shops, outdoor entertainment, a concert hall (Hard Rock Live), and the Universal Cineplex 20 movie theater. CityWalk has a number of combination restaurants and clubs. Open to families with kids until 9 p.m., many of the venues offer live entertainment. Teens can sample a taste of the club scene and still be in bed by 10 p.m.

Liliane

If you want to have a good time at one of the clubs or a calm dinner, consider sending your teen to the movies or to Teen Night at The Groove. The movie theater, restaurants, and clubs are all centrally located, and it is easy to have a "controlled" night out.

For mom's and dad's night out, great entertainment is available at Rising Star, a karaoke bar where a live band backs the singers; reggae at Bob Marley—A Tribute to Freedom; Pat O'Brien's dueling-piano club; Jimmy Buffett's Margaritaville; the Latin Quarter for Nuevo Latino music; the Red Coconut Club, an upscale lounge with cocktails and dancing; and The Groove, a club with high-tech lighting and visual effects. If you want to go clubbing, $12 plus tax admits you to all of the clubs.

In June, on designated nights, teens ages 15–19 (school ID or driver's license is required for admission) can get into the teen spirit at Teen Night at The Groove. A DJ spins the latest hits, admission is $10, and a first soft drink is included. For details and a schedule, call Universal CityWalk information at ☎ 407-224-2691.

How To Make it Work

CityWalk is open daily 11 a.m.–2 a.m., and parking is available in the same garages that serve the theme park at the rate of $14 a day; parking is $3 6 p.m.–10 p.m. If you stay at one of the Universal resorts, it's a short walk, but water taxi and bus transportation are also available to transport you to CityWalk. For added fun, try one of the pedi-cabs that will take you from CityWalk to your resort for a modest tip. Call ☎ 407-224-FOOD for dinner reservations. Visit **universalorlando.com** and select "At CityWalk" under "Events" for special events.

SEAWORLD

MANY DOZENS OF READERS HAVE WRITTEN to extol the virtues of SeaWorld. The following are representative. An English family writes:

The best-organized park [is] SeaWorld. The computer printout we got on arrival had a very useful show schedule, told us which areas were temporarily closed due to construction, and had a readily understandable map. Best of all, there was almost no queuing. Overall, we rated this day so highly that it is the park we would most like to visit again.

A woman in Alberta, Canada, gives her opinion:

We chose SeaWorld as our fifth day at "The World." What a pleasant surprise! It was every bit as good (and in some ways better) than WDW itself. Well worth the admission, an excellent entertainment value, educational, well run, and better value for the dollar in food services. Perhaps expand your coverage to give them their due!

Discount coupons for SeaWorld admission are available in the free visitor magazines found in most (but not Disney) hotel lobbies.

Bob

FAVORITE EATS AT SEAWORLD		
LAND	SERVICE LOCATION	FOOD ITEM
KEY WEST AT SEAWORLD	Captain Pete's Island Eats	Hot dogs and fresh funnel cakes
THE WATERFRONT	Voyager's	Barbecue ribs and chicken
PENGUIN PLAZA	Mama's Kitchen	Sandwiches & salads
SHARK ENCOUNTER*	Sharks Underwater Grill	Floor-to-ceiling glass allows guests to dine and observe some 50 sharks and other fish.
WILD ARTIC	Mango Joe's	Fajitas
FRONT GATE PLAZA	Sweet Sailin' Candy Shop	Candies & hand-dipped chocolate turtles

* table service only

If you don't purchase your admission in advance, take advantage of the automatic admission machines located to the right of the main entrance. The machines are a pain in the rear, asking for your name, age, home zip code, and billing zip code, but if you have a credit card, the machines are a lot faster than standing in line at the ticket windows.

OK, here's what you need to know (for additional information, call ☎ 407-351-3600, 888-800-5447, or visit **seaworld.com**). SeaWorld is a world-class marine-life theme park near the intersection of I-4 and the Beachline Expressway. It's about 10 miles east of Walt Disney World. Opening daily at 9 a.m. and closing between 6 p.m. and 11 p.m., depending on the season, SeaWorld charges about $79 admission for adults and $69 for children ages 3–9. Five-park Combination Passes (called the Orlando Flex Ticket), which include admission to SeaWorld, Universal Studios, Islands of Adventure, Wet 'n Wild, and Busch Gardens, are also available. Sea World offers some super advance purchase discounts on its Web site.

Figure 8–9 hours or more to see everything, 6 or so if you stick to the big deals. Discovery Cove is directly across the Central Florida Parkway from SeaWorld. Parking at Discovery Cove is free.

SeaWorld is about the size of the Magic Kingdom and requires about the same amount of walking. In terms of size, quality, and creativity, it's unequivocally on par with Disney's major theme parks. Unlike Walt Disney World, SeaWorld primarily features stadium shows or walk-through exhibits. This means that you will spend about 80% less time waiting in line during 8 hours at SeaWorld than

STAR RATINGS FOR SEAWORLD ATTRACTIONS

★★★★½   *Believe* (high-tech Shamu and killer-whale show)

★★★★   *A'lure: The Call of the Ocean* (Cirque du Soleil–type presentation)

★★★★   *Clyde and Seamore Take Pirate Island* (sea lion, walrus, and otter show)

★★★★   Kraken (roller coaster)

★★★★   Manta (roller coaster)

★★★★   Shamu's Happy Harbor (children's play area)

★★★★   Shark Encounter

★★★★   Wild Arctic (simulation ride and Arctic wildlife viewing)

★★★½   *Blue Horizons* (whale, dolphin, and bird show)

★★★½   Key West at SeaWorld (dolphin, stingray, and turtle viewing)

★★★½   Pacific Point Preserve (sea lions and seals)

★★★½   Penguin Encounter

★★★½   *Pets Ahoy!* (show with performing birds, cats, dogs, and a pig)

★★★   Journey to Atlantis (combination roller coaster–flume ride)

★★★   Manatee Rescue (manatee viewing)

★★   Sky Tower (400-foot-tall observation tower)

you would for the same-length visit at a Disney park.

But, you'll notice immediately as you check the performance times that the shows are scheduled so that it's almost impossible to see them back to back. A Cherry Hill, New Jersey, visitor confirms this rather major problem, complaining:

The shows were timed so we could not catch all the major ones in a 7-hour visit.

Much of the year, you can get a seat for the stadium shows by showing up 10 or so minutes in advance. When the park is crowded, however, you need to be at the stadiums at least 20 minutes in advance (30 minutes in advance for a good seat). All of the stadiums have "splash zones," specified areas where you're likely to be drenched with ice-cold saltwater by whales, dolphins, and sea lions. Finally, SeaWorld has two of the best coasters, Manta and Kraken, in the county. If you're a coaster lover, be on hand before park opening and ride Manta, then Kraken, as soon as the park opens.

DISCOVERY COVE

SEAWORLD'S INTIMATE PARK, Discovery Cove, is a welcome departure from the hustle and bustle of other Orlando parks; its slower pace could be the overstimulated family's ticket back to mental health.

With a focus on personal guest service and one-on-one animal encounters, Liliane Discovery Cove admits only 1,000 guests per day.

The main draw at Discovery Cove is the chance to swim with their troupe of 25 Atlantic bottlenose dolphins. The 90-minute experience is open to visitors age 6 and up who are comfortable in the water. Discovery Cove is located across the street from SeaWorld.

Other exhibits at Discovery Cove include the Coral Reef and the Aviary. Snorkel or swim in the Coral Reef, which houses thousands of exotic fish, as well as an underwater shipwreck and hidden grottoes. In the Aviary, you can touch and feed gorgeous tropical birds. The park is threaded by a "tropical river" in which you can float or swim, and dotted with beaches that serve as pathways to the attractions.

Discovery Cove is open 9 a.m.–5:30 p.m. daily. Admission is limited, so purchase tickets well in advance; call ☎ 877-4-DISCOVERY or visit **discoverycove.com.** Prices vary seasonally from $199 per person to $319, tax not included (no children's discount). Admission includes the dolphin swim, self-parking, one meal, and use of beach umbrellas, lounge chairs, towels, lockers, and swim and snorkel gear. Discovery Cove admission also includes a 14-day pass to SeaWorld Orlando, Aquatica, or Busch Gardens Tampa. If you're not interested in the dolphin swim, you can visit Discovery Cove for the day for $99–$199 per person, depending on the season.

The price is high, but the prize is right. Swimming with a dolphin Liliane across the bay was one of the most amazing things I have ever done in my life.

PART TWELVE

THE REST *of* *the* WORLD

The **WATER THEME PARKS**

WALT DISNEY WORLD HAS TWO SWIMMING THEME PARKS. Typhoon Lagoon is the most diverse Disney splash pad, while Blizzard Beach takes the prize for the most slides and most bizarre theme (a ski resort in meltdown). Blizzard Beach has the best slides, but Typhoon Lagoon has a surf pool where you can bodysurf. Both parks have excellent and elaborate themed areas for toddlers and preschoolers.

During summer and holiday periods, Typhoon Lagoon and Blizzard Beach fill to capacity on weekdays and close their gates before 11 a.m.

Disney water parks allow one cooler per family or group, but no glass and no alcoholic beverages. Both parks charge the following rental prices: towels, $2; lockers are $8 small, $10 large (plus $5 refundable deposit); life jackets are available at no cost. Strollers are welcome but are not available for rent. Admission costs for each park is $45 per day for adults and $39 per day for children (ages 3–9).

The best way to avoid standing in lines is to visit the water parks when they're less crowded. We recommend going on a Saturday or Sunday, when most visitors are traveling, or on a Monday—very few guests go to a water park on their first day at Walt Disney World. Like the four major Disney parks, the water parks participate in the Extra Magic Hours program. Note that Disney is cutting costs left and right. Don't be surprised if Extra Magic Hours at the water parks goes the way of the dodo.

If you are going to Blizzard Beach or Typhoon Lagoon, get up early, have breakfast, and arrive at the park 30 minutes before opening. Wear your bathing suit under shorts and a T-shirt so you don't need to use lockers or dressing rooms. Wear shoes. The paths are relatively easy on bare feet, but there's a lot of ground to cover. If you or your children have tender feet, wear your shoes as

If you have a car, drive instead of taking a Disney bus.

you move around the park, removing them when you raft, slide, or go into the water. Shops in the parks sell sandals, Reef Runners, and other protective footwear that can be worn in and out of the water.

You will need a towel, sunblock, and money. Carry enough money for the day and your Disney resort ID (if you have one) in a plastic bag or Tupperware container. Though nowhere is completely safe, we felt comfortable hiding our plastic money bags in our cooler. Nobody disturbed our stuff, and our cash was easy to reach. However, if you're carrying a wad or worry about money anyway, rent a locker. Another great device is a water-proof card case with a lanyard to hold park tickets, a credit card, some cash, and your hotel key. You can buy them at the water parks for about $8; more sophisticated versions are available at any good outdoors or sport shop.

Lost children stations at the water parks are so out of the way that neither you nor your child will find them without help from a Disney cast member. Liliane Explain to your children how to recognize a Disney cast member (by their distinctive name tags) and how to ask for help.

Personal swim gear (fins, masks, rafts, and so on) is not allowed. Everything you need is either provided or available to rent. If you forget your towel, you can rent one (cheap!). If you forgot your swimsuit or lotion, they're available for sale. So are disposable, waterproof cameras, which are especially fun to have at Typhoon Lagoon Shark Reef.

Establish your base for the day. Many beautiful sunning and lounging spots are scattered throughout both swimming parks. Arrive early, and you can have your pick. The breeze is best along the beaches of the lagoon at Blizzard Beach and the surf pool at Typhoon Lagoon. At Typhoon Lagoon, if children younger than age 6 are in your party, choose an area to the left of Mount Mayday near the children's swimming area.

Though Typhoon Lagoon and Blizzard Beach are huge parks with many slides, armies of guests overwhelm them almost daily. If your main reason for going is the slides and you hate long lines, try to be among the first guests to enter the park. Go directly to the slides and ride as many times as you can before the park fills. When lines for the slides become intolerable, head for the surf or wave pool or the tube-floating streams.

Both water parks are large and require almost as much walking as the major theme parks. Add to this wave surfing, swimming, and climbing to reach the slides, and you'll definitely be pooped by day's end. Consider a low-key activity for the evening.

While I do not feel any better on a water roller coaster than I do on the dry thing, I love the water parks. My all-time favorite water ride is Team-boat Springs, the Liliane 1,200-foot white-water raft flume at Blizzard Beach.

Ian

Grab an inner tube and go on Cross Country Creek or Castaway Creek. It's best when you go with a group like your family. Sometimes I hop off the tube and find an underwater jet on the side of the bank. If you go underwater, the jet will shoot you out really fast. It's a blast! Don't worry; the water isn't deep. A good trick to play on someone in your family is to push their inner tube under a cave waterfall. The water is ice cold. It's fun to watch them freak out.

It's as easy to lose a child or become separated from your party at one of the water parks as it is at a major theme park. On arrival, pick a very specific place to meet in the event you are separated. If you split up on purpose, establish times for checking in.

Children under age 10 must be accompanied by an adult. The water parks are great fun for the whole family, but if you have very young children or if you are not a thrill-seeking water puppy, the pool of your hotel might serve just as well. The water parks, however, were made to order for teens. Note that during the winter months, Disney closes Blizzard Beach and Typhoon Lagoon for refurbishing, alternating maintenance in such a way that one water park will be open at all times. If it is very wintry, Disney will close both parks. Call ☎ 407-824-4321 for current information.

HOW TO MAKE IT WORK

JUST LIKE AT THE MAJOR THEME PARKS, the key to a successful visit to the water parks is to arrive early. Plan to arrive a half hour before the scheduled opening time. If you are a Disney resort guest, visit on a day the water park of your choice offers Extra Magic Hours. Remember, in high season the parks fill up quickly and often reach capacity by 11 a.m.

Decide if you need the locker or not. If you do, send one member in your party to stake out a base for the day while you take care of the locker business. It is easier to lose a child or become separated from your party at one of the water parks than it is at the major theme parks. Upon arrival, pick a specific place to meet in the event you get separated.

Remember to have fun. Experience the must-do thrill slides right away but don't overdo it; the lazy rivers at both parks are perfect for relaxation. Float through caves, beneath waterfalls, past gardens, and under bridges. Life is beautiful and the water is soothing. Did you know that in the winter months Disney actually heats all the water park pools?

BEFORE YOU GO

1. Call ☎ 407-824-4321 or visit **disneyworld.com** the day before you go to find out the official park opening time.
2. Purchase admission tickets online before you arrive.
3. Decide if you want to picnic or not, and then plan or pack accordingly. Pets are not allowed at the water parks.

Blizzard Beach

ATTRACTION | HEIGHT REQUIREMENT | WHAT TO EXPECT

CHAIR LIFT UP MT. GUSHMORE | 32 inches | Great ride even if you only go up for the view. When the park is packed, use the single-riders line.

CROSS COUNTRY CREEK | None | Lazy river circling the park; grab a tube.

DOWNHILL DOUBLE DIPPER | 48 inches | Side-by-side tube-racing slides. At 25 mph, the tube races through water curtains and free falls. It's a lot of fun but rough.

MELT-AWAY BAY | None | Wave pool with gentle, bobbing waves. The pool is great for younger swimmers.

RUNOFF RAPIDS | None | Three corkscrew tube slides to choose from. The center slide is for solo raft rides; the other two slides offer one-, two-, or three-person tubes. The dark, enclosed tube makes the ride feel as if you've been flushed down a toilet.

SKI PATROL TRAINING CAMP | Ages 5–11 | Preteens can train here for the big rides.

SLUSH GUSHER | 48 inches | A 90-foot double-humped slide. Ladies, cling to those tops—all others hang on to live.

SNOW STORMERS | None | Three mat-slide flumes; down you go on your belly.

SUMMIT PLUMMET | 48 inches | A 120-foot free fall at 60 mph. This ride is very intense. Make sure your child knows what to expect. Being over 48 inches tall does not guarantee an enjoyable experience. If you think you'd enjoy washing out of a 12th-floor window during a heavy rain, then this slide is for you.

TEAMBOAT SPRINGS | None | 1,200-foot white-water group raft flume. Wonderful ride for the whole family.

TIKE'S PEAK | 48 inches and under only | Kid-size version of Blizzard Beach. This is *the* place for little ones.

TOBOGGAN RACERS | None | Eight-lane race course. You go down the flume on a mat. The ride is less intense than Snow Stormers.

A WORD FROM THE WEATHERMAN

THUNDERSTORMS ARE COMMON in Florida. On summer afternoons such storms often occur daily, forcing the water parks to close temporarily while the threatening weather passes. If the storm is severe and prolonged, it can cause a great deal of inconvenience. The park may actually close for the day, launching a legion through the turnstiles to compete for space on the Disney resort buses. If you depend on Disney buses, leave the park earlier, rather than later, when you see a storm moving in. Most important though, instruct your children to immediately return to "home base" at the sight of lightning or when they hear the first rumble of thunder.

The Slush Gusher at Blizzard Beach is really cool. It's really steep and wavy on the way down. You have to cross your arms and legs because water will rush up your swimsuit. Stay as still as possible, and you will go really fast. A speed sign at the bottom shows how fast you came down. Be careful, because if you try to open your eyes, water goes in, and sometimes water goes up your nose.

Typhoon Lagoon

ATTRACTION | HEIGHT REQUIREMENT | WHAT TO EXPECT

CASTAWAY CREEK | None | Half-mile lazy river in a tropical setting. Wonderful!

CRUSH 'N' GUSHER | 48 inches | Water roller coaster where you can choose from among three slides: Banana Blaster, Coconut Crusher, and Pineapple Plunger, ranging 410–420 feet long. This thriller leaves you wondering what exactly happened—if you make it down in one piece, that is. It's not for the faint of heart. If your kids are new to water-park rides, this is not the place to break them in, even if they're tall enough to ride.

GANG PLANK FALLS | None | White-water raft flume in a multiperson tube.

HUMUNGA KOWABUNGA | 48 inches | Speed slides that hit 30 mph. A five-story drop in the dark rattles the most courageous rider. Ladies should ride this in a one-piece swimsuit.

KEELHAUL FALLS | None | Fast white-water ride in a single-person tube.

KETCHAKIDDEE CREEK | 48 inches and under only | Toddlers and preschoolers love this area reserved only for them. Say "splish splash" and have lots of fun.

MAYDAY FALLS | None | The name says it all. Wild single-person tube ride. Hang on!

SHARK REEF | None | After you're equipped with fins, mask, snorkel, and a life vest, you get a brief lesson in snorkeling. Then off you go for about 60 feet to the other side of the saltwater pool, where you swim with small colorful fish, rays, and very small leopard and hammerhead sharks. If you don't want to swim with the fish, visit the underwater viewing chamber anytime during the day. Surface Air Snorkeling—a SCUBA-like pursuit involving a "pony" tank, a small regulator, and a buoyancy vest—is also offered. Participants must be at least 5 years old. To sign up and get more information, visit the kiosk near the entrance to Shark Reef.

STORM SLIDES | None | Three body-slides down and thru Mount Mayday.

SURF POOL | None | World's largest inland surf facility with waves up to 6 feet high. Adult supervision required. Four times a week at 5:45 a.m. during the summer and three times a week at 6:45 a.m. during other seasons (before the park opens), surfing lessons are offered (surfboard provided). Cost is $150 for 2½ hours; minimum age is 8; class size is 12. Call ☎ 407-WDW-PLAY. The price does *not* include park admission.

We recommend that you monitor the local weather forecast the day before you go, checking again in the morning before leaving for the water park. Scattered thunderstorms are to be expected and usually cause no more than temporary inconvenience, but moving storm fronts are to be avoided.

SAFETY FIRST

TOO MUCH FUN IN THE SUN isn't a good thing if you get sunburned or become dehydrated. Drink lots of fluids, use sunscreen, and bring a T-shirt and a hat for extra protection. Read all signs and follow the rules. Lifeguards are on duty throughout the parks. At Typhoon Lagoon, a first-aid station is located behind Leaning

FAVORITE EATS AT THE WATER PARKS

LAND | SERVICE LOCATION | FOOD ITEM

BLIZZARD BEACH | Avalunch | Hot dogs and cheesecake
Cooling Hut | Popcorn, nachos, and Itzakadoozie
Lottawatta Lodge | Pizza, burgers, salads, and kids' meals
Warming Hut | Hot dogs and chicken wraps

TYPHOON LAGOON | Happy Landings | Ice cream, cookies, and waffle cone.
Garbage pail: Ice cream pieces, fudge, nuts, and sprinkles in pail with shovel.

Leaning Palms | Pizza and kids' meals inside sand pail with shovel
Lowtide Lou's (seasonal) | Chicken wrap, tuna sandwich
Typhoon Tilly's | Fish, barbecued pork, and kids' meals inside sand pail with shovel

Refillable mugs: If you or the kids enjoy soda, your best bet is to get a refillable mug, available at both water parks. For the price of the mug ($10), you are entitled to free refills throughout the day (only on the day of purchase). Select locations.

Palms. The Blizzard Beach first-aid station is between Lottawatta Lodge and Beach Haus.

WET 'N WILD

WET 'N WILD (ON INTERNATIONAL DRIVE IN ORLANDO, one block east of I-4 at Exit 75A; ☎ 800-992-WILD or 407-351-1800; **wetnwildorlando.com**) is a non-Disney water-park option. If you are looking for a colorful atmosphere, Wet 'n Wild will not deliver; however, the park is packed with incredible slides, flumes, and activities for all ages. Water puppies will get their fill, and kids can go wild.

Tickets with tax at the main gate are $48 for adults and $42 for kids ages 3–9. Always check for special deals and discounts (especially for AAA members, Florida residents, and members of the military). An annual pass is $90 (plus tax; includes parking), and an annual pass for weekdays runs $50 (plus tax; does not include parking). In recent years Wet 'n Wild has offered unlimited admission for the rest of the year or the rest of your stay for the price of a one-day ticket. The park also regularly offers half-price admission in the afternoon. Parking fees are $10 for cars and vans and $12 for RVs. Lockers can be rented for $5–$10 depending on size, and towel rental is $4; both require a refundable deposit of $3. Life vests are provided for free. Pets are not allowed inside the park, and there is no kennel.

Mears Transportation operates a shuttle to Wet 'n Wild that stops three times a day at Disney hotels. It's the same shuttle that commutes between Walt Disney World and Universal Orlando. Cost is $18 for

Wet 'n Wild

ATTRACTION | HEIGHT REQUIREMENT | WHAT TO EXPECT

THE BLACK HOLE | 48 inches if riding alone; 36 inches if riding with an adult | Two-person tube; 1,000 gallons of water per minute; all this in the dark. Do we need to say more? While not the wildest ride in town, it sure is dark in there.

THE BLAST | 48 inches if riding alone; 36 inches if riding with an adult | Two-person tube ride inside a waterworks where all the pipes are broken. You cannot get any wetter.

THE BOMB BAY | 48 inches | You stand on a pair of doors that open, dropping you down a 76-foot slide. You're gonna need a lot of nerve to stand on those doors and wait for the drop.

BRAIN WASH | 48 inches | Extreme six-story tube ride with a 53-foot vertical drop into a 65-foot funnel; tube holds two or four riders.

BUBBA TUB | 48 inches if riding alone; 36 inches if riding with an adult | Long straight track with three hummocks to impede momentum.

DER STUKA | 48 inches | Speed flume descending from a six-story tower.

DISCO H2O | 48 inches if riding alone; 36 inches if riding with an adult | Four persons in a raft are ushered down a tube into a 1970s-era nightclub complete with lights, music, and a disco ball.

THE FLYER | 48 inches if riding alone; 36 inches if riding with an adult | A calmer toboggan-style ride more suitable for families with smaller children.

MACH 5 | 48 inches | Mat slide. For a really fast ride, grab a newer mat.

THE STORM | 48 inches | Half slide, half toilet bowl. This ride is exhilarating and disorienting; when the lifeguard begins hollering, just stumble toward his voice and give him a thumbs-up.

THE SURGE | 48 inches if riding alone; 36 inches if riding with an adult | Four-person raft ride sends you flying down 600 feet of banked turns. Wild!

guests age 3 and older. There is no transportation to Wet 'n Wild from Disney property. If you are staying in Walt Disney World, in Lake Buena Vista, or along US 192, you will need a car. If you are staying on International Drive, you can take the International Drive trolley (visit **iridetrolley.com** for schedules and fees). As with all thrill slides, lines can become unbearably long, so arrive early. Also keep in mind that most slides are geared more toward older children. All the slides outside the Kids' Park have a 48-inch height requirement, except for multipassenger slides, for which the minimum height is 36 inches if an adult accompanies the short rider. The only exceptions to this policy are the rides at Wake Zone, with a height requirement of 51 inches (The Wild One) and 56 inches (Knee Ski and Wake Skating).

Other Wet n' Wild attractions include a 3,200-square-foot **Kids' Park** with a smaller-scale version of the adult menu. It's located to the left of the main gate; look for the oversize sandcastle capped off with a big blue bucket. The bucket actually fills with water and tips over, soaking the people in front of the castle. The area has slides, a mini-wave pool, a kid-size climbing net, a junior river ride, and two very short zip lines.

Much fun for the younger crowd is **Bubble Up**—a large, wet, inflated bubble made just for kids to climb, bounce, and slide down into 3 feet of water. Kids must be 42–64 inches tall and under 13 years of age to ride this attraction.

The 17,000-square-foot wave pool at **Surf Lagoon** is perfect for body bobbing. If you prefer to ride the waves with tubes, you can rent those at the main rental stand. Another great way to relax is the **Lazy River.** Be forewarned though: The circuit is short and the current fast. If you lose your tube, swim down the river or wait patiently until an empty one passes within reach.

Wake Zone, situated on a lake roughly the same size as the rest of the park, offers wakeboarding, knee-boarding, and tubing. The lines can be considerable, especially since the attraction only runs from noon until dusk and is open on weekends only from mid-March to June, daily during the summer, and weekends only from September to mid-October. Be sure to call before going to Wet 'n Wild to see if the area is open on the day of your visit.

When you get hungry, the main food pavilions are the centrally located **Bubba's BBQ, Manny's Pizza,** and **Surf Grill,** together offering such staples as burgers, pizza, and barbecued-pork sandwiches, as well as more-nutritious (and nontraditional) items such as veggie burgers and tabbouleh. Wait times are long, and prices are high but not outrageous. Guests may bring a picnic, but alcohol and glass containers are not allowed (although beer can be purchased inside the park).

> What I like best about Wet 'n Wild is that the park is open 9:30 a.m.– 9 p.m. daily throughout the summer. This is a huge advantage over the Disney water parks that generally close between 6–7 p.m.
>
> Liliane

HOW TO MAKE IT WORK

YOU CAN TAKE IN all the attractions at Wet 'n Wild in one day, especially in the summer when the park is open until 9 p.m. It is a huge park, and a whole day playing in the water under the hot Florida sun will poop you out. Try to get back to the hotel for a midday nap, and don't plan on dragging already tired kids to a restaurant for a sit-down dinner.

BEFORE YOU GO

1. Call ☎ 800-992-WILD or 407-351-1800, or visit **wetnwildorlando. com,** the day before you go to find out the official park opening time.

2. Purchase admission tickets online before you arrive.

3. Visit the Web site to determine what attractions are appropriate for the kids in your party.

AQUATICA *by* SEAWORLD

AQUATICA, ORLANDO'S FIRST NEW SWIMMING PARK to open in more than a decade, is located across International Drive from the backside of SeaWorld. From Kissimmee, Walt Disney World, and Lake

Aquatica by SeaWorld

ATTRACTION | HEIGHT REQUIREMENT* | WHAT TO EXPECT

CUTBACK COVE AND BIG SURF SHORES | None | One cove serves up bodysurfing waves, while the other puts out gently bobbing floating waves. A spacious beach arrayed around the coves is the park's primary sunning venue. Shady spots, courtesy of beach umbrellas, ring the perimeter of the area for sun-sensitive guests.

DOLPHIN PLUNGE | Guests must be at least 48 inches tall and be able to maintain proper riding position unassisted | Corkscrewing romp through a totally arced tube until you blast through the clear tube at the end. The viewing of the dolphins is nearly impossible because you're flushed through the clear tube so fast and with so much water splashing in your face, the ride is over before you've seen anything.

HOOROO RUN | 42 inches | A six-story open-air run down a steep, straight, undulating slide.

KATA'S KOOKABURRA COVE | 48 inches and under only | Wading pool and slides for the preschool crowd.

LOGGERHEAD LANE | Guests must be in a single or double tube | Take a tube and enjoy this lazy river, which at one point passes through the Fish Grotto, a tank populated by hundreds of exotic tropical fish.

ROA'S RAPIDS | Guests under 51 inches are required to wear a life vest | Floating stream with a very swift current but without any rapids. There is only one place to get in and out.

TASSIE'S TWISTERS | Guests must be able to maintain proper riding position while holding on to both handles unassisted | An enclosed slide tube spits you into an open bowl, where you careen around the bowl's edge much in the manner of the ball in a roulette wheel.

TAUMATA RACER | Guests must be at least 42 inches tall and be able to maintain proper riding position unassisted | A high-speed mat ride down a steep hill.

WALHALLA WAVE | Guests must be at least 42 inches tall and be able to maintain proper riding position unassisted | Circular raft that can accommodate up to four people and splashes down a six-story enclosed twisting tube.

WALKABOUT WATERS | Guests must be 36–42 inches for slides into main pool and over 42 inches tall for larger slides | 15,000-square-foot children's adventure area. If your children are under the age of 10, this alone may be worth the admission price. It's impossible not to get wet and impossible not to have fun!

WHANAU WAY | Guests must be able to maintain the proper riding position while holding on to both handles unassisted | Tubes carry one or two passengers down one of four slides with a few twists and one corkscrew.

Guests under 48 inches are required to wear a life vest.

Buena Vista, take I-4 East, exit onto the Central Florida Parkway, and then bear left on International Drive. From Universal Studios, take I-4 West to FL 528 and from there exit onto International Drive. Admission costs about the same as at the Disney water parks and at Wet 'n Wild. If you don't want to wait in a queue to purchase tickets, buy them in advance at **aquaticabyseaworld.com** or use the credit-card ticket machines to the left of Aquatica's main entrance.

Aquatica is comparable in size to other water theme parks in the area. Attractively landscaped with palms, ferns, and tropical flowers, it's far less themed than Disney's Typhoon Lagoon and Blizzard Beach but much greener and more aesthetically appealing than Wet 'n Wild. You can take in all the attractions in one day but, as with all water parks, remember that an entire day of action in the Florida sun will wear out the most active kids and most grownups too.

As at other water parks, there are lockers, towels, wheelchairs, and strollers to rent, gift shops to browse, and places to eat. The three restaurants at Aquatica are **WaterStone Grill,** offering specialty sandwiches, fried fish, wraps, and salads; **Banana Beach Cookout,** an all-you-can-eat venue dishing up burgers, hot dogs, and chicken; and **Mango Market,** a diminutive eatery serving pizza and chicken tenders. WaterStone Grill and Mango Market serve beer.

BEFORE YOU GO

1. Call ☎ 888-800-5447 or 407-351-3600, or visit **aquaticaby seaworld.com** the day before you go to find out the official park opening time.
2. Purchase admission tickets online before you arrive.
3. Visit the Web site to determine what attractions are appropriate for the kids in your party.

DOWNTOWN DISNEY

DOWNTOWN DISNEY COMPRISES THE Disney Village Marketplace, Pleasure Island, and Disney's West Side. All three are shopping, dining, and entertainment complexes. You can roam, shop, and dine without paying any sort of entrance fee.

If you have a car, use it. There is bus transportation from all the Disney resorts to Downtown Disney, and some resorts (Old Key West and Port Orleans) offer boat transportation. The problem is that buses make stops at a number of locations at Downtown Disney, so you might sit on the bus for 20 minutes or more before you finally depart for your destination. The boats are better than the buses but take about four times as long as driving your car. The boat route, however, is very pretty and a good choice if you're not in a hurry. Shops open as early as 9:30 a.m., but there is really no reason to arrive at the crack of dawn—for once.

Downtown Disney

Downtown Disney West Side

Parking

1. Cirque du Soleil *La Nouba*
2. DisneyQuest
3. House of Blues
4. Ridemakerz *(open through fall 2010)*
5. Wolfgang Puck Grand Cafe
6. Specialty shopping:
   Disney's Candy Cauldron
   D-Street
   Hoypoloi
   littlemissmatched
   Magic Masters
   Magnetron Magnetz
   Mickey's Groove
   Pop Gallery
   Sosa Family Cigars
   Sunglass Icon
7. Bongos Cuban Cafe
8. AMC Pleasure Island 24 Theatres
9. Wetzel's Pretzels/Häagen-Dazs
10. Characters In Flight
11. Planet Hollywood
12. Curl by Sammy Duvall
13. Paradiso 37
14. Orlando Harley-Davidson
15. Fuego by Sosa Cigars
16. Raglan Road/Cookies of Dublin

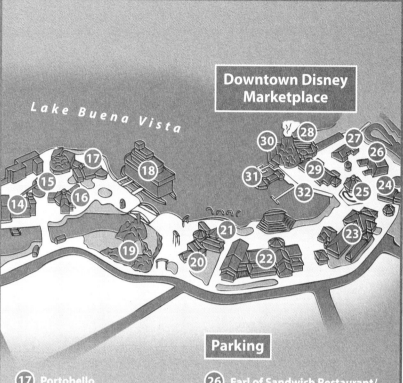

Downtown Disney Marketplace

Lake Buena Vista

Parking

(17) Portobello

(18) Fulton's Crab House

(19) T-REX

(20) Pollo Campero

(21) LEGO Imagination Center

(22) World of Disney

(23) Specialty shopping:
   Arribas Brothers
   Basin
   Ghirardelli Soda Fountain
     & Chocolate Shop
   Team Mickey
   Tren-D

(24) Once Upon a Toy

(25) Disney's Pin Traders

(26) Earl of Sandwich Restaurant/
   Mickey's Pantry

(27) Wolfgang Puck Express Cafe

(28) Specialty shopping:
   The Art of Disney
   Disney's Design A Tee
   Disney's Wonderful World
     of Memories

(29) Specialty shopping:
   Goofy's Candy Co.
   Mickey's Mart
   Pooh Corner

(30) Rainforest Cafe

(31) Cap'n Jack's Restaurant

(32) Cap'n Jack's Marina

I love the LEGO Imagination Center at Downtown Disney. You can make your own LEGO cars and drop them down a slope. Better watch out because it gets crowded with kids. One kid ran off with my car. There are cool LEGO statues outside and a LEGO dragon on the lake. It's a good place to take pictures.

— Ian

My all-time favorite toy at Once Upon a Toy is a miniature version of Wilderness Lodge made of Lincoln Logs.

— Liliane

I say go for the hairstyle and makeup only and take your own pictures. Disney princess costumes are available at a reasonable rate at your hometown Halloween shop (best buys just after the holiday) or on eBay. While the salon also offers a "cool dude" makeover for boys, Bibbidi Bobbidi Boutique is a serious girl's thing.

— Liliane

MARKETPLACE HIGHLIGHTS

KIDS WILL PARTICULARLY ENJOY the **LEGO Imagination Center**. You'll know you're there when you see the 30-foot sea serpent made out of more than a million LEGO blocks that lives in the lake right in front of the store. Outside the store is a play area filled with LEGO blocks for children to enjoy.

Once Upon a Toy is a joy. The biggest draws at this 16,000-square-foot store are classic toys with a Disney twist. Here you can find Mr. Potato Head with Mickey Ears or a sorcerer's hat and the classic game Clue set in The Haunted Mansion.

Bibbidi Bobbidi Boutique transforms your little girl into a princess, albeit for a price. A Fairy Godmother-in-training (the shop owner) and her helpers offer salon services for princesses age 3 and up. Hairstyle and makeup cost $53, adding a manicure will cost you $58, and the royal makeover (including your choice of a princess costume with accessories and a photo shoot with imaging package) starts at $202. Prices include tax.

THE WEST SIDE HIGHLIGHTS

THE BEST THING AT DOWNTOWN DISNEY and probably in all of Walt Disney World is **Cirque du Soleil's *La Nouba*.** Mesmerizing, thrilling, superb, and beautiful hardly do the show justice, but it's all of those and more. Tickets range $91–$128 for adults and $74–$104 for kids ages 3–9 (tax included). Florida residents are eligible for a 20% discount. If you are not familiar with Cirque du Soleil, visit the Web site at **cirquedusoleil.com.** You can book online or call ☎ 407-939-7600.

The place for wannabe magicians is **Magic Masters,** where the store interior is a re-creation of Houdini's personal library. If you buy a magic trick, you are taken behind a hidden panel in the bookcase to learn its secret. **Pop Gallery** is the place to go for high-end paintings and sculpture.

Catch all the latest box office hits at the **AMC Pleasure Island** state-of-the-art, 24-movie theater complex, all under one roof and offering flicks in an Art Deco setting. For information on showtimes and tickets, log on to **amctheatres.com** and select Orlando Pleasure Island 24.

Restaurants include the **House of Blues,** which serves Cajun specialties; **Planet Hollywood,** offering movie memorabilia and basic American fare; **Bongos**

Cuban Cafe, serving Cuban favorites; and **Wolfgang Puck Cafe,** featuring California cuisine.

DISNEYQUEST If your children are age 11 or older, DisneyQuest on Disney's West Side is a special treat you might want to consider. DisneyQuest is Disney's pioneering prototype of a theme park in a box, or more literally, in a modest five-story building.

> Weekdays before 4 p.m. are least crowded at DisneyQuest.
>
>
> Bob

Opened in the summer of 1998, DisneyQuest contains all the elements of the larger Disney theme parks. An entrance area facilitates your transition into the park environment and leads to the gateways of four distinct themed lands, referred to here as zones. As at other Disney parks, everything is included in the price of your admission.

It takes about 2–3 hours to experience DisneyQuest once you get in. Disney limits the number of guests admitted to ensure that queues are manageable and that guests have a positive experience.

DisneyQuest is aimed at a youthful audience, say 8–35 years of age, though younger and older patrons will enjoy much of what it offers. The feel is dynamic, bustling, and noisy. Those who haunt the electronic games arcades at shopping malls will feel most at home at DisneyQuest.

From the turnstile, you enter the Departure Lobby and a "Cyberlator"—a sort of "transitional attraction" (read: elevator) hosted by the genie from *Aladdin*—that delivers you to an entrance plaza called Ventureport. From here you can enter the four zones: Explore Zone, Score Zone, Create Zone, and Replay Zone. As in the larger parks, each zone is distinctively themed. Some zones cover more than one floor, so looking around, you can see things going on both above and below you. In addition, DisneyQuest offers two restaurants and the inevitable gift shop.

Each zone offers several attractions, most based on technologies such as simulators that work well in confined spaces. The Explore Zone is representative. You enter through a re-creation of the tiger's-head cave from *Aladdin*. The headline attraction in Explore Zone is the Virtual Jungle Cruise, where you paddle a six-person raft. The raft is a motion simulator perched on top of blue air bags that replicate the motion of water. Responding to the film of the river projected before you, you can choose several routes through the rapids. The motion

> You've got to try Cyberspace Mountain at DisneyQuest! Ride the roller coaster you design on a computer. You can choose to ride in space, the jungle, or inside a volcano. Space is the coolest. I picked barrel rolls, backflips, a dive into a black hole, twists and turns, and a dip down under the track. You sit in a simulator and feel like an astronaut flying through space. And don't miss the Virtual Jungle Cruise. It's totally wild! I worked up a sweat on this one. Feels like you're in a real video game. It's a simulator raft ride and you paddle through river rapids with a group of people. Everybody is yelling and screaming as you try to paddle in the right direction. Watch out for dinosaurs and waterfalls. You will get wet, really, but not too much.
>
> Ian

Pinball wizard, here I come! Seriously, DisneyQuest is great for a rainy day or arrival and departure days.

Liliane

simulator responds to sensors on your paddle. As if navigating the river isn't enough, man-eating dinosaurs and a cataclysmic comet are tossed in for good measure.

Some DisneyQuest attractions tap your imagination. In the Create Zone, for example, you can use a computer to design your own roller coaster, including 360-degree loops, and then take a virtual reality ride on your creation in a motion simulator. Sid's Make-a-Toy, also in the Create Zone, lets you design a toy and receive the parts to actually construct it at home. Other creative attractions include virtual beauty salon makeovers and painting on an electronic canvas.

Like all things Disney, admission to DisneyQuest is not cheap. But especially for teens and technology junkies, it's an eye-opening experience and a fun time.

A one-day admission ranges $35–$41. Children under age 10 must be accompanied by a responsible person 16 years and older. Kids under the age of 3 are admitted free of charge, but strollers are not permitted inside DisneyQuest. You can leave and re-enter anytime you want on the day of your visit: Just make sure your wrist gets stamped upon arrival. Annual passes are available.

Believe it or not, there are height restrictions at DisneyQuest, and here is the countdown: **Cyberspace Mountain:** 51 inches; **Pirates of the Caribbean—Battle for Buccaneer Gold:** 35 inches; and **Buzz Lightyear's Astro Blasters:** 51 inches.

No need to leave DisneyQuest when hunger strikes. Wonderland Cafe and FoodQuest serve the usual fare, and once you are ready to leave, the exit is through the obligatory gift shop.

The Rainforest Cafe is like having dinner in a tree house. Tree branches are everywhere. Birds are chirping, and there are humongous mushrooms. Monkeys, orangutans, and gorillas are all around too. Don't worry; they're not real. While you're eating, every once in a while thunder and lightning appear and a rainstorm happens. The ribs are very good. You have to get the chocolate volcano for dessert. It's incredible!

Ian

PLEASURE ISLAND HIGHLIGHTS

AFTER A 20-YEAR RUN, Disney all but shut down the Pleasure Island nighttime entertainment complex. For the time being, the focus is on family-friendly shops and restaurants, including **Raglan Road,** an Irish pub and restaurant featuring live Celtic music; **Fuego by Sosa Cigars,** a posh cigar bar; **Curl by Sammy Duval,** a surf shop; a Harley-Davidson apparel store; and several outdoor food-and-beverage locations.

HOW TO MAKE IT WORK

IT REALLY DOES NOT MATTER if you make Downtown Disney your destination for the day or if you decide to go on the spur of the moment. Fun can be had by all anytime. Family restrooms (with a changing and nursing area) are located in the Marketplace near Once Upon a Toy and the Art of Disney.

SHOPPING There are five ATMs at Downtown Disney. All major credit cards are accepted, and if you are a Disney resort guest, you can have your shopping purchases delivered to your hotel (this only works if you are not checking out the next day). Pickup is usually at the primary gift shop of your resort (no room delivery), but even so, it sure beats lugging stuff around.

BEFORE YOU GO

1. Determine in advance what all members in your party want to do. Pick up a map at Guest Relations and enjoy the area.

2. Downtown Disney is a great place to give your teenagers some space. Agree on a time and place to reunite and turn them loose. While teens enjoy DisneyQuest or the latest flick at the AMC movie theater, mom and dad can have a peaceful dinner at the Portobello Yacht Club or Wolfgang Puck Cafe.

3. Pets are not allowed at Downtown Disney. Best Friends Pet Care (**bestfriendspetcare.com**) is located near Port Orleans Resort.

Ian's tip gives you a good example of how most kids feel about the Downtown Disney Rainforest Cafe. Getting a table during normal dinner hours, however, is only slightly less diffi- cult than eloping with Daisy Duck. If the kids are all over you to go, try the saner, more manageable Rainforest Cafe at the Animal Kingdom. You'll be done and out the door in less time than it takes to get seated at the Downtown Disney location.

FAVORITE EATS AT DOWNTOWN DISNEY		
AREA	FOOD ITEM	WHERE THEY CAN BE FOUND
MARKETPLACE	Earl of Sandwich	Sandwich paradise
	Ghirardelli Soda Fountain & Chocolate Shop	Ice cream and chocolate treats
	Wolfgang Puck Express	Soups, salads, and pizza
	Rainforest Cafe	Burgers & kids' menu in Jurassic setting with T-Rex dinosaurs
WEST SIDE	Forty-Thirst Street	Mini-doughnuts and coffee
	Wetzel's Pretzels	Pretzels with a twist
	FoodQuest	Pizza, pasta, and salads
	House of Blues	Cajun food and kids' menu.* For shows in the music hall next door, check out **hob.com.**
	Planet Hollywood*	Burgers.* Great for teens who will love checking out the Hollywood memorabilia.
PLEASURE ISLAND	Raglan Road	Irish food and live music

* table service only

The **BEST** *of the* **REST**

UNLESS YOU'RE A GAMBLER OR A NUDIST, you'll probably find your favorite activity offered at Walt Disney World. You can fish, canoe, hike, bike, boat, play tennis and golf, ride horses, work out, take cooking lessons, and even drive a real race car or watch the Atlanta Braves' spring training.

Your kids will go nuts for the **Wilderness Lodge Resort,** and so will you. While you're there, have a family-style meal at the children-friendly Whispering Canyon restaurant and rent bikes for a ride on the paved paths of adjacent Fort Wilderness campground. The outing will be a great change of pace. The only downside is that your kids might not want to go back to their own hotel.

More fun is available at **The ESPN Wide World of Sports,** a 220-acre competition and training complex. During late winter and early spring, the venue is the spring training home of the Atlanta Braves. Disney guests are welcome at the sports complex as paid spectators, but none of the facilities are available for guests to use.

To learn what events, including Major League Baseball exhibition games, are scheduled during your visit, call ☎ 407-939-GAME or visit **disneyworldsports.com.** Admission is $13.50 for adults, $10 for children ages 3–9. Some events carry an extra charge, and dining options are available.

Located 40–60 minutes south of Walt Disney World is the **Disney Wilderness Preserve,** a wetlands-restoration area operated by the Nature Conservancy in partnership with Disney. There are hiking trails, an interpretive center, guided outings on weekends, and buggy rides. Trails wind through grassy savannas, beneath ancient cypress trees, and along the banks of pristine Lake Russell. The preserve is open daily 9 a.m.–5 p.m., closed on Thanksgiving and Christmas days. General admission is $3 for adults and $2 for children ages 6–17. Guided trail walks are offered on Saturday at no extra cost. Reservations are highly recommended. Disney cast members and information operators don't know squat about the Wilderness Preserve, so if you're interested, call the preserve directly at ☎ 407-935-0002.

GOLF

IF GOLF IS YOUR THING, call ☎ 407-938-GOLF for tee times and greens fees at Palm Golf Course (★★★★), Magnolia Golf Course (★★★½), Lake Buena Vista Golf Course (★★★), or Oak Trail Golf Course (★★½). For more information call ☎ 407-938-GOLF.

There is, of course, golf beyond Mickey's Kingdom. The greater Orlando area has enough high-quality courses to rival better-known golfing meccas, such as Scottsdale and Palm Springs. But unlike these destinations with their endless private country clubs, Orlando is unique because almost all its courses are open for some sort of public

ARNOLD PALMER'S BAY HILL CLUB & LODGE ★★★★ **bayhill.com** or
☎ 407-876-2429

CHAMPIONSGATE INTERNATIONAL COURSE ★★★★ ☎ 407-787-4653

CHAMPIONSGATE NATIONAL COURSE ★★★½ ☎ 407-787-4653

CROOKED CAT ★★★★ ☎ 407-656-2626

GRAND CYPRESS GOLF CLUB ★★★★½ **grandcypress.com** or
☎ 407-239-4700

INDEPENDENCE ★★★★ ☎ 407-662-1100

LEGACY ★★★★½ ☎ 407-662-1100

METROWEST GOLF CLUB ★★★½ **metrowestgolf.com** or ☎ 407-299-1099

PANTHER LAKE ★★★★½ ☎ 407-656-2626

play. We compiled a list of off-Disney golf courses for **dad's or mom's special day off** (see the chart above).

The 900-page *Unofficial Guide to Walt Disney World,* by Bob Sehlinger and Len Testa, contains an entire chapter on Walt Disney World and Orlando-area golf with in-depth profiles of all the best courses.

MINIATURE GOLF

CONSIDER MINIATURE GOLF FOR THE WHOLE FAMILY at **Fantasia Gardens Miniature Golf,** located across the street from the Walt Disney World Swan or at **Winter Summerland** right next to Blizzard Beach. Fantasia Gardens Miniature Golf is a beautifully landscaped garden with fountains, animated statues, topiaries, and flower beds. At Winter Summerland the Christmas holiday theme is prevalent, with ornaments hanging from palm trees. At Castle Hole watch out for a snowman that sprays water on unsuspecting guests when their golf balls pass beneath him.

Fantasia Gardens is quite demanding and not nearly as whimsical as Winter Summerland. Adults and older teens will enjoy the challenge of Fantasia Gardens, but if your group includes children younger than 12, head to Winter Summerland. Another Winter Summerland plus is that it can be reached easily via Disney transportation. To access Fantasia Gardens you must take a bus to the Walt Disney World Swan Resort and walk to the course from there. Admission with tax to both courses is $12 for adults and $10 for children ages 3–9. Opening hours are 10 a.m.– 11 p.m. For more information call ☎ 407-WDW-PLAY.

THEME PARK TRIVIA QUIZ ANSWERS

MAGIC KINGDOM

1. (C) 2. (C) 3. (D) 4. (D) 5. (C) 6. (D) 7. (A) 8. (C) 9. (B)
10. (B) 11. (A)

EPCOT

1. (D) 2. (B) 3. (B) 4. (D) 5. (D) 6. (C) 7. (A) 8. (C) 9. (C)
10. (B) 11. (C) 12. (B)

DISNEY'S ANIMAL KINGDOM

1. (C) 2. (A) 3. (D) 4. (B) 5. (D) 6. (B) 7. (B) 8. (D) 9. (C)
10. (D)

DISNEY'S HOLLYWOOD STUDIOS

1. (A) 2. (A) 3. (C) 4. (A) 5. (B) 6. (A) 7. (C) 8. (A) 9. (B)
10. (C) 11. (B) 12. (A)

INDEX

Magic Kingdom Happy Family One-Day Touring Plan

1. If you are a Disney resort guest, arrive at the entrance to the Magic Kingdom 30 minutes prior to opening. Guests staying off-site should arrive at the Ticket and Transportation Center 40 minutes prior to opening. Obtain park maps and a copy of the daily entertainment schedule when you pass through the turnstiles. Stroller rentals are under the train station on Main Street.
2. PARENTS: As soon as the park opens, ride Dumbo the Flying Elephant in Fantasyland.
3. TEENS: As soon as the park opens, ride Space Mountain in Tomorrowland.
4. FAMILY: Ride The Many Adventures of Winnie the Pooh in Fantasyland.
5. FAMILY: Ride the Mad Tea Party in Fantasyland.
6. FAMILY: Ride Peter Pan's Flight in Fantasyland.
7. FAMILY: See *Mickey's PhilharMagic* in Fantasyland.
8. PARENTS: Ride The Magic Carpets of Aladdin in Adventureland.
9. TEENS: Ride Splash Mountain in Frontierland. If the wait exceeds 30 minutes, use Fastpass.
10. TEENS: Ride Big Thunder Mountain Railroad in Frontierland. Tip: Get Fastpasses for Splash or Big Thunder now if you want to ride again later.
11. FAMILY: Ride Pirates of the Caribbean in Adventureland.
12. FAMILY: See *The Enchanted Tiki Room.*
13. FAMILY: Eat lunch. Good nearby dining choices include Pecos Bill Tall Tale Inn and Cafe and the top floor of the Columbia Harbour House.
14. PARENTS: After lunch, return to your hotel for a break. We recommend allowing at least 3 hours.
15. TEENS: Ride Splash Mountain again in Frontierland. If you have Fastpasses, use those. Otherwise, obtain Fastpasses if the wait exceeds 30 minutes.

16. TEENS: Ride Big Thunder Mountain Railroad again in Frontierland. If you have Fastpasses, use those. Otherwise, obtain Fastpasses (if you can) if the wait exceeds 30 minutes.
17. TEENS: See The Haunted Mansion in Liberty Square.
18. TEENS: Explore the rest of the park, or revisit favorite attractions until the rest of the family returns.
19. PARENTS: Return to the Magic Kingdom and take the WDW Railroad from Main Street to Frontierland.
20. FAMILY: Tour Tom Sawyer Island. Allow at least 30–45 minutes to run around the island. Be sure to try the barrel bridges and tour Fort Langhorn.
21. FAMILY: Eat dinner.
22. FAMILY: See *Monsters, Inc. Laugh Floor* in Tomorrowland.
23. FAMILY: Ride Buzz Lightyear's Space Ranger Spin.
24. PARENTS: In Fantasyland, ride The Barnstormer. Note: The Barnstormer will be located in Toontown through 2010 and possibly into 2011; look for it near the Mad Tea Party in the upper right corner of the park map.
25. PARENTS: If time permits, check the daily entertainment schedule for locations and times to meet Disney characters. The most common character greeting locations are Main Street and Fantasyland.
26. FAMILY: See the evening parade and/or fireworks on Main Street. A good viewing location for the fireworks is on the right-hand side of the central hub, near the walkway to Tomorrowland.
27. FAMILY: Depart the Magic Kingdom.

If you have a Web-enabled cell phone, you can view current and future wait times for every attraction—and add the times you see in the parks—at m.touringplans.com.

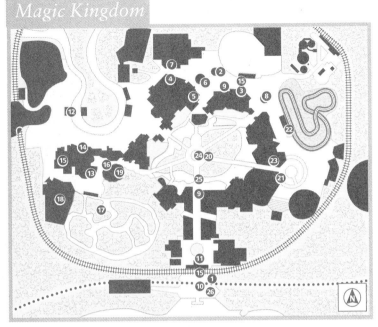

Magic Kingdom

Magic Kingdom One-Day Touring Plan for Grandparents with Small Children

1. If you are a Disney resort guest, arrive at the entrance to the Magic Kingdom 30 minutes prior to opening. Guests staying off-site should arrive at the Ticket and Transportation Center 40 minutes prior to opening. Obtain park maps and a copy of the daily entertainment schedule when you pass through the turnstiles. Stroller rentals are under the train station on Main Street.

2. As soon as the park opens, ride Dumbo the Flying Elephant in Fantasyland. To get to Fantasyland, go down Main Street and either through or around the castle.

3. Ride The Many Adventures of Winnie the Pooh.

4. Ride Peter Pan's Flight.

5. See *Mickey's PhilharMagic*.

6. Take a spin on Prince Charming's Regal Carrousel.

7. Take the It's a Small World boat ride.

8. Give the Mad Tea Party a spin. It's located near the Winnie the Pooh ride.

9. If your grandkids are interested in meeting Disney characters, princesses, or fairies, do so now. Check the daily entertainment schedule for times and locations of each character. The most common locations are in Fantasyland and on Main Street.

10. Eat lunch outside of the park and return to your hotel for a break of 3–4 hours.

11. Return to the Magic Kingdom and take the WDW Railroad from Main Street to Frontierland.

12. Tour Tom Sawyer Island. Allow at least 30–45 minutes to run around the island. Be sure to try the barrel bridges and tour Fort Langhorn.

13. Return to Frontierland for the Frontierland Shootin' Arcade. Cost is $1 per play.

14. See the *Country Bear Jamboree*. If possible, send one member of your party into Adventureland to

check on Fastpasses for Jungle Cruise. If they're available for return in around an hour, get Fastpasses for everyone.

15. Eat dinner if you've not already done so. The nearest counter-service restaurant is Pecos Bill Tall Tale Inn and Cafe in Frontierland.

16. Ride The Magic Carpets of Aladdin.

17. Take the Jungle Cruise if lines are short or you have Fastpasses; otherwise, see *The Enchanted Tiki Room*.

18. Ride Pirates of the Caribbean.

19. Tour the Swiss Family Treehouse.

20. If the evening parade or fireworks will start within the next hour, find a spot on Main Street for the evening parade and fireworks. Grab the kids an ice cream and take a break. Otherwise, try the next few steps in Tomorrowland.

21. Try Buzz Lightyear's Space Ranger Spin in Tomorrowland, and then ride the Tomorrowland Transit Authority, across from Buzz in the center of Tomorrowland.

22. Take a spin on the Tomorrowland Speedway.

23. See *Monsters, Inc. Laugh Floor*.

24. See the evening parade and fireworks from Main Street. The right side of the central hub on Main Street is a good viewing location.

25. If time permits and you've not already done so, obtain character autographs for any characters your grandchildren wish to meet.

26. Depart the Magic Kingdom.

If you have a Web-enabled cell phone, you can view current and future wait times for every attraction—and add the times you see in the parks—at m.touringplans.com.

Magic Kingdom

Magic Kingdom One-Day Touring Plan for Tweens and Their Parents

1. If you are a Disney resort guest, arrive at the entrance to the Magic Kingdom 30 minutes prior to opening. Guests staying off-site should arrive at the Ticket and Transportation Center 40 minutes prior to opening. Obtain park maps and a copy of the daily entertainment schedule when you pass through the turnstiles.
2. As soon as the park opens, ride Space Mountain in Tomorrowland.
3. Ride Buzz Lightyear's Space Ranger Spin.
4. Ride The Many Adventures of Winnie the Pooh in Fantasyland.
5. Ride the Mad Tea Party. Parents can abstain. Really.
6. Ride Peter Pan's Flight.
7. See The Haunted Mansion in Liberty Square.
8. Ride Splash Mountain. If the wait exceeds 30 minutes, consider using Fastpass.
9. Ride Big Thunder Mountain Railroad.
10. Ride Pirates of the Caribbean.
11. Eat lunch. Good nearby counter-service restaurants include Pecos Bill Tall Tale Inn and Cafe in Frontierland and the Columbia Harbour House in Liberty Square.
12. Ride the Jungle Cruise in Adventureland. If the wait exceeds 30 minutes, use Fastpass.
13. Tour the Swiss Family Treehouse.
14. See *The Enchanted Tiki Room*.
15. See the *Country Bear Jamboree* in Frontierland.
16. Try the Frontierland Shootin' Arcade. Cost is $1 per play.
17. Experience *The Hall of Presidents*.
18. See *Mickey's PhilharMagic* in Fantasyland.
19. Eat dinner. The closest sit-down restaurant is Cinderella's Royal Table (reservations required). For counter-service, try Pinocchio Village Haus in Fantasyland.
20. Take a ride on the Walt Disney World Railroad. Stations are located in Frontierland and on Main Street.
21. If time permits, see *Monsters, Inc. Laugh Floor* in Tomorrowland.
22. See the evening parade on Main Street.
23. See the evening fireworks on Main Street. A good viewing spot is to the right of the central hub, on the walkway toward Tomorrowland.
24. Depart the Magic Kingdom.

If you have a Web-enabled cell phone, you can view current and future wait times for every attraction—and add the times you see in the parks—at m.touringplans.com.

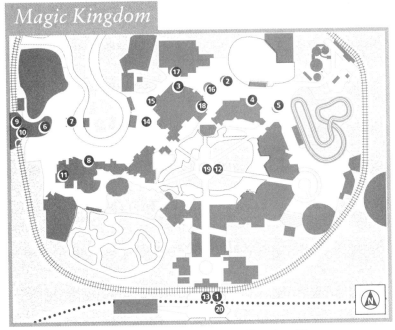

Magic Kingdom

Magic Kingdom Two-Day Touring Plan
for Parents with Small Children—Day 1
(Review the Small-child Fright-potential Chart on pages 182–185)

1. If you are a Disney resort guest, arrive at the entrance to the Magic Kingdom 30 minutes prior to opening. Guests staying off-site should arrive at the Ticket and Transportation Center 40 minutes prior to opening. Obtain park maps and a copy of the daily entertainment schedule when you pass through the turnstiles. Stroller rentals are under the train station on Main Street.
2. As soon as the park opens, ride Dumbo the Flying Elephant in Fantasyland.
3. Ride Peter Pan's Flight.
4. Ride The Many Adventures of Winnie the Pooh.
5. Ride the Mad Tea Party.
6. Obtain Fastpasses for Splash Mountain in Frontierland.
7. Tour Tom Sawyer Island. Allow 30–45 minutes to run around the island. Be sure to try the barrel bridges and tour Fort Langhorn.
8. See the *Country Bear Jamboree*.
9. Take a round-trip on the Walt Disney World Railroad from the Frontierland station. The station is accessed by stairs located to the right of the entrance to Splash Mountain.
10. Ride Splash Mountain.
11. Eat lunch. Good nearby dining choices include Pecos Bill Tall Tale Inn and Cafe, with ample seating and air-conditioning. In Liberty Square, the top floor of the Columbia Harbour House is usually less crowded.
12. After lunch, return to your hotel for a mid-afternoon break. We recommend allowing at least 3 hours,

including transportation—4 hours would be better.
13. Return to the Magic Kingdom.
14. Experience *The Hall of Presidents* and the *Liberty Belle* riverboat in Liberty Square. These attractions are located across from each other in Liberty Square; see first the attraction that begins soonest, then see the other.
15. Eat dinner. The closest counter-service restaurant is Pinocchio Village Haus in Fantasyland. The nearest sit-down restaurant is Liberty Tree Tavern in Liberty Square.
16. Enjoy Prince Charming's Regal Carrousel in Fantasyland.
17. Ride It's a Small World.
18. See *Mickey's PhilharMagic*. This is the last attraction in today's touring. Use extra time to revisit favorite attractions or explore the rest of the park.
19. See the evening parade and/or fireworks. A good viewing location for the fireworks is on the right-hand side of the central hub, near the walkway to Tomorrowland.
20. Depart the Magic Kingdom.

If you have a Web-enabled cell phone, you can view current and future wait times for every attraction—and add the times you see in the parks—at m.touringplans.com.

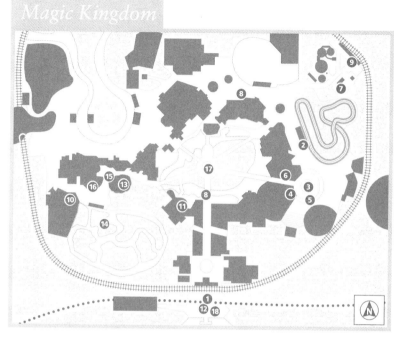

Magic Kingdom Two-Day Touring Plan for Parents with Small Children—Day 2

(Review the Small-child Fright-potential Chart on pages 182-185)

1. If you are a Disney resort guest, arrive at the entrance to the Magic Kingdom 30 minutes prior to opening. Guests staying off-site should arrive at the Ticket and Transportation Center 40 minutes prior to opening. Obtain park maps and a copy of the daily entertainment schedule when you pass through the turnstiles. Stroller rentals are under the train station on Main Street.

2. As soon as the park opens, ride the Tomorrowland Speedway in Tomorrowland.

3. Ride the Astro Orbiter.

4. Ride Buzz Lightyear's Space Ranger Spin. If the wait exceeds 30 minutes, obtain Fastpasses for each member of your party.

5. Ride the Tomorrowland Transit Authority.

6. See *Monsters, Inc. Laugh Floor*.

7. In Fantasyland, ride The Barnstormer. Note: The Barnstormer will be located in Toontown through 2010 and possibly into 2011; look for it near the Mad Tea Party in the upper right corner of the park map.

8. If your children are interested in meeting Disney characters, princesses, or fairies, do so now. Check the daily entertainment schedule for times and locations of each character. The most common locations are in Fantasyland and on Main Street.

9. Make your way to Adventureland. Check the park map to see whether the Toontown/Fantasyland train station is open. If so, take the railroad to Frontierland. If you've rented a Disney stroller, remove your personal possessions, name card, and

rental receipt from the stroller. You'll be issued a new stroller in Frontierland.

10. Ride Pirates of the Caribbean in Adventureland. While most children will take this attraction in stride, the skeletons in some of the scenes may frighten a few children.

11. Eat lunch. Good sit-down restaurants include Liberty Tree Tavern in Liberty Square and the Crystal Palace on Main Street. For burgers, try Pecos Bill Tall Tale Inn and Cafe in Frontierland.

12. Return to your hotel for a mid-day break. Allow at least 3 hours for your break—4 hours would be better.

13. Return to the Magic Kingdom and explore the Swiss Family Treehouse in Adventureland.

14. Ride the Jungle Cruise. If the wait time exceeds 30 minutes, use Fastpass.

15. Ride The Magic Carpets of Aladdin.

16. See *The Enchanted Tiki Room*. This is the last attraction in today's touring. Use extra time to revisit favorite attractions or explore the rest of the park.

17. If you have not already done so, see the evening parade and/or fireworks.

18. Depart the Magic Kingdom.

If you have a Web-enabled cell phone, you can view current and future wait times for every attraction—and add the times you see in the parks—at m.touringplans.com.

Magic Kingdom

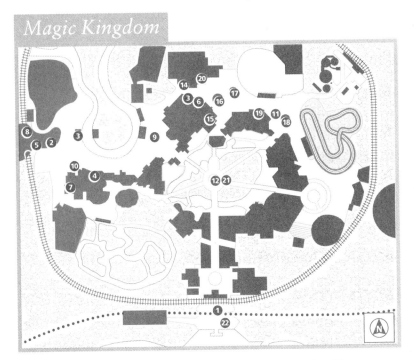

Magic Kingdom Two-Day Sleepyhead Touring Plan for Parents with Small Children—Day 1

(Review the Small-child Fright-potential Chart on pages 182–185)

1. Arrive at the entrance to the Magic Kingdom around 11 a.m. Obtain park maps and a copy of the daily entertainment schedule when you pass through the turnstiles. Stroller rentals are under the train station on Main Street.
2. Obtain Fastpasses for Splash Mountain in Frontierland.
3. Tour Tom Sawyer Island. Allow at least 30–45 minutes to see the island, including the barrel bridges and Fort Langhorn.
4. See the *Country Bear Jamboree*.
5. Ride Splash Mountain. Use the Fastpasses obtained in Step 2.
6. Send one member of your party to obtain Fastpasses for Peter Pan's Flight in Fantasyland.
7. Eat a late lunch. Good nearby dining choices include Pecos Bill Tall Tale Inn and Cafe, with ample seating and air-conditioning. In Liberty Square, the top floor of the Columbia Harbour House is usually less crowded.
8. Take a round trip on the Walt Disney World Railroad from the Frontierland station. The station is accessed by stairs located to the right of the entrance to Splash Mountain.
9. Experience The Hall of Presidents and the Liberty Belle riverboat in Liberty Square. These attractions are located across from each other in Liberty Square; see first the attraction that begins soonest, then see the other.
10. See the afternoon parade from Frontierland or Liberty Square.

11. Send one member of your party to obtain Fastpasses for The Many Adventures of Winnie the Pooh in Fantasyland. Check your Fastpasses for Peter Pan's Flight for the exact time you can obtain Fastpasses for Pooh.
12. Take a 1-hour break inside the park. Good rest areas include the second floor of the Columbia Harbour House in Liberty Square and the walkway near the candy store in Frontierland.
13. Ride Peter Pan's Flight using the Fastpasses obtained in Step 6.
14. Ride It's a Small World.
15. See *Mickey's PhilharMagic*.
16. Enjoy Prince Charming's Regal Carrousel.
17. Ride Dumbo the Flying Elephant.
18. Ride the Mad Tea Party.
19. Ride The Many Adventures of Winnie the Pooh using the Fastpasses obtained in Step 11.
20. Eat dinner. Nearby choices include Pinocchio Village Haus (counter-service) and Cinderella's Royal Table (sit-down; reservations required).
21. See the evening parade and fireworks from Main Street. A good viewing location for the fireworks is on the right-hand side of the central hub, near the walkway to Tomorrowland.
22. Depart the Magic Kingdom.

If you have a Web-enabled cell phone, you can view current and future wait times for every attraction—and add the times you see in the parks—at m.touringplans.com.

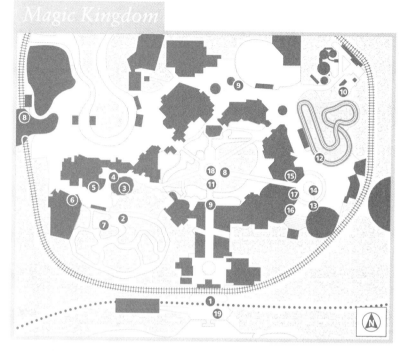

Magic Kingdom Two-Day Sleepyhead Touring Plan for Parents with Small Children—Day 2

(Review the Small-child Fright-potential Chart on pages 182–185)

1. Arrive at the entrance to the Magic Kingdom around 11 a.m. Obtain park maps and a copy of the daily entertainment schedule when you pass through the turnstiles. Stroller rentals are under the train station on Main Street.
2. Obtain Fastpasses for the Jungle Cruise in Adventureland.
3. Explore the Swiss Family Treehouse.
4. Ride The Magic Carpets of Aladdin.
5. See *The Enchanted Tiki Room.*
6. Ride Pirates of the Caribbean.
7. Ride the Jungle Cruise using the Fastpasses obtained in Step 2.
8. Eat lunch. Good nearby dining choices include Pecos Bill Tall Tale Inn and Cafe, with ample seating and air-conditioning. In Liberty Square, the top floor of the Columbia Harbour House is usually less crowded.
9. If your children are interested in meeting Disney characters, princesses, or fairies, do so now. Check the daily entertainment schedule for times and locations of each character. The most common locations are in Fantasyland and on Main Street.
10. In Fantasyland, ride The Barnstormer. Note: The Barnstormer will be located in Toontown through

2010 and possibly into 2011; look for it near the Mad Tea Party in the upper right corner of the park map.
11. Take a 1-hour break inside the park. A good resting spot is inside Cosmic Ray's Starlight Café in Tomorrowland. If possible, send one member of your family to obtain Fastpasses for Buzz Lightyear's Space Ranger Spin in Tomorrowland.
12. Ride the Tomorrowland Speedway.
13. Ride the Tomorrowland Transit Authority.
14. Ride the Astro Orbiter.
15. See *Monsters, Inc. Laugh Floor.*
16. Ride Buzz Lightyear's Space Ranger Spin using the Fastpasses obtained in Step 11.
17. Eat dinner. The closest counter-service restaurant is Cosmic Ray's Starlight Café in Tomorrowland. Or try The Plaza Restaurant on Main Street.
18. See the evening parade on Main Street.
19. Depart the Magic Kingdom.

If you have a Web-enabled cell phone, you can view current and future wait times for every attraction—and add the times you see in the parks—at m.touringplans.com.

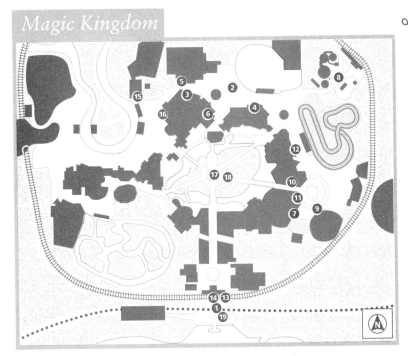

Magic Kingdom

Parent's Magic Kingdom Plan—One Afternoon and One Full Day (Full Day)

(Review the Small-child Fright-potential Chart on pages 182–185)

1. If you are a Disney resort guest, arrive at the entrance to the Magic Kingdom 30 minutes prior to opening. Guests staying off-site should arrive at the Ticket and Transportation Center 40 minutes prior to opening. Obtain park maps and a copy of the daily entertainment schedule when you pass through the turnstiles. Stroller rentals are under the train station on Main Street.

2. As soon as the park opens, ride Dumbo the Flying Elephant in Fantasyland.

3. Ride Peter Pan's Flight.

4. Ride The Many Adventures of Winnie the Pooh. Unless the wait exceeds 30 minutes, do not use Fastpass.

5. Ride It's a Small World.

6. See *Mickey's PhilharMagic*.

7. If possible, send one member of your party to obtain Fastpasses for Buzz Lightyear's Space Ranger Spin in Tomorrowland.

8. Ride The Barnstormer. Note: The Barnstormer will be located in Toontown through 2010 and possibly into 2011, after which it will be located in Fantasyland; look for it near the Mad Tea Party in the upper right corner of the park map.

9. Ride the Tomorrowland Transit Authority in Tomorrowland.

10. See *Monsters, Inc. Laugh Floor*.

11. Ride Buzz Lightyear's Space Ranger Spin, using the Fastpasses obtained in Step 7.

12. Eat lunch. The nearest counter-service restaurant is Cosmic Ray's Starlight Café, across from the Tomorrowland Speedway. Good sandwiches can be found at The Plaza Restaurant on Main Street.

13. Leave the park for a nap back at your hotel. Allow at least 3 hours for this break—4 would be better.

14. Return to the park. If you want to experience any ride again, see if Fastpasses are still available for it. Good evening rides include Splash Mountain in Frontierland and Prince Charming's Regal Carrousel in Fantasyland.

15. See The Haunted Mansion in Liberty Square.

16. Eat dinner if you have not already done so. Most kids will find something they like at the sit-down Liberty Tree Tavern. Reservations are recommended.

17. See the evening parade on Main Street. Liberty Square is a good alternate viewing location if you're already there.

18. See the evening fireworks on Main Street. A good viewing spot is to the right of the central hub, on the walkway toward Tomorrowland.

19. Depart the Magic Kingdom.

If you have a Web-enabled cell phone, you can view current and future wait times for every attraction—and add the times you see in the parks—at m.touringplans.com.

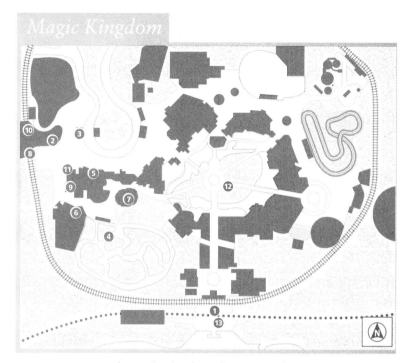

Parent's Magic Kingdom Plan—One Afternoon and One Full Day (Afternoon)

(Review the Small-child Fright-potential Chart on pages 182–185)

1. Arrive at the entrance to the Magic Kingdom around 2 p.m. Obtain park maps and a copy of the daily entertainment schedule when you pass through the turnstiles. Stroller rentals are under the train station on Main Street.

2. Obtain Fastpasses for Splash Mountain in Frontierland. If the wait is 20 minutes or less, ride now instead of using Fastpass.

3. In Frontierland, take the raft over to Tom Sawyer Island. Be sure to explore the barrel bridges and Fort Langhorn. If your kids are especially adventurous, explore the caves too!

4. Ride the Jungle Cruise in Adventureland. If the wait exceeds 30 minutes, use Fastpass.

5. See the *Country Bear Jamboree*. It's a short walk from the Jungle Cruise if you cut through Adventureland to Frontierland. Keep *The Enchanted Tiki Room* on your left, Magic Carpets of Aladdin on your right, and walk straight toward Frontierland. *CBJ* will be on your left.

6. Ride Pirates of the Caribbean in Adventureland.

7. Explore the Swiss Family Treehouse.

8. Ride Splash Mountain, using the Fastpasses obtained in Step 2.

9. Eat dinner. The closest counter-service restaurant is Pecos Bill Tall Tale Inn and Cafe in Frontierland. The closest sit-down restaurant is the Liberty Tree Tavern in Liberty Square. Reservations are recommended.

10. If you want to leave the park now, take the Walt Disney World Railroad from Frontierland to Main Street. The Frontierland station is located just above the entrance to Splash Mountain.

11. See the evening parade from Frontierland. Good viewing spots are along the storefronts of Frontierland—try in front of the candy store.

12. See the evening fireworks on Main Street. A good viewing spot is to the right of the central hub, on the walkway toward Tomorrowland.

13. Depart the Magic Kingdom.

If you have a Web-enabled cell phone, you can view current and future wait times for every attraction—and add the times you see in the parks—at m.touringplans.com.

Epcot One-Day Touring Plan for Parents with Small Children

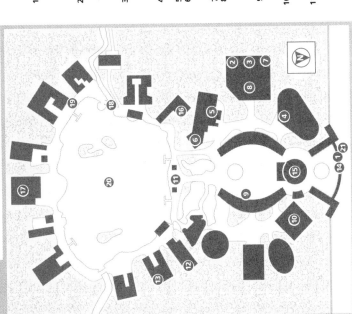

1. Arrive at the entrance to Epcot 30 minutes prior to opening. Pick up a park map and daily entertainment schedule when entering the park. Stroller rentals are just inside the main entrance and to the left.

2. If your children are tall enough, ride Soarin' at the Land pavilion in Future World West. If your children aren't yet tall enough, skip this step and continue to Living with the Land.

3. Ride Living with the Land, also at the Land pavilion. Use Fastpass if the wait exceeds 30 minutes. Exit the pavilion and turn left to get to the Seas pavilion.

4. See The Seas with Nemo and Friends. Be sure to catch *Turtle Talk with Crush.*

5. Ride Journey Into Your Imagination.

6. See the film at the Imagination pavilion, to the right after you exit the post-show area for Journey Into Your Imagination.

7. See *The Circle of Life* in the Land pavilion.

8. Eat lunch. The closest (and best) restaurant will be Sunshine Seasons in the Land pavilion. For burgers, try the Electric Umbrella in Future World East.

9. If your kids are tall enough, try the Sum of All Thrills roller coaster simulator at Innoventions East in Future World East.

10. Ride Universe of Energy in Future World East. This ride can also be seen after Spaceship Earth later today.

11. Sign up for a Kim Possible World Showcase Adventure on the way to World Showcase. Look for the Kim Possible booth on the left side of the main walkway from Future World to World Showcase. The Mexico and Norway adventures will be the closest to the next few steps; France and the United Kingdom will be better choices for the afternoon.

12. Ride the Gran Fiesta Tour at Mexico in World Showcase.

13. Ride Maelstrom at Norway. If the wait exceeds 30 minutes, consider using Fastpass.

14. Return to your hotel for a mid-day break.

15. Return to Epcot and ride Spaceship Earth.

16. See the *O Canada!* film at Canada in World Showcase. Eat dinner. Le Cellier, Canada's sit-down restaurant, is a popular choice. Reservations are required.

17. See *The American Adventure* at the United States pavilion.

18. If you've not already done so, try a Kim Possible World Showcase Adventure. The closest sign-up booth is between France and the United Kingdom in World Showcase.

19. If time permits, explore the Morocco, France, and United Kingdom pavilions.

20. See *IllumiNations.* Excellent viewing locations can be found along the walkway between Canada and France in World Showcase.

21. Depart Epcot.

If you have a Web-enabled cell phone, you can view current and future wait times for every attraction—and add the times you see in the parks—at m.touringplans.com.

Epcot One-Day Sleepyhead Touring Plan for Parents with Small Children

1. Arrive at the entrance to Epcot around 11 a.m. Pick up a park map and daily entertainment schedule when entering the park. Stroller rentals are just inside the main entrance and to the left.

2. If your children are tall enough, obtain Fastpasses for Soarin' at the Land pavilion in Future World West. If the wait is 25 minutes or less, ride now instead of using Fastpass.

3. Ride Living with the Land at the Land pavilion.

4. See The Seas with Nemo and Friends, and then tour the Seas pavilion. Be sure to try Turtle Talk with Crush.

5. Ride Journey into Your Imagination.

6. See the film at the Imagination pavilion, to the right after you exit the post-show area for Journey into Your Imagination.

7. If you have not already done so, eat lunch. Sunshine Seasons at the Land pavilion offers the best selection in Future World.

8. Ride Soarin' using the Fastpasses obtained in Step 2.

9. If your children are tall enough, try the Sum of All Thrills roller coaster simulator at Innoventions East in Future World East.

10. Ride Universe of Energy in Future World East.

11. Ride Spaceship Earth.

12. Sign up for a Kim Possible World Showcase Adventure mission on the way to World

Showcase. A Kim Possible sign-up station is on the left side of the main walkway leading from Future World to World Showcase.

13. Ride the Gran Fiesta Tour boat ride at Mexico.

14. Ride Maelstrom at Norway. Because of the walk back, we do not recommend using Fastpass unless the wait exceeds 45 minutes.

15. See The American Adventure at the United States pavilion. The Liberty Inn is a convenient counter-service restaurant.

16. Eat dinner. Good sit-down restaurants include Restaurant Marrakesh in Morocco and Le Cellier in Canada. Reservations are strongly recommended for Le Cellier.

17. See the O Canada! film at Canada in World Showcase.

18. See IllumiNations. The best viewing spots are along the border between World Showcase and Future World, and between Canada and France in World Showcase.

19. Depart Epcot.

If you have a Web-enabled cell phone, you can view current and future wait times for every attraction—and add the times you see in the parks—at m.touringplans.com.

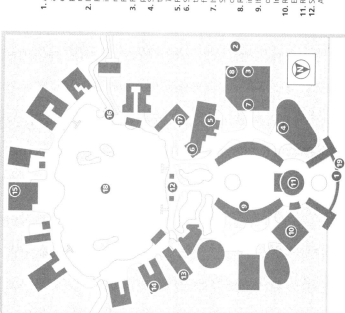

Epcot

Epcot One-Day Touring Plan for Tweens and Their Parents

1. Arrive at the entrance to Epcot 30 minutes prior to opening. Pick up a park map and daily entertainment schedule when entering the park.

2. As soon as the park opens, obtain Fastpasses for Soarin' at the Land pavilion in Future World West.

3. In Future World East, ride Test Track.

4. Ride Mission: SPACE. Do not use Fastpass.

5. In Innoventions East, ride Sum of All Thrills.

6. Ride Living with the Land in the Land Pavilion.

7. Now might be a good time to pick up a second Fastpass for Soarin', if available.

8. See The Seas with Nemo and Friends and Turtle Talk with Crush.

9. Ride Journey into Imagination.

10. See the film at the Imagination pavilion, to the right after you exit the post-show area for Journey Into Your Imagination.

11. Ride Soarin' using the Fastpasses obtained in Step 2.

12. Eat lunch. Sunshine Seasons has the best food in Future World. The Garden Grill in the Land pavilion is the closest sit-down restaurant.

13. Ride Spaceship Earth.

14. Ride Universe of Energy in Future World East.

15. Tour the remaining exhibits in Innoventions East.

16. Sign up for the Kim Possible World Showcase Adventure on the walk to World Showcase.

17. Experience the Gran Fiesta Tour boat ride a Mexico. This begins a clockwise tour of World Showcase.

18. Ride Maelstrom and tour the stave church in Norway.

19. See *Reflections of China*.

20. Tour Germany.

21. Visit Italy.

22. See *The American Adventure*.

23. Explore Japan.

24. Visit Morocco, including the small museum on the left side of the pavilion.

25. See *Impressions de France* at the France pavilion. Children give the film average marks, but the film is shown in an air-conditioned theater with comfortable seating, and everyone might need this kind of break about now.

26. Eat dinner. Good sit-down restaurants include Le Cellier at Canada and the Rose and Crown at the United Kingdom. Reservations are strongly recommended.

27. Visit the United Kingdom.

28. Tour Canada and see O *Canada!*

29. See *IllumiNations*. Prime viewing spots are along the lagoon between Canada and France.

30. Depart Epcot.

If you have a Web-enabled cell phone, you can view current and future wait times for every attraction—and add the times you se in the parks—at m.touringplans.com.

Epcot

Parent's Epcot Touring Plan for an Afternoon and a Full Day (Full Day)

1. Arrive at the entrance to Epcot 30 minutes prior to opening. Pick up a park map and daily entertainment schedule when entering the park.

2. As soon as the park opens, obtain Fastpasses for Soarin' at the Land pavilion in Future World West.

3. In Future World East, ride Test Track.

4. Ride Mission: SPACE. Do not use Fastpass.

5. In Innoventions East, ride Sum of All Thrills.

6. Ride Living with the Land in the Land Pavilion.

7. Now might be a good time to pick up a second Fastpass for Soarin', if available.

8. Ride Journey into Imagination.

9. See the film at the Imagination pavilion, to the right after you exit the post-show area for Journey Into Your Imagination.

10. Ride Soarin' using the Fastpasses obtained in Step 2.

11. Eat lunch. Sunshine Seasons has the best food in Future World. The Garden Grill in the Land pavilion is the closest sit-down restaurant. Or try the counter-service restaurant at Mexico in World Showcase.

12. Sign up for the Kim Possible World Showcase Adventure on the walk to World Showcase.

13. Experience the Gran Fiesta Tour boat ride at Mexico. This begins a clockwise tour of World Showcase.

14. Ride Maelstrom and tour the stave church in Norway.

15. See *Reflections of China.*

16. Tour Germany.

17. Visit Italy.

18. See *The American Adventure.*

19. Explore Japan.

20. Visit the Morocco pavilion.

21. Depart Epcot.

If you have a Web-enabled cell phone, you can view current and future wait times for every attraction—and add the times you see in the parks—at m.touringplans.com.

Epcot

Parent's Epcot Touring Plan for an Afternoon and a Full Day (Afternoon)

1. Arrive at Epcot at 1 p.m. Pick up a park map and daily entertainment schedule when entering the park. Make dining reservations by calling (407) WDW-DINE if you have not already done so.
2. Ride Spaceship Earth.
3. Tour the remaining attractions in Future World East.
4. See the Universe of Energy.
5. See The Seas with Nemo and Friends in Future World West. If you have young children, also see *Turtle Talk with Crush* at the Seas pavilion.
6. See *The Circle of Life* at the Land pavilion in Future World West.
7. If you have not already done so, sign up for the Kim Possible World Showcase Adventure on the walk to World Showcase.
8. See *O Canada!* at the Canada pavilion in World Showcase.
9. Visit the United Kingdom pavilion.
10. In France, see *Impressions de France*.
11. Eat dinner. Good nearby restaurants include Le Cellier at Canada, Restaurant Marrakesh at Morocco, and Teppan Edo at Japan. Reservations are recommended.
12. See *IllumiNations*. Good viewing spots can be found along the waterway between France and Canada.
13. Depart Epcot.

If you have a Web-enabled cell phone, you can view current and future wait times for every attraction—and add the times you see in the parks—at m.touringplans.com.

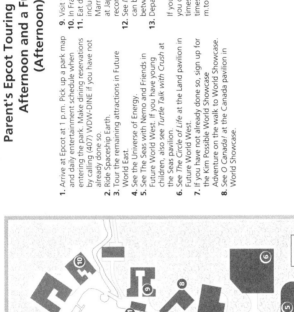

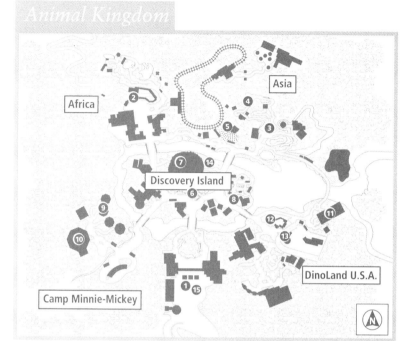

Animal Kingdom One-Day Touring Plan
for Parents with Small Children

1. Arrive at the entrance to Disney's Animal Kingdom 25 minutes prior to opening. Pick up a park map and entertainment schedule. Stroller rentals are just past the entrance, to the right.
2. As soon as the park opens, experience the Kilimanjaro Safaris in Africa.
3. Ride Kali River Rapids in Asia. You will get wet. Use ponchos or plastic bags to keep dry.
4. Walk the Maharajah Jungle Trek.
5. See *Flights of Wonder*. Check the daily entertainment schedule for performance times.
6. See *It's Tough To Be a Bug* in Discovery Island. If the wait exceeds 30 minutes, use Fastpass.
7. See the exhibits at the Tree of Life.
8. Eat lunch. Good nearby locations include Flame Tree Barbecue and Pizzafari.
9. Explore the Camp Minnie-Mickey Character Trails in Camp Minnie-Mickey.

10. See the *Festival of the Lion King*.
11. Check the next performance time of *Finding Nemo: The Musical* at the Theater in the Wild in DinoLand. If the next show is within 25 minutes, see *Nemo* now. Otherwise, see The Boneyard in DinoLand.
12. Check out The Boneyard in DinoLand.
13. Ride TriceraTop Spin in DinoLand.
14. If it's near parade time, find a good viewing spot on Discovery Island for the Afternoon Parade from Discovery Island. The parade is usually performed around 4 p.m.
15. Depart Disney's Animal Kingdom.
    The Animal Kingdom is a theme park to be savored. Take time to explore the exhibits and speak with the cast members.

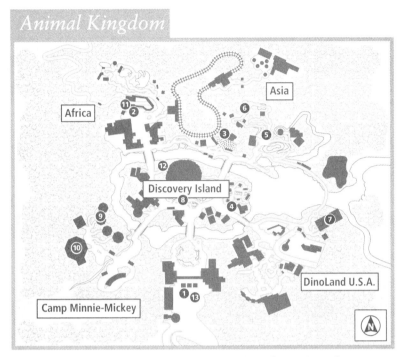

Animal Kingdom

Asia

Africa

Discovery Island

Camp Minnie-Mickey

DinoLand U.S.A.

Animal Kingdom One-Day Sleepyhead Touring Plan for Parents with Small Children

1. Arrive at the entrance to Disney's Animal Kingdom around 11 a.m. Pick up a park map and entertainment schedule. Stroller rentals are just past the entrance, to the right.
2. Send one member of your party to obtain Fastpasses for the Kilimanjaro Safari in Africa.
3. See *Flights of Wonder*. Check the daily entertainment schedule for show times.
4. Eat lunch. The nearest counter-service restaurants are the Flame Tree Barbecue on Discovery Island, and Anandapur Local Foods Cafés in Asia.
5. Ride Kali River Rapids in Asia. You can leave this step for last if you'd rather not walk around the park wet.
6. Walk the Maharajah Jungle Trek in Asia.

7. Check the next performance time of *Finding Nemo: The Musical* at the Theater in the Wild in DinoLand. If the next show is within 25 minutes, see *Nemo* now. Otherwise, see *It's Tough to Be a Bug* first, then see *Nemo*.
8. See *It's Tough To Be a Bug*. Also see the exhibits at the Tree of Life in Discovery Island.
9. Explore the Camp Minnie-Mickey Character Trails in Camp Minnie-Mickey.
10. See the *Festival of the Lion King*.
11. Experience the Kilimanjaro Safaris in Africa using the Fastpasses from Step 2.
12. If desired, see the Afternoon Parade.
13. Depart Disney's Animal Kingdom.

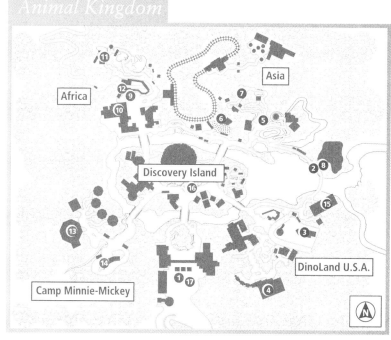

Animal Kingdom One-Day Touring Plan
for Tweens and Their Parents

1. Arrive 40 minutes before official opening mid-June through mid-August and during all holiday periods. At other times arrive 30 minutes early.
2. As soon as the park opens, send one member of your party to get Fastpasses for Expedition Everest in Asia. The shortest route to Everest is from Discovery Island through Asia, not DinoLand U.S.A.
3. Ride Primeval Whirl in DinoLand U.S.A.
4. Ride DINOSAUR.
5. Ride Kali River Rapids in Asia. You will get wet. Ponchos or plastic bags are advised. If you don't feel like getting soaked right now, skip this attraction or obtain Fastpasses for later in the day.
6. See *Flights of Wonder* in Asia if the next show is within 20 minutes from now. Otherwise, walk the Maharajah Jungle Trek, and then see the show.
7. Walk the Maharajah Jungle Trek in Asia if you have not already done so.
8. Ride Expedition Everest in Asia. Don't worry if your Fastpass times have past; Disney rarely enforces the times, as long as you're not trying to get in early.
9. If possible, send one member of your party to obtain Fastpasses for the Kilimanjaro Safaris in Africa.
10. Eat lunch. The closest counter-service restaurant is Tusker House in Africa.
11. Walk the Pangani Forest Exploration Trail.

12. Experience Kilimanjaro Safaris using the Fastpasses obtained earlier. Don't worry if the Fastpass return times have past; Disney rarely enforces them.
13. See the *Festival of the Lion King* in Camp Minnie-Mickey.
14. Meet the characters at Camp Minnie-Mickey.
15. Check the next performance time of *Finding Nemo: The Musical* at the Theater in the Wild in DinoLand. If the next show is within 25 minutes, see *Nemo* now. Otherwise, see *It's Tough to Be a Bug* first, then see *Nemo*.
16. See *It's Tough to Be a Bug* on Discovery Island. Use Fastpass if the wait exceeds 30 minutes. Also check out the exhibits at the Tree of Life.
17. Shop, snack, or repeat any attractions you especially enjoyed. Visit the zoological exhibits in The Oasis, and depart the Animal Kingdom. This plan should work well with Extra Magic Hour mornings. The only exception might be Kali River Rapids, which may open later than the rest of the attractions in Asia. If that happens, skip the attraction and return to it after all the other Asia attractions are done.

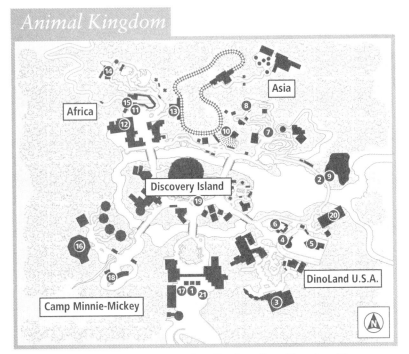

Animal Kingdom

Animal Kingdom Happy Family One-Day Touring Plan

1. **FAMILY:** Arrive 40 minutes before official opening mid-June through mid-August and during all holiday periods. At other times arrive 30 minutes early.

2. **TEENS:** As soon as the park opens, obtain Fastpasses for Expedition Everest in Asia. The fastest way to Everest is through Asia, not DinoLand.
   PARENTS: Don't feel the need to rush to an attraction. Explore The Oasis on Discovery Island, pointing out any unusual animals. Hungry? Look for the Royal Anandapur Tea Company in Asia between Kali River Rapids and Expedition Everest.

3. **TEENS:** Ride DINOSAUR in DinoLand U.S.A.

4. **PARENTS:** Ride TriceraTop Spin in DinoLand U.S.A.

5. **TEENS:** Ride Primeval Whirl in DinoLand U.S.A.

6. **PARENTS:** Check out The Boneyard in DinoLand.

7. **FAMILY:** If everyone's up for it, ride Kali River Rapids in Asia. You will get wet. Ponchos or plastic bags are advised. If you don't feel like getting soaked right now, save this attraction for later in the day.

8. **FAMILY:** Walk the Maharajah Jungle Trek.

9. **TEENS:** Ride Expedition Everest, using the Fastpasses obtained earlier. Don't worry if your Fastpass times have past; Disney rarely enforces the times, as long as you're not trying to get in early.

10. **PARENTS:** See *Flights of Wonder*. If the next show time is too far away, check out other nearby exhibits.

11. **FAMILY:** Send one member of your party to obtain Fastpasses for the Kilimanjaro Safaris in Africa.

12. **FAMILY:** Eat lunch. The closest counter-service restaurant is Tusker House in Africa.

13. **FAMILY:** Take the Wildlife Express train to Rafiki's Planet Watch/Conservation Station. See the exhibits. Note the writing on the bathroom walls. Take the train back to Africa when you're done.

14. **FAMILY:** Walk the Pangani Forest Exploration Trail. If teens want to, they could obtain more Fastpasses for Expedition Everest now. Meet back at the entrance to Kilimanjaro Safaris.

15. **FAMILY:** Experience Kilimanjaro Safaris using the Fastpasses obtained earlier. Don't worry if the Fastpass return times have past; Disney rarely enforces them.

16. **PARENTS:** See the *Festival of the Lion King* in Camp Minnie-Mickey.

17. **TEENS:** Free time. Revisit favorite attractions or explore the rest of the park.

18. **PARENTS:** Meet the characters at Camp Minnie-Mickey.

19. **FAMILY:** See *It's Tough to Be a Bug* on Discovery Island. Use Fastpass if the wait exceeds 30 minutes. Also check out the exhibits at the Tree of Life.

20. **FAMILY:** See *Finding Nemo: The Musical*.

21. **FAMILY:** Shop, snack, or repeat any attractions you especially enjoyed. Visit the zoological exhibits in The Oasis, and depart the Animal Kingdom.

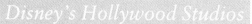
Disney's Hollywood Studios

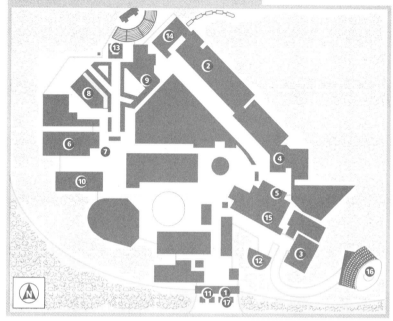

Disney's Hollywood Studios One-Day Touring Plan
for Parents with Small Children

1. Arrive at the entrance to Disney's Hollywood Studios 30 minutes prior to opening. Grab a park map and daily entertainment schedule when you enter the park. Rent strollers as needed at the gas station on the right side of the park entrance, just past the turnstiles.
2. As soon as the park opens, ride Toy Story Mania! at Pixar Place near the back center of the park.
3. If your kids are up for it, ride the Tower of Terror on Sunset Boulevard.
4. See *Voyage of the Little Mermaid.*
5. See *Playhouse Disney—Live on Stage!* Check the daily entertainment schedule for show times.
6. Ride Star Tours. Use Fastpass if the wait exceeds 25 minutes.
7. See the Jedi Training Academy show near Star Tours, either before or after you ride. Check the entertainment schedule for show times.
8. See *Muppet-Vision 3-D.*
9. Explore the *Honey, I Shrunk the Kids* Movie Set.
10. Eat lunch. The Backlot Express and Mama Melrose's are good nearby choices.

11. Take a midday break of around 3 hours.
12. Return to the park and see *Beauty and the Beast.* Check the daily entertainment schedule for show times.
13. See the *Lights, Motors, Action! Extreme Stunt Show* or the *Indiana Jones Epic Stunt Spectacular.* Check the daily entertainment schedule for show times.
14. If time permits, take the Studio Backlot Tour.
15. Eat dinner. Good nearby selections include the counter-service eateries on Sunset Boulevard. The Hollywood Brown Derby and the 50's Prime Time Café are the closest sit-down choices. Reservations are recommended.
16. See *Fantasmic!* if it's playing. Plan on arriving 30–40 minutes early to get decent seats, and up to an hour in advance for good seats.
17. Depart Disney's Hollywood Studios.

If you have a Web-enabled cell phone, you can view current and future wait times for every attraction—and add the times you see in the parks—at m.touringplans.com.

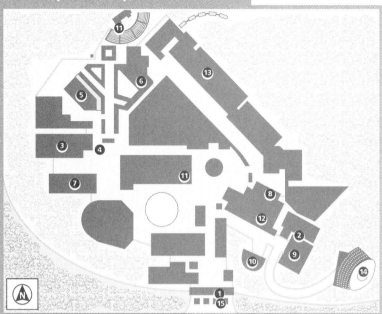

Disney's Hollywood Studios

Disney's Hollywood Studios Sleepyhead Touring Plan for Parents with Small Children

1. Arrive at the entrance to Disney's Hollywood Studios around 11 a.m. Grab a park map and entertainment schedule when you enter the park. Rent strollers as needed at the gas station on the right side of the park entrance, just past the turnstiles.
2. If your kids are up for it, obtain Fastpasses for the Tower of Terror on Sunset Boulevard.
3. Ride Star Tours. Use Fastpass if the wait exceeds 25 minutes.
4. See the Jedi Training Academy show near Star Tours, either before or after you ride. Check the entertainment schedule for show times.
5. See *Muppet-Vision 3-D.*
6. Explore the *Honey, I Shrunk the Kids* Movie Set.
7. Eat lunch. The Backlot Express and Mama Melrose's are good nearby choices.
8. See *Playhouse Disney—Live on Stage!* Check the daily entertainment schedule for show times.
9. Ride the Tower of Terror using the Fastpasses obtained in Step 2.

10. See *Beauty and the Beast.* Check the daily entertainment schedule for show times.
11. See *The American Idol Experience* or the *Indiana Jones Epic Stunt Spectacular.* Check the daily entertainment schedule for showtimes.
12. Eat dinner. Good nearby selections include the counter-service eateries on Sunset Boulevard. The Hollywood Brown Derby and the 50's Prime Time Café are the closest sit-down choices. Reservations are recommended.
13. Ride Toy Story Mania! at Pixar Place at the back of the park.
14. See *Fantasmic!* if it's playing. Plan on arriving 30–40 minutes early to get decent seats, and up to an hour in advance for good seats.
15. Depart Disney's Hollywood Studios.

If you have a Web-enabled cell phone, you can view current and future wait times for every attraction—and add the times you see in the parks—at m.touringplans.com.

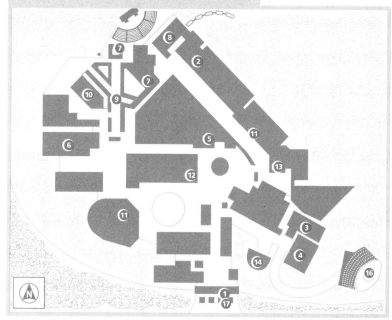

Disney's Hollywood Studios

Disney's Hollywood Studios One-Day Touring Plan for Tweens and Their Parents

1. Arrive at the park 30–40 minutes prior to opening. Grab a park map and entertainment schedule when you enter the park.
2. As soon as the park opens, ride Toy Story Mania! at Pixar Place.
3. Ride Rock 'n' Roller Coaster.
4. Ride the Tower of Terror. Use Fastpass if wait exceeds 30 minutes.
5. Ride The Great Movie Ride.
6. Ride Star Tours. If you have small children, check the daily entertainment schedule for the next performance of the Jedi Training Academy and work Star Tours in around that show. Use Fastpass for Star Tours if wait exceeds 20 minutes.
7. Check your entertainment schedule for the next performance of the *Lights, Motors, Action! Extreme Stunt Show*. Either see the show or eat lunch. Good nearby restaurants include Backlot Express and Mama Melrose's.
8. Take the Studio Backlot Tour.

9. Explore the rest of the Streets of America on the way to *Muppet-Vision 3-D*.
10. See *Muppet-Vision 3-D*.
11. Head toward Echo Lake. Check your entertainment schedule for the next performance of the *Indiana Jones* show. If the next show is within 25 minutes, get in line now. See *Walt Disney: One Man's Dream* between *Little Mermaid* and Toy Story Mania!
12. Check your entertainment schedule for the next performance of *The American Idol Experience*.
13. Work in *Voyage of the Little Mermaid!* if you have small children and time permits.
14. See *Beauty and the Beast.*
15. Tour Hollywood and Sunset boulevards.
16. Enjoy *Fantasmic!* if it's playing.

If you have a Web-enabled cell phone, you can view current and future wait times for every attraction—and add the ones you see in the parks—at m.touringplans.com.

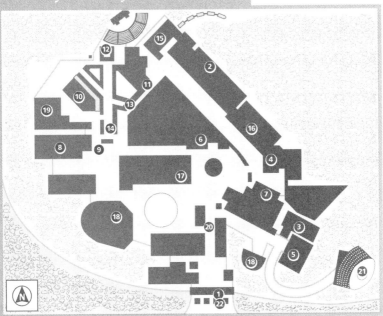

Disney's Hollywood Studios

Disney's Hollywood Studios
One-Day Happy Family Touring Plan

1. Arrive at the park 30–40 minutes prior to opening. Grab a park map and entertainment schedule when you enter the park. Rent strollers or wheelchairs as needed at the gas station on the right side of the park entrance, just past the turnstiles.
2. **FAMILY:** As soon as the park opens, ride Toy Story Mania! at Pixar Place.
3. **TEENS:** Ride Rock 'n' Roller Coaster. Consider using the single-rider line or Fastpass if the standby wait exceeds 25 minutes.
4. **PARENTS:** *See Voyage of the Little Mermaid* in the Animation Courtyard.
5. **TEENS:** Ride the Tower of Terror. Use Fastpass if wait exceeds 30 minutes.
6. **FAMILY:** Ride The Great Movie Ride.
7. **PARENTS:** See *Playhouse Disney—Live on Stage!* Check the daily entertainment schedule for show times.
8. **TEENS:** Ride Star Tours.
9. **PARENTS:** Check the daily entertainment schedule for the next performance of the Jedi Training Academy near Star Tours.
10. **FAMILY:** See *Muppet-Vision 3-D.*
11. **FAMILY:** Eat lunch. The best nearby counter-service restaurant is the Studio Catering Co. Now would be a good time to check the daily entertainment schedule for show times for *Lights, Motors, Action!, Beauty and the Beast, Indiana*

Jones, and *The American Idol Experience.*
12. **TEENS:** See the *Lights, Motors, Action!* stunt show.
13. **PARENTS:** Explore the *Honey, I Shrunk the Kids* Movie Set.
14. **FAMILY:** Explore the Streets of America if you didn't get enough on the way to the *Muppets.*
15. **FAMILY:** Take the Studio Backlot Tour.
16. **FAMILY:** See *Walt Disney: One Man's Dream* near Toy Story Mania! at Pixar Place.
17. **FAMILY:** See the next showing of *The American Idol Experience.* For any show except the last of the day, plan on arriving around 15 minutes in advance to get a seat. Arrive 25 minutes early for the last show.
18. See *Beauty and the Beast* or the *Indiana Jones Epic Stunt Spectacular.*
19. Eat dinner. Good sit-down choices include Mama Melrose's and The Hollywood Brown Derby.
20. Tour Hollywood and Sunset boulevards.
21. Enjoy *Fantasmic!* if it's playing.
22. Depart Disney's Hollywood Studios.

If you have a Web-enabled cell phone, you can view current and future wait times for every attraction—and add the ones you see in the parks—at m.TouringPlans.com.

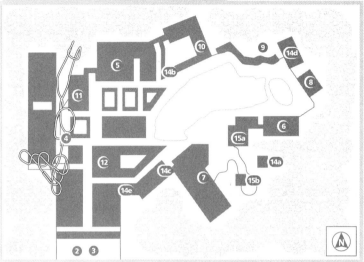

Universal Studios Florida
One-day Touring Plan

1. Call ☎ 407-363-8000 the day before your visit for the official opening time.

2. Arrive 50 minutes before opening and pick up a map and entertainment schedule.

3. Line up at the turnstile. Ask if any rides or shows are closed, and adjust touring plan.

4. Ride Hollywood Rip Ride Rockit.

5. Ride Revenge of the Mummy.

6. Ride The Simpsons Ride.

7. Ride E.T. Adventure (expendable if there are no young kids in your group).

8. Ride Men in Black Alien Attack.

9. Ride JAWS.

10. Experience *Disaster!*

11. See *TWISTER . . . Ride It Out.*

12. See *Shrek 4-D.*

13. Take a break for lunch.

14. See *Animal Actors on Location* **(14a)**, *Beetlejuice's Graveyard Revue* **(14b)**, *Universal Orlando's Horror Make-Up Show* **(14c)**, and *Fear Factor Live* **(14d)** as convenient according to the daily entertainment schedule. See *Terminator 2: 3-D* **(14e)** after 3:30 p.m.

15. Take preschoolers to see Barney **(15a)** after riding E.T., and then head for Woody Woodpecker's KidZone **(15b).**

16. Revisit favorite rides and shows. See any live performances you may have missed.

If you have a Web-enabled cell phone, you can view current and future wait times for every attraction—and add the ones you see in the parks—at **m.touringplans.com.**

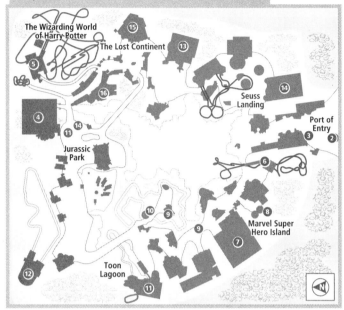

Universal's Islands of Adventure
One-day Touring Plan

1. Call ☎ 407-363-8000 the day before your visit for the official opening time.

2. Arrive 60 minutes before opening time, and pick up a map and daily entertainment schedule.

3. Line up at the turnstiles. Ask if any attractions are closed; adjust touring plan accordingly.

4. Hurry to Harry Potter and the Forbidden Journey as soon as you clear the turnstiles, and ride. Be warned that even without much waiting, you'll invest at least 35–40 minutes here.

5. Ride Dragon Challenge if the wait is 30 minutes or less. Otherwise skip to Step 6.

6. At Marvel Super Hero Island, ride The Incredible Hulk Coaster.

7. Exit left and experience The Adventures of Spider-Man.

8. On exiting Spider-Man, backtrack right and ride Doctor Doom's Fearfall. Skip it if the wait exceeds 20 minutes.

9. Depart Super Hero Island and cross into Toon Lagoon.

10. On your right, ride Popeye & Bluto's Bilge-Rat Barges.

11. Continue your clockwise circuit of the park. Ride Dudley Do-Right's Ripsaw Falls.

12. Continue around the lake to Jurassic Park. Ride the Jurassic Park River Adventure.

13. Pass through The Wizarding World to The Lost Continent. Experience *Poseidon's Fury*.

14. Continue clockwise to Seuss Landing and ride The Cat in the Hat.

15. Check the daily entertainment schedule for performances of *The Eighth Voyage of Sindbad Stunt Show* in The Lost Continent. See the show when convenient.

16. Return to The Wizarding World and explore Hogsmeade Village.

17. Revisit favorite rides and check out attractions you may have missed.

If you have a Web-enabled cell phone, you can view current and future wait times for every attraction—and add the ones you see in the parks—at **m.touringplans.com**.

Unofficial Guide Reader Survey

If you would like to express your opinion in writing about Walt Disney World or this guidebook, complete the following survey and mail it to:

> Unofficial Guide Reader Survey
> P.O. Box 43673
> Birmingham, AL 35243

Or fill out the survey online at **touringplans.com.**

Inclusive dates of your visit_____ Your hometown_____

Your e-mail address_____

Members of your party:	Person 1	Person 2	Person 3	Person 4	Person 5
Gender (M or F)	_____	_____	_____	_____	_____
Age	_____	_____	_____	_____	_____

How many times have you been to Walt Disney World? _____

On your most recent trip, where did you stay?_____

Concerning accommodations, on a scale with 100 best and 0 worst, how would you rate:

    The quality of your room? _____   The value for the money? _____

    The quietness of your room?_____   Check-in/checkout efficiency?_____

    Shuttle service to the parks? _____   Swimming pool facilities? _____

What transportation did you use to get to Orlando? (circle one)

        Car / Airplane / Train / Cruise / Other

For your trip going to Orlando, what day(s) of the week did you travel?

      (circle all that apply) Su Mo Tu We Th Fr Sa

What day of the week did you start your trip home?

      (circle all that apply) Su Mo Tu We Th Fr Sa

Did you rent a car? _____   From whom? _____

Concerning your rental car, on a scale with 100 best and 0 worst, how would you rate:

    Pickup processing efficiency?_____   Return processing efficiency?_____

    Condition of the car? _____   Cleanliness of the car? _____

    Airport shuttle efficiency? _____

Concerning your touring:

    Who in your party was most responsible for planning the itinerary?_____

    What time did you normally get started in the morning? _____

    Did you usually arrive at the theme parks before opening? _____

    Did you return to your hotel for rest during the day? _____

    What time did you normally go to bed at night? _____

If you remember the days of the week and times you visited the theme parks, indicate those in the chart below. Use the a.m. column for morning visits, and p.m. for afternoon/evening visits.

	Sun		Mon		Tue		Wed		Thu		Fri		Sat	
	a.m.	p.m.	a.m.	p.m.	a.m.	p.m.	a.m.	p.m.	a.m.	p.m.	a.m.	p.m.	a.m.	p.m.
MK														
Epcot														
AK														
DHS														
Universal														
IOA														

On a scale with 100 best and 0 worst, rate how the touring plans worked:

Park	Name of Plan	Rating
Magic Kingdom	_____	_____
Epcot	_____	_____
Animal Kingdom	_____	_____
Hollywood Studios	_____	_____
Universal Studios	_____	_____
Islds. of Adventure	_____	_____

Concerning your dining experiences:

How many restaurant meals (including fast food) did you average per day? _____

How much (approximately) did your party spend on meals per day? _____

Favorite restaurant outside of Walt Disney World? _____

Did you buy this guide: Before leaving? _____ While on your trip? _____

How did you hear about this guide?

Loaned or recommended by a friend _____ Radio or TV _____

Newspaper or magazine _____ Bookstore salesperson _____

Just picked it out on my own _____ Library _____

Internet _____

What other guidebooks did you use on this trip? _____

On a 100 best and 0 worst scale, how would you rate them? _____

_____

Using the same scale, how would you rate the *Unofficial Guide*? _____

Are *Unofficial Guides* readily available at bookstores near you? _____

Have you used other *Unofficial Guides*? _____ Which one(s)? _____

Comments about your Walt Disney World Vacation or about the *Unofficial Guide:* _____

_____

_____

_____